SECURWARE 2024

The Eighteenth International Conference on Emerging Security Information, Systems and Technologies

November 3rd - 7th, 2024

Nice, France

SECURWARE 2024 Editors

Fatima Hussain, Toronto Metropolitan University, Toronto, Canada

Steffen Fries, Siemens AG, Germany

Printed from e-media with permission by:

Curran Associates, Inc.
57 Morehouse Lane
Red Hook, NY 12571

Printed with permission by Curran Associates, Inc. (2025)

International Academy, Research, and Industry Association (IARIA)
412 Derby Way
Wilmington, DE 19810

Phone: (408) 893-6407
Fax: (408) 527-6351

petre@iaria.org

Additional copies of this publication are available from:

Curran Associates, Inc.
57 Morehouse Lane
Red Hook, NY 12571 USA
Phone: 845-758-0400
Fax: 845-758-2633
Email: curran@proceedings.com
Web: www.proceedings.com

Table of Contents

SECURWARE 2024

Forward

The Eighteenth International Conference on Emerging Security Information, Systems and Technologies (SECURWARE 2024), held on on November 3-7, 2024, continued a series of events covering related topics on theory and practice on security, cryptography, secure protocols, trust, privacy, confidentiality, vulnerability, intrusion detection and other areas related to low enforcement, security data mining, malware models, etc.

Security, defined for ensuring protected communication among terminals and user applications across public and private networks, is the core for guaranteeing confidentiality, privacy, and data protection. Security affects business and individuals, raises the business risk, and requires a corporate and individual culture. In the open business space offered by Internet, it is a need to improve defenses against hackers, disgruntled employees, and commercial rivals. There is a required balance between the effort and resources spent on security versus security achievements. Some vulnerability can be addressed using the rule of 80:20, meaning 80% of the vulnerabilities can be addressed for 20% of the costs. Other technical aspects are related to the communication speed versus complex and time consuming cryptography/security mechanisms and protocols.

Digital Ecosystem is defined as an open decentralized information infrastructure where different networked agents, such as enterprises (especially SMEs), intermediate actors, public bodies and end users, cooperate and compete enabling the creation of new complex structures. In digital ecosystems, the actors, their products and services can be seen as different organisms and species that are able to evolve and adapt dynamically to changing market conditions.

Digital Ecosystems lie at the intersection between different disciplines and fields: industry, business, social sciences, biology, and cutting edge ICT and its application driven research. They are supported by several underlying technologies such as semantic web and ontology-based knowledge sharing, self-organizing intelligent agents, peer-to-peer overlay networks, web services-based information platforms, and recommender systems.

To enable safe digital ecosystem functioning, security and trust mechanisms become essential components across all the technological layers. The aim is to bring together multidisciplinary research that ranges from technical aspects to socio-economic models.

We take here the opportunity to warmly thank all the members of the SECURWARE 2024 technical program committee, as well as all the reviewers. The creation of such a high quality conference program would not have been possible without their involvement. We also kindly thank all the authors who dedicated much of their time and effort to contribute to SECURWARE 2024. We truly believe that, thanks to all these efforts, the final conference program consisted of top quality contributions.

We also thank the members of the SECURWARE 2024 organizing committee for their help in handling the logistics and for their work that made this professional meeting a success.

We hope that SECURWARE 2024 was a successful international forum for the exchange of ideas and results between academia and industry and to promote further progress in the area of security information, systems and technologies. We also hope that Nice provided a pleasant environment during the conference and everyone saved some time to enjoy the historic charm of the city.

SECURWARE 2024 Chairs

SECURWARE 2024 Steering Committee
Steffen Fries, Siemens, Germany
George O. M. Yee, Aptusinnova Inc. / Carleton University, Ottawa, Canada
Ki-Woong Park, Sejong University, South Korea
Rainer Falk, Siemens AG, Corporate Technology, Germany
Hans-Joachim Hof, INSicherheit - Ingolstadt Research Group Applied IT Security, CARISSMA – Center of Automotive Research on Integrated Safety Syst, Germany

SECURWARE 2024 Publicity Chair
Lorena Parra Boronat, Universitat Politecnica de Valencia, Spain
Laura Garcia, Universidad Politécnica de Cartagena, Spain

SECURWARE 2024

Committee

SECURWARE 2024 Steering Committee

Steffen Fries, Siemens, Germany
George O. M. Yee, Aptusinnova Inc. / Carleton University, Ottawa, Canada
Ki-Woong Park, Sejong University, South Korea
Rainer Falk, Siemens AG, Corporate Technology, Germany
Hans-Joachim Hof, INSicherheit - Ingolstadt Research Group Applied IT Security, CARISSMA – Center of Automotive Research on Integrated Safety Syst, Germany

SECURWARE 2024 Publicity Chair

Lorena Parra Boronat, Universitat Politecnica de Valencia, Spain
Laura Garcia, Universidad Politécnica de Cartagena, Spain

SECURWARE 2024 Technical Program Committee

Aysajan Abidin, imec-COSIC KU Leuven, Belgium
Abbas Acar, Florida International University, Miami, USA
Rabin Acharya, University of Florida, USA
Afrand Agah, West Chester University of Pennsylvania, USA
Chuadhry Mujeeb Ahmed, University of Strathclyde, UK
Sedat Akleylek, Ondokuz Mayis University, Samsun, Turkey
Oum-El-Kheir Aktouf, Greboble INP | LCIS Lab, France
Mamoun Alazab, Charles Darwin University, Australia
Asif Ali laghari, SMIU, Karachi, Pakistan
Luca Allodi, Eindhoven University of Technology, Netherlands
Eric Amankwa, Presbyterian University College, Ghana
Prashant Anantharaman, Dartmouth College, USA
Mohammadreza Ashouri, Virginia Tech, USA
Alexandre Augusto Giron, Federal University of Technology - Parana, Brazil
Ilija Basicevic, University of Novi Sad, Serbia
Luke A. Bauer, University of Florida, USA
Malek Ben Salem, Accenture, USA
Smriti Bhatt, Purdue University, USA
Catalin Bîrjoveanu, "Al. I. Cuza" University of Iasi, Romania
Malte Breuer, RWTH Aachen University, Germany
Robert Brotzman, Pennsylvania State University, USA
Francesco Buccafurri, University Mediterranea of Reggio Calabria, Italy
Arun Balaji Buduru, IIIT-Delhi, India
Enrico Cambiaso, Consiglio Nazionale delle Ricerche (CNR) - IEIIT Institute, Italy
Juan-Vicente Capella-Hernández, Universitat Politècnica de València, Spain
Roberto Carbone, Fondazione Bruno Kessler, Trento, Italy
Juan Carlos Ruiz, Universitat Politecnica de Valencia, Spain
Dirceu Cavendish, Kyushu Institute of Technology, Fukuoka, Japan

Christophe Charrier, Nomandie Univ. | UNICAEN | ENSICAEN | CNRS GREYC UMR 6072, France
Bo Chen, Michigan Technological University, Houghton, USA
Liquan Chen, Southeast University, China
Zelei Cheng, Purdue University, USA
Tan Saw Chin, Multimedia University, Malaysia
Jin-Hee Cho, Virginia Tech, USA
Stelvio Cimato, University of Milan, Italy
Jun Dai, California State University at Sacramento, USA
Dipanjan Das, University of California, Santa Barbara, USA
Avani Dave, Intel Corp., USA
Raffaele Della Corte, "Federico II" University of Naples, Italy
Jean-Christophe Deneuville, ENAC | University of Toulouse, France
Jintai Ding, Tsinghua University, Beijing
George Drosatos, Athena Research Center, Greece
Navid Emamdoost, University of Minnesota, USA
Alessandro Erba, Karlsruhe Institute of Technology, Germany
Rainer Falk, Siemens AG, Corporate Technology, Germany
Yebo Feng, University of Oregon, USA
Anders Fongen, Norwegian Defence University College, Norway
Steffen Fries, Siemens Corporate Technologies, Germany
Chrystel Gaber, Orange, France
Clemente Galdi, University of Salerno, Italy
Kevin Gomez Buquerin, Technical University Ingolstadt, Germany
Nils Gruschka, University of Oslo, Norway
Bidyut Gupta, Southern Illinois University, Carbondale, USA
Saurabh Gupta, IIIT-Delhi, India
Emre Gursoy, Koc University, Istanbul, Turkey
Muhammad Shadi Hajar, Robert Gordon University, UK
Amir Mohammad Hajisadeghi, Amirkabir University of Technology (Tehran Polytechnic), Iran
Mohammad Hamad, Technical University of Munich, Germany
Jinguang Han, Southeast University, China
Petr Hanáček, Brno University of Technology, Czech Republic
Dan Harkins, Hewlett-Packard Enterprise, USA
Mohamed Hawedi, École de Technologie Supérieure Montreal, Canada
Andres Hernandez-Matamoros, Meiji University, Japan
Hans-Joachim Hof, INSicherheit - Ingolstadt Research Group Applied IT Security, CARISSMA – Center of Automotive Research on Integrated Safety Syst, Germany
Gahangir Hossain, West Texas A&M University, Canyon, USA
Fu-Hau Hsu, National Central University, Taiwan
Yuncong Hu, Shanghai Jiao Tong University, China
Fatima Hussain, Royal Bank of Canada, Toronto, Canada
Mauro Iacono, Università degli Studi della Campania "L. Vanvitelli", Italy
Ibifubara Iganibo, George Mason University, USA
Sergio Ilarri, University of Zaragoza, Spain
Nikolay Ivanov, Michigan State University, USA
Prasad M. Jayaweera, University of Sri Jayewardenepura, Sri Lanka
Kun Jin, Ohio State University, USA
Hugo Jonker, Open Universiteit, Netherlands

Taeho Jung, University of Notre Dame, USA
Kaushal Kafle, William & Mary, USA
Sarang Kahvazadeh, Centre Tecnològic de Telecomunicacions de Catalunya (CTTC), Spain
Harsha K. Kalutarage, Robert Gordon University, UK
Georgios Kambourakis, University of the Aegean, Greece
Mehdi Karimi, The University of British Columbia, Vancouver, Canada
Georgios Karopoulos, European Commission JRC, Italy
Sokratis K. Katsikas, Norwegian University of Science and Technology, Norway
Basel Katt, Norwegian University of Science and Technology, Norway
Joakim Kävrestad, University of Skövde, Sweden
Hyunsung Kim, Kyungil University, Korea
Paris Kitsos, University of the Peloponnese, Greece
Andreas Kogler, Graz University of Technology (TU-Graz) | Institute of Applied Information Processing and Communications (IAIK), Austria
Harsha Kumara, Robert Gordon University, UK
Hiroki Kuzuno, SECOM Co. Ltd., Japan
Hyun Kwon, Korea Military Academy, Korea
Romain Laborde, University Paul Sabatier Toulouse III, France
Cecilia Labrini, University of Reggio Calabria, Italy
Yosra Lakhdhar, SUP'COM / Digital Research Centre of Sfax, Tunisia
Vianney Lapôtre, Université Bretagne Sud, France
Martin Latzenhofer, AIT Austrian Institute of Technology | Center for Digital Safety and Security, Vienna, Austria
Wen-Chuan Lee, Apple Inc., USA
Ferenc Leitold, University of Dunaújváros, Hungary
Albert Levi, Sabanci University, Istanbul, Turkey
Shimin Li, Winona State University, USA
Wenjuan Li, The Hong Kong Polytechnic University, China
Zhihao Li, Meta Platform Inc., USA
Stefan Lindskog, SINTEF Digital, Norway / Karlstad University, Sweden
Guojun Liu, University of South Florida, Tampa, USA
Shaohui Liu, School of Computer Science and Technology | Harbin Institute of Technology, China
Shen Liu, NVIDIA, USA
Yi Liu, University of Massachusetts Dartmouth, USA
Giovanni Livraga, Universita' degli Studi di Milano, Italy
George Lord, University of Chicago, USA
Jakob Löw, Technische Hochschule Ingolstadt, Germany
Giuseppe Loseto, LUM "Giuseppe Degennaro" University, Italy
Flaminia Luccio, University Ca' Foscari of Venice, Italy
Duohe Ma, Institute of Information Engineering | Chinese Academy of Sciences, China
Rabi N. Mahapatra, Texas A&M University, USA
Mahdi Manavi, Mirdamad Institute of Higher Education, Iran
Anuradha Mandal, University of Arizona, USA
Soundes Marzougui, Technical University of Berlin, Germany
Michele Mastroianni, University of Salerno, Italy
Antonio Matencio Escolar, University of the West of Scotland, UK
Wojciech Mazurczyk, Warsaw University of Technology, Poland
Weizhi Meng, Technical University of Denmark, Denmark

Ulrike Meyer, RWTH Aachen University, Germany
Aleksandra Mileva, University "Goce Delcev" in Stip, Republic of N. Macedonia
Paolo Modesti, Teesside University, UK
Adwait Nadkarni, William & Mary, USA
Vasudevan Nagendra, Plume Design Inc., USA
Priyadarsi Nanda, University of Technology Sydney, Australia
Liang Niu, New York University (NYU) Abu Dhabi, UAE
Jason R. C. Nurse, University of Kent, UK
Rajvardhan Oak, Microsoft, India
Bogdan Oancea, University of Bucharest, Romania
Livinus Obiora Nweke, Norwegian University of Science and Technology, Norway
Catuscia Palamidessi, INRIA, France
Carlos Enrique Palau Salvador, Universitat Politècnica de València, Spain
Lanlan Pan, Guangdong OPPO Mobile Telecommunications Corp. Ltd., China
Brajendra Panda, University of Arkansas, USA
Ki-Woong Park, Sejong University, Republic of Korea
Balázs Pejó, CrySyS Lab - BME, Budapest, Hungary
Wei Peng, University of Oulu, Finland
Travis Peters, Montana State University, USA
Josef Pieprzyk, Data61 | CSIRO, Sydney, Australia / Institute of Computer Science | Polish Academy of Sciences, Warsaw, Poland
Nikolaos Pitropakis, Edinburgh Napier University, UK
Tassilo Pellegrini, St. Pölten University of Applied Sciences, Austria
Bernardo Portela, University of Porto, Portugal
Mila Dalla Preda, University of Verona, Italy
Yiyue Qian, University of Notre Dame, USA
Alvise Rabitti, Università Ca'Foscari - Venezia, Italy
Khandaker "Abir" Rahman, Saginaw Valley State University, USA
Mohammad Saidur Rahman, Rochester Institute of Technology, USA
Keyvan Ramezanpour, ANDRO Computational Solutions LLC, USA
Mohammad A. Rashid, Massey University, New Zealand
Alexander Rasin, DePaul University, USA
Danda B. Rawat, Howard University, USA
Leon Reznik, Rochester Institute of Technology, USA
Martin Ring, Bosch Engineering GmbH, Germany
Vera Rimmer, KU Leuven, Belgium
Heiko Roßnagel, Fraunhofer IAO, Germany
Salah Sadou, IRISA - Universite de Bretagne Sud, France
Nick Scope, DePaul University, USA
Rodrigo Sanches Miani, Universidade Federal de Uberlândia, Brazil
Stefan Schauer, AIT Austrian Institute of Technology | Center for Digital Safety and Security, Vienna, Austria
Stefan Schiffner, University of Münster, Germany
Savio Sciancalepore, Hamad Bin Khalifa University (HBKU), Doha, Qatar
Giada Sciarretta, Fondazione Bruno Kessler (FBK), Trento, Italy
Tanmoy Sen, University of Virginia, USA
Avi Shaked, University of Oxford, UK
Jain Shalabh, Robert Bosch LLC, USA

Haoqi Shan, University of Florida, USA
Amit Kumar Sikder, Georgia Institute of Technology, USA
Christian Skalka, University of Vermont, USA
Rocky Slavin, University of Texas at San Antonio, USA
Christoph Stach, University of Stuttgart, Germany
Dean Sullivan, University of New Hampshire, USA
Shi-Feng Sun, Shanghai Jiao Tong University, China
Zhibo Sun, Drexel University, USA
Sheng Tan, Trinity University, USA
Michael Tempelmeier, Giesecke+Devrient, Germany
Nils Ole Tippenhauer, CISPA Helmholtz Center for Cybersecurity, Germany
Scott Trent, IBM Research - Tokyo, Japan
Yazhou Tu, University of Louisiana at Lafayette, USA
Vincent Urias, Sandia National Labs, USA
Andrea Visconti, Università degli Studi di Milano, Italy
Qi Wang, University of Illinois Urbana-Champaign / Stellar Cyber Inc., USA
Shu Wang, George Mason University, USA
Wenhao Wang, Institute of Information Engineering | Chinese Academy of Sciences, China
Wenqi Wei, Georgia Institute of Technology, USA
Ian Welch, Victoria University of Wellington, New Zealand
Zhonghao Wu, Shanghai Jiao Tong University, China
Ehsan Yaghoubi, University of Beira Interior, Portugal
Limin Yang, University of Illinois at Urbana-Champaign, USA
Ping Yang, Binghamton University, USA
Wun-She Yap, Universiti Tunku Abdul Rahman, Malaysia
Qussai M. Yaseen, Jordan University of Science and Technology, Irbid, Jordan
George O. M. Yee, Aptusinnova Inc. / Carleton University, Ottawa, Canada
Kailiang Ying, Google, USA
Amr Youssef, Concordia University, Montreal, Canada
Chia-Mu Yu, National Yang Ming Chiao Tung University, Taiwan
Wei Yu, Institute of Information Engineering | Chinese Academy of Sciences, China
Thomas Zefferer, Secure Information Technology Center Austria (A-SIT), Austria
Dongrui Zeng, Palo Alto Networks, Santa Clara, USA
Penghui Zhang, Meta Platforms Inc., USA
Tianwei Zhang, Nanyang Technological University, Singapore
Yubao Zhang, Palo Alto Networks, USA
Yue Zheng, Nanyang Technological University, Singapore
Tommaso Zoppi, University of Florence, Italy

Copyright Information

Detecting Denial of Service Attacks in Smart Grids Using Machine Learning: A Study of IEC 61850 Protocols

Antonin Delhomme
National Graduate School of Engineering of Caen (ENSICaen)
Caen, France
e-mail: antonin.delhomme@ecole.ensicaen.fr

Livinus Obiora Nweke
Noroff University College
4612 Kristiansand S, Norway
e-mail: livinus.nweke@noroff.no

Sule Yildirim Yayilgan
Norwegian University of Science and Technology (NTNU)
Gjøvik, Norway
e-mail: sule.yildirim@ntnu.no

Abstract—**The increasing digitalization of power grids, often referred to as smart grids, has revolutionized the efficiency and functionality of electrical infrastructure. Smart grids integrate advanced communication technologies and digital controls to optimize the generation, distribution, and consumption of electricity. However, this digital transformation has also introduced significant cybersecurity challenges. As these grids are critical national infrastructures, ensuring their protection against cyber threats is essential. This study investigates the application of various machine learning algorithms to detect Denial of Service (DoS) attacks within the International Electrotechnical Commission (IEC) 61850 communication protocols, specifically Generic Object-Oriented Substation Event (GOOSE) and Sampled Values (SV). We employed a simulated substation communication environment to generate normal and attack scenarios, utilizing both GOOSE and SV messages. The machine learning models used in our experiment include a Random Forest Classifier, Decision Tree, Support Vector Machine (SVM), Neural Networks, K-Nearest Neighbors (KNN), Logistic Regression, Gradient Boosting, and a Voting Classifier. The results demonstrated that the Random Forest Classifier and Decision Tree models consistently achieved high accuracy and F1 scores, making them effective for DoS detection in IEC 61850 protocols. The Voting Classifier also showed strong performance, leveraging the strengths of multiple models. Despite the generally good performance of these models, the SVM and Voting Classifier provided the best results in a specific instance with reduced data volume. Training time was also considered, highlighting Decision Tree and Logistic Regression as the most efficient models for quick deployment. This study underscores the potential of machine learning-based approaches for enhancing the security of substation communication systems, providing valuable insights for future research and practical applications in the field of smart grid cybersecurity.**

Keywords-Smart Grids; Digital Substation; Machine Learning; Deep Learning; DoS Attacks; Cyber-Attack Detection.

I. INTRODUCTION

The modernization of electrical power systems has led to the integration of advanced communication technologies to enhance the efficiency and reliability of power delivery. Among these technologies, the IEC 61850 standard [1] has emerged as the foundation for substation automation, enabling real-time data exchange and event-triggered messaging through protocols, such as Generic Object Oriented Substation Event (GOOSE) and Sampled Values (SV). These protocols facilitate crucial functions like protection, control, and monitoring of substations, which are the basis of smart grid communications [1]. However, the increasing reliance on digital communications within substations has also exposed these systems to a range of cyber threats. One of the most significant and pervasive threats is the Denial of Service (DoS) attacks, which aim to overwhelm the communication network with a flood of malicious traffic, thereby disrupting normal operations and potentially leading to catastrophic failures in power delivery [2]. The critical nature of these systems necessitates robust and reliable methods for detecting and mitigating such attacks to ensure the security and stability of the power grid.

Despite advancements in substation automation and security measures, detecting DoS attacks within the IEC 61850 protocols remains a difficult task. Tradition Intrusion Detection Systems (IDS) typically rely on predefined thresholds and signatures to identify malicious activity [3]. However, these methods struggle to keep up with sophisticated and evolving attack patterns. Consequently, there is an urgent need for innovative approaches that can dynamically learn and adapt to new threats. To address this need, this study investigates the efficacy of various machine learning algorithms in detecting DoS attacks within the IEC 61850 communication protocols, with a primary focus on the GOOSE and SV protocols.

The main contributions of this paper are as follows:

1) We develop a testbed using the IEC 61850 protocols (GOOSE and SV) to simulate both normal and DoS attack scenarios in a substation environment.
2) We employ a variety of machine learning models, including Random Forest, Decision Tree, SVM, Neural Networks, KNN, and a Voting Classifier, to detect DoS attacks in these protocols.
3) We provide a comprehensive evaluation of these models based on performance metrics like accuracy, F1-score, training time, and computational efficiency, identifying Random Forest and Decision Tree as the best-performing models.
4) We introduce a new feature, "Timediff", which improves the ability of models to distinguish between normal and

attack traffic, further enhancing the detection of anomalies in GOOSE and SV messages.

This study holds significant importance for several reasons. Firstly, it addresses a critical gap in the cybersecurity of smart grids by focusing on the detection of DoS attacks within the IEC 61850 communication protocols. As the adoption of smart grid technologies continues to grow, ensuring the security of these systems becomes paramount to maintaining reliable power delivery and preventing potential blackouts. Secondly, by exploring the application of machine learning algorithms for intrusion detection, this research contributes to the broader field of cybersecurity by demonstrating the potential of advanced analytical techniques in identifying and mitigating cyber threats. Moreover, the insights gained from this research can guide future studies and practical implementations, providing a foundation for ongoing efforts to enhance the resilience of smart grid communications against cyber attacks.

The rest of the paper is structured as follows. Section 2 delves deeper into this topic. Section 3 describes our data collection process. Section 4 outlines the subsequent steps, such as training models and converting data for these models. Section 5 presents our findings and conclusions. Finally, Section 6 provides a concise summary of the results, discusses their implications, and suggests potential areas for future research and improvements in this field.

II. Related Work

The field of cybersecurity, particularly in the context of digital substations and the detection and mitigation of DoS attacks, has garnered significant attention in recent years. Numerous studies have advanced our understanding of the unique challenges and effective solutions for protecting these crucial infrastructures. Our research extends the work in [4], which emphasizes the necessity of realistic simulation environments to test and improve detection mechanisms. The study highlights the critical role of advanced simulators that replicate various attack scenarios, thus enhancing our ability to respond to cyber threats without jeopardizing real power grids. The authors in [5] explore the vulnerabilities inherent in power system automation and protection schemes, providing a detailed analysis of the impacts of cyber-attacks on power system stability and reliability. This work aids in developing robust protection mechanisms against threats like DoS attacks.

The paper in [6] addresses core cybersecurity issues in digital substations, identifying challenges associated with the integration of digital technologies and underscoring the need for specialized cybersecurity measures. Complementary to this, the work in [7] proposes a method for identifying network anomalies using the IEC 61850 standard, which enhances real-time monitoring and detection capabilities. The authors in [8], provide a comprehensive survey of cybersecurity challenges within the smart grid, including digital substations. They outline major threats and evaluate current cybersecurity measures, providing insights into future research directions. Similarly, the authors in [9] review existing Intrusion Detection and Prevention systems (IDPS) for digital substations, assessing their effectiveness against specific threats in these environments. Also, the paper in [10] evaluates security threats to smart grid communication networks, covering a range of potential attacks, including DoS, and assessing their impact on grid operations.

The work in [11] highlights the threat posed by DoS attacks on IEC 61850-based substation automation systems, emphasizing their vulnerabilities and the need for robust detection and mitigation strategies. Likewise, the authors in [12] focus on developing a lightweight and effective Network Intrusion Detection System (NIDS) that balances detection effectiveness with resource efficiency. In the realm of intrusion detection, the paper by [13] introduces a system designed for IEC 61850 automated substations that enhances detection accuracy and response times. This is further supported by work in [2], which presents a novel method for detecting DoS attacks using Auto-Regressive Fractionally Integrated Moving Average (ARFIMA) modeling of GOOSE communication.

Furthermore, the study in [14] addresses the simulation modeling and analysis of DoS attacks, with a particular focus on the SYN-Flood attack method, providing practical insights into various mitigation strategies. In the same way, the authors in [15] investigate how DoS attacks can compromise protection schemes and propose methods to enhance their resilience.

While significant progress has been made in applying machine learning to detect cyber threats in power systems, there remains a need for comprehensive studies that evaluate multiple machine learning models under realistic substation communication scenarios. Most existing research either focuses on a limited set of algorithms or lacks detailed analysis of the performance metrics across different traffic conditions.

This study aims to fill this gap by providing a thorough evaluation of various machine learning algorithms for detecting DoS attacks within IEC 61850 GOOSE and SV protocols. To achieve this, we simulate DoS attacks in a controlled digital substation environment using the emulator described in [16]. We then apply various machine learning methods to detect these attacks. We also compare these multiple machine learning algorithms, offering a comprehensive evaluation of their strengths and weaknesses to identify the most effective approach. This research provides valuable insights into the effectiveness of these models in real-world substation environments.

III. Methodology

This section details the experimental setup, data collection, preprocessing, feature engineering, and the machine learning models used to detect DoS attacks in IEC 61850 protocols (GOOSE and SV messages).

A. Experimental setup

For the simulation environment, we used the SGSim emulator [16] to simulate the substation communication, including devices such as Intelligent Electronic Devices (IEDs), Digital Primary Substations (DPS), and Digital Secondary Substations (DSS), as illustrated in Figure 1. The testbed ran on a system with the following hardware and software specifications:

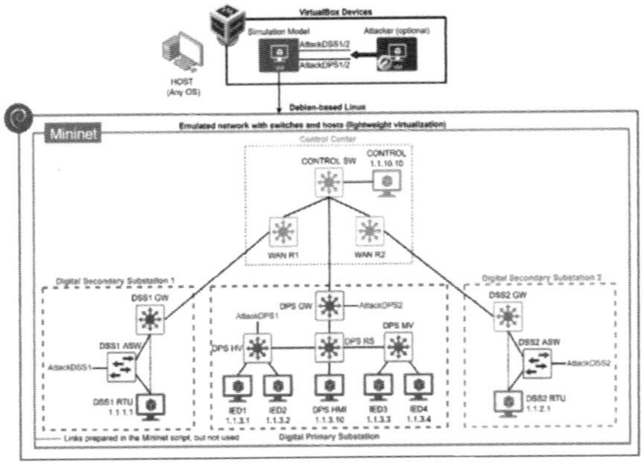

Figure 1. Complete Topology of the Simulator SGSim [16].

- Hardware: Intel Core i7-9700K processor, 16 GB RAM, NVIDIA GTX 1080 GPU.
- Software: The emulator ran on Ubuntu 20.04, and the machine learning algorithms were implemented using Python 3.8 with Scikit-learn 0.24.2 for the model training and evaluation. Wireshark (v3.4.5) and Tshark were used for data capture and conversion to CSV format.

These specifications ensure the results are reproducible in similar environments, and provide a foundation for researchers looking to replicate or extend this work.

B. Data Collection

The dataset used for this experiment was generated based on the topology as shown in Figure 1. It consisted of the components listed in the previous section where the IED communicate with each other using the GOOSE and/or SV protocol defined in the IEC 61850 standard. GOOSE and/or SV network packets were generated to represent normal and attack scenarios. A comprehensive approach was taken to identify and mitigate DoS attacks through machine learning models, setting the stage for experimental findings. By leveraging the unique features of GOOSE and SV messages, it becomes possible to detect anomalies and protect digital substations more effectively.

Table I shows the basic features of a GOOSE message [17]. These features are extracted from network packet headers and can be observed in captured messages, for example, using the Wireshark tool [18]. The first two columns show the feature name and its description, while the last column refers to the protocol analyzer name 'tshark' [19], which reads previously captured network files and decodes those packets to the standard output (Comma-Separated Value (CSV) files). These CSV files are then used in machine learning algorithms, as described in further sections.

Similarly, Table II presents the basic features of an SV message [20]. These features are also extracted from network packet headers and can be observed in captured messages using Wireshark [18]. These features laid the groundwork for analyzing GOOSE and SV messages to identify anomalies

TABLE I
BASIC FEATURES OF GOOSE MESSAGES.

Feature Name	Description	tshark Name
GOOSE APPID	Application identification	goose.appid
GOOSE Length	GOOSE message length	goose.length
GOOSE gocbRef	GOOSE control block reference	goose.gocbRef
GOOSE TTL	Maximum wait time for message	goose.timeAllowedtoLive
GOOSE dataset	Object reference of control block	goose.datSet
GOOSE goID	GOOSE message identification	goose.goID
GOOSE time	Time to stNum increase	goose.t
GOOSE stNum	Status number	goose.stNum
GOOSE sqNum	Sequence number	goose.sqNum
GOOSE confRev	Configuration revision	goose.confRev
GOOSE numDataSetEntries	Number of dataset entries	goose.numDatSetEntries
GOOSE data	Variable sensor data	goose.data
Time of packet	Time of packet recording	frame.time
Time interval	Time interval from the previous packet	frame.time_delta
Interval_between_devices	Time interval between use of field devices	NA
Interval_between_state_info	Time interval between control command or state information retrieval	NA

TABLE II
BASIC FEATURES OF SV MESSAGES.

Feature Name	Description	tshark Name
SV APPID	Application Identification	sv.appid
SV Length	SV message length	sv.length
SV svID	SV message identifier	sv.svID
SV smpCnt	Sample count	sv.smpCnt
SV confRev	Configuration revision	sv.confRev
SV smpSynch	Sample synchronization	sv.smpSynch
SV datSet	Data set reference	sv.datSet
SV smpRate	Sample rate	sv.smpRate
SV time	Time of sample	sv.time
SV data	Sampled data values	sv.data
Time of packet	Time of packet recording	frame.time
Time interval	Time interval from the previous packet	frame.time_delta
Interval_between_devices	Time interval between use of field devices	NA
Interval_between_state_info	Time interval between control command or state information retrieval	NA

and potential DoS attacks. By converting these features into CSV files using 'shark' [19], machine learning algorithms can process them to train and assess models, thus establishing a solid framework for securing IEC 61850-based digital substations. With data collection complete, our next step was to define the scenarios and how to process the data.

C. Scenarios and Data Preprocessing

The GOOSE and SV protocols, part of the IEC 61850 standards, are critical for real-time data exchange and event-triggered messaging, essential for substation automation and control. In this setup, both protocols were utilized to simulate a realistic substation communication environment, with specific scenarios designed to evaluate normal operations and potential attack conditions. These scenarios allowed us to create a comprehensive dataset that includes both normal and attack conditions, ensuring our models could learn and generalize well. The data preprocessing steps were crucial in transforming raw data into a structured format suitable for machine learning.

1) Normal and Attack Scenarios: The following scenarios were developed to assess the performance of machine learning algorithms in identifying DoS attacks within IEC 61850 protocols (GOOSE and SV messages).

a) Normal Scenario: Two types of normal traffic scenarios were utilized to establish baseline data for the models:

- Normal Traffic: This scenario portrays the typical communication load within a substation, including the regular exchange of GOOSE and SV messages between Intelligent Electronic Devices (IEDs), substations, and the control center.
- Increased Traffic (2 times): This scenario simulates a higher load of normal traffic, doubling the amount of regular communication. It tests the performance of the models under heavier but legitimate communication loads. Both traffic scenarios were evaluated by considering three types of messages:
- GOOSE-only: Messages exclusively using the GOOSE protocol, typically employed for event-driven communication like protection relay signaling.
- SV-only: Messages exclusively using the SV protocol, often used for transmitting sampled measurement values from the primary equipment.
- GOOSE + SV: Combined traffic of both GOOSE and SV messages, representing a comprehensive communication environment within a substation.

b) Attack Scenario: Three types of attack scenarios were designed, each characterized by an increasing amount of malicious traffic, to assess the models' ability to detect threats under different levels of stress. These scenarios were:

- 4 times the amount of normal traffic: This scenario represents a moderate DoS attack, with the traffic load quadrupled compared to normal conditions. It tests the models' capability to detect early signs of an attack.
- 5 times the amount of normal traffic: This scenario represents a severe DoS attack, with the traffic load quintupled. It assesses the performance of the models under significant attack conditions.
- 6 times the amount of normal traffic: This scenario represents an extreme DoS attack, with the traffic load increased sixfold. It tests the models' limits in detecting and responding to very high levels of malicious traffic.

Due to simulator constraints, it was nearly impossible to generate combined GOOSE + SV traffic for the 6 times scenario. Each scenario was carefully monitored to ensure the integrity and accuracy of the data collected, providing a robust foundation for the subsequent data preprocessing steps.

2) Data Preprocessing Steps: Once the GOOSE and SV messages features were identified from the literature, the next step in the experiment was to pre-process the data collected using Wireshark [18]. The following are the main steps involved in the experiment for this process:

1) Identify relevant features required for the experiment from GOOSE and SV messages. It was found that in this experiment, only the following features were found relevant: Source, Destination, Timestamp, Length.
2) Use of 'tshark' scripts to convert wireshark files (pcap format) to machine learning readable format (csv).
3) Label data rows (0 for normal and 1 for attack). This labelling is done manually based on the context of the data, if it was during the attack or normal scenario.
4) Use feature engineering. A new feature named Timediff was introduced in the experiment, representing the time difference between two packets from the same protocol. This feature was designed to aid the model in understanding the relationship between these features and the target variable.
5) Scaling the values of each column.
6) Training different algorithms as mentioned in the next section.

These preprocessing steps ensured that the data was in a suitable format for training and evaluating machine learning models. With the data prepared, we then proceeded to the next phase of our experiment: employing machine learning algorithms to detect anomalies.

D. Machine Learning Based Anomaly Detection

Machine learning is a field that focuses on computational algorithms that can learn from their environment by mimicking human intelligence [21]. It can be divided into three modes of operation: Supervised, Unsupervised, and Semi-Supervised. In supervised learning, both the training and test datasets are labeled. The experiment utilized labeled datasets. The primary advantage of using machine learning in this context was that it allows for the detection of attacks without the need for a packet rate threshold. Thus, when raw GOOSE and SV messages were received, the system could extract relevant features and classify them as either an intrusion or normal event based on these trained models.

As mentioned in the previous section, attack-free data was initially generated using the experimental setup. This data was captured using Wireshark, after which the attack data was produced using the same setup. GOOSE and SV messages were extracted from the captured data for training various machine learning algorithms. The effectiveness of the proposed anomaly detection system was evaluated by introducing DoS attacks.

The following machine learning and deep learning models were employed in the experiment:

- Random Forest Classifier (RFC): This is an ensemble learning method for classification, which aggregates the results of multiple decision trees built on different subsamples of the training data.
- Support Vector Machines (SVM): This is a supervised learning algorithm used for classification and regression. It separates data into classes by finding the hyperplane in a high-dimensional space.
- Neural Network: We used the MLPClassifier from scikit-learn, a Neural Network model for Multi-Layer Perceptron (MLP) classification. It has parameters for the number of

hidden layers, activation functions, solver, and regularization, among others.
- K-Nearest Neighbors (KNN): This is a non-parametric, instance-based, supervised learning algorithm that classifies data points based on the majority class of its k-nearest neighbours in the feature space.
- Logistic Regression: This is a statistical method for binary and multi-class classification that models the relationship between the dependent variable and independent variables using a logistic function.
- Gradient Boosting: This is an ensemble machine learning technique that combines the predictions of multiple weak models to make a strong prediction using a gradient descent optimization algorithm.
- Decision Trees (DTs): This is a non-parametric supervised learning method used for classification and regression. It aims to create a model that predicts the value of a target variable by learning simple decision rules inferred from the data features.
- Voting Classifier: This machine learning model trains on a collection of several models and predicts an output (class) based on the class with the highest likelihood of becoming the output. The models used were LogisticRegression, DecisionTreeClassifier, SVC, MLPClassifier, and RandomForestClassifier. These choices will be explained in the results section.

For each machine learning model, we tuned key hyperparameters to optimize performance. For the Random Forest Classifier, we evaluated various values for the number of estimators, ranging from 50 to 200, and found that 100 estimators provided the best balance between accuracy and computational efficiency. Similarly, for Support Vector Machines, we adjusted the kernel function (linear, Radial Basic Function (RBF)), with RBF yielding the best results for our dataset. The hyperparameter tuning process was conducted using a grid search cross-validation, ensuring that each model's configuration was optimized for both accuracy and training time. These choices improved model robustness and reliability in detecting anomalies. Also, the 'train-test-split' function from the 'scikit-learn' library [22] was utilized to test the machine learning algorithms on 20% of the data points, which were randomly selected. The results from testing these algorithms are presented in the following section.

IV. Results

This section presents the outcomes of our experiments, evaluating the performance of various machine learning algorithms in detecting DoS attacks within IEC 61850 protocols. Different datasets were created using a simulated environment that mimics real-world substation conditions, including IEDs, gateways, control centers, and network communication protocols like GOOSE and SV. This setup allows for the introduction and monitoring of cyberattacks, providing a valuable data source for training and testing machine learning models. During the experiment, normal data was classified as 0, while attack data was classified as 1. We compared the best results with other models using various metrics, including training time, precision, recall, F1-Score, and accuracy. These metrics allowed us to evaluate the performance of different machine learning algorithms and identify the most effective approach for detecting DoS attacks in the dataset.

A. Complete dataset

Figure 2 presents the results of the various machine learning and deep learning algorithms described in the previous section, but only for those that produced good results. Some algorithms were biased or unable to draw conclusions. This may be due to the fact that during our experiment, the source and destination IP addresses were the same for each packet, which made class prediction more difficult.

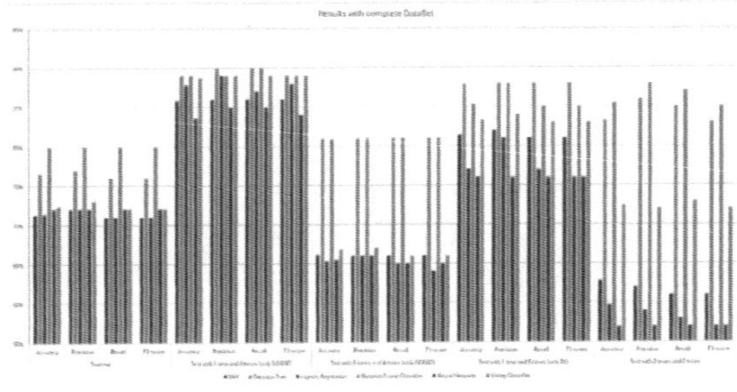

Figure 2. Results of the training and tests for different models.

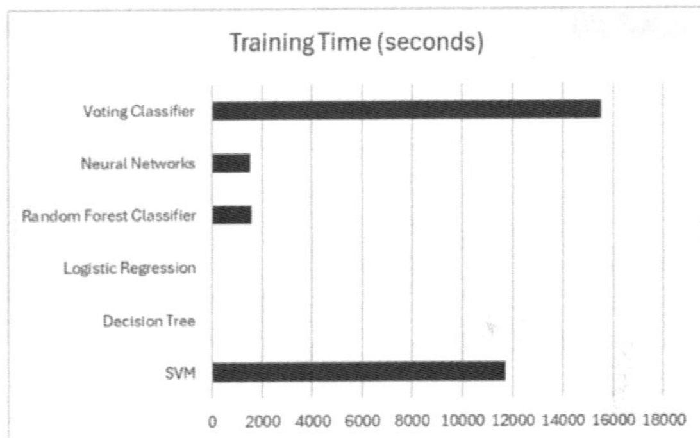

Figure 3. Time needed for different models to train on the dataset.

- Training Performance:
  - Random Forest Classifier: Achieved the highest training accuracy (79.95%) and F1-score (0.80), indicating strong learning capabilities from the training data.
  - Decision Tree: Showed an accuracy of 76.54% and an F1-score of 0.76, performing well but slightly less effective than Random Forest.
  - Voting Classifier: Demonstrated a 72.37% accuracy and a 0.72 F1-score, highlighting the effectiveness of combining multiple models.
  - Neural Networks, SVM, and Logistic Regression: Had similar performances with accuracies around 71-72% and F1-scores of 0.71-0.72.
- Testing Performance:

  - 1 Time and 6 Times GOOSE: Decision Tree and Random Forest led with accuracies of 89.07% and 89.06%, respectively, followed closely by Voting Classifier at 88.73%.
  - 2 Times and 4 Times GOOSE: Decision Tree and Random Forest were again the top performers with accuracies around 80.91%, whereas Voting Classifier dropped to 66.76%. SVM, Neural Networks, and Logistic Regression lagged behind.
  - 1 Time and 5 Times SV: Decision Tree achieved the highest accuracy of 87.86%, with Random Forest closely following at 85.30%. SVM and Neural Networks performed moderately well, while Logistic Regression trailed.
  - 3 Times and 5 Times: Random Forest excelled with 85.40% accuracy, while Decision Tree and Voting Classifier performed moderately.
- Training Time as shown in Figure 3:
  - SVM had the longest training time, making it less practical for quick deployments.
  - Decision Tree and Logistic Regression had the shortest training times, suitable for real-time applications.
  - Random Forest, Neural Networks, and Voting Classifier had moderate training times.

To summarize, Random Forest Classifier and Decision Tree consistently provided the best performance across various test scenarios, making them suitable choices for detecting DoS attacks in IEC 61850 protocols. The Voting Classifier also demonstrated strong performance by combining the strengths of multiple models. Neural Networks performed well in some scenarios but not as consistently as tree-based methods. SVM and Logistic Regression had mixed results and might not be the best choices considering SVM's longer training times and Logistic Regression's lower performance. Training time is a critical factor, with Decision Tree and Logistic Regression offering the quickest training, which can be advantageous for real-time or iterative model updates.

B. Incomplete dataset

For the incomplete dataset scenario, the data was halved to evaluate the models' performance with limited data. This helps assess the robustness of models when less data is available for training and testing. The results are shown in Figure 4. Previous models not represented here are missing because they gave the same results as before.

- Training Performance:
  - Voting Classifier: Achieved higher training accuracy (84.11%) compared to SVM (82.25%), with slightly better precision, recall, and F1-scores.
  - SVM: Although slightly lower in training accuracy, it excelled in testing scenarios.
- Testing Performance:
  - 1 Time and 6 Times GOOSE: SVM showed near-perfect performance with 99.74% accuracy, and perfect precision, recall, and F1-score. Voting Classifier also performed well with 98.18% accuracy.
  - 2 Times and 4 Times GOOSE: SVM outperformed Voting Classifier with 91.51% accuracy, while Voting Classifier struggled significantly in this scenario.
  - 1 Time and 5 Times SV: SVM continued its strong performance with 92.32% accuracy. Voting Classifier was slightly lower but still respectable.
  - 3 Times and 5 Times: SVM maintained good performance with 85.25% accuracy, while Voting Classifier showed a significant drop in performance.
- Training Time as shown in Figure 5:
  - Both models showed efficient training times compared to the complete dataset, with SVM being faster than the Voting Classifier.

SVM is highly recommended for detecting DoS attacks in IEC 61850 protocols due to its consistent high accuracy, precision, recall, and F1-score across various test scenarios. The Voting Classifier also shows potential but may need further tuning to handle specific test scenarios more effectively and reduce the training time. The reduced dataset indicates that SVM can handle limited data availability well, while the Voting Classifier's performance is more variable, potentially overfitting the larger dataset.

The findings from both datasets highlight the importance of

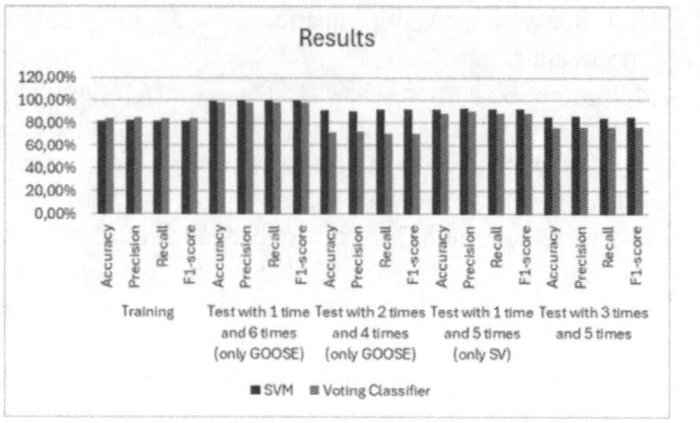

Figure 4. Results of the training and tests for 2 models with incomplete dataset.

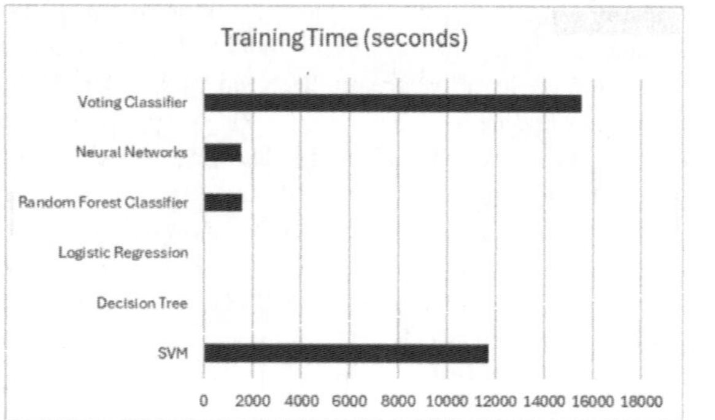

Figure 5. Time needed for models to train on the incomplete dataset.

selecting appropriate machine learning models based on data availability and specific application scenarios. The Random Forest and Decision Tree models perform exceptionally well with a complete dataset, while SVM excels in scenarios with limited data. This suggests that different models may be preferred depending on the operational context and data constraints in digital substations.

V. Discussion

The goal of this study is to evaluate the effectiveness of machine learning models in detecting DoS attacks in digital substations using IEC 61850 protocols. The Random Forest and Decision Tree classifiers showed superior detection capabilities with accuracies of 84.12% and 83.52%, respectively, while SVM excelled with limited data, achieving nearly perfect accuracy in some scenarios. Tree-based models like the Random Forest and Decision Tree are effective in detecting DoS attacks with comprehensive datasets, while SVM shows high accuracy and efficiency with limited data. These findings support the use of tailored intrusion detection systems in digital substations to enhance power grid resilience against cyber threats.

These findings also have several important implications for cybersecurity in smart grid systems. The robust performance of tree-based methods suggests that these should be primary choices for developing intrusion detection systems within smart grid environments. Their ability to perform well consistently across different scenarios also highlights their potential for deployment in diverse operational contexts. The variability observed in ensemble methods like the Voting Classifier points to the potential benefits and challenges of such approaches. While they can offer improved accuracy by combining different models, their effectiveness is highly dependent on the correct alignment and tuning of individual models. Additionally, the significant role of feature engineering, as demonstrated by the inclusion of the TimeDiff feature, cannot be understated. It highlights the need for domain-specific knowledge in enhancing model performance, which is crucial for detecting sophisticated cyber threats.

The computational complexity of the proposed methods was evaluated in terms of both time and space. The Decision Tree and Random Forest models demonstrated relatively efficient training times, with the Decision Tree being the fastest due to its greedy algorithmic approach. Memory consumption, measured during the training phase, showed that ensemble methods like Random Forest and Voting Classifier consumed significantly more memory compared to simpler models like Logistic Regression. However, these methods also provided superior performance in terms of accuracy. The space complexity scales with the depth of trees in tree-based models, where deeper trees require more memory but yield better results. These findings suggest that while the models are computationally more demanding, their enhanced detection capabilities justify the overhead in real-world applications.

Our study's findings align with existing literature that underscores the effectiveness of tree-based methods in network intrusion detection. Studies in [23] and [24] support our observations, noting the superiority of these methods in various cybersecurity applications. However, our research contributes unique insights by focusing specifically on the IEC 61850 protocols and providing a detailed analysis of performance under simulated attack scenarios that mimic real-world conditions. This protocol-specific focus and the comprehensive evaluation of model performance under different traffic conditions offer new contributions to the field of smart grid cybersecurity.

Moreover, our findings align with [5], which analyzed vulnerabilities in power systems. Our study complements the work by providing empirical evidence of the efficacy of machine learning models in mitigating these vulnerabilities, particularly against DoS attacks. Unlike the traditional methods discussed in [6], which focus on cybersecurity challenges at a theoretical level, our approach uses machine learning for practical intrusion detection. This advancement highlights the importance of integrating advanced analytics into cybersecurity frameworks, a theme also echoed by authors in [7], in their exploration of network anomaly detection.

Despite these contributions, our study is not without limitations. The inability to generate combined GOOSE and SV traffic for the most intense attack scenarios due to simulator constraints may have affected the comprehensiveness of our evaluation. Additionally, the potential exists for further enhancing model performance through more extensive feature engineering and the exploration of additional machine learning models, including deep learning architectures which were not included in this study. Lastly, the necessity for real-world validation remains, as our experiments were conducted in a simulated environment, which, while controlled and informative, may not fully capture the complexities of operational smart grid systems.

This study enhances cybersecurity by demonstrating how machine learning models can improve intrusion detection systems in digital substations. It provides a framework for selecting suitable algorithms based on data and context, advancing the understanding of machine learning in cybersecurity and offering practical solutions for protecting critical infrastructure. The demonstrated effectiveness of the Random Forest Classifier and Decision Tree offers a promising avenue for future research and practical implementations aimed at strengthening the cybersecurity postures of smart grid systems.

VI. Conclusion

This study focused on evaluating the performance of various machine learning algorithms in detecting DoS attacks within IEC 61850 protocols, specifically GOOSE and SV messages. The Random Forest Classifier and Decision Tree models were identified as the most effective models due to their high accuracy and reliability in detecting DoS attacks in IEC 61850 protocols, accompanied by reasonable training times. However, the SVM model outperforms others in this comparison due to its robust performance, even when trained with half of the data. The Voting Classifier also holds potential but may require further enhancements to achieve the consistency of the

SVM model. These findings underscore the potential of tree-based methods for real-time anomaly detection in smart grid communications, providing a reliable approach to enhancing cybersecurity measures in substation automation systems.

Future research should focus on overcoming simulator constraints to evaluate models under more extensive attack scenarios, exploring a broader set of machine learning algorithms, and conducting real-world validations. Expanding the feature set and refining model parameters could further enhance detection capabilities. The insights gained from this study offer valuable directions for advancing the security frameworks of smart grid systems, ensuring their resilience against sophisticated cyber threats.

REFERENCES

[1] T. Xu *et al.*, "Analysis on iec 61850 interoperability support", in *2007 IEEE Power Engineering Society General Meeting*, 2007, pp. 1–6. DOI: 10.1109/PES.2007.386057.

[2] G. Elbez, H. Keller, A. Bohara, K. Nahrstedt, and V. Hagenmeyer, "Detection of dos attacks using arfima modeling of goose communication in iec 61850 substations", *Energies*, vol. 13, no. 19, p. 5176, 2020. DOI: 10.3390/en13195176.

[3] L. O. Nweke, "A survey of specification-based intrusion detection techniques for cyber-physical systems", *International Journal of Advanced Computer Science and Applications*, vol. 12, no. 5, 2021, ISSN: 2158-107X. DOI: 10.14569/ijacsa.2021.0120506.

[4] D. Abraham, S. Y. Yayilgan, F. Holík, S. Acevedo, and A. Gebremedhin, "Cyber attack simulation and detection in digital substation", in *2023 IEEE International Conference on Smart Cities, Cybernetics, and Computational Intelligence (ICSCCC)*, 2023, pp. 762–768. DOI: 10.1109/ICSCCC58608.2023.10176955.

[5] V. S. Rajkumar, M. Tealane, A. Ştefanov, A. Presekal, and P. Palensky, "Cyber attacks on power system automation and protection and impact analysis", in *2020 IEEE PES Innovative Smart Grid Technologies Europe (ISGT-Europe)*, 2020, pp. 247–254. DOI: 10.1109/ISGT-Europe47291.2020.9248840.

[6] I. Kolosok and E. Korkina, "Problems of cyber security of digital substations", in *Proceedings of the 3rd International Workshop on Computer Intelligence (IWCI-19)*, 2019, pp. 75–78. DOI: 10.2991/iwci-19.2019.13.

[7] H. Yoo and T. Shon, "Novel approach for detecting network anomalies for substation automation based on iec 61850", *Multimedia Tools and Applications*, vol. 74, pp. 303–318, 2014. DOI: 10.1007/s11042-014-1870-0.

[8] W. Wang and Z. Lu, "Cyber security in the smart grid: Survey and challenges", *Computer Networks*, vol. 57, pp. 1344–1371, 2013. DOI: 10.1016/j.comnet.2012.12.017.

[9] S. Quincozes, C. Albuquerque, D. Passos, and D. Mossé, "A survey on intrusion detection and prevention systems in digital substations", *Computer Networks*, vol. 184, p. 107 679, 2021. DOI: 10.1016/j.comnet.2020.107679.

[10] Z. Lu, X. Lu, W. Wang, and C. Wang, "Review and evaluation of security threats on the communication networks in the smart grid", in *2010 IEEE Military Communications Conference*, 2010, pp. 1830–1835. DOI: 10.1109/MILCOM.2010.5679551.

[11] S. Ashraf, M. H. Shawon, H. M. Khalid, and S. Muyeen, "Denial-of-service attack on iec 61850-based substation automation system: A crucial cyber threat towards smart substation pathways", *Sensors*, vol. 21, no. 19, p. 6415, 2021. DOI: 10.3390/s21196415.

[12] M. Elrawy, L. Hadjidemetriou, C. Laoudias, and M. Michael, "Light-weight and robust network intrusion detection for cyber-attacks in digital substations", in *2021 IEEE Innovative Smart Grid Technologies Asia (ISGT Asia)*, 2022, pp. 1–5. DOI: 10.1109/ISGTAsia49270.2021.9715626.

[13] U. Premaratne, J. Samarabandu, T. Sidhu, R. Beresh, and J.-C. Tan, "An intrusion detection system for iec 61850 automated substations", *IEEE Transactions on Power Delivery*, vol. 25, pp. 2376–2383, 2010. DOI: 10.1109/TPWRD.2010.2050076.

[14] J. Zhang, Y. Chen, N. Jin, L. Hou, and Q. Zhang, "Opnet based simulation modeling and analysis of dos attack for digital substation", in *2017 IEEE Power & Energy Society General Meeting*, 2017, pp. 1–5. DOI: 10.1109/PESGM.2017.8274254.

[15] I. Kharchouf, M. Abdelrahman, A. Alrashide, and O. Mohammed, "Assessment of protection schemes and their security under denial of service attacks", in *2022 IEEE International Conference on Environment and Electrical Engineering and 2022 IEEE Industrial and Commercial Power Systems Europe (EEEIC/I&CPS Europe)*, 2022, pp. 1–6. DOI: 10.1109/EEEIC/ICPSEurope54979.2022.9854745.

[16] F. Holík, S. Y. Yayilgan, and G. Olsborg, "Emulation of digital substations communication for cyber security awareness", *Electronics*, vol. 13, no. 12, p. 2318, 2024. DOI: 10.3390/electronics13122318.

[17] O. Hegazi, E. Hammad, A. Farraj, and D. Kundur, "Iec 61850 goose traffic modeling and generation", in *2017 IEEE Global Conference on Signal and Information Processing (GlobalSIP)*, 2017, pp. 1100–1104. DOI: 10.1109/GlobalSIP.2017.8309131.

[18] Wireshark, *About wireshark*, https://www.wireshark.org/, retrived: October, 2024.

[19] Tshark, *Tshark manual page*, https://www.wireshark.org/docs/man-pages/tshark.html, retrived: October, 2024.

[20] Typhoon Hill, *Iec 61850 sampled values protocol*, https://www.typhoon-hil.com, retrived: October, 2024.

[21] I. El Naqa and M. Murphy, "What is machine learning?", in *Machine Learning in Radiation Oncology*, 2015, pp. 3–11. DOI: 10.1007/978-3-319-18305-3_1.

[22] F. Pedregosa *et al.*, "Scikit-learn: Machine learning in python", *Journal of Machine Learning Research*, vol. 12, pp. 2825–2830, 2011.

[23] M. A. Bouke, A. Abdullah, S. H. ALshatebi, M. T. Abdullah, and H. E. Atigh, "An intelligent ddos attack detection tree-based model using gini index feature selection method", *Microprocessors and Microsystems*, vol. 98, p. 104 823, Apr. 2023, ISSN: 0141-9331. DOI: 10.1016/j.micpro.2023.104823.

[24] A. Coscia, V. Dentamaro, S. Galantucci, A. Maci, and G. Pirlo, "Automatic decision tree-based nidps ruleset generation for dos/ddos attacks", *Journal of Information Security and Applications*, vol. 82, p. 103 736, May 2024, ISSN: 2214-2126. DOI: 10.1016/j.jisa.2024.103736.

[25] D. Faquir, N. Chouliaras, V. Sofia, K. Olga, and L. Maglaras, "Cybersecurity in smart grids, challenges and solutions", *AIMS Electronics and Electrical Engineering*, vol. 5, no. 1, pp. 24–37, 2021. DOI: 10.3934/electreng.2021002.

[26] T. A. Youssef, M. El Hariri, N. Bugay, and O. A. Mohammed, "Iec 61850: Technology standards and cyber-threats", in *2016 IEEE 16th International Conference on Environment and Electrical Engineering (EEEIC)*, Florence, Italy, 2016, pp. 1–6.

[27] P. Srikantha and D. Kundur, "Denial of service attacks and mitigation for stability in cyber-enabled power grid", in *2015 IEEE Power and Energy Society Innovative Smart Grid Technologies Conference (ISGT)*, 2015, pp. 1–5.

Framework for Quantum Identity Wallets

Javaid Iqbal Zahid
Toronto Metropolitan University
Toronto, Canada
Email: javaid.iqbal@torontomu.ca

Dr. Alex Ferworn
Toronto Metropolitan University
Toronto, Canada
Email: aferworn@torontomu.ca

Dr. Fatima Hussain
Toronto Metropolitan University
Toronto, Canada
Email: fatima.hussain@torontomu.ca

Abstract—**Self-Sovereign Identity (SSI) is a relatively new framework for authentication of entities on the Internet. It is based on distributed peer-to-peer networking, a departure from centralized and federated identity management systems currently in practice. Security of SSI, as well as any information exchange using Internet, is based on Public-key cryptography,for example, Rivest-Shamir-Adleman (RSA) algorithm. Emerging Quantum Computing is a threat to public-key cryptography and needs to be upgraded either using post-quantum cryptography or using the principles of quantum computing. In this research, we propose a quantum digital identity storage framework in the form of "quantum digital wallets", using quantum cryptography approach that will be secure from attacks by quantum computers.**
Keywords: Self-Sovereign Identity, Digital Wallet, Verifiable Credentials, Public-key Cryptography, Quantum Cryptography, RSA, Peer-to-Peer Network.

I. Introduction

Digital wallet, an important component of Self-Sovereign Identity (SSI), is a kind of secure storage system along with an agent that facilitates messaging and communication protocols between peers [1]. Digital wallet can contain information belonging to and controlled by its user. The user information might contain, decentralized identifiers, verifiable credentials, digital copies of passports, driving licenses, birth certificates, diplomas, business cards, vaccination certificate/tokens, resumes, biographical information, usernames, passwords, or any other information of interest that a user might like to keep it in the wallet. Digital wallet is designed based on the principles of portability and openness by default, consent-driven, privacy-by-design, and security-by-design. The architecture of digital wallet is based on two major components; Secure Storage and Agent. The functions of these components are shown in Figure 1.

Quantum computing exploits the principles of quantum mechanics to perform information processing and transmission of information. Quantum information processing is an exciting and new research area with numerous applications, including quantum key generation and distribution, quantum teleportation, quantum computing, quantum lithography, and quantum memories. Quantum computers are expected to outperform the existing classical computing as it exploits the quantum principles of linear superposition, entanglement, and quantum parallelism. Linear superposition, contrary to the classical bit where only two distinct values 0 or 1 are allowed, allows quantum bit, or qubit, to take all possible linearly combined values. Quantum parallelism allows a large number of operations in parallel, can process multiple inputs simultaneously

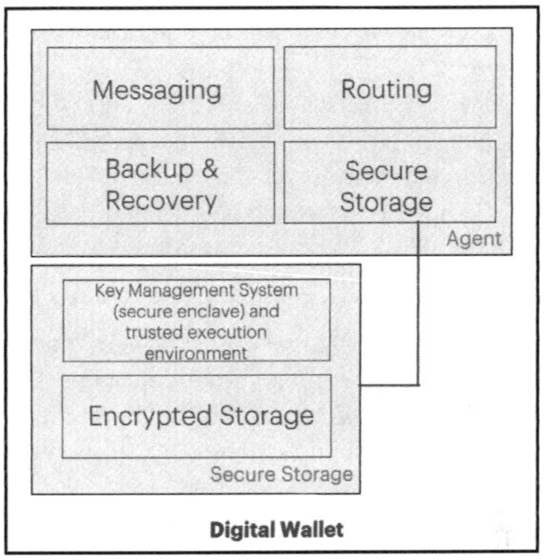

Fig. 1. Architecture of a Digital Wallet.

representing a major difference between classical and quantum [2]. Quantum technology is complex and multidisciplinary in nature, that requires expertise in physics, computer science, materials science, and other fields. We use quantum technology to design digital wallet.

In section II, we outline the objectives of the proposal, and in section III we describe the proposed framework. Finally, we conclude the paper in section IV.

II. Objective and Proposal

The primary objective of the proposed research on Quantum Digital Identity Wallet (QDIW) is to design an architecture and reference framework for promoting trusted digital identities for users to be in control of their own online transactions and presence. SSI and its digital wallet plays an important role to achieve self control. These wallets can be used for identification, authentication, and authorization services by various organizations. Driven by new technologies and standards in cryptography, distributed networks, cloud computing and smart phones, SSI is a paradigm shift for digital identity. The core of SSI security is based on classical public-key cryptosystems (like RSA) [3]. This is provably breakable when universal quantum computing is available [4]. Therefore, it is necessary to direct our research to design quantum digital identity wallet (QDIW) as a preamptive trustworthy service. It will facilitate the creation of encrypted containers or "identity wallets". It is the right time to rethink the design of SSI schemes based on quantum computing. This will ensure a quantum-resistant SSI.

Specific objectives of this research proposal are as follows:

1) Explore and examine proposals, on digital identity wallet (if any) from national or international standards bodies, and draw operational and technical requirements/specifications for implementation of digital wallet using quantum technologies.
2) Develop architectural framework with use cases for prototyping the QDIW that will help is achieving following goals:
   a) Provide consumers with a WDIW that complies with the human rights principles of preserving people's privacy and control over their information.
   b) Counter Cyber Security threats using trusted and secure QDIW.

III. Proposed Quantum Identity Frame work

We intend to develop a set of algorithms that can take advantage of the unique properties of quantum systems to achieve high-security protection using the wallet concept. Essentially, the sequence of our objectives is as follows:

- Create a structure of digital identity
- Convert the structure into classical information bits
- Map the classical information bits into quantum bit (qubits)
- Develop a process (a quantum algorithm) to encrypt and sign this quantum digital identity
- Develop a procedure to securely share the quantum bits (teleportation) between two communicating parties over classical and quantum channels, while maintaining suitable authentication process.

A. Implementation and Test Bed

In table 1, we outline the project activities, milestones, deliverables, and timeline for the project. The software implementation of the quantum digital wallet is based on Python and Qiskit (IBM). The implementation consist of a *class Wallet* with few instance variables related to some personal attributes of people. Objects of *Wallet* are created, sample from the attributes is selected, and is converted to binary format. This binary information is mapped to quantum bits (qubits) in an initialization process. Further processing of qubits is performed to show the possibility of having secure storage using functions, such as; shifting, transposing, encryption and hashing. Some algebraic processing (inner product, outer product, tensor product, finding density matrix, decimal-to-binary, binary-to-decimal conversion, random quantum state generation, calculation of Shannon entropy, and Linear entropy) would also be needed. The process is shown in Figure 2. 2.

TABLE I
Detailed Research Plan

Objectives	Description
Literature Review on SSI	Comprehensive review of existing literature on SSI schemes (strengths and weakness), and quantum computing.
Identification and Evaluation of Relevant Technologies	Process of selecting relevant and suitable quantum computing, quantum communication, and quantum cryptography approaches to implement SSI.
Development of a Proof of Concepts (PoC)	Design and implement a prototype to prove the viability of designed SSI architecture.
Analysis of Results from PoC	Analysis of effectiveness of our architecture based on the results obtained from PoC.
Assessment of Social Impact	Assessment of the impact of technology on data privacy, protection of individual rights, and other consequences.

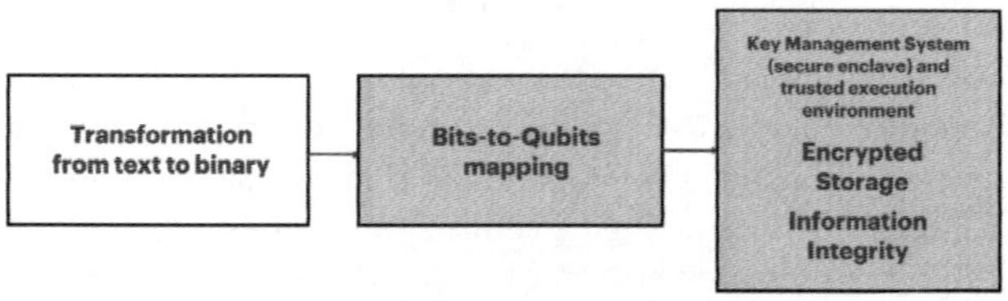

Fig. 2. Quantum Information Processing.

IV. Conclusion

Quantum algorithms hold great promise for solving complex problems, however, many technical and practical challenges need to be overcome before they can be widely adopted. Implementation of quantum algorithms is difficult because of the fragility of quantum systems as quantum hardware and software is still in its early stages of development and is not yet scalable or fault-tolerant enough for practical applications. Furthermore, qubits are highly sensitive to their environment and can easily become de-cohered, resulting in errors and loss of quantum information. Quantum algorithms also require significant expertise in both quantum mechanics and computer science, which is also not very common.

References

[1] A. Preukschat and D. Reed, *Self-Sovereign Identity*. Manning Publishing Co., 2021.

[2] M. A. Nielsen and I. L. Chuang, *Quantum Computing and Quantum Information*. Cambridge University Press, 2010.

[3] A. S. R. L. Rivest and L. Adleman, "A method for obtaining digital signatures and public key cryptosystem," in *Communications of the ACM*, vol. 21, no. 2, 1978, pp. 120–126.

[4] P. W. Shor, "Polynomial-time algorithm for prime factorization and discrete logarithms on a quantum computer," in *SIAM Journal on Computing*, vol. 26, no. 5, October 1997, pp. 1484–1509.

Evaluating the Robustness of Kolmogorov-Arnold Networks against Noise and Adversarial Attacks

Evgenii Ostanin
Toronto Metropolitan University
Toronto, Canada
email:eostanin@torontomu.ca

Nebojsa Djosic
Toronto Metropolitan University
Toronto, Canada
email:nebojsa.djosic@torontomu.ca

Fatima Hussain
Toronto Metropolitan University
Toronto, Canada
email:fatima.hussain@torontomu.ca

Salah Sharieh
Toronto Metropolitan University
Toronto, Canada
email:salah.sharieh@torontomu.ca

Alexander Ferworn
Toronto Metropolitan University
Toronto, Canada
email:aferworn@torontomu.ca

***Abstract*—Kolmogorov-Arnold Networks (KANs) is a new perspective direction in Machine Learning (ML) domain. KANs use spline functions to enhance interpretability and adaptability of the ML models. However, their robustness against Adversarial Attacks (AAs) has not been fully researched. This paper aims to address this gap by evaluating KAN performance under Gaussian noise and AAs, by using the Fast Gradient Sign Method (FGSM) and Projected Gradient Descent (PGD) attacks. The objective of this paper is to assess the comparative robustness of KANs and Multi-Layer Perceptrons (MLPs) when exposed to Gaussian noise and adversarial attacks, aiming to identify areas of improvement for KANs and to provide insights into their performance under real-world, noisy conditions. The results show that KANs achieve higher accuracy than MLPs in a clean environment. At the same time, KANs demonstrate noticeable reduction in accuracy under conditions where increased noise and adversarial perturbations are present. KANs experience a more substantial accuracy drop under FGSM and PGD attacks compared to MLPs, which reveals critical areas for improvement and further research. The sensitivity of KANs to Gaussian noise further highlights their limitations in real-world scenarios. These findings underscore the need for further research to develop more resilient KAN architectures and better understand their role in secure ML systems.**

Keywords-Kolmogorov-Arnold Network, KAN, MLP, FGSM, PGD, MNIST, Classification.

I. INTRODUCTION

The rapid advancement of Machine Mearning (ML) has led to increasingly sophisticated models that perform well across a variety of tasks. Among these developments, Kolmogorov-Arnold Networks (KANs) represent a novel approach based on the Kolmogorov-Arnold representation theorem. KANs bring a promise to enhance models' interpretability and flexibility. However, the robustness of KANs, particularly to Adversarial Attacks (AAs) and noisy data, has not been thoroughly researched.

Traditional Multi-Layer Perceptrons (MLPs) often struggle with capturing complex nonlinear relationships due to their reliance on fixed activation functions and linear weight matrices. This can lead to limitations in model flexibility and interpretability, making them less effective in handling intricate patterns present in real-world data. Moreover, MLPs can be vulnerable to overfitting and may not generalize well to unseen data, especially under adversarial conditions or noise. To address these challenges, KANs introduce learnable activation functions on edges, replacing static weights with parameterized functions. This architectural shift enhances the model's ability to capture complex, nonlinear relationships, offering improved flexibility and interpretability over traditional MLPs [1].

Robustness of the ML models is an important quality for real-world applications, often characterized by suboptimal conditions. AAs, such as the Fast Gradient Sign Method (FGSM) and Projected Gradient Descent (PGD), exploit the models' vulnerabilities by making small perturbations to input data, while noise can obscure key features and degrade performance.

This paper explores the robustness of KANs compared to MLPs, focusing on their resilience to Gaussian noise and AAs like FGSM and PGD. The goal of this paper is to assess the security and practical limitations of KANs by comparing their performance under various perturbations. All experiments are conducted using the Modified National Institute of Standards and Technology dataset (MNIST) [2], [3], a widely recognized benchmark for evaluating image classification models.

MLPs are selected as a benchmark for comparison because they represent one of the most widely used and established neural network architectures in machine learning. Their simplicity, effectiveness in various tasks, and resistance to adversarial conditions provide a useful baseline for evaluating the performance and robustness of newer, more complex architectures like KANs. Focusing on KANs provides an opportunity to assess a novel architecture that could potentially address some limitations of traditional models, thereby justifying its selection over other alternatives.

The primary objective of this paper is to systematically assess the robustness of KANs compared to traditional MLPs under adversarial conditions. Specifically, this study aims to evaluate how KANs and MLPs perform when exposed to Gaussian noise and AAs, such as the FGSM and PGD. By comparing their resilience across key metrics such as accuracy, precision, recall, and F1-score using the MNIST dataset, the paper seeks to identify the strengths and limitations of KANs in real-world, noisy environments. The findings aim to inform further research and development of more robust KAN architectures for secure machine learning systems.

The remainder of this paper is organized as follows: Section II reviews related work and existing approaches in the field. Section III outlines the methodology, including the experimental setup and evaluation metrics. Section IV presents the results of the experiments, followed by a discussion in Section V. Finally, Section VI concludes the paper and suggests directions for future research.

II. Related Work

KANs are a new neural architecture based on the Kolmogorov-Arnold representation theorem, offering an alternative to traditional MLPs. Instead of fixed activation functions on nodes and linear weight matrices, KANs use learnable activation functions on edges, with each weight replaced by a 1D learnable function parameterized as a spline. This new architecture promises improved accuracy and interpretability compared to traditional MLPs and can find application in various domains [1]. Figure 1 provides a comparative visualization of KANs and MLPs. On the left, the KAN architecture is shown, where the edges represent learnable activation functions, unlike traditional networks. In KANs, nodes perform sum operations across these learned functions, enabling greater flexibility and non-linearity. On the right, the MLP architecture is depicted, where the edges correspond to learnable weights and fixed activation functions are applied at each node. This distinction highlights the novel design of KANs, which replace static activations with adaptive spline functions, allowing for potentially better handling of complex relationships in data compared to MLPs.

	Kolmogorov-Arnold Network	Multi-Layer Perceptron
edges	learnable activation function	learnable weights
nodes	sum operation	fixed activation function
model	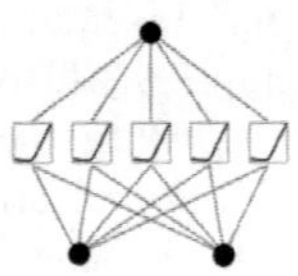	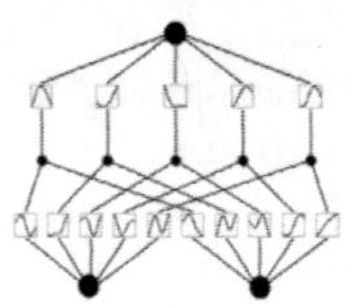

Figure 1. KAN and MLP Architecture, derived from [1]

KANs have been explored in computer vision, where they have been compared to architectures like MLP-Mixer, CNNs, and Vision Transformers. Studies [4]–[6] demonstrate that KANs can achieve competitive accuracy on datasets like CIFAR10 and MNIST while offering benefits in computational efficiency and parameter reduction. However, they sometimes fall short compared to models like ResNet-18, indicating both their potential and limitations.

In time series analysis, KANs have been applied to capture complex temporal patterns and enhance model interpretability. Models like Temporal Kolmogorov-Arnold Transformer (TKAT) [7], Temporal Kolmogorov-Arnold Networks (T-KAN), and Multivariate Temporal Kolmogorov-Arnold Networks (MT-KAN) [8] have shown improved performance in handling multivariate data streams and detecting concept drift. These studies highlight KANs' adaptability and efficiency, particularly in forecasting tasks [9].

However, KANs have limitations that were discussed in several studies. For instance, [10] compares KANs with MLPs and finds that KANs do not always outperform MLPs. KANs can fall behind when dealing with irregular or noisy functions. Both models struggle with noise, and while increasing training data helps, KANs often match, rather than surpass, MLPs in such noisy conditions. [11] further emphasizes KANs' sensitivity to noise, showing that even small amounts can significantly degrade performance. Although oversampling and denoising techniques can mitigate these issues the increased computational cost can become a limiting factor for the practical applications of KANs. Additionally, [12] explores KANs in hardware applications, finding that they fall short of MLPs in complex datasets and require more hardware resources. [5] also concludes that benefits of KANS for more complex datasets like CIFAR-10 are not evident. While KANs excel in capturing complex patterns and promise improvements in interpretability, their vulnerability to noise and ability to handle more complex tasks raises concerns about potential susceptibility to AAs, an area yet to be thoroughly explored.

Recent developments in AAs have focused on refining techniques that exploit vulnerabilities in machine learning models [13]–[16], particularly in computer vision [17], [18]. Two well-researched methods for evaluating model robustness are the FGSM and PGD. FGSM, introduced by [19], generates adversarial examples through small perturbations to input data, which can cause models to make incorrect predictions. PGD, a more iterative and sophisticated method, was introduced by [20] and is now a benchmark for testing resilience against stronger attacks. These methods are particularly impactful in computer vision, where minor input changes can lead to significant shifts in model outputs [21]. Defenses against FGSM and PGD have been explored [22]–[24]. Despite these advancements, FGSM and PGD remain the standard for assessing robustness of ML models.

Tools like the Adversarial Robustness Toolbox (ART) provide methods for crafting adversarial examples and defenses [25], and datasets such as MNIST [2] are frequently used for benchmark adversarial vulnerability across studies. While KANs have been applied to various domains, their resistance to AAs, particularly FGSM and PGD, is largely unexplored. This paper aims to fill that gap, enhancing the understanding of KANs' robustness in adversarial settings.

III. Methodology, Tools and Environment

Methodology: The experiments compare two machine learning models: a KAN and a traditional MLP-based feedforward classifier. Both are trained on the MNIST dataset to maintain consistency. Their robustness is evaluated through various performance metrics under different conditions, including noise and AAs. Model architectures and pre-trained weights remain unchanged throughout the experiments, with only the test data being manipulated for assessment.

Both models are trained using the MNIST dataset [2], [3], which contains samples of handwritten digits. Initial evaluations are conducted on unaltered test data to set a performance baseline. Metrics like accuracy, confusion matrices, precision, recall, and F1-scores are used to assess both models. The same evaluation approach is maintained across all experiments to ensuring uniformity.

Experiments: To test noise sensitivity, Gaussian noise with mean zero and varying standard deviations is added to the test data, with noise levels increasing from 10 to 90 in increments of 10. These standard deviation values represent the intensity of the noise added, simulating conditions from mild to severe distortion. The noise is added to each pixel in the images, introducing variability that can blur edges and obscure important features necessary for accurate classification. This method measures the models' ability to maintain accuracy as the noise level increases, providing insights into each model's robustness in noisy environments To test robustness against FGSM attack, adversarial examples are created by introducing perturbations in input data and applied to both models. The attack's strength is controlled by the epsilon parameter, ranging from 0.1 to 0.8. Models' accuracy degradation is tracked as epsilon increases, showing each model's vulnerability to FGSM attacks. Similarly, the PGD attack, a more iterative adversarial method, is tested with epsilon values between 0.1 and 0.8. This reveals how both models handle stronger attacks. Once the experiments on noise, FGSM, and PGD attacks are completed the results are aggregated to compare the robustness of KAN and the MLP. Table I summarizes a performance comparison of MLP and KAN models under different scenarios. A discussion follows, highlighting key performance strengths and weaknesses under different conditions and further research directions are suggested.

Tools and environment: The MNIST dataset is used throughout the experiments [2], [3], while adversarial examples are generated using the Adversarial Robustness Toolbox (ART) [25]. The KAN implementation is sourced from GitHub repositories [26], [27] and the MLP is implemented using PyTorch and Scikit-learn python libraries. These standardized tools ensure the experiments' reproducibility and reliability.

Models Architectures

The MLP implementation is a feedforward neural network with five hidden layers, each followed by ReLU activation and dropout for regularization. The input is a flattened 28x28 pixel image, resulting in 784 features. The layers progressively reduce in size from 512 to 64 neurons, and the output layer contains 10 neurons for the digit classes. The model uses the AdamW optimizer with a learning rate of 0.001 and weight decay to prevent overfitting. This regularization penalizes larger weight values and encourages the model to maintain smaller weights, which helps prevent overfitting by reducing model complexity and improving generalization to unseen data. An Exponential Learning Rate Scheduler adjusts the learning rate during training, and the CrossEntropyLoss function is used for classification.

The KAN implementation [27] leverages spline-parametrized univariate functions instead of traditional activations, based on the Kolmogorov-Arnold theorem. It begins with a 784-feature input layer, followed by two KANLinear layers, which transform the features using spline-based activations. The first KANLinear layer outputs 1569 units, while the second produces 10 units corresponding to the digit classes. The model includes customizable spline parameters like grid size and spline order, which allow it to learn complex functions. Regularization techniques, including activation and entropy penalties, are applied to maintain model stability. Like the MLP, KAN is optimized with AdamW and trained with the CrossEntropyLoss function, with the learning rate dynamically adjusted by an Exponential Scheduler. Figure 2 provides architectural diagrams for MPL and KAN implementations.

IV. RESULTS

Default models: In the initial experiment on the clean MNIST test dataset, both the MLP and KAN performed similarly well. The MLP achieved an accuracy of 97.40%, while KAN outperformed it with 97.95%. Both models showed comparable precision, recall, and f1-scores, with minor differences in misclassifications (Table II). KAN's slight edge in accuracy and recall suggests better handling of data variability.

Gaussian Noise: When exposed to noisy data, both models showed accuracy degradation as noise levels increased (Figure 3). At a noise level of 90, the MLP showed 94.77% accuracy, while KAN's performance dropped to 88.21%. The MLP showed stronger resistance to noise, achieving higher precision, recall, and f1-scores across all digits. KAN particularly struggled with digits 1 and 8, where performance dropped drastically (Table III). At lower noise levels, KAN outperformed the MLP, but its accuracy deteriorated more quickly at higher noise levels.

Fast Gradient Sign Method: Under the FGSM AA, both models experienced accuracy declines as epsilon increased (Figure 4). At epsilon 0.3, the MLP showed 92.48% accuracy, while KAN's dropped to 63.87%. The MLP retained more consistent precision, recall, and f1-scores, while KAN saw sharp declines, particularly with digits 1 and 8 (Table IV). KAN's accuracy fell rapidly as epsilon increased, indicating a greater vulnerability to adversarial attacks compared to the MLP, which maintained resilience until epsilon values grew larger.

Projected Gradient Descent: During the PGD attack, a more iterative adversarial method, both models again showed performance declines (Figure 5). At epsilon 0.3, the MLP showed 96.29% accuracy, while KAN dropped significantly to 53.12%. The MLP exhibited strong overall precision, recall, and f1-scores, while KAN struggled significantly, particularly with digits 1 and 8, where precision and recall dropped sharply (Table V). KAN's performance deteriorated more rapidly than the MLP as the epsilon value increased emphasizing its greater vulnerability to stronger adversarial attacks.

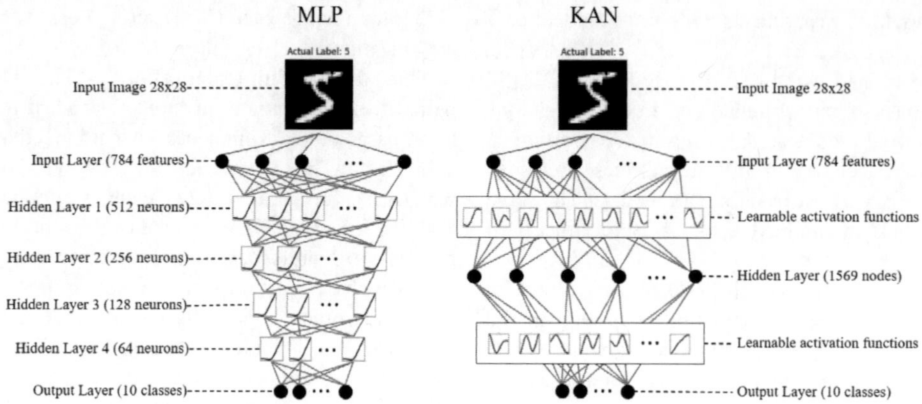

Figure 2. MPL and KAN Implementations

TABLE I
PERFORMANCE COMPARISON OF MLP AND KAN MODELS UNDER DIFFERENT SCENARIOS

Scenario	MLP				KAN			
	Accuracy	Precision	Recall	F1-score	Accuracy	Precision	Recall	F1-score
Default models	0.97	0.97	0.97	0.97	0.98	0.98	0.98	0.98
Gaussian Noise (Level 30)	0.97	0.98	0.98	0.98	0.98	0.98	0.98	0.98
Gaussian Noise (Level 60)	0.97	0.96	0.97	0.96	0.96	0.96	0.96	0.96
Gaussian Noise (Level 90)	0.95	0.95	0.95	0.95	0.89	0.92	0.89	0.89
FGSM (eps. 0.1)	0.97	0.97	0.97	0.97	0.96	0.96	0.96	0.96
FGSM (eps. 0.3)	0.92	0.93	0.92	0.92	0.64	0.77	0.64	0.64
FGSM (eps. 0.6)	0.65	0.67	0.65	0.66	0.20	0.43	0.20	0.19
PGD (eps. 0.1)	0.96	0.96	0.96	0.96	0.97	0.97	0.97	0.97
PGD (eps. 0.3)	0.96	0.96	0.96	0.96	0.53	0.68	0.53	0.55
PGD (eps. 0.6)	0.42	0.46	0.42	0.42	0.07	0.08	0.07	0.02

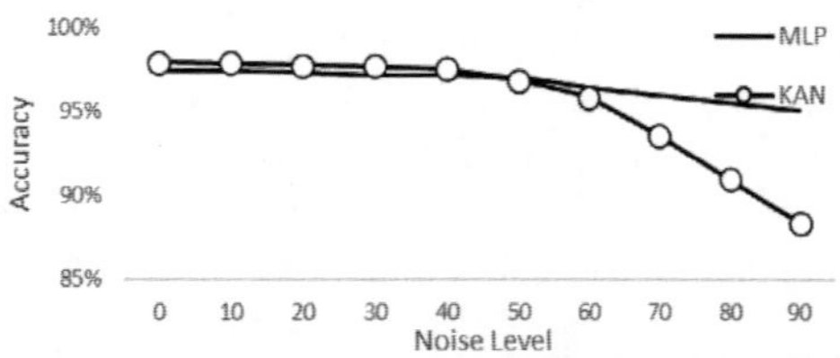

Figure 3. Gaussian Noise: Accuracy by Noise Level

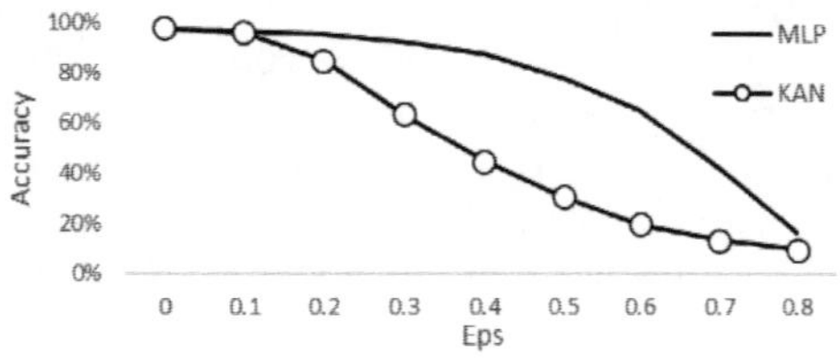

Figure 4. FGSM: Accuracy by Eps Level

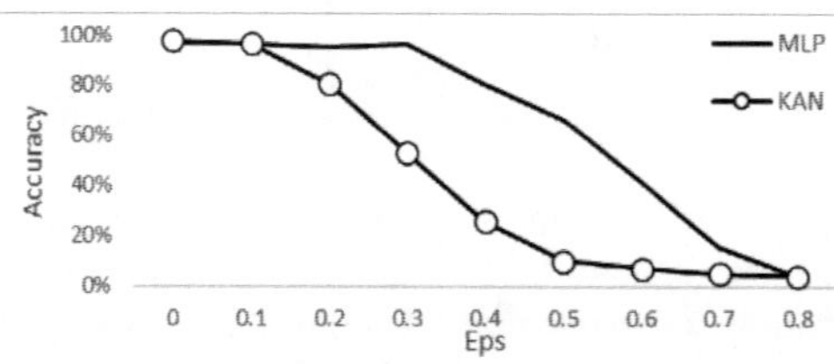

Figure 5. PGD: Accuracy by Eps Level

Discussion: Across all experiments, KAN displayed greater sensitivity to noise and adversarial attacks especially in more challenging conditions, while the MLP showed more stable performance and resilience. The vulnerabilities of KANs to noise and adversarial attacks could be linked to their reliance on spline-based transformations, which may be more sensitive to perturbations compared to the simpler linear activations used in MLPs. KANs' flexibility in modeling complex functions might lead to overfitting, making them less robust when faced with data that deviates from the training distribution, such as noisy inputs or adversarial perturbations. The spline functions used in KANs may also be more prone to distortions from small input changes, explaining their susceptibility to adversarial attacks. Additionally, KANs' complexity might hinder their ability to generalize well in adversarial scenarios, where simpler MLP structures could offer more stability.

V. CONCLUSION AND FUTURE WORK

The results of the experiments show clear differences in how KANs and classic MLPs handle AAs and noise. In clean conditions, both models perform similarly, with KAN slightly outperforming the MLP in accuracy (97.95% vs. 97.40%) and

TABLE II
PERFORMANCE COMPARISON: DEFAULT MODELS.

Class	MLP			KAN		
	Precision	Recall	F1-score	Precision	Recall	F1-score
0	0.99	0.99	0.99	0.99	0.99	0.99
1	0.98	0.99	0.98	0.98	0.99	0.99
2	0.98	0.96	0.97	0.98	0.98	0.98
3	0.97	0.96	0.97	0.98	0.97	0.97
4	0.98	0.97	0.98	0.98	0.98	0.98
5	0.96	0.97	0.97	0.97	0.97	0.97
6	0.98	0.99	0.98	0.98	0.99	0.98
7	0.98	0.97	0.97	0.98	0.98	0.98
8	0.97	0.97	0.97	0.98	0.97	0.98
9	0.96	0.96	0.96	0.96	0.98	0.97

TABLE III
PERFORMANCE COMPARISON: MODELS EXPOSED TO NOISE LEVEL 90.

Class	MLP			KAN		
	Precision	Recall	F1-score	Precision	Recall	F1-score
0	0.98	0.98	0.98	0.98	0.98	0.98
1	0.98	0.97	0.97	1.00	0.58	0.73
2	0.95	0.95	0.95	0.92	0.95	0.94
3	0.93	0.95	0.94	0.94	0.92	0.93
4	0.95	0.94	0.94	0.95	0.91	0.93
5	0.91	0.94	0.93	0.96	0.88	0.92
6	0.97	0.97	0.97	0.97	0.94	0.96
7	0.95	0.96	0.95	0.98	0.85	0.91
8	0.94	0.92	0.93	0.56	0.99	0.72
9	0.92	0.91	0.92	0.90	0.88	0.89

TABLE IV
PERFORMANCE COMPARISON: MODELS EXPOSED TO FGSM, EPS0.3.

Class	MLP			KAN		
	Precision	Recall	F1-score	Precision	Recall	F1-score
0	0.98	0.99	0.98	0.97	0.91	0.94
1	0.98	0.98	0.98	0.67	0.02	0.03
2	0.97	0.94	0.96	0.91	0.78	0.84
3	0.91	0.92	0.91	0.81	0.79	0.80
4	0.86	0.89	0.88	0.77	0.64	0.70
5	0.85	0.95	0.90	0.77	0.56	0.65
6	0.96	0.96	0.96	0.92	0.82	0.87
7	0.92	0.91	0.92	0.96	0.41	0.58
8	0.88	0.88	0.88	0.24	0.96	0.38
9	0.90	0.80	0.85	0.58	0.61	0.60

TABLE V
PERFORMANCE COMPARISON: MODELS EXPOSED TO PGD, EPS0.3.

Class	MLP			KAN		
	Precision	Recall	F1-score	Precision	Recall	F1-score
0	0.98	1.00	0.99	0.96	0.94	0.95
1	1.00	0.98	0.99	0.00	0.00	0.00
2	1.00	1.00	1.00	0.88	0.64	0.74
3	0.93	0.98	0.96	0.90	0.67	0.77
4	0.90	0.97	0.94	0.68	0.34	0.46
5	0.94	0.91	0.93	0.78	0.41	0.54
6	0.99	1.00	0.99	0.90	0.71	0.80
7	0.97	0.93	0.95	1.00	0.33	0.49
8	0.93	0.98	0.95	0.17	0.98	0.29
9	0.96	0.84	0.90	0.52	0.43	0.47

showing marginally better metrics overall. However, KANs struggle when noise is introduced. As noise levels increase, KANs experience a sharper drop in accuracy compared to the MLP. This indicates that while KANs perform better in clean environments, they suffer accuracy degradation under noisy conditions, revealing a weakness in robustness in real-life scenarios. Under FGSM and PGD AAs, KANs demonstrate even greater vulnerability. Their accuracy declines much faster than that of the MLP as the epsilon value rises. For example, at epsilon 0.3, KANs' accuracy falls to 63.87%, while the MLP still shows 92.48%. This trend continues with increasing perturbations, showing that KANs are more vulnerable to AAs than the MLP. Although KANs show high performance in optimal conditions, they face challenges in robustness and security. Their rapid decline in accuracy under noise and adversarial conditions suggests they are more vulnerable than traditional models. This poses risks in security-sensitive applications, where resilience against such attacks is crucial.

Future Research Directions

Improving KANs' robustness could involve exploring advanced regularization methods, adversarial training, or defense mechanisms tailored for KANs. Additionally, designing architectures that better handle noisy inputs and conducting more comprehensive security analyses across diverse attacks and datasets would further enhance KANs' resilience and security.

The future research directions include:

- Investigating and developing advanced robustness techniques tailored for KANs. This may include exploring novel regularization methods, adversarial training, or defensive strategies specifically designed to improve KANs' resilience to noise and AAs. Trying different types of activation functions could provide new insights into improving model performance and robustness. Activation functions based on Fourier transforms, for instance, can capture periodic patterns in data, while Chebyshev and Jacobi polynomials might offer superior approximation capabilities for certain types of functions. Investigating these alternatives could lead to the development of KANs that are more resilient to noise and adversarial attacks by leveraging the mathematical properties of these functions.
- Designing KAN architectures that inherently handle noisy inputs better. This might involve incorporating noise-robust activation functions or more sophisticated noise-handling mechanisms within the network. One approach could be to employ regularization methods that penalize overly sensitive spline functions, making the network less reactive to small perturbations in the input. Another strategy is to integrate preprocessing steps or layers within the KAN that filter out noise before it propagates through the network.
- Conducting a thorough security analysis of KANs across a broader range of AA methods and datasets is imperative, as it can provide deeper insights into KANs vulnerabilities and help in devising more effective defense strategies. Future work will involve testing KANs against more

sophisticated attacks like the Carlini & Wagner attack, DeepFool, and black-box attacks to evaluate their robustness comprehensively. Additionally, experimenting with diverse datasets such as CIFAR-10, ImageNet, or domain-specific datasets will help assess the generalizability of KANs' resilience across different types of data.

REFERENCES

[1] Z. Liu *et al.*, *Kan: Kolmogorov-arnold networks*, retrieved: September 2024, Apr. 2024.

[2] L. Deng, "The mnist database of handwritten digit images for machine learning research", *IEEE Signal Processing Magazine*, vol. 29, pp. 141–142, 6 2012, ISSN: 10535888. DOI: 10.1109/MSP.2012.2211477.

[3] OpenML, "Mnist handwritten digit dataset", retrieved: September 2024, [Online]. Available: https://www.openml.org/d/554.

[4] M. Cheon, *Demonstrating the efficacy of kolmogorov-arnold networks in vision tasks a preprint*, retrieved: September 2024, 2024.

[5] B. Azam and N. Akhtar, *Suitability of kans for computer vision: A preliminary investigation*, retrieved: September 2024, Jun. 2024.

[6] A. D. Bodner, J. N. Spolski, A. S. Tepsich, and S. Pourteau, *Convolutional kolmogorov-arnold networks*, retrieved: September 2024, 2024.

[7] R. Genet and H. Inzirillo, *A temporal kolmogorov-arnold transformer for time series forecasting*, retrieved: September 2024, Jun. 2024.

[8] K. Xu, L. Chen, and S. Wang, *Kolmogorov-arnold networks for time series: Bridging predictive power and interpretability*, retrieved: September 2024, Jun. 2024.

[9] C. J. Vaca-Rubio, L. Blanco, R. Pereira, and M. Caus, *Kolmogorov-arnold networks (kans) for time series analysis*, retrieved: September 2024, May 2024.

[10] C. Zeng, J. Wang, H. Shen, and Q. Wang, *Kan versus mlp on irregular or noisy functions*, retrieved: September 2024, 2024.

[11] H. Shen, C. Zeng, J. Wang, and Q. Wang, *Reduced effectiveness of kolmogorov-arnold networks on functions with noise*, retrieved: September 2024, Jul. 2024.

[12] V. D. Tran *et al.*, *Exploring the limitations of kolmogorov-arnold networks in classification: Insights to software training and hardware implementation*, retrieved: September 2024, Jul. 2024.

[16] K. Sadeghi, A. Banerjee, and S. K. Gupta, "A system-driven taxonomy of attacks and defenses in adversarial machine learning", *IEEE Transactions on Emerging Topics in Computational Intelligence*, vol. 4, pp. 450–467, 4 Aug. 2020, ISSN: 2471285X. DOI: 10.1109/TETCI.2020.2968933.

[17] B. Xi, "Adversarial machine learning for cybersecurity and computer vision: Current developments and challenges", *Wiley Interdisciplinary Reviews: Computational Statistics*, vol. 12, p. 1511, 5 Sep. 2020, ISSN: 19390068. DOI: 10.1002/wics.1511.

[13] L. Huang, A. D. Joseph, B. Nelson, B. I. Rubinstein, and J. D. Tygar, "Adversarial machine learning", in *Proceedings of the ACM Conference on Computer and Communications Security*, Oct. 2011, pp. 43–58. DOI: 10.1145/2046684.2046692.

[14] D. Dasgupta, Z. Akhtar, and S. Sen, "Machine learning in cybersecurity: A comprehensive survey", *Journal of Defense Modeling and Simulation*, vol. 19, pp. 57–106, 1 Jan. 2022, ISSN: 1557380X. DOI: 10.1177/1548512920951275.

[15] G. Apruzzese, L. Ferretti, M. Colajanni, and M. Marchetti, "Addressing adversarial attacks against security systems based on machine learning", in *2019 11th international conference on cyber conflict (CyCon)*, vol. 900, 2019, pp. 1–18.

[18] G. R. Machado, E. Silva, and R. R. Goldschmidt, *Adversarial machine learning in image classification: A survey towards the defender's perspective*, retrieved: September 2024, Sep. 2020. DOI: 10.1145/3485133.

[19] I. J. Goodfellow, J. Shlens, and C. Szegedy, *Explaining and harnessing adversarial examples*, retrieved: September 2024, Mar. 2015.

[20] A. Madry, A. Makelov, L. Schmidt, D. Tsipras, and A. Vladu, *Towards deep learning models resistant to adversarial attacks*, retrieved: September 2024, Jun. 2017.

[21] W. Villegas, A. Jaramillo-Alcázar, and S. Luján-Mora, "Evaluating the robustness of deep learning models against adversarial attacks: An analysis with fgsm, pgd and cw", *Big Data and Cognitive Computing*, vol. 8, p. 8, Jan. 2024. DOI: 10.3390/bdcc8010008.

[22] G. Sriramanan, S. Addepalli, A. Baburaj, and R. V. Babu, "Guided adversarial attack for evaluating and enhancing adversarial defenses", in *Advances in Neural Information Processing Systems*, vol. 33, 2020, pp. 20 297–20 308.

[23] Y. Jang, T. Zhao, S. Hong, and H. Lee, "Adversarial defense via learning to generate diverse attacks", in *In Proceedings of the IEEE/CVF International Conference on Computer Vision*, 2019, pp. 2740–2749.

[24] S. Mohandas, N. Manwani, and D. P. Dhulipudi, "Momentum iterative gradient sign method outperforms pgd attacks", in *International Conference on Agents and Artificial Intelligence*, vol. 3, Science and Technology Publications, Lda, 2022, pp. 913–916. DOI: 10.5220/0010938400003116.

[25] M.-I. Nicolae *et al.*, *Adversarial robustness toolbox v1.0.0*, retrieved: September 2024, 2019.

[26] Z. Liu, "Kolmogorov-arnold networks (kans)", retrieved: September 2024, [Online]. Available: https://github.com/KindXiaoming/pykan.

[27] H. Cao, "An efficient implementation of kolmogorov-arnold network (kan)", retrieved: September 2024, [Online]. Available: https://github.com/Blealtan/efficient-kan.

KAN vs KAN: Examining Kolmogorov-Arnold Networks (KAN) Performance under Adversarial Attacks

Nebojsa Djosic
Toronto Metropolitan University
Toronto, Canada
email: nebojsa.djosic@torontomu.ca

Evgenii Ostanin
Toronto Metropolitan University
Toronto, Canada
email: eostanin@torontomu.ca

Fatima Hussain
Toronto Metropolitan University
Toronto, Canada
email: fatima.hussain@torontomu.ca

Salah Sharieh
Toronto Metropolitan University
Toronto, Canada
email: salah.sharieh@torontomu.ca

Alexander Ferworn
Toronto Metropolitan University
Toronto, Canada
email: aferworn@torontomu.ca

***Abstract*—Recent interest in applying Kolmogorov-Arnold Networks (KANs) to the Machine Learning (ML) domain has grown significantly. Different KAN implementations leverage various architectures, with the primary distinction being their use of different learnable activation functions. While recent studies have benchmarked and evaluated the performance of different KAN models, little attention has been given to their robustness against Adversarial Attacks (AAs). In our previous work, we compared the performance of a single KAN model to a Multi-Layer Perceptron (MLP) classifier under Gaussian noise and AAs, using the Fast Gradient Sign Method (FGSM) and Projected Gradient Descent (PGD) attacks on the MNIST dataset. In this paper, we extend that analysis by comparing several popular KAN implementations subjected to the same attacks. We evaluate standard metrics, including accuracy, precision, recall, and F1-scores, using the MNIST dataset as in prior research. The aim is to empirically investigate how different activation functions influence the robustness of KAN models under AAs. Our results reveal substantial differences in accuracy loss across KAN models when exposed to AAs.**

Keywords-FGSM; MNIST; Kolmogorov-Arnold Networks; KAN; PGD; Classification.

I. INTRODUCTION

The fast-paced growth of Machine Learning (ML) has led to the development of increasingly advanced models that excel in various tasks. Among these innovations, Kolmogorov-Arnold Networks (KANs) introduced a novel framework grounded in the Kolmogorov-Arnold representation theorem [1]. KANs hold great potential for mobile device applications since they require less computation, memory, and thus energy to run. They also show potential for applications where interpretability is important. In addition, KAN models could be incrementally and continuously trained, although the initial training time is generally (significantly) longer for KANs, when compared to MLP models.

The increasing sophistication of adversarial attacks poses significant challenges for deep learning models, especially in safety-critical applications such as autonomous systems and cybersecurity. In addition, the growing use of ML in real-life applications are increasingly running into environmental noise that is not present during training. Despite their potential, the robustness of KANs, especially against Adversarial Attacks (AAs) and noisy data, remains mostly underexplored in spite of several recent papers [2], [3]. Robustness is a critical aspect of machine learning models in real-world applications, which often operate under less-than-ideal conditions [4]. Adversarial attacks, such as the Fast Gradient Sign Method (FGSM) and Projected Gradient Descent (PGD) exploit weaknesses in models by introducing subtle alterations to input data, while noise can obscure important features, leading to performance degradation [5].

In our previous paper [6], we compare the robustness of one of the first KAN to that of MLP Classifier. In this paper we compare different KAN implementations each using a different learnable function. We utilize adversarial attacks such as the FGSM and PGD, which fall under the category of white-box, evasion attacks, where the attacker has full knowledge of the model and seeks to degrade performance by introducing carefully crafted perturbations to the input data. Additionally, we employ Gaussian noise as a form of non-adversarial perturbation, which can obscure critical features and simulate natural noise, further impacting model robustness. By aligning these attack methods within widely recognized taxonomies of adversarial attacks, we provide a structured approach to evaluating model vulnerabilities under both adversarial and stochastic noise conditions.

The objective of this paper is to assess the impact of these activation functions on the robustness of KAN models. The key contributions of this work include a detailed evaluation of robustness using metrics such as accuracy, precision, recall, and F1-score, a comparative analysis of model performance under various adversarial attack scenarios, and comprehensive charts and figures that visually highlight the performance differences between the models.

Paper Structure: The remainder of this paper is organized as follows. In Section II, we provide an overview of the related work, discussing key contributions and architecture of KAN. Section III outlines the methodology, detailing the models architecture, implementation and parameters used in experiments. In this section we also describe the details and tools used for AAs. The experimental results are presented and analyzed in Section IV. Section V concludes the paper, summarizing the main findings, and potential directions for future work.

II. Related Work

A. Kolmogorov-Arnold Representation Theorem

The Kolmogorov-Arnold Representation Theorem, or the superposition theorem, was introduced by Andrey Kolmogorov in 1957 and later extended and refined by Vladimir Arnold in 1963. The theorem proposes that any multivariate continuous function $f(x_1, ..., x_n)$ within a bounded domain can be represented as a superposition of continuous single-variable functions, which is typically written as:

$$f(x) = f(x_1, ..., x_n) = \sum_{q=1}^{2n+1} \Phi_q \left(\sum_{p=1}^{n} \phi_{q,p}(x_p) \right)$$

where $\phi_{q,p} : [0,1] \to \mathbb{R}$ and $\Phi_q : \mathbb{R} \to \mathbb{R}$.

B. KAN Architecture

KANs is a novel neural network architecture based on the Kolmogorov-Arnold representation theorem, presenting an alternative to traditional multilayer perceptrons (MLPs). Unlike MLPs, which use fixed activation functions on nodes and linear weight matrices, KANs introduced learnable activation functions along edges. Each weight in KANs is replaced by a one-dimensional learnable function, often parameterized as a spline. However, other alternatives to splines can also be used. This architectural shift promises enhanced accuracy and interpretability compared to MLPs, making KANs suitable for diverse applications in various fields [1]. An especially interesting aspect is the reduced demand for resources and the increased interpretability.

KANs and MLPs share a similar approach and architecture. Figure 1 from [1] shows KAN and MLP architectures compared side by side.

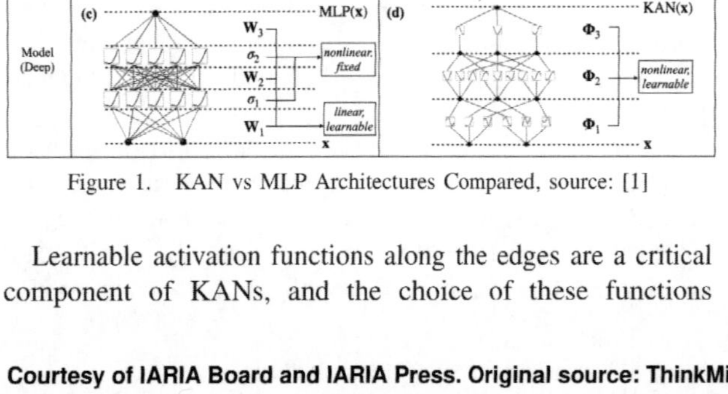

Figure 1. KAN vs MLP Architectures Compared, source: [1]

Learnable activation functions along the edges are a critical component of KANs, and the choice of these functions has a significant impact on the robustness of the model against adversarial attacks. While splines are well established for approximating the one-dimensional functions required by KAN decomposition, there are other methods capable of representing any continuous multivariate function as a finite sum of continuous univariate functions, as outlined by the Kolmogorov-Arnold theorem. Selecting the optimal one-dimensional functions is one of the most important decisions when implementing KANs, as it directly influences efficiency and model performance.

Splines are a natural choice because of their capacity to approximate continuous functions with a low number of parameters and smooth transitions between data points. This smoothness is particularly advantageous in interpolation tasks, where data changes are handled efficiently, making splines more computationally efficient compared to high-degree polynomials. Their efficiency is crucial for both the training phase and inference in KANs [1].

Beyond splines, there are several other alternative choices for learnable activation functions. Each alternative offers different trade-offs in performance and computational complexity. NNs, for instance, are capable of approximating non-linear functions with high accuracy, although training NNs for each one-dimensional function introduces longer training times. This trade-off may be beneficial for more complex tasks, where increased accuracy is needed. Polynomial function approximations are computationally straightforward and may be suitable for simpler tasks where minimal approximation is required. Fourier series offers another alternative, especially for periodic or smooth functions, using sine and cosine terms to capture the essential properties of continuous functions [7]. Chebyshev Polynomial would be another alternative to the use of splines [8].

KANs have demonstrated potential in computer vision tasks. In [9], KANs were evaluated on several well-known benchmarks, and their performance was compared to models like MLP-Mixer, Convolutional Neural Networks (CNNs), and Vision Transformers (ViTs). KANs surpassed MLP-Mixer, however, they were outperformed by the ResNet-18 model [10].

KANs sensitivity to noise is featured in [2] and [3], where authors show that even relatively small noise perturbations are causing significant degradation in KANs performance. In [11], authors show KANs weaknesses compared to MLPs in hardware applications using complex datasets requiring additional resources. Some authors like [10] claim that using KANs for more complex datasets, like CIFAR-10, shows no benefits.

C. Adversarial Attacks

Refining techniques that exploit vulnerabilities in ML models has been the focus of recent research in AAs domain [5], [12]–[14], and particularly in computer vision [4], [15]. The FGSM and PGD emerged as the two most prominent methods for evaluating model robustness. Introduced by [16], FGSM generates adversarial examples by adding small perturbations to input data, which can induce incorrect predictions. PGD, a more iterative and sophisticated approach developed by [17], has become a benchmark for testing resilience against stronger attacks. In computer vision, where minor changes to input images can lead to significant shifts in the model outputs, these methods are especially effective [18]. Several different defenses against FGSM and PGD have been proposed [19]–[21]. However, FGSM and PGD still remain the state of the art for assessing the robustness of ML models which is why we selected these methods to evaluate KANs in our research presented in this paper.

The Adversarial Robustness Toolbox (ART) [22] is one of many similar tools which offer techniques for generating adversarial examples and defences, while datasets like MNIST [23] are commonly used to benchmark adversarial vulnerability across studies. Although KANs have been applied in various domains, their resistance to AAs, specifically FGSM and PGD, remains largely unexamined. In this paper, we examine and compare different KAN architectures under AA attacks in an attempt to provide insights into KANs' robustness relative to the chosen architecture.

III. METHODOLOGY

The primary objective of this study is to evaluate the relative change in performance metrics when models are subjected to adversarial attacks, rather than focusing on achieving optimal performance. While we acknowledge that each model could be fine-tuned for better results through parameter optimization and enhanced training techniques, this paper assumes that the relative impact of adversarial attacks on model performance will remain consistent. This assumption will have to be examined in future research to validate if it can be confirmed and generalized.

KAN architecture is illustrated in Figure 1. We selected four different KAN implementations available on GitHub each using a different activation function, but otherwise the same architecture as in Figure 1. All models are subjected to one noise and two AA: the FGSM, and PGD. AA are administered using ART [22]. Metrics like accuracy, precision, recall, and F1 scores are used to assess models' robustness. MNIST dataset [23], which contains 33,600 training samples and 8,400 test samples of handwritten digits, is used for all training and evaluation experiments. For a baseline, a control, we use a simple, typical MLP Classifier based on a feed forward NN. The four KAN implementations we selected to examine are: *Linear (Efficient) KAN* [24], *Naive Fourier KAN* [25], *Jacobi KAN* [26], *Chebyshev KAN* [27]

A. Model Architectures

We used an AdamW optimizer for all models with a learning rate of 0.001 and weight decay to prevent over-fitting. During the training Exponential Learning Rate Scheduler is used to regulate the learning rate. The CrossEntropyLoss function is used for classification.

All selected KAN models follow the same basic architecture illustrated in Figure 1 except for the activation function. The code is provided by their respective authors on GitHub and most of the code stems from the original KAN implementation introduced in [1] and available on GitHub [28].

Linear KAN [24] is based on the original KAN implementation pykan [28] which is the repo behind the paper [1]. This model uses splines. It was trained using the $(n * n) * 2 + 1$ formula derived from the Kolmogorov-Arnold theorem. The KAN NN needs to map the n-dimensional input space in this case $n = (28 * 28)$ corresponding to the MNIST image size used as input, into one-dimensional functions, which are then summed up to recover the multivariate structure. The factor of 2 in the formula corresponds to the fact that each variable influences the other in the decomposition. Adding 1 captures the residuals, or bias, that pairwise terms may not be able to capture. The total 784 * 784 * 2 + 1 = 1,229,377 gives the model capacity to represent patterns in the MNIST data.

Naive Fourier KAN [25] replaces spline with single dimension Fourier coefficients. The authors argue that this approach would lead to a simplification since the Fourier representations are more compact and dense. The naive version uses memory proportional to the grid size parameter which is typically related to the resolution of images in our case 28 x 28. Apart from the grid size this model uses bias which we set to true to allow for a flexible fit and the *smooth_init* parameter is also set to true to help with weights initialization.

Chebyshev KAN [27] called *ChebyKAN* replaces spline with Chebyshev polynomials. According to the authors B-splines lead to poor performance and are not intuitive which lead to the use of the use of Chebyshev polynomials, which are widely used for approximations and polynomial interpolation since they provide close approximation to a continuous function. The simplification leads to a reduction in model parameters. Apart from the image size 28 x 28 and the number of classes, digits 0-9, we only have the degree of the polynomial.

Jacobi KAN [26] called *JacobiKAN* is based on the Chebyshev KAN [27] and it is also using orthogonal polynomials this time Jacobi. They are similar but have two extra parameters α and β to control the upper and lower ends of the interval which is typically $[-1, 1]$. When these parameters are both 0 it is a special case of Jacobi, the Legendre polynomials. This is typically used for MNIST classifications. The other parameters are the same as in ChebyKAN, that is input, output, and degree.

MLP Classifier is a feed-forward NN in the following formation:

$$(28 * 28) \rightarrow 512 \rightarrow 256 \rightarrow 128 \rightarrow 64 \rightarrow 10$$

where (28 * 28) represents the input layer corresponding to MNIST image size. Each layer is followed by ReLU activation and dropout for regularization. The layers decrease in size leading to the output layer containing 10 neurons, one for each digit 0-9.

B. Attack Architecture

Noise Attack: We conducted Gaussian noise attacks at a noise level of 100 to evaluate the robustness of the models under extreme conditions. This high noise level was deliberately chosen to highlight the performance degradation, enabling a clear comparison between different KAN architectures and a baseline multi-layer perceptron (MLP) model used as a control. In our prior work, we assessed the performance of a single KAN model across progressively increasing noise levels to analyze its sensitivity to noise attacks in comparison to the MLP. In this study, our focus shifts to a comparative analysis of various KAN models, while maintaining the MLP model as a reference for evaluating performance robustness.

Fast Gradient Sign Method Attack: ART [22] was utilized to generate adversarial examples and implement the FGSM attack on each model. Perturbations were introduced to the MNIST test data to create adversarial samples, with the epsilon parameter, typically ranging from 0.1 to 0.8, controlling the degree of perturbation. Higher epsilon values increase the likelihood of visible distortions in the images. For this study, we selected an epsilon value of 0.5, which was sufficient to degrade model performance while avoiding noticeable visual alterations to the images.

Projected Gradient Descent Attack: For this attack we also used the ART to prepare and run the test. The PGD attack works by progressively making small random perturbations to the input to increase (maximize) loss. In each iteration step, perturbation level is increased by a parameter while maintaining imperceptibility to the human eye through the control of the max size of perturbations. This attack is considered one of the strongest first-order adversarial attacks because of this iterative process, in contrast to the FGSM attack. We also used the 0.5 level for this attack as well, to keep it at a reasonable, realistic level.

Tools and environment: All KAN implementations are sourced from GitHub repositories [25]–[28] as well as The ART [22] while the MLP is implemented by us using PyTorch and Scikit-learn Python libraries. Google Colab cloud hardware and software environment is used to develop and run all experiments using Python. These standardized tools and environments along with the above listed model parameters ensure that the experiments are reproducible.

Experiments: All models were first trained using Google Colab free tear environments. We evaluated all models before adversarial attacks including the MLP Classifier. In each adversarial attack, we measured the change in the performance for each metric relative to the performance metrics before the attack. We also compared the performance of each KAN relative to that of MLP.

IV. RESULTS

Before Attacks: A comparison of models' accuracy scores before attacks is visualized in the bar graph from Figure 2. It shows that MLP and Linear KAN have nearly identical accuracy. However, the other three KAN models in our experiments didn't achieve the same level of accuracy. Since we are only interested in relative changes in metrics this was not of critical importance, however, this is something we will be looking into exploring in the future. Although not the primary focus of this paper, we observed that KAN models took significantly more time to train. The training time in Google Colab T4 GPU free tear improved about tenfold, however, training KAN models still took more time in relatively the same proportion.

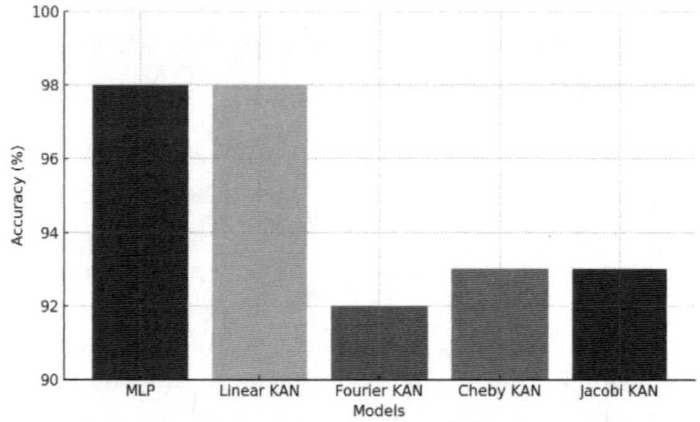

Figure 2. Model Accuracy Comparison Before Attacks

Another interesting observation is that KAN models are not as well balanced as MLP as illustrated in the graph Figure 3. Linear KAN also achieves nearly the same F1 scores across all classes except for the last, digit 9, where it significantly drops. All other KAN model F1 scores follow the same pattern. Confirming and exploring this imbalance further would be important as it may lead to interesting new directions. All these observations are left for future research.

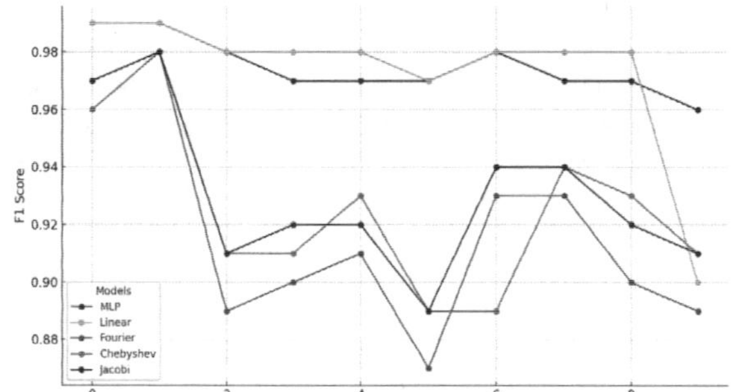

Figure 3. Model F1 Score Comparison Before Attacks

Gaussian Noise Attack Results: All models showed accuracy degradation when exposed to noisy data at level 100. The MLP model showed only a slight decrease followed closely by the Linear KAN model. However, the other KAN models suffered a catastrophic drop in accuracy. Figure 4 shows the before and after accuracy scores for each model. Only the Linear KAN suffered minimal accuracy degradation, although still more than double the MLP loss.

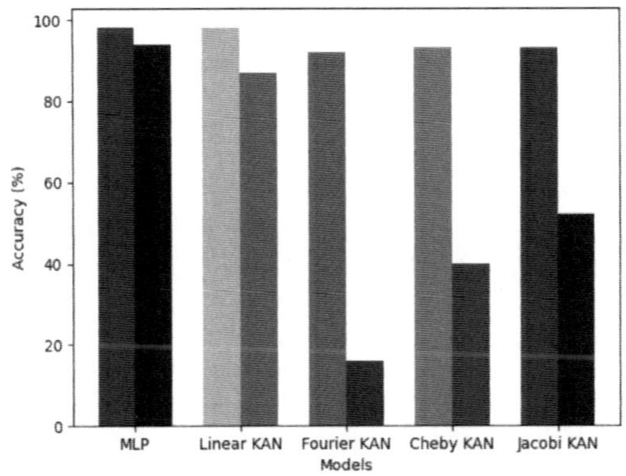

Figure 4. Model Accuracy Comparison After Noise Attack

Fast Gradient Sign Method Attack Results: As expected under the FGSM attacks (at 0.5 level) all models lost accuracy more than under noise attacks. Figure 5 shows the comparison between accuracy scores before and after FGSM attacks for each model. The MLP model, again, suffered the least among the models, however, this time the drop is significant. The Linear KAN model sustained even greater loss of accuracy although performed better than the rest of the KAN models. The most interesting observation following the FGSM attack is that the Fourier KAN, that suffered the worst under the noise attack, performed the best amongst KAN models, except Linear, under FGSM attack.

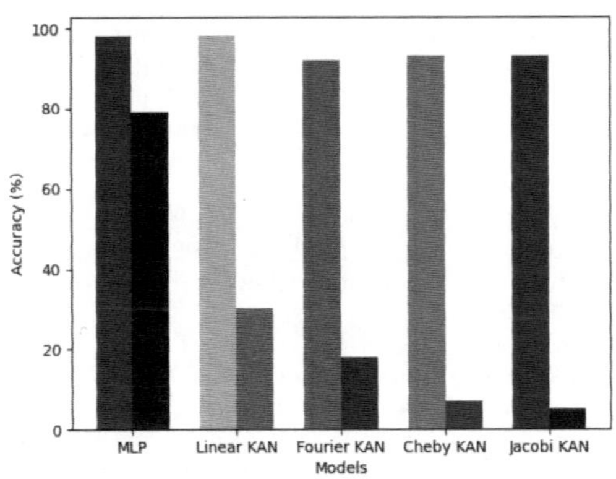

Figure 5. Model Accuracy Comparison After FGSM Attack

Projected Gradient Descent Attack Results: Under PGD attacks at an intensity level of 0.5, all models experienced a catastrophic degradation in performance. Figure 6 shows the comparison of accuracy scores before and after PGD attack for each model.

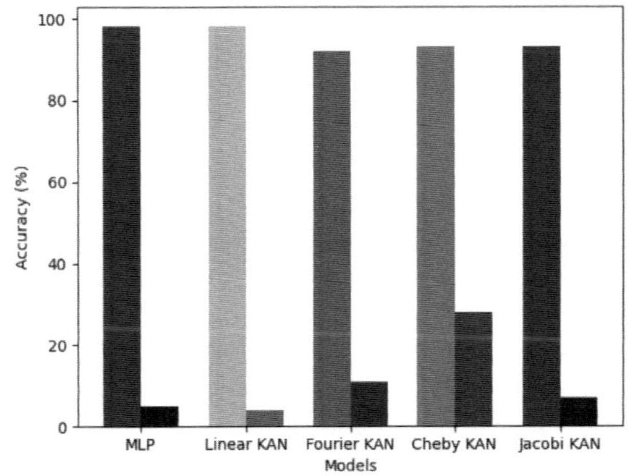

Figure 6. Model Accuracy Comparison After PGD Attack

We also observed that the accuracy for all models for the majority of digit classes dropped to zero. In the few cases where some accuracy was retained, the performance remained below 10%. What is interesting here is that all KAN models except Linear KAN, showed better overall resilience than MLP, with Cheby KAN leading the pack. Of course, the caveat is that the results are still catastrophic. The best-performing model, Cheby KAN achieved a score of just below 0.3. Still, it showed the least loss of accuracy compared to all other models.

V. Conclusion and Future Work

The results demonstrate a significant variation in how different KAN models handle AA attacks and how they compare to MLP. Consistent with our previous findings [6], we confirmed that the MLP classifier is generally more resilient than the KAN classifiers under AAs. However, under PGD attacks, we see this reversed. Specifically, the Cheby KAN model surpassed the MLP, while both the Fourier and Jacobi KAN models also achieved better performance than the MLP. We shouldn't forget that all these results are poor. Nevertheless, these preliminary empirical results highlight the need for further investigations into theoretical and empirical differences between KAN models using different activation functions, and between MLP and KAN models. Understanding these differences could offer valuable theoretical insights for both KANs and MLPs. It could potentially open new avenues for developing AA attack-resilient ML model architectures.

We also observed that KAN models have a higher class imbalance, as illustrated in Figure 3. Looking further into the reasons behind this could also unveil some interesting new insights.

In this paper, we did not prioritize training efficiency or performance optimization. However, investigating the relationship between training efficiency and robustness against AA attacks could be a valuable direction for future work, especially since KAN models offer various optimization opportunities. One notable finding is that the Cheby KAN model, despite starting with a slightly lower accuracy score of 0.93 before attacks, compared to 0.98 for both the MLP and Linear KAN models, under PGD attacks exhibited significantly less accuracy degradation. The Cheby KAN model retained an accuracy score of 0.3, while the MLP and Linear KAN models' accuracy dropped to 0.05 and 0.04, respectively. This substantial difference warrants further exploration and could lead to important insights.

Future research directions include:

- Investigating the observed differences further and developing robustness training techniques better suited for KANs.
- Looking into training KAN models specifically aimed at handling AA.
- Looking into improving AA methods given that they were less successful attacking KAN models specifically PGD attacking the Cheby KAN model.
- Looking into the resistance of KAN models using different AA methods, and using different datasets would be a priority given our findings.

REFERENCES

[1] Z. Liu *et al.*, "Kan: Kolmogorov-arnold networks", retrieved: September 2024, Apr. 2024, [Online]. Available: http://arxiv.org/abs/2404.19756.

[2] C. Zeng, J. Wang, H. Shen, and Q. Wang, "Kan versus mlp on irregular or noisy functions", retrieved: September 2024, 2024, [Online]. Available: https://arxiv.org/abs/2408.07906.

[3] H. Shen, C. Zeng, J. Wang, and Q. Wang, "Reduced effectiveness of kolmogorov-arnold networks on functions with noise", retrieved: September 2024, Jul. 2024, [Online]. Available: http://arxiv.org/abs/2407.14882.

[4] B. Xi, "Adversarial machine learning for cybersecurity and computer vision: Current developments and challenges", *Wiley Interdisciplinary Reviews: Computational Statistics*, vol. 12, p. 1511, 5 Sep. 2020, ISSN: 19390068. DOI: 10.1002/wics.1511.

[5] D. Dasgupta, Z. Akhtar, and S. Sen, "Machine learning in cybersecurity: A comprehensive survey", *Journal of Defense Modeling and Simulation*, vol. 19, pp. 57–106, 1 Jan. 2022, ISSN: 1557380X. DOI: 10.1177/1548512920951275.

[6] E. Ostanin, N. Djosic, F. Hussain, S. Sharieh, and A. Ferworn, *Evaluating the robustness of kolmogorov-arnold networks against noise and adversarial attacks*, to appear in 2024 IARIA SECURWARE 2024, ECSTAI, 2024.

[7] J. Xu *et al.*, "Fourierkan-gcf: Fourier kolmogorov-arnold network – an effective and efficient feature transformation for graph collaborative filtering", retrieved: September 2024, 2024, arXiv: 2406.01034 [cs.IR], [Online]. Available: https://arxiv.org/abs/2406.01034.

[8] S. Sidharth, A. Keerthana, R. Gokul, and K. Anas, "Chebyshev polynomial-based kolmogorov-arnold networks: An efficient architecture for nonlinear function approximation", retrieved: September 2024, 2024, arXiv: 2405.07200 [cs.LG], [Online]. Available: https://arxiv.org/abs/2405.07200.

[9] M. Cheon, "Demonstrating the efficacy of kolmogorov-arnold networks in vision tasks a preprint", retrieved: September 2024, 2024, [Online]. Available: https://arxiv.org/abs/2406.14916.

[10] B. Azam and N. Akhtar, "Suitability of kans for computer vision: A preliminary investigation", retrieved: September 2024, Jun. 2024, [Online]. Available: http://arxiv.org/abs/2406.09087.

[11] V. D. Tran *et al.*, "Exploring the limitations of kolmogorov-arnold networks in classification: Insights to software training and hardware implementation", retrieved: September 2024, Jul. 2024, [Online]. Available: http://arxiv.org/abs/2407.17790.

[12] G. Apruzzese, L. Ferretti, M. Colajanni, and M. Marchetti, "Addressing adversarial attacks against security systems based on machine learning", in *2019 11th international conference on cyber conflict (CyCon)*, vol. 900, 2019, pp. 1–18.

[13] L. Huang, A. D. Joseph, B. Nelson, B. I. Rubinstein, and J. D. Tygar, "Adversarial machine learning", in *Proceedings of the ACM Conference on Computer and Communications Security*, Oct. 2011, pp. 43–58. DOI: 10.1145/2046684.2046692.

[14] K. Sadeghi, A. Banerjee, and S. K. Gupta, "A system-driven taxonomy of attacks and defenses in adversarial machine learning", *IEEE Transactions on Emerging Topics in Computational Intelligence*, vol. 4, pp. 450–467, 4 Aug. 2020, ISSN: 2471285X. DOI: 10.1109/TETCI.2020.2968933.

[15] G. R. Machado, E. Silva, and R. R. Goldschmidt, "Adversarial machine learning in image classification: A survey towards the defender's perspective", retrieved: September 2024, Sep. 2020, [Online]. Available: http://arxiv.org/abs/2009.03728%20http://dx.doi.org/10.1145/3485133.

[16] I. J. Goodfellow, J. Shlens, and C. Szegedy, "Explaining and harnessing adversarial examples", retrieved: September 2024, Mar. 2015, [Online]. Available: https://arxiv.org/abs/1412.6572.

[17] A. Madry, A. Makelov, L. Schmidt, D. Tsipras, and A. Vladu, "Towards deep learning models resistant to adversarial attacks", retrieved: September 2024, Jun. 2017, [Online]. Available: http://arxiv.org/abs/1706.06083.

[18] W. Villegas, A. Jaramillo-Alcázar, and S. Luján-Mora, "Evaluating the robustness of deep learning models against adversarial attacks: An analysis with fgsm, pgd and cw", *Big Data and Cognitive Computing*, vol. 8, p. 8, Jan. 2024. DOI: 10.3390/bdcc8010008.

[19] Y. Jang, T. Zhao, S. Hong, and H. Lee, "Adversarial defense via learning to generate diverse attacks", in *In Proceedings of the IEEE/CVF International Conference on Computer Vision*, 2019, pp. 2740–2749.

[20] G. Sriramanan, S. Addepalli, A. Baburaj, and R. V. Babu, "Guided adversarial attack for evaluating and enhancing adversarial defenses", in *Advances in Neural Information Processing Systems*, retrieved: September 2024, vol. 33, 2020, pp. 20 297–20 308.

[21] S. Mohandas, N. Manwani, and D. P. Dhulipudi, "Momentum iterative gradient sign method outperforms pgd attacks", in *International Conference on Agents and Artificial Intelligence*, vol. 3, Science and Technology Publications, Lda, 2022, pp. 913–916. DOI: 10.5220/0010938400003116.

[22] M.-I. Nicolae *et al.*, "Adversarial robustness toolbox v1.0.0", retrieved: September 2024, 2019, [Online]. Available: https://arxiv.org/abs/1807.01069.

[23] L. Deng, "The mnist database of handwritten digit images for machine learning research", *IEEE Signal Processing Magazine*, vol. 29, pp. 141–142, 6 2012, ISSN: 10535888. DOI: 10.1109/MSP.2012.2211477.

[24] H. Cao, "An efficient implementation of kolmogorov-arnold network (kan)", retrieved: September 2024, 2024, [Online]. Available: https://github.com/Blealtan/efficient-kan.

[25] G. Noesis, "Pytorch layer for fourierkan", retrieved: September 2024, 2024, [Online]. Available: https://github.com/GistNoesis/FourierKAN/tree/main.

[26] SpaceLearner, "Jacobi polynomials kan", retrieved: September 2024, 2024, [Online]. Available: https://github.com/SpaceLearner/JacobiKAN.

[27] SynodicMonth, "Chebyshev polynomials kan", retrieved: September 2024, 2024, [Online]. Available: https://github.com/SynodicMonth/ChebyKAN/.

[28] Z. Liu, "Python kolmogorov-arnold networks (kans)", retrieved: September 2024, 2024, [Online]. Available: https://github.com/KindXiaoming/pykan.

An AI-based Cognitive Architecture for Augmenting Cybersecurity Analysts

Salvatore Vella
Department of Computer Science
Toronto Metropolitan University
Toronto, Ontario
e-mail: sal.vella@torontomu.ca

Moussa Noun
Royal Bank of Canada
Toronto, Ontario
e-mail: moussa.noun@rbc.com

Salah Sharieh
Department of Computer Science
Toronto Metropolitan University
Toronto, Ontario
e-mail: salah.sharieh@torontomu.ca

Alex Ferworn
Department of Computer Science
Toronto Metropolitan University
Toronto, Ontario
e-mail: aferworn@torontomu.ca

Abstract—**We present a Generative Artificial Intelligence (AI) based cognitive architecture and an agent specifically developed for the complexities of Cybersecurity analysis. White-collar roles, exemplified by Cybersecurity analysts, are multifaceted and rely on declarative knowledge, procedural understanding, and diverse tools. The ability to learn and adapt to the nuances of the job is crucial. This paper introduces CorpIA, a cognitive architecture that provides an agent with knowledge, tools, and the capacity to acquire on-the-job experience. This system enhances human performance by providing suggested solutions and continuous mentoring. Our research demonstrates that the CorpIA agent can learn from interactions using Bloom's Taxonomy. We provide the source code for these experiments.**

Keywords-AI Agents; Cybersecurity; Automation.

I. Introduction

Digital systems and the Internet are critical to our everyday lives. Cyber threats from bad actors require robust Cybersecurity measures.

Cybersecurity analysts are prototypical white-collar professionals who rely on large amounts of knowledge and data and use their experience and skills to collaborate with others in the workplace. Moreover, there is lifelong learning as security threats, methods, tactics, techniques, and tools evolve.

The challenges for Cybersecurity analysts are numerous. There are skill requirements to be proficient in many tools and technologies which also change over time. There are challenges to ongoing learning with emerging threats.

There is a need for advanced Artificial Intelligence (AI) support for Cybersecurity analysts. We have identified the need for Generative AI solutions specifically tailored for these professions [1], [2].

Large Language Models (LLMs) are Generative AI models that implement transformer models to generate text and other content. They can automate tasks previously done by humans [3]. Since ChatGPT became available, many white-collar professionals have been using these tools [4]. These evolved into more general frameworks such as ChatDev [5] and Autogen [6], allowing users to create multiple autonomous agents which can run through workflows. ChatDev specializes in software development roles, and Autogen provides for the creation of more general roles.

Our proposed approach is described next.

- Use the CorpIA architecture to create a cybersecurity analyst agent and show that the agent can use declarative and procedural knowledge and can learn and apply additional information from the chat.
- Apply Bloom's Taxonomy [7] to help measure the AI agent's levels of understanding and application of that knowledge.
- Explore the use of Human AI collaboration to design systems that mentor professionals.

In continuation of our proposed approach, the following are our contributions in this paper:

- Introduction of the CorpIA architecture for creating AI agents for knowledge workers. This novel architecture simplifies the creation of a knowledge worker agent. We demonstrate several knowledge worker agents developed in the accompanying GitHub repository.
- Enhancement of Human Performance. We demonstrate how AI agents can help human professionals in complex tasks.
- On The Job Learning of AI Agents. We show how AI agents are able to learn from interactions. We show that these agents can progress through Bloom's taxonomy in practical scenarios.
- Source Code. We offer the CorpIA source code for replication, validation and further development.

Starting with the Introduction in Section I, the rest of the paper is organized in this manner. A Literature Review is presented in Section II followed by the CorpIA architecture in Section III. Section IV discusses Results and the Conclusion is drawn in Section V.

II. Literature Review

In this section, we will review various topics discussed in this paper.

A. Digital Labour

Digital labour represents an emergent form characterized by value production through interaction with information and communication technologies such as digital platforms or artificial intelligence [8]. With the emergence of Generative AI agents comes the possibility of augmentation agents acting as assistants for white-collar professionals.

We can emulate the best professionals in the field. For example, the best Cybersecurity analyst agent with the best knowledge acts with the most successful experiences and presents the best personality for the specific client.

Work on enhancing human intellect has also evolved. Engelbart [9] is one of the most influential and prolific inventors of devices we use today. He focused mainly on physical aids to augment humans. We have now evolved to digital aids to augment professionals. Vella and Sharieh [10] have introduced a framework that defines knowledge workers as a set of knowledge, experience and skills.

B. Autonomous Agent Frameworks

Building on simple graphical tools such as OpenAI's ChatGPT [11], autonomous agent frameworks have been built using the underlying APIs. Autogen [6] is an example of such a framework that allows for the definition of agents and workflows between those AI agents.

There are many such agent frameworks and some excellent summaries of their construction. Two good sources are Cheng et al. [12] and Wang et al. [13]. These frameworks allow for the definition and creation of agents to perform tasks and interactions. They include memory, tools, and a workflow engine.

C. Memory and Learning

There is extensive research on memory add-ons for autonomous agent systems. A good summary of the research areas is found in [13]. Most frameworks include systems for short—and long-term memory and various options for moving short-term memories into long-term memory. We can additionally learn from other work on memory.

The Soar and ACT-R (Adaptive Character of Thought - Rational) models discussed by Nuxoll et al. [14] and Anderson [15] are also relevant as additional memory models to emulate. Memory is crucial for augmentation agents as on-the-job learning is critical to learning institutional knowledge and continuing learning in the specific role.

ACT-R introduces the concepts of the following:

- Declarative memory consists of facts such as Canada is a country in North America.
- Procedural memory is made of productions. Productions represent knowledge about how we do things, such as how to get information from the Internet.

Both are important to any white-collar augmentation agent, especially to this work, which focuses on gaining job experience while on the job.

Bloom's Taxonomy [7], [16] is a valuable framework for categorizing educational goals. This taxonomy represents a progression from basic information remembering through a series of steps to the ability to create new, original work.

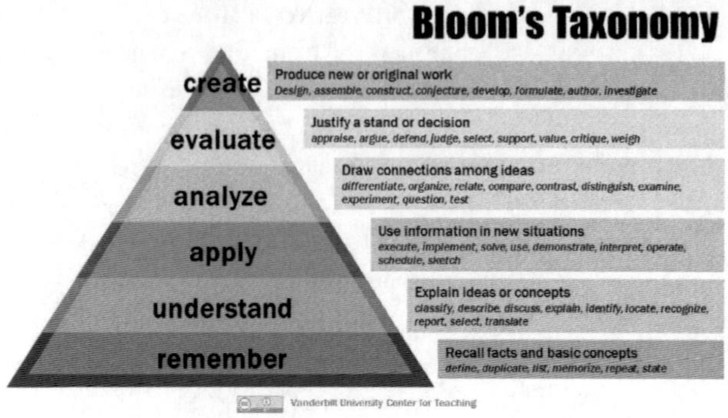

Figure 1. Bloom's Taxonomy.

Bloom's Taxonomy has six cognitive skills levels, from low-level skills requiring less cognitive processing to high-level skills requiring more cognitive processing. Figure 1 shows the hierarchy of cognitive skills.

- Remember refers to the ability to retain discrete pieces of information.
- Understand refers to the ability to classify, describe, and explain the ideas or concepts.
- Apply refers to the ability to use information in a new situation.
- Analyze refers to the ability to compare, contract, and draw connections between ideas.
- Evaluate refers to the ability to be able to appraise, judge or critique a decision
- Create refers to the ability to produce new or original work.

In this way, we measure the on-the-job learning that a knowledge professional will experience. They learn new facts, they can apply them to the workplace, and eventually, they can create original work based on their learning.

We use Bloom's Taxonomy to devise questions and exercises to test an agent's learning and cognitive abilities.

D. Use Cases

Cybersecurity is an area where Generative AI is having an impact both from an attack and a defence perspective [17]. With its ability to analyze large amounts of data, Gernative AI can help with threat detection, incident response and with cyber security reporting. These are all tasks that Cybersecurity analysts perform today in an environment with massive data growth [18]–[20].

Miller [21] and Davenport [22] discuss the concept of Augmentation versus Automation, where humans prefer augmentation (helping the human) versus automation (replacing the human). Miller provides a good set of guidelines for companies implementing AI to ensure they keep humans in the loop.

III. The CorpIA Cognitive Architecture

This section introduces and describes the cognitive architecture of CorpIA (Corporate Intelligence Augmentation), using a Cybersecurity analyst as an example. We define an augmentation agent as an AI that helps a white-collar professional. It can provide answers, learn on the job, and provide ongoing mentoring advice.

The CorpIA cognitive architecture allows an augmentation agent to be taken through a perceive, reason, act, and learn loop.

1) Perceive. This is the collection of information needed to perform the tasks. The following data sources are used:
   a) Role Definition. This defines the role, experience and personality that the agent has.
   b) Declarative Knowledge. These are the facts that the agent knows.
   c) Procedural Knowledge. These are the procedures for how to do things.
   d) Learned Knowledge. This is acquired knowledge and is queried for information relevant to the question. Specific listening cues can be specified to isolate particular pieces of information types that are relevant for the role.
2) Reason. This is the formation of the execution plan based on the information collected. In this step, a Critic agent is used to double-check the step-by-step plan created by the augmentation agent.
3) Act. This is the actual execution of the plan created in the Reasoning step.
   The Act step uses teammate agents if applicable. The possible teammates are listed in the definition of the agent. For example, if "Lawyer" is specified as one of the possible helpful agents to be used and the execution plan calls for a legal review in one of its steps, then the Lawyer helpful agent will be dynamically created and answer that part of the execution plan.
   Finally, the Cybersecurity agent is asked to answer the question based on the information collected in the Perceive step and the plan from the Reason step.
4) Learn. Once the answer is provided, learning can occur for further conversations. These are:
   a) Mentor feedback for the human. This is advice from an expert agent on what was learned from this question and what could be applied to future situations.
   b) Specific learning for future. These are based on cues specific to the definition of the augmentation agent.

As the augmentation agent moves through these loops, it learns about the job and its environment. In essence, this is the augmentation agent's on-the-job training.

Figure 2 shows the CorpIA augmentation agent.

A. Methodology

We will use the role of a Cybersecurity analyst to demonstrate the operation of the augmentation agent as an aid for the white-collar professional. A Cybersecurity analyst has both declarative and procedural knowledge and, over time, gains a set of episodic memories. This role has the challenges of a white-collar role where learning on the job is essential, and we can show the augmentation agent improving over time. Moreover,

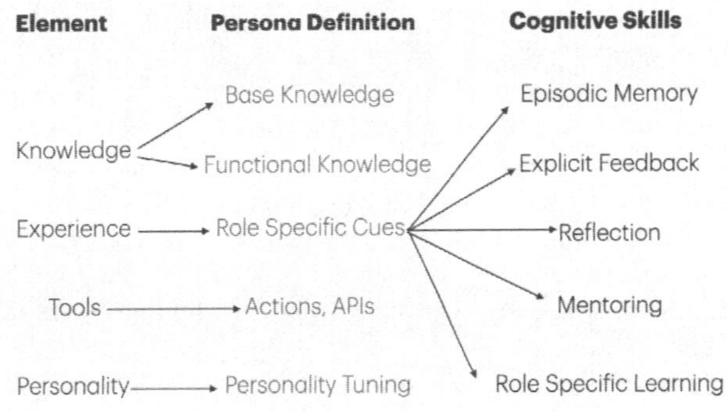

Figure 2. Basic elements of an Augmentation Agent.

the augmentation agent provides an ongoing mentoring dialogue with the Cybersecurity analyst.

B. Exercising the Cybersecurity Analyst Augmentation Agent

We synthesize a set of conversations between the Cybersecurity analyst and the agent to show the agent's ability to go through the Perceive-Reason-Act-Learn cycle for each interaction. Over a set of interactions, the agent becomes more proficient and learns based on the listening cues for the role.

C. Evaluating the Cyber Security Analyst Augmentation Agent

We will measure the performance of the augmentation agent using Bloom's Taxonomy, a method for classifying learning objectives. Bloom's Taxonomy provides a way to measure learning, ranging from remembering facts to organizing facts, and to use these face-ups to create novel content.

IV. Results

A Cybersecurity analyst is an expert in computer security, vulnerabilities, and remediation of those vulnerabilities. They possess a deep knowledge of computer security issues and can translate them into their working environment. As the computer security landscape changes often, they are lifelong learners.

A. Defining the Cyber Security Analyst Augmentation Agent

We start with the role definition of the Cybersecurity analyst, which includes a description of the role, the knowledge - declarative and procedural, the skills of the role, the tools used, and the personality of the role.

We have given an in-depth report on the Log4j vulnerability [23] as its declarative knowledge and a NIST manual on responding to computer security incidents [24] as its procedural knowledge. We have the agent listening for computer threats and ABC Bank to build its episodic memory, and we have a lawyer and an IT specialist as possible helper agents.

B. Exercising the Cyber Security Advisor Augmentation Agent

Bloom's Taxonomy [16] is used to create student learning outcomes. We will use the framework to measure the learning ability of the Cybersecurity augmentation agent. We will look at the outcomes of a conversation with the augmentation agent to determine if the agent has demonstrated that level of Bloom's Taxonomy.

The Cybersecurity agent will go through a series of steps while storing the additional information in a persistent store to help serve the customer later. Using a simulated client conversation with the Cybersecurity analyst, we demonstrate the agent's ability to learn and retain relevant information. Cybersecurity analysts have a set of knowledge, are given a set of skills, and develop their experience through a set of cognitive skills.

In the first request (Figure 3), we add information about the client. Having specified "ABC Bank" as one of the listening cues, CorpIA extracts information about the client and stores this for later use.

Prompt:
ABC Bank information:
- large multinational bank
- 10 data centres across 4 countries
- cloud and on-premise data centres
- 20,000 servers
- 3,000 applications
- 10 million customers

How do I know if Log4j affects our organization?

Figure 3. Augmentation Agent Prompt.

C. Evaluating the Cybersecurity Analyst Augmentation Agent

After the augmentation agent has been exercised with several queries, we ask it a set of questions to see how well it has learned the materials using Bloom's taxonomy.

After joining a firm, this on-the-job learning is familiar to all human Cybersecurity analysts. Starting with basic knowledge, they learn about the company and its specific configurations and processes as they do their job.

Figure 4 shows an example of the output created. Only a portion of the output is shown here. Still, one can see that information learned about the client - including the bank's IT landscape information- is incorporated into the answer.

To determine if Log4j affects ABC Bank, a systematic and thorough approach should be taken, particularly given the scale of your organization, which includes 10 data centers across 4 countries, 20,000 servers, and 3,000 applications. Here's how you can assess the situation effectively:

Steps to Assess the Impact of Log4j (CVE-2021-44228) on ABC Bank:

Step 1: Formulate a Cross-Functional Team
- Action: Assemble a team comprising members from IT, Cybersecurity, application development, compliance, and operations departments.
- Purpose: A diverse team ensures a comprehensive evaluation of the bank's operations and assessment capabilities.

...

Figure 4. Augmentation Agent Output.

Figure 5 exemplifies the mentoring feedback provided. This would be helpful advice for the white-collar professional to review and use in future interactions.

As a mentor guiding you in your role as a Cybersecurity Analyst, I want to emphasize the importance of structured processes like the one you've outlined for assessing the impact of Log4j at ABC Bank. Here are some tailored pieces of advice to enhance your effectiveness in this role:

1. Emphasize Collaboration in Your Cross-Functional Team

While you mentioned forming a cross-functional team, actively foster collaboration among team members. Encourage open communication and regular meetings to discuss progress, hurdles, and insights. This will create a sense of ownership and encourage knowledge sharing, which is invaluable in a complex environment such as yours.

...

Figure 5. Augmentation Agent Mentoring.

We show that information is assimilated over time. We demonstrate that the agent can understand what information is essential to store for later use additional information about the client, its performance, and information about how the client wishes to be served—and does that in long-term memory across chat sessions.

We use Bloom's Taxonomy to test the augmentation agent as a final exam. These are questions to validate the learning. We provide a qualitative evaluation here, and the full transcript is available at [25].

TABLE I. BLOOM'S TAXONOMY EVALUATION.

Bloom's Taxonomy Step	**Question / Exercise**	**Evaluation**
Remembering	What is the IT profile for ABC Bank	The agent is able to recall the IT profile the user provided.
Understanding	Describe the aspects of ABC Bank that are vulnerable to Log4j	The agent can use the information in the profile to provide an answer.
Analyzing	Creating a strategy for ABC Bank to deal with the Log4j vulnerability	The agent can create a strategy integrating the profile and its understanding of the bank's vulnerability.
Applying	What are the potential impacts for ABC Bank of Log4j, including legal impacts	The agent provides a comprehensive answer.
Understanding	What should ABC Bank have done in preparation for the Log4j vulnerability? Talk about the people, process and tools.	The agent provides a complete retrospective.
Creating	What is the long-term strategy for ABC Bank to ensure similar vulnerabilities are promptly identified and addressed in the future?	The agent provides a structured and comprehensive set of recommendations.

We have shown that we can use the CorpIA framework to create an autonomous agent that enhances the Cybersecurity analyst's performance. We have used Bloom's Taxonomy to test the agent's learning.

D. Discussion

Using the CorpIA framework, an agent is created, which allows for the parameter-based definition of a white-collar role.

We evaluated the ability of the agent to learn using Bloom's Taxonomy to design a set of questions that tested the agent's ability to remember facts all the way to being able to create novel content.

The AI agent is especially important for Cybersecurity analysts. With the growing severity of threats, the time to respond is greatly reduced. AI can help automate and assist with the planning and data collection elements. At the same time, the volume of information is growing, and tools such as AI can help human professionals sift through the information and summarize key pieces.

V. Conclusion

Integrating AI into white-collar roles is a key area of research that needs focus. This work has demonstrated that an AI agent can assist a Cybersecurity analyst. We have shown that this agent produces output that is useful and highly regarded by professionals in the field. Additionally, we have shown that the agent can learn over time. For this, we have used Bloom's Taxonomy, and we have shown that the agent can pass a set of tests to demonstrate it can move from remembering new facts to creating novel content. The amount of information white-collar professionals need to deal with increases dramatically. AI agents like the one presented in this paper can greatly assist white-collar professionals. Additionally, the AI agent has a mentoring function that provides advice for the professional in addition to just the answer to the question.

The CorpIA cognitive architecture represents a promising step toward fully realizing AI's potential to enhance a Cybersecurity analyst's capabilities. It offers a way to create AI agents for white collar professionals, which can then be used to study how these can be made more valuable in real work workplaces.

Future work will be to evaluate the tool in professional settings to evaluate its usefulness with practicing cybersecurity professionals.

References

[1] D. Townsend, "Leveraging Generative AI tools like ChatGPT for startups and small business growth", *Entrepreneur and Innovation Exchange*, 2023.

[2] V. Jüttner, M. Grimmer, and E. Buchmann, "ChatIDS: Explainable cybersecurity using Generative AI", *ArXiv*, vol. abs/2306.14504, 2023, Accessed: 2024-10-10.

[3] E. Brynjolfsson, D. Li, and L. Raymond, "Generative AI at work", *SSRN Electronic Journal*, 2023.

[4] Q. Gallea, "From mundane to meaningful: AI's influence on work dynamics - evidence from ChatGPT and Stack Overflow", *arXiv*, 2023. DOI: 10.48550/arxiv.2308.11302.

[5] C. Qian *et al.*, "ChatDev: Communicative agents for software development", in *Annual Meeting of the Association for Computational Linguistics*, 2023.

[6] Q. Wu *et al.*, "AutoGen: Enabling next-gen LLM applications via multi-agent conversation", 2023, Accessed: 2024-10-10. arXiv: 2308.08155 [cs.AI].

[7] N. E. Adams, "Bloom's taxonomy of cognitive learning objectives.", *Journal of the Medical Library Association : JMLA*, vol. 103 3, pp. 152–3, 2015.

[8] Z. Saleem, A. M. Hanif, U. Sumayya, M. S. Vohra, and H. Raza, "Productivity in the virtual office: Unpacking the role of digital tools and work-life harmony", *International Journal of Social Science & Entrepreneurship*, 2023.

[9] D. C. Engelbart, *Augmenting Human Intellect: A Conceptual Framework*, Air Force Office of Scientific Research, AFOSR-3233, www . bootstrap . org / augdocs / friedewald030402 / augmentinghumanintellect/ahi62index.html, 1962.

[10] S. Vella and S. Shariah, "All you need is knowledge, experience and tools: A framework for integrating digital labour with white collar work", *2024 4th Interdisciplinary Conference on Electrics and Computer (INTCEC)*, pp. 1–7, 2024.

[11] OpenAI, *ChatGPT*, https://chat.openai.com, Accessed: 2024-10-10, 2024.

[12] Y. Cheng *et al.*, "Exploring large language model based intelligent agents: Definitions, methods, and prospects", *ArXiv*, vol. abs/2401.03428, 2024, Accessed: 2024-10-10.

[13] L. Wang *et al.*, "A survey on large language model based autonomous agents", *ArXiv*, vol. abs/2308.11432, 2023, Accessed: 2024-10-10.

[14] A. Nuxoll and J. E. Laird, "Enhancing intelligent agents with episodic memory", *Cognitive Systems Research*, vol. 17, pp. 34–48, 2012.

[15] J. Anderson, *The Architecture of Cognition*, 1st. Psychology Press, 1996. DOI: 10.4324/9781315799438.

[16] P. Armstrong, "Bloom's Taxonomy. Vanderbilt University center for teaching", Accessed: 2024-10-28.

[17] M. Gupta, C. Akiri, K. Aryal, E. Parker, and L. Praharaj, "From ChatGPT to ThreatGPT: Impact of Generative AI in cybersecurity and privacy", *IEEE Access*, vol. 11, pp. 80 218–80 245, 2023.

[18] S. Metta, I. Chang, J. Parker, M. P. Roman, and A. F. Ehuan, "Generative AI in cybersecurity", *ArXiv*, vol. abs/2405.01674, 2024, Accessed: 2024-10-10.

[19] Y. Yigit, W. J. Buchanan, M. G. Tehrani, and L. A. Maglaras, "Review of Generative AI methods in cybersecurity", *ArXiv*, vol. abs/2403.08701, 2024, Accessed: 2024-10-10.

[20] I. Prieto and B. Blakely, "Proposed uses of Generative AI in a cybersecurity-focused SOAR agent", in *Proceedings of the AAAI Symposium Series*, vol. 2, 2023, pp. 386–390.

[21] S. M. Miller, "AI: Augmentation, more so than automation", *Asian Management Insights (Singapore Management University) Vol. 5 Iss. 1 (2018) p. 1 - 20 ISSN: 2315-4284*, 2018.

[22] T. Davenport and J. Kirby, *Only Humans Need Apply: Winners & Losers in the Age of Smart Machines*. HarperCollins, 2016, ISBN: 9780062438607.

[23] R. Silvers *et al.*, *Review of the December 2021 Log4j event*, en, 2022. DOI: https://doi.org/10.6028/NIST.SP.800-61r2.

[24] P. Cichonski, T. Millar, T. Grance, and K. Scarfone, *Computer security incident handling guide*, en, 2012-08-06 2012. DOI: https://doi.org/10.6028/NIST.SP.800-61r2.

[25] S. Vella, *Corpia*, GitHub repository, accessed: 2024-10-25, 2024.

Validating Damage Assessment: A Simulation-Based Analysis of Blind Write Lineage in Fog Computing

Mariha Siddika Ahmad
Electrical Engineering and Computer Science Department
University of Arkansas
Fayetteville, AR 72701 USA
ma135@uark.edu

Brajendra Panda
Electrical Engineering and Computer Science Department
University of Arkansas
Fayetteville, AR 72701 USA
bpanda@uark.edu

Abstract— **In order to solve problems like temporal lag, communication overhead, and the requirement for computational and storage resources to be closer to both the ground and end users, the idea of fog computing evolved as an extension of cloud computing. Due to its large number of interconnected nodes, this system is susceptible to cyberattacks. Damage from the attack swiftly spreads to other nodes and their data items when valid transactions cause modifications using the value of a compromised object, thus impairing the system's real-time functions. This research proposes a fast damage assessment approach to provide users access to unaffected nodes while accelerating system recovery. In this paper, we provide various algorithms along with simulated results to efficiently identify and mitigate damage, ensuring the system's resilience and continuity. Our proposed method demonstrates significant improvements in damage assessment speed and efficiency compared to traditional approaches, with simulation results consistently showing substantially fewer data item reads required during the recovery process across various scenarios.**

Keywords- Fog computing security; blind write; data dependency; damage assessment; malicious transaction.

I. INTRODUCTION

While cloud computing brought advantages like processing power and communication, it also raised concerns about data security and user experience due to delays. Fog computing was developed as an extension of cloud computing to tackle these issues. It brings the needed resources closer to users but inherits security and privacy risks from traditional cloud systems. In fog environments, the interconnected nature and vast amount of data create a bigger attack surface, allowing damage to spread rapidly. This is especially worrisome for real-time processing, where breaches can have a swift and significant impact. For critical systems like those used by emergency services, hospitals, and police, fast recovery of compromised data is essential. Unfortunately, traditional recovery methods, which involve shutting down systems for analysis and restoration, are not suitable for real-time fog systems.

Traditional logs struggle to track data access during attacks, hindering recovery. Blind write operations are those that update data without reading it. These can be handily used to accelerate recovery. This research builds on prior work on blind write's role in recovery efficiency [1]. We explore the damage assessment process and present the effectiveness of our approach through simulation. We show that by using blind writes, data recovery can be automated and becomes significantly faster, eliminating manual data checks.

This paper is structured as follows: the following section will explore the motivation behind this research. Section 3 will examine relevant past research connected to this endeavor. In Section 4, we will delve into the specifics of the model. Section 5 will provide a broad discussion of damage assessment for blind write lineage along with their corresponding algorithms. Then, in Section 6, the simulated results are shown. Finally, Section 7 will wrap up the paper with the conclusion.

II. MOTIVATION

Distributed fog systems strategically store large amounts of data near users, enabling real-time services in critical areas. Their speed and reliability make them ideal for essential computing infrastructure across various organizations, from local emergency services to large enterprises. However, the sensitive data they store makes them attractive targets, and their inherent vulnerabilities pose significant security challenges.

Fog systems' strength lies in their interconnectedness, but this very feature creates a vulnerability. Like a chain breaking at its weakest link, a single compromised node can trigger a domino effect, crippling interconnected systems. These systems are also heterogeneous, meaning different nodes have varying software and data. Additionally, the sheer volume of data across all connected nodes makes recovery extremely complex after an attack. This complexity leads to significant delays, a major issue considering the real-time nature of the services fog systems provide.

A successful attack on a single fog node can wreak havoc beyond its local database. Corrupted data can spread like a virus as legitimate transactions unknowingly read tainted information and update healthy data based on these bad values. This domino effect rapidly infects other interconnected nodes, creating a snowballing problem. Recovering from such an attack becomes a race against time, as these systems rely on real-time functionality. A swift and accurate recovery mechanism is essential, not just for system survival but also to minimize service disruptions.

The potential impact on critical infrastructure includes:

- **Emergency Services**: A compromised fog node could lead to incorrect dispatch of information, delaying response times and potentially costing lives.

- **Healthcare Systems**: Corrupted patient data could result in misdiagnosis or improper treatment plans.
- **Financial Institutions**: Tainted transaction data could cause widespread financial losses and erode customer trust.
- **Smart City Infrastructure**: Compromised traffic management systems could lead to gridlock or increased accident risks.

Traditional recovery methods, which often involve system-wide shutdowns and time-consuming manual checks, are simply not feasible for these real-time, mission-critical systems. The need for a solution that can rapidly assess damage, isolate compromised data, and restore system functionality is paramount.

This paper proposes a novel method for recovering data in fog computing systems that manage vital information. We highlight the urgency of real-time recovery during cyberattacks, leveraging the concept of blind writes to accelerate the damage assessment process. Our approach aims to minimize downtime, reduce the spread of corrupted data, and ensure the continuity of essential services even in the face of sophisticated attacks.

By addressing these critical challenges, our research contributes to building more resilient fog computing infrastructures capable of withstanding and swiftly recovering from cyber threats, ultimately safeguarding the vital services that modern society increasingly depends upon.

III. RELATED WORK

Following the success of cloud computing, fog and edge computing are emerging as the next frontier. Research on fog computing's role in the Internet of Things is well-established by Bonomi et al. in [2] as well as several insightful surveys exploring its key issues and potential by Mouradian et al. in [3] and Vaquero et al. in [4]. Security remains a major concern, as evidenced by various studies by Sun et al. [5] and Mukherjee et al. [6]. In addition, in reference [7], Wu et al. explore security vulnerabilities in critical infrastructure data storage and management systems. Additionally, research by Viganò et al. in [8] highlights vulnerabilities specific to critical infrastructure data management systems.

Beyond general security, researchers like Kotzanikolaou et al. [9] have investigated targeted risk assessment models for cascading failures in critical infrastructure. Others have emphasized how Cyber-Physical Systems introduce new attack vectors in data-rich environments like Ding et al. in [10]. Notably, Rehak et al. [11] propose a valuable model depicting interconnected elements within an infrastructure system. This model's focus on dependencies closely resembles the interconnected nature of fog computing systems, offering insights into potential cascading damage from attacks.

Database attacks can have a ripple effect, corrupting healthy data through seemingly valid transactions unaware of the compromise. Post-attack recovery is crucial, relying heavily on system logs to identify affected data and initiate recovery procedures. The concept of blind writes, updating data without reading them, has been explored by various researchers. Stearns et al. [12] define it as writing data without a prior read request, highlighting the lack of a preliminary check. Mendonca et al. [13] emphasize that during a blind write operation, data copies are modified regardless of their original values. Similarly, Burger et al. [14] focus on the absence of a pre-write read operation inherent to blind writes.

Rapid damage assessment is vital for fog system recovery. Existing methods leverage transaction or data dependencies for this purpose by Ammann et al. in [15] and Tripathy et al. in [16]. Recovery is equally important, as evidenced by research on database recovery after attacks by Panda et al. [17] and efficient damage assessment algorithms by Haraty et al. [18]. Notably, Haraty et al. [18] presents a memory and time-efficient algorithm that effectively handles blind writes, minimizing attack impact and enabling swift, accurate recovery.

The field of damage assessment has seen prior research exploring the potential of blind writes for faster identification of compromised data [1]. This paper takes that concept a step further. We introduce a new model specifically tailored for fog computing systems, a domain where rapid damage assessment is paramount due to their interconnected nature and the potential for swift propagation of attacks. Our proposed model leverages blind writes for efficient damage assessment, and we will further validate its effectiveness through the inclusion of simulated results. By incorporating simulations, we aim to demonstrate the model's ability to quickly pinpoint compromised data after a cyberattack in a fog computing environment.

Fog computing's distributed nature compels us to explore damage assessment techniques from distributed systems research. Existing work in this area offers promise for fog computing. For instance, Alshehri et al. [19] outline a blockchain-based method designed to prevent a malicious fog node from affecting other nodes in the network. The authors propose a model that uses blockchain technology and Ciphertext-Policy Attribute-Based Encryption (CP-ABE) to create fog federations that enable secure and distributed authorization among fog nodes. This approach aims to reduce time delays and communication overhead between fog nodes and cloud servers by allowing fog nodes within the same federation to conduct distributed authorization processes using smart contracts on the blockchain. By adapting these techniques, specifically by integrating blockchain-based authorization mechanisms and encryption methods such as CP-ABE, fog systems can enhance their defense against cyberattacks while maintaining system performance and scalability. This approach enables more secure and efficient damage recovery in fog computing environments, where timely and coordinated responses to threats are crucial for resilience.

Our research introduces the concept of blind write lineage to address security challenges in fog computing. This model efficiently traces data dependencies and rapidly assesses damage by leveraging the characteristics of blind writes. Unlike traditional methods that rely on log analysis, our approach offers a more effective solution for real-time damage assessment in interconnected fog systems, which are particularly vulnerable to cascading failures and rapid damage propagation.

IV. BLIND WRITE LINEAGE MODEL

The previous research [1] leverages blind writes for rapid damage assessment in fog computing systems. Blind writes update data without first reading their existing values. A key concept is data dependency, where one data item relies on the value of another for its update.

[1] introduces the concept of blind write lineage, which tracks data items solely dependent on a blindly written item or its descendants. To facilitate damage assessment and recovery, two crucial data structures are maintained:

Blind Write (BW) List: List which includes blindly written data items, timestamps, and transaction numbers.

Blind Write Lineage (BW Lineage) List: Tracks the lineage of data items solely dependent on blindly written items or their descendants. Represented as [Parent_node → Child_node].

Blind write lineage is a method for swift damage assessment in fog computing systems. It capitalizes on blind writes, where data updates occur without first retrieving the existing value. The previous paper [1] explored two primary scenarios within blind write lineage:

Case 1: Single-parent/Single-child Lineage (Simpler Scenario)

This case represents a simpler scenario where data items are updated sequentially, with each item relying on a single predecessor. The lineage of affected data items can be efficiently traced back to the original blindly written item.

Case 2: Multipath Lineage (More Complex Scenario)

This case presents a more intricate scenario where a child node might have multiple parent nodes, and vice versa. Data items can also be updated by leveraging multiple arguments. This complexity necessitates a more refined approach to damage assessment.

In a fog computing system, the integrity of data relies heavily on the relationships between various data items. When an attack occurs, it is crucial to identify how data has been compromised by analyzing transaction logs. These logs store the sequence of operations performed on data items, including read and write operations. In the context of blind writes, where data is updated without reading its prior value, it becomes especially challenging to trace which items are affected by compromised data.

To efficiently perform damage assessment, the system needs to track how data dependencies unfold. Each time a data item is blindly written, its dependent items—those that rely on it for updates—become potential candidates for compromise. By analyzing the transaction logs, the system can trace these dependencies and organize them into subgraphs, which represent different clusters of related data items.

The analysis of transaction logs in a fog computing system can reveal complex data dependencies. These dependencies can be visualized as a graph, where:

- Nodes represent data items
- Edges represent dependencies between data items (i.e., one data item being used to update another)

However, this overall graph is not necessarily fully connected. Instead, it often consists of multiple disconnected subgraphs. Each of these subgraphs (G_1, G_2, G_3, etc.) represents a distinct "blind write lineage" - a chain of data updates originating from a blindly written data item.

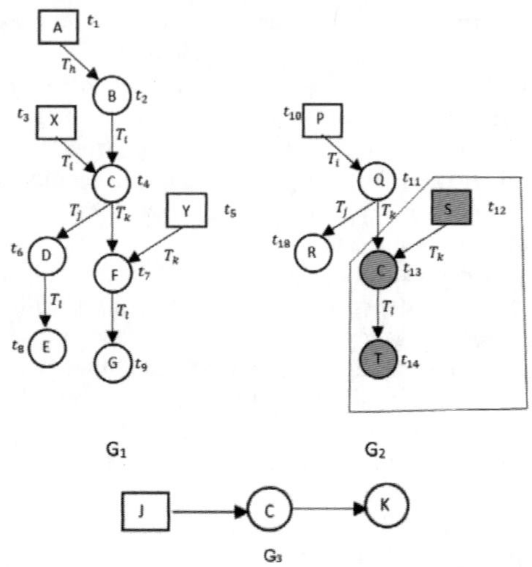

Figure 1. Multiple subgraphs in the data dependency (G) [1].

The analysis of transaction logs can reveal multiple disconnected subgraphs within the overall data dependency graph (Figure 1). These subgraphs, denoted as G_i (where i represents a specific subgraph), collectively form the set G. Each subgraph (G_i) represents a distinct blind write lineage. For Figure 1, G would be: G: {G_1, G_2, G_3}. This structure allows for efficient assessment of damage even in scenarios with multiple attack points.

One algorithm focuses on the simpler scenario of single-parent/single-child lineage. It operates by first checking if the initially compromised data item is present on the Blind Write (BW) list. If found, the algorithm leverages the Blind Write Lineage (BW Lineage) list to identify all subsequent data items affected by the attack. The final output is a comprehensive list of Damaged Data Items that require remediation.

The next algorithm tackles the more general scenario of multipath lineage. It achieves this by first identifying distinct subgraphs within the overall data dependency graph. For each subgraph, the algorithm defines three crucial sets:

Blind Write Set (*BWS_i*): This set encompasses all blindly written data items within the subgraph, along with their corresponding timestamps. These blindly written items serve as the root cause of potential damage.

Children Data Set (*CDS_i*): This set comprises all data items that are dependent on one or more elements within the ***BWS_i*** of the same subgraph. It also includes timestamps for each data item's update. These data items are considered potentially compromised due to their dependency on blindly written elements.

Damaged Set (*D*): These items are considered damaged because they were created by an attacker transaction. The damaged set is like a family tree, where each data item is a parent node in their respective subgraphs. This is because the assumption is that attacker transactions create data blindly.

By meticulously constructing these sets for each subgraph based on transaction data, the last algorithm lays the groundwork for effective damage assessment. The resulting subgraphs, along with the BWS_i and CDS_i sets, provide valuable insights into the extent of the attack and the data items that require further investigation or restoration.

V. Damage Assessment

For damage assessment, time (t_a) as in attack time and for every data item last updated time ($t_{last\ updated\ time}$) and graph(G) must be taken into consideration for damage assessment. As was mentioned in the previous paper [1], the same data item can be updated in different transactions at different times. So, time is very crucial here to find the damaged data items and if that damaged item has been used before or after the attack, depending on the time, it can be decided if the damaged item should be recovered or not. Again, the damaged graph is needed as in to differentiate if the same data item is updated at the same time, it would be much easier for assessment. For this purpose, the final updated time for each data item and their corresponding subgraph would be listed in a table (Table II). There would be one table for Graph set G_i (Table I). Suppose for this example let's check the final updated timetable and the BWSi and CDSi set:

TABLE I. Sets

G_i	G_1	G_2	G_3
BWS_i	{(A,t_1), (X,t_3), (Y,t_5)}	{(P,t_{10}), (S,t_{12})}	{(J,t_{15})}
CDS_i	{(B,t_2), (C,t_4), (D,t_6), (E,t_8), (F,t_7), (G,t_9)}	{(Q,t_{11}),(C,t_{14}), (T,t_{15})}, (R,t_{18})}	{(C,t_{16}), (K,t_{17})}
D	{(S,t_{12})}		

TABLE II. Final Updated Time Table

Data Items	A	B	X	Y	D	E	F	G
$t_{\text{Last Updated}}$	t_1	t_2	t_3	t_5	t_6	t_7	t_8	t_9
Graph	G_1	G_1	G_1	G_1	G_1	G_1	G_1	G_1

Data Items	P	Q	S	T	J	C	K	R
$t_{\text{Last Updated}}$	t_{10}	t_{11}	t_{12}	t_{14}	t_{15}	t_{16}	t_{17}	t_{18}
Graph	G_2	G_2	G_2	G_2	G_3	G_3	G_3	G_2

In all three subgraphs (Figure 1), C is found to be updated at t_4, t_{13} *and* t_{16}. But in Table II, the final update of C is listed which is t_{16} and it appears in subgraph G_3 (shaded part).

It is possible for the same data items to be blindly written by multiple transactions. For instance, let's consider the data item S, which could be blindly written in all the subgraphs (G_1, G_2, and G_3). In such a scenario, all the Blind Write Sets (BWS_i) for these subgraphs would contain "*S*." However, if the update time is not considered within the set, all the subgraphs will be deemed damaged. So, the time of the update of each data item has been included in the BWS_i and CDS_i as an ordered pair. Thus, in this example, when the initial damaged set D, {(S,t_{12})}, is intersected with the Blind Write Sets (BWS_i) of all the subgraphs in the system, only G_2 would be identified as damaged, as the ordered pairs match.

In the case of G_1 and G_2, G_1 has used a non-damaged *C*. Since it is in a different graph it has no connection with subgraph G_2 hence this value is independent of that value of *C* there. It is evident that data item *C* is a child of *S*, the initially maliciously modified data item, implying that *C* is damaged. However, in G_3, *C* has been modified using a blindly written data item, *J*. Given that these subgraphs are isolated and unrelated to each other, it is deduced that *C* in G_3 has already been recovered and can be released for use.

Upon establishing that a specific graph is affected, the time of update for every child of the initial damage is referred to as the affected time. For instance, in G_2, if *S* is the initial damage, then the time of update for *C* is denoted as t_{13}, which represents the affected time for *C*, and for T, the affected time is t_{14}. These affected times can also be found in the CDS_i. Another case to be mindful of is the possibility of a specific data item being recovered within the same damaged graph. Let's illustrate this scenario with an example to provide clarity:

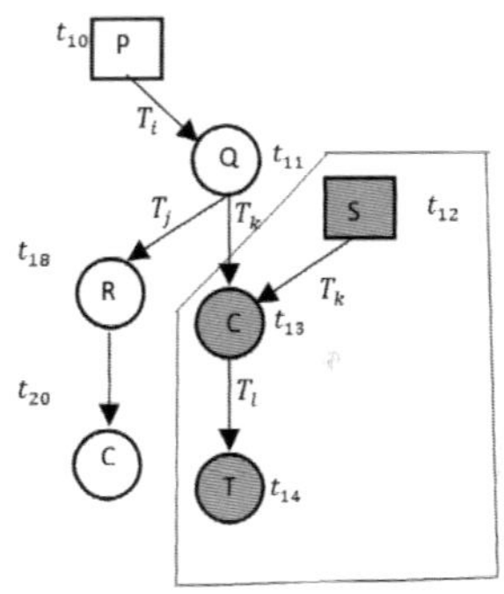

Figure 2. An example showing a data item being damaged and recovered in the same Subgraph G_2.

In Figure 2, it is evident that data item *C* was initially damaged at t_{13}. However, it undergoes modification again at t_{20}, transpiring within the same damaged graph. Notably, this time, *C* has a parent data item *R* that remains undamaged. Consequently, *C* is successfully recovered within the same damaged graph.

In a damage assessment scenario using the following algorithm for case 2, imagine we have a subgraph where the initial damaged data item is *A*, which belongs to the Blind Write Set (BWS) of the subgraph. The system starts by identifying that the subgraph is compromised because *A* intersects with the BWS. Next, it evaluates the Child Data Set (CDS), which contains dependent data items, such as *C* and *DD*. Since *C* depends on *A*, it is flagged for potential damage and added to the Potential Damaged List (PDL). Moving further, *D* depends on *C*, and as *C* is already marked for damage, *D* is also added to the PDL. The algorithm then checks the final updated times for *C* and *D* against the attack time and the affected time. If the last updated time of an item is equal to the affected time (e.g., *C*), it is confirmed as damaged and retained for further evaluation. For items like *D*, if its last update is after the affected time, the algorithm checks if its parent (in this case, *C*) is damaged. Since *C* is indeed compromised, *D* is also classified as damaged. Finally, the algorithm outputs a list of damaged data items (*C* and *D*) for further recovery processes. This structured approach efficiently isolates and assesses damage propagation through data dependencies.

Algorithm: (Evaluate Subgraph Damage)

Input:

D: The initial damaged set of data items.
BWS_i: The Blind Write set of a specific subgraph.
CDS_i :The Child Data Set of a specific subgraph.
G: The data structure or graph representing the subgraphs.
t_a: Attack time
t_{aff}: Affected time
t_{last}: last/final updated time
Rl: released data item list that contains the released data items would be kept after process
PDl: potential damaged list
damaged_data_items: A list of data items within the subgraph to retain for further evaluation.

Procedure:

1. **Assess Subgraph for Damage considering each Gi:**
   1.1. If $D \cap BWS_i$!=NULL for Gi
      1.1.1. indicating there's at least one common data item.
      1.1.2. Gi is damaged.
2. **Identify Data Items for Further Evaluation (if damaged):**
   2.1. If Gi is damaged:
      2.1.1. For each data items y in CDS_i:
         2.1.1.1. if y= f(z) where z∈ D or z∈ descendant of D
            2.1.1.1.1. Add y to the PDl
      2.1.2. For each data item x in PDl
         2.1.2.1. Check table Final_updated_timetable
         2.1.2.2. If t_last(x)=t_aff
            2.1.2.2.1. Add x to the damaged_data_items list
         2.1.2.3. Elif t_last(x)> t_aff
            2.1.2.3.1. if the Gi = the subgraph containing the initial damaged data item
               2.1.2.3.1.1. check parents of x
               2.1.2.3.1.2. if x=f(z) where z∈D or z∈ descendant of D
                  2.1.2.3.1.2.1. Add x to the damaged_data_items list
               2.1.2.3.1.3. Else
                  2.1.2.3.1.3.1. Release x
            2.1.2.3.2. Else
               2.1.2.3.2.1. Release x
3. if $D \cap BWS_i$ =NULL for G_i
   3.1. Release all the data items in G_i
4. **Output Result:**
   4.1. return the damaged_data_items list for further evaluation.

Comment:

2.1.2.2. to 2.1.2.2.1.1: If the last update time is after the damaged time, only then it is checked if they belong to same graph or in the different graph. If they belong to same graph, then they could be affected depending on if one of there are damaged or not and if they belong to different graph then they can be released. This scenario can be explained in the following section.

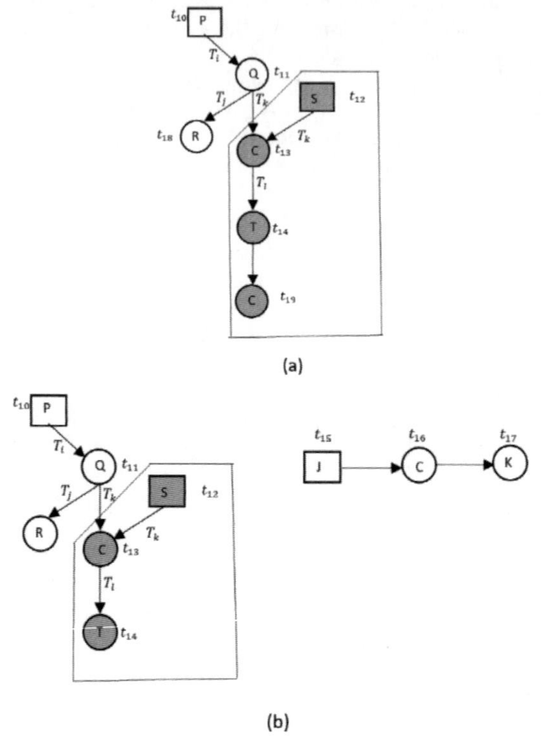

Figure 3. Multiple subgraphs in the data dependency (G).

TABLE III. FINAL UPDATED TIMETABLE (FOR SCENARIO (A))

Data Items	P	Q	S	T	C	R
$t_{\text{Last Updated}}$	t_{10}	t_{11}	t_{12}	t_{14}	t_{19}	t_{18}
Graph	G_2	G_2	G_2	G_2	G_2	G_2

TABLE IV. FINAL UPDATED TIMETABLE (FOR SCENARIO (B))

Data Items	P	Q	S	T	J	C	K	R
$t_{\text{Last Updated}}$	t_{10}	t_{11}	t_{12}	t_{14}	t_{15}	t_{16}	t_{17}	t_{18}
Graph	G_2	G_2	G_2	G_2	G_3	G_3	G_3	G_2

In Figure 3, two scenarios are discussed using G_2 and G_3. Tables III and IV display the final updated timetables for scenario (a) and (b), respectively.

When examining all the children for a particular graph, if it is discovered that the final updated time of a specific child is after the attack, the graph undergoes scrutiny. If the graph is distinct from the damaged graph, then the child data item is deemed safe for release. Because it belongs to a different graph that means it has no connection with the damaged items in the previous graph. Had there been a connection it would have been in the same graph. Since it is not in the same graph that guarantees there is no connection with any of the previously damaged values. However, if it belongs to the same damaged graph, it could be considered as damaged depending on its' parents. If it's one of the parents is damaged, then definitely that data item is damaged. And if none of its parents are damaged then it can be said that even after being damaged it recovered in the same graph. For example, in scenario (a), checking Table III reveals that the child data item *C* was finally updated at t_{19}, transpiring in the damaged graph G_2 (shaded part). Conversely, from the shaded area of Table IV (scenario (b)), even though *C* is a child of the initial damaged data item S, its last update occurred at t_{16} in the separate graph G_3, signifying that *C* is safe for release.

Our algorithm systematically processes each data item in the database to ascertain its affected status. If deemed affected, the data item is forwarded for recovery; if not, it is released. This comprehensive approach involves checking every graph, ensuring that each data item within that graph undergoes examination.

It is essential to note that there will be no data item existing outside of a graph. This assurance stems from the inherent nature of data item creation, where it is either generated blindly or based on another data item. In both scenarios, the data item is bound to be part of a graph.

As the algorithm meticulously examines each graph and subsequently categorizes every data item within as damaged or undamaged, the guarantee is established that the algorithm checks and classifies every data item as damaged or not damaged without exception.

VI. Simulation Results

In our simulation study, we consider five variables, which are as follows:

1. **Number of Transactions**: This represents the quantity of transactions executed per experiment.
2. **Number of Data Items**: Denotes the total count of data items utilized per experiment.
3. **Maximum Number of Operations per Transaction**: This parameter can vary and is randomly selected within the program.
4. **Maximum Write Operations**: Specifies the maximum number of write operations permitted per transaction, which can also vary.
5. **Number of Blind Writes**: Indicates the number of blind writes permitted in each experiment, calculated as 5% of the total number of transactions.

For consistency, we will maintain the following base values throughout the experiments:

- Number of Transactions = 200
- Number of Data Items = 1000
- Maximum Number of Operations per Transaction = 5
- Maximum Write Operations = 2
- Number of Blind Writes per Transaction = (Number of Transactions * 5%)

In each scenario, we will manipulate one variable while keeping the others constant. We will execute the program 25 times for each case and compute the average number of data readings using our blind writing method, as well as in normal transactions after identifying the malicious blind write.

A. *Varying the number of transactions*

In this scenario, we will be altering the number of transactions, ranging from 200 to 900, while maintaining the other variables (Number of data items, Maximum number of operations per transaction, Maximum write operations, Number of blind writes per transaction) constant.

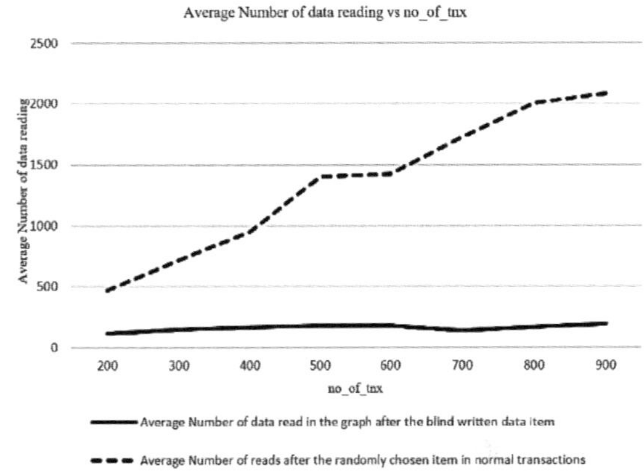

Figure 4: Varying the number of transactions.

As observed (Figure 4), when the number of transactions increases, the average data item reads after identifying malicious data in the usual log gradually rises. However, in our method, the average data item reads from the graph remains relatively constant but significantly lower compared to the usual scenario. This trend is attributed to the increasing number of transactions, which consequently leads to a higher number of blind writes and subsequently more graphs. Despite this, the average dependency per graph remains consistent. Hence, the graph representing our method appears almost flat due to this consistent average dependency per graph.

B. *Varying the number of data items*

In this scenario, we will be adjusting the number of data items, ranging from 500 to 3000, while keeping the other variables (Number of transactions, Maximum number of operations per transaction, Maximum write operations, Number of blind writes per transaction) constant.

In this scenario, we observe a significant reduction in the average reading of data items after identifying the damaged data in our method compared to the normal case (Figure 5). However, the graph remains relatively consistent. This consistency can be attributed to the fixed number of blind-written data items and the fixed number of written data items per transaction in our method. Since, the reading of data items is dependent on the data items written previously which means previously written data items are mostly read later on to write another data item, leading to consistent behavior even with variations in the number of data items.

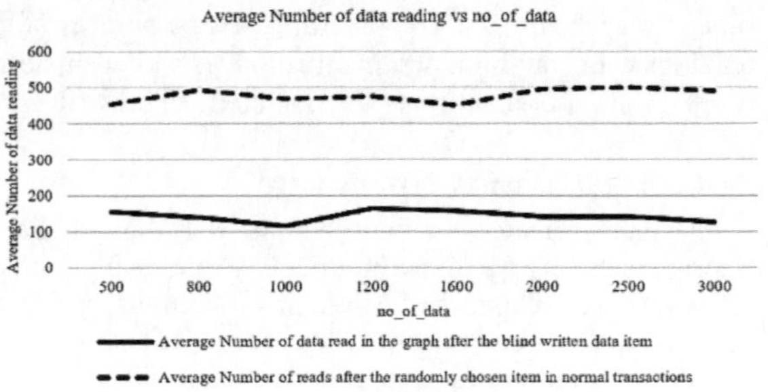

Figure 5: Varying the number of data items.

C. *Varying the Max number of operations per transaction*

In this scenario, we will be adjusting the maximum number of operations per transaction, ranging from 3 to 12, while maintaining the other variables (Number of transactions, Number of data items, Maximum write operations, Number of blind writes per transaction) constant.

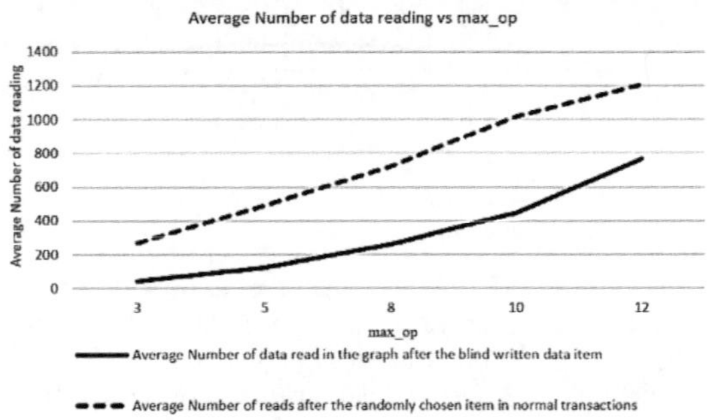

Figure 6: Varying the Max number of operations per transaction.

While both cases exhibit a gradual increase, the average read in our method remains significantly lower compared to normal transactions (Figure 6). However, the average read in our method increases gradually due to the higher number of operations per transaction. Since the number of write operations per transaction is fixed, more operations per transaction result in more read items, leading to increased dependency and consequently more data to read. This explains the gradual increase observed in the graph.

D. *Varying the Number of blind write per transaction*

In this scenario, we will be adjusting the number of blind writes per transaction, ranging from 1% to 10% of the number of transactions, while keeping the other variables (Number of transactions, Number of data items, Maximum number of operations per transaction, Maximum write operations) constant.

In this case, we observe a gradual decrease in the average reading in our method, while the average reading remains relatively constant in normal transactions (Figure 7). This difference can be attributed to the effect of varying the number of blind-written data items. In normal transactions, this variation has no impact. However, in our method, as the number of blind writes increases, the number of graphs also increases. Consequently, the number of data items depending on each graph decreases, leading to a decrease in the average reading.

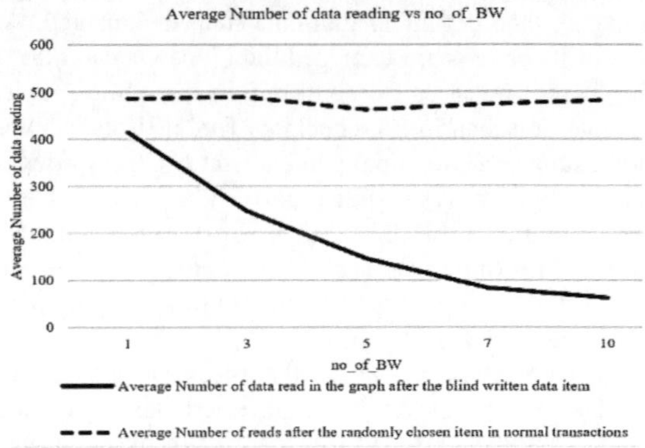

Figure 7: Varying the Number of blind writes per transaction.

It is important to note that in the first scenario where the number of transactions was varied, the graph representing our method remained constant. This was because the number of blind writes increased proportionally with the number of transactions. However, in the current scenario where the number of transactions and other factors are fixed, while the number of blind writes was varied, we observe a gradual decrease in the average number of data items read to recover after identifying the malicious data.

E. *Varying the Max write operations*

In this scenario, we will manipulate the number of maximum write operations, ranging from 1 to 5, while keeping the other variables constant (Number of transactions, Number of data items, Maximum number of operations per transaction, Number of blind write per transaction).

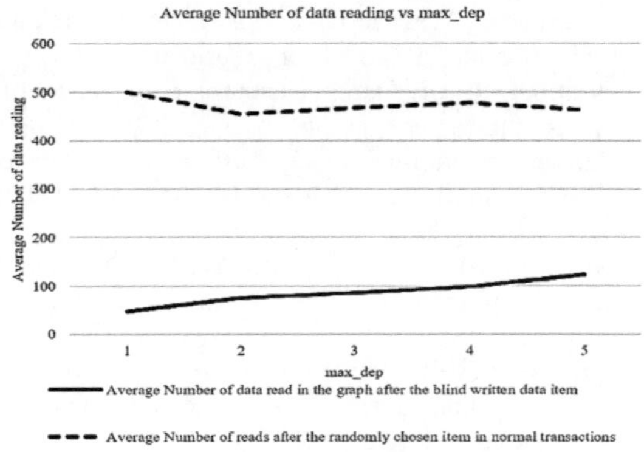

Figure 8: Varying the Max write operations.

In this case, it can be observed that in the normal case, the average reading remains somewhat constant (Figure 8). However, in our method, it increases gradually. This occurs because, with more write operations, the dependency also increases, given that blind writes are fixed in this scenario. Although blind writings are fixed, the process involves writing more data items after reading them, leading to increased dependency. Consequently, the graph shows a slight increase over time.

VII. CONCLUSION

This research proposes a novel technique for swiftly assessing damage caused by malicious attacks in fog computing systems. Traditional methods relying on log analysis are slow, hindering real-time data access. This model addresses this issue by leveraging blind write lineage, efficiently tracing the impact of blindly written data. The model constructs three key data structures during ongoing transactions: a Blind Data Set to track blindly written items, a Children Data Set to identify dependent data items, and Sub-dependency Graphs to represent intricate data relationships. When an attack is detected, the algorithm analyzes affected sub-dependency graphs and evaluates data items within them. This evaluation considers time parameters, release criteria, and potential damage to generate a final list of compromised data items. The simulation results show that the model offers advantages in speed, efficiency, and accuracy compared to traditional methods. However, applying this approach to real-world fog systems presents several requirements. These include the need for robust transaction logging, real-time dependency tracking mechanisms, and synchronization across distributed nodes. One key lesson learned is the critical role of data dependency management in preventing the propagation of damage. However, the diversity of fog systems introduces challenges, particularly the need to balance performance with accuracy in environments with heterogeneous node configurations and complex multipath dependencies. Future work will focus on refining the model to address attacks within specific time ranges, optimizing memory consumption through more efficient data structures, and ensuring scalability across diverse fog architectures. Additionally, exploring blockchain integration for immutable logging of transactions will further enhance the system's security and resilience. Overall, this research offers a significant contribution towards building more robust fog computing systems capable of maintaining real-time data access and swift recovery in the face of cyberattacks.

ACKNOWLEDGMENT

This work has been supported in part by grant H98230-22-1-0321 issued by the National Security Agency as part of the National Centers of Academic Excellence in Cybersecurity's mission to expand cybersecurity research and education for the Nation.

REFERENCES

[1] M. S. Ahmad and B. Panda, "Damage Assessment in Fog Computing Systems: A Blind Write Lineage Approach." In 2024 IEEE 24th International Symposium on Cluster, Cloud and Internet Computing Workshops (CCGridW), pp. 50-55. IEEE, 2024.

[2] F. Bonomi, R. Milito, J. Zhu, and S. Addepalli. "Fog computing and its role in the internet of things," In Proceedings of the first edition of the MCC workshop on Mobile cloud computing, pp. 13-16. 2012.

[3] C. Mouradian et al., "A Comprehensive Survey on Fog Computing: State-of-the-art and Research Challenges", IEE Communications Surveys Tutorials, vol. 20, pp. 416-464. 2018.

[4] L. M. Vaquero and L. Rodero-Merino, "Finding Your Way in the Fog: Towards a Comprehensive Definition of Fog Computing", ACM SIGCOMM Computer Communication Review, vol. 44., No. 5, pp. 27-32, 2014.

[5] G. Sun et al., "Security and privacy preservation in fog-based crowd sensing on the internet of vehicles," Journal of Network and Computer Applications, vol. 134, pp. 89–99, 2019.

[6] M. Mukherjee et al., "Security and Privary in Fog Computing: Challenges", IEEE Access, vol. 5, pp. 19293-19304, 2017.

[7] D. Wu and N. Ansari, "A Cooperative Computing Strategy for Blockchain-Secured Fog Computing," in IEEE Internet of Things Journal, vol. 7, no. 7, pp. 6603-6609, July 2020, doi: 10.1109/JIOT.2020.2974231.

[8] E. Viganò, M. Loi, and E. Yaghmaei, "Cybersecurity of Critical Infrastructure," In The Ethics of Cybersecurity; Springer: Cham, Switzerland, 2020, pp. 157–177.

[9] P. Kotzanikolaou, M. Theoharidou, and D. Gritzalis, "Cascading Effects of Common-Cause Failures in Critical Infrastructures," In: J. Butts and S. Shenoi (eds) Critical Infrastructure Protection VII. ICCIP 2013. IFIP Advances in Information and Communication Technology, vol 417. Springer, Berlin, Heidelberg. Communications, 2017, pp. 1-9.

[10] J. Ding, Y. Atif, S. F. Andler, B. Lindström, and M. Jeusfel, "CPS-based threat modeling for critical infrastructure protection," ACM SIGMETRICS Performance Evaluation Review, 45(2), pp.129-132, 2017.

[11] D. Rehak, J. Markuci, M. Hromada, and K. Barcova, "Quantitative evaluation of the synergistic effects of failures in a critical infrastructure system," International Journal of Critical Infrastructure Protection, *14*, pp.3-17, 2016.

[12] R. E. Stearns and D. J. Rosenkrantz, "Distributed Database Concurrency Controls using Before-values," Proceedings of the 1981 ACM SIGMOD International Conference on Management of Data, pp. 74-83, 1981.

[13] N. das Chagas Mendonca and R. de Oliveira Anido, "Using Extended Hierarchical Quorum Consensus to Control Replicated Data: from Traditional Voting to Logical Structures," Proceedings of the Twenty-Seventh Hawaii International Conference on System Sciences, vol. 27. pp. 303–312, 1994.

[14] A. Burger, V. Kumar, and M. L. Hines, "Performance of Multiversion and Distributed Two-Phase Locking Concurrency Control Mechanisms in Distributed Databases," Inf. Sci., vol. 96, no. 1-2, pp. 129-152, 1997.

[15] P. Ammann, S. Jajodia and Peng Liu, "Recovery from malicious transactions," in IEEE Transactions on Knowledge and Data Engineering, vol. 14, no. 5, pp. 1167-1185, Sept.-Oct. 2002, doi: 10.1109/TKDE.2002.1033782.

[16] S. Tripathy and B. Panda, "Post-Intrusion Recovery Using Data Dependency Approach," In Proceedings of the 2001 IEEE Workshop on Information Assurance and Security, pp. 156-160, 2001.

[17] B. Panda and P. Ragothaman, "Database Recovery in Information Warfare Scenario," Handbooks in Information Systems, vol. 4, Information Assurance, Security and Privacy Services, pp. 73-97, H. Raghav Rao 12 and Shambhu Upadhyaya (Editors), Emerald Publications, United Kingdom, July 2009.

[18] R. A. Haraty, S. Kaddoura, and A.S. Zekri, "Recovery of business intelligence systems: Towards guaranteed continuity of patient centric healthcare systems through a matrix-based recovery approach," Telematics and Informatics, 35(4), pp. 801-814, 2018.

[19] M. Alshehri et al., "A Novel Blockchain-based Encryption Model to Protect Fog Nodes from Behaviors of Malicious Nodes," Electronics, vol. 10, pp. 313, 2022.

Theoretical and Practical Aspects in Identifying Gaps and Preparing for Post-Quantum Cryptography

Jörn-Marc Schmidt
IU International University of Applied Science
Erfurt, Thüringen, Germany
joern-marc.schmidt@iu.org

Alexander Lawall
IU International University of Applied Science
Erfurt, Thüringen, Germany
alexander.lawall@iu.org

***Abstract*—In cryptographic security, quantum computing poses a significant challenge to traditional cryptographic protocols. This study investigates the landscape of Post-Quantum Cryptography (PQC), focusing on the transition from theoretical underpinnings, over standardization efforts to practical implementations. The primary research question that guides this contribution is: What mechanisms can be implemented to safeguard applications? This question is answered by the current state of standards supporting PQC and the ongoing preparation efforts. Thereby, not only the standards for the cryptographic algorithms, but also the protocols relying on them are considered. Furthermore, the status of (open-source) implementations is considered. This study contributes to the ongoing efforts to strengthen cryptographic systems against the challenges posed by quantum computing and provides insights into the available possibilities.**

Keywords-Post Quantum Cryptography (PQC); PQC Standards; PQC Implementations.

I. Introduction

Quantum computers will influence many fields. They will improve biological and chemical simulations, can be applied for risk modeling, and improve solving of optimization problems. In addition to those constructive improvements, they have the potential to impact the security of cryptographic algorithms. Especially, asymmetric algorithms that rely on the hardness factorization or the discrete logarithm problem cannot be considered secure when a Cryptographic Relevant Quantum Computer (CRQC) is available. Hence, use cases relying on such algorithms will be impacted by CRQCs. Moreover, even data transmitted today can be endangered by attackers recording the transmission and decrypting it as soon as CRQCs are available. This is referred to as harvest now and decrypt later attack.

This challenge, i.e. Post-Quantum (PQ) security, is already picked up by security researchers, developers, several government agencies, and companies. In order to drive the readiness of post-quantum cryptographic algorithms and their adoption in standard applications forward, many activities are underway. They include various working groups, like the Internet Engineering Task Force (IETF) working group *Post-Quantum Use In Protocols* [1], and the European Telecommunications Standards Institute (ETSI) *Quantum-Safe Cryptography (QSC)* working group [2]. Further activities are driven by various companies like Google [3], IBM [4], and Microsoft [5], and Utimaco [6].

This paper provides an overview of those activities. Its scope includes enterprise use cases, not the implementations that are provided to end-users directly. Thereby, its focus is on use cases for asymmetric cryptography due to the expected high impact of CRQC on this type of algorithm. The paper highlights the status of standardization processes and the production-readiness of implementations. As such, it gives guidance on what can be done today to protect applications and data.

The paper is structured as follows. Section II discusses the general preparation process and security protocols. Section III summarizes the status of the standardization of new cryptographic algorithms, while Section IV looks into the status of protocol standards. Libraries that support PQC algorithms, as a foundation for implementations, are presented in Section V. Finally, conclusions are drawn in Section VI.

II. Building Blocks

The transition to post-quantum cryptography, given the widespread use of the algorithms, is a huge undertaking. As a first step, it is important to understand where susceptible algorithms are employed and how valuable the protected data is. Hence, for a company to prepare, a risk assessment of its application portfolio is required. The first step in such an endeavor is creating a cryptographic inventory, providing insights on where which algorithms, protocols and related parameters are used. Various tools can help creating an inventory [7].

Afterwards, a sound risk model that integrates into the company's risk management procedures is required. For the financial industry, the Financial Services Information Sharing and Analysis Center (FS-ISAC) provides a white paper on modeling the risk [8]. This helps to create a profound strategy and to decide where the highest risks and the biggest benefits are expected. Finally, a maturity index helps judging and comparing where a company is on its journey to post-quantum security [9] [10].

A. Data Protection

Generally speaking, data requires protection at rest, in transit, and in use.

Data at rest commonly relies on symmetric cryptography, where limited impact of quantum computers is expected. Solutions that employ asymmetric cryptography can make

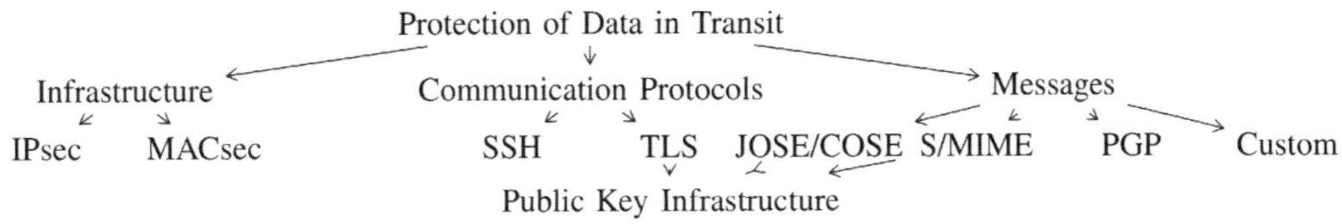

Figure 1. Overview of protocols used in different scenarios to protect data in transit.

use of Key Encapsulation Mechanisms (KEMs) discussed in Section III.

Encryption of data in use is not yet widely used. An available possibility is to rely on processor extensions like Intel Software Guard Extensions (SGX) [11] / Trust Domain Extensions (TDX) [12] or AMD Secure Encrypted Virtualization (SEV) [13]. Especially the attestation, i.e., proving that the protected environment is in a trustworthy state, relies on asymmetric cryptography. Solutions are discussed in [14].

In particular, when focusing on harvest now and decrypt later attack scenarios, security of encryption in transit against attacks with quantum computers is the most pressing scenario. In order to protect data in transit, it is possible to

- protect the underlying infrastructure by ensuring that the communication is PQ-secure. While this has large impact, it is restricted to endpoints that are in direct control; protecting the connections to end-users might not be possible. Commonly, protocols like IPsec and MACsec are employed in such scenarios.
- ensure that the communication protocols are PQ-secure. Common protocols are Transport Layer Security (TLS) and Secure Shell (SSH). Both protocols allow to negotiate the used ciphers with a handshake. This enables using PQC whenever both parties support it without preventing non-PQC-secure communication in case one endpoint is not able to use such a cipher.
- encrypt the transferred message in a quantum-secure way. By using a method that ensures that the data is encapsulated with post-quantum cryptography, a sound protection against adversaries can be achieved. This can be achieved either via standards suitable to the application, like Secure/Multipurpose Internet Mail Extensions (S/MIME) for emails/web-pages, Javascript Object Signing and Encryption (JOSE)/Concise Binary Object Representation (CBOR) Object Signing and Encryption (COSE) for JSON-based messages and Pretty Good Privacy (PGP) for encrypting arbitrary data including files. Another option is to rely on self-defined, custom protocols, e.g. by employing implementations discussed in Section V directly.

The different options that are discussed in the following sections are given in Figure 1.

B. Public Key Infrastructure (PKI) and Certificates

Methods for authentication and ensuring the authenticity of data are required as soon as a CRQC is available. Collecting data today, as in the harvest and decrypt scenario, does not represent a current threat. However, a lack of being ready in time will have devastating consequences as well, as an adversary can impersonate every identity that is not protected and forge any non-PQC signature. A foundation for many protocols and signatures is a valid certificate. Hence, a PQ-secure Public Key Infrastructure (PKI) is required. It can be the foundation for TLS authentication, for re-signing documents, like contracts, and for secure authentication of devices.

III. The Quest for new Cryptographic Algorithms

The basis of all protocols and building blocks is quantum-secure algorithms. Hence, it is essential to develop and standardize new (asymmetric) cryptographic algorithms to replace the current ones.

A key activity in this regard was launched by National Institute of Standards and Technology (NIST) end of 2016. The NIST issued a call for papers for new post-quantum cryptographic algorithms [15]. Out of 69 initial submissions, three were selected to become Federal Information Processing Standards (FIPS). The following documents have recently (at the time writing this paper) been finalized:

- FIPS 203, Module-Lattice-Based Key-Encapsulation Mechanism Standard (ML-KEM), based on Cryptographic Suite for Algebraic Lattices (CRYSTALS)-Kyber [16]
- FIPS 204, Module-Lattice-Based Digital Signature Standard (ML-DSA), based on CRYSTALS-Dilithium [17]
- FIPS 205, Stateless Hash-Based Digital Signature Standard (SLH-DSA), based on SPHINCS+ (for practical stateless hash-based signatures) [18]

Moreover, the process is continuing with a fourth round. Remaining candidates are the Key-Encapsulation Mechanisms (KEMs) Bit Flipping Key Encapsulation (BIKE), Classic McEliece, Hamming Quasi-Cyclic (HQC), and Supersingular Isogeny Key Encapsulation (SIKE). As there is no algorithm for digital signatures left from the initial submissions, NIST launched another Call-for-Proposals on *Post-Quantum Cryptography: Digital Signature Schemes*, which is currently in the first round. Hence, despite there are NIST standards already finalized, further algorithms are under consideration.

Naturally, the NIST process and its contributions from researchers all over the world are closely followed by government agencies from other nations.

The British National Cyber Security Center (NCSC) published a white paper recommending the use of the NIST standards or the hash-based signatures Leighton-Micali Hash-Based Signatures (LMS) or eXtended Merkle Signature Scheme (XMSS) [19].

In terms of post-quantum algorithms, the German Bundesamt für Sicherheit in der Informationstechnik (BSI) recommends in its technical policy TR-02102-1 Version 2024-01 using FrodoKEM or Classic McElice as a post-quantum cryptographic algorithm for encryption/key-agreement [20]. It recommends FrodoKEM as a more conservative choice compared to the ML-KEM that is standardized by NIST. While FrodoKEM is not planned to be part of a NIST standard, its specification was submitted to International Organization for Standardization (ISO) for standardization [21]. However, the policy states that ML-KEM will be included in a future version based on the publication of the related NIST standard.

For digital signatures, the policy recommends (among non-PQC-algorithms) Merkle-Signatures, in detail XMSS or LMS, including Multi-Tree-Variants as described in [22]. In addition, it mentions the intent to include SLH-DSA (SPHINCS+) and ML-DSA (CRYSTALS-Dilithium) in future versions.

In general, the policy recommends combining a PQC approach and a classical one. The combination needs to ensure to stay secure, as long as one of the used schemes is secure. Hash-based signatures are an exception in case they are properly implemented, i.e., the do not require a hybrid approach.

In contrast to the German BSI, the French Cybersecurity Agency (ANSSI) states in their PQC position paper, that the *ANSSI traditionally does not provide any closed list of recommended algorithms in order to avoid proscribing innovative state-of-the-art algorithms that could be well-suited for some particular use cases* [23]. However, a list of post-quantum algorithms together with recommendations is given. For KEM, they include ML-KEM and FrodoKEM. The list of digital signature algorithms contains ML-DSA, Falcon (FN-DSA), XMSS/LMS and SLH-DSA. In terms of combining PQC and classical algorithms, the ANSSI states their alignment with the position of the BSI recommending a hybrid approach.

Overall, the process of standardization results in the publication of various recommendations and draft standards. The analysis, including research on secure implementations, is still ongoing, leading to new attacks, cf. [24]. While the NIST is driving the most prominent competition, the government bodies of UK, Germany, and France are basically in line with the recommendations and have not announced any plans for running another competition.

Concluding, the current state, especially in a hybrid setting with a classic algorithm, provides a solid foundation for building and implementing protocols and further post-quantum secure solutions.

IV. Protocols

In addition to developing and standardizing quantum-secure algorithms, protocol standards need to be adopted.

A. *Infrastructure*

Common communication protocols to connect hosts to networks in a secure fashion or to establish a secure connection between networks are MACsec [25] and IPsec [26].

1) MACsec: As MACsec relies only on symmetric algorithms during the key agreement, using a 256-bit key is sufficient for post-quantum security. In addition, it is important to ensure that the key distribution is quantum-secure. Especially, since the session keys do not provide forward secrecy, i.e., a compromise of the long-term key material affects past session keys [27].

2) IPsec: For IPsec, Request For Comments (RFC) 8784 [28] defines a method to use pre-shared keys to achieve post-quantum security. This provides a viable solution already today. Potential adoptions of PQC for the Internet Key Exchange Protocol Version 2 (IKEv2) are in draft status. For example, the document specifying a Hybrid Key Exchange with ML-KEM [29] is currently an individual submission without IETF endorsement.

B. *Communication Protocols*

Common communication protocols include Transport Layer Security (TLS) and Secure Shell (SSH).

1) Transport Layer Security (TLS): The Transport Layer Security (TLS) protocol allows a secure end-to-end connection between applications. Various research has been conducted on how to best integrate post-quantum cryptography in the protocol and related performance, e.g., [30] [31].

All this research focuses on the actual TLS 1.3 version. For TLS 1.3, a draft specifies a hybrid use of algorithms [32]. This ensures that the connections remain secure even if used algorithms are broken. An experimental implementation of this draft is available in the Botan library [33] since version 3.2. Another implementation of the draft is provided by the Open Quantum Safe project [34] in the form of an OpenSSLv3 provider and an integration into a BoringSSL fork. However, those two implementations should not be considered *production quality* according to the project.

Note that a recent IETF draft states that TLS 1.2 will not be further enhanced, which implies, it will not support PQC, despite TLS 1.2 is still widespread [35].

Further experiments on challenges when using PQC-TLS at a large scale were conducted by Google [3]. Their tests revealed incompatibilities in network products that will be fixed via firmware updates. Similar PQC-support is enabled by Cloudflare [36], targeting support of all outbound connections by March 2024. This can be used with browsers supporting the hybrid cipher suite consisting of X25519 and Kyber-768, like Chrome, where it has been enabled since version 116 [37].

Hence, a draft standard and first implementations are available, and some widespread experiments have been conducted successfully. Stable and standardized support of PQC for TLS 1.3 is expected to build on the released NIST standards.

2) Secure Shell (SSH): Secure Shell (SSH) is a protocol for secure execution of remote commands. A very prominent implementation is OpenSSH, which is part of many major Linux distributions. OpenSSH made a hybrid key exchange method that combines Number Theory Research Unit (NTRU)-Prime with an Elliptic-curve Diffie–Hellman (ECDH) key exchange default in version 9.0/9.0p1 [38]. However, this implementation relies on an individual IETF draft submission that has already expired [39]. Other, at the time of writing, active drafts of individual IETF submissions are [40] and [41]. The ladder one is implemented and used by Amazon Web Services (AWS) [42]. The Open Quantum Safe project [34] also provides an implementation of this draft, but it is currently inactive.

Overall, with OpenSSL, that uses a hybrid approach per default, and the AWS implementation, there are real-world possibilities for PQC key-agreement, despite there being no final standard yet.

C. Message Security

On the message layer, the application can choose to encrypt/sign the transferred data, depending on the use case. Potential solutions include JOSE/COSE for sharing data between applications, S/MIME for mail/web pages and PGP for arbitrary data, including file exchange.

1) JOSE/COSE: JSON and CBOR are formats for data exchange between applications. The related signing and encryption standards are JOSE and COSE. For COSE, hash-based signatures are defined in RFC 8778 [43]. Active IETF drafts exist to support Dilithium [44] and SPHINCS+ signatures [45]. In addition to those working group drafts, other individual drafts have been submitted to the IETF as well.

2) S/MIME: The S/MIME standard [46] mandates the support of RSA-based and EC-based ciphers for signing and encryption. Preparing the standard for the quantum-age is part of the *Limited Additional Mechanisms for PKIX and SMIME (lamps)* working group charta [47]. Nevertheless, the possibility of integrating PQC-ciphers into the mail client Thunderbird is briefly discussed in [48], and a demo integration was done by the MTG AG [49].

3) PGP: The options for using post-quantum ciphers in PGP were analyzed by Wussler [50], leading to an IETF draft [51]. A former version of this draft was formally analyzed by Tran et al. [52].

While there is work underway for all three standards, there is still a lack of practical implementations and experiments that will lead to solutions that can be used in production environments.

D. Public Key Infrastructures (PKIs) and Certificates

Public Key Infrastructures (PKIs) are essential for ensuring trust in the digital world. Ranging from communication protocols to digitally signed documents - a reliable PKI is required to ensure the identity of the counterpart. For trustworthy certificates in the presence of quantum computers, the whole chain, starting from the root certificate must be quantum-secure.

The draft [53] defines a composite certificate combining ML-DSA with traditional signature algorithms. This solution ensures that the certificate remains secure even in case one of the algorithms is broken. A similar approach is used for KEM solutions [54] in the context of PKI-related profiles and protocols like Cryptographic Message Syntax (CMS) [55] and Public Key Infrastructure for X.509 (PKIX).

Various drafts are already published to be ready to proceed now the NIST standards are finalized. They include certificates using stateless hash-based digital signatures [56], Kyber [57], and Dilithium [58].

During the transition phase, it is important that also legacy systems that might not support post-quantum cryptography can verify a certificate with classic algorithms. The specifications above cannot be used in such a scenario, as they require the verifying system process PQC signatures. A possible approach in the transition scenario is using related certificates, as laid out in the draft specifications [59] and [60]. The impact of hybrid certificates on current implementations was investigated in [61]. The authors concluded the certificates can be processed by the tested solutions without or with minor modifications.

Another option is specified in by the International Telecommunication Union Telecommunication Standardization Sector (ITU-T) [62], namely to include an alternative signature in a certificate. This allows clients that are not capable of processing PQC algorithm to ignore this signature, while others can benefit from it. However, the drawback of this approach is the increased certificate size for all consuming entities.

When it comes to commercial products, PKI solution vendors are working towards addressing the upcoming challenges, preparing examples [63], offering experimental suites [6], [64] or solutions [65].

Despite various activities that are underway, neither the majority of the standardization work nor the related implementations have been concluded yet. As especially the root certificates are commonly valid for several years, it is important to plan their replacement together with a sound transition approach.

V. Foundations and Libraries

Together with research and standardization of PQC algorithms, their implementation is progressing. A popular project to support *the transition to quantum-resistant cryptography* is Open Quantum Safe [34]. It is part of the Linux Foundation's Post-Quantum Cryptography Alliance. Its main working items are a C library for post-quantum algorithms, called liboqs, and prototype integration into protocols and applications. Currently, liboqs supports Kyber, Dilithum, Falcon and SPHINCS+ algorithms selected by NIST, the round 4 candidates Classic McEliece, BIKE and HQC, as well as, FrodoKEM and NTRU-Prime. The project provides several language wrappers to allow using it for example in C++, JAVA, Go, and Python. However, the project page does recommend refraining from using the library in production environments, as it has not undergone a thorough audit/analysis process yet.

Another popular library that provides PQC support is Bouncy Castle for Java and C# [66]. Its implementation includes all algorithms supported by liboqs, plus the NIST round 3 candidates Saber, NTRU, Picnic, Rainbow and Great Multivariate Short Signature (GeMSS). The project states that those algorithms can be used for experiments as they are still subject to change and that the provided KEM algorithms are suited for short-term protection in a hybrid setting, not for long-term protection.

Overall, there are two aspects to consider about using PQC algorithms today: (1) First standards have recently been finalized and the security research is ongoing. They also do not have the benefit of a long history of intensive security research that current standards possess. Therefore, the Bouncy Castle team, in line with the BSI, recommends using the current PQC algorithms in a hybrid mode. (2) In addition to the security of the algorithms, quality [67] and security of its implementations are important. This includes sufficient quality assurance and auditing to prevent vulnerabilities and security bugs as well as resistance against potential side-channel attacks like [68]–[70].

VI. Conclusions and Recommendations

Quantum computers endanger the security cryptographic algorithms. Especially asymmetric algorithms are affected. This requires new algorithms as well as updated standards to make use of those new algorithms. Various efforts from research over standardization to implementation are currently under way to address this challenge. This paper started by looking at possibilities to secure the underlying network infrastructure. As IPsec and MACsec can rely on secret-key cryptography, the remaining challenge is secure key management.

In order to achieve end-to-end security, SSH can be used with post-quantum security, e.g., via OpenSSH, whereas TLS implementations are still in an experimental state. Standards for message encryption are still at a comparably early stage. However, libraries, especially BouncyCastle for JAVA and C#, provide algorithms that can already integrated into applications; given the required expert knowledge is available.

Overall, the transition will require thorough planning. This paper highlighted where first steps can be done already today. Depending on the use case, hybrid approaches can protect against quantum attacks while preventing risks due to attacks on comparably new PQC algorithms. Furthermore, becoming crypto-agile, in the sense that algorithms can be exchanged easily, will not only help in addressing the current PQC challenge, but also reduce the effort of future transitions of cryptographic algorithms.

References

[1] "Post-Quantum Use In Protocols (pquip)," retrieved: September, 2024. [Online]. Available: https://datatracker.ietf.org/wg/pquip/about/

[2] "Quantum-Safe Cryptography (QSC)," retrieved: September, 2024. [Online]. Available: https://www.etsi.org/technologies/quantum-safe-cryptography

[3] Googe, "How Google is preparing for a post-quantum world, note = retrieved: September, 2024." [Online]. Available: https://cloud.google.com/blog/products/identity-security/how-google-is-preparing-for-a-post-quantum-world

[4] IBM, "Make the world quantum safe," retrieved: September, 2024. [Online]. Available: title={https://www.ibm.com/quantum/quantum-safe},

[5] Microsoft, "Post-quantum cryptography," retrieved: September, 2024. [Online]. Available: https://www.microsoft.com/en-us/research/project/post-quantum-cryptography/

[6] Utimaco, "Post Quantum Cryptography," retrieved: September, 2024. [Online]. Available: https://utimaco.com/solutions/applications/post-quantum-cryptography

[7] ETSI, "ETSI TR 103 619 V1.1.1 (2020-07) - CYBER; Migration strategies and recommendations to Quantum Safe schemes ." [Online]. Available: https://www.etsi.org/deliver/etsi_tr/103600_103699/103619/01.01.01_60/tr_103619v010101p.pdf

[8] Post-Quantum Cryptography (PQC) Working Group, "Risk model technical paper," FS-ISAC, Tech. Rep., 2023, retrieved: September, 2024. [Online]. Available: https://www.fsisac.com/hubfs/Knowledge/PQC/RiskModel.pdf

[9] T. Patterson, "Moving toward a Quantum Security Maturity Index," retrieved: September, 2024. [Online]. Available: https://pkic.org/events/2023/pqc-conference-amsterdam-nl/pkic-pqcc_tom-patterson_accenture_moving-toward-a-quantum-security-maturity-index.pdf

[10] DigiCert, "Post-Quantum Cryptography (PQC) Maturity Model," retrieved: September, 2024. [Online]. Available: https://www.digicert.com/resources/post-quantum-cryptography-maturity-model.pdf

[11] Intel, "Intel® Software Guard Extensions (Intel®SGX)," retrieved: September, 2024. [Online]. Available: https://www.intel.de/content/www/de/de/products/docs/accelerator-engines/software-guard-extensions.html

[12] ——, "Intel® Trust Domain Extensions (Intel® TDX)," retrieved: September, 2024. [Online]. Available: https://www.intel.com/content/www/us/en/developer/tools/trust-domain-extensions/overview.html

[13] AMD, "AMD Secure Encrypted Virtualization (SEV)," retrieved: September, 2024. [Online]. Available: https://www.amd.com/de/developer/sev.html

[14] G. Caruso, "Post-quantum algorithms support in Trusted Execution Environment," Ph.D. dissertation, Politecnico di Torino, 2024.

[15] NIST, "NIST CFP," retrieved: September, 2024. [Online]. Available: https://csrc.nist.gov/Projects/post-quantum-cryptography/post-quantum-cryptography-standardization/Call-for-Proposals

[16] N. I. of Standards and Technology, "Module-lattice-based key-encapsulation mechanism standard," U.S. Department of Commerce, Washington, D.C., Tech. Rep. Federal Information Processing Standards Publication (FIPS) 203, 2024.

[17] ——, "Module-lattice-based digital signature standard," U.S. Department of Commerce, Washington, D.C., Tech. Rep. Federal Information Processing Standards Publication (FIPS) 204, 2024.

[18] ——, "Stateless hash-based digital signature standard," U.S. Department of Commerce, Washington, D.C., Tech. Rep. Federal Information Processing Standards Publication (FIPS) 205, 2024.

[19] National Cyber Security Center, "Next steps in preparing for post-quantum cryptography," 2023-11-039 2023. [Online]. Available: https://www.ncsc.gov.uk/whitepaper/next-steps-preparing-for-post-quantum-cryptography

[20] Federal Office for Information Security, "Kryptographische Verfahren: Empfehlungen und Schlüssellängen," Bonn, Deutschland, 2024. [Online]. Available: https://www.bsi.bund.de/SharedDocs/Downloads/DE/BSI/Publikationen/TechnischeRichtlinien/TR02102/BSI-TR-02102.pdf

[21] E. Alkim et al., "FrodoKEM - Practical quantum-secure key encapsulation from generic lattices." [Online]. Available: https://frodokem.org/

[22] D. Cooper, D. Apon, Q. Dang, M. Davidson, M. Dworkin, and C. Miller, "Recommendation for Stateful Hash-Based Signature Schemes," 2020. [Online]. Available: https://nvlpubs.nist.gov/nistpubs/SpecialPublications/NIST.SP.800-208.pdf

[23] ANSSI, "ANSSI views on the Post-Quantum Cryptography transition (2023 follow up)," 2023. [Online]. Available: https://cyber.gouv.fr/sites/default/files/document/follow_up_position_paper_on_post_quantum_cryptography.pdf

[24] P. Ravi, D. Jap, S. Bhasin, and A. Chattopadhyay, "Machine Learning based Blind Side-Channel Attacks on PQC-based KEMs - A Case Study of Kyber KEM," Cryptology ePrint Archive, Paper 2024/169, 2024, https://eprint.iacr.org/2024/169. [Online]. Available: https://eprint.iacr.org/2024/169

[25] M. Seaman, "IEEE Standard for Local and metropolitan area networks–Media Access Control (MAC) Security." [Online]. Available: https://1.ieee802.org/security/802-1ae/

[26] S. Frankel and S. Krishnan, "IP Security (IPsec) and Internet Key Exchange (IKE) Document Roadmap," RFC 6071, Feb. 2011. [Online]. Available: https://www.rfc-editor.org/info/rfc6071

[27] ETSI, "ETSI TR 103 617 V1.1.1 (2018-09) - Quantum-Safe Virtual Private Networks." [Online]. Available: https://www.etsi.org/deliver/etsi_tr/103600_103699/103617/01.01.01_60/tr_103617v010101p.pdf

[28] S. Fluhrer, P. Kampanakis, D. McGrew, and V. Smyslov, "Mixing Preshared Keys in the Internet Key Exchange Protocol Version 2 (IKEv2) for Post-quantum Security," RFC 8784, Jun. 2020. [Online]. Available: https://www.rfc-editor.org/info/rfc8784

[29] P. Kampanakis and G. Ravago, "Post-quantum Hybrid Key Exchange with ML-KEM in the Internet Key Exchange Protocol Version 2 (IKEv2)," Internet Engineering Task Force, Internet-Draft draft-kampanakis-ml-kem-ikev2-03, Mar. 2024, work in Progress. [Online]. Available: https://datatracker.ietf.org/doc/draft-kampanakis-ml-kem-ikev2/03/

[30] J. I. E. Pablos, M. E. Marriaga, and A. P. d. Pozo, "Design and Implementation of a Post-Quantum Group Authenticated Key Exchange Protocol With the LibOQS Library: A Comparative Performance Analysis From Classic McEliece, Kyber, NTRU, and Saber," *IEEE Access*, vol. 10, pp. 120 951–120 983, 2022.

[31] J. Henrich, A. Heinemann, A. Wiesmaier, and N. Schmitt, "Performance Impact of PQC KEMs on TLS 1.3 Under Varying Network Characteristics," in *Information Security*, E. Athanasopoulos and B. Mennink, Eds. Cham: Springer Nature Switzerland, 2023, pp. 267–287.

[32] D. Stebila, S. Fluhrer, and S. Gueron, "Hybrid key exchange in TLS 1.3," Internet Engineering Task Force, Internet-Draft draft-ietf-tls-hybrid-design-10, Apr. 2024, work in Progress. [Online]. Available: https://datatracker.ietf.org/doc/draft-ietf-tls-hybrid-design/10/

[33] Botan, "Botan - Release Notes," retrieved: September, 2024. [Online]. Available: https://botan.randombit.net/news.html#version-3-2-0-2023-10-09

[34] "Open Quantum Safe Project," retrieved: September, 2024. [Online]. Available: https://openquantumsafe.org/

[35] R. Salz and N. Aviram, "TLS 1.2 is in Feature Freeze," Internet Engineering Task Force, Internet-Draft draft-ietf-tls-tls12-frozen-00, Apr. 2024, work in Progress. [Online]. Available: https://datatracker.ietf.org/doc/draft-ietf-tls-tls12-frozen/00/

[36] W. Evans, B. Westerbaan, C. Patton, P. Wu, and V. Gonçalves, "Post-quantum cryptography goes GA," retrieved: September, 2024. [Online]. Available: https://blog.cloudflare.com/post-quantum-cryptography-ga/

[37] D. O'Brien, "Protecting Chrome Traffic with Hybrid Kyber KEM," retrieved: September, 2024. [Online]. Available: https://blog.chromium.org/2023/08/protecting-chrome-traffic-with-hybrid.html

[38] OpenSSH, "Openssh 9.0 release notes," retrieved: September, 2024. [Online]. Available: https://www.openssh.com/txt/release-9.0

[39] M. Friedl, J. Mojzis, and S. Josefsson, "Secure Shell (SSH) Key Exchange Method Using Hybrid Streamlined NTRU Prime sntrup761 and X25519 with SHA-512: sntrup761x25519-sha512," Internet Engineering Task Force, Internet-Draft draft-josefsson-ntruprime-ssh-02, Sep. 2023, work in Progress. [Online]. Available: https://datatracker.ietf.org/doc/draft-josefsson-ntruprime-ssh/02/

[40] S. Josefsson, "Secure Shell Key Exchange Method Using Hybrid Classic McEliece and X25519 with SHA-512: mceliece6688128x25519-sha512," Internet Engineering Task Force, Internet-Draft draft-josefsson-ssh-mceliece-00, Dec. 2023, work in Progress. [Online]. Available: https://datatracker.ietf.org/doc/draft-josefsson-ssh-mceliece/00/

[41] P. Kampanakis, D. Stebila, and T. Hansen, "PQ/T Hybrid Key Exchange in SSH," Internet Engineering Task Force, Internet-Draft draft-kampanakis-curdle-ssh-pq-ke-02, May 2024, work in Progress. [Online]. Available: https://datatracker.ietf.org/doc/draft-kampanakis-curdle-ssh-pq-ke/02/

[42] AWS Security Blog, "Post-quantum hybrid SFTP file transfers using AWS Transfer Family," retrieved: September, 2024. [Online]. Available: https://aws.amazon.com/de/blogs/security/post-quantum-hybrid-sftp-file-transfers-using-aws-transfer-family

[43] R. Housley, "Use of the HSS/LMS Hash-Based Signature Algorithm with CBOR Object Signing and Encryption (COSE)," RFC 8778, Apr. 2020. [Online]. Available: https://www.rfc-editor.org/info/rfc8778

[44] M. Prorock, O. Steele, R. Misoczki, M. Osborne, and C. Cloostermans, "ML-DSA for JOSE and COSE," Internet Engineering Task Force, Internet-Draft draft-ietf-cose-dilithium-03, Jun. 2024, work in Progress. [Online]. Available: https://datatracker.ietf.org/doc/draft-ietf-cose-dilithium/03/

[45] ——, "SLH-DSA for JOSE and COSE," Internet Engineering Task Force, Internet-Draft draft-ietf-cose-sphincs-plus-02, Jan. 2024, work in Progress. [Online]. Available: https://datatracker.ietf.org/doc/draft-ietf-cose-sphincs-plus/02/

[46] J. Schaad, B. C. Ramsdell, and S. Turner, "Secure/Multipurpose Internet Mail Extensions (S/MIME) Version 4.0 Message Specification," RFC 8551, Apr. 2019. [Online]. Available: https://www.rfc-editor.org/info/rfc8551

[47] R. Housley and T. Hollebeek, "Limited Additional Mechanisms for PKIX and SMIME (lamps)." [Online]. Available: https://datatracker.ietf.org/wg/lamps/about/

[48] C. Döberl et al., "Quantum-resistant End-to-End Secure Messaging and Email Communication," in *Proceedings of the 18th International Conference on Availability, Reliability and Security*, ser. ARES '23. New York, NY, USA: Association for Computing Machinery, 2023, pp. 1–8. [Online]. Available: https://doi.org/10.1145/3600160.3605049

[49] MTG AG, "PQC Anwendungen jetzt testen!" retrieved: September, 2024. [Online]. Available: https://www.mtg.de/de/post-quantum-kryptografie/pqc-demo/#PQC_Testanwendungen

[50] A. Wussler, "Post-Quantum cryptography in OpenPGP," Master's thesis, Wien, 2023.

[51] S. Kousidis, J. Roth, F. Strenzke, and A. Wussler, "Post-Quantum Cryptography in OpenPGP," Internet Engineering Task Force, Internet-Draft draft-ietf-openpgp-pqc-03, May 2024, work in Progress. [Online]. Available: https://datatracker.ietf.org/doc/draft-ietf-openpgp-pqc/03/

[52] D. D. Tran, K. Ogata, and S. Escobar, "A formal analysis of OpenPGP's post-quantum public-key algorithm extension," in *Proceedings of the 2nd International Workshop on Formal Analysis and Verification of Post-Quantum Cryptographic Protocols (FAVPQC), 2023*. Brisbane, Australia: JAIST Press, 2023, pp. 22–35.

[53] M. Ounsworth, J. Gray, M. Pala, J. Klaußner, and S. Fluhrer, "Composite ML-DSA for use in Internet PKI," Internet Engineering Task Force, Internet-Draft draft-ietf-lamps-pq-composite-sigs-01, Jun. 2024, work in Progress. [Online]. Available: https://datatracker.ietf.org/doc/draft-ietf-lamps-pq-composite-sigs/01/

[54] ——, "Composite ML-KEM for Use in the Internet X.509 Public Key Infrastructure and CMS," Internet Engineering Task Force, Internet-Draft draft-ietf-lamps-pq-composite-kem-03, Mar. 2024, work in Progress. [Online]. Available: https://datatracker.ietf.org/doc/draft-ietf-lamps-pq-composite-kem/03/

[55] R. Housley, J. Gray, and T. Okubo, "Using Key Encapsulation Mechanism (KEM) Algorithms in the Cryptographic Message Syntax (CMS)," Internet Engineering Task Force, Internet-Draft draft-ietf-lamps-cms-kemri-08, Feb. 2024, work in Progress. [Online]. Available: https://datatracker.ietf.org/doc/draft-ietf-lamps-cms-kemri/08/

[56] K. Bashiri, S. Fluhrer, S.-L. Gazdag, D. V. Geest, and S. Kousidis, "Internet X.509 Public Key Infrastructure: Algorithm Identifiers for HSS and XMSS," Internet Engineering Task Force, Internet-Draft draft-ietf-lamps-x509-shbs-01, Jun. 2024, work in Progress. [Online]. Available: https://datatracker.ietf.org/doc/draft-ietf-lamps-x509-shbs/01/

[57] S. Turner, P. Kampanakis, J. Massimo, and B. Westerbaan, "Internet X.509 Public Key Infrastructure - Algorithm Identifiers for Module-Lattice-Based Key-Encapsulation Mechanism (ML-KEM)," Internet Engineering Task Force, Internet-Draft draft-ietf-lamps-kyber-certificates-03, Mar. 2024, work in Progress. [Online]. Available: https://datatracker.ietf.org/doc/draft-ietf-lamps-kyber-certificates/03/

[58] J. Massimo, P. Kampanakis, S. Turner, and B. Westerbaan, "Internet X.509 Public Key Infrastructure: Algorithm Identifiers for ML-DSA," Internet Engineering Task Force, Internet-Draft draft-ietf-lamps-dilithium-certificates-03, Feb. 2024, work in Progress. [Online]. Available: https://datatracker.ietf.org/doc/draft-ietf-lamps-dilithium-certificates/03/

[59] A. Becker, R. Guthrie, and M. J. Jenkins, "Related Certificates for Use in Multiple Authentications within a Protocol," Internet Engineering Task Force, Internet-Draft draft-ietf-lamps-cert-binding-for-multi-auth-05, Apr. 2024, work in Progress. [Online]. Available: https://datatracker.ietf.org/doc/draft-ietf-lamps-cert-binding-for-multi-auth/05/

[60] C. Bonnell, J. Gray, D. Hook, T. Okubo, and M. Ounsworth, "A Mechanism for Encoding Differences in Paired Certificates," Internet Engineering Task Force, Internet-Draft draft-bonnell-lamps-chameleon-certs-03, Jan. 2024, work in Progress. [Online]. Available: https://datatracker.ietf.org/doc/draft-bonnell-lamps-chameleon-certs/03/

[61] J. Fan et al., "Impact of post-quantum hybrid certificates on PKI, common libraries, and protocols," *International Journal of Security*

and Networks, vol. 16, no. 3, pp. 200–211, 2021. [Online]. Available: https://www.inderscienceonline.com/doi/abs/10.1504/IJSN.2021.117887

[62] Telecommunication Statdardization Sector of ITU, "Directory Information technology – Open Systems Interconnection – The Directory: Public-key and attribute certificate frameworks," Oct. 2019.

[63] GlobalSign, "Post Quantum Computing - Future-proofing digital trust with safe certificates," retrieved: September, 2024. [Online]. Available: https://www.globalsign.com/en/post-quantum-computing

[64] Keyfactor, "Post-Quantum Cryptography Keys and Signatures," retrieved: September, 2024. [Online]. Available: https://doc.primekey.com/ejbca/ejbca-operations/ejbca-ca-concept-guide/certificate-authority-overview/post-quantum-cryptography-keys-and-signatures

[65] Entrust, "Post-Quantum Cryptography," retrieved: September, 2024. [Online]. Available: https://www.entrust.com/solutions/post-quantum-cryptography

[66] "Bouncy Castle," retrieved: September, 2024. [Online]. Available: https://www.bouncycastle.org/

[67] M. J. Kannwischer, P. Schwabe, D. Stebila, and T. Wiggers, "Improving software quality in cryptography standardization projects," in *IEEE European Symposium on Security and Privacy, EuroS&P 2022 - Workshops, Genoa, Italy, June 6-10, 2022.* Los Alamitos, CA, USA: IEEE Computer Society, 2022, pp. 19–30.

[68] P. Ravi, A. Chattopadhyay, J. P. D'Anvers, and A. Baksi, "Side-channel and Fault-injection attacks over Lattice-based Post-quantum Schemes (Kyber, Dilithium): Survey and New Results," *ACM Trans. Embed. Comput. Syst.*, vol. 23, no. 2, pp. 1–54, mar 2024. [Online]. Available: https://doi.org/10.1145/3603170

[69] C. Mujdei et al., "Side-channel Analysis of Lattice-based Post-quantum Cryptography: Exploiting Polynomial Multiplication," *ACM Trans. Embed. Comput. Syst.*, vol. 23, no. 2, pp. 1–23, mar 2024. [Online]. Available: https://doi.org/10.1145/3569420

[70] A. T. Hoang et al., "Deep Learning Enhanced Side Channel Analysis on CRYSTALS-Kyber," in *2024 25th International Symposium on Quality Electronic Design (ISQED)*, 2024, pp. 1–8.

Riskpool – A Security Risk Management Methodology

Martin Ring*, Paul Duplys*, Sven Köhler†
*Robert Bosch GmbH
email:{martin.ring, paul.duplys}@de.bosch.com
†ITK Engineering GmbH
email:{sven.koehler}@itk-engineering.de

Abstract—**Risk management is widely defined as a process during product development. As an example, the International Organization for Standardization (ISO) 31000 family of standards defines risk management as *coordinated activities to direct and control an organization with regard to risk*. While necessary, process-related aspects cover only one part of a risk management system since processes usually specify *that* something must be done, but not how to do it. In this paper, we propose a new methodology for implementing risk management in commercial software engineering, over the complete product lifetime. We illustrate our method by showing how it can be applied to address cyber security risks. We argue that our method has significant advantages over classical risk management techniques especially in domains like cyber security where new regulations and laws are being introduced.**

Keywords-security; risk management; cyber security.

I. Introduction

Traditionally, risk management methodologies for product development were designed with the (implicit) assumption that products do not change after being deployed in the field. As a result, these methodologies have limited means to address maintenance and support – including keeping the product's software up-to-date – over the entire lifetime of a product as mandated by new regulations like [1]–[6].

Conceptually, risk management methodologies from other industries, e. g., insurance, can be applied to product development. In practice, however, there is no industry consensus how to estimate the initial risk of all active products and, in particular, the *cost* associated with this risk. In addition, insurance companies typically adjust their risk assessment and the corresponding insurance fee on a yearly basis. For cyber-physical products, on the other hand, such adjustments are impractical because substantial price variations from year to year are unacceptable from the customers' perspective. Consequently, the initial risk assessment needs to be more precise and the risk management methodology has to take into account that the cost-risk function must remain valid over a multi-year period.

In this paper, we describe a new methodology that allows to derive a more reliable initial risk assessment and a sustainable cost function. In addition, we give hints for the recurring assessment. In Section II, we present the state of the art in risk management and risk assessment, and describe the challenges faced by companies offering products that include software or are themselves software-based. In Section III, we introduce our approach to generating and maintaining a holistic risk management system. Additionally, we provide an example and discuss the results in detail. Section IV concludes the paper by summarizing our approach and offering an outlook for future developments.

II. State of the Art

In the following sections, we want to introduce the background information necessary and to further motivate the presented approach.

A. Risk Management

Risk management became more and more the risk management of everything, but the focus shifted in the mid 1990's from managing first order risks (risks directly stemming from the developed product, e. g., radiation in mobile phones or food quality) to second order risks (the public perception of the company when first order risks manifest) [7]. With this paper, we want to lay the focus on first order risk management. For most domains, the definition and probability for these risks can be calculated, e. g., for safety mechanisms in the automotive domain, there are a priori known probabilities for failures, these have to be minimized below an acceptable level and these ratings or levels do not change over lifetime of the product and will not degrade. On the contrary, cyber security risks can change over the life time of a product and need constant effort to keep a connected product safe and secure, as new vulnerabilities are discovered and hacker capabilities increase, e. g., with increased computing power. So, not only is it necessary to reevaluate the associated risk of such a product, but laws and regulations [1]–[3] mandate that known vulnerabilities need to be addressed, at least in part, by updates to the product software over the *customer expected lifetime*. Discussion regarding this definition is ongoing, but lifetimes for consumer products are expected to be between two and ten years, depending mainly on their price.

B. Common Vulnerabilities and Exposures (CVE) + Code

To get a ballpark figure of how many vulnerabilities over the course of a product's lifetime might need to be fixed, we take a look at a diverse set of software projects and their assigned vulnerabilities. The overview is summarized in Table I, while Figure 1 gives an overview over typical sizes of code bases for different products. The table was created with CVEs over a time span of 10 years (2012-2022). Depending on the company planning to apply this methodology, the time span can be adjusted, but a general trend is visible in constantly increasing code bases and, with that, at least a similar increase

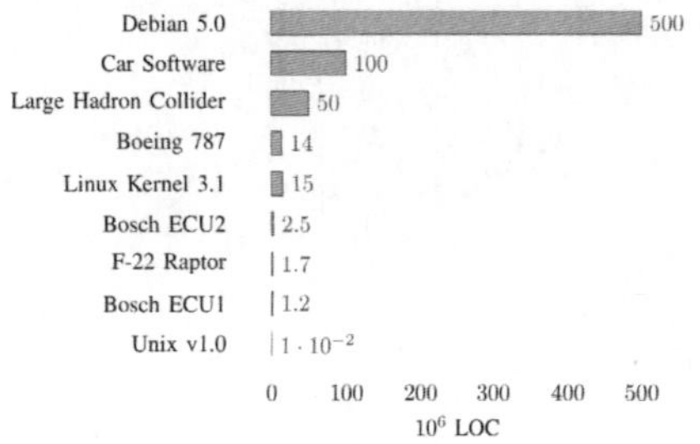

Figure 1. Lines of code of different software projects [10].

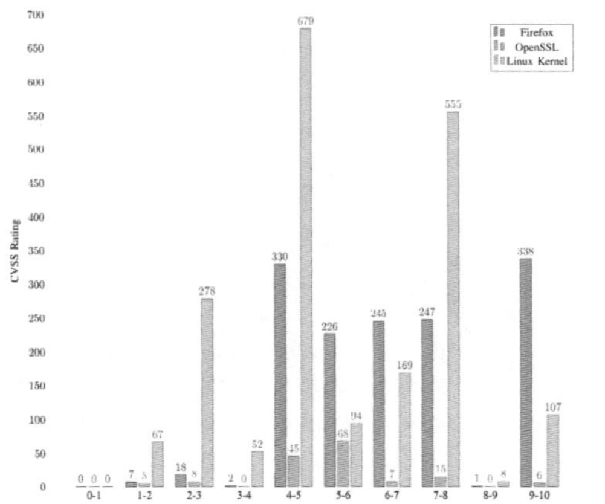

Figure 2. CVSS Ratings for three software projects 2011-2021 [11].

in vulnerabilities is expected. Other sources put the defect rate of software as industry average in the range of 1 to 25 defects per 1,000 Lines Of Code (LOC) [8]. Not all these defects will result in vulnerabilities, but they all potentially can lead to a vulnerability. When we take a cautious estimation of 100,000,000 (LOC) in a modern car [9] and take some of the best (lowest number of CVEs per 1,000 LOC) software as basis for our assumption (firefox) we come to a total of at least 5,766 exploitable vulnerabilities over the supported lifetime (ten years) of a modern car. These vulnerabilities have no impact rating at the moment assigned to them. The distribution of Common Vulnerability Scoring System (CVSS) ratings is plotted for the sample projects in Figure 2. The ratings are from 2011 to 2021, because 2022 still had a lot of unrated CVEs. As can be seen, no clear distribution is visible, thus we can learn from this overview, that there is a typical bandwidth of vulnerabilities per LOC, and this value depends also on the period under review, but there is no generally applicable distribution of vulnerability distribution regarding their risks (CVSS ratings). To come to a reasonable risk estimation, we need further information from the project, the basis for which will be presented in the next section.

C. Threat Analysis and Risk Assessment

A Threat Analysis and Risk Assessment (TARA) is standard for almost all modern software projects, but not limited to those. A TARA strives to formally enumerate all possible threats to a product (e. g., based on attack trees [3]). There are multiple norms, standards and publications that target this specific topic [3], [13], [14]. Only most recently the ISO 21434 provided a way to rate vulnerabilities with safety implication, while, e. g., the common criteria approach solely focuses on the attack potential, and CVSS ratings only partially address the impact ratings, especially in cyber-physical-systems, as highlighted before [15], [16]. The CVSS version 4.0 now includes safety aspects but does not include them in the final scoring. The ISO 21434 proposes a rather simple matrix, where impact and feasibility are rated from negligible to severe, and very low to high, respectively, see Table II - resulting in a single dimension risk value. This risk value (points) will be one of the values that defines the inequation of the risk pool we introduce below.

TABLE I. OVERVIEW OF BIG AND DIVERSE SOFTWARE PROJECTS, THEIR NUMBER OF CODE LINES, REPORTED AND CVE ASSIGNED NUMBER OF VULNERABILITIES [11], [12].

Software	Vulnerabilities per 1,000 LOC	LOC (2023)	$\sum$ CVEs 2012-2022
Google Chrome	0.08	25,600,000	2,154
Firefox	0.06	25,300,000	1,459
Linux Kernel	0.07	33,600,000	2,230
OpenSSL	0.11	1,540,000	163
Python	0,06	1,320,000	77
PHP	0.23	1,510,000	349

TABLE II. RISK MATRIX EXAMPLE [3].

		Attack Feasibility Rating			
		Very Low	Low	Medium	High
Impact Rating	Severe	2	3	4	5
	Major	1	2	3	4
	Moderate	1	2	2	3
	Negligible	1	1	1	1

Risk in general can be *avoided*, *reduced - impact/likelihood*, *shared* and *retained*. Risk avoidance and reduction is possible, e. g., with the introduction of further mitigations, that possibly increase the LOC count, but reduce at the same time the sum of residual risks of the TARA. Risk sharing is not in the focus of this publication, although it is possible to distribute the fallout of a defect. Risk retention is the acceptance of certain risks, as the costs of fixing them would outweigh the possible costs of defects in the field [17].

III. A RISK POOL AS RISK MANAGEMENT METHODOLOGY

The general idea of this methodology consists of the risks associated with all products that are not at the end of their lifetime on one hand and a risk pool, representing the available capacity to fix defects in a product over its lifetime on the other hand, described in more detail with Equation (1)

$$\sum_i (\text{Project}_i \cdot \text{TARA Residual Risks}_i \cdot \text{Weight}_i) \quad \leq$$
$$\sum \text{Developers} \cdot \text{Fixing Capability} \cdot \text{Capacity} \quad (1)$$

Where:

- i: i is the number of all projects in the period under review (i. e., the lifetime of the product associated with the project). Each project with a different risk, lifetime or changed code base has to be counted individually.
- *TARA Residual Risks*: As described before, the vulnerabilities of different projects follow no common distribution, but to get to a good first estimation we take the residual risks as basis for our inequation to determine the risk pool.
- *Weight*: These residual risks will be weighted with an additional value based on five properties (LOC, code age, innovation level, update capability & known defects [17]). The weight can be set between 0.02 and 0.1. This weight allows a scaling according to the aforementioned properties, and thus a weight regarding exploitability, i. e., a new and unreleased product that might be of high interest to adversaries should be weighted with 0.1.
- *Developers*: The number of software developers in the considered company
- *Fixing Capability*: this capability will depend on the risk evaluation methodology and the product.
- *Capacity*: How much of the work force or how much of their time should or can be assigned to fixing defects that resulted in vulnerabilities.

A. Example

For demonstration purposes, we will look into the fictitious company ExCom; this company has two products, ECU 1 – an Automotive Safety Integrity Level (ASIL) D and ECU 2 – an ASIL B ECU. We will have a look at these two products including their risk rating and we will look at how a risk pool would look like for this company.

1) ECU 1 - ASIL D ECU: This product is of the highest safety category for automotive applications, but it is a rather simple ECU with a smaller code base. The innovation level of this ECU is low, the code base is older and some deviations are already in production and in the field, so the code base is well tested and proven. Furthermore, the connectivity is low, as it has only the capability for low range external communication. The risk was determined according to ISO 21434 and as depicted in Table II. The sum in this project according to this method is a weighted TARA residual risk value of 29 points, with a weight of 0.02, based on the aforementioned terms.

2) ECU 2 - ASIL B ECU: This product has a medium safety category, it is a completely new product, with a high innovation level. The connectivity is low, as it has no wireless external communication interfaces. The TARA residual risk value for this product is 116 points, with a weight of 0.05, based on its complexity, innovation level, and connectivity.

B. Discussion

ExCom employs 1,000 developers. For their products and employees, we know that an average developer is capable of fixing the equivalent of 30 points (as introduced in Table II) vulnerabilities per year. The company has the equivalent of 1,000 developer years available. Not more than 5% of development time shall be appointed to fixing vulnerabilities. This results in an available risk pool of 1,500 points:

$$\sum \text{Developers} \cdot \text{Fixing Capability} \cdot \text{Capacity} = 1,000 \cdot 30 \cdot 0.05 = 1,500$$

ExCom has 500 projects each year going into production, equally distributed across its two products. The support period today is the one year warranty period. With these information we come to the inequation as follows:

$$\sum_{i=0}^{250}(29) \cdot 0.02 + \sum_{i=250}^{500}(116) \cdot 0.02 \overset{?}{\leq} \sum 1,000 \cdot 30 \cdot 0.05 \tag{2}$$

$$1,595 \overset{!}{>} 1,500 \tag{3}$$

With Equation (3) showing the Inequality (2) being false, the company in the example is exceeding its available risk pool. A possible solution might be limiting the amount of projects with higher risk, or the expansion of allocated fixing time for the developers, e. g., from 5 % to 6 % (Resulting in an available pool of 1,800 points), which would necessitate a price increase of the sold products. If the products need to be supported over a longer period, additional developer capacity is needed and needs to be paid for, e. g., by a maintenance contract with the potential customers. If the introduced new regulations come into effect, the price of the product needs to increase, as the support has to be provided without additional contracts, when dealing with end customers.

This approach might not fit the bill over every period under review, but is supposed to average out over time. When fixing capabilities are vacant, these shall be used to reduce technical debt and refactoring older code bases to reduce the future possibility of found defects or reduce the needed capacity to fix them.

IV. Conclusion

Using the riskpool methodology, we enhanced risk assessment for software. Companies can now transition from abstract numbers to practical tools that guide their risk appetite, including resource management and pre-planning: understand the risk → manage the risk. A company is thus able to control the maximum amount of projects that they can handle with their assigned riskpool. For a limited time, additional risks can be taken by stretching the riskpool but this risk can be quantified, not only for single projects but for the sum of all ventures a company has. If the riskpool is depleted, the company can take measures, e. g., by shifting capacities. The weight factor allows to tailor the method to individual products and business cases. Until now, risk estimations were confined to individual projects. With this risk pool approach, companies can gain a comprehensive view of their combined risks across all projects and calculate resilience based on their organization's capacity to address these risks.

REFERENCES

[1] Council of European Union, *Directive 2019/771 of the european parliament and of the council of 20 may 2019 on certain aspects concerning contracts for the sale of goods, amending regulation 2017/2394 and directive 2009/22/ec, and repealing directive 1999/44/ec*, https://eur-lex.europa.eu/legal-content/EN/TXT/?uri=CELEX:32019L0771, Accessed: 2024-10-02, 2019.

[2] Deutscher Bundestag, *Gesetz zur umsetzung der richtlinie über bestimmte vertragsrechtliche aspekte der bereitstellung digitaler inhalte und digitaler dienstleistungen [in english: Act implementing the directive on certain aspects of contract law aspects of the supply of digital content and digital services]*, https://www.bmj.de/SharedDocs/Gesetzgebungsverfahren/Dokumente/Bgbl_Digitale_Inhalte.pdf?__blob=publicationFile&v=2, Accessed: 2024-10-02, 2021.

[3] International Organization for Standardization, "ISO/SAE 21434:2021 - Road vehicles – Cybersecurity engineering," Standard, 2021.

[4] International Organization for Standardization, "ISO/IEC 27005:2022 - Information security, cybersecurity and privacy protection – Guidance on managing information security risks," Standard, 2022.

[5] Council of European Union, *Directive 2022/2555 of the european parliament and of the council of 14 december 2022 on measures for a high common level of cybersecurity across the union, amending regulation no 910/2014 and directive 2018/1972, and repealing directive 2016/1148 (nis 2 directive)*, https://eur-lex.europa.eu/eli/dir/2022/2555/oj, Accessed: 2024-10-02, 2022.

[6] International Society of Automation, "ISA/IEC 62443 Industrial communication networks - Network and system security," Standard, 2021.

[7] M. Power, "The risk management of everything," *The Journal of Risk Finance*, 2004.

[8] S. McConnell, *Code complete*. Pearson Education, 2004.

[9] R. N. Charette, "This car runs on code," *IEEE spectrum*, vol. 46, no. 3, p. 3, 2009.

[10] D. McCandless, *Lines of code overview for different software projects, incl. sources*, https://docs.google.com/spreadsheets/d/1s9u0uprmuJvwR2fkRqxJ4W5Wfomimmk9pwGTK4Dn_UI/, Accessed: 2024-10-02.

[11] SecurityScorecard, *Cve details - the ultimate security vulnerability datasource*, https://www.cvedetails.com, Accessed: 2024-10-02.

[12] Synopsis, *Synopsys - black duck open hub*, https://www.openhub.net, Accessed: 2024-10-02.

[13] Common Criteria Working Group, "Common methodology for information technology security evaluation," Technical report, Common Criteria Interpretation Management Board, Tech. Rep., 2017.

[14] A. Shostack, *Threat modeling: Designing for security*. John Wiley & Sons, 2014.

[15] M. Ring, "Systematische security-tests von kraftfahrzeugen [in english: Systematic security testing of motor vehicles]," Ph.D. dissertation, Universität Ulm, 2019.

[16] E. Kovacs, *Cvss scores often misleading for ics vulnerabilities: Experts*, https://www.securityweek.com/cvss-scores-often-misleading-ics-vulnerabilities-experts/, Accessed: 2024-10-02.

[17] E. Kovacs, *Siemens drives rise in ics vulnerabilities discovered in 2022: Report*, https://www.securityweek.com/siemens-drives-rise-in-ics-vulnerabilities-discovered-in-2022-report/, Accessed: 2024-10-02.

Device Onboarding Transparency – Supporting Initial Trust Establishment

Steffen Fries, Rainer Falk
Siemens AG
Technology
Munich, Germany
e-mail: {steffen.fries|rainer.falk}@siemens.com

Abstract—**Device onboarding is the process of introducing devices into target systems and target domains, and further on to bring them into operational state. This has a direct relation to cybersecurity, as it establishes trust between the device and the domain based on identities and associated cryptographic parameters. Different technologies for automated device onboarding have been specified. Having information on performed onboarding is important during operation, in which the identities and cryptographic parameters are maintained as part of device lifecycle management. Current onboarding approaches do not explicitly consider binding this information to the device management information used during operation. The binding information may be specifically important if attacks occur, as it can support the root cause analysis to derive immediate measures to further maintain the attacked service. This supports addressing requirements from existing and currently developed regulations. This paper proposes enhancements to current onboarding approaches that provide this transparency.**

Keywords–communication security; onboarding; trust establishment; industrial automation and control system; cybersecurity; Internet of Things.

I. INTRODUCTION

Device onboarding can be described as introduction of a new device into an operational environment. This introduction typically comprises different exchanges of information about the identity of the onboarding device and its capabilities, as well as the provisioning of the device with operational parameters of the deployment environment to serve the intended purpose. This typically comprises also domain specific security parameters, like a locally assigned device identity and associated credentials.

New devices in a system may have an influence on the security status of the overall operational environment. Therefore, the introduction of new devices needs to be performed in a trusted and auditable way, which supports also root cause analysis in case of failures in the system.

Technically, there have already several solutions been specified that support the onboarding of devices in new deployment environments in a secure way. While they differ in their detailed functionality, they can be used to ensure that only known and devices are put into operation as intended. Solutions range from Trust-On-First-Use (TOFU), which focuses on the initial use of a device in its new operational environment implicitly assumed to be trustworthy during onboarding, up to automated, mutually trusted introduction of devices into the system to ensure that not only the system trusts the new device, but also to ensure the device trusts the operational environments likewise.

As the onboarding of new devices directly relates to the security of the overall system, it is in the interest of the operator of the system to safeguard the continuous and reliable service provisioning during operation. Besides the business continuity requirements of an operator (e.g., an automation service provider), there are also more and more regulative requirements defined that require the operator of specifically critical systems to operate the system in a resilient and secure way. This obviously affects the processes of the operator to maintain the system and components used in his operational environment. As a precondition, it already requires product manufacturers to support security in a holistic way, from the development of the product from an idea to the final product, covering the processes and the technical features of the product. Meanwhile there are regulative requirements for both, system operators and product manufacturers to consider security as integral part of operation and manufacturing. As onboarding concerns the introduction of devices into an operational domain, it supports asset management and thus also supports keeping track of the security state of devices.

This paper is structured in the following way. Section II provides an overview about related work. It concentrates on regulative boundary conditions and standardized system security requirements. Section III gives an overview about device onboarding in general, the relation to product lifecycle and the supply chain interaction. Moreover, it provides examples of existing technologies to perform onboarding. Section IV outlines potential onboarding enhancements that provide improvements specifically to support the auditing of trust establishment and maintenance started with the introduction of new devices into an operational environment. This in turn contributes to a consistent security view of an operational environment. Section V concludes the paper and provides an outlook to potential future work.

II. RELATED WORK

As stated in the introduction, several regulative requirements have been defined that have to be fulfilled by operators of critical infrastructures, by integrators, or by product manufacturers. They relate to the security of the products and systems and also their interaction and operation and have a clear relation to being able to monitor the security state of components, as well as their operational security parameters. The introduction of devices into operational environments is considered as onboarding and thus constitutes an important point in the ability to monitor system security.

A. *Regulative Boundary Conditions*

Examples from Europe are provided by the NIS2 directive [1] that describes minimum cybersecurity means to be realized by entities operating critical infrastructures in 18 different sectors (application domains). The Radio Equipment Directive (RED) [2] and also the EU Cyberresilience Act [3], which are currently defined, target product manufacturers and pose specific cybersecurity requirements on the products and the related product development process.

An example from US is provided by the executive order EO 14028 [4], requiring operators beyond others to maintain a dedicated security level, obligate incident reporting, and specifically address the security in the supply chain.

B. *Requirements Engineering Standards*

Various requirement standards for procedural and technical requirements have been specified. Here, two holistic frameworks are referenced as examples to show how they address device security, as well as credential and trust management throughout the lifecycle of devices. Both frameworks are broadly applied in industry.

A holistic cybersecurity framework defining specific requirements for automation system operators, integrators, and manufacturers is provided by IEC 62443 [5]. While it has been developed with the focus on industrial automation and control systems, it has already been adopted in the power system industry, railway industry, and healthcare for cybersecurity requirement specification. Moreover, it is the main base for creating harmonized standards to address the requirements from regulation and to provide means to show conformity. Besides providing requirements to operational and development processes, it specifically describes technical requirements on system and component level, targeting four different security levels, which relate to the strength of a potential attacker. Also, it contains requirements regarding security of devices and the lifecycle management of their security credentials in operative environments.

The NIST Cybersecurity Framework (CSF) 2.0 [6] provides general guidance on managing cybersecurity risk along the operation, including the identification of risks, the detection of potential attacks, but also the recovery to addresses resilience for normal and adverse situations.

III. ONBOARDING – OVERVIEW AND APPROACHES

Device onboarding is considered as process to introduce devices into a target domain and to bring them into operational state. This process has direct relation to cybersecurity, as it includes the trust establishment of the domain into the device in the first step. There may be situations, in which it is also required to support the trust establishment of the device into the domain to ensure that a device is operated in its intended environment. Approaches, which do not require the device to verify the domain are often called "trust-on-first-use", while approaches in which an explicit trust establishment is performed may be understood as mutually trusted onboarding.

Key for the trust establishment are identities and corresponding cryptographic key material, which is imprinted into devices during product manufacturing. Identity information of the device is provided, along the supply chain as shown in Figure 1. It is issued by the manufacturer together with cryptographic information, as X.509 certificate [7] and known as IDevID (Initial Device Identity).

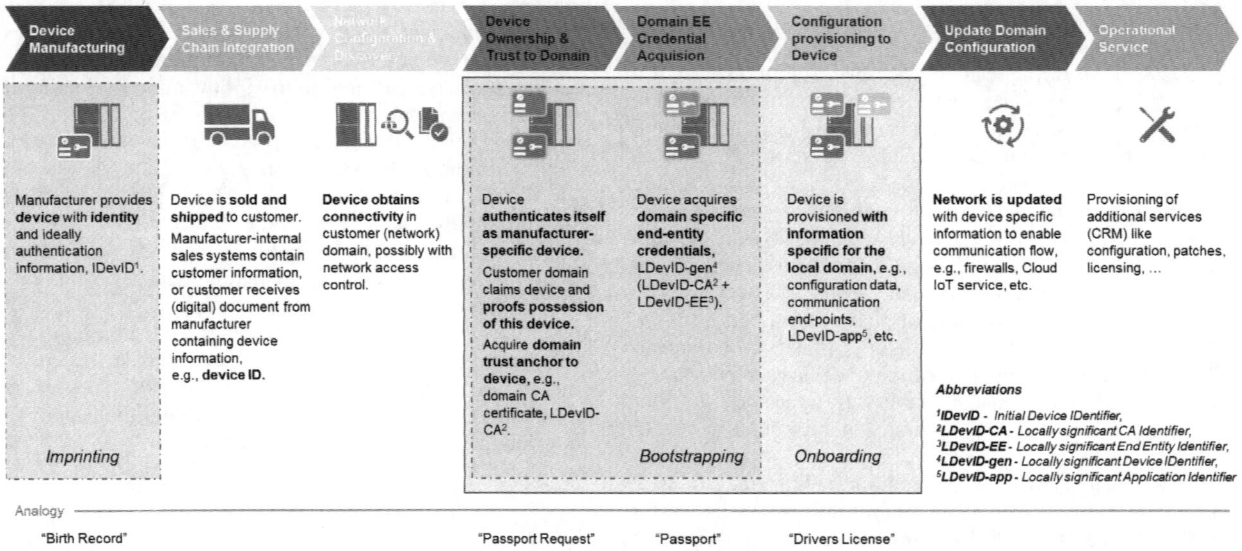

Figure 1. Onboarding Overview: From Imprinting in Factory to Operation.

In the target domain, it can be used to bootstrap mutual trust in an automated way and to support issuing domain-related identities and associated cryptographic keys, known as LDevID (Locally significant Device Identity), as operational credentials.

Based on the established trust relations and credentials, further operational data, like configuration and engineering information including security parameters, can be provided to the device. To achieve this, several technical approaches for onboarding and provisioning already exist. Examples for onboarding are specified as:

- Bootstrapping Remote Secure Key Infrastructure (BRSKI, [8]) provides a standardized way to establish a mutually trusted relation between a device and a new network domain supported by a manufacturer service known as Manufacturing Authorized Signing Authority (MASA) based on a so-called voucher, a signed statement containing the domain certificate. Once trust is established, domain specific security credentials (LDevIDs) can be enrolled be used to secure the further system interaction. The enrollment utilizes Enrollment over Secure Transports (EST, [9]) as main approach. Enhancements to BRSKI exist, supporting alternative enrollment protocols (BRSKI-AE, [10]) using the Certificate Management Protocol (CMP, [11]) or scenarios, in which the joining device acts as server, rather than as client (BRSKI-PRM, [12]).
- Secure Zero Touch Provisioning Protocol (SZTP, [13]) specifies a further approach employing a so-called ownership voucher, which accompanies a device along its lifecycle. It supports the mutual trust establishment and enrollment of domain specific credentials and further operational information.
- FIDO Device Onboarding (FDO, [14]) enables building a trust relation of a device into a new owner, based on the trust into the previous owner, also supported by an ownership voucher. As the manufacturer is only involved at the beginning the interaction with the voucher is facilitated by a rendezvous server instead of a service of the manufacturer.
- OPC-UA Device Onboarding (Part 21, [15]) provides mechanisms to verify the authenticity of devices to be onboarded, to set up their security and to maintain their configuration. For this it uses so-called tickets, which can be understood as vouchers.

As stated above, part of the onboarding is typically the enrollment of operational certificates. As for onboarding, also for enrollment, there exists a variety of approaches, two of them, EST and CMP, have already been named.

In addition to pure onboarding or provisioning standards, further standards support the propagation of security relevant data. Specifically for the enrollment as part of the onboarding, certificate transparency [16] is known that provides an extension to PKI services for publicly logging issued certificates. This is intended to identify certificates that have been issued inappropriately.

IV. PROPOSED ONBOARDING ENHANCEMENTS

As discussed in Section II, there are several onboarding approaches known and applied. It is very likely that a device may only support one onboarding approach, while the infrastructure likely supports multiple approaches. This will ensure that in environments utilizing different standards, products from different vendors can be easily integrated. To select the appropriate onboarding approach at the earliest point in time, the supported technical onboarding approach may be contained in the IDevID certificate, which can be analyzed by the first network component during network attachment. As the IDevID certificate is essentially an X.509 certificate, it can be enhanced by so called extensions. An `extension` is added as certificate component similar to other certificate components like the `subject` or the `issuer`.

To provide information about supported onboarding and provisioning approaches, a new extension is defined as shown in Figure 2.

```
supportedProvisioningMethods EXTENSION ::= {
  SYNTAX SupportedProvisioningMethods
  IDENTIFIED BY id-ce-SupportedProvisioningMethods }

SupportedProvisioningMethods ::= ProvisioningDescription
{{ ProvisioningMethod }}

ProvisioningMethod::= SEQUENCE {
  provisioningMethod    Name,
  provisiningId         OBJECT IDENTIFIER OPTIONAL,
  provisioningVersion   integer OPTIONAL
}

ProvisioningMethod ::= {CMP, SCEP, EST, CMC, ACME, FDO,
OMA-DM, OPC-UA-P21, BRSKI, SZTP, …}
```

Figure 2. Proposed Provisioning Certificate Extension

Out of the listed `ProvisioningMethod`, a device may support one or multiple options. As an example, a device with an IDevID certificate containing the information `ProvisioningMethod ::= {EST, BRSKI}` provides the information that it supports BRSKI for onboarding and EST for certificate management. The proposed enhancement is independent of the specific chosen onboarding method as it relies only on the X.509 certificate utilized to carry the transparency information.

A target network infrastructure may be designed in a way to have different virtual LANs (VLAN) defined for different onboarding approaches, to keep new devices contained within a separate network zone until they have received their LDevID. If the IDevID carries the extension with the onboarding and provisioning information, the device can be assigned to the appropriate VLAN based on its supported provisioning methods. This is depicted in Figure 3 below.

The figure shows an example with two devices (IoT Dev 1, IoT Dev 2). Depending on the provisioning methods supported by the respective device, they are connected by the network access switch to the onboarding VLAN1 (for local onboarding, e.g., OPC-UA-P21) or to VLAN2 (for infrastructure-based onboarding, e.g., BRSKI).

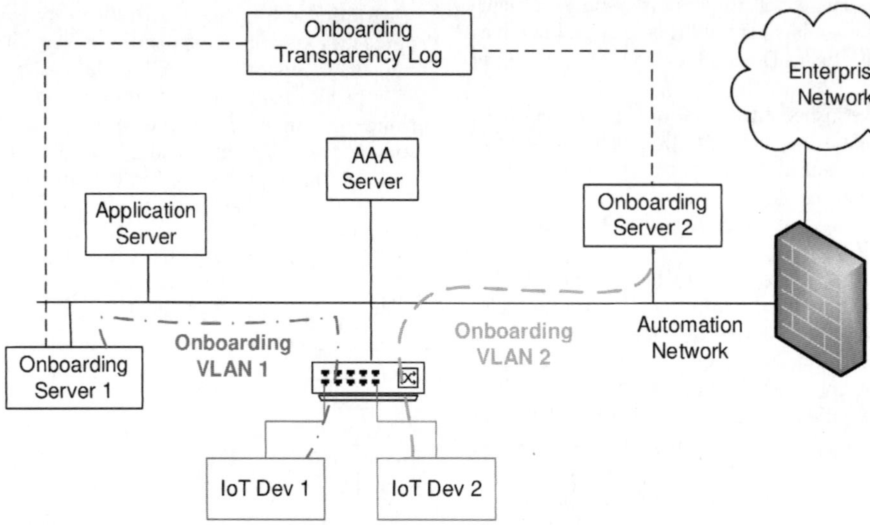

Figure 3. Onboarding Decision Support and Onboarding Transparency.

The check of the supported provisioning methods and the decision is made here by the AAA server to which the IoT device authenticates itself during network access. It is also possible for the AAA server to provide information on the provisioning method to be used by the device if multiple methods are supported. This has the advantage that the device does not have to try several provisioning methods to determine one that is supported by the connected network and that the device can continue to temporarily block other provisioning methods so that they cannot be misused.

While the proposed method eases the automated assignment of devices to the correct onboarding VLANs, the finally chosen onboarding variant may be logged in an onboarding transparency service. This is specifically helpful in case of security breaches, as the root cause may be related to the method how the device has been introduced into the network.

The information about onboarding may be provided as data structure encoded in different formats like XML or JSON and is ideally signed by the onboarding server. This structure may contain different sets of information like

- Device identification (e.g., product serial number, fingerprint of the IDevID certificate of the device or the IDevID certificate directly)
- Time stamp of the actual onboarding
- Voucher issued during the onboarding. The voucher shows which device from which manufacturer was put into operation in which target domain.
- Number of successful onboarding processes: Information on the history of the device can be provided, e.g., how often the device has already been put into operation in other domains.
- Issued LDevID certificate for the device (or a fingerprint of the LDevID certificate). This information can also be linked to the known approach of Certificate Transparency [16].

As stated, the information may be helpful in performing root cause analysis in case of discovered anomalies in an operational network.

V. CONCLUSION AND OUTLOOK

This paper provides an overview on onboarding and provisioning as part of introducing devices into a network and to provide the devices with information to securely communicate with other devices. This is done from a general viewpoint and by investigating different standardized technical approaches. In addition, it proposes enhancements to the currently known approaches and processes to leverage information about supported onboarding and provisioning methods of new devices, as well as the actually chosen onboarding approach during network introduction.

The novel contribution of this paper is the usage of the onboarding method information to perform access decisions as well as in the aftermath of a security event, e.g., if the device or the network has been compromised. The onboarding information may support the identification which network element caused the breach, which in turn can be used to provide a fast remediation.

While the described approach has been investigated from a conceptual point of view, it is planned to investigate into a proof of concept to verify effectiveness of the proposed approach. Such a proof of concept requires enhancements during the issuing of IDevIDs and LDevIDs to include the supported and chosen onboarding method in the extension of the utilized X.509 certificates. Moreover, it also requires enhancements in the evaluation of the additional onboarding information during security decisions in the operational phase and the consideration in potential post-event analysis.

References

[1] "Directive (EU) 2022/2555 of the European Parliament and of the Council of 14 December 2022 on measures for a high common level of cybersecurity across the Union", Document 02022L2555-20221227, Dec. 2022, [Online]. Available from: https://eur-lex.europa.eu/eli/dir/2022/2555, [retrieved: September, 2024]

[2] "Directive 2014/53/EU of the European Parliament and of the Council of 16 April 2014 on the harmonisation of the laws of the Member States relating to the making available on the market of radio equipment and repealing Directive 1999/5/EC Text with EEA relevance", 10/2023, [Online]. Available from: https://eur-lex.europa.eu/legal-content/EN/TXT/?uri=celex%3A32014L0053 [retrieved: September, 2024]

[3] "Proposal for a Regulation of the European Parliament and of the Council on horizontal cybersecurity requirements for products with digital elements and amending Regulation (EU) 2019/10202", COM/2022/454 final, Document 52022PC0454, Sep. 2022, [Online]. Available from: https://eur-lex.europa.eu/legal-content/EN/TXT/?uri=celex:52022PC0454 [retrieved: September, 2024]

[4] "Executive Order 14028: Improving the Nation's Cybersecurity", May 2017, [Online]. Available from https://www.federalregister.gov/documents/2021/05/17/2021-10460/improving-the-nations-cybersecurity [retrieved: September, 2024]

[5] IEC 62443, "Industrial Automation and Control System Security" (formerly ISA99), [Online]. Available from: http://isa99.isa.org/Documents/Forms/AllItems.aspx [retrieved: September, 2024]

[6] NIST CSF, "The NIST Cybersecurity Framework (CSF) 2.0", Feb. 2024, [Online]. Available from: https://doi.org/10.6028/NIST.CSWP.29 [retrieved July, 2024]

[7] ITU-T X.509 ISO/IEC 9594-8:2020, Rec. ITU-T X.509 (2019), Information technology – Open systems interconnection – The Directory: Public-key and attribute certificate frameworks, [Online]. Available from: https://www.itu.int/rec/T-REC-X.509-201910-I/en, [retrieved: September, 2024]

[8] M. Pritikin, M.Richardson, T. Eckert, M. Behringer, and K. Watson, IETF RFC 8995, "Bootstrapping Remote Secure Key Infrastructure (BRSKI)", May 2021, [Online]. Available from: https://datatracker.ietf.org/doc/html/rfc8995, [retrieved: September, 2024]

[9] M. Pritikin, P. Yee, and D. Harkins, IETF RFC 7030, "Enrollment over Secure Transport", October 2013, [Online]. Available from https://datatracker.ietf.org/doc/html/rfc7030, [retrieved: September, 2024]

[10] D. von Oheimb, H. Brockhaus, and S. Fries IETF Draft, "Alternative Enrollment Protocols in BRSKI (BRSKI-AE)", Work in Progress, [Online]. Available from: https://datatracker.ietf.org/doc/draft-ietf-anima-brski-ae/, [retrieved: September, 2024]

[11] C. Adams, S. Farrell, T. Krause, and T. Mononen, IETF RFC 4210, "Internet X.509 Public Key Infrastructure Certificate Management Protocol (CMP)", September 2005, [Online]. Available from https://datatracker.ietf.org/doc/html/rfc4210, [retrieved: September, 2024]

[12] S. Fries, T. Werner, E. Lear, and M. Richardson., IETF Draft, "BRSKI with Pledge in Responder Mode (BRSKI-PRM)", Work in Progress, [Online]. Available from: https://datatracker.ietf.org/doc/draft-ietf-anima-brski-prm/, [retrieved: September, 2024]

[13] K. Watsen, M. Abrahamsson, and I. Farrer, IETF RFC 8572, "Secure Zero Touch Provisioning (SZTP)", June 2021, [Online]. Available from: https://datatracker.ietf.org/doc/rfc8572, [retrieved: September, 2024]

[14] FIDO Device Onboarding, [Online]. Available from https://fidoalliance.org/device-onboarding-overview/, [retrieved: September, 2024]

[15] OPC Foundation, "OPC 10000-21: UA Part 21: Device Onboarding", Nov. 2022, [Online]. Abailable from: https://reference.opcfoundation.org/Onboarding/v105/docs/, [retrieved: September, 2024]

[16] B. Laurie, E. Messeri, and R. Stradling, IETF RFC 9162, "Certificate Transparency Version 2.0" Dec. 2021, [Online]. Available from: https://datatracker.ietf.org/doc/html/rfc9162, [retrieved: September, 2024]

Fast Charging Communication and Cybersecurity: A Technology Review

Jakob Löw, Kevin Mayer, Hans-Joachim Hof
CARISSMA Institute of Electric, Connected and Secure Mobility
University of applied sciences Ingolstadt
Ingolstadt, Germany
e-mail: {jakob.loew | kevin.mayer | hof}@thi.de

Abstract—**With the increasing amounts of electric vehicles on the road, the demand for public charging stations increases as well. While alternating current (AC) is used for charging at home, direct current (DC) fast charging is commonly used when traveling long distances. Since DC fast charging requires higher level communication between vehicle and charging station, it provides an increased attack surface to both sides. This paper reviews communication standards and their implementations used in fast charging scenarios. Focusing on cybersecurity aspects of these communications, we cover current and future security measures built into the communication standards between vehicles and charging stations.**

Keywords-charging; fast charging; ccs; iso15118; DC charging; electric vehicle; vehicle charging.

I. Introduction

Many countries are currently transitioning away from combustion engine vehicles towards battery electric vehicles. This transition is happening at a rapid rate, because buying an electric vehicle often gets incentivised through tax reductions or straight refunds [1]. With people buying more and more electric vehicles, the demand for charging infrastructure rises. In Germany, not only electric vehicles, but also the buildup of charging infrastructure got heavily subsidized by the government. This high demand and government incentives resulted in a rapid growth in charging station numbers, suppliers and operators [2]. Due to the rushed development, the cybersecurity of current charging stations is below average compared to other cyberphysical systems [3]–[5]. Recently, cybersecurity researchers investigating charging backend infrastructure have found a range of textbook vulnerabilities, such as SQL injection, cross site scripting or unauthenticated remote update procedures [3].

This paper focuses on DC fast charging stations. Because of their functional design, described in Section II-B, they have a demand for complex two-way communication with the vehicle for exchanging charging parameters and limits. While other works, such as Tu et al. [6] have already covered electrical and other aspects of fast charging stations, this paper will focus on communication aspects. The ISO15118 standards [7], [8] was created for communication between charging stations and vehicles, enabling interoperability between stations and vehicles from different manufacturers. This high level communication protocol provides a larger attack surface compared to other charging techniques, making it more interesting for cybersecurity research.

This paper will first lay out the communication principles and handshake flow of ISO15118 and related standards in Section II. Afterwards, a review of today's charging station vendors and architectures is given in Sections III and IV, respectively. Lastly, different attack vectors and research gaps of charging communication are discussed in Section V.

II. Charging Station Communication

Electricity generally comes in two forms: Alternating Current (AC) and Direct Current (DC). While power grids are running on AC, batteries need to be charged using DC. Therefore, the AC needs to be converted to DC either in the car or in the charging station itself. Cars usually come with an onboard AC to DC converter for charging the onboard battery, their power is usually limited to 7 to 22 kW. In order to achieve higher charging powers, a fast charging station provides a stationary AC to DC converter. Placing it outside of the car removes weight requirements, simplifies cooling and thus allows higher charging currents.

In general, charging stations can be divided into three categories: Unmetered AC charging (often used in residential buildings), Commercial AC charging stations and DC fast charging stations. The following subsections describe the communication and payment mechanisms of these three kinds of charging stations as well as the included security concepts.

A. Low Level Communication

AC charging stations usually supply power from the grid directly, making them just sockets with some very basic communication to the vehicle. In the early days of electric vehicle adoption, mainly these kind of charging stations were built. Because charging a modern vehicle using an AC charging station can take multiple hours, they usually are not used for long distance traveling. Because of their low price and low electrical requirements, they are however still widely used and newly installed, especially for home and office charging as well as on park and ride parking lots.

The most common plug for AC charging by far is the type 2 connector shown in Figure 1. It is used not only as the standard charging plug in Europe, but also in China and other parts of Asia. Apart from the typical connections of a 3-phase power socket, the connector incorporates two additional pins: Charge Pilot (CP) and Proximity Pilot (PP). These two pins are used for a very simple resistor based signaling scheme defined in IEC 61851 [9] and explained by [10]: The charging cable includes a resistor between proximity pilot and Protective Earth (PE), which signals the maximum current for this cable. The charging station supplies a +12V/-12V Pulse

Width Modulation (PWM) signal between CP and PE. The vehicle contains both a diode and a resistor between CP and PE, such that the charging station can detect the presence of a vehicle based on the negative voltage being dropped by the diode and the positive voltage being reduced by the resistor. As soon as the vehicle is ready to charge, it connects a second resistor between CP and PE further reducing the voltage. For unmetered AC charging this is sufficient to start a charging session. For public AC charging infrastructure usually external means of payment, such as mobile app activation or contactless payment have to be used before the session is started. During the charging session the charging station tells the vehicle the maximum allowed current through changing the duty cycle of the +12V/-12V PWM signal between CP and PE. There exists a special PWM duty cycle of 5%, which can be used by the charging station to tell the vehicle to use the high level ISO15118 protocol for communication rather than the low level communication described in IEC 61851 [9].

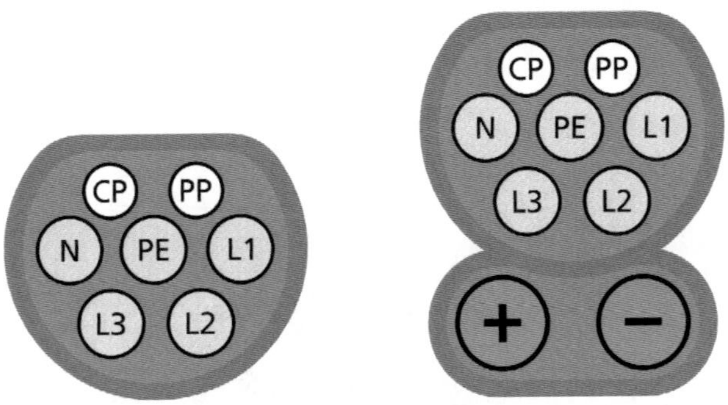

Figure 1. Schematic diagrams type 2 (left) and combined charging system (right) connectors [11]

B. High Level Communication

While charging a vehicle with AC requires little to no communication, DC charging stations on the other hand are required to communicate to the vehicle for properly supplying the correct voltage and power to the battery. For this high level communication, the industry standard ISO15118 [7] was created, enabling interoperability between different vehicle manufacturers and charging station vendors. The standard is based on more or less common standards for all layers of the Open System Interconnect (OSI) model: After the initial handshake of the low level communication, as described in the previous section, the charging station signals the vehicle to use high level communication by supplying a PWM duty cycle of 5%. Afterwards, a powerline communication is modulated on top of the PWM signal between the charge pilot and protective earth. To prevent crosstalk problems [12]–[14] usually arising with powerline communication, ISO15118-3 [8] describes "Signal Level Attentuation Characterization" (SLAC). SLAC measures the interference on the powerline communication line as well as matches vehicles with their nearest charging station connected to the powerline and exchanges a network key for encryption. Once powerline communication is established, IPv6 with link-local stateless autoconfigured addresses is used on top for communication between the charging station and the vehicle. While the ISO15118-2 standard [7] itself is based on the Transmission Control Protocol (TCP), first a User Datagram Protocol (UDP) broadcast service discovery is used for exchanging IPv6 addresses as well as the port to connect to. Afterwards the TCP connection is established, and from there on used for transmitting actual payloads required for starting a charging session and controlling charging limits. For encoding payloads on this TCP connection the standard defines a "Vehicle to Grid Transfer Protocol" (V2GTP) packet format, which apart from some metadata contains one large payload blob encoded in the "Efficient XML Interchange" (EXI) format.

The ISO15118-2 standard defines a list of request messages sent from the vehicle to the charging station and corresponding response messages sent from the charging station to the vehicle. Before charging can start, payment and precharging have to be performed. For payment, the vehicle first asks the charging station for supported payment methods. As of today, mostly the `external` payment method is used, which requires the user to pay through an app, RFID card or electronic cash. The standard also supports certificate based authentication, which will be covered in the next section.

After payment was successful, the charging station performs insulation checks on the charging cable. Afterwards, the precharge procedure is initiated. During precharge, the charging station supplies a voltage to the charging cable, without the main battery contactor relay being closed in the vehicle. The precharging procedure makes sure the voltage present at the cable matches the battery voltage, reducing in rush current and reducing wear on the contactor relay.

After precharging the main charge loop is initiated, consisting of two packets used repeatedly: `CurrentDemandReq` and `CurrentDemandRes`. The first one is sent by the vehicle to request a specific voltage and current flowing into the vehicles battery. The latter one is sent by the charging station informing the vehicle about currently measured voltage and current as well as the charging stations limits. For example, the car might request a voltage of $369V$ and a maximum current of $400A$ resulting in a desired charging power of $148kW$. While the voltage has to be met, depending on the charging stations maximum output power the current might be lower than the requested value, resulting in a slower charging speed.

This main charge loop is repeated until one of the two parties terminates the charging session, opening the main contactor and disabling all current flowing into the battery.

C. ISO15118 Security Concepts

While the most commonly used scheme for the charging communication is based on plain TCP, the ISO15118 standard also allows to use Transport Layer Security (TLS) for encrypted communication. Using the UDP broadcast packet, the vehicle can signal support for TLS encrypted communication. If the charging station also supports TLS encryption it signals

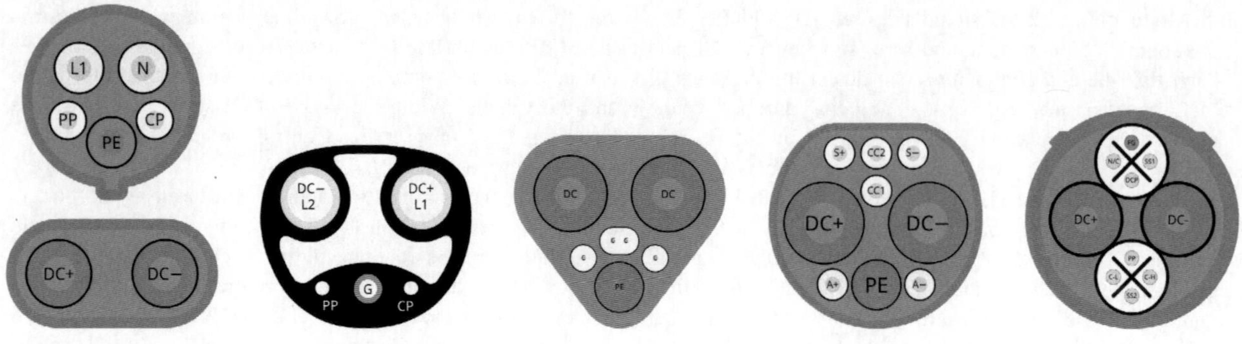

Figure 2. Schematic diagrams of other fast charging connectors. From left to right: Type 1 CCS [15], NACS [16], MCS [17], GB-T [18], Chademo [19]

this to the vehicle in the UDP response including a port to connect to using TLS. While TLS provides a secure way of communication, in order to handle authentication, it requires a Private Key Infrastructure (PKI) to sign and distribute certificates. ISO15118 describes a potential layout of this PKI handing out certificates to vehicle manufacturers and charge point operators, but does not name a specific entity managing this PKI.

D. Other Communication Standards

While type 2 and combined charging standard (CCS) are the most used plugs for passanger cars in Europe, there do exist some other plugs and charging standards for fast charging battery electric vehicles. In total there are five other major plugs used for fast charging around the globe, listed below and shown schematically in Figure 2:

1) Type 1 CCS formerly used in North America
2) NACS future north american charging standard
3) Megawatt Charging System (MCS)
4) GB/T charging standard used in China
5) CHAdeMO used in Japan

While Europe has the type 2 connector for three phase AC charging, America uses a different connector called type 1, since their power grid is usually not based on three phases. There exists a type 1 CCS connector, adding two pins for DC charging, similarly to type 2 CCS. Since communication is identical they can both be referred to as "CCS connectors", or specified as "CCS1 connector" for the American version and "CCS2 connector" for the European version. Similarly the megawatt charging system is also based on ISO15118, but uses a different connector, allowing higher currents and thus faster charging intended for trucks and buses. After Tesla open sourced their proprietary connector in 2022 [20] it became quickly adopted by car manufacturers and charging station operators for vehicles sold in America. While its socket is different, it is also based on ISO15118 communication described above.

GB/T and CHAdeMO are the charging standards used in China and Japan, respectively. They use CAN bus for communication rather than powerline making their implementation easier and cheaper, while disallowing advanced use cases ISO15118 provides. Since electric vehicle sales are much higher in Asia than in Europe and North America [21], the worldwide market share of vehicles with GB/T and CHAdeMO sockets remains significant nevertheless their usage only in China and Japan. According to Blech [22] at the end of 2019 the combined market share of GB/T and CHAdeMO was 55%. Figure 3 shows the market share of all connectors.

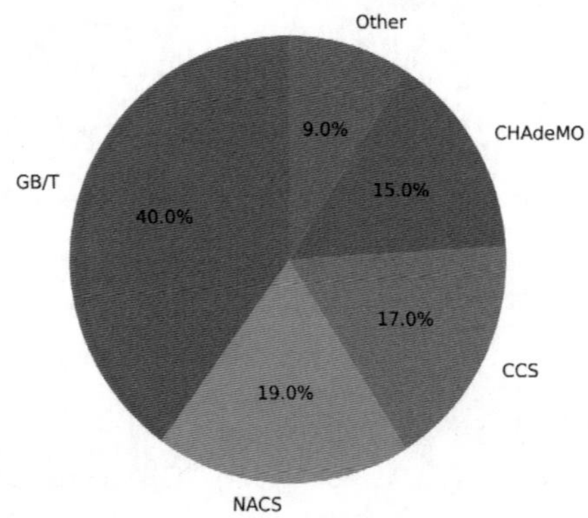

Figure 3. Charging socket market share at the end of 2019, based on Blech [22]

III. CHARGING STATION VENDORS

After the standardization of the type 2 connector in 2009 and even after the introduction of CCS in 2014 most charging stations built offered only AC charging. Since AC charging stations include mostly components also found in home and industrial electric installations, companies active in the field of electric components and installations, such as Mennekes, Hager and E.ON, started building AC charging stations [10].

After CCS connectors became more popular in electric vehicles and the demand for high power fast charging grew [23], some companies started developing and producing DC fast charging stations. While AC charging stations rely on

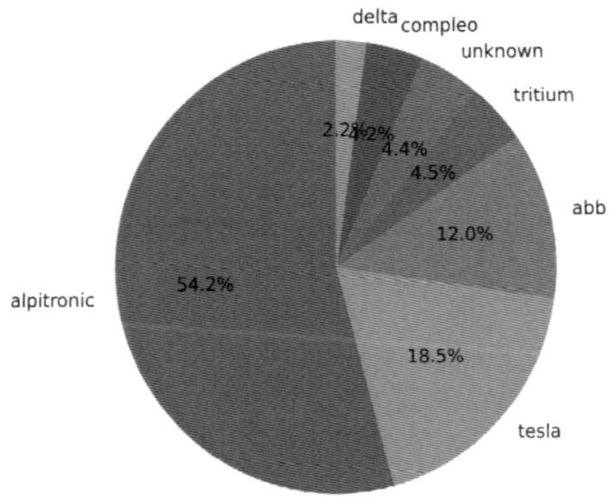

Figure 4. DC charging station vendor market share in Germany

simple components, DC charging stations are more complex, incorporating AC to DC conversion, high level communication and cooling equipment. While the market of AC charging station manufacturers is quite diverse, the complexity of DC charging causes only a handful of companies to produce significant numbers of high power charging stations.

As a part of this research we analyzed the current market share of DC charging stations in Germany. The largest registry of charging stations in Germany is goingelectric.de. This community led effort manages an interactive map as well as an API to fetch positions and metadata for each charging point. Each datapoint in the goingelectric database includes information about the manufacturer and model of the corresponding charging station. By analyzing the counts of all CCS based charging stations in Germany per manufacturer, we calculated the relative market share for each manufacturer.

With currently over 6000 DC charging points Alpitronic manufactured over 50% of todays DC charging stations in Germany. Second place is Tesla with its own supercharger devices and self managed charging network making up 18.5%. ABB is the only traditional electric installation company active not only in the AC charging station market, but also producing DC charging stations, making up 12.0% of all DC charging stations currently installed in Germany. With only three other companies having above 1% market share and Tesla not selling to third parties, the current DC charging station market is dominated by Alpitronic leaving behind well known companies like Siemens, Volkswagen and Porsche Engineering below the 1% mark. Figure 4 shows the market share of all manufacturers currently used in Germany, which have more than 1% market share.

IV. Charging Station Architectures

While the interface between vehicle and charging station is standardized, the communication with other electric components making up a charging park is not. Other research has already extensively covered different electrical aspects and their attributes in regard to battery charging [6], [23], [24]. While the details of high power electronics are hardly relevant to this technology review, some of their attributes influence charging station architecture as well as communication aspects with other systems.

Since electric vehicle power demand is not linear during a charging cycle [25], DC charging stations often share AC to DC power conversion electronics between multiple outlets. For example, Alpitronic chargers contain two to four AC to DC power conversion modules and typically include two CCS outlets. When two cars are being charged at once, rather than statically assigning conversion modules to outlets, the modules are dynamically switched between outlets. This switching allows the charge power to be distributed unevenly between both vehicles based on the demand of each vehicle, effectively increasing the maximum output per outlet without increasing the total amount of conversion modules.

The first three generations of Tesla superchargers used a similar load sharing technique. The new v4 superchargers feature larger conversion modules converting AC grid power to DC and one DC to DC conversion module for each supercharger outlet.

Apart from the internal communication and power management required to service multiple vehicles from one charging station, most charging stations are essentially independent systems, with no external communication. While integration with external power providers such as solar and stationary battery storage promises to be beneficial for grid optimization [24], we could find only little evidence of charging stations communicating with external devices other than through standardized charging protocols.

V. Attack Vectors and Impact

There already exists some research regarding the security of charging stations. Most of them however focus either on high level risk assessments [5], [26]–[31] or target aspects of vehicle charging other than DC fast charging communication [3], [32]–[34]. The following subsection describes some of the few attacks successfully carried out against DC charging communications. Afterwards, general problems with implementing the security concepts defined in ISO15118 are discussed.

A. Low Level Communication Attacks

One attack vector of the ISO15118 standard is targeting the low level powerline communication used as a physical layer. Baker et al. [35] first described an attack on the powerline communication, eavesdropping electromagnetic interference produced by the modulated powerline packets on top of the PWM signal described in Section II-B. While their approach was not reliable enough to capture all of the traffic between charging station and vehicle, they were able to extract the powerline network key exchanged during SLAC, allowing to decrypt further communication.

Another attack on the powerline communication demonstrated by [36] performs a denial of service by jamming the powerline communication signal. Since this attack effectively terminates the currently running charging session, the user has to re-authenticate and restart charging manually afterwards.

B. ISO15118 Security Implementation

As described in Section II-C, the ISO15118 standard uses TLS for securing communication and even for payment authentication.

Support for TLS is signaled by the vehicle and confirmed by the charging station during the UDP based discovery and handshaking. Since this initial communication is neither encrypted nor authenticated, a potential attacker can easily perform a TLS-downgrading attack, effectively disabling encryption in all further communication.

Another problem with the standard lies in it not naming a company or institute handing out certificates required for TLS communication. As of today there are at least four different companies that created a PKI and allow third parties to acquire certificates [37]–[40]. Normally a certificate authority simply provides certificates for a service provider, for example for a website. With ISO15118 however, the vehicle requires a matching client certificate for authenticating. Thus while having multiple certificate authorities is generally a good idea, it creates a maintenance overhead for both vehicle manufacturers and charging station operators in order to support all authorities. Because of this complexity, as of today the vast majority of all charging communication sessions is not encrypted at all. Since TLS is required in order to use plug and charge (PnC), users have to use external payment menthods such as smart cards or apps rather than PnC. While PnC promises to improve usability and thus overall technology acceptance, the nature of the TLS implementation details set by the ISO15118 charging standard hinder its spread and is thus rarely used today.

VI. Conclusion

As discussed in this paper, the market of both AC and DC charging stations is growing rapidly. Even though DC fast charging stations come with additional security implications, cybersecurity has not been a focus of the charging station industry in the past, leading to many textbook vulnerabilities in charging infrastructure. In the recent past this situation is starting to improve, with various institutions publishing guidelines and plans on securing charging infrastructure [41], [42].

While this is a step in the correct direction, a lot of low hanging fruits in regard to security research of DC charging stations remain untouched. This is underlined by the fact, that most scientific publications covering cybersecurity of charging communication are purely theoretical. While some AC charging stations and some web based services have been targets of security research, little research has been done targeting DC fast charging stations nor their communication with vehicles.

In future work, our plan is to perform penetration testing on charging station communication implementations both manually and using automated pentesting techniques. The goal of our future research will be to not only identify vulnerabilities in implementations, but also identifying general problems with the ISO15118 standard. One promising approach we are currently working on is to use state of the art fuzzing techniques for automatically identifying edge cases in the protocol and its implementations.

Acknowledgment

This work was created in the research project "Elektromobiles Sicheres Laden" (ESiLa) funded by the Bavarian Ministry of Economic Affairs, Regional Development and Energy under grant DIK0512/01.

References

[1] Kraftfahrtbundesamt (English: Federal Motor Transport Authority), *Anzahl der Elektroautos in Deutschland von 2006 bis Januar 2024 (English: Number of electric cars in Germany from 2006 to January 2024)*, https://www.kba.de/SharedDocs/Downloads/DE/Pressemitteilungen/DE/2024/pm_08_2024_bestand_01_24_merkmale_excel.xlsx?__blob=publicationFile&v=6, Mar. 2024.

[2] Bundesnetzagentur (English: Federal Network Agency), *Anzahl der öffentlichen Ladepunkte in Deutschland von Januar 2017 bis Oktober 2023 (English: Number of public charging points in Germany from January 2017 to October 2023)*, https://www.bundesnetzagentur.de/SharedDocs/Downloads/DE/Sachgebiete/Energie/Unternehmen_Institutionen/E_Mobilitaet/Ladesaeuleninfrastruktur.xlsx?__blob=publicationFile&v=5, Feb. 2024.

[3] T. Nasr, S. Torabi, E. Bou-Harb, C. Fachkha, and C. Assi, "Power jacking your station: In-depth security analysis of electric vehicle charging station management systems," *Computers & Security*, vol. 112, p. 102 511, Jan. 2022, ISSN: 0167-4048. DOI: 10.1016/j.cose.2021.102511.

[4] J. Johnson, T. Berg, B. Anderson, and B. Wright, "Review of Electric Vehicle Charger Cybersecurity Vulnerabilities, Potential Impacts, and Defenses," *Energies*, vol. 15, no. 11, p. 3931, Jan. 2022, Number: 11 Publisher: Multidisciplinary Digital Publishing Institute, ISSN: 1996-1073. DOI: 10.3390/en15113931.

[5] A. Ahalawat, S. Adepu, and J. Gardiner, "Security Threats in Electric Vehicle Charging," in *2022 IEEE International Conference on Communications, Control, and Computing Technologies for Smart Grids (SmartGridComm)*, Singapore, Singapore: IEEE, Oct. 2022, pp. 399–404, ISBN: 978-1-66543-254-2. DOI: 10.1109/SmartGridComm52983.2022.9961027.

[6] H. Tu, H. Feng, S. Srdic, and S. Lukic, "Extreme Fast Charging of Electric Vehicles: A Technology Overview," *IEEE Transactions on Transportation Electrification*, vol. 5, no. 4, pp. 861–878, Dec. 2019, Conference Name: IEEE Transactions on Transportation Electrification, ISSN: 2332-7782. DOI: 10.1109/TTE.2019.2958709.

[7] ISO/IEC, *ISO/IEC DIS 15118-2: Road vehicles - Vehicle to grid communication interface – Part 2: Network and application protocol requirements*, http://www.iso.org/iso/iso_catalogue/catalogue_ics/catalogue_detail_ics.htm?ics1=43&ics2=120&ics3=&csnumber=55366, 2012.

[8] ISO/IEC, *ISO/IEC DIS 15118-3: Road vehicles - Vehicle to grid communication interface – Part 3: Physical and data link layer requirements*, http://www.iso.org/iso/home/store/catalogue_ics/catalogue_detail_ics.htm?ics1=43&ics2=120&ics3=&csnumber=59675, 2012.

[9] IEC, *IEC 61851-1 ed2.0: Electric vehicle conductive charging system - Part 1: General requirements*, http://webstore.iec.ch /webstore/webstore.nsf/Artnum_PK/44636, 2010.

[10] M. Dalheimer, *Ladeinfrastruktur für Elektroautos: Ausbau statt Sicherheit (English: Charging infrastructure for electric cars: Expansion instead of safety)*, https://media.ccc.de/v/34c3-9092-ladeinfrastruktur_fur_elektroautos_ausbau_statt_sicherheit, Dec. 2017.

[11] Chris828, *Type 2 charging socket, VDE-AR-E 2623-2-2 plug*, https://commons.wikimedia.org/w/index.php?curid=89574378, Apr. 2020.

[12] A. Li, Q. Liu, J. Yang, and N. Zhou, "Crosstalk Analysis between Power Lines and Signal Lines Based on the Finite Difference-Time Domain Method," in *2019 IEEE 8th International Conference on Advanced Power System Automation and Protection (APAP)*, Xi'an, China: IEEE, Oct. 2019, pp. 638–641, ISBN: 978-1-72811-722-5. DOI: 10.1109/APAP47170.2019.9224975.

[13] N. Theethayi, R. Thottappillil, Yaqing Liu, and R. Montano, "Parameters that influence the crosstalk in multiconductor transmission line," in *2003 IEEE Bologna Power Tech Conference Proceedings,*, vol. 1, Bologna, Italy: IEEE, 2003, pp. 388–395, ISBN: 978-0-7803-7967-1. DOI: 10.1109/PTC.2003.1304162.

[14] D. J. T. Ngo Bisse, D. B. G. Onana Essama, D. J. Koko Koko, P. J. Atangana, and P. S. Ndjakomo Essiane, "Crosstalk Characterization and Reduction in Power Lines," *International Journal of Inventive Engineering and Sciences*, vol. 10, no. 9, pp. 1–11, Sep. 2023, ISSN: 23199598. DOI: 10.35940/ijies.C7883.0910923.

[15] Mliu92, *Drawing of J1772 (CCS1 Combo) connector, with labeled pinouts.* https://commons.wikimedia.org/w/index.php?curid=108177318, Aug. 2021.

[16] RickyCourtney, *Drawing of North American Charging Standard connector, with labeled pinouts.* https://commons.wikimedia.org/w/index.php?curid=133111353, Jun. 2023.

[17] Mliu92, *Speculative diagram of Megawatt Charging System, version 3.2.* https://commons.wikimedia.org/w/index.php?curid=119080953, Jun. 2022.

[18] Mliu92, *GBT-20234.3 electric vehicle connector pinout for DC charging.* https://commons.wikimedia.org/w/index.php?curid=108206603, Aug. 2021.

[19] Mliu92, *CHAdeMO connector (viewed facing the plug that interfaces with the vehicle)*, https://commons.wikimedia.org/w/index.php?curid=108209697, Aug. 2021.

[20] *Opening the North American Charging Standard*, https://www.tesla.com/blog/opening-north-american-charging-standard.

[21] *Trends in electric cars – Global EV Outlook 2024 – Analysis*, en-GB, https://www.iea.org/reports/global-ev-outlook-2024/trends-in-electric-cars.

[22] T. Blech, "Project ChaoJi: The background and challenges of harmonising DC charging standards," *CHAdeMO Europe*,

[23] H. S. Das, M. M. Rahman, S. Li, and C. W. Tan, "Electric vehicles standards, charging infrastructure, and impact on grid integration: A technological review," *Renewable and Sustainable Energy Reviews*, vol. 120, p. 109 618, Mar. 2020, ISSN: 1364-0321. DOI: 10.1016/j.rser.2019.109618.

[24] N. Deb, R. Singh, R. R. Brooks, and K. Bai, "A Review of Extremely Fast Charging Stations for Electric Vehicles," *Energies*, vol. 14, no. 22, p. 7566, Jan. 2021, Number: 22 Publisher: Multidisciplinary Digital Publishing Institute, ISSN: 1996-1073. DOI: 10.3390/en14227566.

[25] *Audi e-tron models with high charging performance.* https://www.audi-mediacenter.com/en/press-releases/audi-e-tron-models-with-high-charging-performance-12758.

[26] S. Acharya, Y. Dvorkin, H. Pandžić, and R. Karri, "Cybersecurity of Smart Electric Vehicle Charging: A Power Grid Perspective," *IEEE Access*, vol. 8, pp. 214 434–214 453, 2020, Conference Name: IEEE Access, ISSN: 2169-3536. DOI: 10.1109/ACCESS.2020.3041074.

[27] A. Sanghvi and T. Markel, "Cybersecurity for Electric Vehicle Fast-Charging Infrastructure," in *2021 IEEE Transportation Electrification Conference & Expo (ITEC)*, Chicago, IL, USA: IEEE, Jun. 2021, pp. 573–576, ISBN: 978-1-72817-583-6. DOI: 10.1109/ITEC51675.2021.9490069.

[28] C. Assi, "Ensuring a Resilient and Secure EV Charging Infrastructure for Sustainable Transportation," in *2023 International Conference on Information and Communication Technologies for Disaster Management (ICT-DM)*, Cosenza, Italy: IEEE, Sep. 2023, pp. 1–1, ISBN: 9798350319514. DOI: 10.1109/ICT-DM58371.2023.10286958.

[29] M. Mahrukh and M. S. Thomas, "Load Altering Attacks-a Review of Impact and Mitigation Strategies," in *2023 International Conference on Recent Advances in Electrical, Electronics & Digital Healthcare Technologies (REEDCON)*, May 2023, pp. 397–402. DOI: 10.1109/REEDCON57544.2023.10150456.

[30] Y. Park, O. C. Onar, and B. Ozpineci, "Potential Cybersecurity Issues of Fast Charging Stations with Quantitative Severity Analysis," in *2019 IEEE CyberPELS (CyberPELS)*, Knoxville, TN, USA: IEEE, Apr. 2019, pp. 1–7, ISBN: 978-1-72812-925-9. DOI: 10.1109/CyberPELS.2019.8925069.

[31] K. Bao, H. Valev, M. Wagner, and H. Schmeck, "A threat analysis of the vehicle-to-grid charging protocol ISO 15118," *Computer Science - Research and Development*, vol. 33, no. 1, pp. 3–12, Feb. 2018, ISSN: 1865-2042. DOI: 10.1007/s00450-017-0342-y.

[32] T. Nasr, S. Torabi, E. Bou-Harb, C. Fachkha, and C. Assi, "ChargePrint: A Framework for Internet-Scale Discovery and Security Analysis of EV Charging Management Systems," in *Proceedings 2023 Network and Distributed System Security Symposium*, San Diego, CA, USA: Internet Society, 2023, ISBN: 978-1-891562-83-9. DOI: 10.14722/ndss.2023.23084.

[33] K. Sarieddine, M. A. Sayed, S. Torabi, R. Atallah, and C. Assi, "Investigating the Security of EV Charging Mobile Applications as an Attack Surface," *ACM Transactions on Cyber-Physical Systems*, vol. 7, no. 4, 26:1–26:28, Oct. 2023, ISSN: 2378-962X. DOI: 10.1145/3609508.

[34] T. Nasr, "Large-Scale Study of Internet-Connected Electric Vehicle Charging Station Management Systems: Discovery, Security Analysis and Mitigation,"

[35] R. Baker and I. Martinovic, "Losing the Car Keys: Wireless {PHY-Layer} Insecurity in {EV} Charging," 2019, pp. 407–424, ISBN: 978-1-939133-06-9.

[36] S. Köhler, R. Baker, M. Strohmeier, and I. Martinovic, "Brokenwire : Wireless Disruption of CCS Electric Vehicle Charging," in *Proceedings 2023 Network and Distributed System Security Symposium*, arXiv:2202.02104 [cs], 2023. DOI: 10.14722/ndss.2023.23251.

[37] CharIN, *CharIN V2G PKI goes live!* https://www.charin.global/news/charin-v2g-pki-goes-live/, 2022.

[38] Hubject, *Download Public Key Infrastructure (PKI) | Hubject*, https://www.hubject.com/download-pki.

[39] nexusgroup, *Identities for Plug and Charge/vehicle-to-grid - V2G PKI*, https://doc.nexusgroup.com/pub/identities-for-vehicle-to-grid-v2g-pki.

[40] irdeto, *Irdeto Launches North American V2G Trusted Root CA to Accelerate Plug & Charge Adoption*, https://irdeto.com/news/irdeto-launches-north-american-v2g-trusted-root-ca-to-accelerate-plug-charge-adoption.

[41] J. McCarthy *et al.*, "Cybersecurity framework profile for electric vehicle extreme fast charging infrastructure," National Institute of Standards and Technology (U.S.), Gaithersburg, MD, Tech. Rep. NIST IR 8473, Oct. 2023, NIST IR 8473. DOI: 10.6028/NIST.IR.8473.

[42] ENCS, "Security test plan for EV charging station," *European Network for Cyber Security*, 2019.

Enhanced Arbiter PUF Construction Model to Strengthening PUF-based Authentication

Rizka Reza Pahlevi
Graduate School of Informatics
Nagoya University
Nagoya, Japan
e-mail: pahlevirr@net.itc.nagoya-u.ac.jp

Hirokazu Hasegawa
Center for Strategic Cyber
Resilience Research and Development
National Institute of Informatics
Tokyo, Japan
e-mail: hasegawa@nii.ac.jp

Yukiko Yamaguchi
Information Technology Center
Nagoya University
Nagoya, Japan
e-mail: yamaguchi@itc.nagoya-u.ac.jp

Hajime Shimada
Information Technology Center
Nagoya University
Nagoya, Japan
e-mail: shimada@itc.nagoya-u.ac.jp

***Abstract*—In recent years, ensuring robust security in digital systems has become increasingly challenging, particularly in the realm of authentication. Physical Unclonable Functions (PUFs) have emerged as a promising solution due to their intrinsic ability to leverage manufacturing variations to produce unique and unpredictable responses. This paper presents a novel arbiter PUF construction designed to enhance authentication. The proposed PUF incorporates a cyclic model with four crossed lines in the signature generator to improve overall security. Extensive evaluations on six different Field Programmable Gate Array (FPGA) boards demonstrate that the proposed arbiter PUF achieves ideal levels of uniqueness (40.52% to 58.17%), bit aliasing (48.52% to 60.03%), reliability (80.98% to 96.49%), and balanced uniformity (47.95% to 61.40%). Additionally, the False Acceptance Rate (FAR) and False Rejection Rate (FRR) are maintained within acceptable limits (1.59% to 2.49% for FAR and 1.13% to 2.35% for FRR). Compared to existing arbiter PUF designs, our proposed model shows significant improvements in key security metrics, underscoring its potential for robust and secure authentication applications.**

Keywords-physical unclonable functions; authentication; arbiter PUF.

I. Introduction

In recent years, the domain of security has encountered increasingly challenging issues, particularly in the realm of authentication [1]–[4]. As technological advancements continue to accelerate, the methods employed by malicious entities have also evolved, necessitating the development of more robust security solutions. One promising area of research that has garnered substantial attention is the utilization of PUFs. PUFs capitalize on the inherent randomness introduced during the manufacturing processes of physical devices [2], [5]–[11]. This randomness results in unique and unpredictable responses when a device is queried, rendering it difficult to replicate or predict. Therefore, these distinctive characteristics theoretically position PUFs as a viable solution for generating secure authentication token.

Silicon-based PUFs represent a prominent subset of PUF technologies, offering solutions that can be seamlessly integrated with other systems. Among silicon-based PUFs, delay-based PUFs are particularly notable for their reduced bias compared to memory-based PUFs and their ability to exploit a wider range of manufacturing variables [1], [2], [10]–[16]. A prime example of delay-based PUFs is the arbiter PUF, developed in 2004 [17], [18], which exemplifies a delay-based PUF construction model. The arbiter PUF is classified as a weak PUF and is frequently targeted by various attacks. One common vulnerability is its susceptibility to statistical model attacks, which exploit the correlation between the Challenge-Response Pairs (CRPs) of the arbiter PUF, underscoring its inadequate security properties. Several studies have explored methods to improve the security of arbiter PUFs. One approaches employed an efficient XOR arbiter PUF to bolster uniqueness and security [3]. This efficient XOR arbiter PUF resulting in significant improvements in uniqueness. However, when evaluating PUFs, it is crucial to consider both their intended applications and their security characteristics. Consequently, a significant body of research focuses on designing or enhancing PUFs to meet these stringent security requirements [16], [19].

This study proposed arbiter PUF construction. While it may initially appear similar to other delay-based PUFs, our research demonstrates its capability to enhance and maintain nearly ideal secure PUF attributes. Compared to other arbiter PUF models, such as the XOR arbiter PUF, flip-flop arbiter PUF, and traditional arbiter PUF, our proposed arbiter PUF exhibits superior or nearly ideal security features. For a thorough security assessment, we propose a comprehensive PUF security evaluation. This evaluation measures the level of protection provided by the PUF, encompassing metrics such as FAR, FRR, uniqueness, reliability, uniformity, and bit aliasing. Additionally, we implemented our PUF construction on six different FPGA boards to validate its effectiveness and reliability across varied hardware environments.

The remaining part of this article is organized as follows. Section II discusses previous research aimed to improved arbiter PUF. Section III describes the construction of the proposed arbiter PUF and evaluation metrics. Section IV discusses the collection of the dataset, the experimental results and provides further discussion about the proposed arbiter PUF. Finally, Section V concludes the work and outlines the future research plan.

II. RELATED WORK

Arbiter PUF is a primer example of delay-based PUF, which was developed in 2004 [17], [18], that notable for their reduced bias compared to memory-based PUFs. The arbiter PUF is typically constructed using two lines, each consisting of a number (N) of 2-1 multiplexers (MUX gates). Several studies have been conducted to enhance the performance of arbiter PUFs. Machida et al. [20] proposed a arbiter PUF construction aimed at improving unpredictability. This unpredictability was measured through prediction rate, uniqueness, randomness, and steadiness. They introduced both conventional arbiter PUFs and double arbiter PUFs. The double arbiter PUFs were constructed by XORing the outputs of multiple conventional arbiter PUFs. Their research, tested on three FPGAs, found that the conventional arbiter PUFs exhibited better steadiness compared to the double arbiter PUFs. However, both types generally achieved near-ideal randomness and uniqueness. Mahalat et al. [21] proposed a Path-Changing Switch (PCS) based arbiter PUF to address the low uniqueness issue in conventional arbiter PUFs. The PCS comprised four inverters and three MUXes. Implemented on fifteen Xilinx FPGAs, the PCS-based arbiter PUF achieved 49.81% uniqueness, 49.77% uniformity, and 98.19% reliability (steadiness). Anandakumar et al. [3] introduced an efficient XOR arbiter PUF to tackle poor uniqueness. This design consisted of three blocks of XOR PUFs, with each block's output captured by an arbiter. The arbiter outputs were stored in a 15-bit shift register, and the final response was obtained by XORing the golden responses from each shift register. Their efficient XOR arbiter PUF achieved 48.69% uniqueness, 50.73% uniformity, and 99.41% reliability. Yang et al. [22] proposed a arbiter PUF using improved switch components to address poor uniqueness and high resource consumption on FPGAs. To optimize resource usage, they introduced Programmable Delay Lines (PDLs) and MUXes. Their PDL + MUX arbiter PUF achieved 45.2% uniqueness and 0.357% steadiness (with the ideal steadiness value being 0%).

To ensure PUFs can be used for security purposes, such as authentication, they must be thoroughly evaluated. We categorize the evaluation into two types: classical PUF evaluations and PUF authentication-specific evaluations. The classical PUF evaluations include uniqueness, uniformity, and steadiness. The PUF authentication-specific evaluations include bit-aliasing, FAR, and FRR. Uniqueness, one of the most commonly used metrics, measures the correlation between chips using the same CRP and evaluates the differences between one chip and others. Achieving an ideal uniqueness value is crucial to avoid misidentification of the CRP from a particular chip. However, measuring uniqueness alone is not sufficient. Bit-aliasing complements uniqueness by ensuring no shared variable or systemic bias affects both chips similarly. This metric guarantees that input from a PUF to different chips will produce distinct output patterns, reducing security risks like brute force and replay attacks. Nevertheless, addressing bias alone is not enough; the composition of the PUF output must also be evaluated.

Uniformity measures the balance between bits '1' and '0' in the PUF output, ideally aiming for equal distribution to enhance security by reducing the likelihood of brute force attacks. Ensuring that PUF outputs are unique, free of bias, and uniform is necessary, but these metrics must be supported by reliability. Steadiness evaluates how consistent the output is when the same input is applied, often measured by the Hamming distance. Ideally, steadiness should be zero, meaning no bit errors occur; however, due to inherent noise during the PUF process, achieving zero steadiness is challenging, necessitating error correction mechanisms. To measure authentication performance, FAR and FRR are used. FAR measures how often incorrect PUF outputs are accepted in authentication systems, while FRR measures how often correct PUF outputs are rejected. In biometric systems, FAR and FRR below 2.5% are considered acceptable, and this benchmark is used for PUFs as well. Balancing FAR and FRR is challenging because reducing one often increases the other.

III. IMPROVED ARBITER PUF CONSTRUCTION FOR ROBUST AUTHENTICATION

A. PUF Construction Model

The proposed arbiter PUF consists of two main components: the signature generator and the arbiter. The signature generator is responsible for producing the signal and comprises four lines, each containing a series of MUX gates. At first glance, the proposed arbiter PUF resembles the double arbiter PUF proposed by Machida et al. [20], but it incorporates significant differences. The proposed arbiter PUF consists of four sets of lines instead of two sets. The increased number of lines is intended to maintain circuit delay, thereby reducing bias caused by some paths having minimal circuit delay. Additionally, the cyclic model aims to ensure fair circuit delay by evenly distributing the signal across all paths. This crossing pattern facilitates a more efficient and manageable physical design process while ensuring that signal travel times from inputs to outputs are balanced across all four paths. By maintaining circuit delay through fair path creation and signal distribution, the PUF quality is potentially enhanced. The circuit topology of the proposed arbiter PUF is illustrated in Figure 1. For the arbiter component, we utilized elements from conventional

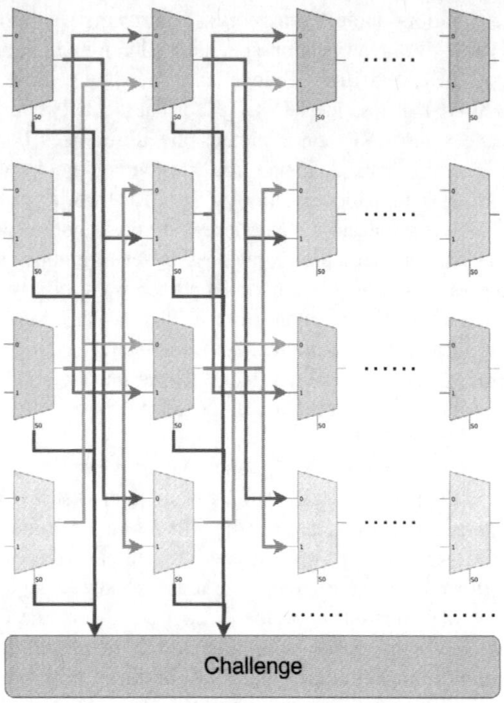

Figure 1. Signature generator of proposed arbiter PUF

arbiter PUF. The final MUX gates in the series of signature generators produce a spike signal, which is then distributed to multiple D Flip-Flops.

B. Security Evaluation Metric

1) Uniqueness: Ideally, the Hamming distance between responses to the same challenge from different chips should average around 50% of the total response size. To quantify this, a cross-measurement of the Hamming distance between responses from different chips is necessary. The uniqueness is calculated using (1).

$$Uniqueness = \frac{2}{n(n-1)} \sum_{i=1}^{n-1} \sum_{j=i+1}^{n} \frac{HD(R_i, R_j)}{m} \quad (1)$$

In (1), n represents the number of responses obtained from the same challenge across different chips. R_i and R_j denote the PUF responses from the i-th and j-th chips, respectively, while $HD(R_i, R_j)$ is the Hamming distance between these responses. The term m is the bit length of the PUF response.

2) Bit aliasing: Ideally, the bit-aliasing value should be close to 50%, indicating a balanced distribution and enhancing security. Equation (2) is used to calculate bit-aliasing.

$$BA(n) = \frac{1}{N} \sum_{i=0}^{R-1} r_{i,n} \quad (2)$$

In (2), N represents the number of challenges used to generate responses from the PUF chip, and $r_{i,n}$ denotes the *n-th* bit of the response generated from the *i-th* challenge. The index i ranges from 0 to R-1, where R is the total number of collected responses.

3) Uniformity: Ideally, the distribution should be equal, with each bit appearing 50% of the time. Equation (3) is used to measure uniformity.

$$Uniformity = \frac{1}{n} \sum_{l=1}^{n} R_{i,l} \quad (3)$$

In (3), n represents the number of repeated responses taken for the same challenge, and $R_{i,l}$ denotes the *i-th* bit of the response generated in the *l-th* repetition. The index l ranges from 1 to n, covering all repetitions of the collected responses.

4) Steadiness: Ideally, a PUF chip should always provide a consistent and reliable response to the same challenges. The bit deviation in response can be quantified using intra-class Hamming Distance (HD_{intra}). The intra-class Hamming distance is calculated using (4).

$$HD_{\text{intra}} = \sum_{i=1}^{k} |x_i - x_i'| \quad \text{where} \quad D = \begin{cases} 0 & \text{if } x = x' \\ 1 & \text{if } x \neq x' \end{cases} \quad (4)$$

In (4), k is the length of the PUF response, x_i represents the i-th bit of the response, and $x\prime_i$ represents the corresponding i-th bit from another response to the same challenge.

5) FAR and FRR: Ideally, both FAR and FRR should be zero, indicating that the PUF responses are perfectly unambiguous. If the distribution of the intra-class and inter-class Hamming distances follows a Gaussian distribution, FAR and FRR can be statistically determined. The FRR is calculated using (5).

$$FRR = \frac{1}{\sigma_{\text{intra}}\sqrt{2\pi}} \int_{HD_{\text{max}}}^{\infty} \exp\left(-\frac{1}{2}\left(\frac{x-\mu_{\text{intra}}}{\sigma_{\text{intra}}}\right)^2\right) dx \quad (5)$$

In (5), HD_{max} represents the maximum Hamming distance allowed to accept a response, μ_{intra} denotes the mean of the intra-class Hamming distances, and σ_{intra} is the standard deviation of the intra-class Hamming distances. Similarly, the FAR is calculated using (6).

$$FAR = \frac{1}{\sigma_{\text{inter}}\sqrt{2\pi}} \int_{-\infty}^{HD_{\text{max}}} \exp\left(-\frac{1}{2}\left(\frac{x-\mu_{\text{inter}}}{\sigma_{\text{inter}}}\right)^2\right) dx \quad (6)$$

In (6), μ_{inter} represents the mean of the inter-class Hamming distances, and σ_{inter} represents the standard deviation of the inter-class Hamming distances.

IV. Result and Discussion

A. Collection of Dataset

For this study, we implemented our proposed arbiter PUF construction on six different FPGA boards. The specific boards used are as follows: Cyclone V SE 5CSEMA4U23C6N (referred to as CHIP 1), Cyclone V SE 5CSEBA6U23I7 (referred to as CHIP 2), Cyclone V GT 5CGTFD9E5F35C7N (referred to as CHIP 3), Cyclone V SE 5CSEBA6U23I7 (a second board, referred to as CHIP 4), MAX10 10M04SCE144C8 (referred to as CHIP 5), and Cyclone IV EP4CE22F16C6 (referred to as CHIP 6). To evaluate the performance and reliability of the PUFs, we sent 10,052 different challenges to each board. For every challenge, 1,000 response samples were collected, resulting in a comprehensive dataset. In total, we gathered 10,052,000 response samples per chip, amounting to a grand total of 60,312,000 dataset entries across all six chips.

B. Security Evaluation Result

1) Uniqueness: Utilizing (1), the average Hamming distance observed was close to the ideal uniqueness, indicating a high level of uniqueness and distinctiveness between the responses from different chips. Table I shows the results of the uniqueness measurements from the six FPGA boards.

The results show that the average Hamming distances between the chips were mostly above 50%. This indicates a high level of uniqueness and distinctiveness in the PUF responses across different chips. Notably, the Hamming distances ranged from 40.52% (between CHIP 3 and CHIP 6) to 58.17% (between CHIP 1 and CHIP 6), thereby supporting the effectiveness of our PUF design in providing unique responses.

2) Bit aliasing: Utilizing (2), the bit-aliasing value was found to be close to the ideal 50%, demonstrating that the responses are unbiased and originate from inherent manufacturing variations. Table II shows the results of bit aliasing for the proposed arbiter PUF.

The bit aliasing results reveal that the values are generally close to the ideal 50%. The values range from 48.52% (between CHIP 1 and CHIP 5) to 60.03% (between CHIP 3 and CHIP 6), with most values clustering around the 50% mark. These results confirm that the randomness in the PUF responses is primarily due to inherent manufacturing variations, thereby supporting the robustness of the PUF design.

3) Uniformity: Utilizing (3), the uniformity was found to be close ideal. Table III shows the results of the uniformity measurements for the proposed arbiter PUF. The uniformity results show that the average result is generally close to the ideal 50%. CHIP 2, with an average of 47.95%, is the closest to this ideal value, indicating a well-balanced distribution. On the other hand, CHIP 3 has the highest average at 61.40%, which is further from the ideal but still demonstrates a reasonable level of uniformity.

4) Steadiness: Utilizing (4), the steadiness was found to be close to ideal. Table III shows the results of the steadiness measurements for the proposed arbiter PUF. The results indicate a range of average intra-class Hamming distances across different chips, suggesting varying levels of steadiness. CHIP 3 exhibited the lowest average intra-class Hamming distance at 4.4920 (96.49%), indicating the highest level of consistency among the tested chips. In contrast, CHIP 2 had the highest average intra-class Hamming distance at 24.3330 (80.98%), suggesting more variability in its responses.

5) FAR and FRR: Utilizing (6), the FAR was found to be under 2.5%. Tables IV present the detailed results of FAR for the proposed arbiter PUF. The FAR results in range from 1.5940% (between CHIP 3 and CHIP 6) to 2.4940% (between CHIP 4 and CHIP 5), indicating a relatively low rate of false acceptances. Utilizing (5), the FRR was found to be under 2.5%. Table IV is shown the result of FRR. The values range from 1.1281% (CHIP 3) to 2.3465% (CHIP 2). Both FAR and FRR values are below 2.5%, which is considered acceptable for robust authentication systems.

C. Discussion

The evaluation of the proposed arbiter PUF across various metrics demonstrates its effectiveness and robustness. The uniqueness metric, measured by the Hamming distance between responses from different chips to the same challenge, yielded values close to the ideal 50%, indicating distinct and distinguishable responses across different chips (Table I). This high level of uniqueness reduces the likelihood of misidentification and enhances system security. Bit aliasing, assessed to ensure no systemic bias, showed values close to the ideal 50%, ranging from 48.52% to 65.61%, indicating minimal bias and confirming the randomness in the PUF responses originates from inherent manufacturing variations shown in Table II. The average uniformity values were generally close to the ideal 50% as shown in Table III, with CHIP 2 achieving the closest average at 47.95%. This balanced uniformity enhances the security against brute force attacks and contributes to the reliability of the PUF.

The results of steadiness, shown in Table III, reveal varying levels of steadiness across different chips. CHIP 3 exhibited the highest consistency of 4.492 (96.49%), while CHIP 2 showed more variability of 24.333 (80.98%). These findings highlight areas for improvement in ensuring more uniform steadiness across different chips, which is crucial for enhancing the reliability of the PUF. The FAR and FRR metrics are critical for assessing the authentication performance of the PUF. As detailed in Tables IV, the FAR values ranged from 1.5940% to 2.5145%, and the FRR values ranged from 1.1281% to 2.3465%. The low rates of false acceptances and rejections confirm that the system effectively distinguishes between valid and invalid responses, thereby enhancing the overall security and usability of the PUF. The high level of uniqueness, minimal bit aliasing, balanced uniformity, consistent steadiness, and low FAR and FRR values collectively underscore the superior performance of our PUF design. These results compare favorably with other arbiter PUF research, highlighting the advancements and contributions of our work to the field of PUF-based security solutions.

D. Comparison from previous research

To contextualize our findings, we compared our results with previous arbiter PUF research as summarized in Table V. The table shows that our proposed PUF achieves favorable results across various metrics. Specifically, our PUF demonstrates a FAR range of 1.5940% to 2.5145% and an FRR range of

TABLE I
UNIQUENESS OF THE PROPOSED ARBITER PUF

	CHIP 1	CHIP 2	CHIP 3	CHIP 4	CHIP 5	CHIP 6
CHIP 1	–	56.02%	54.19%	55.12%	53.64%	58.17%
CHIP 2	56.02%	–	51.05%	52.61%	50.01%	48.42%
CHIP 3	54.19%	51.05%	–	51.75%	53.78%	40.52%
CHIP 4	55.12%	52.61%	51.75%	–	52.99%	50.58%
CHIP 5	53.64%	50.01%	53.78%	52.99%	–	50.23%
CHIP 6	58.17%	48.42%	40.52%	50.58%	50.23%	–

TABLE II
BIT ALIASING OF THE PROPOSED ARBITER PUF

	CHIP 1	CHIP 2	CHIP 3	CHIP 4	CHIP 5	CHIP 6
CHIP 1	–	50.56%	53.74%	52.39%	48.57%	49.89%
CHIP 2	49.73%	–	54.53%	53.81%	51.41%	55.85%
CHIP 3	53.14%	56.08%	–	57.02%	49.28%	60.03%
CHIP 4	51.91%	54.09%	56.85%	–	49.98%	56.82%
CHIP 5	48.52%	53.60%	51.38%	51.47%	–	54.57%
CHIP 6	49.38%	57.79%	65.61%	57.33%	52.31%	–

TABLE III
UNIFORMITY AND STEADINESS OF THE PROPOSED ARBITER PUF

Chip	Uniformity (average)	Steadiness(HD_{intra}) (average)
CHIP 1	61.16%	88.63%
CHIP 2	47.95%	80.98%
CHIP 3	61.40%	96.49%
CHIP 4	53.04%	87.18%
CHIP 5	43.29%	86.88%
CHIP 6	51.94%	93.60%

1.1281% to 2.3465%, which are comparable to or better than those reported in other studies. In terms of uniqueness, our PUF's range of 48.52% to 65.61% is slightly higher than the ideal 50%, but still within an acceptable range. This indicates a high level of distinctiveness in our PUF responses. Reliability, measured through steadiness, showed a range of 96.49% to 80.98%, which is competitive with other designs. While the 4-1 Double APUF by Machida et al. [20] achieved nearly ideal uniformity values, our design maintains a reasonable balance, further enhancing security against brute force attacks. The results from Lin [23], Aknesil [24], and Yang [22] provide additional benchmarks, where our PUF consistently shows competitive performance.

V. CONCLUSION

The proposed arbiter PUF construction model presents significant advancements in the field of PUF-based authentication solutions. By integrating a cyclic crossing pattern within the signature generator, our design effectively increase the security, leading to more secure for authentication purpose. Comprehensive testing on six FPGA boards has validated the effectiveness of our design, demonstrating ideal performance in uniqueness (40.52% - 58.17%), reliability (96.49%), uniformity (47.95% - 61.40%), and bit aliasing (48.52% - 60.03%) compared to traditional arbiter PUF models. The measured FAR and FRR further confirm the robustness of our PUF in secure authentication applications. We found the FAR in range of 1.59% - 2.494%, and FRR in range 1.13% - 2.35%. In conclusion, our proposed arbiter PUF construction offers a promising solution for enhancing digital security through improved authentication mechanisms. The advancements presented in this paper contribute significantly to the development of more secure and reliable PUF technologies, paving the way for their widespread adoption in various security-critical applications. Despite these achievements, there are still areas for potential improvement. Future work could focus on optimizing the PUF architecture for even lower FAR and FRR values and introducing a method to increase the reliability. Additionally, implementing our PUF design in a broader range of hardware environments could provide deeper insights into its versatility and scalability.

ACKNOWLEDGMENT

This research has been supported by the Kayamori Foundation of Informational Science Advancement with grand number K35 Research XXVIII No. 632

REFERENCES

[1] M. Barbareschi, A. De Benedictis, E. La Montagna, A. Mazzeo, and N. Mazzocca, "A PUF-based mutual authentication scheme for Cloud-Edges IoT systems," *Future Gener. Comput. Syst.*, vol. 101, pp. 246–261, Dec. 2019.

[2] M. Barbareschi, A. De Benedictis, and N. Mazzocca, "A PUF-based hardware mutual authentication protocol," *J. Parallel Distrib. Comput.*, vol. 119, pp. 107–120, Sept. 2018.

[3] N. N. Anandakumar, M. S. Hashmi, and M. A. Chaudhary, "Implementation of efficient xor arbiter puf on fpga with enhanced uniqueness and security," *IEEE Access*, vol. 10, pp. 129832–129842, 2022.

[4] R. R. Pahlevi, P. Sukarno, and B. Erfianto, "Secure MQTT PUF-Based key exchange protocol for smart healthcare," *Jurnal Rekayasa Elektrika*, vol. 17, pp. 107–114, June 2021.

[5] Y. Guo, T. Dee, and A. Tyagi, "Barrel shifter physical unclonable function based encryption," *Cryptography*, vol. 2, p. 22, Aug. 2018.

[6] I. Papakonstantinou and N. Sklavos, "Physical unclonable functions (PUFs) design technologies: Advantages and trade offs," in *Computer and Network Security Essentials*, pp. 427–442, Cham: Springer International Publishing, 2018.

[7] A. Tsuneda, "Various auto-correlation functions of m-bit random numbers generated from chaotic binary sequences," *Entropy*, vol. 23, no. 10, 2021.

TABLE IV
FAR AND FRR OF THE PROPOSED ARBITER PUF

	FAR						FRR
	CHIP 1	**CHIP 2**	**CHIP 3**	**CHIP 4**	**CHIP 5**	**CHIP 6**	
CHIP 1	–	2.1825%	1.8879%	2.0153%	2.4738%	1.8380%	1.7899%
CHIP 2	2.1825%	–	2.2582%	2.3246%	2.4935%	2.4553%	2.3465%
CHIP 3	1.8879%	2.2582%	–	1.8419%	2.4910%	1.5940%	1.1281%
CHIP 4	2.0153%	2.3246%	1.8419%	–	2.4940%	1.8631%	2.2095%
CHIP 5	2.4738%	2.4935%	2.4910%	2.4940%	–	2.5077%	1.9949%
CHIP 6	1.8380%	2.4553%	1.5940%	1.8631%	2.5077%	–	1.4496%

TABLE V
COMPARISON OF PROPOSED PUF TO PREVIOUS ARBITER PUFS

Arbiter PUF Research	PUF Security Evaluation					
	FAR	FRR	Uniqueness	Steadiness(HD_{intra})	Uniformity	Bit Aliasing
Ideal	0%	0%	50%	100%	50%	50%
Conventional APUF [20]	–	–	4.72% / 4.96% / 4.44%	99.24% / 99.17% / 99.55%	53.81% / 56.53% / 54%	–
2-1 Double APUF [20]	–	–	41.36% / 49.70% / 48.06%	92.21% / 88.8% / 89.95%	55.19% / 31.4% / 50.63%	–
4-1 Double APUF [20]	–	–	50.46% / 51.34% / 48.78%	65.04% / 81.01% / 74.15%	55.67% / 54.76% / 54.59%	–
Path Changing Switch (PCS) [21]	–	–	49.81% / 51.34%	Avg 0.35% / Avg 1.49%	Avg **49.77%** / Avg 57.64%	–
APUF [23]	–	–	42.7%	96%	–	–
APUF [24]	–	–	15.15%	0.45% - 0.5%	98%	–
APUF [22]	–	–	45.2%	–	–	–
FOXFFAPUF [25]	–	–	42% / 44%	–	–	–
Efficient XOR APUF [3]	–	–	48.69%	99.41%	50.73%	–
Our Proposed PUF	**1.5940% - 2.4940%**	**1.1281% - 2.3465%**	**40.52%** - 58.17%	**96.49%** to 80.98%	47.95% - 61.40%	**48.52%** - 60.03%

[8] T. Ichiki and A. Tsuneda, "Study on security enhancement of 64-bit NFSR-based block cipher systems with ring structure," in *2018 International Conference on Information and Communication Technology Convergence (ICTC)*, pp. 842–844, Oct. 2018.

[9] A. Shamsoshoara, A. Korenda, F. Afghah, and S. Zeadally, "A survey on physical unclonable function (puf)-based security solutions for internet of things," *Computer Networks*, vol. 183, p. 107593, 2020.

[10] H. Xu, J. Ding, P. Li, F. Zhu, and R. Wang, "A lightweight RFID mutual authentication protocol based on physical unclonable function," *Sensors*, vol. 18, no. 3, p. 760, 2018.

[11] M. N. Aman, K. C. Chua, and B. Sikdar, "Mutual authentication in IoT systems using physical unclonable functions," *IEEE Internet of Things Journal*, vol. 4, pp. 1327–1340, Oct. 2017.

[12] H. Kang, Y. Hori, T. Katashita, and M. Hagiwara, "The implementation of fuzzy extractor is not hard to do: An approach using puf data," in *Proceedings of the 30th Symposium on Cryptography and Information Security, Kyoto, Japan*, pp. 22–25, 2013.

[13] C. Bohm and M. Hofer, *Physical Unclonable Functions in Theory and Practice*. Springer Science & Business Media, Oct. 2012.

[14] K. Mahmood, S. Shamshad, M. Rana, A. Shafiq, S. Ahmad, M. A. Akram, and R. Amin, "PUF enable lightweight key-exchange and mutual authentication protocol for multi-server based D2D communication," *Journal of Information Security and Applications*, vol. 61, p. 102900, Sept. 2021.

[15] W. Xiong, A. Schaller, N. A. Anagnostopoulos, M. U. Saleem, S. Gabmeyer, S. Katzenbeisser, and J. Szefer, "Run-time accessible DRAM PUFs in commodity devices," in *International Conference on Cryptographic Hardware and Embedded Systems*, pp. 432–453, 2016.

[16] J. R. Wallrabenstein, "Implementing authentication systems based on physical unclonable functions," *2015 IEEE Trustcom/BigDataSE/ISPA*, vol. 1, pp. 790–796, 2015.

[17] J. Lee, D. Lim, B. Gassend, G. Suh, M. van Dijk, and S. Devadas, "A technique to build a secret key in integrated circuits for identification and authentication applications," in *2004 Symposium on VLSI Circuits. Digest of Technical Papers (IEEE Cat. No.04CH37525)*, pp. 176–179, 2004.

[18] D. Lim, J. Lee, B. Gassend, G. Suh, M. van Dijk, and S. Devadas, "Extracting secret keys from integrated circuits," *IEEE Transactions on Very Large Scale Integration (VLSI) Systems*, vol. 13, no. 10, pp. 1200–1205, 2005.

[19] Y. Nozaki and M. Yoshikawa, "Secret sharing schemes based secure authentication for physical unclonable function," in *2019 IEEE 4th International Conference on Computer and Communication Systems (ICCCS)*, pp. 445–449, 2019.

[20] T. Machida, D. Yamamoto, M. Iwamoto, and K. Sakiyama, "A new arbiter puf for enhancing unpredictability on fpga," *The Scientific World Journal*, vol. 2015, no. 1, p. 864812, 2015.

[21] M. H. Mahalat, S. Mandal, A. Mondal, B. Sen, and R. S. Chakraborty, "Implementation, characterization and application of path changing switch based arbiter puf on fpga as a lightweight security primitive for iot," *ACM Trans. Des. Autom. Electron. Syst.*, vol. 27, nov 2021.

[22] J. Yang, X. Yu, and R. Wei, "A low resource consumption arbiter puf improved switch component design for fpga," *Journal of Physics: Conference Series*, vol. 2221, p. 012011, may 2022.

[23] L. Lin, S. Srivathsa, D. K. Krishnappa, P. Shabadi, and W. Burleson, "Design and validation of arbiter-based pufs for sub-45-nm low-power security applications," *IEEE Transactions on Information Forensics and Security*, vol. 7, no. 4, pp. 1394–1403, 2012.

[24] C. Aknesil and E. Dubrova, "An fpga implementation of 4x4 arbiter puf," in *2021 IEEE 51st International Symposium on Multiple-Valued Logic (ISMVL)*, pp. 160–165, 2021.

[25] R. Sushma and N. Murty, "Feedback oriented xored flip-flop based arbiter puf," in *2018 International Conference on Electrical, Electronics, Communication, Computer, and Optimization Techniques (ICEECCOT)*, pp. 1444–1448, 2018.

Towards a Stakeholder-Centric Trust Management Approach for the Automotive Ecosystem

Marco Michl, Hans-Joachim Hof
Technische Hochschule Ingolstadt
Carissma Institute of Electric, Connected and Secure Mobility
Ingolstadt, Germany
email: marco.michl@carissma.eu,
hof@thi.de

***Abstract*—The rise of connected services in modern vehicles, combined with the target of software-defined vehicles, makes new approaches to secure the automotive ecosystem necessary. One of these approaches is implementing computational trust models within vehicles to secure interactions in a way inspired by the intuitive concept of trust. Involved stakeholders and their relations are essential to creating a system representing trust. We identified relevant stakeholder groups involved in the communication of modern cars and characterized them based on their lifecycle phase, the user agents and devices used to communicate, and their relations and roles. Furthermore, we describe the necessity for trust in the automotive ecosystem, the connection between trust and authorization, and the trust relations between the stakeholders. The results are thus a basis for designing general trust management systems for the automotive ecosystem.**

Keywords-automotive; ecosystem; trust; authorization; stakeholder.

I. Introduction

Modern vehicles offer various services to their passengers and the surrounding area. The interaction with devices and infrastructure outside of the vehicle is essential for these connected services that use different technologies like Vehicular Ad-Hoc Networks (VANETs) or mobile networks. With the integration of these technologies, the vehicle is no longer an isolated device. It becomes part of the Internet of Vehicles (IoV), a term inspired by the Internet of Things (IoT) to describe the ecosystem built by interconnected vehicles that makes use of an IoT-like architecture [1]–[3]. The functions aim to provide traffic functions or increase traffic safety by contributing to driver assistance or autonomous driving functions.

Different stakeholders interact with the ecosystem in this network to use functions or fulfill services. In this context, a stakeholder is defined as a person or organization that is in some way affected by decisions or actions, influences them, or even considers itself to be affected [4][5]. As multiple stakeholders are involved in the automotive ecosystem, it is a multi-stakeholder system.

In this multi-stakeholder system, trust is a relevant concept necessary for cooperation. Although trust is more a sociological and psychological concept that eases or enables decision-making between persons, it can be stretched to interactions with non-natural entities [6][7]. It describes the relation between two entities: a truster that places trust in services, data, or the general behavior of a trustee. Therefore, the stakeholders and their relations must be known to evaluate and define trust in a system. This also involves relations in automotive use cases, where misplaced trust can have severe consequences due to safety implications.

In computer science, computational trust is closely related to authorization systems. This is reasonable, as trust is a concept to decide about cooperation, and authorization is similar to such a decision. Especially use cases where a truster has to determine whether or not to use data provided by a trustee is comparable to a trustful decision process [8]. Use cases similar to this model get more common with the rise of IoV.

For this purpose, this work aims to identify relevant stakeholders in the automotive ecosystem, assign appropriate characteristics, and describe their trust relationships. This builds a basis for trust models in automotive systems that secure communication between stakeholders and automotive systems. Therefore, the focus is on stakeholders that use electronic communication, excluding, e.g., contractual relations between stakeholders. Furthermore, only standard series vehicles are in scope, and no special vehicles, like emergency, driving school, or shared vehicles with specific adaptions, are included. A further restriction concerns the focus on vehicles in the scope of UNECE R155 regulation that introduces mandatory measures to handle cyber security in the automotive domain [9]. This restriction is applied as we use the lifecycle introduced by this regulation. However, the results are not significantly affected by this limitation.

The rest of this paper is organized as follows. In Section 2, related work is presented. This review shows that no comparable analysis exists. The necessary characteristics to describe the collected stakeholders are developed in the third section. Based on these parameters, the stakeholders are presented in Section 4. The results of the trust relation analysis are followed in the next section before an evaluation of the results based on exemplary use cases is carried out in Section 6. The last section summarizes the content of this work and gives an overview of its further use and limitations.

II. Related Work

Originating from project management, a stakeholder describes a person or organization that can affect or is affected by a decision or an activity [4][5]. This involves all entities that interact with the system in any way. Following Kosch [10], automotive stakeholders are connected to this specific environment in different steps, like the development, production, or usage phase. Furthermore, stakeholders can be categorized into different groups. Marner et al. [11] conducted a stakeholder analysis that mainly involves different stakeholders within an Original Equipment Manufacturer (OEM).

A comparable analysis was performed by Gomez et al. in [12] with a focus on automotive digital forensics. The involved entities are necessary in this domain as their requirements are fundamental to answering forensic questions. This study presents two general stakeholder survey approaches: the brainstorming method based on Bryson [13] and snowballing as introduced by King et al. [14]. Only the first seems applicable, as the stakeholders in automotive digital forensics involve criminals, making a snowballing method including all stakeholders impossible. Using various brainstorming sessions with experts, a list of relevant stakeholders and a Venn diagram describing their main interests were created.

Mansor collected stakeholders regarding security in the automotive ecosystem [15]. This work also proposes a trust model for the automotive ecosystem incorporating the three stakeholders OEM, service or application provider, and vehicle driver or owner. The trust relations between these entities are described. This model does not focus on trust relations on a technical level but instead on an interpersonal level.

Knauss et al. [16] collected a list of stakeholders and their relations in the automotive ecosystem. They gathered their information in interviews at an OEM and mainly focused on the interactions during vehicle development. As such, they did not focus on the electronic communication between stakeholders in the automotive ecosystem.

To our knowledge, a collection of stakeholders in the automotive domain and their trust relations and communication interactions does not yet exist. For this reason, this paper aims to fill this gap.

III. Automotive Stakeholder Characteristics

Appropriate characteristics are necessary to describe and characterize the collected stakeholders. For this work, three factors are considered necessary to describe stakeholders in the automotive domain. These consist of the lifecycle phase of vehicles the stakeholder is involved in, the user agents or devices used for communication, and the stakeholders' rights and responsibilities.

A. Automotive Lifecycle

Vehicle and vehicle projects are divided into several lifecycle phases. These phases are suitable to describe stakeholders, as several only appear in specific phases and because they also take on different roles in different phases [10]. In this work, we combine two different methods to structure the automotive lifecycle. The first describes the *vehicle lifecycle* whereas the latter focuses on the *vehicle project lifecycle*.

Hawkins et al. conducted a lifecycle analysis of battery-electric vehicles and used the three lifecycle phases *production, use,* and *end of life* [17]. Their approach is aimed at

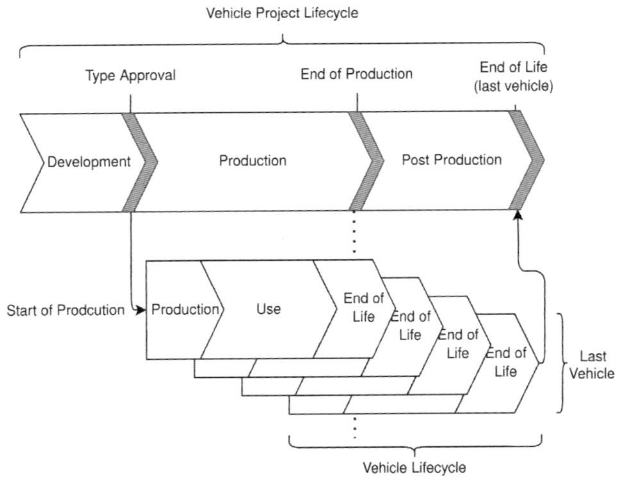

Figure 1. Vehicle Project and Vehicle Lifecycle in comparison.

individual vehicles that are produced, used, and ultimately reused or disposed of, describing the *vehicle lifecycle*.

The second approach targets vehicle projects, as the UN Regulation 155 does. In this regulation, the three phases *development, production,* and *post-production* are distinguished [9]. The phases seem similar to Hawkins' approach. Still, they cut the lifecycle of vehicle projects that are differentiated by the date of the type approval (between *development* and *production phase*) and the end of production date (between *production* and *post-production*). Individual end-user vehicles are only produced in the *production phase*. The last individual vehicle entering its *end of life phase* according to the *vehicle lifecycle* defines the end of the R155 *post-production phase*.

For this work, we assume that stakeholders in both vehicle individual and vehicle project-related lifecycle phases are relevant. Therefore, the generic lifecycle phases *development, production, use,* and *end-of-life* are utilized. We note that during the *development phase* no publicly visible and customer-used vehicles are available. The *post-production phase* used in UN R155 is a phase to structure activities regarding the cyber security of cars after the *end-of-production* while vehicles are still in use. We argue that no additional stakeholders are involved in this phase compared to the *production phase*. Therefore, that phase is not considered explicitly in this work. Figure 1 overviews the used lifecycle phases.

B. User Agents used by Automotive Stakeholders

This work focuses on the security of the automotive ecosystem. As such, the electronic communication between the stakeholders and the communication within the automotive ecosystem is of central interest. As the presented stakeholders are natural, organizational, or legal entities, they use devices or interfaces for their electronic communication. As proposed by Kuschel in [18], we expand the vehicle to an interconnected automotive ecosystem that is used by various stakeholders to fulfill their workflows. This ecosystem consists of connected and communicating devices, which the stakeholders can use

TABLE I. USER AGENTS USED FOR COMMUNICATION IN THE AUTOMOTIVE ECOSYSTEM

User Agent	Description
Vehicle	Systems and ECUs contained inside the vehicle
Backend	Applications on servers accessed online, often operated by the OEM or service providers. This user agent is distinct from frontends in the way that, in this case, the specific operator of the backend service accesses the service.
Diagnostic Devices	Devices used to interact with the vehicle's diagnostic system. Operations going beyond the legally prescribed actions like OBD [19] often require vehicle-specific information, which the OEM must also provide to non-affiliated workshops [20]
Frontends	Frontends for services accessed through the internet, including mobile apps
RSUs	Devices located near street infrastructure that directly communicates to vehicles using VANETs
Charging Station	Infrastructure to charge electric or hybrid vehicles

to interact with the ecosystem and other stakeholders. The ecosystem does not only consist of devices, therefore we use the term user agents for the relevant components of the automotive ecosystem, as stakeholders can utilize them for their communication.

These agents are listed in Table I and form a part of the automotive ecosystem. The list was created based on the stakeholder analysis and the evaluation of exemplary use cases originating in different lifecycle phases, like vehicle usage by end-users, online- and workshop updates, setup of new vehicles by customers, and so on.

User agents must enable stakeholders to take on different roles based on their respective rights, which depend on the lifecycle phase.

C. Responsibilities and Rights in the Automotive Ecosystem

Interactions in the automotive ecosystem should only be possible if the acting stakeholder is allowed to make them. This authorization depends on the stakeholder, action, and context. One part of the context is the lifecycle phase the vehicle (project) is in. As such, the responsibilities and rights of automotive stakeholders are relevant characteristics and are, therefore, added to the stakeholder's description.

A simple but frequently discussed example of authorization is the application of software updates. While only the OEM can release and publish software for a vehicle, it is up to the owners of the cars to have it installed, as it entails a permanent change to the vehicle's condition. However, this division of tasks is only relevant in the use phase, as during development, the OEM itself has all rights to the pre-series vehicles and can, therefore, decide on changes to the condition itself. In the use phase, the authorizations to release and install software are divided among stakeholders, where the OEM maintains its products, but the owner decides on their property.

The vehicle ecosystem has to handle the relevant roles and responsibilities and consider changes within them if the lifecycle phase or, e.g., the ownership of the vehicle changes. Otherwise, the ecosystem might not be able to correctly reflect contractual or business relations, leading to possible vulnerabilities. As this work provides an overview, such specific vulnerabilities are not in scope.

IV. AUTOMOTIVE ENVIRONMENT STAKEHOLDERS

The set of stakeholders, their relations, and interactions presented here was created using a comparable method as Gomez et al. [12] based on Bryson [13] as multiple brainstorming and discussion sessions including various participants were conducted. The stakeholders involved in the different lifecycle phases were collected within these sessions, and their roles were discussed. The participants included several employees of an automotive supplier, two employees of a start-up in the domain of decentralized identities with connections to OEMs and various suppliers, members of an automotive security research group partially with a background at different OEMs as well as a Professor researching in the automotive security domain.

Table II provides an overview of the stakeholders in the automotive ecosystem, the lifecycle phase they are active in, and the user agents they are using. The following section discusses the rights and responsibilities in each stakeholder's description.

a) OEM: During the development phase, the OEM is the driving force behind the development project, is responsible for its overall success, and bears the risk. This responsibility also means that the OEM has all the rights regarding communication and authorization in the ecosystem. These rights change when the vehicle is handed over to the customer. After that, the OEM no longer has direct physical access to the vehicle and can only communicate with connected vehicles via its backend. Indirect access is possible using the workshops, which receive instructions and tools for maintenance and repair from the OEM. The authorization to release changes to the vehicle, for example, through updates or modifications, can only lie with the OEM, as it must ensure compliance with regulations. The OEM remains involved after the utilization phase, as the reuse of components must be planned, for example, for second-life applications of batteries [21] or the use of spare parts from old vehicles, which may have to be approved for reuse in other vehicles [22].

For development, the OEM uses all clients that will be used in the later usage phase, even if only for testing purposes, as with RSUs. In later phases, direct communication between the OEM and the vehicle is only possible via the manufacturer-specific backend.

b) Supplier: OEMs develop new cars with the help of multiple suppliers. As supply chains get more complex, a distinction between different suppliers (Tier 1-3) is commonly used [16][23]. Suppliers get the task of developing, integrating, and supplying certain vehicle parts according to the requirements of the OEM. Their deliverable includes hardware (e.g.,

TABLE II. STAKEHOLDERS INVOLVED IN THE AUTOMOTIVE ECOSYSTEM. AN "X" MARKS THE LIFECYCLE PHASES THIS STAKEHOLDER IS INVOLVED IN AS WELL AS THE USER AGENTS THAT ARE UTILIZED.

Stakeholder	Phases				User Agents						Description
	Development	Production	Use	End of Life	Vehicle	Backend	Diagnostic Device	Frontends	RSUs	Charging Stations	
OEM	X	X	X	X	X	X	X	X		X	Develops, produces and sells the vehicle and is furthermore responsible for providing updates, service instructions, and service access
Supplier	X	X			X		X			X	Develops, manufactures, and delivers hard- or software for the product according to the OEM's requirements
Development Service Provider	X				X	X	X	X		X	Supports the OEM during the development by taking on specific tasks, especially testing
Service and Content Providers or Operators	X	X	X			X			X	X	Offer, adapt or develop services, that are integrated into the later product
Owner			X					X			Legally owner of the vehicle
Driver			X		X			X		X	Entity using the vehicle to drive
Workshops			X	X	X		X	X			Authorized and free workshops offering maintenance and repairs for vehicles
Authorized Test Organizations			X				X				Organizations authorized to verify the conformity of vehicles, e.g. in the PTI
Recycler				X	X		X				Manages recycling and disposing process

mechanical parts, ECUs) or software. With the shift from hard- to software-defined functions in vehicles [24] and the target of software-defined vehicles, together with the shift to more centralized E/E architectures [25], different suppliers need to work closely together to develop their functions.

How suppliers interact with the automotive ecosystem depends on the function they provide. There is no communication between the supplier and the ecosystem for mechanical parts, and there is no further interaction after the part's delivery during the production phase. For software functions, there are often additional activities for updates provided by the supplier or even direct interactions with the ecosystem in case of connected functions if the supplier operates backend services or cooperates with service and content providers. The final diagnostic devices are utilized while developing the development interfaces of ECUs, especially in later development steps. This interface is provided by the OEM to enable suppliers to fulfill their tasks.

The limited communication between suppliers and the ecosystem reflects the supplier's rights in the use phase. As the vehicles' later users mainly interact with the OEM, and the OEM covers its suppliers, they do not have explicit, own rights or responsibilities in the ecosystem.

c) Development Service Provider: For certain activities during development, OEMs commission Development Service Providers to execute tasks, e.g., to test functions or devices regularly. For their activities during the development, the OEM grants them access to necessary parts of the ecosystem that can include all the systems an OEM also uses. They do not have explicit rights or responsibilities, especially not in later lifecycle phases.

d) Serivce and Content Provider or Operator: Modern, connected vehicles consume information from outside the vehicle and deliver their data to external services, forming the automotive ecosystem. To do so, data is provided by service providers, and infrastructure, such as mobile networks, RSUs or charging stations, are utilized that are operated by its operators. For the development of the connected services and the integration into vehicles, these stakeholders are involved in the development and production phase. During the use phase, they provide services, communicate with the vehicles, and are part of the vehicle ecosystem. Services are then mostly offered to the vehicle user, including specific rights and responsibilities according to their services.

e) Owner: Owners of vehicles are a heterogeneous group of stakeholders. Vehicles are owned either privately or for business. Business owners may again use cars for their business or provide them to others, e.g., car rental or sharing companies. Owners are distinct from the driver or user of the vehicle. Therefore, only fleet owners are considered in this study, as they can use special fleet services to manage their vehicles although not directly using them. In this case, access to the vehicle ecosystem is possible through the frontends of fleet services. Furthermore, in the context of this work, the owner is regarded as the primary holder of the rights to his vehicle during the use phase, so the owner must authorize any changes. This assumption is subject to a restriction if the owner is the lessor of the vehicle and transfers it to the lessee in its entirety. An overview of vehicle owner types is given in Figure 2.

f) Driver: Drivers are the actual users of the vehicle. They directly interact with the vehicle, its interfaces, and the frontends intended for end-users. Due to the distinction with owners, drivers have permission to use and drive the vehicle as intended, but they are, e.g., not allowed to manipulate or change the vehicle permanently.

g) Workshop: During the use phase, vehicles require workshops for maintenance and repairs. Electronic communication between the workshop and the vehicle becomes

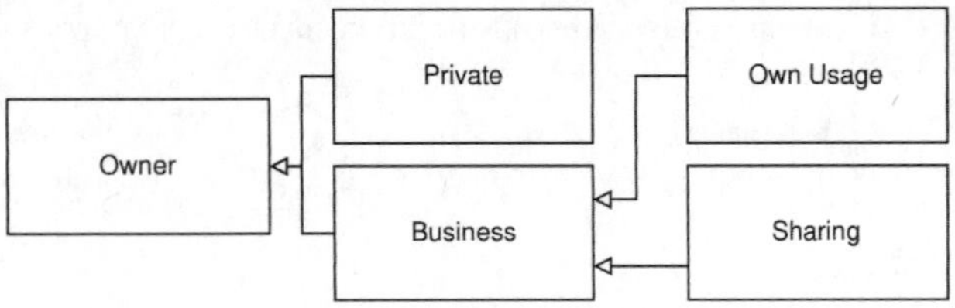

Figure 2. Different types of vehicle owners are divided into private and business owners. Business owners can use the vehicle for their own mobility or provide it as a rental or sharing company

vital with more software functions. OEMs provide special equipment to access the necessary diagnostic interfaces. Due to legal reasons, access to these tools has to be given to independent workshops and must not be restricted to OEM partner workshops [20]. The owner authorizes the workshops to conduct repairs and maintenance, although this authorization is not currently represented in electronic communication.

h) Authorized Test Organization: To ensure the safety of vehicles on public roads, in various countries PTIs are legally required. Authorized Test Organizations carry these out. Communication with the vehicle is necessary during the test procedures, e.g., to access emission-related data via OBD [26].

i) Recycler: At the end of a vehicle's life, recyclers take care of its disposal and reuse. This also requires communication with the vehicle, for example, to trigger the end-of-life function of airbags, which releases the pyrotechnic elements and thus renders them harmless. This is done either via the vehicle's diagnostic system or by direct communication with the airbag control unit [27].

V. Trust Relations in the Automotive Ecosystem

Trust is a characteristic of the relationship between two entities. In the computational trust domain, these entities are not restricted to be humans or organizations, they can also be devices equiped with algorithms that enable them to make decisions based on trust inspired algorithms. In the automotive domain, three types of trust relations exist: trust between two stakeholders, which are natural or organizational entities; one stakeholder and a device within the automotive ecosystem, and two devices of the automotive ecosystem.

The target of trust is to make decisions for or against cooperation, although the own welfare depends on the decision and the behavior of another entity that can neither be controlled nor whose behavior can be predicted with certainty [6]. As such, it is closely related to authorization.

In the automotive ecosystem, such a mechanism can be embedded in an ECU that checks, e.g., the signature of a firmware update before installing it. In this case, the policy tests whether the firmware was signed with a specific key. For example, the OEM controls the necessary private key. This is reasonable, as the OEM is responsible for providing updates and keeping a vehicle safe and secure. The vehicle, therefore, trusts the OEM to provide firmware updates. In this simple use case with only one stakeholder, the OEM is also responsible for specifying and implementing the trust relation. The OEM must also include other relations, providing a particular gatekeeper position.

Trust always has to be considered in a specific context. As the vehicle trusts the OEM in the example above to provide valid software updates, the OEM is not authorized to open the vehicle in the use phase. The vehicle should not trust or follow a request by the OEM to open the car unless it was authorized to do so by the owner or driver of the vehicle. Such a use case becomes relevant if vehicles include functions to unlock it remotely.

Both examples describe an authorization scenario in which the vehicle, as part of the vehicle ecosystem, trusts a stakeholder in different contexts. The stakeholders' responsibilities and roles clearly define the trust relation.

For the sake of completeness, two examples of relations between stakeholders and between devices are given. The function "plug and charge" is considered for the first mentioned. This function allows payment to be processed without the user's additional authentication. The user stores their data in the vehicle, which authorizes the charging station operator to process the payment. For the second category, direct communication between vehicles in VANETs can be considered, in which vehicles exchange information. No stakeholder is directly involved, and a trusting relationship arises between the two vehicles.

The following gives trust relations between the relevant stakeholders for each lifecycle phase.

a) Development Phase: The various stakeholders in the development phase are all authorized by the OEM responsible for the development process. Therefore, the OEM alone has the right to allow other stakeholders to communicate with the automotive ecosystem. The connections within the automotive ecosystem are also governed by the OEM that has complete control over the ecosystem in this phase. Trust relations between stakeholders and the ecosystem devices of all categories are managed by the OEM.

b) Production Phase: The structure of responsibilities in the production phase is similar to the development phase. The OEM is responsible for orchestrating the cooperation of involved suppliers and service and content providers that might have to cooperate during production. For example, a Mobile Network Operator (MNO) might have to prepare the cellular network module during production. Again, the relations and the access are managed by the OEM.

c) Use Phase: When the vehicle is handed to the owner, there is a shift in the responsibilities and role structure. The OEM no longer has control over the entire ecosystem. Instead, the owner has extensive rights over its property and can, therefore, also determine which other stakeholders should interact with it. Beyond the scope of this work, it is necessary to discuss the extent to which vehicle ownership and physical control also justify exclusive rights concerning electronic interactions and to what extent a manufacturer may legitimately restrict these rights through End-User Licence Agreements (EULAs), particularly for services offered. Relations in the other direction are also possible, as service providers can authorize drivers to consume their services based on subscriptions.

More complex relations are possible as well. If we consider an OEM that releases maintenance instructions that have to be performed, the workshop usually receives them within their diagnostic systems. The owner can then authorize the workshop to execute these tasks.

As the rights in this phase are more distributed between stakeholders, this can lead to conflicts. An example of such a conflict led to the right-to-repair movement, where OEMs were forced to provide repair instructions and tools to free workshops alongside their partner workshops [20]. The regulation stated that the owner can decide which workshop should perform maintenance and repair tasks. In contrast, some OEMs wanted to restrict them to authorized workshops by withholding necessary tools. The access to the automotive ecosystem for third parties, as, for example, test organizations are, is often only possible by regulations that force OEMs to provide interfaces. As these interfaces are provided by regulation, there is no real trust or authorization connection between different stakeholders. From the automotive ecosystem perspective, all interactions compliant with the regulations are authorized.

d) End of Life: During the end-of-life phase, the disposal and reuse of the vehicle are the focus. OEMs have to enable the reuse of electronic vehicle parts that workshops can reinstall. Recyclers are responsible for safely disposing of parts that are not directly reusable and, therefore, need to communicate with the vehicle to disengage the airbags. The necessary interface for this interaction is based on regulation and, therefore, does not have to be authorized by the OEM, and there is no real trust relation.

VI. EVALUATION

The results from this work are evaluated in two ways. First, stakeholders were discussed in different groups consisting of people working in the automotive domain and researchers in the automotive security domain. Secondly, exemplary scenarios were considered, and the stakeholders involved and their interactions were compared with the previous results. An excerpt of these scenarios is briefly presented below.

a) Online Software Updates: In an online software update, the OEM provides new software for vehicle components that is usually downloaded over a backend connection and is installed without additional diagnostic equipment at the customer's location. In this case, the OEM is responsible for the overall process and approves the software before it is made available. Software may be supplied by suppliers but is tested and released by the OEM. Infrastructure operators are also included in the scenario to provide necessary services. Either the vehicle's owner or an authorized user usually approves the installation. Finally, workshops are involved in case the installation fails. Additionally, inspired by the terms of dis- and untrust introduced by Marsh et al. [28], a trust relation between the owner and the OEM might not even be necessary, as the owner may not have a choice other than installing mandatory updates, otherwise risking the shut down of the vehicle.

b) Plug and Charge: The plug and charge scenario has already been briefly discussed in the trust section. In this case, the OEM has to provide necessary functions in the vehicle and the connected services (back- and front-end) to store the required information of a financial service provider that handled the payment. The driver then authorizes a charging station provider to request charging fees from the financial service provider.

c) VANETs: VANETs are a special network in which vehicles, RSUs and other devices like mobile devices owned by Vulnerable Road Users (VRUs) communicate directly to exchange information about the current environment to enable cooperative driving functions or to increase road safety. In this scenario, devices within the automotive environment may communicate without the participation of a stakeholder. Involvement of service and infrastructure providers, operators, and drivers is possible, as advertised services are contained in the standardization of VANETs. Trust relations are interesting in this scenario, as no clear and pre-defined interactions exist in this ad-hoc network. Because of this, many automotive trust management systems concentrate on VANET applications [29].

VII. CONCLUSION AND FUTURE WORK

Trust is an essential concept necessary for decision-making between people. The stakeholders involved and their relations must be known to evaluate trust and develop trust management systems in the automotive domain. As a comparable analysis did not yet exist, the relevant stakeholders have been collected in multiple sessions with different people working or researching in the automotive and automotive security domain. The interactions and trust relations between the collected stakeholders were determined by analyzing relevant use cases. To charcterize the stakeholders, the lifecycle phase of vehicles they are involved, the user agents or devices they utilize to communciate in the automotive ecosystem as well as their roles and responsibilities were used.

The stakeholders and their descriptions are general to provide an overview of the automotive domain. Although this was necessary for this work, it is a limitation, as in some scenarios, the same stakeholder groups are involved multiple times. A more in-depth analysis is required for specific scenarios. This also applies to the description of the automotive ecosystem, which can be considered in much more detail. Furthermore, the evaluation of the proposed stakeholder set can be extended to close possible gaps and ease the model's application in other studies. Despite the limitations, the insights gained can be used to define requirements for a trust management system that can map different use cases in the automotive ecosystem.

ACKNOWLEDGMENT

This work was created in the research project TRADE funded by the German Federal Ministry of Research and Education under grant 16KIS1409.

References

[1] F. Yang, S. Wang, J. Li, Z. Liu, and Q. Sun, "An overview of Internet of Vehicles," *China Communications*, vol. 11, no. 10, pp. 1–15, Oct. 2014, ISSN: 1673-5447. DOI: 10.1109/CC.2014.6969789.

[2] A. Rehman *et al.*, "CTMF: Context-Aware Trust Management Framework for Internet of Vehicles," *IEEE Access*, vol. 10, pp. 73 685–73 701, 2022, ISSN: 2169-3536. DOI: 10.1109/ACCESS.2022.3189349.

[3] Y. Kuang, H. Xu, R. Jiang, and Z. Liu, "GTMS: A Gated Linear Unit Based Trust Management System for Internet of Vehicles Using Blockchain Technology," in *2022 IEEE International Conference on Trust, Security and Privacy in Computing and Communications (TrustCom)*, Wuhan, China: IEEE, Dec. 2022, pp. 28–35, ISBN: 978-1-66549-425-0. DOI: 10.1109/TrustCom56396.2022.00015.

[4] *ISO 9000: Quality management systems – Fundamentals and vocabulary*, Geneva, Switzerland, Dec. 2005.

[5] *DIN-69901: Project management Project management systems Part 5: Concepts*, Jan. 2009.

[6] N. Luhmann, M. King, and C. Morgner, *Trust and Power*. Malden, MA: Polity, 2017, 231 pp., ISBN: 978-1-5095-1945-3.

[7] E. Pöll, "Engineering the trust machine. Aligning the concept of trust in the context of blockchain applications," *Ethics and Information Technology*, vol. 26, no. 2, p. 37, Jun. 2024, ISSN: 1388-1957, 1572-8439. DOI: 10.1007/s10676-024-09774-6.

[8] A. Jøsang, R. Ismail, and C. Boyd, "A survey of trust and reputation systems for online service provision," *Decision Support Systems*, Emerging Issues in Collaborative Commerce, vol. 43, no. 2, pp. 618–644, Mar. 1, 2007, ISSN: 0167-9236. DOI: 10.1016/j.dss.2005.05.019.

[9] *UN Regulation No. 155 - Uniform provisions concerning the approval of vehicles with regards to cyber security and cyber security management system*, UN Regulation, Mar. 4, 2021.

[10] T. Kosch, Ed., *Automotive Internetworking* (Intelligent Transportation Systems). Hoboken, N.J: Wiley, 2012, 377 pp., ISBN: 978-0-470-74979-1.

[11] K. Marner, S. Wagner, and G. Ruhe, "Stakeholder identification for a structured release planning approach in the automotive domain," *Requirements Engineering*, vol. 27, no. 2, pp. 211–230, Jun. 2022, ISSN: 0947-3602, 1432-010X. DOI: 10.1007/s00766-021-00369-x.

[12] K. Gomez Buquerin and H.-J. Hof, "Identification of Automotive Digital Forensics Stakeholders," SECUREWARE 2021, p. 7, 2021.

[13] J. M. Bryson, "What to do when Stakeholders matter: Stakeholder Identification and Analysis Techniques," *Public Management Review*, vol. 6, no. 1, pp. 21–53, Mar. 2004, ISSN: 1471-9037, 1471-9045. DOI: 10.1080/14719030410001675722.

[14] C. S. King, K. M. Feltey, and B. O. Susel, "The Question of Participation: Toward Authentic Public Participation in Public Administration," *Public Administration Review*, Public Administration Review, vol. 58, no. 4, pp. 317–326, Jun. 1998.

[15] H. Mansor, "Security and Privacy Aspects of Automotive Systems," Ph.D. dissertation, Royal Holloway, University of London, London, Jul. 19, 2017.

[16] E. Knauss and D. Damian, "Towards Enabling Cross-Organizational Modeling in Automotive Ecosystems," in *MD²P² 2014 – Model-Driven Development Processes and Practices*, Valencia, Spain, Sep. 28–Oct. 3, 2014.

[17] T. R. Hawkins, B. Singh, G. Majeau-Bettez, and A. H. Strømman, "Comparative Environmental Life Cycle Assessment of Conventional and Electric Vehicles," *Journal of Industrial Ecology*, vol. 17, no. 1, pp. 53–64, Feb. 2013, ISSN: 1088-1980, 1530-9290. DOI: 10.1111/j.1530-9290.2012.00532.x.

[18] J. Kuschel, "The Vehicle Ecosystem," in *Open IT-Based Innovation: Moving Towards Cooperative IT Transfer and Knowledge Diffusion*, G. León, A. M. Bernardos, J. R. Casar, K. Kautz, and J. I. De Gross, Eds., vol. 287, Boston, MA: Springer US, 2008, pp. 309–322, ISBN: 978-0-387-87502-6 978-0-387-87503-3. DOI: 10.1007/978-0-387-87503-3_18.

[19] ISO, *ISO 15031-3: Road vehicles - Communication between vehicle and external equipment for emission-related diagnostics - Part 3: Diagnostic connector and related electrical circuits: Specification and use*, Geneva, Switzerland, Feb. 2023.

[20] H.R.1449 — 112th Congress (2011-2012), "Motor Vehicle Owners Right to Repair Act of 2011," Apr. 18, 2011, [Online]. Available: https://www.congress.gov/bill/112th-congress/house-bill/1449 (visited on 05/22/2024).

[21] J. Blümke, K. Mayer, and H.-J. Hof, "An Analysis of Security Concerns in Transitioning Battery Management Systems from First to Second Life," in *Proceedings of the 19th International Conference on Availability, Reliability and Security*, Vienna Austria: ACM, Jul. 30, 2024, pp. 1–11, ISBN: 9798400717185. DOI: 10.1145/3664476.3671010.

[22] Volkswagen AG, "Notes about theft protection and application of a FAZIT/ GeKo authorization < Volkswagen AG erWin Online," Notes about theft protection and application of a FAZIT/ GeKo authorization, [Online]. Available: https://erwin.volkswagen.de/erwin/showOnlineServices.do (visited on 09/27/2024).

[23] A. Bucaioni and P. Pelliccione, "Technical Architectures for Automotive Systems," in *2020 IEEE International Conference on Software Architecture (ICSA)*, Salvador, Brazil: IEEE, Mar. 2020, pp. 46–57, ISBN: 978-1-72814-659-1. DOI: 10.1109/ICSA47634.2020.00013.

[24] G. Gut, C. Allmann, M. Schurius, and K. Schmidt, "Reduction of Electronic Control Units in Electric Vehicles Using Multicore Technology," in *Multicore Software Engineering, Performance, and Tools*, V. Pankratius and M. Philippsen, Eds., red. by D. Hutchison *et al.*, vol. 7303, Berlin, Heidelberg: Springer Berlin Heidelberg, 2012, pp. 90–93, ISBN: 978-3-642-31201-4 978-3-642-31202-1. DOI: 10.1007/978-3-642-31202-1_11.

[25] J. Dobaj, G. Macher, D. Ekert, A. Riel, and R. Messnarz, "Towards a security-driven automotive development lifecycle," *Journal of Software: Evolution and Process*, Nov. 24, 2021, ISSN: 2047-7473, 2047-7481. DOI: 10.1002/smr.2407.

[26] *ISO 27145: Road vehicles - Implementation of World-Wide Harmonized On-Board Diagnostics (WWH-OBD) communication requirements - Part 1: General information and use case definition*, Standard, Geneva, Switzerland, Aug. 2012.

[27] *ISO 26021-1:2022: Road vehicles – End-of-life activation of in-vehicle pyrotechnic devices – Part 1: Application and communication interface*, Standard, version 2, Geneva, Switzerland, Mar. 10, 2022.

[28] S. Marsh and M. R. Dibben, "Trust, Untrust, Distrust and Mistrust – An Exploration of the Dark(er) Side," in *Trust Management*, P. Herrmann, V. Issarny, and S. Shiu, Eds., red. by D. Hutchison *et al.*, vol. 3477, Berlin, Heidelberg: Springer Berlin Heidelberg, 2005, pp. 17–33, ISBN: 978-3-540-26042-4 978-3-540-32040-1. DOI: 10.1007/11429760_2.

[29] R. Hussain, J. Lee, and S. Zeadally, "Trust in VANET: A Survey of Current Solutions and Future Research Opportunities," *IEEE Transactions on Intelligent Transportation Systems*, vol. 22, no. 5, pp. 2553–2571, May 2021, ISSN: 1524-9050, 1558-0016. DOI: 10.1109/TITS.2020.2973715.

Enhancing Phishing Detection: An Eye-Tracking Study on User Interaction and Oversights in Phishing Emails

Meret Kristen, Fabian Engl, Jürgen Mottok
Software Engineering Laboratory for Safe and Secure Systems
OTH Regensburg
Regensburg, Germany
email: {meret.kristen | fabian.engl | juergen.mottok}@oth-regensburg.de

Abstract—**Phishing remains a significant threat to organizational security, necessitating effective countermeasures. This paper presents findings from an in-depth eye-tracking study with 103 participants, evaluating the effectiveness of phishing awareness tools and trainings. The study examines how a phishing awareness system influences user behavior, efficiency, and the ability to identify phishing attempts. By analyzing eye movements, the study reveals real-time interactions and oversights, providing insights into the decision-making process. Results indicate that while the system improves the efficiency of users already proficient in phishing detection, it does not universally enhance recognition rates. Notably, participants using the tool spent significantly less time looking at attachment-related phishing markers, indicating partial efficiency improvements. Since phishing attempts containing suspicious attachments were successful in 19% of cases, as compared to an overall phishing success rate of 15%, the phishing awareness tool is particularly useful here. A usability evaluation revealed that users reporting a higher perceived usability score profited more from the help of the tool. Additionally, no improvement in phishing detection rates was observed in users who had completed prior IT-security training, highlighting the necessity for a paradigm shift in phishing training to adequately prepare users for phishing attempts.**

Keywords-Phishing; Security Awareness; Eye-Tracking; IT-Security; Usability and UX.

I. INTRODUCTION

In information security, various components must work together to form a robust and secure system, with one of the biggest vulnerabilities in this chain being the end user [1]. Regardless of the amount of time and money an organization invests in cybersecurity, the risk of an incident increases significantly if an end user clicks on a compromised link or opens a hazardous attachment. For this reason, the ISO 27001 clause 7.2.2 states 'All employees of the organization and, where relevant, contractors should receive appropriate awareness education and training and regular updates in organizational policies and procedures, as relevant for their job function' [2]. But how effective are these trainings and procedures? Can tools help the end user to distinguish between ordinary emails and phishing attempts? And if they fall for a phishing attack, what relevant information did they ignore?

Publications, such as [3], show that, in contrast to existing works on phishing training, such as [4], voluntary contextual phishing trainings can have the opposite effect, making employees even more susceptible to phishing attacks. While incorporating warnings into email software improves effectiveness, the extent of the warnings — whether short or detailed — does not significantly influence their effectiveness. However, it is unclear to what degree users used the supplied warnings or how it changes the user's behaviour when interacting with emails. Such interactions are difficult to measure as only considering the end results of phishing studies does not paint a clear picture of the subconscious intentions of users when analysing phishing emails.

It has been proven that technologies like eye-tracking enable the measurement of such interactions in real time, showing that eye movements are directly related to thought processes when users view specific information [5]. This is particularly helpful when trying to evaluate the usability and effectiveness of tools, such as phishing awareness software. By analysing the eye movements of participants when working with such tools a pool of further metrics can be measured revealing real time information about decision making, whether users observe every part of the email and which areas were overlooked when participants fail to recognise a phishing attempt. For these reasons this paper proposes a phishing email study based on eye-tracking data and analyses whether supportive security awareness tools can help users to identify phishing emails.

The paper is structured as follows: first, a systematic literature review in Section II identifies the current state of knowledge and research gaps, followed by the formulation of research questions and corresponding hypotheses. This is followed by the study design in Section III, results in Section IV, usability results in Section V, limitations in Section VI and conclusion and future work in Section VII.

II. LITERATURE REVIEW

Having established the benefits of incorporating eye movements in phishing research, a systematic literature review based on the methods given by Kitchenham and Charters in [6] was performed. To establish a broad overview of the status quo of eye-tracking research in the field of security awareness and phishing emails lead to the following research question:

RQ1 What is the state of the art in eye-tracking research for detecting and analyzing user interaction with phishing emails?

As the study of phishing emails and security awareness is a critical part of engineering safe and secure systems, three of the main academic search engines in software engineering were employed: IEEE Xplore, ACM Digital Library and Web of Science. To study the aforementioned research question, a search string was developed based on the methods given in [7]. The partial search string on eye-tracking should thus include the terms for method and device each in the two common spelling variants with and without hyphens (i.e. "eye tracking", "eye-tracking", "eye tracker", and "eye-tracker"). The partial search string on phishing emails and security awareness was chosen to include only terms that are directly related to phishing emails ("phishing", "security awareness", "spam", "social engineering"). Since the term "email" always appears together with one of the search terms stated above in the context of phishing emails, it was not explicitly included in the search string.

("eyetracking" OR "eye-tracking" OR "eyetracker" OR "eye-tracker" OR "eye movement" OR "eye movements") AND ("phishing" OR "security awareness" OR "spam" OR "social engineering")

Due to the different search engines needing different input syntax, the actual search queries used differ slightly in syntax, but not in semantics. The search queries used are shown in Figure 1.

The search yielded three results in ACM, twelve in Web of Science and six in IEEE XPLORE as of February 2024, including one duplicate, giving 20 results in total.

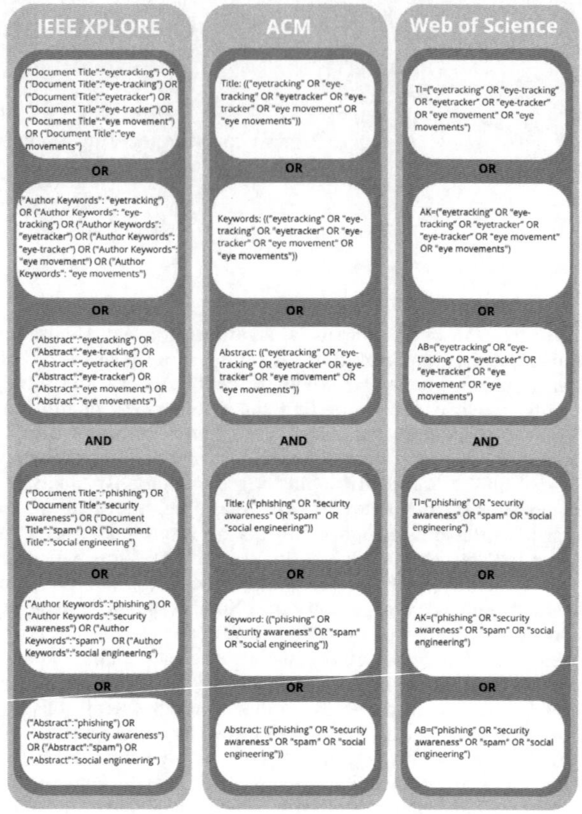

Figure 1. Search strings by data base.

A. Inclusion and Exclusion Criteria

Inclusion and exclusion criteria were defined as follows: Papers need to

1) study email phishing attempts, and
2) conduct eye-tracking studies or evaluate existing eye-tracking data and
3) be accessible with licenses held by OTH Regensburg or University of Regensburg.

After applying the inclusion and exclusion criteria, a total of eight papers and an additional four papers after backward and forward search remained. The found papers are described in the following list.

1) *ADVERT: An Adaptive and Data-Driven Attention Enhancement Mechanism for Phishing Prevention* [8]: This paper presents a study evaluating the effectiveness of generating adaptive visual aids in real-time to prevent user inattentiveness and reduce susceptibility to phishing attacks. The study was conducted with a sample size of 160 students and involved twelve emails.
2) *Evaluation of Contextual and Game-Based Training for Phishing Detection* [9] A study with 41 participants tasked with identifying phishing emails, divided into three groups: without prior training, with game-based training, and with Context-Based Micro-Training (CBMT). The research shows that both training methods can support users towards secure behavior and that CBMT does so to a higher degree than game-based training. In line with [3], the paper also shows that most participants were susceptible to phishing, even after training.
3) *Understanding Phishing Email Processing and Perceived Trustworthiness Through Eye Tracking* [10] In this pilot study, a group of 22 volunteers saw a sequence of emails that included or did not contain signs of phishing emails, all the while having their eye movements monitored. Despite the fact that the phishing signs demanded a higher attentional investment, the study demonstrates that less time was spent viewing them.
4) *Investigating Gaze Behavior in Phishing Email Identification* [11] A preliminary study including 28 students revealing that specialists perform better at identifying phishing emails and that experts and non-experts use different techniques for email examination.
5) *Perceiving and Using Genre by Form – An Eye-Tracking Study* [12] A study with 24 participants tasked with classifying emails into genres (calls for papers, newsletters, spam) demonstrated that genre analysis based on purpose and form is an effective method for identifying the characteristics of these emails. This paper is not specific to phishing emails.

6) *You have e-mail, what happens next? Tracking the eyes for genre* [13] A follow-up paper to the previous eye-tracking study by Clark, with further insight on how users classify emails into genres.
7) *Prediction of Phishing Susceptibility Based on a Combination of Static and Dynamic Features* [14] The user phishing susceptibility prediction model (DSM) presented in this paper is built on a combination of static and dynamic variables. A study involving 50 participants in eye-tracking was carried out to confirm that the model correctly predicts the behavior.
8) *Eyes wide open: The role of situational information security awareness for security-related behaviour* [15] Provides thorough literature research on empirical phishing research and conducts a study with 107 participants to examine how individual-level and system-level factors influence awareness. The findings highlight the significance of situational information security awareness and demonstrate that, whereas contextual relevance and misplaced salience in phishing emails reduce awareness, prior exposure to phishing and security warnings increases awareness.
9) Further papers on [8] with more detailed statistical analyses of the same study
10) *Where the User Does Look When Reading Phishing Mails - An Eye-Tracking Study* [16] A study with 25 participants that were shown emails and decided whether they were phishing. The findings indicate that two critical elements in identifying phishing emails are time and expertise.
11) *Email Reading Behavior-Informed Machine Learning Model to Predict Phishing Susceptibility* [17] A prototype tested with 25 participants to collect eye-tracking data in real time and notify users when they are on the brink of falling for phishing.
12) *Revealing the Hidden Effects of Phishing Emails: An Analysis of Eye and Mouse Movements in Email Sorting Tasks* [18], An online study with 39 participants using mouse movements and gaze patterns. The study shows that when interacting with phishing versus non-phishing emails, there are notable changes in mouse movements and eye gaze.

B. Results of the Literature Review

The literature review shows that while there are previous empirical studies on user interaction with phishing emails that analyze eye movements, the papers found either have a relatively small sample size, or study adaptive mechanisms meant to improve the users phishing recognition. A clear research gap in studying how participants use the provided tools and warnings and which phishing markers that should have raised suspicion were overlooked when users fall for a phishing attempt can be identified. These questions need to be studied in order to develop tools and strategies to prevent phishing attacks. Based on this literature review, the following research questions were developed:

RQ2 How does the use of an additional phishing awareness system influence the effectiveness of recognition of phishing emails?

RQ3 How does the use of an additional phishing awareness system influence the efficiency of the recognition of phishing emails?

RQ4 How does the existence of the phishing awareness system influence the amount of time spent looking at phishing markers?

RQ5 Which phishing markers of an email are most commonly overlooked when a user falls for a phishing attempt?

Based on these research questions, the following hypothesis were developed:

H1 Participants with the phishing awareness system will correctly identify a higher percentage of emails compared to the group not using the sidebar.

H2 Participants with the phishing awareness system need less time to classify the email.

H3 Participants with the phishing awareness system spend less time looking at the relevant phishing markers before making a decision.

H4 Participants with the phishing awareness system that recognise a phishing attempt spent less time proportionally looking at phishing markers compared to participants with the phishing awareness system that fall for a phishing attempt.

III. STUDY DESIGN

The study included 18 different stimuli: twelve phishing emails and six harmless control emails. All emails were real, with minor modifications made to obscure personal details. Furthermore, one email was translated from English to German to eliminate potential language barriers. The twelve phishing emails were further divided evenly into the following categories, to cover a wide spectrum of typical phishing emails:

1) containing a suspicious attachment
2) containing a link to an external website and an injunction to click on said link
3) containing an injunction to send money or items of value (e.g., gift cards, sensitive data)

Each of the three categories is split into two subgroups containing two emails each. This separation is based on the quality of the phishing email, which is measured by the amount of phishing markers within an email. Phishing markers are defined as elements that indicate phishing emails, such as spelling errors, cryptic text, misleading domains or suspicious attachments like *.exe* or *.docm*. For this study, a well-made phishing email is defined as containing a maximum of two subtle phishing markers, such as a slightly altered domain name like *@spotfy.com*. In contrast, poorly written phishing emails are characterized by having more than two markers or very obvious signs, such as cryptic sender addresses. Due to the subjectivity of the interaction with the email, it has to be noted that these categories are not always precisely distinguished and may overlap. The control group also consists

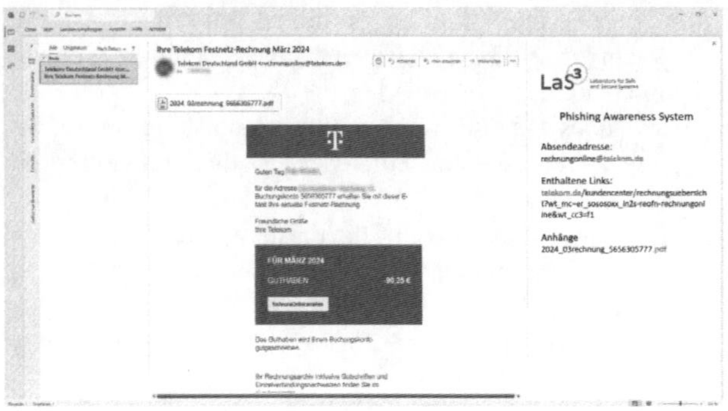

Figure 2. A phishing email with the Phishing Awareness Sidebar (PAS).

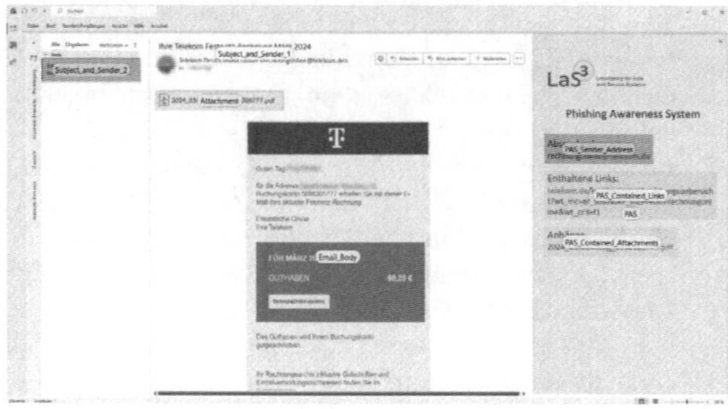

Figure 3. Defined AOIs on an email with the PAS.

of six emails, two for each of the categories names above. The emails were presented in random order.

A. Phishing Awareness System (PAS)

In order to study the research questions mentioned above, a prototype for a Phishing Awareness System (PAS) that is similar to ones already on the market was build. It was embedded into Microsoft Outlook (see Figure 2), as it is a commonly used email client in an office environment. The prototype was designed to help user identify the most common phishing markers by highlighting them. These markers include suspicious links, attachments and the address of the sender. Participants using the system were informed about the existence of the PAS and its functions beforehand.

An in-between-subjects design was used in this study, where half of the participants were provided with an Outlook environment that included the PAS, while the other half used a standard Outlook environment. Group assignment was done randomly to ensure unbiased distribution.

B. Participants

A total of 120 participants were recruited from various local small and medium enterprises, as well as public sector organizations, to ensure a representative real-world dataset. Eleven participants chose not to answer the questionnaire and were subsequently excluded from the dataset. An additional six participants did not meet the calibration and validation requirement of 0.75°, primarily due to extreme visual impairments. Despite this, these six participants still wished to participate in the study for personal interest but were informed that their data would not be considered in the final study. Of the remaining 103 participants, 51 performed the study with the PAS and 52 without. The mean age was 35 for the PAS group and 34 for the group without PAS. In the PAS group, 69% of the participants were male and 31% were female, whereas in the group without the sidebar, 58% of the participants were male and 42% were female. In both groups, over 90% of users (92% with the PAS and 90% without) reported knowing what phishing emails can look like and being able to identify suspicious features. Additionally, 57% of participants in the PAS group and 71% in the group without the sidebar indicated that they receive phishing emails daily or several times per week. In the PAS group, only 49% of participants had previously participated in phishing training, compared to 71% in the no-sidebar group. While the age distribution and prior knowledge were nearly identical across both groups, there were significant differences in gender distribution, prior exposure to phishing, and experience with phishing training, which can influence the final results.

C. Eye-Tracking Setup and Data Collection

Nine mobile Tobii Pro Fusion eye-trackers running at 250 Hz were used for data collection, attached to modular 21-inch screens and each equipped with dedicated laptops. Participants were calibrated with a 65 cm distance to the eye-tracker and asked to sit still during the recording. A nine point calibration and four point validation was chosen to ensure optimal accuracy. To further ensure an accurate dataset, a quality threshold for calibration and validation was set to 0.75°.

The recording locations varied, as the study was conducted across a range of companies. In each location, the eye-trackers were set up in dedicated rooms, with blinds closed whenever possible to minimize direct natural light interference. Before the study, participants were informed about the procedures and asked to sign a consent form approved by the Joint Ethics Committee of the Bavarian Universities (GEHBa). Participation was voluntary and each participant was assigned an anonymous identifier. No additional phishing warnings or trainings were provided, as participants were aware they were participating in phishing research, which could lead to priming effects.

After being briefed on the study, participants were paired with a researcher and seated in front of a Tobii Pro Fusion eye-tracker equipped with a keyboard and a mouse. The eye-tracker was calibrated to each participant before the session began. Participants were initially shown two slides containing instructions with the group with the PAS receiving an additional slide explaining the sidebar's purpose. Participants could start the study at their own pace and had no maximum time to finish. Before each email, a centering cross appeared on the left side of the screen to ensure that participants started viewing the stimulus from a neutral point. If they identified an email as phishing, they were instructed to press the "S" key; if they believed it was not phishing, they were to press the "Right" key. The two keys were purposely selected as the distance between them minimized the risk for accidental presses. Pressing either key would proceed to the next email stimulus.

After the eye-tracking experiment, each participant was given a questionnaire collecting demographic data, prior knowledge of IT-security topics and their familiarity with the companies mentioned in the emails. The participants with the PAS were also asked to rate the tool using the short version of the User Experience Questionnaire (UEQ-S) and the System Usability Scale (SUS).

D. Areas of Interest (AOIs)

Areas of Interest (AOIs) are regions predefined by the researchers that hold particular significance for the research subject. They represent various metrics, such as fixations occurring within a specific area [19]. In this study, the AOIs correspond to phishing markers present in emails and were drawn to match the areas containing these phishing markers, including the sender's email address, the email's subject line, the main body of the email, and any attachments. An illustration of these AOIs can be seen in Figure 3.

IV. RESULTS

For the first hypothesis H1, it was found that participants who used the sidebar generally did not perform better in the emails sorting task.

Figures 4 and 5 show that the sidebar group was overall less effective in correctly identifying emails, as well as less effective in identifying phishing emails. A Shapiro-Wilk test [20] showed that the samples are non-normally distributed, proving the need for non-parametric tests to be performed. A Mann-Whitney U-test with approximated p-value on the number of correctly identified emails in both groups fails to show a difference in distribution between the groups: at $\alpha = 0.05$ it results in $z = 1216.00$, $p = .460$, $r = .07$. A similar result holds for the number of correctly identified phishing emails; here, a Mann-Whitney U-test delivers $z = 1201.50$, $p = .396$, $r = .08$, showing no significant difference at $\alpha = 0.05$ between the two groups. This leads to having to reject H1, showing that there is no significant difference between the group with the sidebar and the group without when it comes to correctly identifying emails.

To test the second hypothesis H2, a Shapiro-Wilk test on the dependent variable 'total time' showed no normal distribution within both groups. This means again that a non-parametric test should be used. A Mann-Whitney U-test yields $z = 1518.00$, $p = .205$, $r = .12$ and thus revealing no significant difference between groups at $\alpha = 0.05$ with small effect. This can also be seen in Figure 6. Testing instead only the time spent to sort phishing emails gives a similar result: no significant difference between the group with PAS and the group without. Looking only at the time spent on emails of specific types (with attachment, with links or with an injunction to send money) also showed no significant difference between the two groups. Neither could a difference be found when looking only at good phishing emails, bad phishing emails or only the control group. Hypothesis 2 thus also has to be rejected.

Hypothesis H3 is the first hypothesis based on the col-

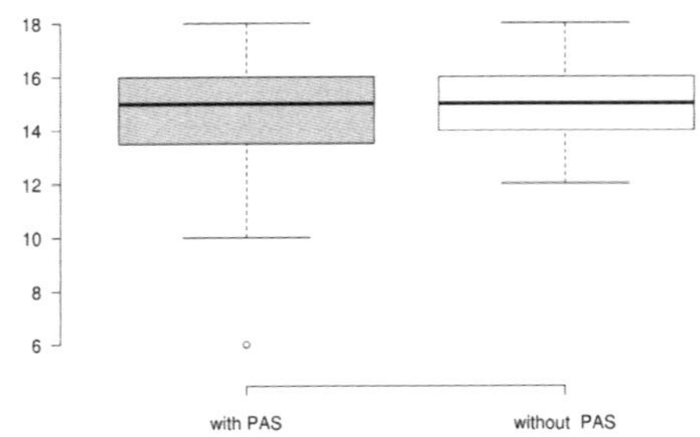

Figure 4. Total number of correctly identified emails with and without sidebar tool.

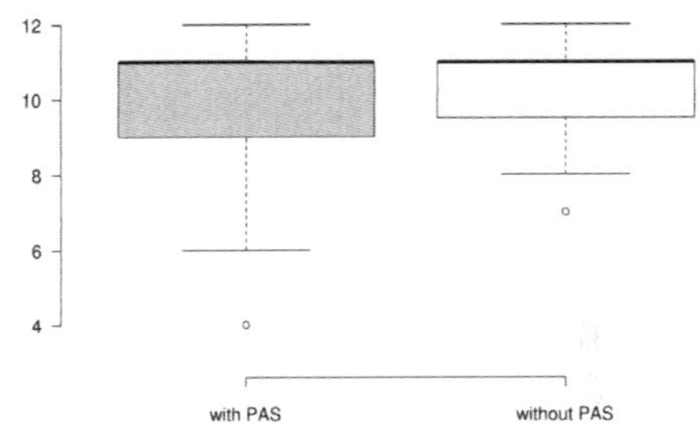

Figure 5. Total number of correctly identified phishing emails with and without sidebar tool.

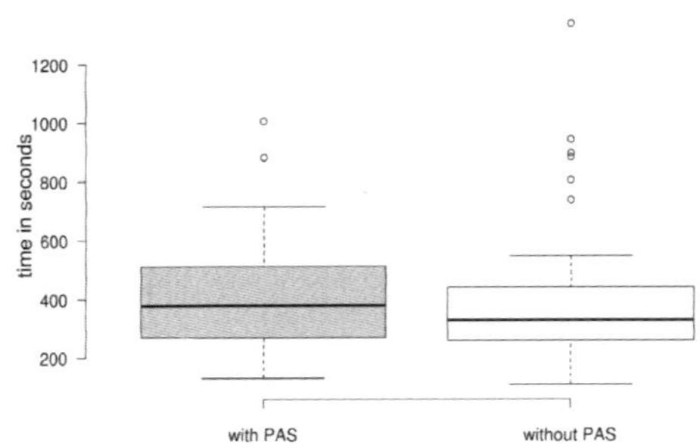

Figure 6. Total time spent on the email sorting task for groups with and without sidebar tool.

TABLE I. MANN-WHITNEY U-TEST RESULTS FOR AOI HITS BETWEEN THE GROUP WITH PAS AND THE GROUP WITHOUT PAS.

	z	p	r
Subject and Sender	1546.00	.147	.14
Attachments	1786.00	.002	.3
Email Body	1290.00	.812	.02

lected eye-tracking data, focusing on three different AOIs: fixations on the main body of the email, the attachments, and the sender's address along with the email's subject line. In Microsoft Outlook, the sender's address and subject line are displayed twice (once on the left side and once above the email) which have been consolidated into a single AOI for this analysis. For the group using the PAS, fixations on relevant phishing markers in both the tool and within Microsoft Outlook were combined. As before a Shapiro-Wilk test on the dependent variable 'AOI hits' showed no normal distribution within both groups. Hence, Mann-Whitney U-tests were applied to assess the number of AOI hits in both groups, as shown in Table I.

Both the number of AOI hits within the subject and sender information, as well as the email body, show no significant differences between the two groups at $\alpha = 0.05$ with small to neglectable effect sizes of .14 and .02, respectively. These small effect sizes indicate minimal differences between the groups. However, for the attachments, the p-value of .002 is well below the $\alpha = 0.05$ threshold, indicating a statistically significant difference in the number of AOI hits and, consequently, the amount of time spent looking at the attachments between the groups. The effect size r of .30 suggests a small to medium effect, indicating that the difference is not only statistically significant but also has moderate practical significance. As shown in Figure 7, the group with the PAS has significantly less AOI hits on the attachment ($M = 1435.58$) compared to the group without the assisting sidebar ($M = 2527.78$). In terms of time, the PAS group spent an average of 5.74 seconds looking at the attachments, compared to 10.11 seconds for the group without the tool.

Based on these findings, Hypothesis 3 can only be partially accepted. While there is no statistically significant difference between the two groups in viewing phishing markers in the email body or sender's address and subject line, there is a significant difference in AOI hits and therefore viewing time for attachments. This indicates that the presence of the PAS significantly reduces the time spent analyzing attachment types. These results underscore the relevance of eye-tracking technology in capturing not only easily measurable metrics, such as completion time which stayed the same between the two groups, but also subconscious interactions and relevant regions revealed by users' eye movements. This data is particularly valuable for understanding how users interact with phishing emails and for identifying which phishing markers attract the most attention or are overlooked.

The observation that participants using the PAS showed no significant difference in the overall time spent classifying

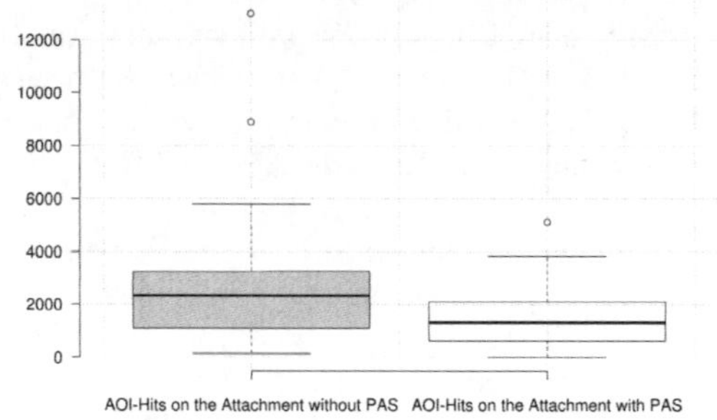

Figure 7. AOI hits on the attachment with and without the PAS.

emails with attachments, despite spending nearly half as much time looking at the attachments and their types, may be due to several explanations. For instance participants might not fully trust the tool and therefore seek to verify their decisions by examining additional phishing markers. Alternatively, the time difference might be attributed to the need to process the additional information provided by the tool.

To answer RQ5, it is necessary to look separately at the group with PAS and the group without. The reason for this is that certain phishing markers, such as sender address, attachments and contained links, are repeated in the PAS and thus participants might divide their attention between the phishing markers in the email and in the PAS. Another reason is that the PAS, being a new tool that participants have not used before, can attract attention from participants. In order not to skew the results, the evaluation was performed separately for the two groups.

For the group without the tool, looking at all 12 phishing emails, it was studied whether participants that classified the email correctly spent less time looking at the phishing markers contained in the AOIs "subject and sender", "email body" and "attachments" than participants that did not classify the email correctly. There was no statistically significant difference in the AOI hits for "subject and sender" and "attachments" found between the group that sorted the emails correctly and the group that did not, as proven by two Mann-Whitney U-tests at $\alpha = 0.05$ that delivered p-values of .202 and .392, respectively. However, there was a significant difference in AOI hits on the email body. A Mann-Whitney U-test delivered values of $z = 27738.00$, $p < .001$ and $r = .22$, showing a significant difference at $\alpha = 0.05$ with small effect. Figure 8 shows that participants without PAS who correctly identified a phishing email had less AOI hits on the email body than participants without PAS who fell for a phishing email. This indicates that users with the ability to correctly identify a phishing attempt need less time to extract the relevant information from the email body.

But the interesting results happen in the group with PAS. In order to test H4, as before, for all 12 phishing emails it was studied whether AOI hits differ between participants

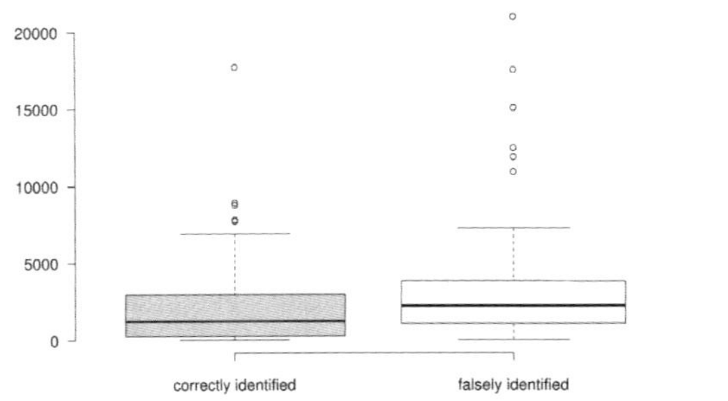

Figure 8. AOI hits on the email body for participants without PAS that correctly identified the phishing email and those that did not.

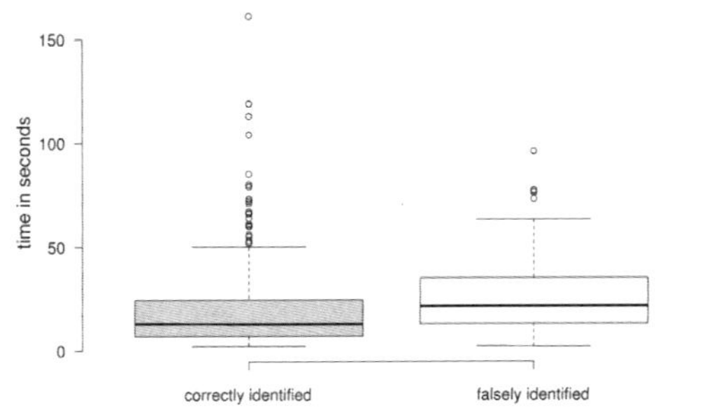

Figure 9. Time needed to identify phishing emails for users with PAS.

who correctly identified the email and participants who did not. Since samples are again non-normally distributed, Mann-Whitney U-tests at $\alpha = 0.05$ were employed, see Table II below.

TABLE II. MANN-WHITNEY U-TEST RESULTS FOR AOI HITS BETWEEN PARTICIPANTS WHO CORRECTLY IDENTIFIED A PHISHING EMAIL VERSUS THOSE THAT DID NOT, IN THE GROUP WITH PAS.

	z	p	r
Subject and Sender	32799.00	$< .001$	.18
Email Body	35047.00	$< .001$	.24
Attachment	25642.00	.973	.00
PAS total	31171.50	$< .001$	.14
PAS contained attachments	30966.50	$< .001$	.16
PAS contained links	31016.00	$< .001$	.14
PAS sender address	30642.50	.001	.13

PAS contained attachments, links and sender address refer to the specific areas in the PAS where the phishing markers are highlighted. They are included separately here to allow for a more detailed evaluation.

These results show significant differences with small effect between the two groups in the number of AOI hits on all AOIs except for the attachment.

TABLE III. MEDIANS OF AOI HITS FOR THE GROUP WITH PAS THAT IDENTIFIED A PHISHING EMAIL CORRECTLY VERSUS THE GROUP WITH PAS THAT FELL FOR THE PHISHING ATTEMPT.

	Median Group Correct	Median Group False
Subject and Sender	103.50	457.00
Email Body	838.00	2034.00
PAS total	242.50	439.50
PAS contained attachments	0.00	26.00
PAS contained links	0.00	74.50
PAS sender address	45.00	114.50

It can be seen in Table III that in the group with PAS, participants who correctly identified a phishing email spent less time looking at phishing markers than participants who fell for the phishing attempt. In the group without PAS, this effect could only be seen in regards to the email body. This indicates that, while the PAS does not make all users more effective in identifying phishing emails, it does make users more efficient that have the sufficient knowledge to identify phishing attempts. A likely interpretation of this result is that users who are proficient in identifying phishing emails benefit from the clarity and overview provided by the PAS and are thus enabled to make their decision faster. The r-values for all phishing markers in which a significant difference was found are of similar size, indicating that the PAS highlights all necessary information except for attachments equally. The same effect can be seen when only looking at the processing time per email instead of the individual AOIs, as seen in Figure 9.

Users with the PAS spent less time on phishing emails that were identified correctly as opposed to phishing emails that were identified falsely. This indicates again a gain in efficiency through the PAS when users are already confident in their decision, but no gain in visibility for individual phishing markers. Hypothesis 4 can thus be accepted, but it remains to say that no satisfying answer to RQ5 could be found. While there is a significant difference in time between participants that recognise a phishing attempt and those that do not in the group with PAS, no definitive statement can be made on which phishing markers are overlooked when a user falls for a phishing attempt.

Overall, participants fell for a phishing attempt with a suspicious attachment in 19% of cases, for a phishing attempt containing a suspicious link in 15% of all cases and for a phishing attempt containing an injunction to send money or other items of value in 11% of cases. This highlights the dangers of phishing attacks and the susceptibility of users to fall especially for phishing attempts with attachments. To counteract this effect, an organization-wide attachment blocker can be used, only allowing attachments of certain file types. To prevent users from clicking on a phishing link, a generic phishing warning on emails containing links is effective [3]. Participants were least likely to fall for a phishing attempt involving an injunction to send items of value, however, at 11% the failure rate is still quite high. Here, again, it is crucial to invoke warnings on emails from external senders [3].

Similar to the findings in [3], this study could not find a significant difference in phishing detection between participants who stated they had already taken part in IT-security training and those who did not. There is a need to distinguish here between this study and the referenced paper: one examined voluntary, contextual training, while the other only asked if participants had ever taken part in any IT-security training, however long ago. Still, this results highlights the necessity for further study to achieve innovative, tailored, and effective training methods.

A. Summary of results

The use of an additional phishing awareness system did not improve phishing recognition or the efficiency of phishing recognition. However, using the PAS leads to less time needed to gather information regarding the attachments of a suspicious email. Additionally, users with the PAS who correctly identified a phishing email spent less time looking at all phishing markers except for attachments, compared to users with the PAS who fell for the phishing attempt. This result could not be seen in the group without PAS, indicating that its existence helps users who already have the necessary knowledge to identify phishing emails to make their decision faster. By adapting the tool using existing human-computer interaction guidelines, one can hope to achieve a benefit to all users, not just the experts, in the future. Previous phishing training was proven to have no effect on how likely a participant is to fall for a phishing attempt. Participants fell most often for phishing emails with suspicious attachments and least often for phishing emails with injunctions to send items of value.

V. Usability Results

Although the PAS prototype did not lead to an overall improvement in the effectiveness or efficiency of detecting phishing emails, it did help specific user groups identify phishing markers more quickly. Generally, participants rated the tool's usability as relatively good. The SUS questionnaire yielded an average score of $M = 75,15$, indicating a good usability score. The UEQ-S confirmed these findings, with the measured pragmatic quality — strongly related to usability [21] — scoring $M = 1,53$, indicating a "Good" to "Above Average" result. However, the hedonic quality, which measures non-task-related experience, scored "Below Average". The detailed results of the UEQ-S are provided in Figure 10. This suggests that while the tool meets users' functional requirements, it does not deliver an outstanding experience.

Furthermore, analyzing the SUS scores revealed that users rating the usability as good (68 and higher, as defined by [22]) were able to correctly identify more emails in total and phishing emails compared to users rating the usability of PAS as below average. The p-values and effect sizes indicated statistically significant differences between the two groups with a medium effect. The results of the Mann-Whitney U-test can be seen in Table IV.

Both the UEQ-S and SUS results should be further investigated to explore potential connections between the efficiency and effectiveness of phishing detection and the perceived usability and user experience.

TABLE IV. Mann-Whitney U-test results between users giving a good usability rating and users giving a below average usability rating.

	z	p	r
Total number of correctly identified emails	157.50	.018	.33
Number of correctly identified phishing emails	155.00	.014	.35

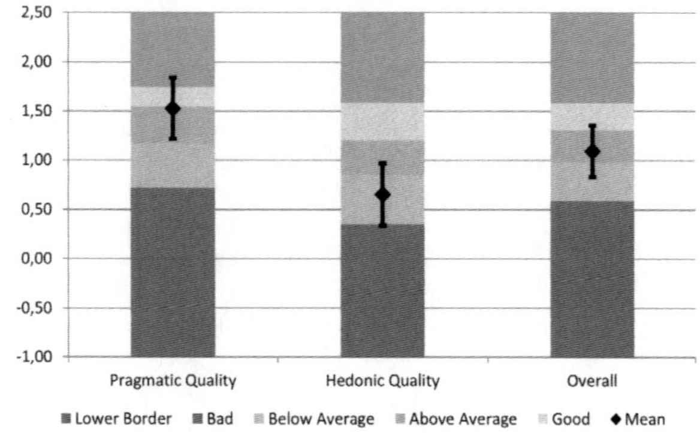

Figure 10. Results of the UEQ-S Questionnaire.

VI. Limitations

The uneven distribution in gender, prior training and exposure to phishing emails between the two groups is to be considered a limiting factor. The effect of prior training is thought to be negligible, since no effect of training could be found in this study. However, only 57% of participants in the PAS group receive phishing mails daily or several times a week, compared to 71% in the group without PAS. This could certainly be an influence as to why no difference in effectiveness between the two groups could be found. Secondly, none of the usability and UX-related questions addressed the participants trust in the tool. Scepticism towards an unfamiliar tool may have been a factor that lead to no measurable difference in efficiency being found between both groups. Understanding and addressing the human elements can enhance the overall effectiveness of security awareness campaigns, ensuring that users are better prepared to recognize and respond to potential threats [23]. Lastly, while the varied recording locations allowed for a diverse and representative set of participants, this also meant that external factors unique to each location could influence the data quality. These include differing levels of natural light, varying background noise levels and differences in posture due to variations in tables and seating heights. As a result, the data quality cannot be compared to eye-tracking studies conducted under laboratory settings. To determine whether these factors influenced the final results, a smaller follow-up study could be conducted to compare the study design in both controlled and uncontrolled environments.

VII. Conclusion and Future Work

This study demonstrates that relying solely on task-related efficiency and effectiveness metrics, such as the number of correctly identified emails and completion time, does not provide a complete picture of the effectiveness of cybersecurity tools. Significant insights come from understanding users subconscious interactions with the system, which eye-tracking technology can reveal. Understanding these interactions is crucial because systems are only as secure and robust as their weakest link. The collected eye-tracking data is comprehensive and warrants further examination in subsequent studies.

Especially RQ4 and RQ5 have shown that the PAS tool was able to help users with sufficient knowledge in detecting phishing markers more quickly. If an influence on one group can be measured, it is likely that the system can be adjusted to help other user groups as well. The PAS prototype could be tailored to fit a wider audience by, for example, supplying additional information that users susceptible to phishing attacks might need. Given the broad debate on the effectiveness of security training and tools [3][4][23], the fact that the evaluated PAS tool was able to support specific user groups and received positive ratings from users can be considered a success. Further developing the tool to be more user-centered could not only lead to a higher perceived hedonic quality but also an increase in overall effectiveness for all user groups [24].

Cybersecurity and information security depend on robust technological systems, physical defenses against attacks, and the security awareness of end users. While phishing attacks using harmful attachments can be effectively countered with suitable blockers, phishing attacks targeting the end user persist. While phishing training alone seems not to be the sole solution to phishing prevention, the problem of security awareness needs to be addressed in some form. A combination of suitable tools and adequate training on the use of these tools, as well as on the broader topic of security awareness, could help companies reduce the total number of successful phishing attacks.

Acknowledgments

This study was conducted as part of the EU-funded EDIH *Digital Innovation Ostbayern (DInO)*. DInO is funded by the European Union (Project Reference 101083427) and the European Funds for Regional Development (EFRE) (Project Reference 20-3092.10-THD-105). The eye-tracking study was approved by the Joint Ethics Committee of the Bavarian Universities (GEHBa) with the reference number GEHBa-202312-V-155-R.

Data

The eye-tracking and questionnaire data collected and evaluated in this study is free to use and can be found on Zenodo under the following link doi.org/10.5281/zenodo.13171791.

References

[1] N. S. Sulaiman *et al.*, "Cyber–information security compliance and violation behaviour in organisations: A systematic review," *Social Sciences*, vol. 11, no. 9, p. 1, 2022, ISSN: 2076-0760. DOI: 10.3390/socsci11090386.

[2] ISO27001, "Information technology, security techniques, information security management systems, requirements," *International Organization for Standardization ISO*, 2005.

[3] D. Lain, K. Kostiainen, and S. Capkun, "Phishing in organizations: Findings from a large-scale and long-term study," *2022 IEEE Symposium on Security and Privacy (SP)*, p. 9, 2022.

[4] A. Heinemann and G. Schembre, "Zur Wirksamkeit von Security Awareness Maßnahmen [on the effectiveness of security awareness measures]," ger, in *DACH Security Tagungsband 2017: Bestandsaufnahme, Konzepte, Anwendungen, Perspektiven*, P. Schartner and A. Baumann, Eds., Klagenfurt (Österreich): Alpen-Adria-Universität, 2017, ISBN: 978-3-00-057290-6.

[5] J. L. Orquin and K. Holmqvist, "Threats to the validity of eye-movement research in psychology," *Behavior Research Methods*, vol. 50, no. 4, pp. 1645–1656, Aug. 2018, ISSN: 1554-3528. DOI: 10.3758/s13428-017-0998-z.

[6] B. Kitchenham and S. Charters, "Guidelines for performing systematic literature reviews in software engineering," vol. 2, Jan. 2007.

[7] L. Grabinger, F. Hauser, C. Wolff, and J. Mottok, "On eye tracking in software engineering," *SN Computer Science*, vol. 5, no. 6, p. 729, Jul. 26, 2024, ISSN: 2661-8907. DOI: 10.1007/s42979-024-03045-3.

[8] L. Huang, S. Jia, E. Balcetis, and Q. Zhu, "Advert: An adaptive and data-driven attention enhancement mechanism for phishing prevention," *IEEE Transactions on Information Forensics and Security*, vol. 17, pp. 2585–2597, 2022. DOI: 10.1109/TIFS.2022.3189530.

[9] J. Kävrestad *et al.*, "Evaluation of contextual and game-based training for phishing detection," *Future Internet*, vol. 14, no. 4, 2022, ISSN: 1999-5903. DOI: 10.3390/fi14040104.

[10] J. McAlaney and P. J. Hills, "Understanding phishing email processing and perceived trustworthiness through eye tracking," *Frontiers in Psychology*, vol. 11:1756, 2020, ISSN: 1664-1078. DOI: 10.3389/fpsyg.2020.01756.

[11] F. Pietrantonio *et al.*, "Investigating gaze behavior in phishing email identification," in *2023 7th Network Traffic Measurement and Analysis Conference (TMA)*, 2023, pp. 1–4.

[12] M. Clark, I. Ruthven, and P. O. Holt, "Perceiving and using genre by form – an eye-tracking study," *Libri*, vol. 60, no. 3, pp. 268–280, 2010. DOI: doi:10.1515/libr.2010.023.

[13] M. Clark, I. Ruthven, P. O. Holt, D. Song, and S. Watt, "You have e-mail, what happens next? tracking the eyes for genre," *Information Processing & Management*, vol. 50, no. 1, pp. 175–198, 2014, ISSN: 0306-4573. DOI: https://doi.org/10.1016/j.ipm.2013.08.005.

[14] R. Yang, K. Zheng, B. Wu, C. Wu, and X. Wang, "Prediction of phishing susceptibility based on a combination of static and dynamic features," *Mathematical Problems in Engineering*, p. 2884769, 2022. DOI: https://doi.org/10.1155/2022/2884769.

[15] L. Jaeger and A. Eckhardt, "Eyes wide open: The role of situational information security awareness for security-related behaviour," *Information Systems Journal*, vol. 31, no. 3, pp. 429–472, 2021. DOI: https://doi.org/10.1111/isj.12317. eprint: https://onlinelibrary.wiley.com/doi/pdf/10.1111/isj.12317.

[16] K. Pfeffel, P. Ulsamer, and N. H. Müller, "Where the user does look when reading phishing mails – an eye-tracking study," in *Learning and Collaboration Technologies. Designing Learning*

Experiences, P. Zaphiris and A. Ioannou, Eds., Cham: Springer International Publishing, 2019, pp. 277–287, ISBN: 978-3-030-21814-0.

[17] N. Xu, J. Fan, and Z. Wen, "Email reading behavior-informed machine learning model to predict phishing susceptibility," *Lecture Notes in Computer Science, vol 14509. Springer, Singapore*, pp. 579–592, 2024.

[18] Y. Abdrabou *et al.*, *Revealing the hidden effects of phishing emails: An analysis of eye and mouse movements in email sorting tasks*, 2023. arXiv: 2305.17044.

[19] C. Blake, "Eye-Tracking: Grundlagen und Anwendungsfelder [Eye-Tracking: Foundations and Applications]," ger, in *Handbuch standardisierte Erhebungsverfahren in der Kommunikationswissenschaft*, W. Möhring and D. Schlütz, Eds., Wiesbaden: Springer Fachmedien Wiesbaden, 2013, pp. 367–387, ISBN: 978-3-531-18776-1. DOI: 10.1007/978-3-531-18776-1_20.

[20] S. S. Shapiro and M. B. Wilk, "An analysis of variance test for normality (complete samples)†," *Biometrika*, vol. 52, no. 3-4, pp. 591–611, Dec. 1965, ISSN: 0006-3444. DOI: 10.1093/biomet/52.3-4.591. eprint: https://academic.oup.com/biomet/article-pdf/52/3-4/591/962907/52-3-4-591.pdf.

[21] M. Hassenzahl, A. Platz, M. Burmester, and K. Lehner, "Hedonic and ergonomic quality aspects determine a software's appeal," in *Proceedings of the SIGCHI Conference on Human Factors in Computing Systems*, ser. CHI '00, The Hague, The Netherlands: Association for Computing Machinery, 2000, pp. 201–208, ISBN: 1581132166. DOI: 10.1145/332040.332432.

[22] J. R. Lewis and J. Sauro, "Item Benchmarks for the System," en, *Journal of Usability Studies*, vol. 13, no. 3, pp. 158–167, 2018.

[23] M. Bada, A. M. Sasse, and J. R. Nurse, "Cyber security awareness campaigns: Why do they fail to change behaviour?" *arXiv preprint arXiv:1901.02672*, 2019.

[24] M. A. Sasse, S. Brostoff, and D. Weirich, "Transforming the 'weakest link' — a human/computer interaction approach to usable and effective security," *BT Technology Journal*, vol. 19, no. 3, pp. 122–131, Jul. 1, 2001, ISSN: 1573-1995. DOI: 10.1023/A:1011902718709.

Countermeasure against Insider Threat Regarding Psychological State of Organizational Members and Business Impact of Information Resources

Yuki Kodaka *
*Department of Informatics
The Graduate University
for Advanced Studies
Tokyo, Japan
e-mail: y_kodaka@nii.ac.jp

Hirokazu Hasegawa †
†Center for Strategic Cyber
Resilience Research and Development
National Institute of Informatics
Tokyo, Japan
e-mail: hasegawa@nii.ac.jp

Hiroki Takakura †
†Center for Strategic Cyber
Resilience Research and Development
National Institute of Informatics
Tokyo, Japan
e-mail: takakura@nii.ac.jp

Abstract—**Compared to external cyberattacks, insider threats caused by organizational members can spread more widely within the organization even at an early stage, leading to significant impacts, such as business interruptions. When illicit activities are disguised as routine operations, it becomes difficult to detect them from behavioral records, such as violations of access privileges to information resources. Therefore, this paper proposes a countermeasure against insider threats regarding the psychological state of organizational members and the business impact of information resources. In addition to system operation record, the psychological state of each member is estimated using Human Resource data, such as stress tests, demotions, and salary reductions, which are held by the organization. Based on these assessments, we assess the risk of potential insider threats. Additionally, we assess the impact on the organization if information resources are leaked or become unusable, based on their operational usage. To mitigate these risks, we propose implementing countermeasures to prevent staged sabotage activities or automatically roll back executed sabotage actions. This approach aims to minimize business downtime and suppress further malicious activities, reducing the impact on business operations. However, not all Human Resource data can be used due to legal, ethical, and privacy concerns that vary across countries. Future work should examine how the accuracy of risk assessment changes when the number of assessment items is reduced.**

Keywords-insider threat; psychological state analysis; business impact analysis.

I. INTRODUCTION

Nowadays, information systems face several security threats. Among them are insider threats, which originate from internal elements, such as members of the organization that are supposed to be trusted. Traditional security measures were focused on external intruders, such as hackers. However, due to the significant impact and difficulty of countering insider threats, addressing these threats has become a pressing issue.

Insider threats are perpetrated by individuals with knowledge of systems and business processes, as well as authorised access privileges. Unlike external threats, insiders have easy access to an organization's information systems and information resources, making them more likely to cause widespread damage. According to a study by the Ponemon Institute [1], the cost of lost sales and technology due to business interruption caused by insider threats is \$8.3 million in 2018 and \$15.38 million in 2022, an increase of 85%.

According to the Vormetric insider threat report [2], 89% of respondents expressed concern about insider threats, whereas only 11% of respondents believed they were adequately prepared to address these threats. An effective countermeasure against insider threats involves detecting signs of unauthorized activities in advance or promptly responding when such activities occur. Insider threats are usually accompanied by unusual or suspicious activities before the actual attack [3]–[5]. However, it is challenging to distinguish between normal and malicious activities based solely on system activity. Furthermore, insider threats may intentionally hide their actions, making it even more difficult to detect the early signs of an attack. Additionally, since a huge amount of access records are generated on the system, it is difficult to manually or automatically detect malicious activities among them. Consequently, it is necessary to limit the access records to a manageable volume that allows for effective analysis.

Therefore, this paper proposes a countermeasure against insider threat regarding the psychological state of organizational members and the business impact of information resources. Since the members of an organization are potential sources of insider threats, they possess extensive knowledge about the organization. On the other hand, the organization also has a lot of information about its members, which is utilized for the countermeasures against insider threats. The risk assessment of potential insider threats is conducted for the organization's members, taking into account their psychological states. Specifically, risk assessments are conducted for each of the two categories of insider threats, i.e., sabotage activities against systems and data. Based on the results, any operation seen as progressing sabotage activities is monitored within the target information system. As a countermeasure, if sabotage activities are progressing step-by-step while hiding malicious actions, the proposed system prevents them at the previous step. If sabotage activities are suddenly executed, the proposed system quickly rolls back the executed operations to minimize downtime. The contaminated data by operations that cannot be rolled back, such as deletion, tampering, and encryption, is replaced using backup data.

This paper is organized in the following sections. Section II refers to related work to this paper. Section III describes the assumptions of the proposed system. After that, we explain the design of the proposed system. Section IV describes the challenges in realizing implementation of the proposed system. Section V concludes this paper and presents future work.

II. RELATED WORK

A. Insider Threat Detection

There are works on insider threat detection methods based on access logs and access order to files. Gates et al. proposed a method to create profiles from user activities to files and use them for insider threat detection and risk mitigation [6]. Toffalini et al. proposed a masquerader detection method that measures the similarity between user access history and newly recorded accesses [7]. These studies utilize only information available on the system for insider threat detection.

In addition to the information obtained from the system, there are works on insider threat detection methods that take into account the psychological state of the user. Greitzer et al. proposed a framework that utilizes psychological data in addition to traditional security audit logs to make the prediction of potential insider threats possible [8]. In subsequent research, they proposed a method for modeling psychological predictors of potential insider threats and identifying high-risk employees [9]. Kandias et al. proposed a method for predicting insider threats based on narcissism, a personality trait identified as a sign of insider threat [10]. In subsequent research, they explored the prediction of insider threats from social media, considering psychological aspects [11]. Additionally, they proposed a method for predicting insider threats based on users' negative comments on videos, viewing these comments as indications of malevolent insiders to law enforcement and authorities [12]. Taylor et al. proposed an insider threat detection method based on changes in the English language in emails [13]. While previous studies have focused on risk assessments related to members, they have not addressed the risks associated with information resources. Additionally, no classification or analysis has been conducted regarding the varying motives and targets of insider threats based on their objectives. Our approach evaluates risks by considering both member attributes and behaviors, while also incorporating assessments of information resources. This allows us to identify high-value or business-critical assets likely to be targeted, enabling proactive monitoring. Furthermore, we propose countermeasures to prevent insider attacks, going beyond mere detection.

B. Case Studies of Insider Threats

There are works on insider threat cases that investigate the motives and background of the insiders. In sabotage activities against systems, it was often observed that technical staff members used administrative privileges to carry out these actions [14]. The motives cited included job-related stress, dissatisfaction with the organization, and a desire for revenge. The causes of stress and dissatisfaction were financial issues, such as annual salary and bonuses, as well as missed promotions and advancement opportunities. Demotion or dismissal was specifically mentioned as a cause of seeking revenge [15]. Mental illnesses, such as alcoholism, drug addiction, panic disorder, and seizure disorder, along with family circumstances, like relationships with spouses, were found to influence the offender's behavior. Additionally, some offenders had a history of previous arrests.

In sabotage activities against data, it was often non-technical members of the workforce who carried out these actions [16]. The motives included financial gain to cover medical expenses related to addiction problems and financial assistance for family and friends [15]. Additionally, some activities were driven by emotional reasons, such as desire and need [16].

III. PROPOSED SYSTEM

In order to prevent activities that pose a threat to organizational operations, the proposed system performs a risk assessment of potential insider threats using information on members. Based on the results, the system monitors the operations of members with high insider threat risk. As countermeasures, the system prevents staged sabotage activities by these members and swiftly rolls back unexpected sabotage activities to minimize damage. For the contaminated data, the system uses backup data to provide replacements.

A. Assumption

First, this subsection explains the insider threats targeted by the proposed system and the assumptions about information used held by the organization for risk assessment.

1) Two categories of insider threats: This system focuses on preventing electronic sabotage of information resources by insiders. Sabotage means making resources unusable for others. Preventing physical sabotage is beyond the scope of this paper because it is difficult to protect information resources once physical access is gained. Additionally, since the theft of information assets cannot be undone once it occurs, theft prevention is also out of scope.

Insider threats are divided into two categories: data sabotage and system sabotage. Since the expected sabotage activities differ between these two categories, the proposed system provides specific countermeasures for both data sabotage and system sabotage.

In the case of data sabotage activities, examples include deletion, modification, and encryption of the contents. Additionally, modifying access privileges and operations on upper-level directories (deletion, modification of access privileges) are also considered sabotage activities against data because they render the data unusable by other members.

On the other hand, in the case of system sabotage activities, activities, such as system shutdown, Operating System destruction, and network blocking are considered sabotage, as well as the deletion, modification, and embedding of malicious code in the system's source code.

2) *Information held by the organization:*

- Information about members
  In general, Asian countries have been slow to implement background checks, whereas many countries in Europe and the United States have adopted them. In the U.S., employers are legally required to conduct background checks before hiring due to the liability for negligent hiring, which refers to the failure to properly investigate an employee's background. Background checks can include debt and credit checks, health checks, nationality verification, criminal background checks, and social media and internet checks [17]. It is assumed that organizations possess this information at the time of hiring or during employment.
  The organization is assumed to collect information about the personality traits of its members through aptitude tests or other methods during the recruitment process. For instance, a five-factor personality test can provide information on traits, such as openness, honesty, extroversion, cooperativeness, and neuroticism [18].
  Furthermore, the organization is assumed to have information on stress check tests conducted periodically on its members, possibly in the form of an Employee Assistance Program (EAP) [19].
- Information about information resources
  In order for an organization to protect and effectively utilize its information resources, appropriate risk management commensurate with their value is necessary. ISO/IEC 27001 recommends that, as a first step in risk management, an organization should understand its information assets. Information resources are selected data and systems that an organization manages, such as information systems, databases, software, personnel information, customer information, financial information, and product technology information. The information asset register is used to identify these information resources. The register includes details, such as asset name, asset description, asset owner, asset location, and asset value. As an example of the method for calculating asset value, there is an approach that evaluates the asset from the perspectives of confidentiality, integrity, and availability, with each aspect being rated on three levels, making a total of nine levels [20]. It is assumed that the organization maintains an information resource management ledger for risk management purposes.

B. *Outline of Proposed System*

To detect and counter sabotage activities by insider threats, the proposed system conducts three types of risk assessments. Figure 1 shows the conceptual diagram of the insider threat risk assessment performed by the proposed system. Member risk assessment evaluates the potential risk of members becoming insider threats. Information resource risk assessment evaluate the impact when targeted and destroyed. Insider threat risk assessment combines the results of the member risk assessment and the information resource risk assessment to evaluate overall insider threat risk.

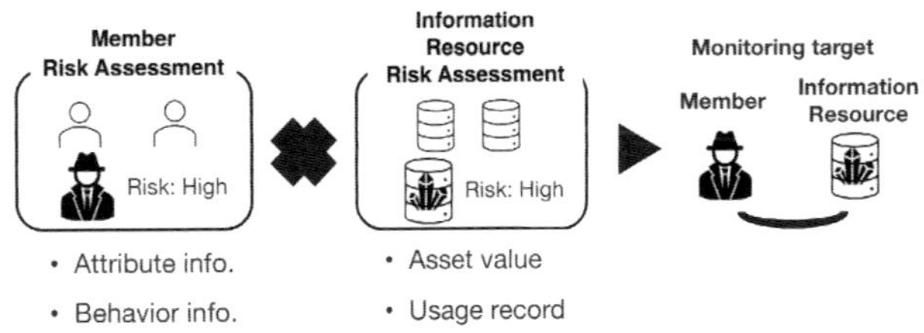

Figure 1. Conceptual Diagram of Internal Threat Risk Assessment.

C. *Architecture of Proposed System*

The architecture of the proposed system is shown in Figure 2. The proposed system consists of five modules: member risk assessment, information resource risk assessment, insider threat risk assessment, operation monitoring, and detection and action, as well as two databases: directory service and sabotage activity operation path database. The sabotage activity operation path database stores operation paths to achieve sabotage activities for each of the two threat categories. The following section describes the system processing procedure using Figure 2, and the details of member risk assessment, information resource risk assessment, insider threat risk assessment, and operation monitoring are explained in Sections III-D, III-E, III-F, and III-G.

1) The member risk assessment module evaluates the risks of each member based on the assessment items described in Section III-D and sends the results to the insider threat risk assessment module
2) The information resource risk assessment module evaluates the risk of each information resource based on its asset value and usage as recorded and sends the results to the insider threat risk assessment module
3) The insider threat risk assessment module evaluates the insider threat risk based on the member risk assessment and the information resource risk assessment
   If judged as an potential insider threat, it sends the combination of members and information resources to the operation monitoring module
4) The operation monitoring module identifies the operations required to execute the insider threat from the sabotage activity operation path database and sends those operations to the detection and action module
5) The detection and action module monitors target log records generated by the directory service and servers, and takes certain actions
   As countermeasures, it takes actions, such as changing privileges to prevent sabotage activities and rolling back operations after they have occurred

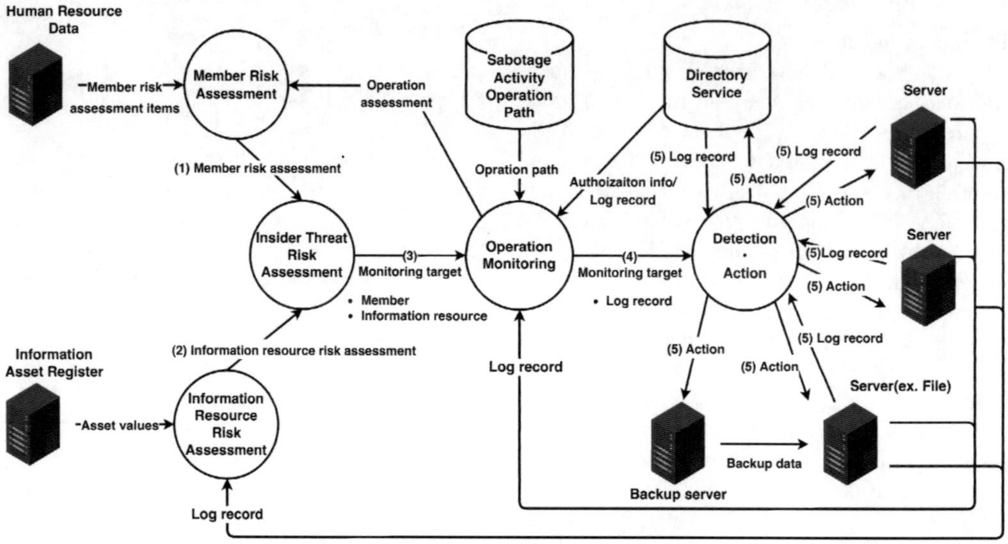

Figure 2. Architecture of Proposed System.

D. Member Risk Assessment

The member risk assessment module evaluates the risks of each member by two categories of insider threats from the information held by the organization.

a) Member risk assessment items: Based on a survey of multiple references analyzing case studies on insider threats, it was found that there are distinctive attributes common to organizational members who committed insider threats. The following assessment items are to be used for assessing the risk of insider threats among organizational members.

- Financial status (annual income, debt, credits) [3][5][8][21]
- Lifestyle status (family issues) [3][14]
- Health status (drug addiction, alcoholism, mental illness) [14]
- Criminal record (arrests) [3][21]
- Personality characteristics (excitement, neurotic tendency, hostility, lack of co-ordination, lack of conscience, self-love tendency) [3][5][21]
- Emotions (stress, lack of job satisfaction, anger, vengeance, lack of belonging to the organization) [3][5][21]
- Personnel (demotion, termination, job change) [5][14][21]
- Job type (technical position) [14]
- Privilege (administrative privileges) [16]

b) Member risk assessment items by two categories of insider threat: Using the above assessment items, member risk assessment is conducted for each of the two categories of insider threats. Based on the case studies of insider threats in Section II-B, we picked up the assessment items that are not identical but are considered to relevant as assessment items for each category of insider threats.

- System sabotage activities (18 items)
  Financial status (annual income, debt, credits), Life status (family issues), Health status (drug addiction, alcoholism, mental illness), Criminal record (arrests), Emotions (stress, lack of job satisfaction, anger, vengeance, lack of belonging to the organization), Personnel (demotion, termination, job change), Job type (technical position), Privilege(administrative privileges)
- Data sabotage activities (13 items)
  Financial status (annual income, debt, credits), Health status (drug addiction, alcoholism, mental illness), Personality traits (excitement, neurotic tendency, hostility, lack of co-ordination, lack of conscience, self-love tendency), Job type (technical position)
  Since the job type is non-technical position, the value needs to be inverted in the next step of binarization.

c) Binary conversion of risk assessment items: Each item is marked as 1 if applicable, otherwise as 0. For annual income, it is marked as 0 if above the industry, occupation, and age average, and 1 if below. For credits, a long-term payment delay is marked as 1, otherwise as 0.

d) Member risk assessment: Based on the attributes of each member, the risk assessments of sabotage activities against systems and data by member i are defined as follows:

$$R_{\text{system\_attribute\_member\_i}} = \frac{1}{n_{\text{system\_attribute}}} \sum_{x} v_{x,\text{system\_attribute\_member\_i}} \cdot w_{x,\text{system\_attribute}} \quad (0 \leq R_{\text{system\_attribute\_member\_i}} \leq 1) \tag{1}$$

$$R_{\text{data\_attribute\_member\_i}} = \frac{1}{n_{\text{data\_attribute}}} \sum_{x} v_{x,\text{data\_attribute\_member\_i}} \cdot w_{x,\text{data\_attribute}} \quad (0 \leq R_{\text{data\_attribute\_member\_i}} \leq 1) \tag{2}$$

where $n_{\text{system\_attribute}}$ is the number of assessment items related to system sabotage activities, $v_{x,\text{system\_attribute\_member\_i}}$ is the score of assessment item x for member i related to system sabotage activities, $w_{x,\text{system\_attribute}}$ is the weight of the assessment item x related to system sabotage activities, $n_{\text{data\_attribute}}$ is the number of assessment items related to data sabotage activities, $v_{x,\text{data\_attribute\_member\_i}}$ is the score of assessment item x for member i related to data sabotage activities, and $w_{x,\text{data\_attribute}}$ is the weight of the assessment item x related to data sabotage activities.

The weights are determined by the person in charge, based on the usability of the items and impact of the item on evaluation results. We set the total weight assigned to all assessment items to always be 1.

Based on the behavior of each member, the risk assessments of sabotage activities against systems and data by member i are defined as follows:

$$R_{\text{system\_behavior\_member\_i}} = \frac{1}{n_{\text{system\_behavior}}} \sum_{y} v_{y,\text{system\_operation\_member\_i}} \quad (0 \leq R_{\text{system\_behavior\_member\_i}} \leq 1) \tag{3}$$

$$R_{\text{data\_behavior\_member\_i}} = \frac{1}{n_{\text{data\_behavior}}} \sum_{y} v_{y,\text{data\_operation\_member\_i}} \quad (0 \leq R_{\text{data\_behavior\_member\_i}} \leq 1) \tag{4}$$

where $n_{\text{system\_behavior}}$ is the number of operations related to system sabotage activities, $v_{y,\text{system\_operation\_member\_i}}$ is the score of each operation y by member i related to system sabotage activities, $n_{\text{data\_behavior}}$ is the number of operations related to data sabotage activities, and $v_{y,\text{data\_operation\_member\_i}}$ is the score of each operation y by member i related to data sabotage activities. $v_{y,\text{system\_operation\_member\_i}}$ and $v_{y,\text{data\_operation\_member\_i}}$ are explained in the Subsection *G. Operation Monitoring*.

By integrating assessments based on attributes and behaviors, the risk assessment of sabotage activities against systems and data by member i is defined as follows:

$$R_{\text{system\_member\_i}} = \frac{1}{2} (R_{\text{system\_attribute\_member\_i}} + R_{\text{system\_behavior\_member\_i}}) \quad (0 \leq R_{\text{system\_member\_i}} \leq 1) \tag{5}$$

$$R_{\text{data\_member\_i}} = \frac{1}{2} (R_{\text{data\_attribute\_member\_i}} + R_{\text{data\_behavior\_member\_i}}) \quad (0 \leq R_{\text{data\_member\_i}} \leq 1) \tag{6}$$

E. Information Resource Risk Assessment

The information resource risk assessment module evaluates the impact when targeted and destroyed based on asset values and usage as recorded, and sends the assessment results to the insider threat risk assessment module. Information necessary for the assessment is obtained from the information asset register and log records of each server.

Assessment items for information resource risk assessment:

- Information asset value
  Normalize the asset value of each information resource obtained from the information asset register to a value between 0 and 1
- Number of users
  Number of users of each system/data within a certain period (e.g., 1 day, 1 week)
- Use frequency
  Use frequency of each system/data within a certain period (e.g., 1 day, 1 week)

The number of users and the use frequency are normalized from 0 to 1 by dividing each value of the system data by the total number of users and frequency of use within a certain period.

Based on the above assessment items, the risk assessment of information resource j are defined as follows:

$$R_{\text{resource\_j}} = \frac{1}{n_{\text{resource}}} \sum_{z} v_{z,\text{resource\_j}} \cdot w_{z,\text{resource}} \quad (0 \leq R_{\text{resource\_j}} \leq 1) \tag{7}$$

where n_{resource} is the number of assessment items included in the information resource risk assessment, $v_{z,\text{resource\_j}}$ is the score of each assessment item z of information resource j, and $w_{z,\text{resource}}$ is the weight assigned to the assessment item z.

The proposed system sets the weights based on key factors such as the type of information resource and its usage characteristics. The weight settings are adjusted differently for systems and data, with more importance assigned to items that have a greater impact on risk: For systems, the impact of destruction tends to align with the static asset value, as their usage patterns are relatively stable. Therefore, the information asset value is given a higher weight in the risk assessment. For data, the impact can fluctuate depending on timing and usage patterns, making items like the number of users and usage frequency more critical. As a result, these items are assigned higher weights in the assessment. The total weight assigned to all assessment items is always set to 1.

The calculations are based on log records collected over a certain period. If there is a large volume of log records, the computation can be costly. Additionally, since usage patterns are unlikely to change drastically in real-time, we plan to update the calculations outside of business hours. Given the time required for these computations, the information resource risk assessment is updated periodically, such as daily.

F. Insider Threat Risk Assessment

The insider threat risk assessment module performs an insider threat risk assessment based on the scores of the member risk assessment and the information resource risk assessment by the two categories of insider threats. If judged as an potential insider threat, it sends the combination of members, and information resources to the operation monitoring module.

Insider threat risk scores for system and data are defined as follows:

$$R_{\text{system\_insider\_i,j}} = R_{\text{system\_member\_i}} \times R_{\text{resource\_j}} \quad (0 \leq R_{\text{system\_insider\_i,j}} \leq 1) \tag{8}$$

$$R_{\text{data\_insider\_i,j}} = R_{\text{data\_member\_i}} \times R_{\text{resource\_j}} \quad (0 \leq R_{\text{data\_insider\_i,j}} \leq 1) \tag{9}$$

Note that $R_{\text{resource\_j}}$ in $R_{\text{system\_insider\_i,j}}$ refers to the system's information resource risk assessment, while $R_{\text{resource\_j}}$ in $R_{\text{data\_insider\_i,j}}$ refers to the data's information resource risk assessment.

If the insider threat risk score $R_{\text{system\_insider\_i,j}}$ or $R_{\text{data\_insider\_i,j}}$ exceeds the threshold $T_{\text{system\_insider}}$ or $T_{\text{data\_insider}}$, it is considered as an insider threat and becomes a monitoring target. These thresholds are set by the proposed system, based on the number of operations that are detected.

G. Operation Monitoring

The operation monitoring module identifies operations to be monitored based on members, and information resources received from the insider threat assessment module. Specifically, it identifies the operations necessary for the member to achieve the sabotage activity of the threat categories for the information resource in the sabotage activity operation path. The sabotage activity operation path database stores the operation paths required to carry out sabotage activities. It is created based on the company's own cases as well as domestic and international examples, and is organized into two categories of insider threats.

An example of the sabotage activity operation path data for file data is shown in Figure 3. The number of operation steps required to achieve the sabotage activity is indicated by s. Operation $s = 1$, when executed, immediately completes the sabotage activity on the information resource. Operation $s \geq 2$ represents a preparatory operation to affect the target. After this operation is performed, the next operation $s = 1$ completes the sabotage activity. The higher the number in s, the more operation steps are required before the sabotage activity is accomplished.

The operation monitoring module obtains the authorization information of each member from the directory service. From this information, the module identifies the next operation on the path that is necessary to achieve the sabotage activity.

The operation monitoring module identifies the operations $s = 1, 2$ to be monitored and sends target operations to the detection and action module. Therefore, if a high-risk member plans sabotage activities step-by-step starting from step 3 or higher, the proposed system can prevent the sabotage activities

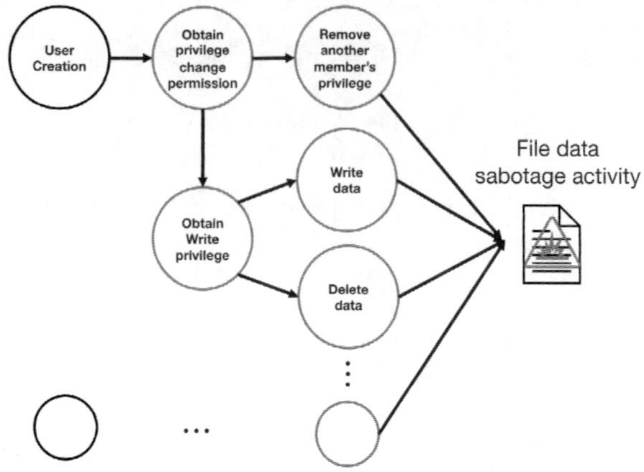

Figure 3. Example of Operation Path for Achieving Objectives.

at $s = 2$. On the other hand, if a high-risk member suddenly executes $s = 1$ operations to carry out sabotage activities, the system quickly rolls back the completed operations to minimize the damage. The contaminated data by operations that cannot be rolled back, such as deletion, tampering, and encryption, is replaced using backup data.

Various paths can be considered, and there may be unexpected paths on the sabotage activity operation path. Therefore, the proposed system cannot predict and monitor all possible paths. If a high-risk member reaches $s = 2$ despite having taken countermeasures on possible paths beforehand, it is necessary to identify the path taken up to that point and reflect that path in the sabotage activity operation path database. Additionally, it is necessary to infer paths that lead to $s = 1$ from that point and take measures, such as containing the impact of the attack.

Operations with $s \geq 3$ are used for member risk assessment as part of their behavioral information. When an operation that suggests advancing sabotage activities is performed, it affects the member's risk assessment. This allows for dynamic risk assessment of the members. The assessment of the operation on system and data by member i is defined as follows:

$$v_{y,\text{system\_operation\_member\_i}} = \frac{1}{2}\left(\frac{1}{s} \times D\right) \quad (0 \leq v_{y,\text{system\_operation\_member\_i}} \leq 1) \tag{10}$$

$$v_{y,\text{data\_operation\_member\_i}} = \frac{1}{2}\left(\frac{1}{s} \times D\right) \quad (0 \leq v_{y,\text{data\_operation\_member\_i}} \leq 1) \tag{11}$$

where s is the number of steps to achieve sabotage activity and D is the number of connected operations. Operations with many connected operations can significantly increase the number of possible achievement paths, thus increasing risk. These activities can be seen as actions leading to potential sabotage.

D is normalized to a value between 0 and 1 by dividing the number of links from the operation at step $s = n$ to the next step $s = n - 1$ by the total number of such links connecting from all operations at step $s = n$. For the operation "obtain write privilege" in Figure 3, since theare are 2 links from $s = 2$ to $s = 1$, and and the total number of such links is 3, the value is $2/3$.

IV. CHALLENGES IN REALIZING IMPLEMENTATION

National laws and organizational attitudes toward privacy and ethics vary, making it difficult to address all assessment items in this paper. In Japan, the Act of Protection of Personal Information (APPI) requires consent from members for the use of their personal information. Similarly, in Europe, the General Data Protection Regulation (GDPR) mandates strict data protection and privacy, while in the United States, laws like the California Consumer Privacy Act (CCPA) provide consumer privacy rights. Employee information is included in these regulations. On the other hand, some countries have security clearance to evaluate the eligibility of individuals who access security-related information. Considering the significant impact and actual damage by insider threats can cause, the need for systems to evaluate eligibility based on various information held by organizations is increasing. The need to explore criteria and methods that enable the effective use of information about members while balancing security and privacy is also crucial.

It is essential to detect the early signs of an attack, but insider threats may hide their activities. The system aims to prevent step-by-step sabotage activities, even if malicious actions are concealed. However, since some activities may evade detection, countermeasures are also needed for when sabotage activities are successfully executed.

The proposed system would replace contaminated data with backup data. However, replacing only part of the data may cause inconsistency issues with other data. This could potentially affect the overall system operation and data reliability. Additionally, if the extent of the contaminated data is unclear, it can be challenging to implement appropriate replacement procedures. This uncertainty complicates the process of ensuring data integrity. Therefore, further consideration is needed regarding the scope and methods of data replacement.

Due to the page limitation, the formulas used for assessment were written without in-depth analysis. They need to be defined more precisely when implementing our method.

V. CONCLUSION AND FUTURE WORK

In this paper, we propose a countermeasure against insider threat regarding the psychological state of organizational members and the business impact of information resources. The method consists of the member risk assessment, the information resource risk assessment, and the insider threat risk assessment. If a high-risk member operates information resources, we detect the operations and take countermeasures.

Personality traits are innate and cannot be changed. However, other assessment items, such as emotions and human resources, are changeable, and organizations can actively intervene in these areas. For example, through EAP, organizations can address individual issues like dissatisfaction and reduce the risk of insider threats.

Due to varying legal, ethical, and privacy issues in different countries, not all assessment items can be used. Future research should investigate how reducing the number of assessment items affects the accuracy of risk assessment. Additionally, the formulas used for assessment also need clear explanation. The proposed system would replace contaminated data with backup data. However, replacing only parts of the data may cause inconsistency issues. If the extent of contamination is unclear, implementing appropriate replacement procedures is challenging. Therefore, further consideration is needed regarding the scope and methods of data replacement.

REFERENCES

[1] Ponemon Institute, "2022 cost of insider threats global report", [retrieved: September, 2024], 2022, [Online]. Available: https://www.proofpoint.com/us/resources/threat-reports/cost-of-insider-threats.

[2] Harris Poll, "Vormetric insider threat report", [retrieved: September, 2024], 2015, [Online]. Available: https://enterprise-encryption.vormetric.com/rs/vormetric/images/CW_GlobalReport_2015_Insider_threat_Vormetric_Single_Pages_010915.pdf.

[3] E. T. Axelrad, P. J. Sticha, O. Brdiczka, and J. Shen, "A bayesian network model for predictiong insider threats", in *Proceeding of the IEEE symposium on Security and Privacy Workshops*, 2013, pp. 82–89.

[4] M. B. Ahmad, A. Akram, M. Asif, and S. Ur-Rehman, "Using genetic algorithm to minimize false alarms in insider threats detection of information misuse in windows environment", *Mathematical Problems in Engineering*, vol. 2014, pp. 1–12, 2014.

[5] D. M. Cappelli *et al.*, "Management and education of the risk of insider threat(merit): Mitigating the risk of sabotage to employers' information, systems, or network", Carnegie Mellon University Software Engineering Institute, Tech. Rep. no. CMU/SEI-2006-TN-041, 2008, CERT Technical Note.

[6] C. Gates *et al.*, "Detecting insider information theft using features from file access logs", in *Proceedings of the 19th European Symposium on Research in Computer Security*, 2014, pp. 383–400.

[7] F. Toffalini, I. Homoliak, A. Harilal, A. Binder, and M. Ochoa, "Detection of masqueraders based on graph partitioning of file system access events", in *Proceedings of the 39th IEEE Symposium on Security and Privacy Workshops*, 2018, pp. 217–227.

[8] F. L. Greitzer and D. A. Frincke, "Combining traditional cyber security audit data with psychosocial data: Towards predictive modeling for insider threat mitigation", *Insider Threats in Cyber Security. Advances in Information Security*, vol. 49, C. W. Probst, J. Hunker, D. Gollmann, and M. Bishop, Eds., pp. 1–12, 2010.

[9] F. L. Greitzer, L. J. Kangas, C. F. Noonan, A. C. Dalton, and R. E. Hohimer, "Identifying at-risk employees: Modeling psychological precursors of potential insider threat", in *Proceeding of the 45th Hawaii International Conference on System Sciences*, 2012, pp. 2392–2401.

[10] M. Kandias, A. Mylonas, N. Virvilis, M. Theoharidou, and D. Gritzalis, "An insider threat prediction model", in *Proceeding of the International conference on Trust, Privacy and Security in Digital Business*, 2010, pp. 26–37.

[11] M. Kandias, K. Galbogini, L. Mitrou, and D. Gritzalis, "Insiders trapped in the mirror reveal themselves in social media", in *Proceeding of the International conference on Network and System Security*, 2013, pp. 220–235.

[12] M. Kandias, V. Stavrou, N. Bozovic, L. Mitrou, and D. Gritzalis, "Can we trust thie user? Predicting insider's attitude via youtube usage profiling", in *Proceeding of the 10th International conference on Ubiquious Intelligence & Computing and Automatic & Trusted Computing*, 2013, pp. 347–354.

[13] P. J. Taylor *et al.*, "Detecting insider threats through language change", *Law and Human Behavior*, vol. 37, no. 4, pp. 267–275, 2013.

[14] A. P. Moore, D. M. Cappelli, and R. F. Trzeciak, "The "big picture" of insider IT sabotage across US critical insfrastructure", *Insider Attack and Cyber Security, Advances in Information Security*, vol. 39, S. J. Stolfo *et al.*, Eds., 2008.

[15] A. Cummings, T. Lewellen, D. McIntire, A. P. Moore, and R. Trzeciak, "Insider threat study: Illicit cyber activity involving fraud in the US financial services sector", Carnegie Mellon University Software Engineering Institute, Tech. Rep. no. CMU/SEI-2012-SR-004, 2012, CERT Special Report.

[16] I. Homoliak, F. Toffalini, J. Guarnizo, Y. Elovici, and M. Ochoa, "Insight into insiders and IT: A survey of insider threat taxonomoies, analysis, modeling, and countermeasure", *ACM Computing Surveys*, vol. 52, no. 2, pp. 1–40, 2019.

[17] M. Brown, "A global guide to background checks", [retrieved: September, 2024], 2015, [Online]. Available: https://www.mayerbrown.com/files/uploads/Documents/PDFs/Employment/A-Global-Guide-Background-Checks.pdf.

[18] T. A. Judge and J. E. Bono, "Five-factor model of personality and transformational leadership", *Journal of Applied Psychology*, vol. 85, no. 5, pp. 751–765, 2000.

[19] A. K. Kirk and D. F. Brown, "Assistance programs: A review of the management of stress and wellbeing through workplace counselling and consulting", *Australian Psychologist*, vol. 38, no. 2, pp. 138–143, 2000.

[20] S. G. Kassa, "It asset valuation, risk assessment and control implementation model", *ISAKA Journal*, vol. 3, 2017.

[21] F. L. Greitzer, "Insider threats: It's the human, stupid!", in *Proceeding of the Northwest Cybersecurity Symposium*, 2019, pp. 1–8.

Addressing Malware Family Concept Drift with Triplet Autoencoder

Numan Halit Guldemir
Centre for Secure Information Technologies
Queen's University Belfast
United Kingdom
nguldemir01@qub.ac.uk

Oluwafemi Olukoya
Centre for Secure Information Technologies
Queen's University Belfast
United Kingdom
o.olukoya@qub.ac.uk

Jesús Martínez-del-Rincón
Centre for Secure Information Technologies
Queen's University Belfast
United Kingdom
j.martinez-del-rincon@qub.ac.uk

***Abstract*—Machine learning is increasingly vital in cybersecurity, especially in malware detection. However, concept drift —where the characteristics of malware change over time— poses a challenge for maintaining the efficacy of these detection systems. Concept drift can occur in two forms: the emergence of entirely new malware families and the evolution of existing ones. This paper proposes an innovative method to address the former, focusing on effectively identifying new malware families. Our approach leverages a supervised autoencoder combined with triplet loss to differentiate between known and new malware families. We create clear and robust clusters that enhance the accuracy and resilience of malware family classification by utilizing this metric learning technique and the Density-Based Spatial Clustering of Applications with Noise (DBSCAN) algorithm. The effectiveness of our method is validated using an Android malware dataset and a Windows Portable Executable (PE) malware dataset, showcasing its capability to sustain model performance within the dynamic landscape of emerging malware threats. Our results demonstrate a significant improvement in detecting new malware families, offering a reliable solution for ongoing cybersecurity challenges.**

Keywords*-*Concept drift; Windows PE malware; temporal analysis; triplet loss; autoencoder; metric learning.

I. Introduction

Machine learning has become a key tool in cybersecurity, particularly for detecting malware. These systems, when well-trained, are highly effective at identifying threats. However, the effectiveness of these systems is continually challenged by the dynamic nature of malware. As cyber threats rapidly evolve, machine learning models that were once effective can quickly become obsolete — a phenomenon known as concept drift [1]. Concept drift in malware detection is often driven by two major factors: developing entirely new malware and modifying existing malware to evade detection systems. A report by AV-Test indicates approximately 320,000 new malware samples emerge daily, underscoring the need for continuous model adaptation to unseen threats [2].

Retraining models frequently is one common strategy to fight against concept drift, but it has problems. Firstly, in cybersecurity, accurately labeling data is essential but costly, as it often requires experts to examine and classify new threats [3]. Moreover, determining the precise timing for updating or retraining a model is not straightforward [4]. Frequently retrained models might fail to keep up with the latest malware without a reliable method to decide when updates are necessary, resulting in security gaps.

Labeling unknown samples is crucial to ensure that the model does not misclassify them and can be accurately analyzed by experts. Machine learning models typically generate a probability distribution over the known class labels, always selecting the most likely class. Ideally, for an unknown input, all classes should exhibit low probabilities, and setting a threshold based on uncertainty should reject these unknown classes. However, recent studies have shown that even inputs far from any known class can produce high probability/confidence scores [5]. This leads to misleadingly high confidence scores even when the model's predictions are incorrect. Neural networks, in particular, tend to produce overly confident predictions in such scenarios, creating a false sense of reliability [6].

This paper addresses the challenges associated with concept drift in malware family detection by proposing a novel neural architecture and training paradigm tailored to this issue. It is important to clarify that this work focuses solely on analyzing and differentiating between malware samples. Thus, we assume that all input samples are malware, and the goal is to identify and address variations within malware families rather than distinguishing between malicious and benign software. To achieve this, we leverage metric learning to map input samples to their respective families based on their proximity to the centroids of known classes. This method enhances the model's generalization ability by constructing a feature space that accurately reflects the similarities and differences between samples. Additionally, we incorporate triplet loss to refine this feature space further, forming distinct, compact clusters that improve the accuracy of assignments. This approach ensures that samples from the same family are closely grouped, while those from different families are pushed apart. Importantly, our work specifically addresses concept drift in detecting new, unknown malware families, rather than focusing on the evolution of existing malware families. This distinction is critical because a related, yet underexplored, aspect of concept drift involves the automated detection of emerging malware families for multi-class classification purposes. While existing approaches may employ drift signaling techniques to determine when to retrain binary classification models, the automatic identification of new malware families —those that significantly deviate from historical data— poses a more intriguing challenge [7].

Our experiments demonstrate the effectiveness of the proposed approach in detecting newly emerging malware families, offering valuable insights into maintaining robust defense mechanisms against rapidly evolving cyber threats. The results show a significant improvement in detection performance for new malware, providing a reliable and adaptive solution to keep pace with the dynamic landscape of cyber threats.

The main contributions of this paper are as follows:

- We present a method that leverages metric learning and DBSCAN for family clustering to address concept drift in malware analysis.
- We propose a neural network architecture that utilizes an autoencoder and triplet loss for robust malware family detection.
- We extensively evaluate our approach using two relevant benchmark datasets for Android and Windows PE malware detection, as commonly used in the literature.

The rest of the paper is organized as follows: Section II covers related work, discussing existing approaches in malware detection, metric learning, and concept drift. Section III explains our proposed method, detailing how we effectively utilize an autoencoder with triplet loss to differentiate between known and new malware families. Section IV details the datasets we used and the experimental setup. Section V presents our experiments' results and evaluates our approach's effectiveness. Section VI discusses the limitations of our study, highlighting potential areas for improvement. Finally, Section VII concludes the paper and discusses potential future work.

II. RELATED WORK

A. Machine Learning in Malware Detection

Numerous studies have leveraged machine learning techniques to enhance the detection of malware and its various families by utilizing a range of features. These include static features, which are extracted from the malware without executing it to reveal the underlying code structure, such as Application Programming Interface (API) function calls [8][9], bytes [10][11] and opcodes [12]–[14]. Additionally, some research has focused on using a set of these static features [15]–[17]. Dynamic features, on the other hand, capture the behavior of malware during its execution and include data, such as API call traces [18][19], instruction traces [20], and network traffic [21]. Some studies have furthered this approach by converting these inputs into visual formats, aiding in recognizing malicious patterns [8][22]. Machine learning thus plays a crucial role in strengthening cybersecurity measures against diverse threats.

B. Metric Learning

Recent advancements in metric learning have demonstrated their efficacy in learning high-quality data representations for tasks involving object differentiation and semantic similarity across various fields, such as computer vision [23]–[25], audio processing [26]–[28], and bioinformatics [29][30]. Metric learning has also garnered significant attention from security researchers due to its potential to enhance malware detection capabilities. Wu *et al.* [31] introduce IFDroid, a system that leverages contrastive learning to enhance the robustness and accuracy of Android malware family classification. IFDroid trains an encoder to extract features resilient to code obfuscation by converting function call graphs into images. Similarly, Jureček and Lórencz [32] employ Particle Swarm Optimization to optimize feature weights for a weighted Euclidean distance metric, improving the accuracy of k-Nearest Neighbors (k-NN) classification. Building on these concepts, Liu *et al.* [33] model the execution behavior of malware as heterogeneous graphs, capturing interactions between entities, such as APIs, processes, and files. This approach uses data augmentations and graph attention networks to generate robust positive and negative samples, enabling effective few-shot detection of malware variants without extensive labeled data. Andresini *et al.* [34] present a method for network intrusion detection that combines autoencoders and triplet networks to improve predictive accuracy by addressing data imbalance and enhancing the separation of normal and malicious network traffic.

C. Concept Drift

In recent years, various approaches have been proposed to address concept drift in different domains, particularly in malware and intrusion detection systems. Singh *et al.* [35] explored concept drift in malware detection by introducing new tracking methods and examining different types of malware evolution. Building on this, Jordaney *et al.* [4] developed the TRANSCEND framework, which identifies concept drift in classification models through statistical metrics and a conformal evaluator to assess model credibility and confidence. The framework was further refined in TRANSCENDENT [36], which formalized the theoretical foundation of conformal evaluation and introduced new evaluators to enhance robustness. Additionally, CADE [37] employed contrastive learning to detect outliers and explain concept drift by mapping data samples into a low-dimensional space. In the realm of intrusion detection, Andresini *et al.* [38] proposed the INSOMNIA framework, which integrates incremental, active, and transfer learning to adapt to non-uniform data distribution over time, thus maintaining the efficacy of intrusion detection models through continuous updates and active learning strategies. Moreover, Zola *et al.* [39] conducted a temporal analysis of distribution shifts in malware classification, proposing a three-step forensic exploration approach to understand model failures caused by concept drift. These diverse methodologies highlight the evolving landscape of concept drift management in cybersecurity applications.

Many approaches do not adequately consider the issue of concept drift, which can lead to a decline in detection accuracy over time [8][13][31]. Additionally, some methods overlook the complexity of dealing with multiple clusters within a single malware family and fail to address the presence of outliers effectively [4][37]. These gaps highlight the need for more robust and adaptive solutions in malware family detection.

III. METHOD

Our method enhances the robustness and performance of detection models through a structured approach to address the challenges posed by concept drift in malware family classification. Initially, high-dimensional feature vectors are extracted from the malware samples. These vectors are then processed using an autoencoder, trained with triplet loss to reduce dimensionality while ensuring that similar points are closer together and dissimilar points are further apart in the latent space. Subsequently, clustering in the latent space using the DBSCAN algorithm is performed to identify sub-clusters within malware families and exclude outliers. Finally, centroids of these clusters are calculated to determine the classification of new samples based on their proximity to the closest centroid, compared against a pre-calculated threshold for cluster membership. The high-level process of the method is illustrated in Figure 1. This section outlines the approach and techniques we employed to maintain reliable classification performance in the face of the constantly evolving nature of malware.

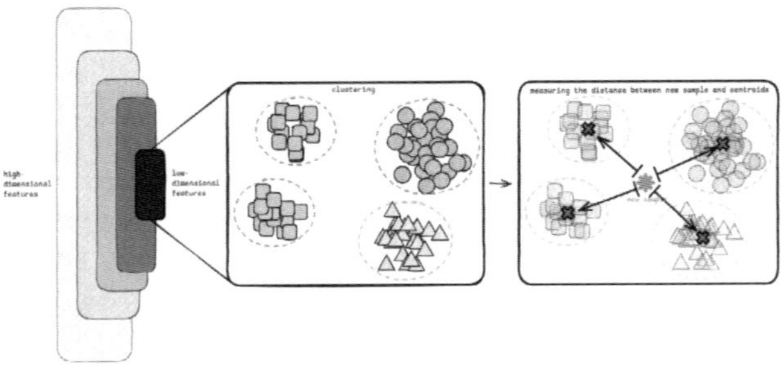

Figure 1. An overview of the method.

We employ metric learning, a machine learning approach that focuses on defining a distance metric between data points to transform the data space. This method aims to bring similar points closer together while pushing dissimilar points further apart [40]. In our implementation, we utilize triplet loss, which simultaneously considers pairs of similar and dissimilar points, enhancing the model's capability to learn meaningful representations. Triplet loss operates by using triplets of data points: an anchor, a positive sample that is similar to the anchor, and a negative sample that is dissimilar [23]. The objective is to ensure that the distance between the anchor and the positive sample is smaller than the distance between the anchor and the negative sample by at least a specified margin. This margin enforces a separation between similar and dissimilar pairs, driving the model to learn a more discriminative feature space. Additionally, working with high-dimensional feature vectors introduces the challenge of the curse of dimensionality. In high-dimensional spaces, distances between data points become less informative, complicating the task of distinguishing between different classes [41]. To overcome this, we incorporated an autoencoder to reduce the dimensionality of the data, thereby mitigating the effects of the curse of dimensionality and making distance measures more reliable. The autoencoder compresses the high-dimensional data into a lower-dimensional latent space, preserving the most critical features while discarding redundant information. This compression not only enhances the efficiency of distance computations but also helps in capturing the underlying structure of the data, making it easier to identify and distinguish between different classes.

After samples are projected into the latent space, samples from the same malware family are grouped, facilitating easier classification. However, since our goal is to analyze new malware families, a more fine-grained analysis is required. To achieve this, clustering in the latent space is used to group samples belonging to subgroups of the same malware families. This approach allows us to project new samples during testing and not only classify them as belonging to an existing or new family but also measure their deviation from existing families. Building on this foundation, we employed the DBSCAN [42] clustering algorithm to identify multiple clusters within each class in the latent space obtained from the bottleneck of the autoencoder. Although we know the number of classes from the training data, DBSCAN helps us identify sub-clusters within these classes, which is crucial since a single class can contain multiple distinct clusters.

Ignoring these sub-clusters can result in misleadingly large distances between data points and their centroids. By employing DBSCAN, we can accurately detect these sub-clusters, leading to precise centroid calculations. This clustering process allows us to determine whether a new sample fits within existing classes or should be considered a new malware family or variant, pending expert verification. Additionally, DBSCAN effectively handles outliers, ensuring that anomalies do not distort the centroid calculations.

To further refine our classification approach, we calculate the centroids of each cluster. Given that we use the DBSCAN algorithm, which does not include every point in a cluster and filters out outliers, we compute the centroids more accurately. The centroids are calculated by taking the mean of the data points within each cluster. This method benefits from DBSCAN's ability to handle outliers effectively, ensuring that these outliers do not distort the centroid calculations.

Once the clusters and their centroids are established, we determine whether a new sample belongs to an existing family by locating the closest centroid in the latent space and noting the family to which this centroid belongs. The distance between the new sample and the closest centroid is then calculated and compared with a pre-calculated threshold for the identified family. Each family's threshold is determined by the distance from the centroid to the furthest point within the cluster (excluding outliers). This threshold acts as a boundary to decide cluster membership. If the calculated distance for the new sample is less than or equal to the threshold, the sample is classified as belonging to that family. Otherwise, it is considered as not belonging to any existing family and may be flagged as a potential new family or variant.

The threshold for each family is calculated during the clustering process with DBSCAN. For each cluster, the threshold is defined as the distance from the centroid to the furthest point within the cluster. This is feasible because DBSCAN effectively excludes outliers, ensuring that the threshold represents the maximum distance within the core points of the cluster.

By employing DBSCAN and centroid calculation, our method can accurately determine whether a new sample fits within existing classes or should be considered a new malware family or variant, pending expert verification. This approach not only enhances detection performance but also provides a reliable mechanism to handle the dynamic nature of malware, maintaining the model's robustness over time.

Impact of triplet loss

The triplet loss function is a powerful technique used in machine learning to enhance the discriminative ability of models [23]. It operates by optimizing the distance between samples in such a way that similar samples (belonging to the same class) are brought closer together, while dissimilar samples (belonging to different classes) are pushed farther apart.

Given an anchor sample x_a, a positive sample x_p of the same class, and a negative sample x_n of a different class, the triplet loss function aims to ensure that the distance between the anchor and positive samples is less than the distance between the anchor and negative samples by at least a margin α. The triplet loss function L can be defined as:

$$L(x_a, x_p, x_n) = \max\{0, D(x_a, x_p) - D(x_a, x_n) + \alpha\} \quad (1)$$

where:

$$D(x_i, x_j) = \|f(x_i) - f(x_j)\|^2 \quad (2)$$

represents the squared Euclidean distance between the embedding vectors of two samples, produced by the embedding function f. The margin α defines the desired separation between positive and negative pairs.

In practice, the loss is computed over a batch of triplets, an anchor input (input pair), a positive input (similar pair), and a negative input (dissimilar pair), and the objective is to minimize the total loss across the batch. In triplet loss, a margin enforces a distinct separation, where distances smaller than the margin do not contribute to the loss function. Assuming we have a set of triplets $\{(x_{a_i}, x_{p_i}, x_{n_i})\}_{i=1}^{N}$, the overall triplet loss can be defined as:

$$L_{\text{batch}} = \frac{1}{N}\sum_{i=1}^{N} L(x_{a_i}, x_{p_i}, x_{n_i}) \quad (3)$$

This formulation forces the network to learn an embedding space where positive pairs (anchor and positive samples) are closer than negative pairs (anchor and negative samples), with a margin α separating them.

Impact of DBSCAN

Selecting an appropriate clustering algorithm is crucial for accurate identification and analysis. Popular clustering methods like K-means were not suitable for our needs due to several reasons. Firstly, K-means require the number of clusters to be specified beforehand, which is challenging in our scenario because the number of clusters is unknown and can vary significantly. A single class could potentially have multiple clusters due to intraclass variants. Secondly, K-means tries to include all data points in a cluster, which is not ideal for real-world data where outliers, such as incorrectly labeled data or genuine anomalies, are present. These outliers can distort the clustering results and reduce the overall accuracy. Additionally, K-means assumes that clusters are spherical and equally sized, which is rarely the case in malware datasets [43]. Malware families can exhibit diverse and complex structures that do not fit the spherical assumption.

Given these limitations, we considered DBSCAN [44] as a potential solution. DBSCAN is effective in identifying clusters of arbitrary shapes and sizes and is robust in detecting outliers. It operates on the principle that regions of high data density are separated by regions of low density. DBSCAN requires two parameters: epsilon ε, which defines the radius for neighborhood search, and minPts, the minimum number of points required to form a dense region. The challenge with DBSCAN lies in setting these parameters correctly, especially for datasets with varying densities. To address this, we employed several heuristics and techniques discussed in the literature. Firstly, we set the minPts parameter based on the dimensionality of the data. A common heuristic is to set minPts to twice the number of dimensions, i.e., $minPts = 2\times dim$ [42]. Choosing the appropriate value for ε is more challenging. One effective method is to use the k-distance plot, where we plot the distance to the k-th nearest neighbor for each point in the dataset. A sharp bend in this plot, known as the "knee" or "elbow," often indicates a good choice for ε. In practice, the value of ε should be chosen as small as possible to capture the most relevant clusters without merging distinct ones.

In our case, there is another advantage of using DBSCAN. One crucial parameter to decide is the distance threshold metric, which helps us determine whether samples exceed or fall within the distance threshold. We utilized the DBSCAN algorithm to establish this distance threshold. The DBSCAN algorithm identifies clusters in the provided data, finding one or multiple clusters if they exist. Importantly, it does not force every point into a cluster; instead, it marks points that do not belong to any cluster as noise or outliers. This feature is advantageous for determining a robust threshold that accounts for outliers. We set the highest distance between a point and a centroid within a cluster as the threshold.

To demonstrate the effectiveness of DBSCAN, we present Figure 2 where multiple clusters within a single class are shown. Specifically, using DBSCAN, we detected two clusters in one of the classes, FakeInstaller. This approach decreased the mean distance between a sample and its centroid by

26%, from 1.46 to 1.07. This significant reduction in mean distance highlights the effectiveness of DBSCAN in accurately separating clusters within a class, ultimately improving the clustering performance.

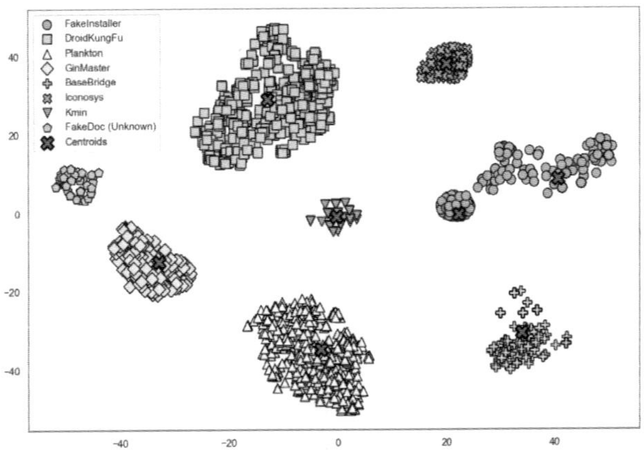

Figure 2. Clustering results using DBSCAN algorithm.

IV. Dataset and Setup

A. Drebin dataset

We utilized the Drebin dataset, an Android malware dataset containing 5,560 malware samples and 123,453 benign applications compiled between August 2010 and October 2012 [15]. Drebin extracts features from the Android Manifest file, such as hardware components, requested permissions, app components, and filtered intents, as well as features from the app's disassembled code, including restricted API calls, used permissions, suspicious API calls, and network addresses.

For our analysis, we selected families with a minimum of 100 malware samples, reducing the dataset to 8 families and a total of 3,317 samples (Table I). We followed a previous study's strategy of splitting the dataset into training and testing sets using an 80:20 ratio, based on the malware creation timestamps [37]. This temporal split ensures that our evaluation reflects real-world scenarios, where models encounter newer malware after being trained on older data, thus providing a robust evaluation against established benchmarks.

TABLE I. Sample Distribution of Drebin Dataset.

Family	Number of Samples
FakeInstaller	925
DroidKungFu	667
Plankton	625
GingerMaster	339
BaseBridge	330
Iconosys	152
Kmin	147
FakeDoc	132

B. BODMAS dataset

We utilized the BODMAS dataset, originally consisting of 57,293 malware samples and 77,142 benign samples, for a total of 134,435 samples [17]. Each sample is represented by a 2,381-dimensional feature vector, extracted through static analysis. These feature vectors include elements such as general file information (file size, imported/exported functions, and section data like relocations, resources, and signatures), header information (machine type, subsystem, and image versions), imported and exported functions, and section information (section names, entropy, and virtual size). Additionally, byte histograms, byte entropy histograms, and string information (e.g., URLs, registry keys, and string entropy) are included to capture statistical properties. The dataset also records timestamp metadata, indicating when each sample was first seen on VirusTotal.

In our preprocessing, we performed several preprocessing steps to refine the subset used in our analysis. We excluded packed malware samples, as packers encrypt and compress the code, making it difficult to carry out accurate drift detection [35][39][45]. Additionally, we focused only on malware families with more than 1,500 samples, resulting in the inclusion of seven families for our study (Table II).

We split the dataset into training and testing sets in an 80:20 ratio based on the first-seen timestamps to simulate real-world settings and evaluate the model's performance under more realistic conditions. The training data consists of samples from August 2019 to July 2020, while the testing data includes samples from July 2020 to September 2020. This temporal split helps minimize experimental bias and aligns with recommendations from previous work [3].

TABLE II. Sample Distribution of BODMAS Dataset.

Family	Number of Samples
berbew	1741
dinwod	1942
ganelp	1413
mira	1526
sfone	3218
sillyp2p	3012
small	3606

C. Experimental Setup

To evaluate the robustness and accuracy of our proposed method, we designed a comprehensive experimental setup involving preprocessing, model training, and validation stages. This section outlines the procedures and configurations employed to ensure the credibility and reproducibility of our results. The experiments were conducted on two prominent malware datasets, Drebin and BODMAS, each requiring tailored preprocessing steps to handle their specific characteristics.

We began by implementing a variance threshold to filter out features with low variance in both datasets. Data was then split into training and testing sets based on timestamps, utilizing the malware creation time for Drebin and the first-seen date (based

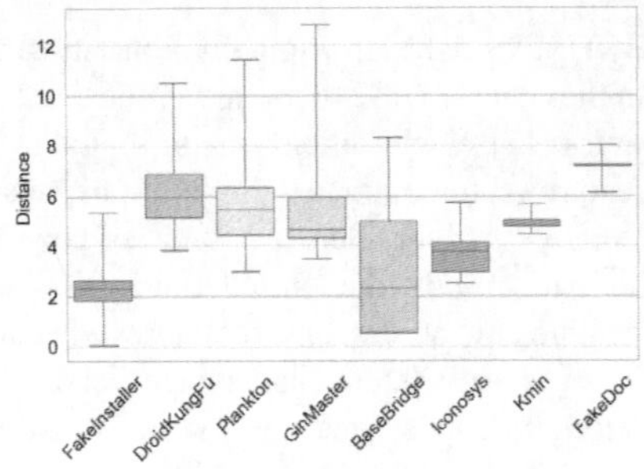

(a) Original feature space.

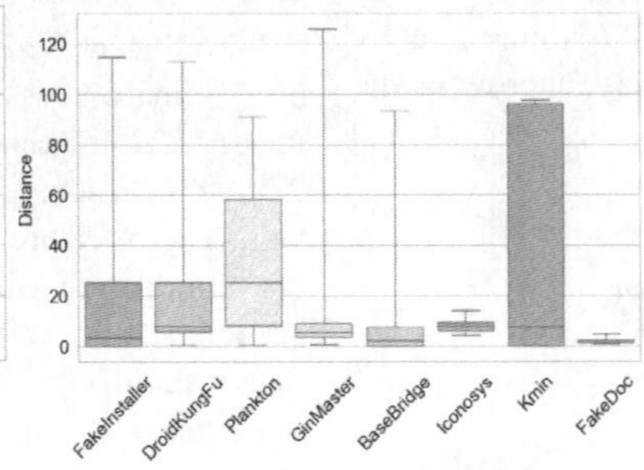

(b) Vanilla AE feature space.

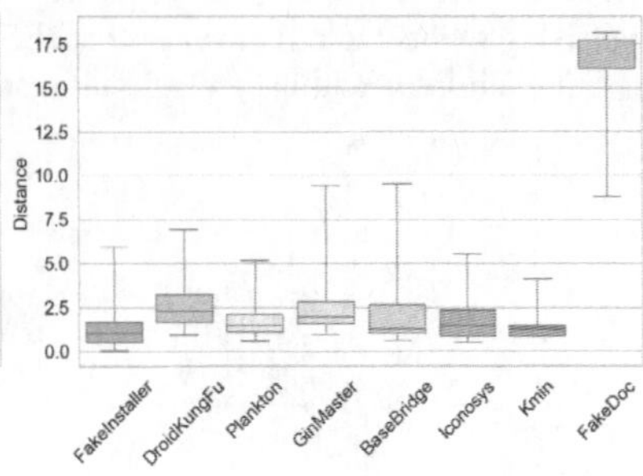

(c) Triplet autoencoder feature space.

Figure 3. Boxplot diagrams showing the distances between samples and their family centroids for three feature representations: original features, vanilla autoencoder features, and triplet autoencoder features.

on VirusTotal) for BODMAS, ensuring a temporal allocation. The Drebin dataset was modeled using neural network layers consisting of 1376 input neurons, followed by 1024, 256, and 32 neurons. The BODMAS dataset's model architecture included layers with 2381, 1024, 256, and 32 neurons. For training, the vanilla autoencoder utilized mean squared error as its loss function, whereas the triplet autoencoder employed a combination of triplet loss and reconstruction loss. Triplets were selected by including one sample from a random class, one sample from the same class, and one from a different class.

To validate our model's performance, we used an 80:20 split for both datasets, with the training set comprising older samples and the testing set consisting of more recent samples. This temporal split simulates real-world scenarios where models are deployed and subsequently encounter new malware.

In our experiments, we simulate the presence of drifting samples by systematically excluding one malware family from the training data in each iteration. For example, if we exclude the FakeInstaller family, the remaining families are used to train the model, and during testing, the previously excluded family (e.g., FakeInstaller) is reintroduced alongside the test sets of the other families. This approach creates a scenario where the model encounters 'unknown' or 'drifting' families, allowing us to evaluate its ability to manage concept drift. This technique aligns with approaches used in previous studies [4][37]. Although this method effectively labels drifted samples (since they are excluded from training), it has a limitation: newer samples from known families in the test set might exhibit drift or initiate drifting, but without specific labels to denote this finer level of drift, they will not be classified as such.

V. EVALUATION

A. Experiment on Android malware dataset (Drebin)

In Figure 3, we present the distance boxplot diagrams of the distance between every sample and its family centroid for three different feature representations: the original features (1376-dimensional features), the vanilla autoencoder (32-dimensional features), and the triplet autoencoder (32-dimensional features). We observe that the distances from centroids are significantly smaller by comparing the original feature space to the triplet autoencoder feature space. This indicates that the samples of the same class are more tightly clustered and closer to each other in the triplet autoencoder feature space.

When comparing the vanilla autoencoder to the triplet autoencoder, we also find that the distances in the triplet autoencoder are more compact. Additionally, we conducted an experiment where one class was designated as an unknown class by excluding any samples from that class during the training phase for both the vanilla autoencoder and the triplet autoencoder. This setup allows us to test the models' ability to handle out-of-distribution samples.

The results show that the distances between the unknown class samples and the closest centroid are much larger, indicating that the unknown class is effectively separated from the known classes. This separation suggests that the triplet autoencoder successfully differentiates between known and unknown classes, enhancing its robustness to data drift and unseen samples.

To further illustrate the separation of classes, we also provide t-distributed Stochastic Neighbor Embedding (t-SNE) graphs of the same data used to generate the boxplots in Figure 4. These t-SNE visualizations offer a clearer picture of how the different feature representations perform in terms of clustering [46]. By comparing the t-SNE plots of the vanilla autoencoder and the triplet autoencoder, it becomes evident that the clusters in the triplet autoencoder are more distinct and tightly packed. This demonstrates the superior capability of the triplet autoencoder in creating a well-defined and separated feature space.

Table III provides comprehensive details about our experiments. The first two columns list the labels of the malware families, along with the family names that were excluded from the training set and reserved solely for testing. The table also presents the F1 scores, which measure the performance of the models in terms of both precision and recall. Three methods are compared in our evaluation, CADE [37], triplet autoencoder with Median Absolute Deviation (MAD) threshold, and

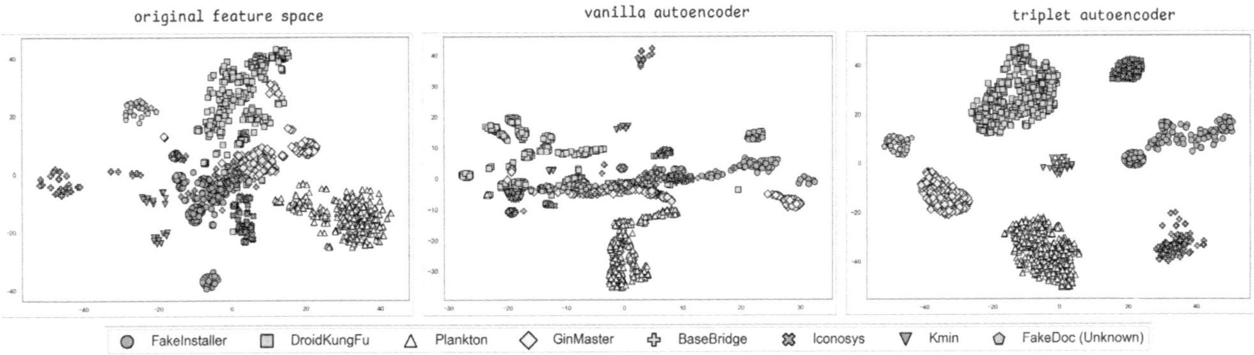

Figure 4. t-SNE diagrams of original features space, vanilla autoencoder and triplet autoencoder.

our proposed approach. MAD, calculated using the formula $MAD = median(|X_i - median(X)|)$, serves as a measure of statistical dispersion, and is used to determine the distance threshold. Including MAD allows us to compare the performance of the threshold using DBSCAN. Since the training model structure is the same for both the MAD and DBSCAN-based methods —both using the triplet autoencoder— the only difference lies in how the threshold is determined to decide whether each sample belongs to existing families. The results in the table demonstrate that the DBSCAN-based method consistently outperforms MAD method in terms of the overall F1 score. Even though in some cases MAD's performance is closer to that of DBSCAN, it is important to note that MAD requires a coefficient determined empirically. In contrast, DBSCAN calculates the threshold automatically without requiring a manual coefficient. When comparing CADE, which uses contrastive loss and MAD threshold, and our method, which employs triplet loss along with the DBSCAN threshold, our method demonstrates superior performance overall.

B. Experiment on Windows PE malware dataset (BODMAS)

We also used the BODMAS dataset to measure the performance of our method. This dataset brings two different advantages: it is a more recent dataset, and it is a Windows PE dataset, representing a different operating system, which helps us measure the generalizability of our method.

The results, summarized in Table IV, show that our method performs well on the Windows PE malware dataset. This performance demonstrates the robustness and generalizability of our method across different types of malware and operating systems. By using the BODMAS dataset, we validated that our approach is not limited to a specific type of malware or operating system but can be effectively applied to various scenarios. This enhances the overall reliability and applicability of our malware detection method, providing a practical and robust solution for cybersecurity challenges across different platforms.

VI. Limitations

While our study provides valuable insights, it is important to acknowledge several limitations. Our analysis considers only one family as the unknown family. However, in real-world scenarios, there can be multiple unknown families, which could affect the clustering results and the interpretation of the data. Moreover, although we automatically determined the parameters of the DBSCAN algorithm based on the method outlined in [42], parameters, such as ε and the minimum number of points (minPts) could be further fine-tuned depending on the specific context and dataset characteristics. Fine-tuning these parameters might lead to more accurate and meaningful clustering results. Additionally, our study did not include any packed samples because the encryption and compression of code by packers make accurate drift detection challenging.

VII. Conclusion and Future Work

This paper presents an approach to addressing concept drift in malware family detection, specifically focusing on the emergence of new malware families. Our method effectively differentiates between known and new malware families by leveraging a triplet autoencoder and the DBSCAN clustering algorithm. We validated our method using two prominent datasets, Drebin and BODMAS, representing Android and Windows PE malware. The results demonstrate that our approach significantly improves the detection performance for new malware families. This robust and reliable solution addresses the dynamic nature of cyber threats, ensuring that detection models remain effective over time. Our contributions include applying metric learning and clustering techniques to improve malware family classification in the face of concept drift, providing a practical framework for ongoing cybersecurity efforts.

Moving forward, we aim to explore retraining strategies to adapt our model to evolving malware behaviors more effectively. This will involve identifying the features and factors contributing to malware drift, allowing us to understand the dynamics of malware evolution better. By incorporating these insights, we aim to develop more robust detection mechanisms to maintain high performance even as malware tactics change.

Acknowledgments

Numan Halit Guldemir is supported by the Republic of Türkiye Ministry of National Education (MoNE-1416/YLSY).

TABLE III. PERFORMANCE OF THE MODELS. THE FAMILY COLUMN INDICATES WHICH MALWARE FAMILY WAS EXCLUDED FROM TRAINING AND KEPT FOR TESTING TO SIMULATE DRIFTING SAMPLES.

Family	No. of known samples	No. of unknown samples	F1 score CADE [37]	F1 score MAD	F1 score DBSCAN
FakeInstaller	478	925	0.86	0.95	**0.95**
DroidKungFu	529	667	0.87	0.89	**0.90**
Plankton	538	625	0.77	0.90	**0.87**
GinMaster	595	339	0.63	0.84	**0.85**
BaseBridge	597	330	0.59	0.97	**0.98**
Iconosys	632	152	0.42	0.46	**0.65**
Kmin	633	147	0.40	0.63	**0.62**
FakeDoc	636	132	0.38	0.56	**0.66**
Overall	**4638**	**3317**	**0.62**	**0.78**	**0.81**

TABLE IV. PERFORMANCE OF THE MODELS. THE FAMILY COLUMN INDICATES WHICH MALWARE FAMILY WAS EXCLUDED FROM TRAINING AND KEPT FOR TESTING TO SIMULATE DRIFTING SAMPLES.

Family	No. of known samples	No. of unknown samples	F1 score
berbew	2817	1741	0.99
dinwod	2634	1942	0.96
ganelp	2636	1413	0.97
mira	2470	1526	0.58
sfone	2231	3218	0.51
sillyp2p	2737	3012	0.83
small	1473	3606	0.96

REFERENCES

[1] J. Lu, A. Liu, F. Dong, F. Gu, J. Gama, and G. Zhang, "Learning under concept drift: A review," *IEEE transactions on knowledge and data engineering*, vol. 31, no. 12, pp. 2346–2363, 2018.

[2] AV-Test, "Malware statistics & trends report," Accessed: 14 July 2024, 2023, [Online]. Available: https://www.av-test.org/en/statistics/malware/.

[3] F. Pendlebury, F. Pierazzi, R. Jordaney, J. Kinder, and L. Cavallaro, "Tesseract: Eliminating experimental bias in malware classification across space and time," in *28th USENIX security symposium (USENIX Security 19)*, 2019, pp. 729–746.

[4] R. Jordaney *et al.*, "Transcend: Detecting concept drift in malware classification models," in *26th USENIX security symposium (USENIX security 17)*, 2017, pp. 625–642.

[5] A. Bendale and T. E. Boult, "Towards open set deep networks," in *Proceedings of the IEEE conference on computer vision and pattern recognition*, 2016, pp. 1563–1572.

[6] K. Lee, K. Lee, H. Lee, and J. Shin, "A simple unified framework for detecting out-of-distribution samples and adversarial attacks," *Advances in neural information processing systems*, vol. 31, 2018.

[7] A. Guerra-Manzanares, "Android malware detection: Mission accomplished? a review of open challenges and future perspectives," *Computers & Security*, p. 103 654, 2023.

[8] M. Ahmadi, D. Ulyanov, S. Semenov, M. Trofimov, and G. Giacinto, "Novel feature extraction, selection and fusion for effective malware family classification," in *Proceedings of the sixth ACM conference on data and application security and privacy*, 2016, pp. 183–194.

[9] A. Sami, B. Yadegari, H. Rahimi, N. Peiravian, S. Hashemi, and A. Hamze, "Malware detection based on mining api calls," in *Proceedings of the 2010 ACM symposium on applied computing*, 2010, pp. 1020–1025.

[10] S. Jain and Y. K. Meena, "Byte level n–gram analysis for malware detection," in *Computer Networks and Intelligent Computing: 5th International Conference on Information Processing, ICIP 2011, Bangalore, India, August 5-7, 2011. Proceedings*, Springer, 2011, pp. 51–59.

[11] Z. Fuyong and Z. Tiezhu, "Malware detection and classification based on n-grams attribute similarity," in *2017 IEEE international conference on computational science and engineering (CSE) and IEEE international conference on embedded and ubiquitous computing (EUC)*, IEEE, vol. 1, 2017, pp. 793–796.

[12] N. McLaughlin *et al.*, "Deep android malware detection," in *Proceedings of the seventh ACM on conference on data and application security and privacy*, 2017, pp. 301–308.

[13] A. G. Kakisim, S. Gulmez, and I. Sogukpinar, "Sequential opcode embedding-based malware detection method," *Computers & Electrical Engineering*, vol. 98, p. 107 703, 2022.

[14] D. Yuxin and Z. Siyi, "Malware detection based on deep learning algorithm," *Neural Computing and Applications*, vol. 31, pp. 461–472, 2019.

[15] D. Arp, M. Spreitzenbarth, M. Hubner, H. Gascon, K. Rieck, and C. Siemens, "Drebin: Effective and explainable detection of android malware in your pocket.," in *Ndss*, vol. 14, 2014, pp. 23–26.

[16] H. S. Anderson and P. Roth, "Ember: An open dataset for training static pe malware machine learning models," *arXiv preprint arXiv:1804.04637*, 2018.

[17] L. Yang, A. Ciptadi, I. Laziuk, A. Ahmadzadeh, and G. Wang, "Bodmas: An open dataset for learning based temporal analysis of pe malware," in *2021 IEEE Security and Privacy Workshops (SPW)*, IEEE, 2021, pp. 78–84.

[18] Z. Salehi, A. Sami, and M. Ghiasi, "Maar: Robust features to detect malicious activity based on api calls, their arguments and return values," *Engineering Applications of Artificial Intelligence*, vol. 59, pp. 93–102, 2017.

[19] D. Uppal, R. Sinha, V. Mehra, and V. Jain, "Malware detection and classification based on extraction of api sequences," in *2014 International conference on advances in computing, communications and informatics (ICACCI)*, IEEE, 2014, pp. 2337–2342.

[20] P. O'kane, S. Sezer, and K. McLaughlin, "Detecting obfuscated malware using reduced opcode set and optimised runtime trace," *Security Informatics*, vol. 5, pp. 1–12, 2016.

[21] A. Boukhtouta, S. A. Mokhov, N.-E. Lakhdari, M. Debbabi, and J. Paquet, "Network malware classification comparison using dpi and flow packet headers," *Journal of Computer Virology and Hacking Techniques*, vol. 12, pp. 69–100, 2016.

[22] E. Rezende, G. Ruppert, T. Carvalho, F. Ramos, and P. De Geus, "Malicious software classification using transfer learning of resnet-50 deep neural network," in *2017 16th IEEE international conference on machine learning and applications (ICMLA)*, IEEE, 2017, pp. 1011–1014.

[23] A. Hermans, L. Beyer, and B. Leibe, "In defense of the triplet loss for person re-identification," *arXiv preprint arXiv:1703.07737*, 2017.

[24] X. Dong and J. Shen, "Triplet loss in siamese network for object tracking," in *Proceedings of the European conference on computer vision (ECCV)*, 2018, pp. 459–474.

[25] B. McCartney, B. Devereux, and J. Martinez-del-Rincon, "A zero-shot deep metric learning approach to brain–computer interfaces for image retrieval," *Knowledge-Based Systems*, vol. 246, p. 108 556, 2022.

[26] A. v. d. Oord, Y. Li, and O. Vinyals, "Representation learning with contrastive predictive coding," *arXiv preprint arXiv:1807.03748*, 2018.

[27] E. Ghaleb, M. Popa, and S. Asteriadis, "Metric learning-based multimodal audio-visual emotion recognition," *IEEE Multimedia*, vol. 27, no. 1, pp. 37–48, 2019.

[28] J. S. Chung *et al.*, "In defence of metric learning for speaker recognition," *arXiv preprint arXiv:2003.11982*, 2020.

[29] Y. Xu, H. Min, H. Song, and Q. Wu, "Multi-instance multi-label distance metric learning for genome-wide protein function prediction," *Computational biology and chemistry*, vol. 63, pp. 30–40, 2016.

[30] H. Luo, J. Wang, C. Yan, M. Li, F.-X. Wu, and Y. Pan, "A novel drug repositioning approach based on collaborative metric learning," *IEEE/ACM transactions on computational biology and bioinformatics*, vol. 18, no. 2, pp. 463–471, 2019.

[31] Y. Wu, S. Dou, D. Zou, W. Yang, W. Qiang, and H. Jin, "Contrastive learning for robust android malware familial classification," *IEEE Transactions on Dependable and Secure Computing*, 2022.

[32] M. Jureček and R. Lórencz, "Application of distance metric learning to automated malware detection," *IEEE Access*, vol. 9, pp. 96 151–96 165, 2021.

[33] C. Liu, B. Li, J. Zhao, Z. Zhen, X. Liu, and Q. Zhang, "Fewm-hgcl: Few-shot malware variants detection via heterogeneous graph contrastive learning," *IEEE Transactions on Dependable and Secure Computing*, 2022.

[34] G. Andresini, A. Appice, and D. Malerba, "Autoencoder-based deep metric learning for network intrusion detection," *Information Sciences*, vol. 569, pp. 706–727, 2021.

[35] A. Singh, A. Walenstein, and A. Lakhotia, "Tracking concept drift in malware families," in *Proceedings of the 5th ACM workshop on Security and artificial intelligence*, 2012, pp. 81–92.

[36] F. Barbero, F. Pendlebury, F. Pierazzi, and L. Cavallaro, "Transcending transcend: Revisiting malware classification in the presence of concept drift," in *2022 IEEE Symposium on Security and Privacy (SP)*, IEEE, 2022, pp. 805–823.

[37] L. Yang *et al.*, "Cade: Detecting and explaining concept drift samples for security applications," in *30th USENIX Security Symposium (USENIX Security 21)*, 2021, pp. 2327–2344.

[38] G. Andresini, F. Pendlebury, F. Pierazzi, C. Loglisci, A. Appice, and L. Cavallaro, "Insomnia: Towards concept-drift robustness in network intrusion detection," in *Proceedings of the 14th ACM workshop on artificial intelligence and security*, 2021, pp. 111–122.

[39] F. Zola, J. L. Bruse, and M. Galar, "Temporal analysis of distribution shifts in malware classification for digital forensics," in *2023 IEEE European Symposium on Security and Privacy Workshops (EuroS&PW)*, IEEE, 2023, pp. 439–450.

[40] M. Kaya and H. Ş. Bilge, "Deep metric learning: A survey," *Symmetry*, vol. 11, no. 9, p. 1066, 2019.

[41] N. Altman and M. Krzywinski, "The curse (s) of dimensionality," *Nat Methods*, vol. 15, no. 6, pp. 399–400, 2018.

[42] E. Schubert, J. Sander, M. Ester, H. P. Kriegel, and X. Xu, "Dbscan revisited, revisited: Why and how you should (still) use dbscan," *ACM Transactions on Database Systems (TODS)*, vol. 42, no. 3, pp. 1–21, 2017.

[43] M. Ahmed, R. Seraj, and S. M. S. Islam, "The k-means algorithm: A comprehensive survey and performance evaluation," *Electronics*, vol. 9, no. 8, p. 1295, 2020.

[44] M. Ester *et al.*, "A density-based algorithm for discovering clusters in large spatial databases with noise," in *KDD*, vol. 96, 1996, pp. 226–231.

[45] D. W. Fernando and N. Komninos, "Fesa: Feature selection architecture for ransomware detection under concept drift," *Computers & Security*, vol. 116, p. 102 659, 2022.

[46] L. Van der Maaten and G. Hinton, "Visualizing data using t-sne.," *Journal of machine learning research*, vol. 9, no. 11, 2008.

Security-risk-mitigation Measures for Automotive Remote Diagnostic Systems

Masaaki Miyashita
The Graduate University for Advanced Studies, Department of Informatics, Graduate School of Interdisciplinary Sciences, Present affiliation is Nissan Motor Corporation
Kanagawa, Japan
e-mail: m-miyashita@nii.ac.jp

Hiroki Takakura
National Institute of Informatics
Tokyo, Japan
e-mail: takakura@nii.ac.jp

Abstract— **Modern automobiles are equipped with numerous electric control units that require an electrical diagnosis system for efficient maintenance. With the emergence of telematics communication in connected cars, remote diagnosis has become possible, allowing for the early detection of electric-system issues. However, remote diagnostic systems, especially those with services requiring special privileges, such as firmware updates or control of vehicle actuators, are vulnerable to cyberattacks. Considering this, we present security-risk-mitigation measures for such systems.**

Keywords-Automotive cybersecurity; Remote diagnosis; UDS.

I. INTRODUCTION

As technology advances, the electronic systems in automobiles are becoming more intricate. These systems consist of numerous components that are connected through in-vehicle communication networks. Diagnostic systems specifically designed for vehicles are required to pinpoint any malfunction. These systems usually require a diagnostic tool to be directly connected to a dedicated connector on the vehicle and must be operated at a garage.

With wireless communication systems increasingly used in vehicles, remote diagnosis systems have become more prevalent. These services enable an operator to read diagnostic trouble codes and data logs through wireless communication. This prompts the driver to bring his/her vehicle to a garage for repairs before the trouble becomes more severe. Diagnostic communications are used not only to read such data but also to write data to in-vehicle parts, such as firmware updates and initial settings of replacement parts.

Studies have indicated that cyberattacks targeting vehicles through diagnostic communications can result in significant damage. For example, it has been demonstrated that some diagnostic Controller Area Network (CAN) messages impacted major critical vehicle control systems, such as the engine, brake, and steering systems [1]. Car theft and privacy breaches are also potential risks of cyberattacks through diagnostic communication [2].

To address these security risks, we present security-risk-mitigation measures for remote diagnostic systems. These systems involve reading diagnostic trouble data and remote firmware-update tasks that were previously only executed at service stations. Our measures aim to reduce the potential security risks associated with these systems.

The rest of the paper is structured as follows. In Section II, we discuss automotive diagnostic communication. In Section III, current status and issues of remote diagnosis are presented. In Section IV, we propose our security-risk-mitigation measures. In Section V, we show how to avoid constraints when implementing proposed measures in vehicle component. Finally, we conclude our work in Section VI.

II. AUTOMOTIVE DIAGNOSTIC COMMUNICATION

The process of remote diagnosis involves the use of wireless communication between a vehicle and a diagnostic server located outside the vehicle. To diagnose the various components implemented in the vehicle, the in-vehicle wireless communication unit, which serves as the entry point to the vehicle, must communicate with other components through the in-vehicle communication network. To achieve this, it is most reasonable from a system-implementation standpoint to use the diagnostic communication protocol typically used for wired-connected diagnostic tools. While this protocol is effective for wired communication, there are security concerns when using it for wireless communication.

With this in mind, we examined the characteristics and issues of automotive diagnostic communications used in the in-vehicle network.

A. *Overview of Diagnostic Communication*

In 1991, the California Air Resources Board mandated the implementation of the On-Board Diagnostics (OBD) connector to standardize vehicle diagnostic communications. Today, the OBD2 connector is the industry standard interface and can use several communication protocols. CAN communication is prevalent in vehicle-embedded processors, and there is a shift towards faster diagnostic communication using Diagnostics over Internet Protocol (DoIP)-based communication with an Ethernet physical layer [3]. To address the need for faster communication and accommodate the increased complexity of automotive software, ISO14229-1 standardized the Unified Diagnostic Service (UDS) Protocol, which is now used as a standard communication protocol by many automotive companies. However, as software complexity increases, so do security concerns, as outlined in previous studies [4] and [5] on DoIP.

B. *Diagnostic Tool*

Advancements in diagnostic-communication hardware and software have brought about changes in diagnostic tools used to identify failures in vehicles. Handheld terminals with basic Liquid Crystal Displays (LCDs) had been commonly used for diagnostic communication before the spread of CAN communication. However, with the increasing number of vehicles supporting diagnostic communication and the complexity of systems due to the introduction of IP communication, developing software for specialized hardware has become inefficient. Thus, it is now common to use a Personal Computer (PC) or tablet in Figure 1 as a diagnostic tool and connect it to an OBD dongle through USB, Bluetooth, wireless LAN, etc.

Figure 1. Diagnostic tools using PC/Tablet.

This approach has the additional benefit of enabling developers of general diagnostic tools that support vehicles from multiple automobile companies to easily acquire diagnostic tool hardware. However, it also raises concerns that these devices, which are essentially PCs and tablets with network connectivity as standard equipment, could be used as gateways for attackers to intrude into vehicles. Since diagnostic communication protocols are standardized and diagnostic tools and software can be purchased inexpensively, attackers can find vulnerabilities through reverse analysis.

C. Security-critical Diagnostic Communication Services

In diagnostic communication, the functionalities offered by a vehicle's Electronic Control Unit (ECU) for using a diagnostic tool are referred to as "services". These services include reading and writing data to operate the ECU as well as diagnostic commands, such as fault code retrieval. The conversation surrounding automotive cybersecurity threats highlights the potential for attacks via the OBD connector by exploiting these services. Previous research [6] and [7] have demonstrated that the following UDS have been susceptible to exploitation.

- Input/Output Control Service: This service controls the input and output signals that are connected to the specified ECU from the diagnostic tool. Its primary function is to identify the failure point. For instance, if the wipers do not operate even after turning on the wiper switch, this service can be used to forcibly drive the wiper motor, and if the wipers start operating, it proves that the motor and its wiring have no problem. This approach helps in efficiently narrowing down the failure point. However, this service can lead to generating hazardous vehicle behavior that the driver did not intend.
- Write Data by Local ID Service: This service is designed for configuring the initial settings and adjusting the parameters of installed components. It can, for example, be used to write the dynamic radius value of a tire to the ECU to calibrate the speedometer or enable/disable optional parts. However, if this service is abused, users may experience adverse effects, such as inaccurate information display or suspension of certain functions.
- Reprogramming Service: This service is for rewriting ECU firmware installed in sold vehicles, usually to correct quality defects in the firmware. However, if this service is abused, it could result in various issues. For instance, the rewritten ECU may behave improperly or even spoof other ECUs, leading to more significant problems, such as sending malicious communication data to other ECUs. Therefore, it is crucial to use this service only for its intended purpose and avoid any abuse.

Decades ago, owners could modify vehicle characteristics by rewriting the ECU firmware or overriding the CAN bus signals. However, due to certain essential services' impact on crucial vehicle features, such services are locked by default within secured ECUs. To grant access to locked services, a process known as "security access (service ID27)" is typically used to verify the legitimacy of the user or diagnostic tool.

D. Authentication by Service ID27 "Security Access"

In diagnostic communication by using UDS, security access communication was generally executed using the following procedure (refer to Figure 2) with a pre-shared symmetric key K.

1. The diagnostic tool to be authenticated sends a seed request (request seed) to the ECU to be unlocked.
2. Upon receiving the request, the ECU sends back seed data X, including random numbers, to the diagnostic tool to avoid the risk of replay attacks.
3. The diagnostic tool processes the obtained X using the key data K and computes the response data Y.
4. The diagnostic tool sends Y to the ECU. ECU calculates Y' from the K & X sent by ECU itself.
5. If Y' and Y are the same value, the authentication is successful and the ECU unlocks the locked critical services.

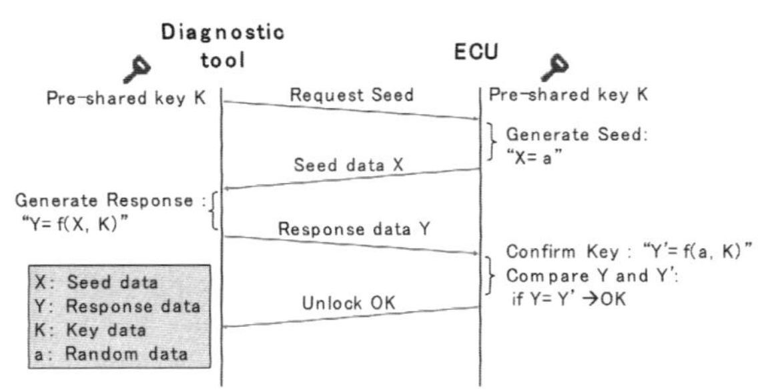

Figure 2. ECU unlock sequence by security access.

If a symmetric key is used for authentication in security access executed by such procedures, an attacker may be able to obtain the key information through reverse analysis of the ECU or diagnostic tools. Therefore, the following solutions have been devised.

- To minimize the risk of reverse key analysis, it is essential to safeguard the private key in asymmetric key authentication. The private key should not be stored in the diagnostic tool. It instead should be kept in the Hardware Security Module (HSM), which is located on the authentication server or in a secure location with restricted access outside the tool. This requires the diagnostic tool to be connected to the authentication server with the HSM. To achieve this, infrastructure development and maintenance are necessary, such as installing a network environment at the garage and managing accounts that enable the diagnostic tool to log into the authentication server.
- Service ID27 does not provide security functions, such as user-privilege management or session key exchange with authentication, requiring each auto manufacturer to develop its own customizations. To remedy these issues, ISO 14229-1 has been updated, and a new UDS service, Authentication (Service ID 29), began in 2020.

E. *Authentication by Service ID 29 "Authentication"*

This new authentication service has the following advantages in terms of security compared with the previously used security access.

- Support for Public Key Infrastructure (PKI)-based authentication mechanisms.
- Support for session key exchange during authentication.
- User-privilege management support.

This service is expected to spread and be implemented into in-vehicle basic software, such as AUTOSAR (AUTomotive Open System ARchitecture). This will make it easier for vehicle manufacturers and component suppliers to implement higher security measures than ever before.

Some automotive ECUs, however, use processors with low processing power, such as 16-bit microprocessors. PKI-based authentication requires certificate parsing, hash calculation, and processing of asymmetric key cryptography, which cannot be afforded by such processors.

To introduce user-privilege management, it is necessary to properly construct and operate a system outside the vehicle that manages the privilege settings for each user and their expiration dates. For example, there is a need for special diagnostic communication during the vehicle-development phase and vehicle-production processes, and the introduction of Service ID 29 will not be effective unless account management for users and production facilities with such special privileges is properly implemented. Therefore, it is necessary to improve not only technical measures, such as the development of ECUs and privilege-management systems, but also the management and operation of the user management process at the same time.

III. CURRENT STATUS AND ISSUES OF REMOTE DIAGNOSIS

A. *What is Remote Diagnostics?*

Section II described wired diagnostic communication. Remote diagnosis refers to diagnostic communication using a wireless communication unit installed in the vehicle, enabling remote diagnosis from a location away from the vehicle. Figure 3 shows a typical configuration for remote diagnosis.

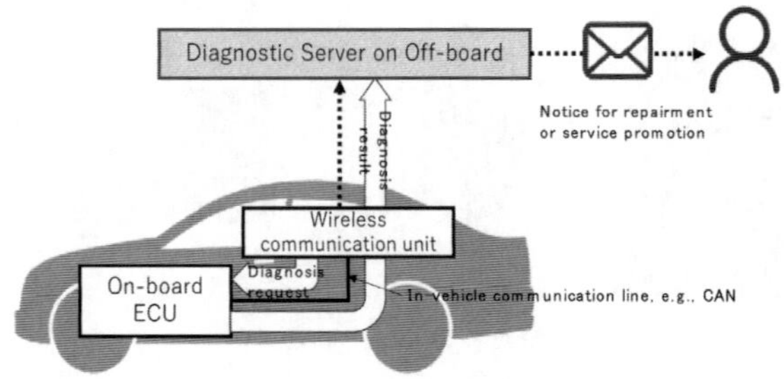

Figure 3. Example of remote diagnostic system.

In remote diagnosis, the wireless communication unit in the vehicle requests the onboard ECU to self-diagnose if any failures occur. The onboard ECU sends back the diagnosis results, which the wireless communication unit forwards to the remote diagnosis server, enabling the diagnosis results to be obtained without entering the vehicle.

If a malfunction occurs, the diagnostic server notifies the user and urges them to repair or go to a garage, preventing the malfunction from becoming a serious problem.

While it is technically possible for the wireless communication unit to transmit requests, such as program rewriting and Input-Output (IO) control, these requests are designed for use under the control of a mechanic only when the vehicle is stopped for maintenance or repair. If operated remotely and unintentionally by the driver while the vehicle is running, they may cause safety-related problems.

In a previous study [8], security measures for remote diagnostic systems were proposed. These measures are based on the assumption that the wireless communication unit (called the telematics module) is correctly installed in the vehicle and properly works. However, the vulnerability of the wireless communication unit can be exploited, making it an entry point for man-in-the-middle attacks through hijacking. This should be assumed as one of the major threats in recent automotive security risk analysis.

With current remote diagnostics, it is assumed that the wireless communication unit can be hijacked, thus the following risk mitigation measures were introduced.

- As illustrated in Figure 4, the communication path used for remote diagnosis and the OBD connector are kept separate by the gateway from the in-vehicle network. The gateway is responsible for forwarding only low-risk services, such as the reading of trouble codes and error log data, while any unauthorized service requests are discarded. In other words, the gateway ensures that only authorized requests are processed and unauthorized ones are discarded.

- The secret keys required to unlock critical services of the ECU are not stored in the diagnostic tool or gateway to which the attacker can obtain physical access by purchasing them.
- The wireless communication unit is not equipped with a function to receive arbitrary diagnostic requests from an off-vehicle server but only push transmission of diagnostic results.
- The wireless communication unit should be able to transmit only predefined low-risk service requests, such as reading trouble codes.

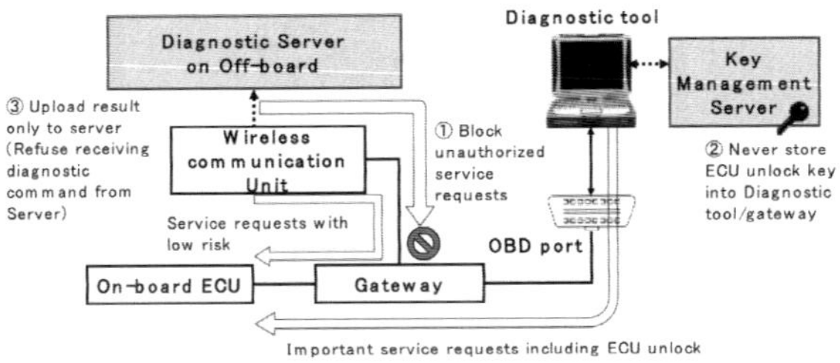

Figure 4. Example of conventional risk-mitigation measures.

B. *Service Expansion Requirements for Remote Diagnosis*

Contrary to the limitations imposed by the risk-mitigation measures described in Section III.A, the following use cases are required for remote diagnosis.

- Remote use of critical commands (e.g., IO control services listed in Section II.C) required for pre-diagnosis to identify parts to bring to a repair place of a vehicle that is stopped on the road due to a malfunction.
- Remote identification and handling of failure caused by senior mechanics (use case similar to telemedicine).

C. *Security Risks from Expansion of Remote Diagnostic Services*

When responding to the need for service expansion as described above, the abuse of critical diagnostic services increases the risk that safety will not be maintained, and fatal incidents will occur.

1) Expanding the impact of incident occurrence: The impact of abusing critical diagnostic services becomes significant because such services can manipulate or illegally modify safety-related vehicle components, for example, the braking or steering system.
2) Failure to confirm the vehicle owner's consent and safe vehicle conditions: Conventionally, the owner's consent could be indirectly obtained by receiving the vehicle key to physically access the OBD connector inside the vehicle. The repair operator had to ensure that the vehicle was in a safe condition, such as by locking the wheels. By allowing work to be done remotely, the above measures cannot be used.
3) Risk of abusing remote operation authority: Conventionally, the OBD connector cannot be accessed unless the vehicle is physically in the hands of the mechanic, so there is no need to worry about workers to whom the owner has entrusted repairs in the past without the owner's permission. Remote operations do not have these restrictions, increasing the risk of insider attack by privilege holders.

To address these risks, the following countermeasures will be necessary

- Countermeasure against risk 1): To prevent the unlocking of critical commands through external communication only requires a special in-vehicle operation to enable remote diagnostics as proof of the vehicle owner's consent.
- Countermeasure against risk 2): In addition to electronically authenticating permission from the vehicle owner, the vehicle receiving the remote diagnostic command also checks the physical condition, indicating that the vehicle is not running but awaiting servicing as one of the conditions for conducting remote diagnosis.
- Countermeasure against risk 3): When authenticating workers who conduct remote diagnosis, a mechanism to check whether the validity period of the work and the authority to carry out the work have been revoked is needed.

IV. PRPPOSED SECURITY-RISK-MITIGATION MEARURES

An overview of the remote diagnostic system operation is shown in Figure 5.

This system can execute remote diagnosis with the following procedure.

A. *Remote Operation Permission*

The vehicle owner who wants to solve a problem with the vehicle or a mechanic who receives a repair request by the owner first conducts owner authentication in the vehicle. The following permission methods are possible.

- The Human Machine Interface (HMI) in the vehicle (navigation-system screen, LCD of cluster meter, etc.) is used to authorize remote diagnosis. This can be done using a PIN or password preset by the vehicle owner to increase the reliability of the authentication.
- The presence of multiple intelligent keys in the vehicle is a condition for starting remote diagnosis permission. This is intended to detect differences from normal driving when only one key is present in the vehicle by the owner bringing a spare intelligent key into the vehicle.
- Pair the owner's smartphone with the vehicle and store the authentication information in the smartphone. The vehicle accepts remote diagnostics only for a certain period after successful Near Field Communication (NFC) authentication.

It is important to combine multiple conditions to increase the reliability of the remote diagnostic authorization described above.

B. Registration of Permitted Operations and Periods

Assuming that part of a vehicle component is malfunctioning, multiple input HMIs should be provided.

1) The owner's smartphone or operator's PC inputs the information and registers the operation information to be allowed to the remote diagnosis server and its validity period.

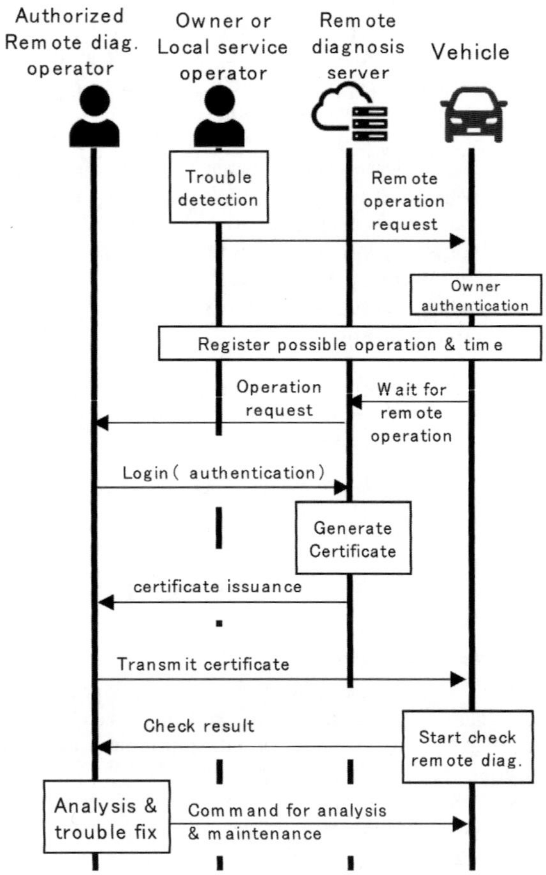

Figure 5. Overview of system operation.

2) Input the information on an HMI in the vehicle and register the operation information to be allowed to the remote diagnosis server via the vehicle's wireless communication unit.

The user can select which operations to allow by using HMI of vehicle infotainment system or Web site of Remote diagnosis server, for example, reprogramming firmware or resetting the ECU.

C. Requesting Analysis via the Diagnosis Server

The remote diagnosis server notifies the registered vehicle that the permitted operations and validity period of the work have been registered. At this time, the vehicle confirms that "permission for remote operation" has been granted in advance and that the vehicle is in a safe maintenance state (e.g., the vehicle is stopped, and the engine hood latch is open), and notifies the remote diagnosis server that it is "waiting for remote diagnosis". The notification data from the vehicle can be supplemented with the vehicle's location information obtained from GPS, etc., and a request can be made to the diagnosis server to limit the locations where remote diagnosis is permitted to the area around the current location. Upon receiving this notification, the remote diagnosis server sends a failure-analysis request to an appropriate operator from among the "authorized remote diagnosis holders" registered in advance.

It is also effective to include a one-time password in the failure-analysis request to increase the reliability of the certificate-issuance process in the next step.

D. Generating and Issuing Certificate of Remote Diagnostic Operations

When an authority holder receives the notification, they log into the remote diagnosis server and request the issuance of a working certificate. To enhance security, it is recommended to require the entry of a one-time password, which is sent only to the authority holder when they receive the notification of the analysis request, as a condition for issuing the certificate.

The issuance of this certificate is also sent to an HMI of the vehicle and the registered smartphone of the vehicle owner. If this notification indicates that a remote diagnostic request was not intended by the driver or vehicle owner in the vehicle, the "waiting for remote diagnosis" status of the vehicle can be canceled, or an instruction can be sent to the remote diagnosis server to stop remote operation for the vehicle in question as a risk-mitigation measure.

The remote diagnosis server issues a certificate to the authority holder as a token that records the expiration date and permitted operating privileges.

E. Access to Vehicles from Remote-diagnostic-authority Holders

The authority holder responsible for remote diagnosis sends a token to the target vehicle. The vehicle checks the token's signature using the remote diagnosis server's pre-shared public key, and if the token is issued by the legitimate remote diagnosis server and is still valid, the vehicle unlocks the remote diagnosis communication and authorized operation rights recorded on the token. The expiration date on the token prevents unauthorized access after the work is completed, which is not intended by the owner.

V. AVOIDING CONSTRAINTS WHEN IMPLEMENTING PROPOSED MEASURES IN VEHICLE COMPONENT

A. *Implementation Constraints to Consider*

The following are constraints in implementing the proposed measures in a vehicle.

- Automobiles are equipped with dozens of ECUs that execute diagnostic communications, and changing all these ECUs to components that implement security measures for remote diagnostics would require large-scale development and take too much time to implement.
- The resources required to adopt enhanced authentication algorithms, user rights management and expiry date management cannot be implemented in components with poor processors, such as 16-bit microcontrollers, which limits their applicability.
- Direct end-to-end communication between the off-vehicle server, which is the connection source for remote diagnosis, and the ECU to be diagnosed, creates a pathway for a direct attack on the ECU inside the vehicle from the off-vehicle server if a vulnerability exists in the ECU communication software, so a workaround is necessary.

B. *Our measures to avoid constraints*

We devised our security-risk-mitigation measures shown in Figure 6 to avoid the constraints described in Section V.A.

To reduce the security risk of remote diagnosis, these measures have the following features that the conventional measures shown in Figure 4 do not have.

1. The in-vehicle gateway is used as the master ECU to manage the remote diagnosis control.
2. The master ECU has a zone for communication with the external server via a wireless communication unit (Zone 1) and another zone for in-vehicle communication (Zone 2), which verifies certificate data for remote diagnosis and sends and receives diagnosis commands to and from multiple ECUs in the vehicle. Zones 1 and 2 are separated by hardware or software, such as a hypervisor, to prevent direct attacks from outside the vehicle to Zone 2, which executes in-vehicle communication processing.
3. Zone 1 of the master ECU communicates with the remote diagnosis server using Transport Layer Security (TLS) to prevent the in-vehicle wireless communication unit from eavesdropping on and falsifying communication data between the master ECU and remote diagnostic server (a countermeasure against man-in-the-middle attacks).
4. The master ECU boots with the remote diagnostics as locked status by default.
5. If the master ECU receives the result of the remote-diagnosis permission correctly executed with an HMI in the vehicle and the "remote diagnosis permission condition" is satisfied within a certain period after that, the master ECU unlocks the remote diagnosis process and enters the "waiting for remote diagnosis" state. The "remote-diagnosis-permission condition" is, for example, all the following conditions are satisfied.
   (1) Successful verification of certificate received from Zone 1.
   (2) The HMI executes remote diagnostic permission in the vehicle and is not canceled.
   (3) No timeout has occurred since the operation in (2).
   (4) The vehicle must be stopped.
   (5) Signals indicating that the vehicle is in a service condition (e.g., engine hood is open) are detected.
6. The target ECU for remote diagnosis connected to the master ECU operates by receiving diagnostic commands from the diagnostic communication process implemented in Zone 2. The master ECU executes the verification process of the certificate data and permission by the HMI, which are necessary as security measures of remote diagnosis, thus avoiding software and hardware changes in the target ECU.
7. Only when remote diagnosis is unlocked, the diagnostic communication process in Zone 2

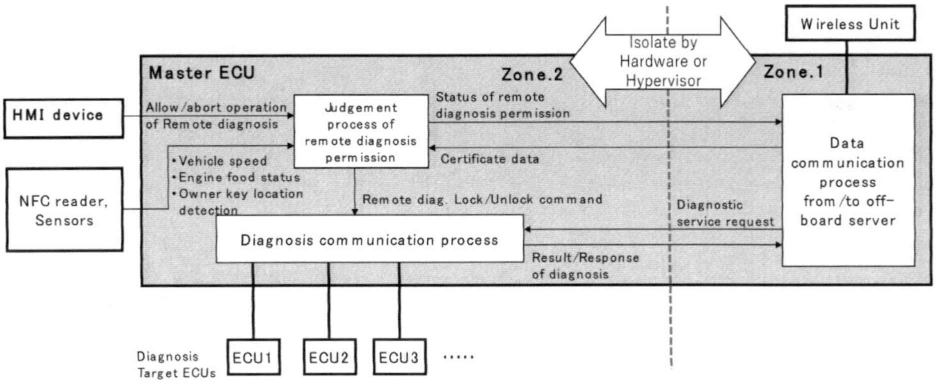

Figure 6. Implementation example using master ECU.

executes diagnostic communication in response to a remote-diagnostic-service request from Zone 1.

8. If the verification of certificate data fails more than once, the time until accepting the next verification is extended.
9. If a diagnostic-service request that is not authorized by the certificate is received, the diagnostic communication process returns a negative response. This history is stored in remote diagnosis sever. The request commands thus rejected are signed and included in the negative-response history data to prevent repudiation by the authorized remote diagnosis operator.

C. *Inspection of Decrease in Communication Speed due to Zone Separation*

To safely separate Zone 1, where communication with the outside of the vehicle takes place, from Zone 2, where important vehicle processing takes place, it is necessary to separate the processors and memory used by the master ECU for processing in each zone and to separate Zone 2 from Zone 1 by using the local network using a different local address from Zone 1. Therefore, a proxy process for address translation is required. The proxy must be implemented before each generic ECU receives data from Zone 1 and is required to relay various types of communications between Zones. Thus, communications that require strict realtime constraints, e.g., vehicle body control, must be properly treated even if other non-realtime communications, e.g., multimedia data, exist. We investigated whether the decrease in communication speed caused by this proxy process is acceptable. For this investigation, we conducted an experiment with the following processor for the master ECU.

Processor name: Renesas R-carS4N-8A
Implemented core:

- ✓ Real-time processor: ARM Cortex R52-1000MHz (1 core)
- ✓ Application processor: ARM Cortex A55-1200MHz (8 core)
- ✓ Microcontroller: RH850 G2MH-400MHz (2 core)

One of the above cores, A55, was allocated for proxy processing. The following cases were assumed for communication between Zones 1 and 2, which require the highest speed and lowest latency, and for the protocols used.

- ✓ Usage: Video transfer between Zone 1 navigation system and Zone 2 components (cluster meter or cameras)
- ✓ Protocol used: Real-time Transport Protocol (RTP)
- ✓ Target throughput 66 Mbps or more, latency 3 ms or less

The experiment was conducted in the environment shown in Figure 7, using 96-Mbps input data, which is higher than the target throughput.

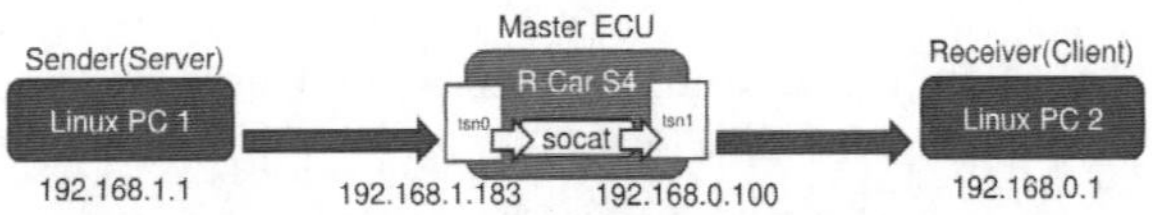

Figure 7. Experimental environment

The operating system used for both R-Car S4 and Linux PC1/PC2 was Ubuntu 20.04.

As shown in Figure 8, the proxy processing using "socat" could output 96-Mbps data without any data loss, and the CPU load at this time was only about 55%, leaving a margin.

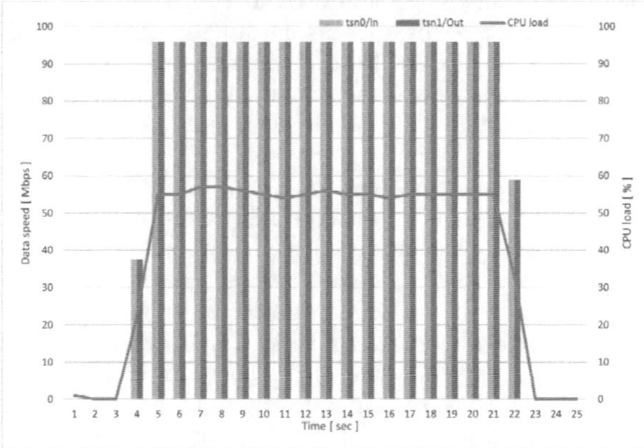

Figure 8. Performance of RTP proxy by socat.

The measured latency was 1.675 ms, achieving the target of less than 3 ms. These results confirm that a general ECU like Renesas R-carS4N-8A has sufficient processing power to function as a master ECU and show the feasibility of the proposed method.

VI. CONCLUSION

Even if a man-in-the-middle attack is carried out by in-vehicle wireless communication unit, our security-risk-mitigation measures can be effective in the following points.

- ✓ TLS communication between the remote diagnosis server in Zone 1.
- ✓ Even if an attacker can forge a certificate to conduct remote diagnostics, it is protected by multiple remote-diagnosis-permission conditions, such as vehicle-side remote-diagnostics-permission operations.
- ✓ To execute malicious code on the master ECU to bypass the remote-diagnostics-permission condition, it is necessary to break into Zone 2, but to do so from Zone 1, it is necessary to break through the separation between Zones 1 and 2.

The network separation between Zones 1 and 2 was a simple proxy using "socat". Since the master ECU processor has sufficient processing power, we will investigate the possibility of enhancing security by, for example, adding an anomaly check for header information.

ACKNOWLEDGMENT

We thank Associate Prof. Hirokazu Hasegawa of NII for his warm advice throughout the research and Mr. Koji Yamada of Renesas Electronics Corporation for his cooperation in evaluating the performance of the master ECU.

REFERENCES

[1] C. Miller and C. Valasek, " Remote Exploitation of an Unaltered Passenger Vehicle", pp. 84–85, Blackhat Aug. 2015.

[2] H. Wen, Q. A. Chen and Z. Lin, "Plug-N-Pwned: Comprehensive Vulnerability Analysis of OBD-II Dongles as A NewOver-the-Air Attack Surface in Automotive IoT", pp. 960–961, Aug. 2020.

[3] S. Robert and J. S. Jayasudha, "Overview of Diagnostic over IP (DOIP), Ethernet Technology and Lightweight TCP/IP for Embedded System", International Journal of Advanced Research in Computer Science, pp. 296–299, 2013.

[4] R. B. Gujanatti, S. A. Urabinahatti and M. R. Hudagi, "Suvey on Security Aspects Related to DoIP", International Research Journal of Engineering and Technology, pp. 2350–2355, 2017.

[5] M. Matsubayashi et al., "Attacks Against UDS on DoIP by Exploiting Diagnostic Communications and Their Countermeasures", 2021 IEEE 93rd Vehicular Technology Conference, pp. 1922–1927, 2021.

[6] C. Miller and C. Valasek, "Remote Exploitation of an Unaltered Passenger Vehicle," in Blackhat USA. Las Vegas, NV, USA: Blackhat Press, pp. 86-88, 2015.

[7] S. Kulandaivel, "Revisiting remote attack kill-chains on modern invehicle networks," PhD thesis, Carnegie Mellon University, pp. 28, 2021.

[8] K. Daimi, "A Security Architecture for Remote Diagnosis of Vehicle Defects", The Thirteenth Advanced International Conference on Telecommunications, pp. 1-7, 2017.

Cyber Threat Response System Design and Test Environment

Taewoo Tak, Young-Jun Lee
Security R&D Team
Korea Atomic Energy Research Institute
Daejeon, Korea
e-mail: ttwispy@kaeri.re.kr, yjlee426@kaeri.re.kr

Taejin Kim
Research Reactor Design and Construction Agency
Korea Atomic Energy Research Institute
Daejeon, Korea
e-mail: taejinkim@kaeri.re.kr

Abstract—**Incidents like the Stuxnet attack, which targeted uranium centrifuges, have proven that systems can be compromised even without direct Internet connectivity. This has underscored the importance of cybersecurity in nuclear facilities. To develop effective detection systems for Nuclear Power Plants (NPPs), it is essential to conduct research on identifying data available for system and device-specific detection based on instrumentation and control systems of NPPs. When analyzing cyberattacks that induce abnormal data and identifying intrusion indicators, the detection of cyber threats is broadly divided into host-based and network-based. This paper describes the design and test environment of cyber threat response systems for NPPs.**

Keywords-cybersecurity in NPP; NPP cybersecurity response system; cybersecurity test environment.

I. INTRODUCTION

The global increase in cyber threats extends beyond Information Technology (IT) to critical infrastructure fields. Historically, the nuclear power field received less attention due to its perceived immunity from cyber threats owing to its closed network environment. However, incidents like the Stuxnet attack, which targeted uranium centrifuges, have proven that systems can be compromised even without direct Internet connectivity [1]. This has underscored the importance of cybersecurity in nuclear facilities. Consequently, NPPs in operation are now integrating additional cybersecurity measures and conducting research to swiftly detect cyber threats for ensuring the safety of nuclear operations.

II. RELATED WORKS

A. *Weakness of Cybersecurity in Nuclear Power Plant*

Nuclear power plants have traditionally employed conservative technologies, largely relying on analog systems in their instrumentation and control systems. These systems were isolated from the internet, which significantly reduced the risk of cyber-attacks and minimized the plants' vulnerability to such threats. As a result, cybersecurity was not a primary concern in the design of these systems. However, with the advance of Information Technology, Instrumentation and Contral (I&C) systems in NPPs have been increasingly implemented with digital control devices, wired communication networks, and software. This shift has introduced new vulnerabilities, making these plants more susceptible to cyber-attacks. As these digital systems become integral to the operation and safety of nuclear facilities, it is crucial to incorporate robust cybersecurity measures to protect against potential threats and ensure the continuous safe operation of nuclear power plants.

Figure 1 provides an overview of the digital systems used in both safety and non-safety systems in the latest Nuclear Power Plant model. As depicted in the figure, the control, monitoring, and protection systems in the safety systems employ Programmable Logic Controller (PLC) platforms. Meanwhile, the non-safety systems utilize Distributed Control System (DCS) platforms. These systems work together to provide integrated Human-Machine Interface (HMI) information to operators in the main control room, enhancing overall plant monitoring and control efficiency [4].

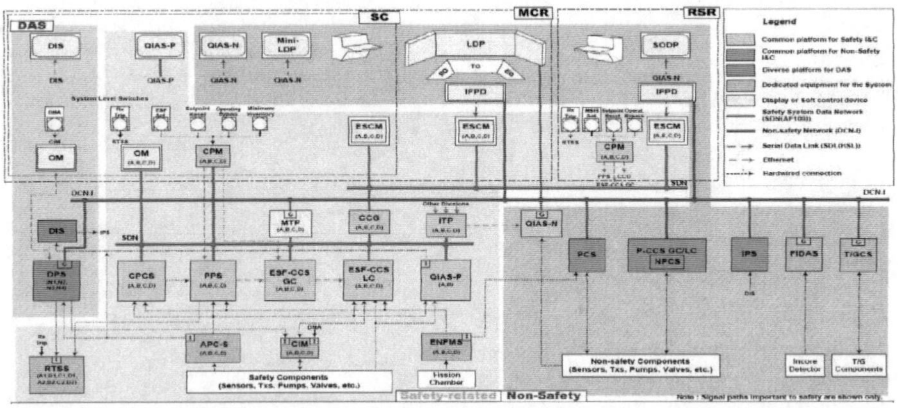

Figure 1. Overview of the digital system.

Recent cybersecurity research has predominantly focused on safety systems like the Plant Protection System (PPS), which are essential for the safe shutdown and protection of nuclear power plants. These systems are critical as they directly influence the plant's operational integrity during emergency situations. However, attention must also be given to non-safety systems, such as the Divers Protection System (DPS). DPS, while classified as non-safety, has the capability to initiate plant shutdowns depending on its functionality. The potential for cyber-attacks to exploit vulnerabilities or induce physical malfunctions in the DPS control system is a matter of significant concern. Such vulnerabilities could prevent the DPS from functioning correctly during critical shutdown phases, posing a substantial risk of severe incidents. As digital systems have increasingly incorporated into NPPs, the importance of securing both safety and non-safety systems against cyber threats becomes paramount to ensuring overall plant safety.

B. The Need for the Design and Testing Technology of Nuclear Power Plant Cyber Threat Response Systems

As cyber intrusion attempts increase, government and public agencies are strengthening their cyber crisis response systems by establishing or expanding dedicated information security teams and conducting cyber-attack response drills [5]. These drills require the development of cyber-attack detection technologies based on intelligent information technology, enabling responses to evolving threats. Modern cyber-attacks are highly sophisticated, involving complex actions, such as control logic manipulation, sensor signal tampering, and HMI display alterations. Detection of such attacks cannot rely solely on IT security measures; nuclear power plants require specialized detection technologies tailored to their systems. Current industrial security measures are insufficient for detecting and countering these advanced cyber threats.

To develop effective detection systems for nuclear power plants, it is essential to conduct research on identifying data available for system and device-specific detection based on nuclear instrumentation and control systems. Additionally, selecting appropriate detection methods and analyzing and verifying detection performance for potential cyber-attacks on the target systems and devices are crucial.

III. Cyber Threat Response System Design and Test Environment

Figure 2 illustrates the configuration of a Nuclear Power Plant digital instrumentation and control (I&C) system [7]. As observed in the figure, while the nuclear power plant digital I&C system does operate some general PCs and servers commonly used in IT, it predominantly utilizes industrial equipment, such as Programmable Logic Controllers (PLCs), Distributed Control Systems (DCS), industrial PCs, and industrial networks. Therefore, directly applying existing cyber security threats identified for general IT systems to this specialized environment is not suitable.

To identify cyber security threats applicable to the nuclear power plant digital I&C system, a comprehensive approach is required. This involves comparing and analyzing the research results and security guidelines on cyber security threats identified in both IT and Industrial Control Systems (ICS). Additionally, an in-depth analysis of the specific functions and characteristics of the target system must be conducted. Based on these analyses, cyber security threats relevant to the nuclear power plant environment can be derived. In nuclear power plants, ensuring the continuous operation and safety of the plant is of utmost importance. This leads to a robust design where safety systems are isolated from any potential vulnerabilities that could arise from communication uncertainties. By adopting a deterministic communication structure, the systems are able to operate with high reliability, ensuring that all commands and data transmissions occur in a predictable and controlled manner. This approach minimizes the risk of unexpected behaviors or failures in the safety-critical functions of the plant, thereby enhancing the overall security and resilience of the nuclear power plant's operations.

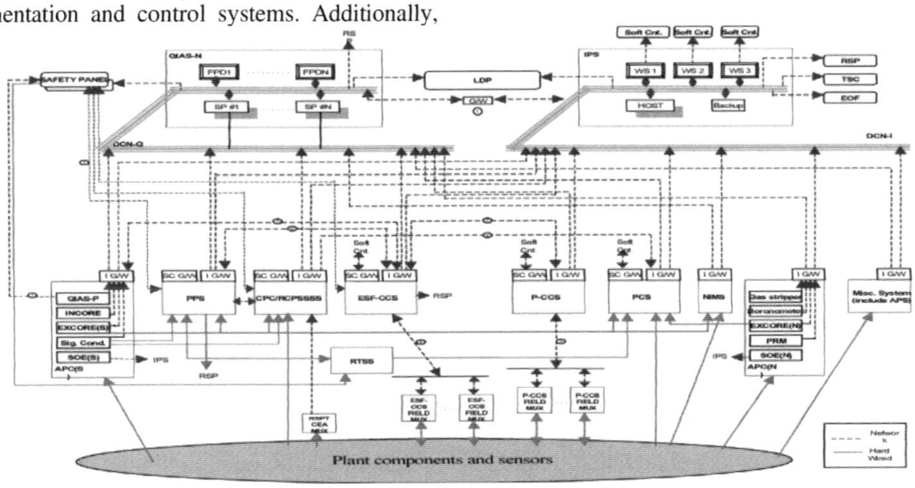

Figure 2. Configuration of a nuclear power plant digital I&C system.

A. *Cyber Threat Response System Design*

The development targets for configuring the cyber threat response system for nuclear power plants are as follows:

- Development of Safety System Applications for Nuclear Power Plants: Design and development of applications for the safety system. Development of simulation applications for normal and abnormal data of the safety system.
- Development of Non-Safety System Applications for Nuclear Power Plants: Design and development of applications for the non-safety system. Development of simulation applications for normal and abnormal data of the non-safety system.
- Design of Cyber Threat Response System: Design and development of the Man Machine Interface Systems (MMIS) cyber threat response system. Development of a system that provides operators with information on threat responses for both safety and non-safety systems in the System Status Overview (SSO) of the MMIS.
- Construction of On-Site Normal/Abnormal Big Data: Design and development of the big data server and interface (REST) for the MMIS. Storage of normal and abnormal state data for both safety and non-safety systems of the MMIS in a database server and development of an interface (REST) for AI learning.
- Development of Test/Verification Technology: Development of abnormal state scenarios through MMIS cyber threats. Development of a system for comparing data of abnormal states induced by MMIS cyber threats with normal state data. Development of a system for comparing simulated data of safety and non-safety systems with database data in the MMIS.

B. *Cyber Threat Response System Test Environment*

Figure 3 shows the configuration of the cyber threat response system design and test environment setup. As illustrated in the figure, the signal simulator is configured to simulate scenario-based input and output signals. The on-site Nuclear Power Plant big data is established using the Testbed owned by the Korea Atomic Energy Research Institute (KAERI), and for the latest non-safety systems not included in the Test-Bed, the big data is constructed using the RTP controller applied to the Shin-Kori Units 5 and 6 CDMS systems.

Experiments for building the on-site Nuclear Power Plant big data are conducted in accordance with KAERI's strict security regulations. Key data from safety and non-safety systems can be simulated as packet signals by developing application software. These packet signals are then used to perform network-based and process-based detection in conjunction with the cyber threat response detection engine server.

The signal simulator reproduces input and output signals based on various scenarios that may occur in the actual operating environment, thus verifying the stability and reliability of the system. This helps ensure that the system operates correctly even in unexpected situations.

Additionally, the on-site Nuclear Power Plant big data construction includes both normal and abnormal state data of the plant, which is used for AI learning and analysis. This data plays a critical role in enhancing the operational efficiency of the plant and applying advanced operational techniques, such as predictive maintenance.

Key data from safety and non-safety systems is converted into network packet signals and analyzed in real-time by the cyber threat detection engine. This process involves both network-based detection and process-based detection, enabling the rapid identification and response to potential cyber threats.

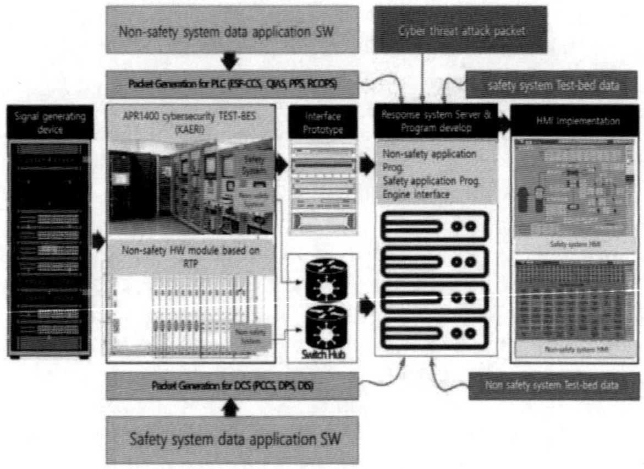

Figure 3. Cyber threat test environment.

C. *Investigation and Analysis of Big Data Utilized in Cyber Threat Response Systems*

Figure 4 shows the Information security Research and Development dataset. The data for cyber threats was utilized by investigating and analyzing the dataset used in the "Network Threat Detection" track of the security challenge competition. Various data were generated and shared according to different purposes, configurations, and network types.

ws.col.UT	ws.col.Prot	ip.src	ip.dst	tcp.srcport	tcp.dstport	tcp.len	tcp.seq	tcp.ack
11:58:59	CDP							
11:59:00	LDAP	192.168.10	192.168.10	33898	389	403	1	1
11:59:00	TCP	192.168.10	192.168.10	33898	389	403	1	1
11:59:00	LDAP	192.168.10	192.168.10	389	33898	316	1	404
11:59:00	TCP	192.168.10	192.168.10	389	33898	316	1	404
11:59:00	TCP	192.168.10	192.168.10	33898	389	0	404	317
11:59:00	TCP	192.168.10	192.168.10	33898	389	0	404	317
11:59:00	LDAP	192.168.10	192.168.10	33904	389	403	1	1
11:59:00	TCP	192.168.10	192.168.10	33904	389	403	1	1
11:59:00	LDAP	192.168.10	192.168.10	389	33904	316	1	404
11:59:00	TCP	192.168.10	192.168.10	389	33904	316	1	404
11:59:00	TCP	192.168.10	192.168.10	33904	389	0	404	317
11:59:00	TCP	192.168.10	192.168.10	33904	389	0	404	317

source ip	source port	destination	destination	attack type
172.16.0.1	32802	192.168.10	80	brute force
172.16.0.1	32822	192.168.10	80	brute force
172.16.0.1	32860	192.168.10	80	brute force
172.16.0.1	32880	192.168.10	80	brute force
172.16.0.1	32900	192.168.10	80	brute force
172.16.0.1	32938	192.168.10	80	brute force
172.16.0.1	32958	192.168.10	80	brute force
172.16.0.1	33016	192.168.10	80	brute force
172.16.0.1	33036	192.168.10	80	brute force

Figure 4. Information security R&D dataset.

TABLE I. VARIOUS NETWORK DATASETS

dataset	Normal traffic	Attack traffic	Meta data	feature	count	Traffic kind	attack
AWID	yes	yes	yes	other	37M packets	emulated	802.11 attack (authentication request, ARP flooding, injection, probe request)
Booters	no	yes	no	packet	250GB packets	real	DDoS attack 9
Botnet	yes	yes	yes	packet	14GB packets	emulated	botnet (Menti, Murlo, Neris, NSIS, Rbot, Sogou, Strom, Virut, Zeus)
CIC DoS	yes	yes	no	packet	4.6GB packets	emulated	application layer Dos attack (executed through ddossim, Goldeneye, hulk, RUDY, Slowhttptest, Slowloris)
CICIDS 2017	yes	yes	yes	packet, bi. flow	3.1M flows	emulated	botnet (Ares), XSS, DoS (executed through Hulk, GoldenEye, Slowloris, and Slowhttptest), DDoS (executed through LOIC), heartbleed, infiltration, SSH brute force, SQL injection
CIDDS-001	yes	yes	yes	uni. flow	32M flows	emulated and real	DoS, port scans (ping-scan, SYN-Scan), SSH brute force
CIDDS-002	yes	yes	yes	uni. flow	15M flows	emulated	port scans (ACK-Scan, FIN-Scan, ping-Scan, UDP-Scan, SYN-Scan)
CTU-13	yes	yes	yes	uni. and bi. flow, paket	81M flows	real	botnet (Menti, Murlo, Neris, NSIS, Rbot, Sogou, Virut)
ISCX 2012	yes	yes	yes	packet, bi. flow	2M flows	emulated	Attack scenario 4
ISOT	yes	yes	yes	packet	11GB packets	emulated	botnet (Storm, Waledac)
KDD CUP 99	yes	yes	no	other	5M points	emulated	DoS, privilege escalation (remote-to-local and user-to-root), probing
Kyoto 2006+	yes	yes	no	other	93M points	real	Honney pot attack (backscatter, DoS, exploits, malware, port scans, shellcode)
LBNL	yes	yes	no	packet	160M packets	real	port scans
NDSec-1	no	yes	no	packet, logs	3.5M packets	emulated	botnet (Citadel), brute force (against FTP, HTTP and SSH), DDoS (HTTP floods, SYN flooding and UDP floods), exploits, probe, spoofing, SSL proxy, XSS/SQL injection
NSL-KDD	yes	yes	no	other	150k points	emulated	DoS, privilege escalation (remote-to-local and user-to-root), probing
PU-IDS	yes	yes	no	other	200k points	synthetic	DoS, privilege escalation (remote-to-local and user-to-root), probing
SANTA	yes	yes	no	other	n.s.	real	(D)DoS (ICMP flood, RUDY, SYN flood), DNS amplification, heartbleed, port scans
SSENET-2011	yes	yes	no	other	n.s.	emulated	DoS (executed through LOIC), port scans (executed through Angry IP Scanner, Nessus, Nmap), various attack tools (e.g. metasploit)
TRAbID	yes	yes	no	packet	460M packets	emulated	DoS (HTTP flood, ICMP flood, SMTP flood, SYN flood, TCP keepalive), port scans (ACKScan, FIN-Scan, NULL-Scan, OS Fingerprinting, Service Fingerprinting, UDP-Scan, XMAS-Scan)
TUIDS	yes	yes	no	packet, bi. flow	250k flows	emulated	botnet (IRC), DDoS (Fraggle flood, Ping flood, RST flood, smurf ICMP flood, SYN flood, UDP flood), port scans (FIN-Scan, NULL-Scan, UDP-Scan, XMAS-Scan), coordinated port scan, SSH brute force
Twente	no	yes	yes	uni. flow	14M flows	real	Open service (FTP, HTTP, SSH) honey pot attack
UGR 2016	yes	yes	some	uni. flow	16900M flows	real	botnet (Neris), DoS, port scans, SSH brute force, spam
Unified Host and Network	yes	n.s.	no	bi. flows, logs	150GB flows (compressed)	real	n.s.
UNSW-NB15	yes	yes	yes	packet, other	2M points	emulated	backdoors, DoS, exploits, fuzzers, generic, port scans, reconnaissance, shellcode, spam, worms

D. *Analysis of Scenarios for Generating Normal/Abnormal Cybersecurity Data*

Normal/abnormal cybersecurity data will be generated through other projects. In order to support the simulation of cybersecurity normal/abnormal data scenarios in the Testbed being built through this project, communication protocols of safety and non-safety systems, as well as configuration information of CPU and IO modules, will be analyzed. This analysis will provide the requirements for the Packet Generator that is planned to be developed.

- The communication protocols for the safety system and DPS are as follows: Physical Layer (Ethernet), Transport Layer (UDP-Unicast), Application Layer (IPS Standard).
- The communication protocols for the non-safety system and DPS are as follows: Physical Layer (Ethernet), Transport Layer (UDP-Unicast), Control Network Transport Layer (TCP/IP), Information Network (UDP-broadcast), Application Layer (DCS Vendor protocol).

Within the CPU and IO module configuration information, there are types of simulated data for both safety system signals and non-safety system signals. The process monitoring data for safety systems requires signal provision by system and node, while state monitoring data requires provision by system and channel. Similarly, process monitoring data for non-safety systems requires signal provision by system and node, and state monitoring data requires provision by system and node. The Packet Generator implements status monitoring data (SSO DB) and class bit information (Class bit Info) for each system.

When analyzing attacks that induce abnormal data and identifying intrusion indicators, the detection of cyber threats is broadly divided into host-based detection and network-based detection. Representative intrusion indicators for both detection methods are illustrated in Table II.

TABLE II. INTRUSION INDACATORS

Category	***Intrusion Indicators***
Host based indicator	Registry key
	File name
	Test string
	Process name
	Mutex
	File hash value
	User account
	Directory path
Network based indicator	IPv4 address
	IPv6 address
	X509 authentication hash value
	Domain name
	Test string
	Communication protocol
	Fil name
	URL

IV. CONCLUSION AND FUTURE WORK

The cyber threat detection system proposed in this paper can be utilized as the technical security measures of cybersecurity plan for NPPs. This system allows for continuous and in-depth response to cyber threats beyond traditional access restriction and prevention strategies. It supports operator' response to cyber threats by integrating with nuclear emergency procedures. Additionally, it enables the acquisition of intelligent information technology-based cyber-attack detection techniques capable of countering sophisticated and intelligent cyber-attacks. This technology can be also applicable to other various areas, such as small modular reactors and nuclear systems in space, polar, and marine environments.

The systematic and consistent development and application of nuclear cybersecurity technologies and devices can enhance the safety, reliability, and operational performance of nuclear power plants. By leading the development of nuclear cybersecurity technologies, which are not yet internationally established, the developed technologies will improve capabilities to detect and respond cyber-attacks in an effective and efficient way for NPPs.

ACKNOWLEDGMENT

This work was supported by the National Research Foundation of Korea (NRF) grant funded by the Korea government (MSIT) (No. 2021M3C1C4039576).

REFERENCES

[1] WIRED, "An Unprecedented Look at Stuxnet, the World's First Digital Weapon," [Online]. Available: https://www.wired.com/2014/11/countdown-to-zero-day-stuxnet/. Accessed: Nov. 3, 2014 .

[2] International Atomic Energy Agency, *Modern Instrumentation and Control for Nuclear Power Plants: A Guidebook*, IAEA, 1999.

[3] Kaspersky ICS CERT, "Threat landscape for industrial automation systems, H2 2019," Kaspersky Lab, 2019.

[4] APR1400 Design Control Document, *Tier 1*, vol. 7, NRC, 2018.

[5] Republic of Korea, *National Cybersecurity Strategy*. Published Aug. 2, 2024.

[6] University of California, Berkeley, *Cyber Security in Nuclear Power Plants: Insights for Advanced Nuclear Technologies*, Sep. 2017, doi:10.13140/RG.2.2.34430.69449.

[7] GENES4/ANP2003, "Advanced MMIS design characteristics of APR1400," presented at GENES4/ANP2003, Kyoto, Japan, Sep. 15-19, 2003.

[8] IAEA, *Computer Security at Nuclear Facilities*, IAEA Nuclear Security Series No. 17, Technical Guidance, 2011.

[9] International Atomic Energy Agency, "Computer Security Incident Response Planning at Nuclear Facilities TDL005 (NST-038)," 2016.

[10] U.S. Nuclear Regulatory Commission (U.S. NRC), *Regulatory Guide 5.71 (R.G 5.71): Cyber Security Programs for Nuclear Facilities*, 2010.

[11] Nuclear Energy Institute (NEI), *NEI 08-09 (Rev. 6): Cyber Security Plan for Nuclear Power Reactors*, 2010.

An Analysis Framework for Steganographic Network Data in Industrial Control Systems

Tom Neubert, Bjarne Peuker, Eric Schueler
Henning Ullrich, Laura Buxhoidt, Claus Vielhauer
Brandenburg University of Applied Sciences
Brandenburg, Germany
e-mail: surname.lastname@th-brandenburg.de

Abstract—**This paper presents a novel analysis framework for steganographic embedding methods in Industrial Control Systems (ICS), which enables the opportunity for a comprehensive comparison of different embedding methods based on a single uncompromized network traffic capture as cover. It is motivated by the observation that industrial control systems are increasingly under attack by stealthy malware, e.g., for reloading malicious code and for data in- and exfiltration. Although multiple detection mechanisms based on published attacks have been developed in recent years, the diversity of steganographic attacks is still a major challenge, and the elaboration of further analysis mechanisms for detection and attribution is a constant arms race. In an exemplary evaluation of three embedding methods by the proposed framework, it is demonstrated that it is possible to assign 88.6% of the samples to a specific steganographic embedding method based on a machine learning approach, proofing the conceptual functionality of the framework. Also, it is shown that different characteristics of payloads can be identified in part. The proposed concept can thus help to derive further detection & defense mechanisms and to differentiate between embedding methods, as well as embedded message types, which increases the potentials for an attribution of attackers in the future, in addition to the detection of incidents.**

Keywords-Information Hiding; Intrusion Detection and Attribution; Network Steganography; Stealthy Malware; Industrial Control Systems; Analysis Framework.

I. INTRODUCTION

During the last several years, information hiding based malware (also stealthy malware) has become more and more popular and is increasingly used by attackers, this can be confirmed by recently presented attack vectors like [1]. Stealthy malware uses completely unobtrusive data to create hidden channels, which are then utilized to embed malicious code or to activate malware for example. Since the Stuxnet-Attack in 2010, it has been clear that also Industrial Control Systems (ICS) are under attack with stealthy malware. In this attack, lnk-files were utilized as cover data and in-memory code injections were used to hide the attack [2]. Additionally, recent attacks like the Ukrainian [3] and the Indian power grid attack [4] demonstrate that attacks with information hiding based malware on ICS become more and more common, especially due to the motivation to stay undetected as long as possible in order to in- and exfiltrate stealthy data.

Currently, several potential information hiding attack vectors for stealthy malware with steganographic embedding techniques and potential defense mechanisms are introduced (e.g., in [5], [6] and [7]). Unfortunately, a framework for comprehensive analysis and comparison of these methods is missing to identify potential similarities, differences, and effects on the cover data and to derive defense mechanisms for specific embedding methods. Additionally, a comprehensive analysis could enable the possibility to distinguish between analyzed embedding methods after a detection, which can lead to the opportunity to identify potential attackers (attribution).

Thus, this work contributes a novel analysis framework, which offers the possibility to compare and analyze multiple steganographic embedding methods based on only a single uncompromized network traffic capture from an exemplary ICS to offer the chance to analyze and evaluate the behaviour of covert information hiding channels (which are used for stealthy steganographic malware). Additionally, the introduced analysis framework for network steganography in ICS is used for an extensive evaluation of three exemplary selected embedding methods (two from state-of-the art and one novel embedding method) to find out, if there is a possibility to differentiate between them and the embedded types of messages (invariant and heterogeneous message) using a machine learning approach based on handcrafted features and a neural network as classification engine.

The paper is structured as follows: In Section II, we present related work and fundamentals. In Section III, we introduce our novel analysis framework. Our evaluation setup to analyze three embedding methods with the novel framework including evaluation goals, data and environment is presented in Section IV. Section V presents the evaluation results and Section VI concludes the paper with a summary and future work.

II. FUNDAMENTALS AND RELATED WORK

In this section, we summarize fundamentals for network steganography in ICS, present recent steganographic attack vectors for network steganography in ICS, and introduce a method to produce synthetic steganographic network data for a fast and easy generation of network data with recent steganographic embedding methods. Furthermore, an overview of methods to analyze steganographic network data for detection and attribution purposes is given.

A. Network Steganography in ICS

"Steganography is the art and science of concealing the existence of information transfer and storage", according to [8]. The subdomain network steganography targets the transfer and storage of hidden information in network communication traffic. From an attacker's perspective, a warden (e.g., intrusion detection system) observes the network traffic and the embedding of stealthy malware should be inconspicuous in a sense that a warden would not be able to differentiate between genuine communication and communication with hidden information embedding [5]. An embedding of hidden information with steganographic techniques can be realized, for example by manipulating the network packets payload on least significant values or by modulating time intervals between specific packets [9].

Network steganography and stealthy malware in ICS are special, due to the lower amount of available data for potential embedding than in traditional Information Technology (IT) networks. Furthermore, the transmitted network packets are usually smaller in ICS since only meta-data or few values (e.g., from sensors) are transferred per packet. Additionally, ICS specific protocols like OPC UA (Open Platform Communications Unified Architecture) [10] or Modbus-TCP [11] are often encapsulated in TCP/IP (or other transport protocols), which enables the opportunity for utilizing the data fields of the ICS specific protocols in addition to TCP/IP protocol headers. It is also not uncommon for the ICS-specific payload to be transmitted unencrypted, because ICS are considered as closed networks and not subject to attacks.

Potential network steganographic embedding patterns and a related terminology is summarized in [12]. A generic taxonomy and overview with the intention of a unified understanding of terms and their applicability for network steganographic methods can be found in [8].

B. Selected Steganographic Embedding Methods for ICS

Two recent and relevant exemplary attack vectors with steganographic embedding techniques in ICS are presented in this section. These Embedding Methods (EM) are selected because both use a timestamp modulation (i.e., timing channel) to embed hidden information, which is a plausible attack vector since every network packet includes them. The presented EM will be analyzed and compared with our novel framework.

1) Selected Embedding Method 1 (EM_1): The approach presented in [5] uses package timestamps (T_i) for embedding while utilizing a dynamic encoding approach based on the hour, minute, and second values, as well as an embedding key and an initialization vector. Similar to the aforementioned approach, low-value-digits of the timestamp are manipulated. This approach is able to hide one *ASCII*-symbol in four of the five highlighted digits of a timestamp in the coding "HH:MM:SS.ffffffff", where H,M,S,f stand for digits of the hour, minute, second and fractional digits of the second of the time value respectively (Example: T_i= 10:00:00.123**456789**). The actual embedding positions are determined using the embedding key and the first digit right of the floating point digit for the fractional second values. Converting a sequence of *ASCII*-symbols to binary values results in a bitstream that is embedded chronologically into every available package. Due to the different modulated values of the variables involved, the encoding of the output values vary in perception.

2) Selected Embedding Method 2 (EM_2): A quite simple and easy to comprehend embedding method is introduced in [6]. The embedding scheme assumes an attack vector with a corrupted Programmable Logical Controller (PLC) via Supply-Chain-Attack. The PLC sends delays in millisecond range ($\mu s_1, \mu s_2, \mu s_3$) to embed a hidden message via timing delays. This means an exemplary timestamp T_i = 10:00:00.123**456**789 is manipulated on the digit positions $\mu s_1 = 4, \mu s_2 = 5, \mu s_3 = 6$. Based on the introduced steganographic taxonomy in [8] (see Section II-A), this represents a *Random State/Value Modulation*. The embedding scheme converts an *ASCII*-message into a bitstream *BS*. For embedding a bit of *BS*, three consecutive PLC OPC UA timestamps are altered (T_i, T_{i+1}, T_{i+2}). To stay inconspicuous, the following three PLC packet timestamps stay untouched (T_{i+3}, T_{i+4}, T_{i+5}). The approach arbitrarily chooses the digit '4' to embed bit = 0 and digit '9' to embed bit = 1.

C. Synthetic Steganographic Data Generation

Diverse and heterogeneous steganographic data for ICS is needed to train and evaluate potential defense mechanisms. But each steganographic embedding needs a mostly sophisticated and complex setup which is very time consuming to assemble and in addition, it raises various security and safety issues. Because of this, the approach of [6] introduces a concept to generate artificial steganographic network data with a limited embedding pace and a specific steganographic embedding technique based on TCP-timestamps. Based on [6], an advanced Synthetic Steganographic Embedding (SSE)-concept is presented in [13]. It offers the possibility to embed hidden information literally everywhere in uncompromized network packet recordings with a embedding pace near real time. This makes it possible to quickly and easily generate test data for many different embedding methods for analysis. In [6], it is assumed that the most important aspects to be simulated in a network traffic are:

1) the physical network including layout and components,
2) the network traffic including types of flows, directions, protocols used, typical payloads, etc., and
3) the type and characteristics of the (steganographic) hidden channel.

Both approaches simulate only the last aspect (3) of this list, the two others are directly used from an uncompromized recording of a physical setup. The SSE-concept has two Synthetic Embedding Options (SEO), one option focuses on a very fast and efficient embedding without accessing structural elements of a packet (called SEO_A), the other option delivers a more comfortable embedding with an easier access to structural elements of a network packet based on json-objects (called SEO_B). In this work, the SSE-concept from [13] is used to generate the steganographic data based on the selected embedding methods in our novel analysis framework, which is presented in the following Section III.

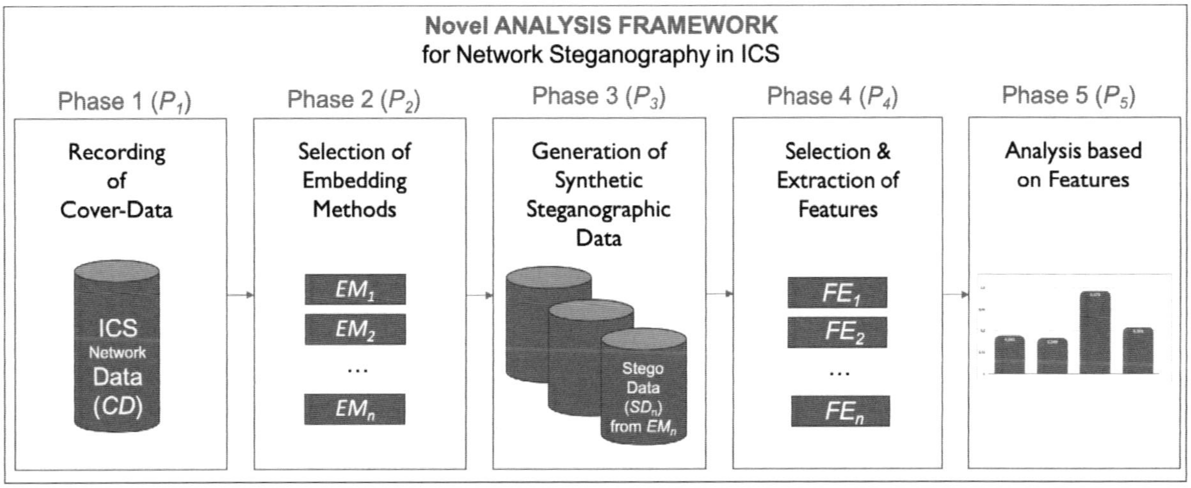

Figure 1. Novel Analysis Framework

D. Analysis of Steganographic Network Data

A basic overview of potential methods to analyze and defend against stealthy malware based on network steganography is presented in [14]. In [15], a novel machine learning based approach is presented to detect network steganography in network recordings based on a handcrafted feature space with an accuracy of 92.9%. The approach analyzes the last six digit positions of a numeric value, because it is best suited for an unobtrusive embedding. The approach performs a frequency analysis of occurrence for the digits 0 to 9 on these six specific positions. This results in 10 features (values) for each digit position between 0.0 and 1.0 representing the percentage of occurrence for each digit 0 to 9. This feature space will be used in this work to analyze the different embedding methods used in this paper for analysis.

III. Novel Analysis Framework

Our novel analysis framework to compare and evaluate different embedding methods to offer the possibility to make a distinction between them for a potential determination or classification of attackers or embedded message types is shown in Figure 1. The concept includes five phases:

- Phase 1 (P_1): the recording of cover-data (see Section III-A),
- Phase 2 (P_2): the selection and formalization of embedding methods (see Section III-B),
- Phase 3 (P_3): the generation of synthetic steganographic data (see Section III-C),
- Phase 4 (P_4): the selection and extraction of features (see Section III-D), and
- Phase 5 (P_5): the analysis based on the features (see Section III-E).

The phases of the framework are described in detail in the following subsections. An exemplary initial evaluation of three embedding methods performed in our evaluation (evaluation setup in Section IV and results in Section V).

A. Recording of Cover Data (P_1)

The framework begins with Phase 1 where network Cover Data (CD) has to be recorded from an uncompromized laboratory ICS setup. CD can be recorded with different capturing tools, we recommend *Wireshark* [16]. The output file is provided in *pcap* or *pcapng* file format for further processing and should contain only relevant traffic for a specific purpose. These file formats are well suited logging protocols for the structural recording of network data. CD is used to build the statistic baseline of the ICS network data to illustrate the impact of the embedding during the analysis and it is also the basis for the steganographic embedding with the selected embedding methods (see Phase 2) to generate the steganographic network data in Phase 3.

B. Selection and Formalization of Embedding Methods (P_2)

Once a network cover data file is recorded, embedding methods for the analysis in Phase 5 have to be selected and should be formalized with a pseudo code representation for a uniform, comparable and comprehensible illustration. In this work, we select two embedding approaches from state-of-the-art and elaborate a novel embedding method. As explained in Section II-B2 all of the algorithms work with an Array A ($A = \{T_1, ..., T_i\}$) that contains all Timestamps T_i of network packet available for manipulation in our pseudo code representation. The specific formalizations for the state-of-the-art approaches EM_1, EM_2, and the novel embedding method EM_3 will be described in the following subsections.

1) Formalization of Embedding Method EM_1: EM_1 takes a dynamic encoding approach while manipulating low value digits of the OPC UA timestamp. An initialization vector I and an encoding key K are used in addition to variables taken from each timestamp to encode the hidden message. D, E,

F, G (meaning: see Figure 2) are all derived directly from the timestamp, as well as H ($H = \{H_0, ..., H_3\}$), which is the 4-digit field in which the encoded message c is embedded. After the encoding process depicted in Figure 2 is finished, the output of S decides the embedding position in H.

Algorithm 1 Steganographic Embedding Method EM_1

```
AM ← A
i ← 0
K ← 4 Digit Key
I ← 4 Digit Initialization Vector
while i < Length(A) do
    D ← Hour value of T_i
    E ← Minute value of T_i
    F ← Second value of T_i
    G ← Value of digit 1 after floating point of T_i
    H ← Value of digit 2−6 after floating point of T_i
    S ← G ⊕ DigitSum(K) mod 2
    O ← D × E × F mod 10000
    K' ← Σ_{n=0}^{3} ((K_n ⊕ (G + I_n)) mod 10) × 10^n
    K'' ← O ⊕ K' mod 10000
    c ← m ⊕ K'' mod 8192
    if S == 0 then
        H_0, H_1, ..., H_3 ← c
    else if S == 1 then
        H_1, H_2, ..., H_4 ← c
    end if
    AM[i] ← T_i
end while
```

Figure 2. Formalized Algorithm for EM_1.

2) *Formalization of Embedding Method EM_2:* Iterating through A, EM_2 embeds a bit of the input bitstream into 3 consecutive timestamps, encoding 0 and 1 by the digital values of 4 and 9, respectively. In the process, three different digits are used for the embedding represented in $\mu_1 - \mu_3$. Manipulated timestamps are then saved in the AM array. This is repeated for each bit in the bitstream until the end of A is reached or all bits are embedded (the algorithm is represented in Figure 3).

Algorithm 2 Steganographic Embedding Method EM_2

```
AM ← A
for Bit in Bitstream do
    for i ← 1 to 3 do
        if Bit_i is 0 then
            T_i[μ_{i mod 3}] ← 4
        else if Bit_i is 1 then
            T_i[μ_{i mod 3}] ← 9
        end if
        AM[i] ← T_i
    end for
end for
```

Figure 3. Formalized Algorithm for EM_2.

3) *Formalization of Embedding Method EM_3:* With the addition of a key used for dynamic encoding and positioning, an advancement of EM_2 is introduced and represented in EM_3. Thus, EM_3 is a novel and sophisticated approach based on EM_2 which has been elaborated for a more unobtrusive embedding. Introducing the dynamic ciphers C_0 and C_1 for the bit values 0 and 1 respectively dynamic encoding is achieved by using K as seed for a random number generator. In cases of collision, the values are generated again. Adding C_0 and C_1 while reducing the sum to a maximum of 3 using the modulo function the position of each bit in the timestamp is calculated (see algorithm representation in Figure 4).

Algorithm 3 Steganographic Embedding Method EM_3

```
AM ← A
i ← 0
K ← "SyntheticStegoKey"
for Bit in Bitstream do
    for i ← 1 to 3 do
        C_0 ← 0
        C_1 ← 0
        while C_1 == C_2 do
            C_0 ← Random(K) mod 9
            C_1 ← Random(K) mod 9
        end while
        j ← C_0 + C_1 mod 3
        if Bit_i is 0 then
            T_i[μ_j] ← C_0
        else if Bit_i is 1 then
            T_i[μ_j] ← C_1
        end if
        AM[i] ← T_i
    end for
end for
```

Figure 4. Formalized Algorithm for EM_3.

C. *Generation of Synthetic Steganographic Data (P_3)*

For the creation and generation of the steganographic network data based on the embedding methods from Phase 2 (EM_1, EM_2, and EM_3), the SSE-concept [13] (introduced in II-C) is used. As mentioned, the SSE-concept offers the possibility to generate steganographic network data synthetically and this results in some obvious advantages for our framework: no matter which embedding method is analyzed, it is not required to elaborate a corrupted, complex ICS setup, which generates the steganographic network data with hidden information. Thus it is well suited because it delivers the opportunity for an easy and fast generation of steganographic network data without the need of a physical setup. The SSE-concept includes four segments:

- Segment I: Record and Pre-Process Network Data,
- Segment II: Synthetic Embedding Option A (SEO$_A$),
- Segment III: Synthetic Embedding Option B (SEO$_B$), and
- Segment IV: Retrieval.

Segment I also deals with the recording of network data, thus Segment Element (SE) I.1 can be skipped for our novel analysis framework since the data capturing is completed after P_1. For the synthetic generation of steganographic network data it offers two synthetic embedding options (Segment II: SEO_A and Segment III: SEO_B, see Section II-C). In the evaluation, this work uses SEO_B since it offers a more comfortable embedding with access to structural elements of a network packet based on json-objects.

D. Selection and Extraction of Features (P_4)

To extract features from pcap or pcapng files, the relevant structural element of the relevant network packets should be converted into csv or txt data to process it afterwards. Therefore, *Tshark* (*Wireshark* console application) [16] with the *-T fields -e field* option can be used to select data fields of network packets that are relevant for feature extraction and analysis. We recommend to use handcrafted statistical feature spaces with as much discriminatory power as possible to analyze steganographic network data. This should lead to comprehensible and plausible analysis results.

In this work, we use the introduced handcrafted feature space from [15], which performs a frequency analysis on least significant digits in timestamps to analyze the three selected exemplary embedding methods (EM_1, EM_2, and EM_3), the approach is briefly described in Section II-D. The selected features shall be extracted for multiple samples from multiple embedding approaches for analysis in P_5.

E. Analysis (P_5)

Based on the extracted features from multiple embedding methods in P_4 a statistical analysis can be carried out. Therefore, various statistical computational techniques such as machine or deep learning based approaches can be taken into consideration based on the selected and extracted features. Thus, for the analysis, different data mining and machine learning tools or libraries, such as *WEKA* [17], *Orange* [18], *Tensorflow* [19] or *Keras* [20], are well suited to analyze differences and commonalities of embedding methods. Generally, the analysis can focus different use case specific aspects, for example: detectability, attributability, embedding scheme, and more depending on goals and objectives of a study.

For our analysis, we train a machine learning based classification approach based on the extracted features to achieve our evaluation goals (presented in Section IV-A).

IV. Evaluation Setup

In our evaluation, we use our presented framework from Section III to compare and analyze the three introduced embedding methods (EM_1, EM_2, and EM_3). In this section, we describe our evaluation goals, as well as the laboratory ICS setup and the resulting evaluation data. Furthermore, we describe our analysis environment to achieve our goals. The evaluation results are presented in Section V.

A. Evaluation Goals

The evaluation has the following goals:

- G_1: Analysis of the three exemplary embedding methods (EM_1, EM_2, and EM_3) based on the extracted features (see Section III-E) to determine whether a potential distinction between the methods is possible for a potential detection of attackers.
- G_2: Analysis of different message types (invariant and heterogeneous) embedded with EM_1, EM_2, and EM_3 to determine whether a potential distinction between embedded messages is possible.

Results for G_1 are presented in Section V-A and for G_2 in Section V-B.

B. Evaluation Data

As mentioned before, to generate synthetic steganographic ICS network data, we have to record cover data from an uncompromized ICS setup (see Section III-A). Thus, we setup a lean laboratory ICS (for better comprehensibility). In our laboratory setup a *Siemens S7-1500* Programmable Logical Controller (PLC) communicates with an Human-Machine-Interface (HMI). On the PLC (server), multiple exemplary automation tasks are running (e.g., traffic light control, binary process status reports, temperature measuring). The HMI (client) requests all PLC outputs every 100 milliseconds. The network traffic on this setup is captured through a mirror port on the connected switch. The laboratory ICS communicates via the ICS specific OPC UA protocol. We have recorded the network communication for around 61 minutes (3,706 seconds). 38,189 network packets (half requests (client, HMI), half responses (server, PLC) were captured and the file size is 7,351,828 Bytes. This capturing builds our steganographic cover data to generate synthetic steganographic network traffic (see the next subsection). The recorded cover data set is called REC_{CD}.

As described previously, our steganographic network data for evaluation is generated with the SSE-concept [13] and the introduced and formalized embedding methods EM_1, EM_2, and EM_3 (see Section III-B). All these embedding methods assume an attack vector with a corrupted PLC via Supply-Chain-Attack. The PLC sends delayed packets in micro- and nanosecond range to embed a hidden message via timing delays with EM_1, EM_2, and EM_3. This means an exemplary timestamp T_i = 10:00:00.123**456789** is manipulated on the bold marked digit positions. Based on the introduced steganographic taxonomy in [8] (see Section II-A) this represents an *LSB state/value modulation*, as mentioned before. The embedding scheme converts an *ASCII*-message into a bitstream *BS*.

For our setup, we embed separately in cover data CD with the three introduced embedding methods. Furthermore, we embed two kinds of messages with each embedding method separately in CD, a heterogeneous message ('$securware2024$') and an invariant message consisting solely of a single character ('a'), both message types are repeated and embedded as often as possible in the data to corrupt all available packets of the cover data. Thus, six steganographic data sets are created and presented in Table I. These data sets and the cover data set (REC_{CD}) are used for feature extraction (see Section IV-C).

TABLE I
NETWORK DATA SETS FOR FEATURE EXTRACTION; STEGANOGRAPHIC DATA IS EMBEDDED SYNTHETICALLY IN REC_{CD}.

Name	Type of Recording	Embedding Method	Message Type	Hidden Message	No. of relevant Packets
REC_{CD}	Cover Data Recording	-	-	-	19,094
$REC_{EM1_{IV}}$	Steganographic Data	EM_1	invariant	a (repeated)	19,094
$REC_{EM1_{HE}}$	Steganographic Data	EM_1	heterogenous	$securware2024$ (repeated)	19,094
$REC_{EM2_{IV}}$	Steganographic Data	EM_2	invariant	a (repeated)	19,094
$REC_{EM2_{HE}}$	Steganographic Data	EM_2	heterogenous	$securware2024$ (repeated)	19,094
$REC_{EM3_{IV}}$	Steganographic Data	EM_3	invariant	a (repeated)	19,094
$REC_{EM3_{HE}}$	Steganographic Data	EM_3	heterogenous	$securware2024$ (repeated)	19,094

C. Analysis Environment

To achieve our goals (G_1 and G_2) presented in Section IV-A, we extract features from the network data sets (see Table I) to train a classifier to determine if we can distinguish between cover data and the different embedding approaches (G_1) and to analyze if we can distinguish between embedded message types (G_2). As mentioned, therefore we use the feature space [15] which performs a frequency analysis on the micro and nanosecond digits of network packet timestamps (as described in Section II-D). To do so, we extract a labeled feature vector (label based on embedding method and message type) from every recorded network data set. We iterate through every recorded network data set and extract a feature vector after 100 relevant packets, which results in 190 samples per data set (since 19,094 relevant packets are included in every data set). Based on the extracted feature space, we train a Multilayer Perceptron (MLP) as classification engine with the feature space as input layer followed by three hidden layers (with 64,32,16 neurons and rectifier activation function) because it is a powerful and modern classification algorithm known for its accurate performance. For evaluation, we perform 5-fold cross-validation to determine the classification accuracy (i.e., results) for G_1 and G_2 (visualized in Figure 5). For G_1, we train a MLP (MLP_{4C}) with 4 classes (cover, EM_1, EM_2, EM_3; represented as 4 neurons in the output layer of the MLP) because the feature vectors extracted from heterogeneous and invariant message types are merged here, because for G_1, we only want to distinguish between cover and embedding types. For G_2 a 7-class-MLP (MLP_{7C}) including all labeled feature vectors from all recordings is trained and the classes are represented as 7 neurons in the output layer of the MLP. An overview of the models and the included feature vectors are presented in Table II.

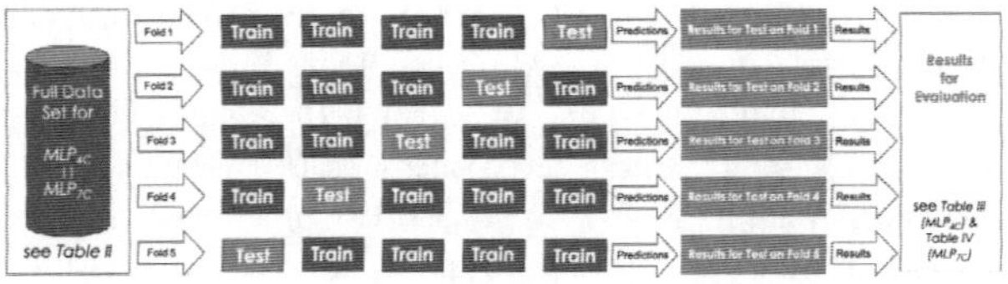

Figure 5. Analysis Environment for Evaluation.

TABLE II
FEATURE VECTORS (I.E., SAMPLES) INCLUDED IN MLP_{4C} AND MLP_{7C} FOR EVALUATION OF G_1 AND G_2

Name	Label of Vectors	In MLP_{4C} included vectors: extracted from:	Number of Vectors	Goal
VEC_{CD}	CD	REC_{CD}	190	G_1
VEC_{EM1}	EM_1	$REC_{EM1_{IV}}$, $REC_{EM1_{HE}}$	380 (2x190)	
VEC_{EM2}	EM_2	$REC_{EM2_{IV}}$, $REC_{EM2_{HE}}$	380 (2x190)	
VEC_{EM3}	EM_3	$REC_{EM3_{IV}}$, $REC_{EM3_{HE}}$	380 (2x190)	
		In MLP_{7C} included vectors:		
VEC_{CD}	CD	REC_{CD}	190	G_2
$VEC_{EM1_{IV}}$	$EM1_{IV}$	$REC_{EM1_{IV}}$	190	
$VEC_{EM1_{HE}}$	$EM1_{HE}$	$REC_{EM1_{HE}}$	190	
$VEC_{EM2_{IV}}$	$EM2_{IV}$	$REC_{EM2_{IV}}$	190	
$VEC_{EM2_{HE}}$	$EM2_{HE}$	$REC_{EM2_{HE}}$	190	
$VEC_{EM3_{IV}}$	$EM3_{IV}$	$REC_{EM3_{IV}}$	190	
$VEC_{EM3_{HE}}$	$EM3_{HE}$	$REC_{EM3_{HE}}$	190	

V. EVALUATION RESULTS

In this section, the classification results of the 5-fold cross validation for G_1 and G_2 are presented and analyzed.

A. Results for G_1

In G_1, we want to determine, if the feature space from [15] in combination with a multilayer perceptron as classification engine (see Section IV-CI MLP_{4C}) is able to distinguish between the selected embedding methods EM_1, EM_2, and EM_3. The presented confusion matrix in Table III shows that most of the samples can be correctly classified (76.84%) during a 5-fold cross validation.

TABLE III
CONFUSION MATRIX OF 5-FOLD CROSS VALIDATION OF MLP_{4C} FOR G_1 (**BOLD**: CORRECT CLASSIFIED SAMPLES)

classified as $->$ Actual	CD	EM_1	EM_2	EM_3
CD (190)	**12**	150	0	28
EM_1 (380)	78	**298**	0	4
EM_2 (380)	0	0	**380**	0
EM_3 (380)	27	21	0	**332**

Especially the results for EM_2 and EM_3 are accurate, MLP_{4C} has correctly classified 100.0% of VEC_{EM2} (i.e., samples from EM_2) and 87.4% correctly classified VEC_{EM3}. Furthermore, we determined an accuracy of 78.4% for VEC_{EM1} (298 of 380 correctly classified). Thus, we can state that MLP_{4C} can distinguish correctly between embedding methods for 88.6% of evaluated samples (1010 of 1140), see Figure 6.

TABLE IV
CONFUSION MATRIX OF 5-FOLD CROSS VALIDATION OF MLP$_{7C}$ FOR G_2
(**BOLD**: CORRECT CLASSIFIED SAMPLES, *italic:* CORRECT CLASSIFIED EMBEDDING METHOD BUT MISCLASSIFIED MESSAGE TYPE)

classified as $->$ / Actual ($\sum$)	CD	$EM1_{IV}$	$EM1_{HE}$	$EM2_{IV}$	$EM2_{HE}$	$EM3_{IV}$	$EM3_{HE}$
CD (190)	**80**	7	8	19	20	39	17
$EM1_{IV}$ (190)	66	**18**	*28*	16	17	31	14
$EM1_{HE}$ (190)	58	*23*	**22**	16	16	38	17
$EM2_{IV}$ (190)	9	0	5	**126**	*35*	15	0
$EM2_{HE}$ (190)	2	0	4	*68*	**107**	9	0
$EM3_{IV}$ (190)	36	2	7	23	26	**62**	*34*
$EM3_{HE}$ (190)	38	1	7	29	22	*69*	**24**

However, the limitations of the approach can not be ignored. It is not able to differentiate between the cover data and EM_1. But this is reasonable, according to [5]. It is related to the size of analyzed packets (100 packets in our setup to extract a feature vector (sample), see Section IV-C), because the embedding becomes more and more unobtrusive the more packets are analyzed (in contrast: EM_2, and EM_3 become more obtrusive according to [15]).

Derived from this, we can state that the approach (feature space from [15] and MLP$_{4C}$ as machine learning based classification engine) is well suited for a usage after a potential anomaly detection in network data for the classification of trained embedding methods to attribute the embedding method used by potential attackers for covered communication.

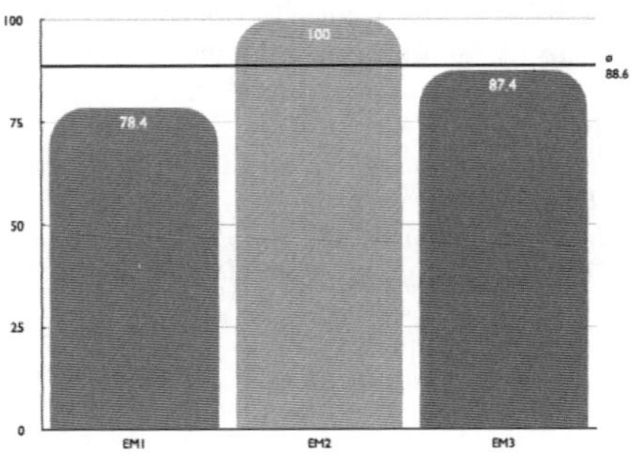

Figure 6. Percentage Share of correctly assigned Samples to Embedding Methods.

B. *Results for G_2*

For evaluation goal G_2, we analyze if our machine learning based approach is able to distinguish between two types of messages (invariant and heterogeneous). As the results in Table IV show, the approach is able to distinguish between embedding methods for most of the extracted feature vectors (samples) which confirms the results from G_1, but the message type can only be distinguished for EM_2 for the majority of samples (61.3% 233 of 380 samples). For EM_1 and EM_3 the message types are mostly misclassified, which means that our used feature space is not able to distinguish it, we also tried it with other classifiers (for example Decision Trees or a Support Vector Machine) but the results were comparable. If we look at the formalization of EM_1 (see Figure 2) and EM_3 (see Figure 4), the classification results are not surprising because the formalizations let us assume that the type of the embedded message should not result in statistically significant differences. Thus, it is plausible that the selected feature space has no discriminatory power to distinguish between embedded message types for these embedding methods. Additionally, the results also show (also from G_1) that our framework is well suited to confirm specific assumption about specific embedding methods and to determine possibilities and limitations which can be taken into account while elaborating novel defense mechanisms.

VI. CONCLUSION AND FUTURE WORK

In this paper, we introduce a novel analysis framework for steganographic network data in ICS. Information hiding techniques embedded with steganographic methods can be used to implement malware, communicating in ICS network traffic. The framework offers the possibility to compare and analyze multiple steganographic embedding methods and to derive defense mechanisms based on the analysis. In this work, we exemplarily analyze three embedding methods based on a straightforward laboratory setup with the novel framework and derive an approach, which is able to distinguish between the evaluated embedding methods after detection with an accuracy of 88.6%. Additionally, we were able to differentiate between invariant and heterogeneous message types for embedding method EM_2 for the majority of samples (61.3%).

These results confirm that the novel framework presented in this paper is well suited to analyze different steganographic embedding methods and it offers an easy and fast possibility to confirm use case specific assumptions about the behaviour of covert information hiding channels, which are used for stealthy malware to elaborate potential detection and defense mechanisms, and to additionally attribute potential attackers.

In future work, the framework will be used to analyze other embedding methods with other payload and embedding places (e.g. sensor values like in [21]). Additionally, we would like to analyze the opportunity to differentiate between message types more accurately with, for example, a novel handcrafted feature space. Furthermore, it should be analyzed if the used machine learning based approach (handcrafted feature space from [15] with MLP as classification engine) is able to attribute more attackers that use different types of steganographic embedding methods and message types that are, for example, not included into training data.

ACKNOWLEDGEMENTS

The research in this work has been performed in context of the project ATTRIBUT (https://omen.cs.uni-magdeburg.de/itiamsl/deutsch/projekte/attribut.html) jointly by a teaching project at "Brandenburg University" in term 2023/2024. This comprises in particular the conceptional design of the experimental analysis framework and embedding method EM_3, software realization in Python of all algorithms for embedding and feature extraction in Section III. It was further supported by the evaluation dataset (Section IV-B) generously contributed by the project "SYNTHESIS", funded by the German Federal Ministry for the Environment, Nature Conservation, Nuclear Safety and Consumer Protection (BMUV, project no. 1501666B) in the framework of the German reactor safety research program.

REFERENCES

[1] MITRE-ATT&CK, "Data obfuscation: Steganography", *https://attack.mitre.org/versions/v14/techniques/T1001/002/, last access: 19/09/24*, 2020.

[2] D. Kushner, "The real story of stuxnet", *https://spectrum.ieee.org/the-real-story-of-stuxnet, last access: 19/09/2024*, 2013.

[3] R. M. Lee, M. J. Assante, and T. Conway, "Analysis of the cyber attack on the ukrainian power grid", SANS Institute, Tech. Rep., 2016.

[4] I. Dragos, "Assessment of reported malware infection at nuclear facility", *https://www.dragos.com/blog/industry-news/assessment-of-reported-malware-infection-at-nuclear-facility/*, 2019.

[5] M. Hildebrandt, K. Lamshoeft, J. Dittmann, T. Neubert, and C. Vielhauer, "Information hiding in industrial control systems: An opc ua based supply chain attack and its detection", IH&MMSec 2020, pp. 115–120, 2020. DOI: 10.1145/3369412.3395068.

[6] T. Neubert, C. Kraetzer, and C. Vielhauer, "Artificial steganographic network data generation concept and evaluation of detection approaches to secure industrial control systems against stegano- graphic attacks", *In The 16th International Conference on Availability, Relia- bility and Security (ARES 2021), August 17–20, 2021, Vienna, Austria. ACM, New York, NY, USA, 9 pages. https://doi.org/10.1145/3465481.3470073*, 2021.

[7] K. Lamshoeft, T. Neubert, J. Hielscher, C. Vielhauer, and J. Dittmann, "Knock, knock, log: Threat analysis, detection & mitigation of covert channels in syslog using port scans as cover", *Digital Investigation 2022 (DFRWS EU 2022)*, 2022.

[8] S. Wendzel *et al.*, "A generic taxonomy for steganography methods", Jul. 2022. DOI: 10.36227/techrxiv.20215373.v1.

[9] W. Mazurczyk, S. Wendzel, and K. Cabaj, "Towards deriving insights into data hiding methods using pattern-based approach.", *ARES 2018, 13th International Conference on Availability, Reliability and Security; Hamburg, Germany, August 27 - August 30, ISBN: 978-1-4503-6448-5*, 2018.

[10] OPC-Foundation, "Unified architecture", *https://opcfoundation.org/about/opc-technologies/OPCUA/, last access: 19/09/24*, 2008.

[11] ACROMAG-Incorporated, "Introduction to modbus tcp/ip", *https://www.prosoft-technology.com/kb/assets/intro_modbustcp.pdf, last access: 19/09/24*, 2005.

[12] S. Wendzel *et al.*, "A revised taxonomy of steganography embedding patterns.", *In the Proceedings of 16th International Conference on Availability, Reliability and Security (ARES 2021), Article No.: 67, Pages 1 - 12, August 17–20, 2021, Vienna, Austria. ACM, New York, NY, USA, 12 pages. https://doi.org/10. 1145/3465481.3470069*, 2021.

[13] T. Neubert, B. Peuker, L. Buxhoidt, E. Schueler, and C. Vielhauer, "Synthetic embedding of hidden information in industrial control system network protocols for evaluation of steganographic malware", *Tech. Report, arXiv, https://doi.org/10.48550/arXiv.2406.19338*, 2024.

[14] L. Caviglione, "Trends and challenges in network covert channels countermeasures", *Applied Sciences*, vol. 11, Feb. 2021. DOI: 10.3390/app11041641.

[15] T. Neubert, A. J. C. Morcillo, and C. Vielhauer, "Improving performance of machine learning based detection of network steganography in industrial control systems.", *In the Proceedings of 17th International Conference on Availability, Reliability and Security (ARES 2022), Article No.: 51, pp. 1 - 8, August 23– 26, 2022, Vienna, Austria. ACM, New York, NY, USA, 8 pages. https://doi.org/10.1145/3538969.3544427*, 2022.

[16] Wireshark-Foundation, "About wireshark", *https://www.wireshark.org/about.html, last access: 19/09/24*, 2024.

[17] M. Hall, "The weka data mining software: An update.", *In SIGKDD Explorations*, 2009.

[18] J. Demšar *et al.*, "Orange: Data mining toolbox in python", *Journal of Machine Learning Research*, vol. 14, pp. 2349–2353, 2013.

[19] M. Abadi *et al.*, *TensorFlow: Large-scale machine learning on heterogeneous systems*, Software available from tensorflow.org, 2015.

[20] F. Chollet *et al.*, *Keras*, https://keras.io, last access: 19/09/24, 2015.

[21] K. Lamshoeft, C. Kraetzer, J. Dittmann, T. Neubert, and C. Vielhauer, "Information hiding in cyber physical systems: Challenges for embedding, retrieval and detection using sensor data of the swat dataset", *In Proceedings of the 2021 ACM Workshop on Information Hiding and Multimedia Security (IHMMSec '21), pp. 113 - 124, June 22–25, 2021, Virtual Event, Belgium. ACM, New York, NY, USA, 12 pages. https://doi.org/10.1145/3437880.3460413*, 2021.

Information Hiding Detection in Industrial Control Systems Statistical Analysis in Modbus TCP/IP

Robert Altschaffel
Advanced Multimedia and Security Lab
Otto-von-Guericke University
Magdeburg, Germany
email: Name.Surname@iti.cs.uni-magdeburg.de

Lennox Lingk
Advanced Multimedia and Security Lab
Otto-von-Guericke University
Magdeburg, Germany
email: Name.Surname@iti.cs.uni-magdeburg.de

Jana Dittmann
Advanced Multimedia and Security Lab
Otto-von-Guericke University
Magdeburg, Germany
email: Name.Surname@iti.cs.uni-magdeburg.de

Abstract—Hidden Communication is a technique increasingly employed by advanced attackers. Attacks performed by such advanced attackers on Industrial Control Systems (ICS) also recently gained relevance. This paper aims at increasing the security of ICS against attacks employing hidden communication. The detection of hidden communication is a necessary foundation to prevent non-legitimate communication within a network – potentially one used within a critical infrastructure. Besides detection, the attribution of such an advanced attack is useful to enhance future security. Therefore, we explore means to detect hidden communication in ICS using statistical methods. We demonstrate an approach based on heuristic methods and show a proof of concept for Modbus Messaging on Transmission Control Protocol/Internet Protocol (Modbus TCP/IP) including the successful evaluation with 37 network captures for ICS.
Keywords-Communication; Steganography; Attribution.

I. INTRODUCTION

Hidden Communication is a technique increasingly employed by advanced attackers; see e.g., the description of the technique Data Obfuscation: Steganography in the MITRE ATT&CK Matrix [1] or the widespread SteganoAmor campaign [2]. Also, Industrial Control Systems (ICS) are a relevant target surface.

The detection of hidden channels is a necessary prerequisite to prevent non-legitimate communication within a network – potentially one used within a critical infrastructure. The detection has to address varying embedding parameters and scenarios. Therefore, we use this paper to show how non-legitimate communication within an ICS can be detected using statistical methods.

Besides detection, the attribution of such an advanced attack is useful to enhance future security. Therefore, we explore means to identify the embedding parameters used by an attacker while hiding communication within the network traff c of an ICS. We demonstrate an approach based on heuristic methods and show a proof of concept.

The paper is structured as follows: Section II provides background information about stegomalware, steganographic terminology, and some information on ICS and Modbus Messaging on Transmission Control Protocol/Internet Protocol (Modbus TCP/IP) addressed in this paper. Section III provides an overview of a concept for the investigation of the use of statistic methods to detect hidden communication in ICS traff c including the essential creation of a test setup. Section IV describes the proof of concept of a statistical approach for the detection of steganographic messages in ICS traff c, while Section V describes the evaluation of the proof of concept. Section VI provides a summary and a discussion of limitations of the presented approach.

II. BACKGROUND

This section provides a brief background on some concepts used within the scope of this paper: the terminology of hidden communication including its potential use in malicious software, ICS and the protocol Modbus TCP/IP, which is commonly employed in such systems.

A. Stegomalware and steganographic terminology

Stegomalware is a composite word of steganography and malware (which is in turn a composite word of malicious and software). Therefore, stegomalware is malicious software that uses steganographic means to hide some communication, be it the initial download of the malicious software or for command and control (C2).

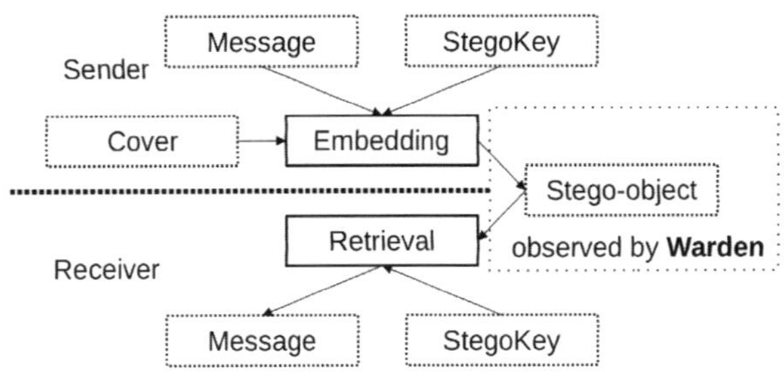

Figure 1. Communication using a steganographic channel.

The general procedure of communication can be seen in Figure 1. On the sender side, a message is embedded into a cover object by using a steganographic key. The embedding parameters vary depending on the channel and generally include information about embedding position, encoding, start or stop sequences. The resulting stego-object is then transferred to the receiver of the message and might be subject to investigation by a warden, the generic term for any security measure trying to detect hidden communication within a cover object. The receiver then uses the knowledge of the steganographic key to obtain the message.

B. Industrial Control Systems (ICS)

ICS control industrial processes. They consist of sensors that measure the physical world, actuators that manipulate the physical world and computing units that calculate, which manipulations achieve the industrial objective based on the readings provided by sensors. These computing units are commonly known as Programmable Logic Controllers (PLCs). The overall system relies on the communication between the components, which is performed using ICS-specific technologies and protocols. Some ICS protocols use Ethernet as transmission medium with Modbus TCP/IP being an example.

C. Modbus TCP/IP

The Modbus protocol is widely used in ICS. Modbus TCP/IP is an adaptation for the use of Ethernet as a carrier. Modbus/TCP uses a client/server model. The protocol itself is quite simple. Modbus/TCP uses a client/server model. The protocol itself has a simple structure as shown in Figure 2, consisting of the Mobdbus Application Protocol (MBAP) Header and the Protocol Data Unit (PDU). The MBAP Header consists of a Transaction Identifier (a sequence number used to tie requests and responses together), a Protocol Identifier (a static field), a length entry and the Unit ID that is used to identify remote peripheral devices that might be attached to a server. The PDU contains a function code, as well as data field of varying length.

Modbus TCP/IP Application Data Unit					
Transaction ID	Protocol ID	Length	Unit ID	Function Code	Data
MBAP Header				Protocol Data Unit	

Figure 2. Modbus TCP/IP Application Data Unit.

D. Modbus TCP/IP and hidden channels

The possibility to use hidden channels in Modbus TCP/IP communications has been explored in [4] by using an extended taxonomy of network information hiding patterns (see [5]) and exploring their application in the specific case of Modbus TCP/IP. It identifies 14 theoretical patterns and evaluated their capacity as well as requirements such as whether they could be implemented on the server and/or the client-side. Furthermore, four patterns are implemented for testing.

The storage pattern *S6 Reserved/Unused* is of special relevance to this paper. It uses the Unit ID field in the Modbus TCP/IP protocol to embed up to one byte of data.

E. Attribution and embedding parameters

Attribution relies on identifying properties of the attacker. These properties include the capabilities of the attacker, the tools and techniques used as well as the parameters used. These parameters include the embedding parameters used by a steganographic method.

F. Usage of statistical methods in computer security

Statistical methods have been used in the scope of computer security in various forms. They act as a foundation for pattern recognition. A primary benefit of using statistical methods in this approach is the fact that approach can be easily explained and understood; especially in contrast to complex machine learning algorithms where the field of explainability currently develops into a relevant research field. Explainability is fundamental for attribution since it allows to comprehend the reasoning over the result of a algorithm.

III. Concept

We want to show that statistic methods can be used to detect hidden communication in ICS traffic as a first step. As the second step we aim to obtain the embedding parameters used by steganographic methods in specific scenarios.

This process is described in detail in Section IV. However, to evaluate the applicability of such an approach, a data set of network recordings with and without steganographic embeddings is necessary.

In this work, we use steganographic embeddings performed within Modbus TCP/IP based on the results presented in [4].

Our approach uses a test set of Modbus TCP/IP traffic without steganographic embedding (*Cover*). Then, we perform steganographic embeddings on these Modbus TCP/IP recordings (*Steganographic Embeddings*) with varying embedding parameters. Finally, we analyse the Modbus TCP/IP traffic in order to detect steganographic embedding and to obtain the embedding parameters. Network recordings in the pcap-file format were used.

A. Cover Data Set: Modbus TCP/IP traffic

As a foundation, the publicly available data sets *MB-Base-1* [6] and *MB-Base-2* [7] are used. Schneider Modicon PLCs were used to create these two data sets. These Schneider PLCs act as client and server, respectively. Data is transferred cyclically between client and server.

MB-Base-1 [6] consists of two subsets. The subset *MB-Base-1-1* consists of 9 recordings of the communication between one client and two servers for about 10 minutes, each. The number of transferred data fields and the cycle time are varied among the recordings. The subset *MB-Base-1-1* contains two recordings of the communication between one client and one server for 10 and 70 minutes, respectively.

MB-Base-2 [7] consists of three recordings of the communication between one client and one server for 2 hours, each.

The number of transferred data fields and the cycle time are varied among the recordings.

B. Steganographic Embeddings: Storage Channel S6

The steganopgrahic pattern S6 from [4] was re-implemented in the tool timeembedder [8]. The goal was to enable a batch processing of various embeddings to create a broad data set by varying the embedding parameters and the embedded message. This implementation of the pattern S6 uses five embedding parameters:

- **startCode** Numeric start code for the embedding process in the packets that mark the start of the message embedding, Length: 3
- **endCode** Numeric end code for the embedding that marks the end of the embedded message, Length: 3
- **skipSize** Number of skipped packets between embeddings
- **oneCode** Numeric code for the embedding of a 1, e.g., 121 could be a code for 1, Length: 3
- **zeroCode** Numeric code for the embedding of a 0, e.g., 122 could be a code for 0, Length: 3

The storage channel S6 uses the field Unit ID of the MBAP header. In addition, this implementation fills the Unit ID with random values to avoid the suspicion that any non-zero values obviously belong to a steganographic transmission.

We use the data set *MB-Embed-1* [9], which was created using this algorithm and are publicly available. In total, this data sets contain 3 captures with steganographic embedding using the pattern S6. The data set also contain additional captures using other steganographic patterns described in [4] that are irrelevant for this paper.

C. Additional data sets for evaluation of detection performance

Due to the general handling of the field Unit ID in the MBAP header, further data sets are required to evaluate the performance of detecting the steganographic embedding. These data sets must mimic the behaviour of the changed Unit ID entries without embedding a steganographic message. Thus, a data set of 11 captures with the changed Unit ID behaviour but without steganographic embedding has been created.

However, traffic captures from general ICS were also used to evaluate the approach presented in this paper. A test set of Modbus TCP/IP network captures was compiled from public sources in [10] (it contains network captures from [11], [12] and [13]). This publicly available test set contains 8 network captures (see [14]).

IV. Statistical analysis to detect steganographic embedding using the storage channel S6 in Modbus TCP/IP

This section describes how steganographic embedding using the storage channel S6 in Modbus TCP/IP can be detected. This detection could be performed by a warden residing on the network of the Modbus TCP/IP communication. At first, a preprocessing is necessary in order to extract the Unit ID fields from the network recordings. Then, statistical analysis is performed following some assumptions about the network recordings, which are discussed in the following.

A. Preprocessing

As a first step, a preprocessing is necessary in order to extract the Unit IDs from the network recordings. The network recordings were available in the pcap-file format (see [15] for specification). The file format contains a file header and the packet records, which include the network packets and timing information.

The tool NWD [16] strips the file header and detects Modbus TCP/IP packets in network recordings and outputs timing information, as well as the MBAP headers, including the field Unit ID that is used by the S6 steganographic pattern.

B. Statistical assumptions

There are some underlying assumptions for the statistical analysis based on the behaviour of hidden channels in network streams:

- A start sequence (StartCode in the implementation of the pattern S6 used in this work; see Section III-B) can only appear to a very limited extend within a given network capture; the retrieval relies on the presence of such start sequence.
- The end sequence (EndCode) should be rare since random occurrences of the end sequence after the start sequence would disrupt the retrieval by cutting a message short.
- Between the start and end sequence, the sequences encoding the message (oneCode and zeroCode) will be overrepresented.

These assumptions hold true whether there is one embedded message or multiple messages using the same embedding key within a given network recording. For the proof of concept presented here, we assume only one embedded message per given network recording. Thus, a start sequence will only occur once.

C. Statistical Analysis

Based on these assumptions, the potential start sequence is identified by processing the network recording and searching for the least occurring instances of the Unit ID. This can be done by creating a histogram over the entire network recording and picking the rarest instance of Unit ID. These are the potential candidates for the start and end sequence.

In the next step, permutations of the specific pairings of start and end sequences are created and checked whether these pairings appear in said ordering within the data set.

If a suspected start sequence - end sequence segment is identified within the network capture, the next step is to extract the segment between these two markers for further statistical analysis.

It is assumed that the sequences encoding the message are overrepresented in the segment between start sequence and end sequence. Therefore, a histogram over the segment is

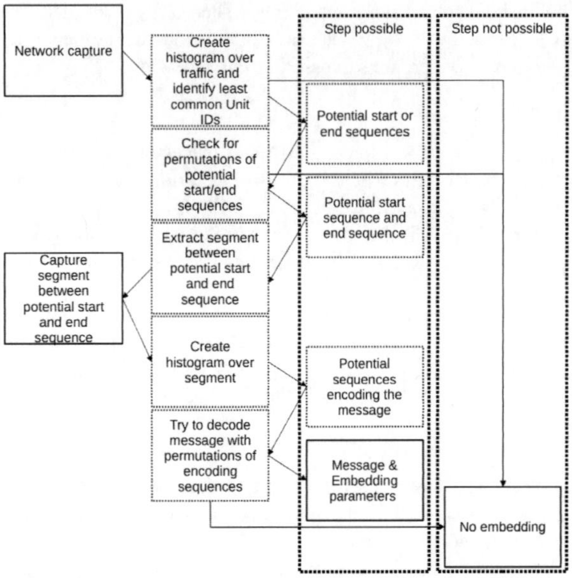

Figure 3. Process for the statistical analysis to find embeddings using the S6 steganographic pattern.

calculated to identify the most common occurrences of Unit IDs as candidates for oneCode and zeroCode, respectively.

At this point, the suspected oneCode and zeroCode can be used to try to retrieve the message. As such, any occurrence of the suspected codes is translated to a zero or a one, respectively. As it is not possible to identify, which of the candidates is the oneCode or the zeroCode at this point, both permutations have to be tried in order to check whether they lead to the retrieval of the message.

In addition, the distance between sequences identified as either oneCode or zeroCode within the segment can be used to calculate the SkipSize from the distance between the respective segments. At this step, the entire embedding key is obtained.

The entire process is visualized in Figure 3.

V. Evaluation

A proof of concept was created from the approach described in Section IV within the tool uidhist.pl [17] for evaluation.

The captures described in Section III-B and Section III-C were used for the evaluation of the detection mechanisms. In total, 37 network captures were used for the evaluation of the detection approach. All instances of the embedding were successfully detected with no false positives. An overview on the evaluation results can be seen in Table I.

Dataset MB-Embed-1 contained recordings with embedded steganographic messages using the S6 steganographic patterns. In these cases, the embedding was identified and the correct embedding parameters were obtained by the use of the presented approach. A screenshot of the exemplary output of the approach can be seen in Figure 4. The embedding parameters were correctly identified as shown in Table II.

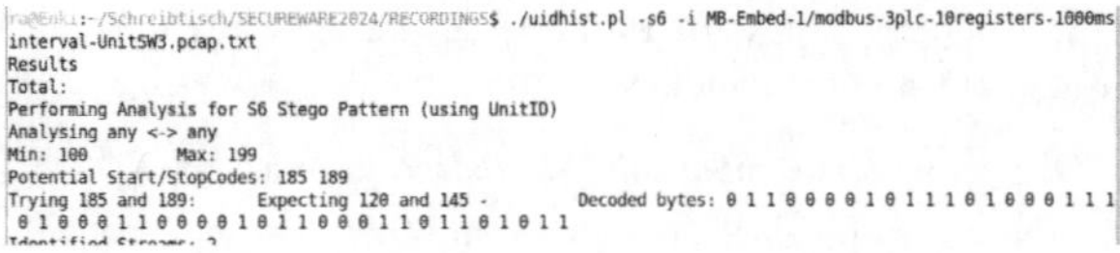

Figure 4. Screenshot from the application of the modified *uidhist.pl* on capture 18. The identified embedding parameters are visible as output.

In the case of the other evaluation data, no steganographic messages were embedded and none were detected. In the case of captures with few packets, potential candidates for the start and end sequence were detected (e.g., with captures 24 and 29). This is due to the fact that these captures do not contain enough packets for the statistical distribution to fully develop. However, in these cases no message could be detected and hence, the no embedding was detected.

This shows that the present approach enables promising results with the data sets used within this research.

VI. Conclusion and Future Work

This paper shows the viability of using statistic means to detect steganographic communication in ICS communications on the example of Modbus TCP/IP traffic. An approach for detection was presented and evaluated with 29 network captures showing promising results. In addition, the identification of embedding parameters was shown to be possible using the same approach. It was successfully evaluated with the network recordings that contained embedded steganographic messages. A clear limitation is that the approach is tied to the specific embedding pattern and to very similar patterns. Similar detection mechanisms can be devised for other parts of the MBAP header or for parts of other protocols. Another limitation is the use of our own data set for testing and evaluation in this work.

Future work is focused on the application of the proposed approach to other ICS protocols and steganographic patterns. In terms of ICS protocols, mainly Open Platform Communications Unified Architecture (OPC UA) and MQ Telemetry Transport (MQTT) are of interest due to their widespread use. So far, the application to MQTT seems promising. In terms of other steganographic patterns, the application to User-data Value Modulation and Reserved/Unused (S10 in [4]) forms the next goal in our research.

Acknowledgment

The work contributed by Lennox Lingk [6], [7], [8], [9], as well as the work on the usage of statistical measures in order to identify parameters of steganographic embedding has been performed in the research project ATTRIBUT (https://omen.cs.uni-magdeburg.de/itiamsl/deutsch/projekte/attribut.html). This work has been supported by the Agentur für Innovation in der Cybersicherheit GmbH. The Agentur für Innovation in der Cybersicherheit GmbH did not interfere in the research process and its results.

The tool NWD [16] was used in an older version created in the scope of the project "SYNTHESIS - Synthetically

TABLE I
RESULTS OF THE EVALUATION OF THE DETECTION APPROACH AGAINST THE VARIOUS DATA SETS.

Number	Filename	Dataset	Duration	Modbus Pakets	Embedding	
					present	detected
1	modbus-3plc-1registers-200msinterval	MB-Base-1	10:02	6024	✗	✗
2	modbus-3plc-5registers-200msinterval	MB-Base-1	10:00	6011	✗	✗
3	modbus-3plc-10registers-200msinterval	MB-Base-1	10:01	6020	✗	✗
4	modbus-3plc-1registers-500msinterval	MB-Base-1	10:05	2420	✗	✗
5	modbus-3plc-5registers-500msinterval	MB-Base-1	10:01	2048	✗	✗
6	modbus-3plc-10registers-500msinterval	MB-Base-1	10:03	2416	✗	✗
7	modbus-3plc-1registers-1000msinterval	MB-Base-1	10:04	1212	✗	✗
8	modbus-3plc-5registers-1000msinterval	MB-Base-1	10:46	1296	✗	✗
9	modbus-3plc-10registers-1000msinterval	MB-Base-1	9:22	1124	✗	✗
10	modbus-2plc-10registers-1000msinterval-70mins	MB-Base-1	1:10:23	33792	✗	✗
12	modbus-2plc-10registers-1000msinterval	MB-Base-1	10:02	4832	✗	✗
13	10_registers_2h_1000ms	MB-Base-2	2:03:00	95762	✗	✗
14	120_registers_2h_1000ms	MB-Base-2	2:12:22	1932985	✗	✗
15	240_registers_2h_1000ms	MB-Base-2	2:35:17	2266247	✗	✗
16	modbus-3plc-1registers-200msinterval-UnitSW1	MB-Embed-1	10:02	6024	✓	✓
17	modbus-3plc-5registers-500msinterval-UnitSW2	MB-Embed-1	10:01	2024	✓	✓
18	modbus-3plc-10registers-1000msinterval-UnitSW3	MB-Embed-1	9:22	1124	✓	✓
19-29	modbus-3plc-1registers-...					
19	...200msinterval-RandomUID-NoMessage	Created	10:02	6024	✗	✗
20	...200msinterval-RandomUID-NoMessage-1	Created	10:02	6024	✗	✗
21	...500msinterval-RandomUID-NoMessage-1	Created	10:05	2420	✗	✗
22	...500msinterval-RandomUID-NoMessage-2	Created	10:05	2420	✗	✗
23	...500msinterval-RandomUID-NoMessage-3	Created	10:00	6011	✗	✗
24	...1000msinterval-RandomUID-NoMessage-3	Created	10:04	1212	✗	✗
25	...200msinterval-RandomUID-NoMessage-4	Created	10:00	6011	✗	✗
26	...1000msinterval-RandomUID-NoMessage-6	Created	10:46	1296	✗	✗
27	...200msinterval-RandomUID-NoMessage-7	Created	10:01	6020	✗	✗
28	...500msinterval-RandomUID-NoMessage-8	Created	10:03	2416	✗	✗
29	...1000msinterval-RandomUID-NoMessage-9	Created	9:22	1124	✗	✗
30	eth2dump-clean-0,5h_1	[11]	0:30:00	35430	✗	✗
31	eth2dump-clean-1h_1	[11]	1:30:00	72150	✗	✗
32	eth2dump-clean-6h_1	[11]	6:00:00	427842	✗	✗
33	mb	[12]	1:30	55800	✗	✗
34	run8	[13]	1:00	72186	✗	✗
35	run11	[13]	1:00	72489	✗	✗
36	run1_3RTU_2s	[13]	1:00	305932	✗	✗
37	run1_6RTU	[13]	1:00	134690	✗	✗

TABLE II
EMBEDDING PARAMETERS OBTAINED BY THE DETECTION APPROACH IN THE CAPTURES THAT CONTAINED EMBEDDINGS.

Number	Filename	StartCode		EndCode		OneCode/ZeroCode	
		used	found	used	found	used	found
16	modbus-3plc-1registers-200msinterval-UnitSW1	185	185	189	189	120; 145	120; 145
17	modbus-3plc-5registers-500msinterval-UnitSW2	185	185	189	189	120; 145	120; 145
18	modbus-3plc-10registers-1000msinterval-UnitSW3	185	185	189	189	120; 145	120; 145

generated data segments with hidden malicious code functions for safety analysis in nuclear control technology" with the grant number FKZ: 1501666A which is funded by the Federal Ministry for the Environment, Nature Conservation, Nuclear Safety and Consumer Protection (BMUV). The tool uidhist.pl [17] which was used as a basis for the evaluation of the detection approach also originates from this project.

In addition, we would like to thank Dr-Ing. Stefan Kiltz for his support with formatting as well as Stefan Seidlitz for presenting the results at the conference.

REFERENCES

[1] MITRE ATT&CK, "Techniques - Data Obfuscation: Steganography ," https://attack.mitre.org/techniques/T1001/002/, 2020, [retrieved: October, 2024].

[2] A. Badaev and K.Naumova, "SteganoAmor campaign: TA558 mass-attacking companies and public institutions all around the world,"

Positive Technologies, https://www.ptsecurity.com/ww-en/analytics/pt-esc-threat-intelligence/steganoamor-campaign-ta558-mass-attacking-companies-and-public-institutions-all-around-the-world/, 2224.
[3] J. Dittmann, C. Kraetzer, J. Alemann, and B. Birnbaum, "Forensic Trace Analysis for MP3 based Stego-Malware: Exemplary Study for Stego-Algorithm and Capacity Attribution to derive YARA Rules for Malware Identification," Proceedings of the 2024 ACM Workshop on Information Hiding and Multimedia Security, pp. 101–112, https://dl.acm.org/doi/10.1145/3658664.3659641, 2024.
[4] K. Lamshoeft and J. Dittmann, "Assessment of Hidden Channel Attacks: Targetting Modbus/TCP," 21st IFAC World Congress, vol. 53, pp. 529–551, https://www.sciencedirect.com/science/article/pii/-S240589632030536X, 2020.
[5] W. Mazurczyk, S. Wendzel, and K. Cabal, "Towards deriving insights into data hiding methods using pattern-based approach," 13th International Conference on Availability, Reliability and Security, pp. 1-10, https://dl.acm.org/doi/10.1145/3230833.3233261, 2018.
[6] MB-Base-1 (Modbus-Schneider-Basis), https://datasets-amsl.cs.uni-magdeburg.de/index.php/s/YEpM7Nx6FPjdWJe, released 05.06.2024, [retrieved: October, 2024].
[7] MB-Base-2 (Modbus-Schneider-Basis), https://datasets-amsl.cs.uni-magdeburg.de/index.php/s/YEpM7Nx6FPjdWJe, released 05.06.2024, [retrieved: October, 2024].
[8] L. Lingk, *timeembedder*, released 26.07.2024, [retrieved: October, 2024].
[9] MB-Embed-1 (Modbus-Schneider-Embed), https://datasets-amsl.cs.uni-magdeburg.de/index.php/s/YEpM7Nx6FPjdWJe, released 05.06.2024, [retrieved: October, 2024].
[10] *[GERMAN]* R. Altschaffel, S. Kiltz, K. Lamshöft, and J. Dittmann, "ICS/OT-Sicherheit: Evaluation und Validierung der Erkennungsleistung von Stego-Malware in industriellen Steuernetzwerken mittels Synthese und Simulation," [Translation: ICS/OT Security: Evaluation and Validation of the Detection Performance against Stegomalware in ICS using Synthesis and Simulation], Kongressdokumentation zum 20. Deutschen IT-Sicherheitskongress des BSI, pp 333-348, 2024.
[11] I. Frazão, P. H. Abreu, T. Cruz, H. Araújo, and P. Simões, "Denial of Service Attacks: Detecting the frailties of machine learning algorithms in the Classification Process," in 13th International Conference on Critical Information Infrastructures Security (CRITIS 2018), ed. Springer, Kaunas, Lithuania, September 24-26, 2018, Springer series on Security and Cryptology , 2018. DOI: 10.1007/978-3-030-05849-4_19
[12] https://github.com/ITI/ICS-pcap/tree/master [retrieved: October, 2024].
[13] A. Lemay and J. M. Fernandez, "Providing SCADA network data sets for intrusion detection research," in 9th Workshop on Cyber Security Experimentation and Test (CSET 16), 2016; https://www.usenix.org/-conference/cset16/workshop-program/presentation/lemay [retrieved: October, 2024]
[14] R. Altschaffel, "Modbus Fingerprints - BSI Paper," https://gitti.cs.uni-magdeburg.de/raltschaffel/modbus-fingerprints-bsi-paper [retrieved: October, 2024]
[15] Network Working Group, "PCAP Capture File Format," https://www.ietf.org/archive/id/draft-gharris-opsawg-pcap-01.html, 2020, [retrieved: October, 2024].
[16] R. Altschaffel and R.Mecke , *nwd* version 0.2, https://gitti.cs.uni-magdeburg.de/raltschaffel/nwd/-/blob/23ae26a3b699b10d0d1df2f9d23d3e2c9c668bac/nwd.c, [retrieved: October, 2024].
[17] R. Altschaffel, *uidhist.pl* version 1.52, https://gitti.cs.uni-magdeburg.de/raltschaffel/nwd, [retrieved: October, 2024].

A Comparative Study of Backbone Architectures for Language Model-Based Intrusion Detection

Benedikt Pletzer and Jürgen Mottok
Laboratory for Safe and Secure Systems (LaS^3)
OTH Regensburg
Regensburg, Germany
email: {benedikt.pletzer, juergen.mottok}@oth-regensburg.de

Abstract—**Network based Intrusion Detection Systems (NIDS) have recently been shown to benefit from techniques developed for Natural Language Processing (NLP). Specifically, pretrained models based upon the ubiquitous Transformer backbone architecture have been shown to outperform other approaches. In recent months, promising research aimed at improving the aforementioned Transformer backbone or even replacing it all together has been published. This includes low bit quantization techniques like BitNet, as well as new model types like Mamba. This study, therefore, evaluates the potential of emerging foundation models, such as BitNet and Mamba, as backbones for NIDS. For this purpose, a comparative study of these models as backbone of an otherwise unchanged Language Model (LM) based NIDS algorithm is performed. Our results indicate that Mamba outperforms all other models in terms of classification performance, as well as in inference latency, if Graphics Processing Unit (GPU) acceleration is available. We also establish that low-bit-quantized models are able to achieve good classification accuracies, making them an auspicious option if their potential in computational efficiency are reached.**

Keywords- IDS; Transformer; BitNet; Mamba; MatMul-Free LM.

I. INTRODUCTION

In times of ever-increasing cybersecurity threats, emanating from state-sponsored entities, as well as criminal groups motivated by profit, countermeasures are in high demand. One of these countermeasures are Network based Intrusion Detection Systems (NIDS). Most NIDS currently deployed in industry use pattern matching methods to compare past attacks in order to detect them and notify system administrators when an attack occurs. These systems, however, struggle with detecting new or evolving threats, making them vulnerable to zero-day exploits or attackers changing their approach to avoid detection. Therefore, various machine learning based approaches to NIDS are researched at present. In [1], Ferrag et al. propose a NIDS that borrows the concepts currently applied in natural language processing to analyze network traffic. The authors report that their approach, based on Language Models (LM), outperforms the state of the art in attack classification accuracy. Aside from its performance in detection and classification, there are other potential upsides of using language modeling techniques in NIDS. These include the semantic interpretation of threat detections and the generation of threat responses in natural language [1][2]. Ferrag et al. utilize the Bidirectional Encoder Representations from Transformers (BERT) [3] Transformer as the backbone of their intrusion detection model. BERT, which has been proposed in 2018, shows strong performance in sequence classification tasks, but a lot of research has been done to improve on the standard Transformer architecture since then. This poses the question whether substituting the BERT backbone of the IDS model with a more modern one could lead to improvements either in classification accuracy, inference, speed or memory consumption. In recent months, various new model architectures and quantization techniques have been proposed to either replace the Transformer or improve it in key characteristics. This publication, therefore, aims to provide a summary of recent advancements in language modeling and to examine the validity of these new architectures and techniques in the field of NIDS. The following four architectures are chosen for this study:

- Transformer++ [4], [5]
- BitNet [6], [7]
- Mamba [8], [9]
- MatMul-Free LM [10]

Transformer++ serves as baseline, representing the state-of-the-art Transformer model. This publication provides reference points of existing implementation of the aforementioned models. Because some of these techniques can not yet meet their full potential, i.e., due to unoptimized implementations in software or the lack of dedicated hardware, the comparison of actually realized results is followed by a discussion of untapped potential. The contributions of this publication can be summarized as follows:

C1: A summary of recent advancements regarding LM backbones is given.
C2: The performance of these backbones in a NIDS task are studied comparatively
C3: The (to our knowledge) first NIDS models using BitNet, and MatMul-Free LM are presented

These three contribution aim to aid with answering the question: Which backbone architecture is most promising for the development of language model based NIDS?

This work is structured into a review of current challenges and recent advances regarding the backbones of language models, aiming to improve Transformers or replace them with more capable models, see Section II. Following this, Section III provides a description of the methodology used to train our models and evaluate them in regard to classification performance and inference speed. In Section IV the results are stated, once again subdivided into classification performance and inference speed. The results are then discussed in Section V, followed by a conclusion and the proposal of future work regarding LM based NIDS and LMs in cybersecurity in general in the final Section VI.

II. Related Work

This section will summarize some chosen advances in language modeling that have been published in recent months. The following paragraphs aim to inform about the basic concepts that drive the recent surge of change in foundational language model architecture. In our view, there are two foundational concepts that drive the publications described in this Section. On the one hand there is the low-bit quantization, on the other there is the emergence of parallelizable recurrent architectures that blend the properties of classical Recurrent Neural Networks (RNNs) and Convolutional Neural Networks (CNNs) [8]. These concepts will now be examined, exploring their implementation in recent models and their potential impact on the field of language modeling.

As language models are being released to the public and used by a wide range of individuals privately, as well as professionally, the cost associated with their inference becomes an increasingly urgent topic. Reducing this cost is therefore a central topic of current language model research. One approach to this topic is reducing the cost of inference by using less resource intensive operations within an otherwise unchanged Transformer model. This process, called quantization, has been standard practice for years. Customary quantization techniques involve replacing the floating point values (for example 16 bit precision floating point) used as weights or activation with integer values, e.g., 8-bit integers. This achieves a reduction in computational cost, and therefore energy consumption, as well as a reduction in consumed memory. Tao et al. show in [11] that low-bit quantized models can maintain good performance while reducing cost, provided quantization-aware training is done right.

The idea of increasing inference efficiency by applying low-bit quantization to the tried and tested Transformer architecture has recently been advanced by H. Wang and S. Ma et al. by proposing BitNet in [7] and further improved in [6]. BitNet uses the same basic building blocks as standard Transformer networks, while replacing its linear feedforward components with the BitLinear layer. This layer uses 1-bit binarized weights, quantizing every element in the weight matrix to either one or minus one, while quantizing the activation to 8-bit. Multiplication of these weight matrices with input vectors can therefore be performed using addition and subtraction only. These changes are not applied outside the Transformer block, meaning input and output components of the network remain unchanged. Wang and Ma show in [6] that the 1 bit-quantized BitNet can produce competitive results with regular Transformers, while significantly improving memory consumption and computational cost of inference.

S. Ma and H. Wang et al. further improve upon the aforementioned findings in [6] proposing BitNet 1.58, a BitNet variant that utilizes ternary instead of binary weights. This extends the values in the weight matrices from $\{-1, 1\}$ to $\{-1, 0, 1\}$. This change increases the information entropy of each weight matrix entry to 1.58 bits, hence the name BitNet 1.58, while maintaining BitNet's main advantage, the omission of multiplication operations. The authors state the ability to filter features as an additional advantage of adding zeros to the weight values. BitNet 1.58 is therefore more expressive than BitNet without additional computational cost.

The previously mentioned Transformer model [12] with Attention [13] as its foundational mechanism has been the dominating network architecture for sequence to sequence tasks in recent years. This success is a consequence of its ability to encode complex relations within a set reference window while maintaining a dense representation of information within its weights and computational efficiency in inference, as well as in training. The Transformer architecture, however, is not without its drawbacks. One of them is the fixed maximum length of its reference window. This drawback is further aggravated by the fact that the computational cost attached to the Transformer scales quadratically with the length of its reference window. A Transformers' ability to extract information from longer sequences is therefore limited, especially in resource-constrained environments.

Another heavily researched area of improvements to language models is the quest for a replacement for the Transformer architecture that remedies the shortcomings of the latter while maintaining the abilities that made Transformers successful. One of the most promising of these alternatives has been proposed by A. Gu and T. Dao in [9]. The authors present Mamba, a variant of State Space Models that scales almost linearly with sequence length while also showing an ability to reason on long sequences that rivals that of Transformer Networks. This model architecture also fulfills the requirement for efficient computations in training and inference because it can be computed either as linear recurrence (for inference) or global convolution (for highly parallelized training) [9]. A NIDS model based on the mamba is described in [14] by Wang et al.

Zhu et al. combine ideas from the previously described papers in [10] to create a language model that eliminates the need for matrix multiplication in inference completely. They achieve this by adapting the ternary BitLinear layer from [6] and combining this with the fundamental concept of Mamba, i.e., replacing the Transformer architecture with a parallelizable recurrent net. Thus avoiding the fundamental scaling issue of attention layers. In addition to their conceptual contribution, they also describe an optimized variant of the BitLinear layer that fuses the RMS (Root Mean Square) Norm with the activation function to be executed as a single block in the faster Static Random-Access Memory (SRAM) of GPUs reducing latency and memory consumption in comparison to the original BitLinear implementation.

Following this summary of chosen publications promising to

improve the current state of language models (**C1**), a description of the methodology used to determine the potential of the aforementioned techniques is given.

III. Test Setup and Methodology

This publication aims to provide a comparison between the aforementioned innovations with the language model like NIDS algorithms in mind. The two most significant criteria in this field are, according to the authors' opinion, the classification performance that can be achieved and the computational cost at inference needed to do so. The former is the most commonly described using metrics like precision, recall and F1-Score as shown in surveys regarding the topic [15][16]. While the latter is especially crucial in application areas with constrained computational resources like the Internet of Things (IoT) [17]. This section is, therefore, structured into a description of the training setup and the classification task used to benchmark model accuracy, and the setup used to measure inference speed.

A. Training and Classification

The dataset used for our tests is the Edge-IIoTset published by Ferrag et al. in [18]. We employ the readily extracted features provided in the CSV format. Due to alignment issues, the rows with the attack labels Man In The Middle (MITM) & Distributed Denial Of Service for User Datagram Protocol (DDOS-UDP) are removed from the dataset, reducing the number of labels, including normal, from fifteen to thirteen. This dataset is chosen to facilitate comparisons with similar, previously published models.

The structure of the NIDS algorithm, as well as the implemented training process, are borrowed from [1]. The model consists of an embedding layer that gets tokens as input, followed by a sequence to sequence model, that is referred to as backbone in this paper. The output of the sequence to sequence model is fed into two different Multi Layer Perceptron (MLP) heads. The first one is a Masked Language Model (MLM) head with an output shape fitting to reproduce the input tokens. The other one is a 13 class softmax head used for attack type classification. Figure 1 shows the previously described structure.

The training process is accordingly split into two stages. The first one, in the following referred to as pretraining, is an unsupervised training stage in which the network is fed with sequences of partially masked tokens from the training set. That means that 15 percent of the tokens are replaced with a mask token and the network is tasked with reproducing the original unmasked sequence. This allows the network to learn inner dependencies of the dataset and thus gain an understanding on how certain tokens relate to each other. In the second training step, the MLM head is replaced with a classification head and trained to classify the attack label associated with the last package in the input sequence in a supervised manner. To combat the heavily biased dataset, random oversampling is deployed, resulting in better classification results for classes with less support. Both training stages take sequences of tokens as input. The process of obtaining those tokens is the

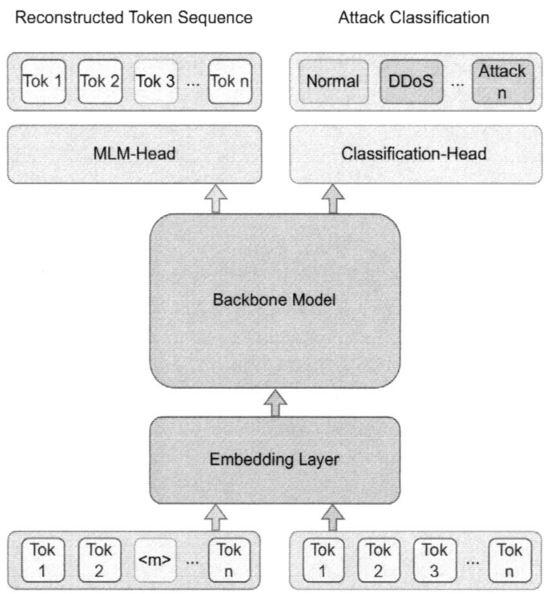

Figure 1. Structure of the Network in pretraining (left) and finetuning (right).

Privacy-Preserving Fixed-Length Encoding (PPFLE) algorithm described in [1]. Each entry in the CSV table is concatenated with the associated column name. The resulting string is then hashed, creating a fixed length string for each column name value combination in each line of the CSV. These are then converted into tokens using the Byte-level-Byte-Pair-Encoding.

The dataset is split into train, test, and validation splits with the respective sizes of 1272242, 381700, and 163600 entries each. The test split is used during training to select the most capable models, while the validation set is used to perform a final assessment of the models' performance, creating the numbers presented in Section IV. Each of the training stages consists of 1200 batches with a batch size of 256. Each element of a batch consists of a sequence of 900 tokens. The learning rate follows a sinus shape overlaid with an exponential decay. This training regime is chosen because it delivers good results with all tested backbone architectures.

Tuning the hyperparameters of each model is done by choosing smaller network sizes as initial reference points. The parameters of the network are later tweaked to enlarge the networks' parameter count. The variations in hyperparameters that result in noticeable improvement in classification performance are kept, and the process is repeated. The enlargement of the networks is stopped when improvements in classification performance are negligible. This approach is derived from LM scaling laws that suggest that a model's performance will increase with increasing parameter count as it's ability to encode complex information increases. For fixed data sizes, this trend can be expected to continue until a threshold based on the available data is reached and a phase of diminishing returns begins. We try to detect this threshold and determine the optimal model size based on the point of diminishing returns.

The backbones included in this comparative study are selected based on the Related Work presented in Section II. The baseline of this comparison will be a standard implementation of a Transformer network, including the improvements described in Transformer++ [4]. The specific implementation of this backbone is taken from the repository published with Meta's LLaMA [5]. Transformer++/LLaMA is commonly used as baseline in other publications, i.e., [6], [7], [9].

For the implementation of the low-bit quantization proposed in [6], [7] the process described in [7] is followed. Therefore, the LLaMA model used as baseline is adapted by interchanging the linear layers within the attention and the feed-forward blocks of the Transformer model with BitLinear layers. As BitLinear layer, the ternary variant described in [6] is used, as it outperforms or ties the binary variant in all regards except for information density in the weight matrices. The implementation of the BitLinear layer is taken from [10], as it is more efficient and already part of the project.

For Mamba, two different implementations are used. The first one is provided by the authors and contains a computationally efficient selective-scan written in CUDA. This, however, limits the algorithm to be used on systems that have GPU acceleration available. In order to also perform tests using CPU, a PyTorch only implementation is used [19].

The implementation for the final backbone architecture examined in this study is provided by Zhu et al., the authors of the paper describing it [10].

B. Inference Benchmarking

The inference speed test runs with CUDA GPU are executed on a virtual machine hosted on a laboratory server. The virtual machine has the following specifications:

- 12 core Intel(R) Xeon(R) Gold 6230R CPU @ 2.10GHz CPU
- NVIDIA A5000 with 24GB GDDR6 memory
- 128GB system memory

All models are implemented in PyTorch and executed using version 2.2.1 in half precision mode.

The implementation of Mamba provided by A. Gu and T. Dao utilizes a memory optimization that reduces copies between the slower HBM (High-Bandwidth-Memory) and the faster but smaller SRAM of GPUs. This optimization speeds up training and inference but requires access to a GPU, preventing the model from being inferred on CPUs. As many NIDS applications rely on low-cost devices, that usually do not have access to a GPU, to perform the classification of network data we deploy a pure python implementation to compare CPU inference latencies of Mamba and Transformer++. These tests are performed on the virtual machine described above but without access to the A5000 GPU. BitNet and MatMul-Free LM are omitted in this test the reasoning for this decision is given in Section IV-B.

IV. RESULTS

This section describes results obtained using the setups described in the previous section. The results are, like the test-setup description, structured into classification performance and inference speed.

A. Classification Results

A collection of metrics comparing the classification performance of the models trained as described in the previous section is shown in Table I. For a more visual comparison, selected key metrics are shown in the radar chart depicted in Figure 2.

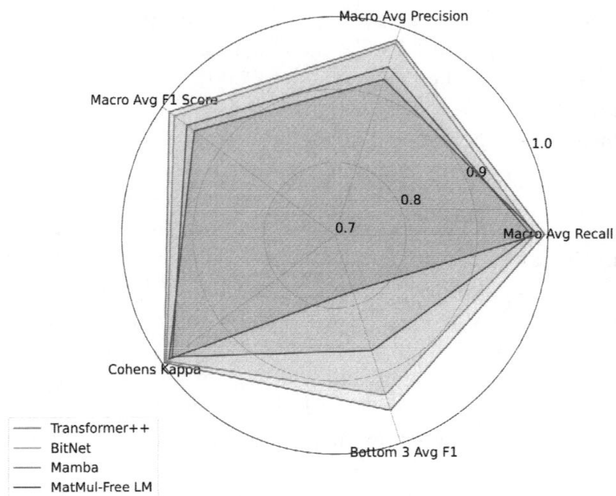

Figure 2. Radar chart showing key classification metrics.

Both charts show that the model using Mamba as backbone performs the best in all chosen metrics. BitNet is second in all metrics except for Macro Avg Recall, in which it comes third. The standard Transformer++ implementation and MatMul-Free LM take last place in all selected metrics. BitNet outperforming Transformer++ is notable as it only differs from Transformer++ by using BitLinear layers instead of 16 bit floating point linear layers. This change is primarily done to reduce the resources necessary to infer it. Comparing the results with the ones published by Ferrag et al. in [1] shows that all backbone models outperform the implementation using BERT as backbone. But it has to be noted that the training process and dataset are not identical to the ones used by Ferrag et al. as for example the sequence window is longer and, as described in Section III-A, two of the classes were removed from our dataset.

B. Inference Speed

Figure 3 shows a violin plot of each networks' inference latency on an Nvidia A5000 GPU using CUDA. The plot shows that Mamba beats the baseline set by Transformer++ by a wide margin. The latency of Mamba is 34 percent lower than the one of Transformer++ despite outperforming it in terms of classification, which makes Mamba the fastest as well as the most capable model in this comparison.

TABLE I
TABULAR OVERVIEW OF THE CLASSIFICATION PERFORMANCE

	Transformer++	BitNet	Mamba	MatMul-Free LM
Macro Avg Recall	0.9759	0.9819	0.9953	0.9851
Macro Avg Precision	0.9429	0.9766	0.9818	0.9245
Macro Avg F1 Score	0.9574	0.9791	0.9882	0.9442
Weighted Avg Recall	0.9926	0.9973	0.9988	0.9950
Weighted Avg Precision	0.9933	0.9974	0.9988	0.9961
Weighted Avg F1 Score	0.9928	0.9973	0.9988	0.9954
Cohens Kappa	0.9834	0.9940	0.9972	0.9888
Top 3 Avg F1	0.9985	0.9993	0.9996	0.9980
Bottom 3 Avg F1	0.8668	0.9303	0.9526	0.7803

The two quantized models, BitNet and MatMul-Free LM, on the other hand, have inference latencies that are larger than Transformer++'s by a factor of 6 and 4, respectively. These results can be explained by the method used to implement the quantized models in PyTorch, which is further discussed in the next section.

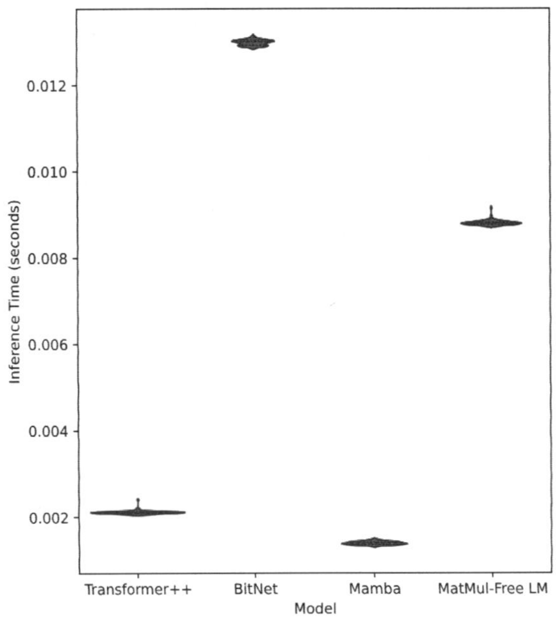

Figure 3. Inference latency on GPU.

Figure 4 shows the violin plots for the CPU inference tests. BitNet and MatMul-Free LM are not included in this test, as the GPU tests have already shown that their implementations are not competitive at the moment. This would not change on CPUs as the underlying cause of it, which is discussed in Section V-B, is the same. The plot shows that the advantage Mamba has over Transformer++ on GPU does not carry over to CPUs.

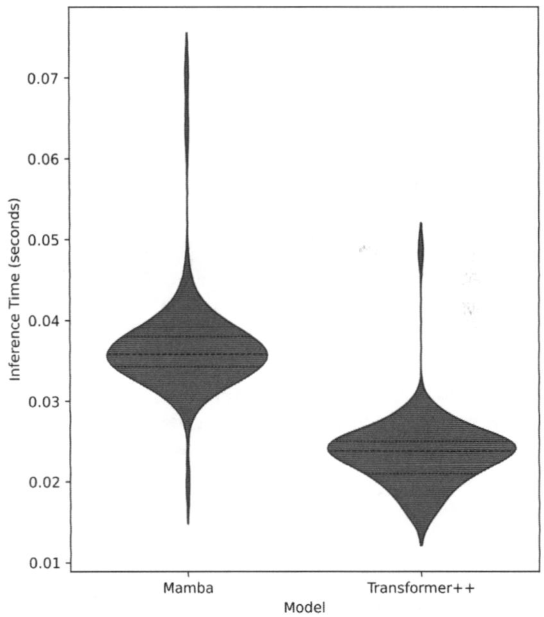

Figure 4. Inference latency without GPU acceleration, using CPU.

V. DISCUSSION

This section discusses the results presented in Section IV. In parallel to the preceding section, it is also subdivided into classification performance and inference latency.

A. Discussion of Classification Performance

The fact that all the models trained for the purpose of this study outperform the model described in [1] should not be solely attributed to the superiority of the more modern backbones used in our models. Attributing this difference to the attack classes removed in our tests seems natural, but does not withstand closer examination. Both classes (MITM & DDOS-UDP) are classified flawlessly by Ferrag et al.'s model. The main differentiator between our models and the reference is the classification performance for the fingerprinting class (F1 score in [1] 0 and .92 in our Mamba model). This discrepancy might be explained by omitting the separation of network traffic into flows. The removal of this step allows networks to draw connections between suspicious packages sent to and from different devices in close temporal proximity. The fingerprinting attack comprised in the Edge-IIoTset [18] aims at identifying the operating systems of potential victims in the Network. The attack therefore likely contains similar messages to different Hosts in the network in short timespans. Thus making detection easier if inputs are not restricted to one flow. The added capability of models creating an understanding of what happens in different parts of a network in combination with the sub-quadratic scaling of models like Mamba in regard to input sequence length suggests that non-flow-based NIDS could be a better choice going forward.

Determining why BitNet outperforms Transformer++ in our tests requires further experimentation. Besides quantization, the most notable difference between BitLinear and nn.Linear layers are the additional RMS Norm added before activation quantization. This added step, originally done for the sake of numerical stability, might contribute to this otherwise counterintuitive finding.

B. Discussion of Inference Latencies

The underwhelming results of BitNet and MatMul-Free LM can be explained by the fact that their default implementation use a technique called fake-quantization. This means that they use standard floating point values that are clipped during inference to behave like ternary/8-bit quantized operation. This is done because it is, due to limitations of the PyTorch library, the most efficient approach. using currently available hard and software. The usage of floating-point operations, however, cancels out the theoretical gains in computational load during inference, and memory requirements. Clipping these floats to get quantized values even introduces additional operations, leading to overall worse performance. In order to harness the full potential, these techniques offer, specialized inference frameworks like BitBlas or even better hardware accelerators tailored to these operations would be necessary.

Zhu et al. describe two approaches to dealing with this problem. One of them is the aforementioned BitBlas library used to generate their performance latency benchmarks, showing a reduction of latency by a factor of 3.65. The fused BitLinear implementation used for these tests are at the moment not publicly available. These results can therefore not be reproduced for this study. It has to be noted that BitBlas is intended for the deployment of large models on powerful hardware. Whether these results are transferable on the much smaller model sizes used in this study is yet to be determined.

The same limitations apply to our BitNet model, as it uses the fused BitLinear layer proposed in [10].

The other approach described in [10] is an implementation on Hardware using Field-Programmable Gate Arrays (FPGA) demonstrating the potential speed up and increase in efficiency that custom hardware tailored to MatMul-Free models would have. Using FPGAs is however out of the scope of this publication.

VI. Conclusion and Future Work

This publication provides a comparison between promising candidates for language model based NIDS backbones. Supposed to give researchers in the field guidance on which backbone to pick for their models. For this purpose, to our knowledge, the first NIDS using BitNet and MatMul-Free LM as backbones are presented (**C3**). A language model based NIDS using Mamba has been proposed by Wang et al. in [14]. Our research confirms their finding that constitutes a capable and efficient backbone for language model NIDS. Making Mamba the foremost choice as backbone if GPU acceleration is available. Our Inference tests on CPU show that basic Transformer++ might still be the best choice if inference on CPU is mandatory (**C2**).

We prove that low-bit quantized backbones can provide good classification performances which makes them an interesting option for low-power or otherwise resource-constrained application, as soon as specialized hardware or better software implementations for inference are available.

Additionally, we report, to our knowledge, the best classification results on the Edge-IIoTset [18] to date, using Mamba as backbone. The other models proposed in this work also outperform the baseline set in [1].

Future work in this direction might include expanding benchmarks by adding different datasets, as well as different representations of network traffic data, i.e., using raw byte data as input for the tokenizer.

Promising directions for future work include the development of better software solutions for low-bit quantized operations. An investigation into the potential upsides of specialized hardware accelerators might unlock new possibilities for the edge deployment of language model based NIDS and language models in general.

Another promising research field is the generation of detailed descriptions of security incidents in natural language. Ferrag et al. propose in [2] a model based on FalconLLM [20] that generates incidence responses using NIDS classification results as prompt. This approach, however, limits the generated incidence responses to general advices on how to counter certain threats. More detailed outputs might be possible if the generating language model has access to information from the hidden states of the NIDS model.

ACKNOWLEDGMENT

The presented work is part of the research project *KRITIS Scalable Safe and Secure Modules* (KRITIS³M), which is funded by the Project Management Jülich (PtJ) and the German Federal Ministry for Economic Affairs and Climate Action (BMWK) under funding code 03EI6089A.

REFERENCES

[1] M. A. Ferrag *et al.*, "Revolutionizing Cyber Threat Detection With Large Language Models: A Privacy-Preserving BERT-Based Lightweight Model for IoT/IIoT Devices", *IEEE Access*, vol. 12, pp. 23 733–23 750, 2024, ISSN: 2169-3536. DOI: 10.1109/ACCESS.2024.3363469.

[2] M. A. Ferrag *et al.*, "Revolutionizing Cyber Threat Detection with Large Language Models", 2023. DOI: 10.48550/ARXIV.2306.14263.

[3] J. Devlin, M.-W. Chang, K. Lee, and K. Toutanova, "BERT: Pre-training of deep bidirectional transformers for language understanding", in *Proceedings of the 2019 Conference of the North American Chapter of the Association for Computational Linguistics: Human Language Technologies, Volume 1 (Long and Short Papers)*, J. Burstein, C. Doran, and T. Solorio, Eds., Minneapolis, Minnesota: Association for Computational Linguistics, Jun. 2019, pp. 4171–4186. DOI: 10.18653/v1/N19-1423.

[4] P. Thapak and P. Hore, *Transformer++*, Mar. 2020. arXiv: 2003.04974 [cs, stat].

[5] H. Touvron *et al.*, *LLaMA: Open and Efficient Foundation Language Models*, Feb. 2023. arXiv: 2302.13971 [cs].

[6] S. Ma *et al.*, *The Era of 1-bit LLMs: All Large Language Models are in 1.58 Bits*, Feb. 2024. arXiv: 2402.17764 [cs].

[7] H. Wang *et al.*, *BitNet: Scaling 1-bit Transformers for Large Language Models*, Oct. 2023. arXiv: 2310.11453 [cs].

[8] T. Dao and A. Gu, *Transformers are SSMs: Generalized Models and Efficient Algorithms Through Structured State Space Duality*, May 2024. arXiv: 2405.21060 [cs].

[9] A. Gu and T. Dao, *Mamba: Linear-Time Sequence Modeling with Selective State Spaces*, Dec. 2023. arXiv: 2312.00752 [cs].

[10] R.-J. Zhu *et al.*, *Scalable MatMul-free Language Modeling*, Jun. 2024. arXiv: 2406.02528 [cs].

[11] C. Tao *et al.*, "Compression of Generative Pre-trained Language Models via Quantization", in *Proceedings of the 60th Annual Meeting of the Association for Computational Linguistics (Volume 1: Long Papers)*, Dublin, Ireland: Association for Computational Linguistics, 2022, pp. 4821–4836. DOI: 10.18653/v1/2022.acl-long.331.

[12] A. Vaswani *et al.*, "Attention is all you need", in *Advances in Neural Information Processing Systems*, I. Guyon *et al.*, Eds., vol. 30, Curran Associates, Inc., 2017.

[13] D. Bahdanau, K. Cho, and Y. Bengio, *Neural Machine Translation by Jointly Learning to Align and Translate*, May 2016. arXiv: 1409.0473 [cs, stat].

[14] T. Wang *et al.*, *NetMamba: Efficient Network Traffic Classification via Pre-training Unidirectional Mamba*, May 2024. arXiv: 2405.11449 [cs].

[15] T. Saranya, S. Sridevi, C. Deisy, T. D. Chung, and M. Khan, "Performance Analysis of Machine Learning Algorithms in Intrusion Detection System: A Review", *Procedia Computer Science*, vol. 171, pp. 1251–1260, 2020, ISSN: 18770509. DOI: 10.1016/j.procs.2020.04.133.

[16] Z. Ahmad, A. S. Khan, C. W. Shiang, J. Abdullah, and F. Ahmad, "Network intrusion detection system: A systematic study of machine learning and deep learning approaches", *Transactions on Emerging Telecommunications Technologies*, vol. 32, no. 1, Jan. 2021, ISSN: 2161-3915, 2161-3915. DOI: 10.1002/ett.4150.

[17] A. Heidari and M. A. Jabraeil Jamali, "Internet of Things intrusion detection systems: A comprehensive review and future directions", *Cluster Computing*, Oct. 2022, ISSN: 1386-7857, 1573-7543. DOI: 10.1007/s10586-022-03776-z.

[18] M. A. Ferrag, O. Friha, D. Hamouda, L. Maglaras, and H. Janicke, "Edge-IIoTset: A New Comprehensive Realistic Cyber Security Dataset of IoT and IIoT Applications for Centralized and Federated Learning", *IEEE Access*, vol. 10, pp. 40 281–40 306, 2022, ISSN: 2169-3536. DOI: 10.1109/ACCESS.2022.3165809.

[19] J. Ma, *Mamba-minimal*, https://github.com/johnma2006/mamba-minimal, Feb. 2024.

[20] E. Almazrouei *et al.*, *The Falcon Series of Open Language Models*, Nov. 2023. arXiv: 2311.16867 [cs].

Fingerprinting and Tracing Shadows: The Development and Impact of Browser Fingerprinting on Digital Privacy

Alexander Lawall
IU International University of Applied Science
Erfurt, Thüringen, Germany
alexander.lawall@iu.org

***Abstract*—Browser fingerprinting is a growing technique for identifying and tracking users online without traditional methods like cookies. This paper gives an overview by examining the various fingerprinting techniques and analyzes the entropy and uniqueness of the collected data. The analysis highlights that browser fingerprinting poses a complex challenge from both technical and privacy perspectives, as users often have no control over the collection and use of their data. In addition, it raises significant privacy concerns as users are often tracked without their knowledge or consent.**

Keywords-browser fingerprinting; device fingerprinting; tracking; privacy.

I. INTRODUCTION

In the increasingly digitized world, the issues of online privacy and data security are becoming more complex. Particularly in tracking — monitoring users and their devices across different web servers — browser fingerprinting has emerged as an effective technique for creating detailed user profiles. Unlike the storage of information via cookies, which requires explicit user consent as mandated by the European General Data Protection Regulations (GDPR) guidelines, fingerprinting does not require such consent. A browser fingerprint can be generated in the background without any obvious signs to the end user, leaving them unaware of whether and to what extent they are being tracked.

It is possible to manipulate a device locally to alter its fingerprint. This is often not feasible for all users, unlike deleting cookies. This invisible threat is not apparent to the general public and raises significant privacy concerns, as individuals can be tracked unnoticed. These profiles can contain private information, depending on the server operators, including age group, ethnic origin, social circles, and interests of the affected person.

Browser fingerprinting poses a threat to the privacy of the general public. Contrary to being a threat, it is an opportunity to provide valuable information to enhance the authentication mechanisms. Both perspectives are explored throughout this paper. The focus will be on the various techniques of fingerprinting to understand how accurate and detailed user profiles can be created. The main research questions that this paper seeks to answer are:

RQ1 *"What methods are used in browser fingerprinting and what user data are collected in the process?"*

RQ2 *"How has the development of browser fingerprinting as a user identification method influenced user privacy and data protection in the digital space?"*

The paper is structured as follows: Section I introduces browser fingerprinting and its privacy implications. In Section II, the theoretical background explains how fingerprinting works and its legal challenges. Section III outlines techniques like HTTP Headers, Canvas, and WebGL Fingerprinting. Section IV examines the impact of fingerprinting on privacy and the regulatory landscape. Section V concludes with a summary of the findings, emphasizing the need for stronger privacy measures and further research on countermeasures.

II. THEORETICAL BACKGROUND

A. Fingerprinting

Browser fingerprinting refers to collecting characteristic information that the browser directly or indirectly reveals about itself. Often used to track users, this technology has also found applications in IT security, such as fraud detection. Unlike tracking methods like cookies, browser fingerprinting does not require storing data on the user's computer, allowing the process to occur secretly and without consent [1, p. 1]. Consequently, creating a new identity, similar to deleting cookies, is not easily achievable, and GDPR privacy laws often provide little protection. Unlike cookie tracking, browser fingerprinting is not explicitly mentioned in the GDPR. It should fall under the collection of identifiable information but website operators frequently claim "legitimate interest", enabling such data collection without the user's consent [2].

Active transmission of data is not required for browser fingerprinting, as loading a webpage can transmit various pieces of information, such as the user's preferred language, within the HTTP headers. This passive data collection provides only a limited amount of information, so it is often supplemented with active data collection methods. An active approach typically employs JavaScript to interface with the browser and gather information, such as screen resolution, installed add-ons, and graphics card data, merging them into a unique fingerprint [3, pp. 1, 3].

Similar to human fingerprints, browser fingerprinting relies on the uniqueness of browser characteristics, which typically do not change significantly with regular use. This allows for accurate user identification over extended periods [3, p. 2]. However, not all collected data points are equally unique or stable, necessitating careful selection of information to achieve accurate results. The fingerprinting algorithm combines both passively and actively collected data into a unique string. Depending on the operator's goals, adjustments can be made;

for instance, using cookies, the fingerprint might be less stable but more unique, while tracking users without cookies requires high stability [4, pp. 1-5]. Eckersley's study showed that participant browsers already had high entropy, indicating many unique characteristics sufficient for accurate fingerprinting, though not stable enough for long-term accuracy. In recent years, potential entropy has increased with new techniques like HTML Canvas, WebGL-based hardware fingerprints, audio API fingerprints, plug-in-based fingerprints, and methods utilizing mouse movements or differences in HTML parsing between browsers, making cross-browser user identification possible [3, pp. 4-5].

B. Concerns for Digital Privacy

Historically, the greatest threat to online tracking was posed by cookies, along with other technologies like Flash cookies, which have lost significance in recent years. Changes by browser manufacturers, such as Mozilla, which rendered many exploited technologies, so-called "super-cookies", ineffective [5], and additional browsers planning to block or eliminate third-party cookies in the coming years [6], have shifted the landscape. Following the GDPR, the use of non-essential cookies has been further restricted and standardized for the first time, defining how users share their data through cookies [7]. In contrast, browser fingerprinting occurs in the background and leaves no stored information on the user's computer. Thus, the use of fingerprints not only circumvents previous issues related to local storage, such as privacy laws and technical limitations but also persists even when local data is deleted or when incognito mode is used.

A 2021 study of the Alexa Top 100,000 websites found that nearly 10% of the sites used scripts to generate fingerprints [8, pp. 11-12]. Comparing this to a similar 2014 study, which recorded 5.5% of the top 100,000 sites using canvas fingerprinting scripts, reveals an almost doubling of usage over seven years [9]. This suggests a shift towards online tracking using this technology, which is much harder to detect and prevent compared to cookies. The creation of a fingerprint is imperceptible to the user, with no simple way to effectively change or delete their fingerprint. Cookie banners give a false sense of security while tracking continues in the background without consent.

Thus, browser fingerprinting poses an active threat to privacy, as users often have no control over the collection and use of their data. This stands in opposition to many current data protection principles, such as the GDPR.

III. Methods of Browser Fingerprinting

In the context of browser fingerprinting techniques, the methods of data collection are varied and comprehensive. Therefore, specific properties and criteria are used to select techniques. The following sections will encompass the explanation of the techniques in terms of their functionality and their applications will be discussed to provide a detailed understanding of their use. An evaluation based on the advantages and disadvantages of each technique is also included to weigh their effectiveness and potential risks. Given the ever-increasing number of techniques, only the most commonly used, established, or novel methods will be presented here.

A. HTTP Header Attributes

1) Definition and Basics: The HTTP request header is a part of every HTTP request exchanged between a client (web browser) and a server, transmitting various functional and compatibility-related information [10]. Although individual attributes are not unique, they can be combined to distinguish a client. This explanation is based on HTTP version 1.1, with HTTP/2 maintaining most attributes within a modified header frame [11].

2) Analysis: HTTP request headers include attributes that differ by browser and version. Effective fingerprinting requires selecting attributes that remain consistent over time. Reliable fields include User-Agent, Accept, Content-Encoding, and Content-Language, which provide valuable identification information [4, p. 5] [12, p. 880]. The User-Agent, despite lacking standardization, offers high uniqueness due to its detailed browser and OS information [13].

3) Advantages: The main advantage of using HTTP headers is their passive information collection, which occurs automatically with each request. This method is efficient, unobtrusive, and compatible with most web servers, processing data on the server side without a noticeable impact on the client.

4) Disadvantages: HTTP header information is limited, as most attributes provide minimal details. The User-Agent, while informative, can be easily altered by browser extensions, reducing its reliability (i.e. User-Agent Switcher for Chrome). Furthermore, using such technologies without consent can violate GDPR regulations, necessitating legal review before implementation [14].

B. Enumeration of Browser Plugins

1) Definition and Basics: Browser plugins, whether pre-installed or user-added, have been a method for recognizing systems, along with font detection. Most browser features are indirectly modified, except for extensions. The demand for accurate enumeration of these extensions is high [12, pp. 878-880].

2) Analysis: Many information-rich plugins, like Flash, have disappeared over the years. Since 2016, most browsers, including Firefox, no longer support the Netscape Plugin Application Programming Interface (NPAPI) plugin interface, leading to the navigator.plugins object in modern browsers showing only standard plugins like PDF viewers [15]. This limitation reduces the impact of plugins on fingerprinting but still allows differentiation between systems and browsers. The direct detection of user-installed add-ons is not possible, limiting the data's significance [12, pp. 886-887]. However, new methods to enumerate extensions have emerged. Chromium-based browsers can access extension settings via a local URL. A GitHub project exploits this to check for over 1,000 extensions by requesting internal resources and checking the status codes [16]. Additionally, ad blockers' behavior in removing unwanted content can be detected by creating elements they typically block and checking for changes, revealing active blocklists [17]. Another method involves reading the status of handler protocols to identify installed programs like Skype and Zoom.

3) Advantages: User-installed extensions offer high uniqueness and stability due to the number of extensions.

4) Disadvantages: Insights into users' privacy, including sensitive information like health conditions, religion, and political views, can be inferred [18, pp. 11-12]. The fingerprinting process relies on limited methods, making it prone to errors, and requires continuous updates to maintain reliability.

C. Canvas Fingerprinting

1) Definition and Basics: Canvas fingerprinting involves generating a digital fingerprint using the Canvas element introduced in HTML5. It utilizes the Canvas API to draw a hidden 2D graphic in the background. Variations in how different browsers and devices handle this image due to differences in hardware acceleration, installed fonts, and graphic libraries result in a highly stable and unique fingerprint [1, pp. 1-3].

2) Analysis: A script embedded in a webpage adds an invisible Canvas element that draws a predetermined 2D graphic in the background. Text can also be drawn using the Canvas context, employing various fonts and sizes. WebFonts enable dynamic loading of fonts from the internet, allowing specific fonts to be chosen to test for uniqueness in font rendering. The resulting image data can be extracted using functions like *getImageData* and *toDataURL*, which can then be hashed to form a fingerprint, typically using a hashing algorithm. This hash is sent via a web request to a server for processing and storage. Besides storing the fingerprint for later identification, another application method involves comparing the fingerprint with an extensive database of known fingerprints and corresponding system configurations, enabling reliable system profiling [1, pp. 2-4].

3) Advantages: Mowery and Shacham demonstrated that implementing Canvas fingerprinting is straightforward, requiring minimal lines of client-side code. It leverages basic JavaScript functions and can be deployed across all major web applications. The fingerprinting process is discrete for users and challenging to block because Canvas operations are common in web applications, making it difficult to distinguish normal operations from fingerprinting scripts. The simplicity of fingerprint creation enables high speed, stability, uniqueness, and entropy, making it particularly valuable for real-time tracking applications [1, pp. 1-5].

4) Disadvantages: Changes in browser environments, such as updates or graphic settings, can affect the stability of the fingerprint. Variability in hardware and software configurations can lead to inconsistencies. As an active technique, executing code on the client side is necessary, posing risks of detection and potential blockage by blocklists targeting known fingerprinting scripts [1, pp. 3-7]. While imperceptible to users, the limited interfaces to retrieve generated Canvas data can be monitored and manipulated by extensions. Add-ons like CanvasBlocker allow users to prevent data retrieval or manipulate Canvas data, continuously generating new fingerprints to prevent identification [19]. Finally, while implementing Canvas fingerprinting is "relatively simple", analyzing and interpreting the data can be complex and may require expertise in the field [1, pp. 6-8].

D. WebGL Fingerprinting

1) Definition and Basics: WebGL fingerprinting is a technique utilizing the WebGL JavaScript API, based on OpenGL ES 2.0, allowing web applications to render both 2D and 3D graphics with high performance by directly accessing the GPU [20]. Unlike Canvas fingerprinting, which focuses on 2D graphics and identifies software differences mainly through fonts and graphic libraries, WebGL fingerprinting provides deeper and more precise detection capabilities. It captures unique hardware information, particularly details about the graphics processor, distinguishing it significantly from Canvas fingerprinting and broadening its application for tracking purposes [1, p. 4].

2) Analysis: WebGL fingerprinting uses a Canvas element to access the API. Similar to Canvas fingerprinting, it creates an invisible element performing 3D operations in the background to collect data without user interaction. A straightforward application involves accessing specific variables, such as *UNMASKED_VENDOR_WEBGL* and *UNMASKED_RENDERER_WEBGL*, using the *getParameter* function in the WebGL context. These variables provide information about the graphics hardware manufacturer (Vendor) and model (Renderer). For example, a Vendor entry like "Intel" indicates an integrated graphics unit, while "Nvidia" combined with "GeForce GTX 970" as Renderer indicates a dedicated graphics card. These details can reveal insights into the system being used [21, p. 17]. Privacy concerns have led browsers like Apple's WebKit to provide generic information instead of specific data to protect user privacy. Since 2020, WebKit has masked Vendor and Renderer information, as well as shading language details [22]. Firefox similarly groups graphics processor models into categories instead of displaying specific models. In practice, this means that a Nvidia card from the 900 series onward, for example, is reported as "GeForce GTX 980". In summary, research investigating hardware fingerprinting using HTML5 demonstrated the capability to identify devices based on GPU performance. It utilizes the graphics processor's clock frequency and clock skew to render complex 3D graphics, measuring GPU performance based on the number of frames rendered within a period, providing insights into the GPU's frequency and core count [23, pp. 3-4].

3) Advantages: As demonstrated by Cao et al., WebGL can offer high uniqueness and stability [24]. Its direct interface with the system ensures consistency across browsers, making it challenging for users to evade identification through simple browser changes or reinstalls. Despite changes to enhance WebGL's resistance to fingerprinting, it reliably identifies users. The successor to WebGL, WebGPU, is currently in development, promising even more privacy risks due to its closer hardware access, allowing for classifications with up to 98% accuracy in 150 milliseconds, a reduction from the 8 seconds WebGL took [25].

4) Disadvantages: The complexity of WebGL fingerprinting is significantly higher compared to previous techniques, necessitating careful consideration whether a simpler Canvas approach combined with other methods might be accurate enough for specific use cases. Intensive tasks in a 3D environment can also strain the target system, leading to longer fingerprint creation times [1, p. 4]. Implementing WebGL requires caution, as shown by the cases of Laperdrix et al. and Cao et al., and opting for a ready-made solution might be advisable. Moreover, WebGL shares Canvas's vulnerability to blocked or misread data if detection methods rely on differences in rendered graphics. Even novel methods like DrawnApart can be mitigated through countermeasures, such as limiting to a single EU [26, p. 12]. WebGL may also not be available or disabled on some devices, necessitating consideration of alternatives, such as using the 2D Canvas.

E. Audio Fingerprinting

1) Definition and Basics: The Web Audio API is a JavaScript interface for processing and synthesizing audio signals in the web browsers, part of the HTML5 standard. It can identify systems through manufacturing differences in audio hardware. Methods analyze signal processing characteristics, hardware differences, and system responses to specific audio signals for fingerprinting [27, pp. 1107-1109].

2) Analysis: Audio fingerprinting involves various acoustic measurements to create a unique device fingerprint. It requires an AudioContext linking an AudioBuffer, Oscillator, and Compressor. The AudioBuffer represents a small audio segment, while the Oscillator generates a waveform at a defined frequency. The Compressor manipulates the audio signal. The unique waveform generated and manipulated reflects system characteristics, allowing a unique fingerprint to be created using a hash function on the final waveform. This method, known as "Dynamic Compressor (DC)", is highly stable, producing the same fingerprint for the user each time using a reliable hash function [27, pp. 1109-1111].

Another method is the "Fast Fourier Transform" (FFT), converting audio signals from the time domain to the frequency domain. It measures hardware implementation differences to identify characteristics. FFT is less stable than DC, often requiring multiple attempts for consistent results. DC and FFT are often used together for more reliable outcomes [27, pp. 1111-1114]. Researchers compared the techniques, including custom-designed ones, alongside DC and FFT. These included creating "Custom Signals", "Merged Signals", and analyzing generated AM and FM waves. All techniques showed good stability, averaging two to four attempts for fingerprint matching [28, pp. 3-5].

3) Advantages: The generated fingerprints are highly stable and can differentiate systems based on their properties. Queiroz and Feitosa showed that mobile devices using Firefox could be consistently recognized and grouped by their stable fingerprints [27, p. 1119]. Techniques like DC are simple to implement and offer high stability. Other promising techniques, especially when used together, could enhance potential but are more challenging to implement [28, pp. 1-3].

4) Disadvantages: While audio fingerprinting offers high stability, it lacks uniqueness and accuracy on its own and should be used with other fingerprinting techniques [27, p. 1119]. Additionally, the Web Audio API can be disabled on devices or manipulated by add-ons like "Canvas Blocker", which also blocks and manipulates Canvas and WebGL.

F. Font Fingerprinting

1) Definition and Basics: Font fingerprinting is a browser fingerprinting technique that identifies devices by recognizing installed fonts. This method creates unique digital fingerprints by combining fonts with other data points, which can be used for tracking and identification purposes [29, p. 314].

2) Analysis: After the end of Adobe Flash, a new method for font recognition was needed. JavaScript uses a fallback mechanism to recognize fonts by comparing the dimensions of texts in specific fonts with expected values. Invisible *div* elements and the canvas element are used to identify installed fonts [29, p. 311] [30, p. 12]. The experimental Local Font Access API requires user consent and is therefore not suitable for fingerprinting [31].

3) Advantages: Font recognition offers high entropy and stability since fonts are rarely changed. This allows the identification of the operating system and installed software packages like Office or Photoshop [3, p. 7].

4) Disadvantages: Without Flash, font recognition is done through "brute-force" methods, reducing accuracy if unknown fonts are installed. Similar fonts can lead to false positives. Extensions and adjustments, such as those in Apple's WebKit, can manipulate or restrict recognition [24, p. 10] [29, p. 311].

G. Screen Fingerprinting

1) Definition and Basics: Screen fingerprinting identifies a device by analyzing various screen-related characteristics, including screen resolution, pixel depth, color depth, and browser window size. This method leverages the uniqueness of screen configurations and browser modifications, which can create rare resolution combinations [32, p. 20].

2) Analysis: JavaScript provides attributes for screen and browser window characteristics through the *window.screen object*, offering details like color depth (*colorDepth*), screen orientation (*screenOrientation*), and screen dimensions (*screenHeight*, *screenWidth*). Values, such as *window.innerWidth* and *window.innerHeight*, determine the browser window's inner area, which can be altered by toolbars or bookmark bars [24, p. 3].

3) Advantages: Screen and window resolution information typically have high entropy, making them useful for stabilizing fingerprints when combined with other techniques. This method is particularly effective for distinguishing between desktop, tablet, and mobile devices, as these have distinct resolutions and aspect ratios compared to standardized desktop screens [27, p. 277].

4) Disadvantages: Since values are derived from browser attributes rather than hardware tests, they can be limited or altered by extensions or privacy settings. Browsers like TOR set the window to a fixed size of 1000x1000 pixels, reducing uniqueness, and browsers like Firefox always report a color depth of 24. Additionally, users with multiple monitors or those using zoom functions can affect the accuracy of screen fingerprinting, as there is no reliable way to determine the zoom factor directly, which reduces entropy [24, p. 10].

H. WebRTC Fingerprinting

1) Definition and Basics: WebRTC is a standard and accessible JavaScript interface available in most browsers. It facilitates real-time communication over stateless HTTP by establishing direct connections between participants, allowing the extraction of local network adapter information. This can reveal private and public IP addresses, which can be used for fingerprinting or identifying users behind proxies or VPNs [30, p. 12]. It also provides information about connected devices, such as microphones, webcams, and speakers.

2) Analysis: Unlike other browser mechanisms like camera or microphone access, establishing a WebRTC connection requires no permissions or user notifications. After connecting to the target computer via a Session Traversal Utilities for NAT (STUN) server, IP addresses can be read from the RTCPeerConnection object as iceCandidates [33, p. 667]. This data can be used for fingerprinting, and WebRTC can further enumerate the local network to build a unique profile of the target's environment. It can also read all local adapter addresses, including those for VPNs and virtual machines [33, p. 667-668]. The DetectRTC project [34] demonstrates WebRTC's capabilities, highlighting information about microphones, webcams, and speakers. While exact device names require permissions, WebRTC can read Media Device IDs, which can contribute to unique fingerprints.

3) Advantages: Extracting private and public IPs provides deep insights, especially for identifying targets behind VPNs or proxies. No other technique can silently reveal addresses behind Network Address Translation (NAT) [35, p. 273]. The collected data is highly unique; a study with 80 devices found over 97% uniqueness using only WebRTC [33, p. 668].

4) Disadvantages: WebRTC might be disabled in the target browser, or extensions might block its usage without user consent. Accessing Media Device IDs requires permission, alerting users to potential background activities, making it unsuitable for stealth operations. Additionally, WebRTC relies on STUN servers, either self-hosted or third-party, adding dependency considerations for its use.

I. CSS Fingerprinting

1) Definition and Basics: Different to the active fingerprinting techniques using JavaScript, CSS fingerprinting is a passive method. CSS is a stylesheet language primarily used to enhance the presentation of HTML elements. Over time, the CSS specification has expanded to include selectors and filters, enabling limited dynamic selections, which this technique leverages [36, p. 10].

2) Analysis: Until 2010, the *:visited* selector could identify if a website had been visited by changing the link color, detectable via JavaScript. After this was patched, researchers explored time-based methods to read user history, but these required JavaScript and were impractical [37, p. 4]. In 2015, Takei et al. introduced a JavaScript-free method using CSS properties and multiple *@media* queries to fetch URLs based on defined rules. The server could then identify system properties like screen dimensions, resolution, touchscreen presence, installed fonts, browser, and OS from the requesting IP address and URL parameters [38, p. 3-5]. A current GitHub project demonstrates this method's practical capabilities [39].

3) Advantages: CSS fingerprinting's independence from JavaScript allows it to identify even cautious users who block JavaScript or use extensions like NoScript. This technique can even detect if JavaScript is disabled via noscript tags [38, p. 2]. Due to its limited use and lesser-known status, no effective user solutions currently exist to prevent it.

4) Disadvantages: Takei et al.'s method provides limited data, which, without JavaScript, can only be supplemented by techniques like header analysis. Oliver Brotchie notes in his project repository that the method is not currently scalable, as each request requires over 1MB of CSS files to be downloaded. However, he warns that upcoming CSS Values 4 implementation could reduce download sizes significantly, making the method more practical. Additionally, font recognition relies on brute-forcing, which can be noticeable in network traffic.

J. Additional JavaScript Attributes

1) Definition and Basics: Most of the previously discussed techniques actively use JavaScript to extract information from various interfaces. Additional possibilities are briefly mentioned here to provide a more comprehensive picture. Since these techniques share many characteristics with other JavaScript-based methods, listing their pros and cons is omitted.

2) Analysis: The *navigator* object in browsers provides information, such as DoNotTrack status, user agent details, platform, languages, cookies usage, granted and available permissions, and time zone [29, p. 9]. JavaScript implementation varies between browsers and versions, and Mowery et al. demonstrated that these differences are measurable and can indicate the software and hardware used [1].

Additionally, there are differences in the availability and execution of functions, which offers an alternative way to detect user agents if manipulated by extensions. Another technique that caused concern among Tor users is the use of the *getClientRects* function to obtain precise DOM element data, even with Canvas disabled. These factors can vary based on implementation, font sizes, and screen resolutions, enabling identification in the otherwise anonymous browser [40]. This vulnerability has been fixed in Tor but remains exploitable in other browsers [41].

3) Advantages: JavaScript-based fingerprinting techniques are highly versatile and widely applicable since JavaScript is essential for web functionality. These methods can collect a broad range of information, such as user agent details, time zones, and system settings, often without requiring user consent or visibility. The stealthy nature of JavaScript fingerprinting allows it to operate in the background, making it difficult for users to detect. Moreover, JavaScript-based attributes work consistently across different browsers, enabling effective cross-browser tracking.

4) Disadvantages: However, JavaScript fingerprinting is limited by browser-specific implementations, which can result in inconsistent data collection. Privacy-focused browsers like Tor or extensions, such as NoScript, actively block or obscure JavaScript-based tracking, reducing its effectiveness. Additionally, users are becoming more aware of privacy risks and increasingly use tools to disable or modify JavaScript functions. Finally, updates to browsers may close vulnerabilities or alter features that JavaScript fingerprinting relies on, decreasing its long-term viability.

K. Advanced Techniques Using Machine Learning

1) Definition and Basics: Most active techniques discussed so far use JavaScript to gather hardware and software information. They rely on unique data combinations based on implementation quirks or directly available information. Newer methods often employ "side-channels", capturing additional data by observing behavioral differences during various operations within the execution environment. Methods like plugin enumeration (cf. Section III-B), font fingerprinting (cf. Section III-F), and CSS fingerprinting (cf. Section III-I) use this approach in simple forms by testing known combinations to gain indirect information. These side-channel methods can be implemented with minimal effort but can also be used in more sophisticated ways with machine learning to gather otherwise unobtainable information [42, p. 1].

2) Analysis: Wang et al. explored using cache usage, memory consumption, and CPU activity to identify visited websites. Previously, CSS selectors were used to reveal browsing history, posing significant privacy risks and leading to prompt fixes. Side-channel techniques employ various tricks to analyze system behavior more accurately. Complex calculations stress the hardware in the background, and machine learning models categorize the results with expected values from known sites. Tests showed 80-90% accuracy in identifying websites [42, p. 3-5]. Further research is needed, but implementations using WebAssembly [43] and the Performance API [44] are conceivable.

3) Advantages: This method is invisible to the user and provides insightful information not available through conventional means. Currently, there are no methods to protect users from such techniques [42, pp. 1-3].

4) Disadvantages: While previous techniques aimed to identify a user over time, this method could offer dangerous insights into the person's behavior behind the screen. However, the technique is still in its initial stage and remains a theoretical approach not yet tested in the real world. It is unlikely to be reliably used by actors in the near future [42, p. 6].

IV. Discussion

Browser fingerprinting can be used positively for security, as shown by technologies like BrFast and private, passive user recognition methods. However, there's a risk of misuse, especially in advertising. Personalized ads significantly impact Generation Z, who discover products primarily through social media. The advertising industry, driven by creating accurate user profiles, heavily invests in digital advertising, with data-driven ads accounting for 60-70% of digital ad revenue in Germany. Traditionally, data collection relied on cookies, but users developed ways to avoid tracking, such as deleting cookies or using incognito mode. Unlike cookies, browser fingerprints are collected in the background and are not easily altered. GDPR regulations mandate user consent for data collection, but enforcement is inconsistent, and compliance with fingerprinting guidelines remains unclear, even with new laws like Germany's TTDSG [45].

Online tracking is ubiquitous, affecting nearly all user groups. A 2016 study of the top 1 million websites revealed extensive tracking, with services like Google and Facebook present on over 10% of sites. Post-GDPR, fingerprinting scripts increased to 68.8% of the top 10,000 sites. A study with 234 participants found that demographics like age, gender, education, IT background, and privacy awareness influenced trackability, with men and those with higher education being less trackable. Despite understanding fingerprinting, many participants believed they could protect themselves from it. The AmIUnique study, with over 100,000 fingerprints, indicated a bias towards more privacy-aware internet users. Current research from Friedrich-Alexander-University shows that most study participants are male and well-educated, suggesting that while almost everyone is affected by browser fingerprinting, only a small, informed group actively researches and understands it [46].

Browser fingerprinting, as explored through various methods in this paper (cf. Table I), represents a comprehensive and evolving threat to digital privacy. Each fingerprinting technique, from HTTP Header Attributes to more sophisticated approaches like Canvas and WebGL Fingerprinting, offers unique data points, but their power lies in their combinatorial use. While individual methods may not be highly unique or stable, their integration enables more persistent and accurate user identification across devices and browsers. Techniques like WebRTC and Font Fingerprinting complement traditional methods by exposing additional layers of system and network data. Furthermore, the advancement of machine learning-based fingerprinting is pushing the boundaries of tracking, allowing for the analysis of side-channel behaviors, such as CPU or memory usage. This convergence of methods creates a powerful, multi-dimensional profiling system that is increasingly resistant to countermeasures, challenging both privacy

TABLE I
OVERVIEW OF FINGERPRINTING METHODS

Fingerprinting Method	Uniqueness	Stability	Entropy	Impact on User Privacy	Defense Techniques
HTTP Header Attributes	Low	Moderate	Low	Moderate impact: limited detail but useful when combined with other methods.	Altering or masking headers (e.g., randomizing User-Agent).
Enumeration of Browser Plugins	Moderate	High	High	High impact: reveals sensitive data, such as installed plugins.	Disabling plugin enumeration, avoiding unnecessary add-ons.
Canvas Fingerprinting	High	Moderate	High	High impact: generates unique fingerprints based on rendering.	CanvasBlocker extension to block or manipulate rendering.
WebGL Fingerprinting	High	High	High	High impact: collects detailed hardware data for tracking.	Block or manipulate WebGL outputs.
Audio Fingerprinting	Moderate	High	Moderate	High impact: captures unique audio processing details.	Disable Web Audio API, use privacy extensions.
Font Fingerprinting	High	High	Moderate	High impact: identifies installed fonts, making it persistent.	Limit font access with privacy-focused browsers (e.g., Tor).
Screen Fingerprinting	Moderate	High	Low	Moderate impact: uses screen resolution and window size but less effective on mobile devices.	Fix window size or limit resolution reporting with privacy browsers.
WebRTC Fingerprinting	Very High	High	Very High	Very high impact: exposes real IP addresses, even behind VPNs.	Disable WebRTC, use extensions that block data collection.
CSS Fingerprinting	Low	Moderate	Low	Low impact: provides limited system and style information.	Limit or disable CSS fingerprinting through extensions or scripts.
JavaScript Attributes	Moderate	High	Moderate	Moderate impact: uses various browser features for tracking.	Disable unnecessary JavaScript functions or use privacy extensions.
Advanced Machine Learning Fingerprinting	Very High	Very High	Very High	Very high impact: uses side-channel data (e.g., CPU/cache) for tracking.	Limit access to Performance API and WebAssembly, emerging defenses needed.

frameworks and user efforts to remain anonymous online. Therefore, the future of browser fingerprinting lies in this synergistic exploitation of both passive and active methods, making it a critical issue in the broader context of digital surveillance and privacy regulation.

V. CONCLUSION

A. Summary of the Research Outcome

This contribution has examined browser fingerprinting, a growing technique in online tracking. It has demonstrated that browser fingerprinting is a sophisticated method for identifying and tracking users online without traditional methods like cookies.

The analysis highlighted that browser fingerprinting poses a complex challenge from both technical and privacy perspectives. While it provides companies and advertisers with detailed insights into user behavior for targeted advertising, it raises significant privacy concerns as users are often tracked without their knowledge or consent. Despite stricter privacy laws like the GDPR in the EU, browser fingerprinting remains a grey area. Anti-fingerprinting techniques are limited and continually evolving to keep up with new tracking methods.

In conclusion, browser fingerprinting plays and will continue to play a significant role in the digital landscape. Both users and regulatory bodies must increase awareness of browser fingerprinting practices and their implications.

B. Implications for Practice

Consent and Cookies: Always accept only the necessary cookies in cookie banners and regularly delete cookies to hinder tracking and fingerprinting. This is particularly important for news sites, which often misuse collected data without user consent.

Blending in with the Masses: Reducing APIs and data sources for fingerprinting can ironically make users more identifiable [47]. Thus, widely adopted browsers and protection mechanisms should be used to stay less conspicuous.

Browser Choice: Choose browsers with robust privacy protections. On iOS, Safari is recommended due to its advanced tracking protection and large user base [48]. For Android, the Mull browser is highly rated for fingerprinting protection, while Brave is a good, widely-used alternative. On desktops, Brave, Librewolf, and Mullvad browsers are recommended for their privacy features and user bases [49].

Browser Extensions: Limit the use of browser extensions, as they can become sources of unique information. While some extensions block known trackers or modify API outputs, these protections are often already built into recommended browsers like Brave and Librewolf [18] [47].

C. Future Research

Future research in browser fingerprinting should focus on several key areas. First, countermeasures and defense mechanisms need to be explored further, especially in mitigating the newer techniques that leverage machine learning and side-channel attacks. These advanced methods can bypass traditional privacy safeguards, such as disabling JavaScript or using incognito modes, making the development of more robust anti-fingerprinting technologies imperative. Additionally, research should explore the ethics and regulatory frameworks surrounding fingerprinting, examining how existing privacy and data protection laws like GDPR can be adapted to better address fingerprinting practices. Another promising direction is improving cross-device tracking prevention by understanding how fingerprinting works across different platforms and hardware. Lastly, investigating user awareness and educational tools on fingerprint privacy risks will help empower the general public to protect their digital identities more effectively. Thus, future research should focus on developing more effective privacy techniques to balance commercial interests and user privacy rights.

REFERENCES

[1] K. Mowery and H. Shacham, "Pixel perfect: Fingerprinting canvas in HTML5," *Proceedings of W2SP*, vol. 2012, 2012.

[2] K. Szymielewicz and B. Budington. (2018) The GDPR and Browser Fingerprinting: How It Changes the Game for the Sneakiest Web Trackers. Accessed: 2024-09-27. [Online]. Available: https://www.eff.org/de/deeplinks/2018/06/gdpr-and-browser-fingerprinting-how-it-changes-game-sneakiest-web-trackers

[3] D. Zhang, J. Zhang, Y. Bu, B. Chen, C. Sun, and T. Wang, "A Survey of Browser Fingerprint Research and Application," *Wireless Communications and Mobile Computing*, vol. 2022, no. 1, p. 3363335, 2022. [Online]. Available: https://onlinelibrary.wiley.com/doi/abs/10.1155/2022/3363335

[4] P. Eckersley, "How unique is your web browser?" in *Privacy Enhancing Technologies*, M. J. Atallah and N. J. Hopper, Eds. Berlin, Heidelberg: Springer Berlin Heidelberg, 2010, pp. 1–18.

[5] S. Englehardt and A. Edelstein. (2021) Firefox 85 Cracks Down on Supercookies. Accessed: 2024-09-27. [Online]. Available: https://blog.mozilla.org/security/2021/01/26/supercookie-protections/

[6] E. Woollacott. (2021) Browser fingerprinting more prevalent on the web now than ever before. Accessed: 2024-09-27. [Online]. Available: https://portswigger.net/daily-swig/browser-fingerprinting-more-prevalent-on-the-web-now-than-ever-before-research

[7] R. Koch. (2019) Cookies, the GDPR, and the ePrivacy Directive. Accessed: 2024-09-27. [Online]. Available: https://gdpr.eu/cookies/

[8] U. Iqbal, S. Englehardt, and Z. Shafiq, "Fingerprinting the Fingerprinters: Learning to Detect Browser Fingerprinting Behaviors," in *2021 IEEE Symposium on Security and Privacy (SP)*. IEEE, 05 2021, pp. 1143–1161.

[9] G. Acar. (2014) Browser Fingerprinting and the Online-Tracking Arms Race. Accessed: 2024-09-27. [Online]. Available: https://www.esat.kuleuven.be/cosic/news/the-web-never-forgets-persistent-tracking-mechanisms-in-the-wild/

[10] "Request header," accessed: 2024-09-27. [Online]. Available: https://developer.mozilla.org/en-US/docs/Glossary/Request_header

[11] "HTTP/2 fingerprinting: A relatively-unknown method for web fingerprinting," accessed: 2024-09-27. [Online]. Available: https://lwthiker.com/networks/2022/06/17/http2-fingerprinting.html

[12] P. Laperdrix, W. Rudametkin, and B. Baudry, "Beauty and the Beast: Diverting Modern Web Browsers to Build Unique Browser Fingerprints," in *2016 IEEE Symposium on Security and Privacy (SP)*, 2016, pp. 878–894.

[13] "User-Agent," accessed: 2024-09-27. [Online]. Available: https://developer.mozilla.org/en-US/docs/Web/HTTP/Headers/User-Agent

[14] B. Wolford. (2024) What are the GDPR consent requirements? Accessed: 2024-09-27. [Online]. Available: https://gdpr.eu/gdpr-consent-requirements/

[15] "Navigator: plugins property," accessed: 2024-09-27. [Online]. Available: https://developer.mozilla.org/en-US/docs/Web/API/Navigator/plugins

[16] "Extension Detector," accessed: 2024-09-27. [Online]. Available: https://github.com/z0ccc/extension-detector

[17] "How ad blockers can be used for browser fingerprinting," accessed: 2024-09-27. [Online]. Available: https://fingerprint.com/blog/ad-blocker-fingerprinting/

[18] S. Karami, P. Ilia, K. Solomos, and J. Polakis, "Carnus: Exploring the Privacy Threats of Browser Extension Fingerprinting," in *27th Annual Network and Distributed System Security Symposium, NDSS 2020, San Diego, California, USA, February 23-26, 2020*. The Internet Society, 2020.

[19] "CanvasBlocker," accessed: 2024-09-27. [Online]. Available: https://github.com/kkapsner/CanvasBlocker

[20] "WebGL: 2D and 3D graphics for the web," accessed: 2024-09-27. [Online]. Available: https://developer.mozilla.org/en-US/docs/Web/API/WebGL_API

[21] T. Stephenson, "A Comparative Study on Analyses of Browser Fingerprinting," Ph.D. dissertation, Wesleyan University, 2023.

[22] "WebKit," accessed: 2024-09-27. [Online]. Available: https://github.com/WebKit/WebKit/commit/ae710d34c23858295b385e3f95ad7f6edd29f9d7

[23] G. Nakibly, G. Shelef, and S. Yudilevich, "Hardware Fingerprinting Using HTML5," *arXiv preprint arXiv:1503.01408*, 03 2015.

[24] Y. Cao, S. Li, and E. Wijmans, "(Cross-)Browser Fingerprinting via OS and Hardware Level Features," in *Network and Distributed System Security Symposium*, 2017.

[25] M. Mantel. (2022) Browser-Fingerprinting: PCs, Smartphones & Co. lassen sich über die GPU tracken. Accessed: 2024-09-27. [Online]. Available: https://www.heise.de/news/Browser-Fingerprinting-PCs-Smartphones-Co-lassen-sich-ueber-die-GPU-tracken-6345233.html

[26] Laor et al., "DRAWNAPART: A Device Identification Technique based on Remote GPU Fingerprinting," *ArXiv*, vol. abs/2201.09956, 2022. [Online]. Available: https://api.semanticscholar.org/CorpusID:246276013

[27] J. S. Queiroz and E. L. Feitosa, "A Web Browser Fingerprinting Method Based on the Web Audio API," *Comput. J.*, vol. 62, pp. 1106–1120, 2019. [Online]. Available: https://api.semanticscholar.org/CorpusID:86644316

[28] S. Chalise and P. Vadrevu, "A Study of Feasibility and Diversity of Web Audio Fingerprints," *arXiv preprint arXiv:2107.14201*, 2021.

[29] A. Gómez-Boix, P. Laperdrix, and B. Baudry, "Hiding in the Crowd: an Analysis of the Effectiveness of Browser Fingerprinting at Large Scale," in *Proceedings of the 2018 World Wide Web Conference*, ser. WWW '18. Republic and Canton of Geneva, CHE: International World Wide Web Conferences Steering Committee, 2018, p. 309–318. [Online]. Available: https://doi.org/10.1145/3178876.3186097

[30] S. Englehardt and A. Narayanan, "Online Tracking: A 1-million-site Measurement and Analysis," in *Proceedings of the 2016 ACM SIGSAC Conference on Computer and Communications Security*, ser. CCS '16. New York, NY, USA: Association for Computing Machinery, 2016, p. 1388–1401. [Online]. Available: https://doi.org/10.1145/2976749.2978313

[31] "Local Font Access API," accessed: 2024-09-27. [Online]. Available: https://developer.mozilla.org/en-US/docs/Web/API/Local_Font_Access_API

[32] P. Laperdrix, N. Bielova, B. Baudry, and G. Avoine, "Browser Fingerprinting: A Survey," *ACM Trans. Web*, vol. 14, no. 2, apr 2020. [Online]. Available: https://doi.org/10.1145/3386040

[33] A. Reiter and A. Marsalek, "WebRTC: your privacy is at risk," in *Proceedings of the Symposium on Applied Computing*, ser. SAC '17. New York, NY, USA: Association for Computing Machinery, 2017, p. 664–669. [Online]. Available: https://doi.org/10.1145/3019612.3019844

[34] "DetectRTC," accessed: 2024-09-27. [Online]. Available: https://github.com/muaz-khan/DetectRTC

[35] V. Bernardo and D. Domingos, "Web-based Fingerprinting Techniques," in *Proceedings of the 13th International Joint Conference on E-Business and Telecommunications*, ser. ICETE 2016. Setubal, PRT: SCITEPRESS - Science and Technology Publications, Lda, 2016, p. 271–282. [Online]. Available: https://doi.org/10.5220/0005965602710282

[36] T. Bujlow, V. Carela-Español, J. Solé-Pareta, and P. Barlet-Ros, "A Survey on Web Tracking: Mechanisms, Implications, and Defenses," *Proceedings of the IEEE*, vol. 105, no. 8, pp. 1476–1510, 2017.

[37] L. Olejnik, C. Castelluccia, and A. Janc, "Why Johnny Can't Browse in Peace: On the Uniqueness of Web Browsing History Patterns," *12th Privacy Enhancing Technologies Symposium (PETS 2012)*, 07 2012. [Online]. Available: https://petsymposium.org/2012/papers/hotpets12-4-johnny.pdf

[38] N. Takei, T. Saito, K. Takasu, and T. Yamada, "Web Browser Fingerprinting Using Only Cascading Style Sheets," in *2015 10th International Conference on Broadband and Wireless Computing, Communication and Applications (BWCCA)*, 2015, pp. 57–63.

[39] "CSS-Fingerprint," accessed: 2024-09-27. [Online]. Available: https://github.com/OliverBrotchie/CSS-Fingerprint

[40] "Advanced Tor Browser Fingerprinting," accessed: 2024-09-27. [Online]. Available: http://jcarlosnorte.com/security/2016/03/06/advanced-tor-browser-fingerprinting.html

[41] "Investigate impact of fingerprinting via getClientRects()," accessed: 2024-09-27. [Online]. Available: https://gitlab.torproject.org/tpo/applications/tor-browser/-/issues/18500
[42] H. Wang, H. Sayadi, A. Sasan, P. D. Sai Manoj, S. Rafatirad, and H. Homayoun, "Machine Learning-Assisted Website Fingerprinting Attacks with Side-Channel Information: A Comprehensive Analysis and Characterization," in *2021 22nd International Symposium on Quality Electronic Design (ISQED)*, 2021, pp. 79–84.
[43] "WebAssembly," accessed: 2024-09-27. [Online]. Available: https://developer.mozilla.org/en-US/docs/WebAssembly
[44] "High precision timing," accessed: 2024-09-27. [Online]. Available: https://developer.mozilla.org/en-US/docs/Web/API/Performance_API/High_precision_timing
[45] "Browser Fingerprinting und das TDDDG: Erlaubt oder nicht? [Browser Fingerprinting and the TDDDG: Allowed or not?]," accessed: 2024-09-27. [Online]. Available: https://dr-dsgvo.de/browser-fingerprinting-und-das-ttdsg/
[46] G. Pugliese, C. Riess, F. Gassmann, and Z. Benenson, "Long-Term Observation on Browser Fingerprinting: Users' Trackability and Perspective," *Proceedings on Privacy Enhancing Technologies*, vol. 2020, pp. 558–577, 05 2020.
[47] N. Al-Fannah and C. Mitchell, "Too little too late: can we control browser fingerprinting?" *Journal of Intellectual Capital*, vol. ahead-of-print, 01 2020.
[48] K. Kollnig, A. Shuba, M. Van Kleek, R. Binns, and N. Shadbolt, "Goodbye Tracking? Impact of iOS App Tracking Transparency and Privacy Labels," in *Proceedings of the 2022 ACM Conference on Fairness, Accountability, and Transparency*, ser. FAccT '22. New York, NY, USA: Association for Computing Machinery, 2022, p. 508–520. [Online]. Available: https://doi.org/10.1145/3531146.3533116
[49] X. Lin, F. Araujo, T. Taylor, J. Jang, and J. Polakis, "Fashion Faux Pas: Implicit Stylistic Fingerprints for Bypassing Browsers' Anti-Fingerprinting Defenses," in *2023 IEEE Symposium on Security and Privacy (SP)*, 2023, pp. 987–1004.

Forensic Analysis of GAN Training and Generation: Output Artifacts Assessment of Circles and Lines

Stefan Seidlitz and Jana Dittmann
Department of Computer Science
Otto-von-Guericke University
Magdeburg, Germany
e-mail: stefan.seidlitz@ovgu.de | jana.dittmann@iti.cs.uni-magdeburg.de

Abstract—**Motivated by the challenges in different forensic detection tasks based on machine learning, this paper evaluates the training behavior, as well as the generation performance of images which are generated by Generative Adversarial Networks (GANs) based on simple geometric shapes using the example of circles and lines. Circles, for example, are relevant for DeepFaceFakes where eyes might be checked for inconsistencies. Therefore, we trained several StyleGAN3 models with different self-created training data sets using geometrical shapes of circles and lines. We use these models to generate fake circles and lines from a random latent vector, which we then forensically analyzed in two different ways: a visual, subjective evaluation based on an observation as well as an automated Circle-Checking approach. In both experiments, we were able to show on the example of StyleGAN3, that generative approaches have difficulties with the generation of geometric shapes: circles are often more comparable to eggs, lines are mostly not linear. Our contribution is to advance the knowledge on what kind of artifacts a Generative Adversarial Network generates. This gives a first tendency for new detection strategies to identify these artifacts, based on geometrical shapes in DeepFake images.**

Keywords-Media Forensic; Generative Adversarial Networks (GAN); DeepFake; Advance and Challenges.

I. INTRODUCTION AND OUR CONCEPT

Motivated by the increasing use of Artificial Intelligence (AI) in media creation and processing, as well as for security incident detection in malicious cases, forensic explainability and reproducibility of the process is necessary for understanding and evaluating the results. In our paper, we propose to use a forensic analysis by using simplified and well-defined shapes on the example of geometric shapes of circles and lines, available as Open Data in [2]. The goal is to train models with a set of simplified and well-defined shape images to measure and study the output from the generation. The well-defined training guides the comparison and allows measuring artifacts in the output, which were not included in the training. In the comparison, we use a visual human-based assessment and a first, straight forward automated analysis on the example of 4 circle data sets. The goal is to show a possible first setting of the idea of simplified and well-defined shapes with a first tendency of results advancing the knowledge.

In particular, we are motivated by the DeepFakes cases. For example, recent methods are AutoEncoders (AEs) based approaches to replace the face or voice from person with the face or voice of another person. Further, we designate full synthetic, non-existing faces which are generated by a Generative Adversarial Network (GAN) also as DeepFakes. To avoid a critical use of DeepFakes a detection of DeepFakes is necessary in specific cases. In addition, the identification of characteristic DeepFake traces improves the examination as an essential part of a forensic investigation and it is required to showcase evidence in court. Nevertheless, full synthetic GAN based DeepFake images consist of a face in the foreground as well as a generated background area. While the faces in a DeepFake usually look deceptively real, the background can often be a strong indication of a DeepFake. Here, often the model is unable to generate geometric patterns, as it is not considered in the original training data. In consequence, there are several background artifacts e.g. letters consisting of curved lines in the background.

Most approaches like [3] or [4] for the detection of DeepFakes fall back to the use of AI, especially Neural Networks (NNs). Guo et al. [5] shows that the shape of the pupils in GAN-generated faces is irregular without giving any explanations of the causes. It is unclear to us whether other shapes in a facial image have an influence on the training behavior of a GAN. But, the observation of Guo et al. motivated us to train a StyleGAN3 [6] only with images of simplified shapes using the GitHub implementation of [1]. The National Institute of Standards and Technology (NIST) [7] suggests explanations in *purposes* and *styles*. Our approach has to address this and we follow the two main objectives: (A) How accurate can a GAN be used to generate perfect shapes? and (B) In a mixed training scenario, has a shape type an influence to another (different) shape type?

First, we summarize the key aspects of the development process of ProgressiveGAN [8], StyleGAN [9] and its extensions and introduce our approach in the next subsections. After a small overview about the implementation in Section II, we describe in Section III our observations on our training iterations separated on general observations as well as specific training observations. Additionally, we compare and discus the Automated Circle-Checking with our visible observations on all circle images. Finally, we conclude our paper in Section V.

A. *Used methods from State of the Art*

Goodfellow et al. [10] create with GANs the fundamentals for the work of Karras et al. [8]. This work allows

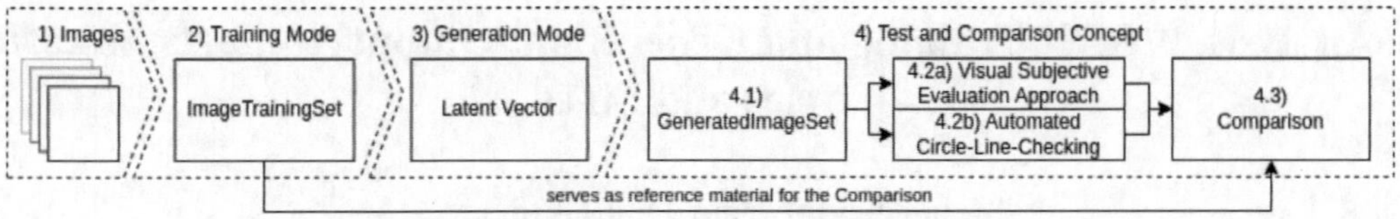

Figure 1. Pipeline for our approach, with StyleGAN3 implementation from [1].

the generation of high-resolution digital images, especially artificial face images. With ProgressiveGAN, they expand the trained image size step by step over the whole training phase. Additionally, they created a new image based high-quality data set named CelebA-HQ. In Karras et al. [9], the authors replaced the traditional generator network with a mapping network followed by a synthesis network, which allows the style transfer between latent vectors. However, the used Adaptive Instance Normalization (AdaIN) within the synthesis networks caused artifacts looking like water droplets in the generated images. Instead of the Instance Normalization, Karras et al. used a demodulation technique which results in normalized weights within the synthesis network [11]. Further, the technique of the progressive growing resolution in [8] results in a strong location preference for details. Instead of the progressive growing approach, the authors of StyleGAN2 used a skip generator and a residual discriminator architecture. Karras et al. [12] stabilized the discriminator of StyleGAN2-ada to avoid overfitting with different augmentation techniques which allows training the GAN with less training data. With StyleGAN3, Karras et al. [6] redesigned the generator network to avoid aliasing artifacts, specific details on its configuration are given in [6].

Those and further DeepFake generation methods like few-shot vid2vid [13] or Collaborative Diffusion [14] are used for the DF40 data set [15]. The aim of this data set is to combine the different DeepFake techniques such as face-swapping, face-reenactment and entire image synthesis. In consequence, the challenging task to tackle the generalization problem in DeepFake detection is opened, because most DeepFake detection strategies are focused to detect specific DeepFake techniques.

B. Our Approach

We divide our approach into three phases which are described in the following sections. Additionally, we highlight the main aspects of our approach in Figure 1.

1) Training Mode: For the *Training Mode*, different data sets called *ImageTrainingSet* are created which are described in Table I and some example images are visualized in Table III. Each data set consists of 50k images which have a shape of 64×64 pixels. Only grayscale images are created. The background color of each image is set to white (color value: 255). All geometric objects use a black color (color value: 0). We mainly decide between 'single' and 'multi' *ImageTrainingSet* which address the amount of geometric objects within the images. Images in a 'single' data set have only one geometric object (Table I: ID 1, 3, 4 and 6) whereas images in a 'multi' data set have between one and ten geometric objects (Table I: ID 2 and 5). Currently, no image has two different kinds of geometric objects (circles and rings or lines). The position of every geometric object is set randomly. But no object was allowed to have connections with the image boundary or with other objects in the same image. In all images of every *ImageTrainingSet*, we define a distance of 2 pixels to the boundary of the image. In the *multi ImageTrainingSet* of circles, we define a minimum distance of 2 pixels to other circles. The size of the circled shapes is between 3 and 60 pixels. Further, we create circled rings with a border size of 1 to 5 pixels, the ring size is the same as full circles. In case of lines, we set the minimal size to 10 pixels, the maximum size is calculated in combination with the boundary pixels and their orientation within the image. Each line has a thickness of

TABLE I. OVERVIEW OF ALL CREATED TESTING DATA SETS FOR STEP 1 (COMPARE TO FIGURE 1).

ID	Type	Content	Image Count	Image Size	Image Color	Number and Type of Shapes per Image
1	single circle	black circles and circled black rings	50.000	64×64	black / white	only one with random size and position, no connection with border
2	multiple circle	black circles and circled black rings	50.000	64×64	black / white	between one and ten with random size and position, no connection between other circles and with border
3	single horizontal line	black horizontal line	50.000	64×64	black / white	only one with random size and position, no connection with border
4	single line	black line	50.000	64×64	black / white	only one with random size, line direction and position, no connection with border
5	multiple lines	black lines	50.000	64×64	black / white	between one and ten with random size, line direction and position, no connection with other lines and with border
6	single circle or line	black circles rings, and lines	circles and rings: 25.000; lines: 25.000	64×64	black / white	only one with random size, direction and position, no connection with border; sub sets are randomized reused from data set 1 and 4

1 pixel. All other parameters for the line data sets are similar to the circle data sets. Please note, in a *multi ImageTrainingSet* the shape size is also defined from other shapes, because in an image no connections to other shapes are allowed. For the *combined ImageTrainingSet* of circles and lines, we reuse subsets of both *multi ImageTrainingSet* for circles and lines. The images of both subsets are selected randomly.

2) Generation Mode: In the *Generation Mode* we differentiate between two generation methods. The first generation method is done during the training process of StyleGAN3. It creates after a defined time of training steps a snapshot of the current training state as well as an overview image of different generated images. This overview image is a grid of 32×32 images, where each image is generated from a random selected latent vector. Separately, from selected snapshots of several models we generate images from a latent vector defined by a seed using the image generation script gen_images.py of [1]. The seed is chosen by randomly generated numbers between 0 and 10000 using a bash script which executes the generation script of StyleGAN3. The script will be available at [2].

3) Test and Comparison Concept: We propose in our concept a **Visual Subjective Evaluation Approach** on circles and lines to support explainability for humans. Our criteria are (derived from Visual Morphing Detection Assessment [16]): (1) How homogeneous are the colors of the background or the generated geometrical objects? (2) Are there visible differences between the generated and the ideal geometrical object (e.g., missing symmetry)? (3) Is the amount of objects within the generated images similar to the specific training set? (4) Are there intersections with other generated objects or the border of the image?

Furthermore, we suggest to use for circles an automated approach (**Automated Circle-Checking**) by using Hough Transform. Here, we show in a first test setting for circles an approach for their detection. The subjective and automated results are compared for a circle test case to show possibilities and limitations by deriving further work.

TABLE II. STYLEGAN3 TRAINING CONFIGURATION (STEP 2, FIGURE 1).

Required		
outdir	*path to the output directory*	
cfg	*stylegan3-t*	
data	*path to the training data set*	
GPUs	1	(proposed values from the Readme file for the training parameter)
batch	32	
gamma	8.2	
Optional features		
mirror	1	
all other parameters are not set, either the default configurations were used or the specific parameter was not used here		
Misc hyperparameters		
those parameters are not set, either the default configurations were used or the specific parameter was not used here		
Misc settings		
kimg	25000 (default value)	
snap	50 (default value) or 10	
all other parameters are not set, either the default configurations were used or the specific parameter was not used here		

II. IMPLEMENTATION

A. Preparation for the data sets

For the creation of our data sets, we use Python and the programming library Pillow, which is needed for the creation of circles and rings (please note: for the creation of circles, the function for the creation of ellipse is needed) or lines. Other geometric shapes are not used for this work. Table I shows the specific content of all available data sets. Note, the data set ID 6 reused randomly 50 % of the images of the data set with the ID 1 and 50 % of the images of the data set with the ID 4. Some example images for each data set are given in Table III. The data sets are available at [2].

All images are created as BMP pixel image without compression. For the training, the data sets need to be preprocessed with the dataset_tool of [1] which converts all images into PNG images. Furthermore, this tool creates a ZIP archive that includes all images of the specific data set.

B. Training approaches and expected outcome

Every data set was used to train two StyleGAN3 models whereby only the snap parameter was changed to store the models more frequently. The reason for this is on the one hand to ensure reproducibility and on the other hand to get a finer view how the models are changing over the training time. Because of the color space of the images, StyleGAN3 automatically chooses the shape $[1, 64, 64]$ where the first value addresses the color space and the last two values the dimensions of the images. In consequence StyleGAN3 identified automatically the correct color space of the training image data set. All other parameters are set on the basis of the "Training" section of the README.md file of the GitHub repository of StyleGAN3 [1]. Compare here also the Table II. Both models from the same data set were trained parallel on one separate GPU card of the same type. The final trained models are available at [2].

Table IV describes the expected results of each training approach to imitate the given image data sets. Note, the snapshot frequency (third column of Table IV) is calculated from the snap parameter with the tick parameter which is default set to the value 4.

For this paper, the evaluation was performed manually by a human with a visual observation of randomly generated images by the StyleGAN3 generator. For this purpose, the automatically generated grid images as well as self generated images are used.

III. EVALUATION

A. Subjective Evaluation Approach: Observations on StyleGAN3 generated shapes

We randomly analyzed samples from every training approach over different training iterations. Thereby, several unexpected not trained lines and circles (defined as errors) in all generated images are observed. We distinguish those errors between general and specific errors which are described in following sections: The general observations describe errors

TABLE III. EXAMPLE IMAGES FOR ALL DATA SETS FROM TABLE I, SEE STEP 1 OF FIGURE 1.

single circles and circled rings; ID 1	single horizontal line; ID 3	single line with random direction; ID 4
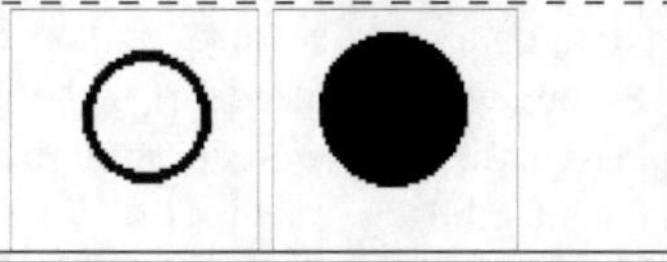	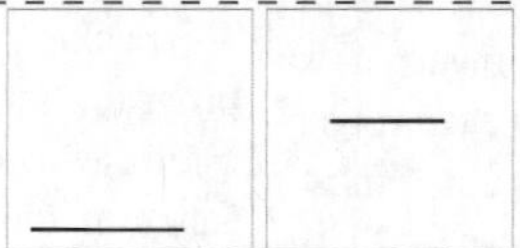	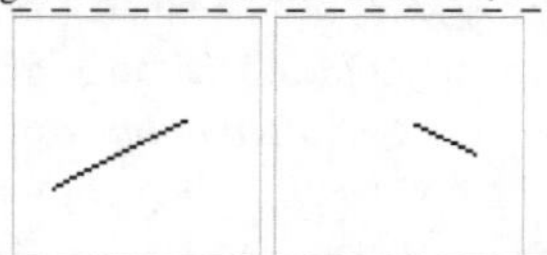
single circle and single line with random direction; ID 6	**multi circle; ID 2**	**multi line; ID 5**
	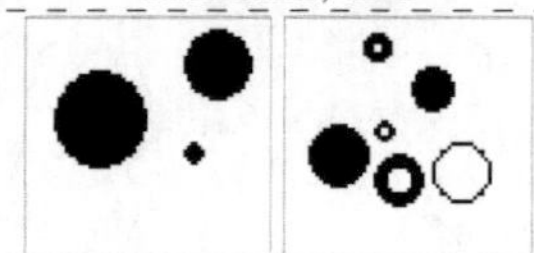	

TABLE IV. TRAINING INTENTIONS, EVERY MODEL IS TRAINED WITH THE CONFIGURATION OF TABLE II, ONLY THE SNAPSHOT SEQUENCE WAS CONFIGURED WHICH IS GIVEN IN THE COLUMN "SNAPSHOTS" (SEE STEP 2 OF FIGURE 1).

ID	used data set	snapshots	training intention / expected training behavior
1	multi: circle & rings; data set id: 2	every 200 kimg	Size, shape and color of circles and ring should be similar to the training data set. The generator should create between 1 and 10 objects (circles and/or rings) to emulate images from the data set. No object should have connections with the border of the image or with other objects.
2		every 40 kimg	
3	single: circle & rings; data set id: 1	every 200 kimg	Size, shape and color of circles and ring should be similar to the training data set. The generator should create only 1 object (circle or ring) to emulate images from the data set. No object should have connections with the border of the image.
4		every 40 kimg	
5	single: horizontal lines; data set id: 3	every 200 kimg	Size, shape, alignment and color of lines should be similar to the training data set. The generator should create only 1 horizontal line to emulate images from the data set. No line should have connections with the border of the image.
6		every 40 kimg	
7	single: lines with a random direction; data set id: 4	every 40 kimg	Size, shape, alignment and color of lines should be similar to the training data set. The generator should create only 1 line with an indifferent alignment to emulate images from the data set. No line should have connections with the border of the image.
8		every 200 kimg	
9	multi: lines with a random direction; data set id: 5	every 200 kimg	Size, shape, alignment and color of lines should be similar to the training data set. The generator should create between 1 and 10 lines with an indifferent alignment to emulate images from the data set. No line should have connections with the border of the image or intersections/connections with other lines.
10		every 40 kimg	
11	single: circles, rings & lines; data set id: 6	every 40 kimg	The behavior of this training test should be similar to the training IDs 3 and 4 in combination to 7 and 8. The influence from specific features of one training set to the other training set is unexpected before the training process starts.
12		every 200 kimg	

which are present in all images over all training approaches and specific observations which are only present in specific training approaches.

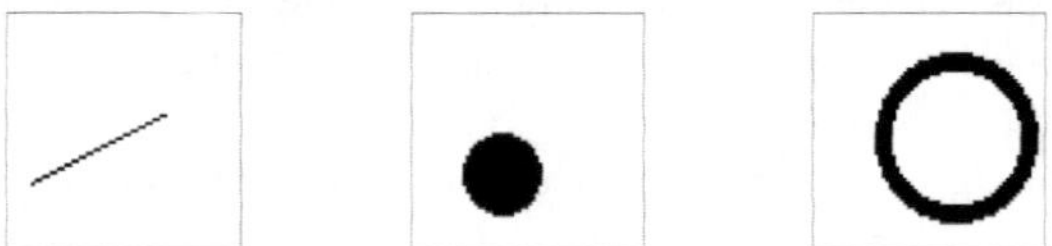

Figure 2. Scaled color scheme on real images using the image processing tool Gimp (which have no effect here).

1) General observations: We noticed in every generated image that areas of the same visible color (e.g., background as well as geometric objects) are not homogeneous. For example, we identified on the white background color areas of bright gray colored pixels which are not visible at the first glance. For visualization reasons and because of comprehensibility aspects, we scale the color values on Figure 2 and Figure 3 using Gimp [17]. Figure 3 visualized these 'invisible' artifacts. Because of the BMP input file type, these artifacts are not explainable with our training data sets (see images in Figure 2).

Figure 3. Scaled color scheme on fake images using the image processing tool Gimp.

In case of all training approaches which used a 'single' data set for the training (Table IV: ID 3 to 8, 11 and 12), some images are generated where more than one geometric object is created. In Table VII there are some images of a 'single' approach shown where not exactly one geometric object was generated; especially for ID 1 image 1 and 3 with two geometric objects, for ID 3 image 2 with no geometric object, for ID 4 image 3 and 4 with two or three geometric objects and for ID 6 image 2 with two geometric objects. The reason for this can be caused by the latent vector or style vector of StyleGAN3. Because of that the influence of the random seeds to the latent vector as well as the latent vector to the image generation process should be analyzed. Further, it is possible that also generated images of all multi training approaches are affected with a similar issue (Table IV: ID 1, 2, 9 and 10). The network is allowed to generate up to ten geometric objects, but it also not able to count the geometric objects which can be result in the generation of more than ten geometric objects. This circumstance is less visually recognizable than on a training approach with a single based data set, why a visual observation is here not effective.

2) Specific observations: The specific observation is divided into shape type of the geometric objects: circles and circled rings, lines and the mixed data set of lines and circles or circled rings (Table IV: ID 11 and 12). A separated observation of single and multi data sets is not useful because we noticed the same errors on both approaches. Compare here also Table V, which summarizes our observations for each training approach, and Table VII, which shows obvious errors.

The training approaches of both circle data sets (Table IV: ID 1 to 4), which will only address circles and circled rings, shows that StyleGAN3 was not able to train with all training iterations perfect circles or circled rings. Most generated circles do not show (because of the gridded circles, even if approximated) a specific rotational symmetry. Also, the sizes of the generated rings are not always the same on every position of the ring.

With respect to the line based data sets (Table IV: ID 5 to 10), only the generated horizontal lines (Table IV: ID 5 and 6) are most similar to their training data set. However, they have the same errors which are introduced in the previous Subsection III-A1: mostly on the line ends the color value is not always 0 (black). Once the lines were randomly rotated in their training data set, StyleGAN3 was not able to create perfectly straight lines. The generated lines (Table IV: ID 7 to 10) are curved, sometimes only one time, sometimes two times.

We also tried to train 25k single random line images with 25k single circle images at the same time (Table IV: ID 11 and 12). On this approach, we identified the same errors which are described before for the other training approaches. Only a transfer of features from circles or rings to lines or vice versa was not determined. Especially small lines and small circles seem to be mixed during the training process of StyleGAN3.

B. Objective Evaluation with the Automated Circle-Checking and its comparison with the Subjective Approach

For the Automated Circle-Checking, we use the Hough Circle Detection on our real- as well as fake Multi Circle data set (Table V, ID 1-4). As this detector is still in its early stages, it is currently unable to distinguish between genuine and fake images. The decision whether it is a real or a fake image is made by the examiner. We evaluate the detected position and size of our circles.

In most cases, the position of our real circles is detectable. Only the size was not always detected correctly. The reason for this could be due to the parameterization of the Hough transformation. Nevertheless, we have also tested our Automated Circle-Checking on our Multi Circle data set with fake circles. Please note that our fake images have a different color distribution: it is possible that the StyleGAN3 generator used any gray value between 0 and 255, while on real images only color values of 0 (circle color) and 255 (background) are possible. This fact has an influence on the circle detection using Hough transform. The circle detector was able to detect many small circles, which are usually a part of a large circle. Detection of the entire circle was rare. In some cases, the detector detects circles on a position where no circle was present. Table VI illustrates the behavior of the Automated Circle-Checking on real images compared to fake images.

IV. Discussion

Using the example of circles and lines, we could see that GANs are not able to generate exact circles or lines from a randomly given latent vector. This statement is further verified by our subjective in case of circles and lines as well as automated evaluation in case of circles. In relation to a more complex scenario, also in real faces specific shapes are given. Best example is the iris and the pupil of the eyes which is shown in the image process pipeline for an iris detection on Figure 4. Are there similar shape artifacts in full synthetic face images given and can our findings be used to identify other artifacts in synthetic face images? A first assessment is given in Figure 5. It is obvious that the extracted iris of a fake face generated by StyleGAN2 (extracted from

TABLE V. Visual observed errors of all trainings (see 4.2a of fig. 1), objective evaluation performed with ID 1-4 and confirm errors.

ID	used data set	human observations
1 2	circle and rings (multi); data set id: 2	no homogeneous geometric area, no given symmetry, no circle shape, objects also in area of border possible
3 4	circle and rings (single); data set id: 1	no homogeneous geometric area, no given symmetry, no circle shape, objects also in area of border possible, sometimes more than one object
5 6	lines (horizontal); data set id: 3	lines have mostly the same horizontal direction, pixel values of lines are mostly homogeneous, only at the line border are different pixel values possible
7 8	lines (single, random direction); data set id: 4	non straight lines, partially one to two turning points on the line, smoother transitions due to gray value change on line segments
9 10	lines (multi, random direction); data set id: 5	same visible observation like ID 7 or ID 8; line alignments are similar to the line alignments of the initial data set (compare table I ID 5)
11 12	circles, rings and lines (single); data set id: 6	shapes have the same errors which are described for the training runs of ID 3, ID 4, ID 7 and ID 8; a feature transfer (or error transfer) from line to circle and vice versa are not visible

thispersondoesnotexist.com in May 2024) does not have a typical circular shape which was confirmed by our automated detection approach.

Figure 4. Circle detection on an eye of a real person using the London Face Set [18].

Figure 5. Circle detection on an eye of a fake person generated by StyleGAN2 using the web page https://thispersondoesnotexist.com/.

At the moment, we evaluate our approach mostly on small images of real or generated geometrical shapes like circles or lines. Against, the experiments on facial images were performed only on a few images which results in new challenges compared to our initial geometrical data sets. In this case, it is necessary to have more pre-processing steps until the geometrical shape evaluation is usable. Furthermore, the image size of synthesized face images is usually larger than the images in our data sets, which requires different parameter settings for the Hough transform than those used for small images.

Additionally, our approach is only tested on images with a small size of 64×64 pixels which limits specific attributes of the geometric shape. Because of the rasterized pixel graphic, circles are limited in their minimum size. If they are too small, they are not distinguishable from squares or rhombuses. On larger images, large rasterized circles are more comparable to real circles than on smaller images. This allows a calculable metric which can be used for an identification of DeepFake images in future work.

TABLE VII. GENERATED EXAMPLE IMAGES (ONLY GRAYSCALE) FOR ALL DATA SETS WHICH ARE SHOWN IN TABLE I (SEE STEP 4.1 OF FIGURE 1).

single circle (circles and circled rings); ID 1
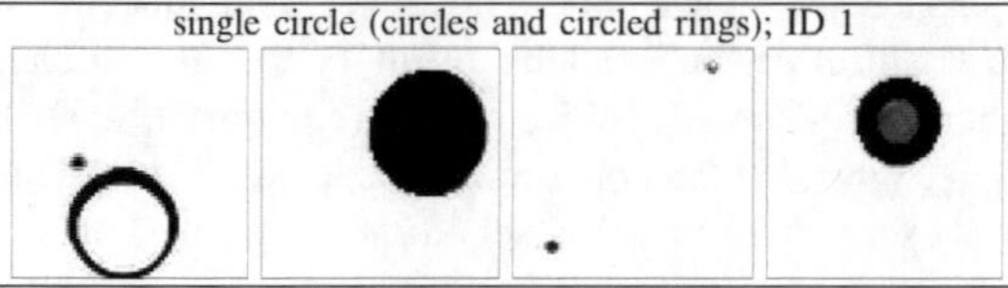
single horizontal line; ID 3
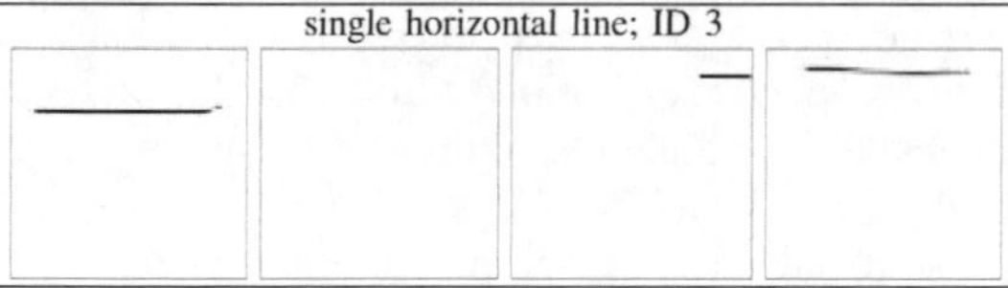
single line with random direction; ID 4
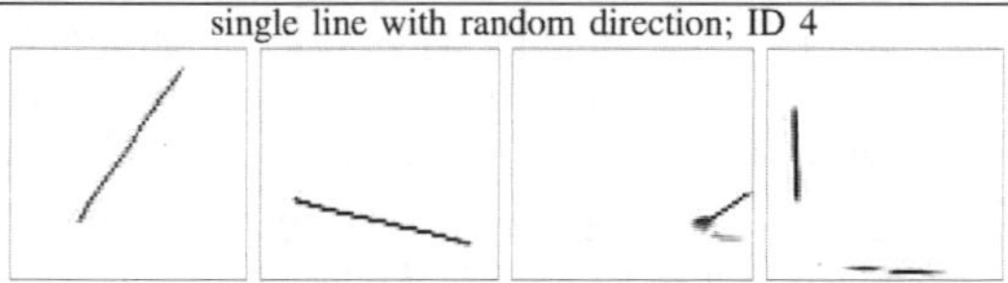
single circle and single line with random direction; ID 6
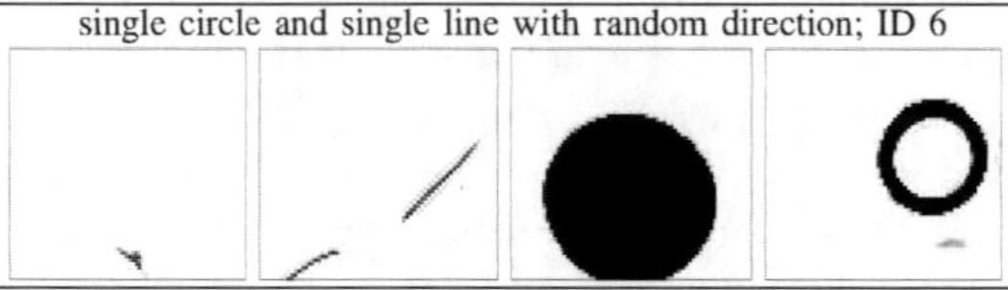
multi circle; ID 2
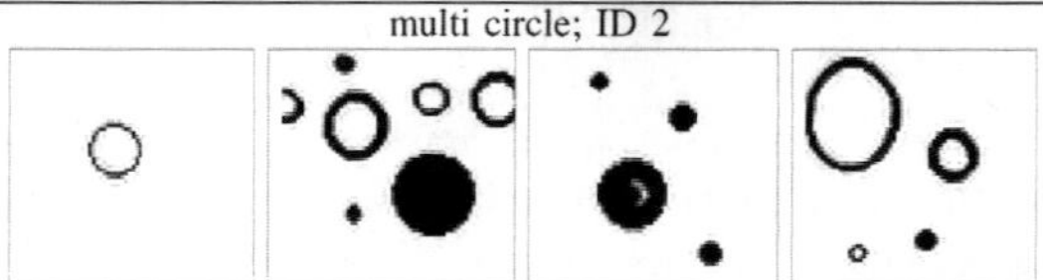
multi line; ID 5
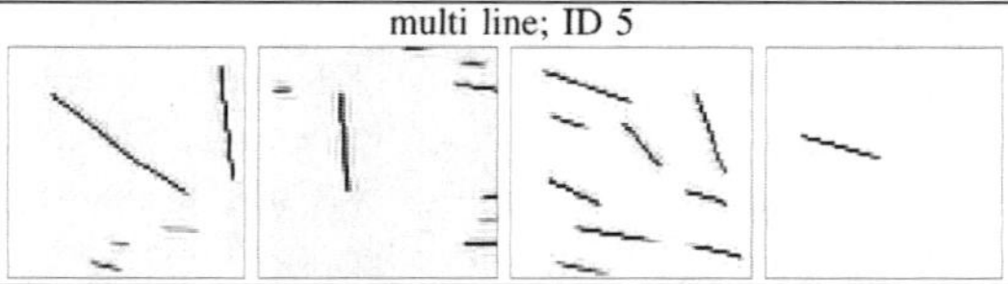

In difference to circles, straight lines within the facial area are very unusual. But the detection is not limited to the face. As introduced, especially for full synthetic DeepFake images also the background can be used for their detection. The probability for possible fake lines is in the background area of DeepFake images higher. Further, the use case of the geometrical shape detection does not need to be restricted to DeepFakes. Han et al. [19] propose a GAN for

TABLE VI. COMPARISON OF AUTOMATED CIRCLE DETECTION (FIG. 1 4.2B) FOR REAL AND FAKE IMAGES, RED LINES HIGHLIGHTS THE DETECTED CIRCLES, HUMAN BASED COMPARISON BETWEEN THE VISUAL AND AUTOMATED APPROACH CONFIRM ERRORS IN GAN IMAGE GENERATION (FIG. 1 4.3).

automated detection on **real** circles and circled rings);	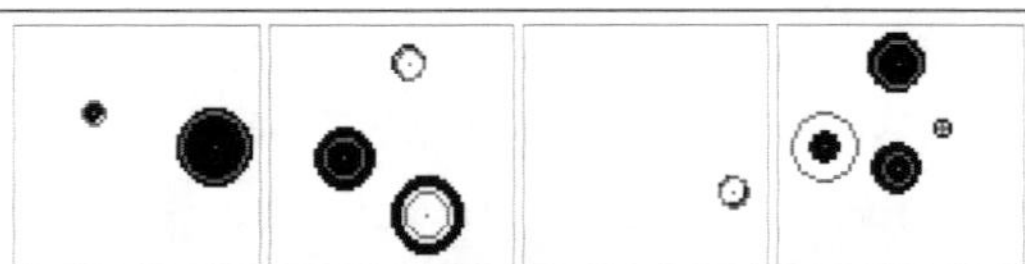	Most circles from training are automated detected correctly in their position and size. In General the detected center position is identical with the given center position. The automated detection of the circle size is not always the same compared to the visual circle.
automated detection on **fake** circles and circled rings);	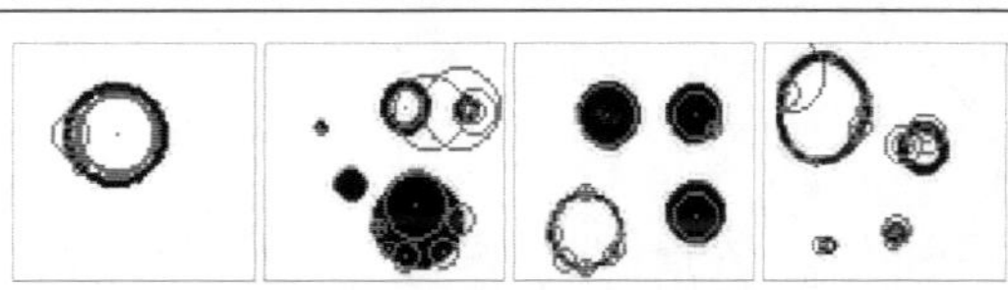	Automated detection of small circles from fake circle generation was mostly correct in their position and size. On bigger circles more than one circle were detected. Specially the detection of big circled rings results in the detection of small circles on the border area of those rings. The detection of the whole ring was not successful. There are also shapes which was not detected as circle, but visually also not identified as circle by the human.

the generation of synthetic license plates of cars. Within the European Union, all license plates follow a specific standard. Our circle and line detection approach offers further applications. For example, the Germany License Plate DIN standard DIN 74069:2022-10 [20] with specific regularities for plate size and position as well as color, font and character size offers an evaluation: Would a GAN be able to correctly reproduce a German license plate and would be a GAN able to be detected a synthetic generated plate as DeepFake?

V. Conclusion

In this work, we introduced a new methodology to bring GANs to their limit by reducing the level of detail of the training material. We follow the challenge to identify issues which are a result of its generation process. To be specific, we train different StyleGAN3 models with different gray scale data sets of images with geometric shapes. On this way, our approach shows the root cause of circle artifacts in GAN generated data and explains therefor findings the artifact results in Guo et al. [5]. For further investigation on this question, we currently enhance our Automated Circle-Checking to an Automated Circle-Line-Checking approach. Additionally, we want to establish our approach to other generative AI technologies such as AEs.

As our approach uses StyleGAN3 implementations from [6] it can also be used in further decision support systems for DeepFake detection purposes. Further, both our generator and detector are provided as open source models and open data [2] to allow transparency in understanding and reproducing the inner processes of models. For future explainability, we plan to introduce on the one hand an improved user based comparison of potential fake and ideal circles and on the other hand a quantitative evaluation method with the definition of scores based on the overlapping areas of original and reproduces circles.

Acknowledgments and Author Contributions

The work in DeepFakes in this paper is funded in part by the German Federal Ministry of Education and Research (BMBF) under grant number FKZ: 13N15736 (project "Fake-ID"). The research for transparency with Open Source and Open Data conducted within this paper was partly funded by the European Union Project "CyberSecurity-Verbund LSA II" (Grant No.: ZS/2023/182058) - "CyberSecurity-Verbund LSA II – Prävention, Detektion und Reaktion mit Open Source-Perspektiven".

Initial idea & methodology: J. Dittmann (JD); Conceptualization: S. Seidlitz (StS) and JD; Modeling & application in the context of DeepFake: StS; Writing – original draft: StS and JD; Writing – review & editing: StS and JD. Thanks to Nischay Purnekar (University of Siena, Italy) for proof reading.

References

[1] T. Karras *et al.*, *GitHub repository of StyleGAN3*, https://github.com/NVlabs/stylegan3, Oct. 29, 2024.

[2] S. Seidlitz and J. Dittmann, *Specific Scripts, Models and Data of this Paper*, https://cloud.ovgu.de/s/sBRWzxSLYikp64x, Oct. 2, 2024.

[3] L. Nataraj *et al.*, "Detecting GAN generated fake images using co-occurrence matrices," *Electronic Imaging*, vol. 31, no. 5, pp. 532-1–532-1, 2019. DOI: 10.2352/ISSN.2470-1173.2019.5.MWSF-532.

[4] F. Marra, C. Saltori, G. Boato, and L. Verdoliva, "Incremental learning for the detection and classification of GAN-generated images," *2019 IEEE International Workshop on Information Forensics and Security (WIFS)*, pp. 1–6, 2019.

[5] H. Guo, S. Hu, X. Wang, M.-C. Chang, and S. Lyu, "Eyes tell all: Irregular pupil shapes reveal GAN-generated faces," in *ICASSP 2022 - 2022 IEEE International Conference on Acoustics, Speech and Signal Processing (ICASSP)*, 2022, pp. 2904–2908. DOI: 10.1109/ICASSP43922.2022.9746597.

[6] T. Karras *et al.*, "Alias-free generative adversarial networks," *CoRR*, vol. abs/2106.12423, 2021. arXiv: 2106.12423.

[7] P. J. Phillips *et al.*, "Four principles of explainable artificial intelligence," Tech. Rep., Sep. 2021. DOI: 10.6028/nist.ir.8312.

[8] T. Karras, T. Aila, S. Laine, and J. Lehtinen, "Progressive growing of GANs for improved quality, stability, and variation," *CoRR*, vol. abs/1710.10196, 2017. arXiv: 1710.10196.

[9] T. Karras, S. Laine, and T. Aila, "A style-based generator architecture for generative adversarial networks," *CoRR*, vol. abs/1812.04948, 2018. arXiv: 1812.04948.

[10] I. J. Goodfellow *et al.*, *Generative adversarial networks*, 2014. arXiv: 1406.2661 [stat.ML].

[11] T. Karras *et al.*, "Analyzing and improving the image quality of stylegan," *CoRR*, vol. abs/1912.04958, 2019. arXiv: 1912.04958.

[12] T. Karras *et al.*, "Training generative adversarial networks with limited data," *CoRR*, vol. abs/2006.06676, 2020. arXiv: 2006.06676.

[13] T.-C. Wang *et al.*, "Few-shot video-to-video synthesis," in *Conference on Neural Information Processing Systems (NeurIPS)*, 2019.

[14] Z. Huang, K. C. Chan, Y. Jiang, and Z. Liu, "Collaborative diffusion for multi-modal face generation and editing," in *Proceedings of the IEEE/CVF Conference on Computer Vision and Pattern Recognition*, 2023.

[15] Z. Yan *et al.*, "Df40: Toward next-generation deepfake detection," *arXiv preprint arXiv:2406.13495*, 2024.

[16] A. Makrushin, D. Siegel, and J. Dittmann, "Simulation of border control in an ongoing web-based experiment for estimating morphing detection performance of humans," in *Proceedings of the 2020 ACM Workshop on Information Hiding and Multimedia Security*, ser. IH&MMSec '20, Denver, CO, USA: Association for Computing Machinery, 2020, pp. 91–96, ISBN: 9781450370509. DOI: 10.1145/3369412.3395073.

[17] The GIMP Development Team, *Gimp*, version 2.10.12, https://www.gimp.org, Jun. 12, 2019.

[18] L. DeBruine and B. Jones, "Face Research Lab London Set," May 2017. DOI: 10.6084/m9.figshare.5047666.v3.

[19] B.-G. Han, J. T. Lee, K.-T. Lim, and D.-H. Choi, "License plate image generation using generative adversarial networks for end-to-end license plate character recognition from a small set of real images," *Applied Sciences*, vol. 10, no. 8, 2020, ISSN: 2076-3417. DOI: 10.3390/app10082780.

[20] DIN 74069:2022-10, "Retroreflektierende Kennzeichenschilder, Stempelplaketten und Plakettenträger für Kraftfahrzeuge und deren Anhängefahrzeuge [in English: Retro-reflective registration plates, seal-sticker and sticker-cover for motor vehicles and their trailers]," DIN Media GmbH, Berlin, Tech. Rep., 2022. DOI: 10.31030/3379383.

Merging Digital Twins and Multi-Agent Systems Approaches for Security Monitoring

Zoé Lagache[†], Annabelle Mercier[*], Oum-El-Kheir Aktouf[*] and Arthur Baudet[*]
[*]Univ. Grenoble Alpes, Grenoble INP, LCIS, 26000 Valence, France
e-mail: {firstname.lastname}@lcis.grenoble-alpes.fr
[†]Univ. Grenoble Alpes, CEA, Grenoble, France zoe.lagache@cea.fr

***Abstract*—This paper proposes a method for designing a model based on the Multi-Agent System (MAS) and Digital Twin (DT) concepts to study the cyber-physical systems security. When Cyber-Physical Systems (CPS) are used in a network to address a complex problem (such as the deployment of smart cities, Industry 4.0, etc.), they present a unique wide vulnerability challenges as their attack surface ranges from hardware and physical attacks to software attacks and even including network attacks. To meet these challenges, we explored several approaches to ally MAS and DT with the aim to benefit from the scalability and adaptability of MASs and the enhanced modelling of DTs. As a result of this exploration, we present a novel approach to tackle networking attacks of CPSs. To showcase our approach, we present its application to detect blackhole attacks (a kind of attack in which one or more nodes attract all communications and not forward them, mimicking an error in the network) in a simulated smart home environment. As results are promising, we conclude and discuss future research perspectives in allying DTs and MASs for managing the security of CPSs.**

Keywords- Multi-Agent Systems, Digital Twins, Cyber Physical Systems, Network Security

I. Introduction

Cyber-Physical Systems (CPSs), defined as the interaction between physical systems and processes using computations and communication abilities with the Cyber-Physical Systems Steering Group [1], can be found everywhere: in vehicles to control safety mechanisms such as airbags and belt tensioners, to monitor in manufacturing plants [2] or acting as sensors and actuators components of smart homes and smart cities [3]. However, these ubiquitous systems can also be vectors of attacks, such as the unauthorized access, manipulation of system controls, and the disruption of critical infrastructure. These risks can have significant consequences, including loss of life, economic damage, and the disclosure of sensitive information [4] [5]. It is important to have robust security measures in place to mitigate these risks and to have available contingency plans to respond to potential security breaches. CPSs can be found in a wide range of applications and could benefit from a stronger degree of security. Our approach, motivated by this need of security, aims at contributing to CPSs security field by combining innovative approaches such as, Multi-Agent System (MAS) and Digital Twin (DT) models.

A MAS is a system composed of agents collaborating with each other in order to achieve a common goal. These agents communicate with their local neighbors and typically possess only a limited and localized view of the overall system. MAS are now a trend in the Internet of Things (IoT) field thanks to its decentralization aspect. Furthermore, a DT is often associated with a way to track and analyze a system in real time, usually in order to predict its behavior. Both MAS and DT hold very useful potential for modeling CPS. These two concepts are complementary in modeling, securing, and preventing cyberattacks on CPS, DT allows for dynamic simulations of system behavior under various scenarios, while MAS provides a deeper understanding of complex interactions between system components. When combined, these models provide a more comprehensive approach to identifying vulnerabilities, testing security measures, and optimizing system design to enhance security. Our contribution introduces a novel method for modeling complex CPSs, facilitating the identification of potential security vulnerabilities and the development of strategies to improve security and protect against cyber threats.

Section II proposes a brief related work. Section III presents the motivations for our study and the main points about CPS vulnerabilities. In Section IV, we introduce the different possibilities for leveraging the DT and MAS models for monitoring CPS and detecting vulnerabilities, and explain the adopted model. In Section IV-D, we discuss the application of our model to the case study of a blackhole attack detection in a smart home setting. Validation of this application is then presented in Section V. Finally, we conclude in Section VI.

II. Related work

DTs are often used in the field of complex system monitoring. For example, they can be used to simulate product quality in a manufacturing process [6], incorporating real-time data from IoT sensors to improve simulation accuracy and reduce uncertainty. As for MASs, they can model distributed and heterogeneous systems [7] which makes them also good candidate for simulating CPS. In terms of security analyses, a framework for evaluating the security of a system is named "cia model" [8] which uses three main criteria to assess the overall security: *Confidentiality* refers to the protection of sensitive information from unauthorized access or disclosure ; *Integrity* refers to the protection of information from unauthorized modification or destruction ; *Availability* refers to the ability of authorized individuals to access the information when they need it. The association of DT and MAS for security is a topic that is not much studied in literature, as evidenced by the scarcity of relevant studies or papers. The available literature is also often highly specialized, making it difficult to find comprehensive information on the topic. For example, work in [9] focuses on the medical field and present an agent-based DT to advise severe traumas, which is their use case. Other examples exist, such as the work in [10] [11] that focus on smart cities and farms management, respectively. Another example is [12] which discuss the existing literature about the extended reality in systems such as CPS, but it does not give any insights on security of such systems. Nevertheless, we can encounter some more general papers in very recent works [13], which is a review on MASs in support of DTs. They present the main challenges like a roadmap for DT and MAS in general context, but this paper does not focus on security issues, and [14] that explore the development of Artificial Intelligence in digital ecosystems and focus on how to make them safer. However, this last paper does not explicitly refer to MAS but to collaborative systems. The work in [15] presents a generic way of modelling DT using the MAS idea, discusses the difficulty in building DTs and creates a method to make this goal easier.

III. CPS VULNERABILITIES

A. Our CPS model

As explained in the introduction, CPSs are the combination of the physical world and the cyberspace interacting with one another through the use of sensors, actuators, communication, and interfaces. The cooperation between the physical and cyber systems is typically achieved through the use of sensors to monitor the physical system and actuators to control it, as seen in [12] [16] [17]. Monitoring refers to the process of gathering data and information about a system, process or environment, by using sensors and virtual models. Figure 1 represents an abstract view of a CPS. We simplified a CPS as two parts: the Physical Process(es) (PP) part and the cybersystem part. Both of these parts are interacting with each other through sensors and actuators, which compose the interface between both worlds. The Cyber System (CS) is composed of computing devices receiving data from the sensors, processing it, and sending the result to the actuators. The green arrows indicate the monitoring interaction, while the red ones represent the communication within the CS. The numbers point to the parts of the CPS that are subject to vulnerabilities.

B. Identification of vulnerabilities

By analyzing and synthesizing the classifications done in [4] [5] [18], we define four attacks classes shown in Table I. First, communication attacks have the potential to be operated on all communication links, i.e., points ②, ④, ⑥ and ⑦. For example, *eavesdropping* is a passive attack where the attacker is listening to a communication between two or more nodes and (Confidentiality criteria is affected) in the *Man-In-The-Middle (MITM)*, the attacker can intercept the communication packets and thus to tamper with them (Confidentiality and Integrity). Second, network or routing attacks are attacks that are the result of a changing behavior from one element of the system that can impact changes in the rest of the network. All parts of the system from ① to ⑤ could be impacted by such attacks. In a *blackhole attack*, the attacker is able

TABLE I
SUMMARY OF CPS VULNERABILITIES.

Attack Class	Attack	Vulnerable Surface	CIA Involved
Communication	Eavesdropping	②, ④, ⑥ & ⑦	Confidentiality
	MITM		Confidentiality, Integrity
Network/Routing	Blackhole	①–⑤	Availability
	Greyhole		Availability
	Wormhole		All
Physical	Side Channel	①,⑤	Confidentiality
	Fault injection		Confidentiality
	Jamming		Availability
Miscellaneous	Malware	③	All
	DOS	② or ③	Availability

to corrupt one or more nodes in the networked system to make them advertise fake routes that are shorter than those of its neighbors. However, once the blackhole nodes receive a packet, they drop it and Availabity is affected. Other attacks in this class are *greyhole attack* and *wormhole attack*. Third, physical attacks can be done on the devices that are the closest to the real world, thus on the actuators or on the sensors (① and ⑤). They can be *side channel attack*, *fault injection attack* where Integrity is affected and all criteria for *jamming attack*. Fourth, miscellaneous attacks have their own locations on the map and are not part of previous classes and could affect all criteria. For example, *a malware spreading attack* is an application attack where the attacker spreads a piece of malicious code into one or more computing devices (③). Another attack can be a *DoS attack* where the attacker disables a device, so it cannot work anymore, which can be located either on point ② or on point ③ and affects availability.

Most of these attacks can be avoided with preventive methods. Eavesdropping and MITM attacks can be prevented by encrypting the communications, the side channel and fault injection ones by the specific algorithms or Trusted Execution Environments, and malwares by computing and comparing checksums of binaries. That is why our work is focused on the detection of routing attacks. More precisely, we chose to work on blackholes detection in Section V because they exist in less diverse and elaborated versions than the other attacks.

IV. A MODEL TO MERGE DT AND MAS FOR MONITORING SECURITY IN CPS

As there are few studies that focus on MAS and DTs at the same time, and even fewer that are concerned with system security, we propose here a study of the different possibilities to compose the MAS and DT models for a scalable solution to manage security in CPSs. In this section, we present different approaches to leverage MAS and DTs solution to secure CPS,

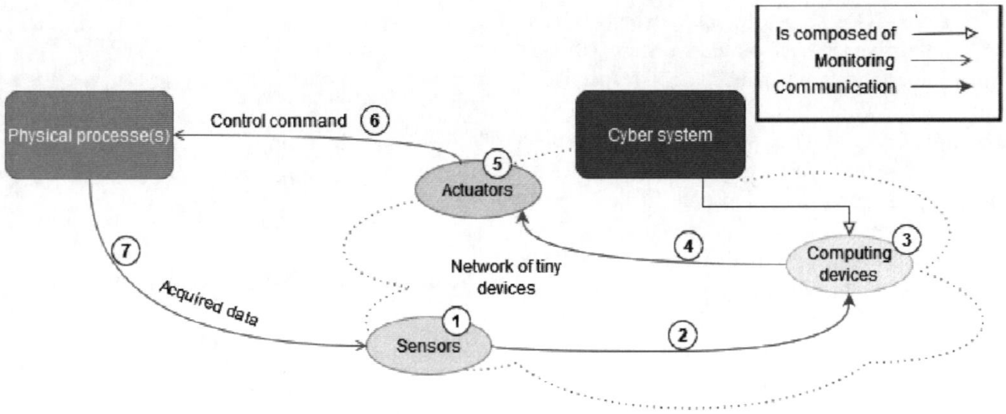

Figure 1. CPS main vulnerabilities

compare them and then present the approach we adopted and implemented, for the validation in the rest of the paper. To understand the models that we propose and to compare them, we will first explain the model architecture elements, and then we will introduce a guiding example to follow the way and processing of a measurement returned by a sensor.

The **Physical system Process(es)** (PP) is composed of sensors and actuators. For example, a sensor measures a room's temperature and an actuator increases or decreases the radiator thermostat. The physical system represents either a single element or is composite by bringing together several objects. The **Cyber System** (CS) is the digital entry point of the PP one. It has a module that receives datas, a module that transmits actions, and a module that processes the information. The CS is configured based on the hardware's organization of the constituting the physical system. We call the combination of CS and PP a Cyber-Physical System (CPS). We define a digital twin as a system that digitises the process and data flow of the physical system, with a feedback loop injecting new information via the cyber system to monitor or improve the physical system. In our study, the digital twin does not possess intelligence, it only digitizes information. The intelligence of the system to process data and audit potential security flaws lies at the agent level. The multi-agent system composed of several agents (upper than 3 agents) constitutes an intelligent virtualization of the system. According to the presented architectures, the physical system consists of sensors and actuators, and the cyber system consists of processing units. To understand the architecture of the proposed models, we use a guiding example with the following nominal scenario. For each model, we will explain the way of the sensored measurement, information processing, and subsequent actions.

In the context of smart home technology, a room is equipped with a physical system consisting of temperature sensors and actuators that can order the adjustment of the thermostat of a heating device or actuator to control the opening of the shutters in a room. The nominal scenario consists of regulating the temperature to maintain 20°C in a given space (room, house). The CPS returns 19°C via a temperature sensor, and the multi-agent system processes the information through the agent associated with the sensor. Depending on the behavior of the agent, an order may be directly sent to the actuator to open the shutters or increase the thermostat of the heating system. However, a more complex behavior involving information exchange in the system can be adopted. In this case, monitoring the security of the system becomes important. The agent may request measurements from its neighbors to obtain additional temperature readings from the physical system and wait for this new data to make a decision. For example, if the neighboring measurements are below 20°C, it could decide to send an order to increase the thermostat of the heating system.

A. A MAS Composed of Digital Twins of Cyber-Physical Systems

In this first approach, we consider a set of CPSs communicating and interacting with each other. Each CPS run DTs of its physical processes, and each CPS is considered an agent of global MAS. This idea is illustrated in Figure 2. Such an approach would allow the CPSs to produce a complete view of their processes thanks to the DTs models and use MAS capabilities to organize and handle the information in an autonomous and dynamic fashion. An example of the application of this approach, as a security framework, would be to deploy embedded systems, monitors, running DTs of sensors and actuators, sharing the information with nearby CPS to compare values to detect attacks on the sensed values. This model is used to manage a set of DT/CS. An agent represents the DT/CS pair and retrieves the sensors' measurements and executes the orders transmitted to the actuators. In our example, a sensor measures 19°C, the DT digitises the information and the associated agent processes the datas, for example by sending measurement requests to neighbouring agents. Once the information has been returned, a decision can be made to wait if the values returned are above 20°C or to ask the CS to send a command to increase the heating thermostat.

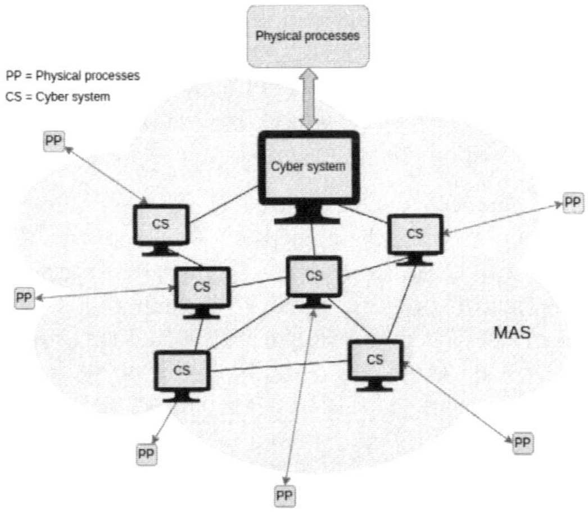

Figure 2. MAS composed of CPSs running Digital Twins of their processes.

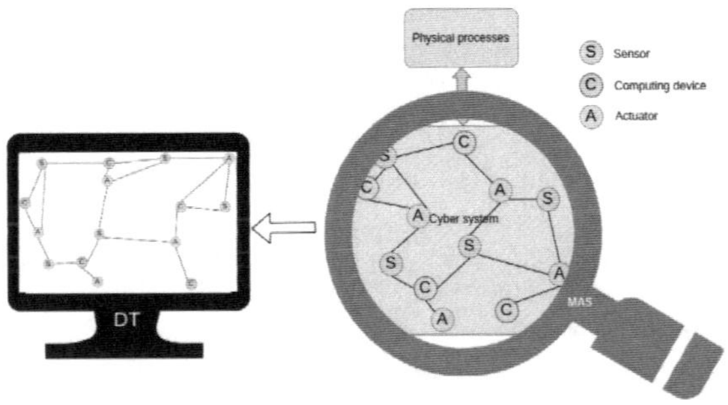

Figure 3. Digital Twin of the CPSs controlled by a Multi-Agent System.

In this approach, the DTs enable a better modelling of the physical processes, including computed information, to provide a better viewpoint of processes handled by the monitors. To not merge all information of the DTs but rather use a MAS approach provides a better scalability as well as better behaviors under changes of the systems: the monitors will first try to coordinate with their neighbors, without overloading the whole systems with a large amount of data, and also be able to re-organize at run-time if a monitor stops working or if new ones are added (including different ones since MASs allow for the cooperation of heterogeneous systems).

The main drawback of this approach is that it creates a "system of systems" which itself brings its one challenge in terms of security [19]. Since the monitors communicate with each other's, their communications or even themselves can be attacked. Moreover, such systems are also difficult to be modelled since they rely on the coordination of multiple systems, which can create numerous possible interactions and states in which the whole system can be.

B. Multi-Agent Algorithm Monitoring a Digital Twins of CPSs

The second approach also focuses on a network of CPSs, but this time, they are only communicating with their respective physical processes and a server, in charge of analyzing the information of the whole system. This server is running DTs for each CPS and a MA algorithm to analyze the modelled system. The output of the MA algorithm is then used to send control commands to the CPS through their DTs. This approach is illustrated in Figure 3.

Such an approach would provide a single, central view of the whole system thanks to the DTs. Unlike the previous approach, the MAS approach does not enable decentralized control but rather enable a more coherent way of analyzing the network of DTs, a distributed system (for example, by attributing an agent to each DT). An example of the application of this approach would be an industry 4.0 plant in which each component (robots, packages) is modelled with a DT and the MA algorithm provides on-line analysis of the DTs to detect incoherent behaviors due to attacks on the production lines [20].

In this model, an agent is associated with the sensors and actuators of the PP and the computing device of the CS. All the sensors, actuators, and processing unit make up a single CPS. The DT provides a snapshot of the system. In our scenario, the sensor reads 19°C, the processing unit and its associated agent process the information and can instruct the actuator to raise the temperature or ask its neighbours for other readings. Here, the DT has a supervisory role; for example, if the system is overloaded or if the data seems inconsistent, the operator, who can see what is happening, can send instructions directly to the CPS system.

This approach is the canonical use of DTs and CPS and benefits from the advantages of DTs, an enhanced view of the whole system execution for an optimal control and CPSs analysis. The MAS provides a natural way of designing the analysis and control algorithms as well as enabling horizontal scaling, some of the agents can be located on different servers to scale to larger numbers of CPSs. Moreover, since the control is centralized, it is possible for an operator to get a global view of the system. However, since it is centralized, the server running the DTs becomes a Single-Point-Of-Failure (SPOF) and needs to be hardened since it will be a target of choice for an attacker. If the server is compromised or its communications prevented, the CPSs will no longer receive commands and attacks will remain undetected due to the lack of information provided by the CPSs.

C. Digital Twin of the Cyber-Physical System seen as a MAS

Unlike the two previous one, the third approach focuses on a single CPS. In this approach, the DTs modelled the sensors and actuators of the CPS and, like the second approach, a multiagent (MA) algorithm is used for analyzing the behavior of the DTs. This approach is illustrated in Figure 4.

This third approach allows for an analysis at the sensors and actuators level, as the first approach, with a central control, as the second approach. An example of the application of this approach could be the fine-grained detection of attacks

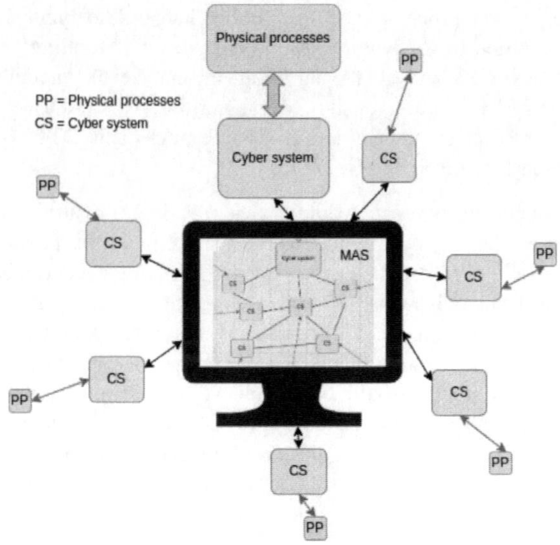

Figure 4. MA algorithm monitoring DTs of the components of a CPS.

in one production line by detecting incoherent values given by the DTs of the sensors and behaviors of the DTs of the actuators, each one an agent of a MAS. In this model, the cyber system and the physical process are able to receive, transmit and process the datas, they form a single CPS. An agent is associated at each CS to a server. The multiagent system on the server is the brain of the system, we obtain the digitalisation of the whole elements of the CPS. The sensored data is sent to the associated agent on the server. The multiagent makes decisions and will transmit the actions to the CPS.

This approach provides an interesting trade-off between the centralization of all the data of a whole network and the complexity of controlling a decentralized system. The analysis is done near at the edge of the network, on each CPS, thanks to the modeling capabilities of the DTs as well as the efficiency of the multi-agent paradigm. While, it may not be possible to run a machine learning and deep learning algorithm on the CPS, a multiagent algorithm may detect incoherent behaviors at a lower computational and energetic cost.

However, this approach only focuses on one CPS at the time, which may not be enough to detect large scale attacks spanning over a whole plant, smart home or network of vehicles. It also does not provide any solution if the whole CPS (and not only the actuators and sensors) is under attack. To summarize, Table II gives a comparison with advantages and drawbacks of the three models.

D. Chosen model for monitoring security issues in CPSs

We propose a new approach which is a compromise to avoid the pitfalls of the systems-of-systems model, while leveraging MAS benefits. We propose a multi-agent algorithm used to analyze information of the DTs of the components of a single CPS, but not running on the CPS itself, but rather on a distant server. This approach is illustrated in Figure 5. It is a trade-off between the three approaches presented above and is a good candidate for a proof-of-concept as it encompasses most of the notions of the approaches while remaining simple enough to be properly validated.

This approach could be used in a smart home system setup: the CPS would be composed of the actuators (heating, lights, kitchen appliances, etc.) and sensors (presence or smoke detector, light sensor, etc.). Each CPS component would send information to a central server, which would then use DTs to model the CPS and a MA algorithm to analyze the behaviors of the components in order to detect attacks on the CPS.

The use of a central server creates a SPOF, which is a major drawback but which also drastically decrease the difficulty of deploying our approach: the MA algorithm has access to all the information on a single device and does not have to rely on coordination between the CPS components to take a decision. Moreover, it is easier to harden the security of the server rather than to each component of the CPS. The DTs can also serve as a monitoring tool for users and operators and can be used to ease the CPS maintenance.

The server that digitises the information constitutes the physical system's DT. Here, we add the notion of sensor twins, which are visualised on the DT diagram. The agents associated with the sensor twins make up the SMA: the granularity can be chosen to process the data in the agents. Thermometers can be combined, humidity sensors or both. Sensors could also be combined by room type (neighbouring, north, south). In this way, the multi-agent system could adopt different processing rules depending on the location of the building or its function. Once a measurement of 19° has been taken, a notification is sent to the DT. The sensor twin updates T°=19. The agent retrieves this information, and can apply its process and decision rules by asking neighbouring agents for the temperature they have recorded, and make the same type of decision as in the previous models.

This approach also works under the assumption that some components can reliably send information to the server. If some components do not send information to the server, we expect that the MA algorithm will detect their absence and adapt accordingly (e.g., raising an alarm, and re-organizing if the loss was expected).

V. Proof of concept: blackhole detection

We have done a general simulation with Mesa framework [21] to simulate communication in a CPS and to test our architecture on a blackhole detection. The source code of the experiments is available on GitHub [22]. As explained in Section III-B, we consider the blackhole attack because it can be detected by a behavior analysis that suits well with the use of a MAS. Only attacks directed toward the CPS will be taken into account. Attacks on the server part in Figure 5, or its communication with the CPS are not investigated. To lead our experiments, we make several hypotheses about the

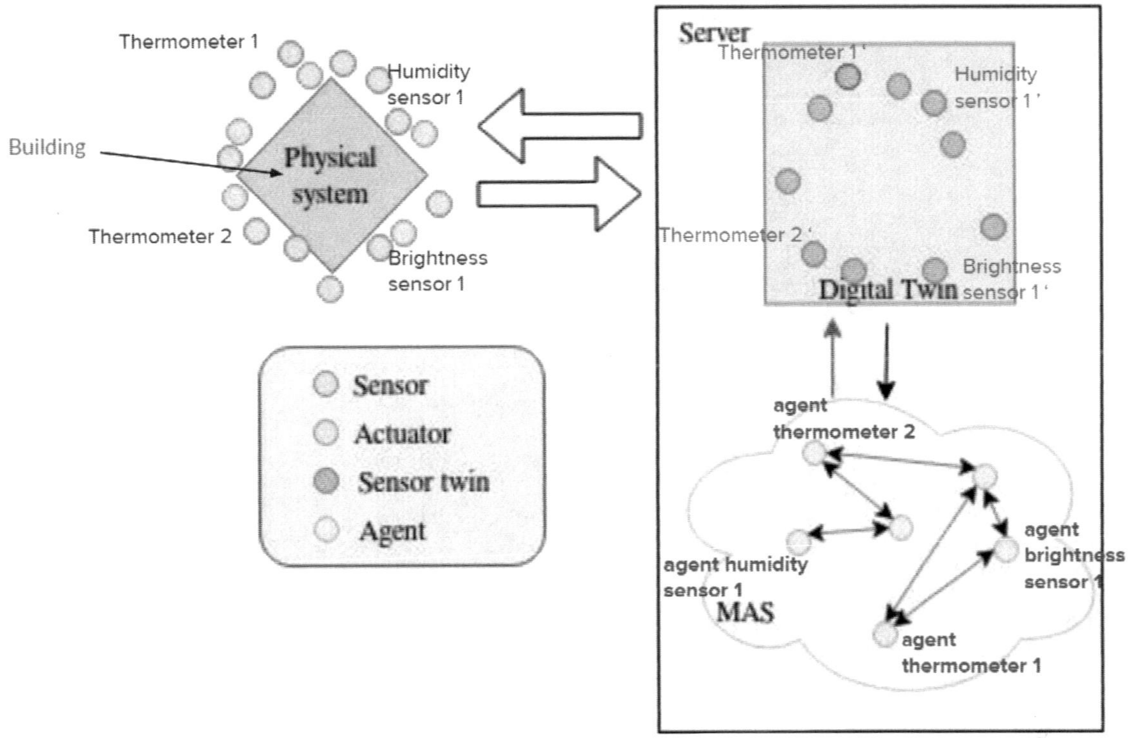

Figure 5. Chosen model: Monitoring the DTs of a CPS using a multi-agent algorithm.

TABLE II
COMPARISON OF THE THREE PROPOSED APPROACHES.

No.	Benefits	Drawbacks
1	• High scalability • High adaptability at run-time	• Hard to maintain • Only provides a global security analysis • Creates new vulnerabilities
2	• Enables part of MAS scalability without the difficulties of the system-of-systems approach • Provide a global view of the system	• Only provide a global security analysis • The server is a single-point-of-failure
3	• Low impact on the system as it runs directly on the CPSs • Highly scalable	• Only provide a local security analysis • No redundancies, if one CPS is under attack, the others will not be able to detect it

attacker's goals, capabilities, and knowledge. The goal of the attacker, in our chosen scenario, is to achieve a blackhole on the CPS network. Thus, to alter the availability of the system through the usage of corrupted nodes that will drop packets and potentially advertise maliciously. Thus, the attacker can add intruder nodes as well as corrupt a victim node. Since some metadata on exchanged packets, such as the source and destination addresses, are important to analyze them. For the experiments, we simulate the CPS by a network of nodes that exchange messages. The requirements on the CPS structure are defined as follows: (1) it is made of sensor nodes communicating with each other forming a network, (2) nodes can be added or removed from the network, and (3) a node cooperates with the DT by sending it notifications. The considered messages to help the blackhole algorithm detection are: (i) `data` messages: messages containing raw datas used by the higher level application, (ii) `advertisement` messages: messages to determine which path must be used between two nodes. In most protocols, the value of this type of message starts from 0 from the sending node and is incremented each time a new node receives it, so the sending node knows its closest neighbors. In order to detect the blackhole of communication between nodes, we also assumed that sensor nodes are sending notification to the server, giving information on messages received and sent. If a node does not cooperate, it is either because it is not part of our system or because it is malicious. In the second case, either the node does not communicate with other nodes of the system, and thus is not harmful to it, or it communicates and will therefore be seen through the notifications from other nodes. The implementation process is defined as follows. The DT block receives the inputs, which are the sensor nodes notifications. Since our tests do not work in real time, a YAML is adopted to simulate data exchange between nodes. A message has a source ID and a destination ID and information on message (message type, datas and

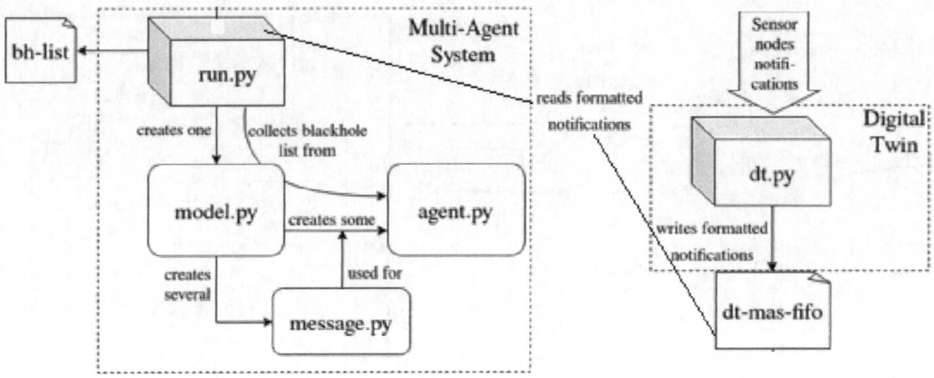

Figure 6. Implementation architecture with Mesa.

source if of previous node) ; when the message could not be sent directly there is the destination ID of the next node and ; when the message can not be sent directly the source ID and destination ID of second message.

Each of the test files contains each notification received by the DT from each node. Thus, they contain all messages sent and received by each sensor. The dt.py python code writes these notifications into a FIFO. On the other side of this FIFO, the run.py python code, which is the entry point of the MAS block, reads the notifications and launches Mesa. The Mesa agents analyze the data and create a blackholes list, which is retrieved by run.py. More precisely, the run.py python code reads the notifications from the FIFO and creates a Mesa model which is our MAS model. The model.py python code is what creates and keeps updated the Mesa agents and messages object, which are respectively described in agent.py and message.py. During running time, Mesa agents will analyze the messages they have and create a list of tags, or states, indicating which node they consider blackhole from their local point of view. Mesa includes a time system based on steps. We write what the agents and the model do each step. Each agent analyses itself and the nodes from which it receives messages at each step. The architecture implementation is shown in Figure 6. The agent behavior checks the three elements to allow the blackhole detection: (1) whether the number of messages of type Data it sends is above the threshold given by the user, (2) whether it forwards messages received that are not destined to it, and, (3) whether it receives advertisement messages of value 0. Indeed, a lot of network protocols use a system of advertisement messages to determine which path must be used between two nodes. The value of this type of message is incremented each time a new node receives it. Thus, it is not possible for a node to receive advertisement messages of value 0. The blackholes lists are then retrieved and merged with the Mesa Model at each step before being put into a file by run.py.

Several tests are leading to evaluate the effectiveness of the proposed solution. We created some data sets in which we deliberately included anomalies, to be able to check the effectiveness of our code. Each of these tests are stored in a YAML file which is read in one go when executed. We made a total of 9 test files, checking if the 3 analysis on a basic configuration network of nodes Figure 7.

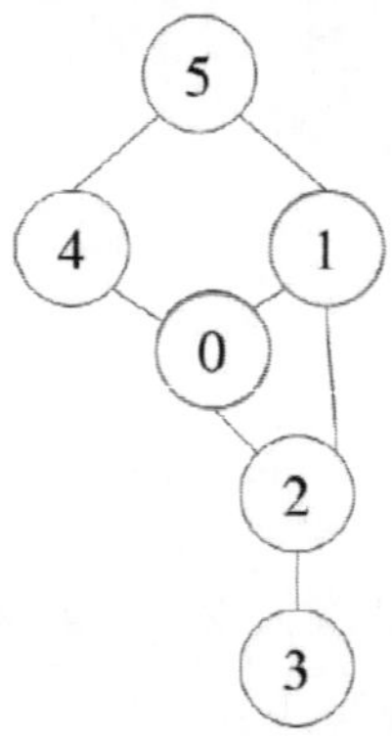

Figure 7. Test configuration network.

```
TagDict:
Step AgentID
1    0            {0: State.Safe}
     1            {1: State.Safe}
     2       {2: State.Blackhole}
     3            {3: State.Safe}
     4       {4: State.Blackhole}
     5            {5: State.Safe}
```

Figure 8. Detection of blackhole.

First, we make one test without any anomaly, to check that nothing is detected in this case. To complete simple cases, we make three other tests to check if a blackhole is detected if (1) a node does not forward a message (2) a node does not send any Data type messages; and (3) a node sending a wrong advertisement. Then, tests are leading to check that detecting a malicious node does not impact the detection of another one in three other cases (1) a node not forwarding and another not sending Data messages; (2) a node not forwarding and another sending wrong advertisement; and (3) a node not sending

Data messages and another sending a wrong advertisement. The last tests have to check that having multiple anomalies in one node does not impact the blackhole detection with the following situations: (1) a node not sending Data messages and sending a wrong advertisement; and (2) a node not forwarding and sending a wrong advertisement. The scenario of testing a situation with two suspicious nodes is as follows: Node 2 does not send any messages except its advertisement. Node 4 does not forward one (or more) message it received that was destined to another node. It is expected that Node 4 detects itself as a blackhole because it did not forward one message or more, and node 2 detects itself because it did not send any Data messages. The obtained results are shown in Figure 8: node 2 detecting that it is not sending any messages, while node 4 detects that it is not forwarding one (or more) message. Thus, they changed their own tag for the blackhole tag.

VI. Conclusion

Our initial investigations revealed that digital twins and multiagent systems for security issues in CPS are rarely explored together, underscoring the need for further research in this area. After analyzing CPS vulnerabilities and outlining MAS and DT, we considered various approaches to integrate both concepts into a cohesive model. The final model was developed by selecting the most relevant components, aligned with our objectives and constraints. To validate our approach, we conducted an experimental implementation using the Mesa framework simulation tool. This implementation featured a basic algorithm for detecting blackholes in a Wireless Sensor Network (WSN)-like environment, along with a preliminary set of tests to evaluate its functionality. However, the lack of access to a real CPS or a comprehensive dataset posed significant limitations, leaving our analysis incomplete. Given these constraints, particularly the absence of benchmarks and an actual CPS, the most promising future work would involve implementing our model on a real CPS capable of sending real-time notifications. This would allow for the collection of realistic data and enable the evaluation of the model's performance, as well as the potential integration of feedback mechanisms into the CPS.

References

[1] CPS Steering Group, "Cyber-Physical Systems Executive Summary," Chicago, IL, USA., 2008.

[2] B. Dafflon, N. Moalla, and Y. Ouzrout, "The challenges, approaches, and used techniques of cps for manufacturing in industry 4.0: a literature review," *The International Journal of Advanced Manufacturing Technology*, vol. 113, no. 7, pp. 2395–2412, 2021.

[3] C.-S. Shih, J.-J. Chou, N. Reijers, and T.-W. Kuo, "Designing cps/iot applications for smart buildings and cities," *IET Cyber-Physical Systems: Theory & Applications*, vol. 1, no. 1, pp. 3–12, 2016.

[4] E. K. Wang, Y. Ye, X. Xu, S. M. Yiu, L. C. K. Hui, and K. P. Chow, "Security Issues and Challenges for Cyber Physical System," in *2010 IEEE/ACM Int'l Conference on Green Computing and Communications & Int'l Conference on Cyber, Physical and Social Computing*, 2010, pp. 733–738.

[5] S. Singh, N. Yadav, and P. K. Chuarasia, "A Review on Cyber Physical System Attacks: Issues and Challenges," in *2020 International Conference on Communication and Signal Processing (ICCSP)*, 2020, pp. 1133–1138.

[6] H. Marah and M. Challenger, "Intelligent agents and multi agent systems for modeling smart digital twins," *Engineering multi-agent systems*, 2022.

[7] M. E. Gregori, J. P. Cámara, and G. A. Bada, "A jabber-based multi-agent system platform," in *Proceedings of the Fifth International Joint Conference on Autonomous Agents and Multiagent Systems*, ser. AAMAS '06, 2006, p. 1282–1284.

[8] NIST, "Security and privacy controls for information systems and organizations," 2020.

[9] A. Croatti, M. Gabellini, S. Montagna, and A. Ricci, "On the integration of agents and digital twins in healthcare," *Journal of Medical Systems*, 2020.

[10] T. Clemen, N. Ahmady-Moghaddam, U. A. Lenfers, F. Ocker, D. Osterholz, J. Ströbele, and D. Glake, "Multi-Agent Systems and Digital Twins for Smarter Cities," in *Proceedings of the 2021 ACM SIGSIM Conference on Principles of Advanced Discrete Simulation*, 2021, pp. 45–55.

[11] V. Laryukhin, P. Skobelev, O. Lakhin, S. Grachev, V. Yalovenko, and O. Yalovenko, "Towards developing a cyber-physical multi-agent system for managing precise farms with digital twins of plants," *Cybernetics and Physics*, pp. 257–261, 2019.

[12] Y. P. Tsang, T. Yang, Z. S. Chen, C. H. Wu, and K. H. Tan, "How is extended reality bridging human and cyber-physical systems in the IoT-empowered logistics and supply chain management?" *Internet of Things*, vol. 20, p. 100623, 2022.

[13] E. Pretel, E. Navarro, V. López-Jaquero, A. Moya, and P. González, "Multi-Agent Systems in Support of Digital Twins: A Survey," in *Bio-inspired Systems and Applications: from Robotics to Ambient Intelligence*, 2022, pp. 524–533.

[14] E. Cioroaica, B. Buhnova, and E. Tomur, "A paradigm for safe adaptation of collaborating robots," in *Proceedings of the 17th Symposium on Software Engineering for Adaptive and Self-Managing Systems*, 2022, pp. 113–119.

[15] H. Marah and M. Challenger, "Madtwin: a framework for multi-agent digital twin development: smart warehouse case study," *Annals of Mathematics and Artificial Intelligence*, vol. 92, pp. 1573–7470, 2023.

[16] L. Chen, F. Hu, S. Wang, and J. Chen, "Cyber-physical system fusion modeling and robustness evaluation," *Electric Power Systems Research*, vol. 213, p. 108654, 2022.

[17] C.-U. Lei, K. Wan, and K. L. Man, "Developing a Smart Learning Environment in Universities Via Cyber-Physical Systems," *Procedia Computer Science*, vol. 17, pp. 583–585, 2013.

[18] M. Wazid, A. K. Das, S. Kumari, and M. K. Khan, "Design of sinkhole node detection mechanism for hierarchical wireless sensor networks," *Security and Communication Networks*, vol. 9, no. 17, pp. 4596–4614, 2016.

[19] A. Baudet, O.-E.-K. Aktouf, A. Mercier, and P. Elbaz-Vincent, "Systematic Mapping Study of Security in Multi-Embedded-Agent Systems," *IEEE Access*, vol. 9, pp. 154 902–154 913, 2021.

[20] T. Horak, P. Strelec, L. Huraj, P. Tanuska, A. Vaclavova, and M. Kebisek, "The vulnerability of the production line using industrial iot systems under ddos attack," *Electronics*, vol. 10, no. 4, 2021.

[21] J. Kazil, D. Masad, and A. Crooks, "Utilizing python for agent-based modeling: The mesa framework," in *Social, Cultural, and Behavioral Modeling*, R. Thomson, H. Bisgin, C. Dancy, A. Hyder, and M. Hussain, Eds., vol. 12268, 2020, pp. 308–317.

[22] Z. Lagache, A. Baudet, A. Mercier, and O.-E.-K. Aktouf, "Ghithub link for experimental." [Online]. Available: https://hal.science/hal-04720424

Vehicle Security Operations Center for Cooperative, Connected and Automated Mobility

Kevin Mayer, Tina Volkersdorfer, Jenny Hofbauer, Patrizia Heinl, Hans-Joachim Hof
CARISSMA Institute of Electric, Connected and Secure Mobility (C-ECOS)
Technical University Ingolstadt
Ingolstadt, Germany
e-mail: {kevin.mayer | tina.volkersdorfer | jeh7703 | patrizia.heinl | hof}@thi.de

Abstract—**Security Operations Centers (SOCs) are well established in the general IT domain. They provide IT security services, including collecting and correlating data, detecting and analyzing cybersecurity incidents, and applying dedicated reactions to such incidents. With the increasing digital capabilities of modern vehicles, appropriate reactions to cybersecurity incidents for vehicles and their ecosystem should be applied, too. Therefore, we propose a novel architecture for a Vehicle Security Operations Center (VSOC) in a Cooperative, Connected, and Automated Mobility (CCAM) environment. The VSOC implements different boxes addressing data storage, analysis capabilities, event-processing procedures, response options, digital forensics capabilities, and threat-hunting activities. The architecture allows the VSOC to communicate with third parties such as manufacturer backends or cybersecurity service providers (e.g., threat intelligence). Furthermore, we evaluate the proposed VSOC against fourteen metrics, which result from related work and our contribution. Examples are autonomy, data aggregation, coverage, inclusion of people, addressing physical assets, and supporting real-time safety.**

Keywords-automotive; cyber security; security operations center; vehicle; vehicle security operations center; defensive; detection.

I. INTRODUCTION

Modern vehicles introduce a variety of different services and features. Examples include smartphone integration in modern infotainment systems, smart-home integration of vehicles, and vehicle-to-infrastructure communication. Those new services pose security risks to modern vehicles. The complexity and exposure of interfaces and the introduction of vehicle services increase by integrating vehicles into an ecosystem of connected entities. The European Parliament refers to the new ecosystem as Cooperative, Connected and Automated Mobility (CCAM) [1]. In this context, vehicles and ecosystem participants are connected, collaborate, and provide automated functionality. Participants in this environment aim to identify issues and join forces to mitigate them automatically. One key element in successfully implementing a CCAM is adapting security practices to mitigate security risks.

As a result, security practices must be evolved and adapted to keep up with these heterogeneous systems in CCAM environments. This adaption includes the area of detection and response tasks such as those implemented in Vehicle Security Operations Centers (VSOCs). In this regard, a VSOC should be capable of providing CCAM-specific services. Those include cooperative, connected, and automated features focusing on automotive-specific qualities such as safety, real-time, privacy, and legacy system characteristics. Based on these unique characteristics and the developments in the CCAM environment, we state the following three research questions:

RQ1: *What data streams are relevant for a VSOC?*

RQ2: *Which components of an VSOC are required in a CCAM environment?*

RQ3: *Which information of a VSOC are beneficial to provide to CCAM participants?*

The research questions focus on implementing and evaluating a VSOC capable of handling a realistic amount of data. The data is within a connected environment (i.e., CCAM) while being heterogeneous and diverse. As a result, we present the following contributions:

- Identification of data streams (RQ1)
- Simplified and adaptable VSOC architecture (RQ2)
- Applicability on CCAM environments (RQ2)
- Identification of outgoing data (RQ3)

The remainder of the publication is structured as follows. Section II focuses on a literature survey showing work that aims to solve parts of our contributions. Next, Section III highlights critical aspects of a VSOCs followed by Section IV presenting our approach in implementing a VSOC for the CCAM environment. Section V evaluates the presented implementation. The publication concludes with suggestions for future research directions and a conclusion in Section VI.

II. EXISTING RESEARCH AND REQUIREMENTS FOR AUTOMOTIVE SECURITY

First, we focus on research and requirements in automotive security. We specify the literature survey on works and regulations that highlight monitoring and defensive techniques in the vehicle ecosystem environment because those tasks are the primary responsibility of a VSOC.

Langer et al. establish an environment similar to a VSOC called "*Automotive Cyber Defense Center*" [2, pp. 98-122]. The authors present a theoretical implementation that aims to protect six layers: (1) Public mobility operation, (2) Original Equipment Manufacturer (OEM) mobility operation, (3) fleet operation, (4) vehicle operation, (5) vehicle network operation, and (6) Electronic Control Unit (ECU) operation. They further set requirements for the defense center by the ISO/SAE 21434 [3] and UN Regulation No. 155 [4] that lead to the following metrics: (a) Reaction time, (b) criticality, (c) autonomy, (d) data aggregation, and (e) control-flow.

Hofbauer et al. identify metrics from IT-focused Security Operations Centers (SOCs) that apply for VSOCs too [5]. Those are (a) coverage of the VSOC, (b) people (including domain knowledge, analyst bias), (c) technical (including limitations, vulnerabilities, risks, safety implications, and incident), and (d) governance as well as compliance topics (e.g., regulations and identity/asset management).

Barletta et al. present a tool called "*V-SOC4AS*", a VSOC for improving automotive security in general [6]. The tool collects Controller Area Network (CAN) logs, converting them to a Syslog representation using the JSON format and sending them to the Security Information and Event Management (SIEM) (in their case, IBM Qradar). The focus of the VSOC implementation is on data from in-vehicle components.

Previous works highlighted the UN Regulation No. 155 [4] that states requirements regarding a Cyber Security Management System (CSMS). Vehicle OEMs must provide monitoring capabilities for their products (i.e., vehicles and backend services). However, the standard does not explicitly highlight the need for a VSOC.

In a whitepaper by NTT DATA, the authors introduce an Intrusion Detection System (IDS) for the in-vehicle CAN bus [7]. The collected data and identified anomalies are transmitted to the NTT DATA VSOC. The whitepaper highlights no additional implementation details. However, the authors indicate that IDS-related data can be valuable for a VSOC.

Menges et al. publish their General Data Protection Regulation (GDPR) compliant SIEM called "*DINGfest*" [8]. The implementation complies with legal requirements for pseudonymization while maintaining detectability. They defined boundaries for GDPR compliant architectures. The protectable data, regarding privacy aspects, are stored in a central repository.

Compared to existing related work, we provide a VSOC architecture that is suitable for diverse CCAM environments and addresses automotive-specific requirements such as moving endpoints (i.e., cars) and the use of proprietary technologies. Existing architectures can not fulfill the requirements one faces in a CCAM environment. Hence, our implementation focuses on the CCAM environment that utilizes in-vehicle data combined with vehicle ecosystem data.

III. Analysis and Design

An effective VSOC should follow principles proven by classical enterprise IT SOCs. Hofbauer et al. present for SOC metrics that should be adopted by effective VSOCs [5]. Those metrics are (a) coverage metrics on how many assets are monitored by a VSOC. (b) People metrics focus on analyst domain knowledge and analyst bias. (c) Technical metrics focus on limitations, vulnerabilities, risk and safety, and incident handling. (d) Governance and compliance metrics focus on compliance, identity, and asset management. In addition, as focused by Menges et al., (e) Data privacy concern metric

TABLE I
Identified metrics for Vehicle Security Operations Centers.

Metric	Source
Reaction time	Langer et al. [2]
Criticality	Langer et al. [2]
Autonomy	Langer et al. [2]
Data aggregation	Langer et al. [2]
Control-flow	Langer et al. [2]
Coverage	Hofbauer et al. [5]
People	Hofbauer et al. [5]
Technical	Hofbauer et al. [5]
Governance and compliance	Hofbauer et al. [5]
Data privacy concern	Menges et al. [8]
Physical assets	Our contribution
Real-time safety	Our contribution
Complex supply chain	Our contribution
Attack vectors	Our contribution

is relevant for an effective VSOC [8]. Vehicles generate vast amounts of data, including sensitive information about occupants and behaviors. Protecting this data from unauthorized access and ensuring compliance with data privacy regulations (such as GDPR or CCPA) is critical to automotive SOC operations.

We further extend the metrics for an effective VSOC with the following: (f) Physical assets metric because automotive ecosystems involve physical assets such as vehicles, sensors, and infrastructure, unlike classical IT environments, which predominantly deal with virtual assets like servers and databases. It means the threats an automotive SOC faces include physical tampering, theft, sabotage, and digital attacks. (g) The real-time safety concerns metric is that security breaches can directly impact safety in automotive environments, leading to potentially life-threatening situations. Therefore, VSOCs must not only focus on data breaches and system compromises but also on ensuring the vehicles' and their occupants' safety and integrity. (h) Complex supply chain metric since the automotive industry involves a complex ecosystem of suppliers, manufacturers, and service providers, leading to a broader attack surface than classical IT environments. SOCs in automotive ecosystems must consider the security implications of the entire supply chain, including third-party components and software. (i) Attack vector metric since automotive systems are susceptible to unique attack vectors such as remote hacking of vehicle electronics, GPS spoofing, and manipulation of connected infrastructure (e.g., traffic lights). SOCs in automotive environments must be equipped to detect and respond to these unconventional threats.

As a result, the metrics from Hofbauer et al., Menges et al., Langer et al., and our extension lead to a foundation for effective VSOCs in a CCAM environment. Hence, instead of collecting in-vehicle data (e.g., from an IDS) only, we suggest extending the coverage of the VSOC to the vehicle ecosystem. All metrics are summarized in Table I.

IV. Implementation

The implementation focuses on fulfilling the proposed metrics. Furthermore, we aim to allow organizations such as

OEMs to adapt the architecture. As a result, the concept must be technology-independent, expandable, modular, and follow the KISS principle to "*keep it simple {and} stupid*" [9, p. 21].

The following sections will highlight the outside and inside views of the proposed VSOC implementation.

A. Outside view

The main interface to exchange information with participants and the VSOC is the VSOC API. It allows the introduction of technology-independent interfaces for communication between vehicle ecosystem participants and the monitoring entity (i.e., VSOC). We use HTTP REST for the proposed CCAM VSOC. HTTP(S) REST is well-documented and allows us to follow best practices. Various APIs from internet services use it. As a result, the VSOC provides three main services to the outside CCAM world:

- VSOC API as a communication interface based on the HTTP REST architecture style.
- Collecting predefined input data through the API based on defined and documented communication channels.
- Providing services for CCAM participants that are communicated through the API.

As highlighted, the communication method is the API. We utilize two specific communication methods while following the KISS principle: (a) CCAM participants implement their own HTTP REST client or server. It allows them to communicate with the VSOC and subscribe to relevant endpoints. (b) CCAM participants install SIEM-specific tooling to exchange information with the VSOC. One example would be the *Splunk Universal Forwarder* if Splunk is used as a SIEM. Figure 1 illustrates the outside view based on the presented technologies.

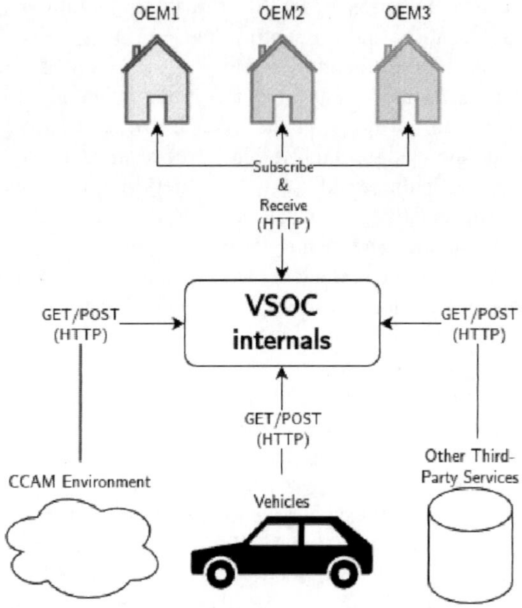

Figure 1. Outside view of the Vehicle Security Operations Center.

B. Inside view

Next, we introduce the inside view of the VSOC. Here, we follow a similar structure from IDSs. Vehicle IDS have been shown as a suitable method to manage cybersecurity events in automotive systems [10, p. 2774-2779] [11, p. 117-123][12, p. 185489-185502][13, p. 2531-2533][14][15, p. 1-9]. Hence, we follow a similar architectural structure in the VSOC.

Figure 2 illustrates the complete inside view and data streams.

Bidou took a similar approach [16]. However, we extend the pure IDS architecture with CCAM specifics such as Digital Forensics (DF) aspects for court-ready (requires an extensive amount of documentation and attributes such as reproducibility of the investigation results) event reconstruction and reporting capabilities. Due to vehicles' safety implications, this aspect is relevant for CCAM environments. As a result, we argue that cybersecurity incidents tend to lead to legal actions. Another extension is the Threat-informed Management System (TiMS) component. This component provides a knowledge foundation to facilitate defense and identification services. The diversity of components in CCAM environments enables the occurrence of complex cyberattacks that can evade typical IDS. Therefore, assisting threat hunting is significant to ensure security in a CCAM ecosystem. Based on the classical IDS structure and an adaption to CCAM, we propose the following components:

- D-box: data repository separated in (raw) data storage and a repository for knowledge in a dedicated format (e.g., ontologies or knowledge graphs).
- A-box: implements analysis capabilities.
- E-box: main system after the events are received. Distribute them accordingly.
- R-box: submits responses to external systems based on A-box results and using D-box data.
- F-box: provides forensic capabilities for investigations.
- TiMS-box: complements the A-box by implementing threat-analysis capabilities based on design information for threat hunting activities.

1) D-box: The D-box, or data box, serves as a repository within the system architecture, encompassing raw data storage and a dedicated repository for structured knowledge organized in formats like knowledge graphs. The primary requirement for the D-box lies in its ability to store vast amounts of data while also providing mechanisms for structuring and organizing this data into meaningful formats. It is the foundational element upon which other components of the VSOC internal architecture rely, necessitating robust storage capabilities and data retrieval mechanisms. Additionally, the D-box must facilitate seamless integration with other boxes, enabling easy access to raw data and structured knowledge for downstream processes.

The D-box's needs revolve around scalability, flexibility, and interoperability. It must be capable of accommodating diverse data types and formats, ranging from structured to unstructured

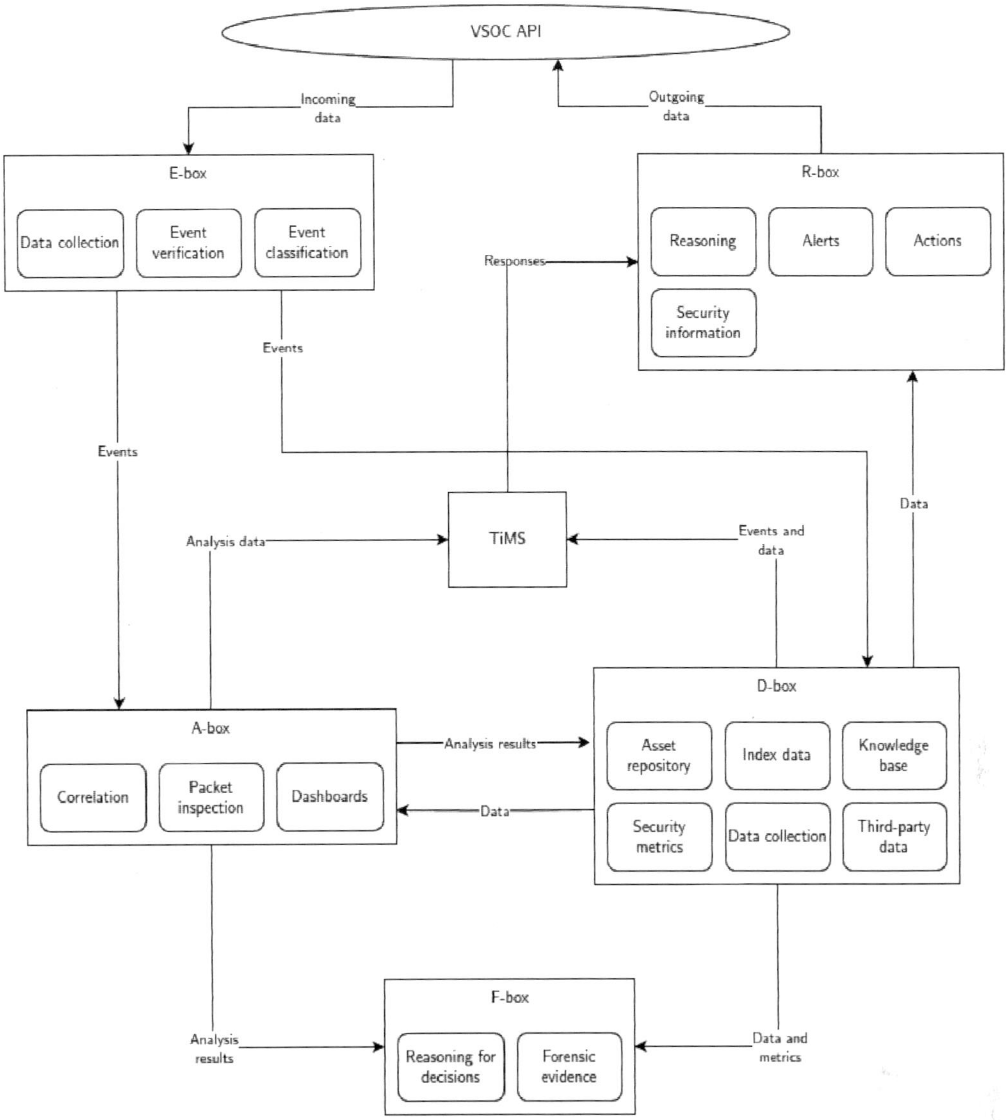

Figure 2. Inside view of the Vehicle Security Operations Center.

data, and scaling seamlessly to handle growing data volumes. Furthermore, the D-box should support interoperability with various data sources and formats, enabling seamless integration with external systems and data streams. Ensuring data quality, security, and privacy is also paramount, necessitating robust data validation, access control, and encryption mechanisms. Privacy principles are adapted by following guidelines from Menges et al. [8][17].

The D-box's capabilities include data storage and retrieval, support for structured knowledge representation, and seamless integration with other system components. It enables semantic querying and reasoning over stored data by leveraging knowledge graphs, facilitating advanced analytics and decision-making processes. Moreover, it is a centralized repository for shared knowledge within the system, enabling consistent interpretation and understanding of data across different components.

The D-box's limitations primarily revolve around scalability challenges, potential performance bottlenecks, and complexities of managing diverse data types and formats. As data volumes grow, the D-box may face scalability limitations, requiring careful design considerations and optimization strategies to ensure optimal performance. Also, managing heterogeneous data sources and formats can introduce integration and interoperability complexities, potentially leading to inconsistencies or data quality issues.

2) A-box: The A-box, or analysis box, constitutes a critical component within the system architecture that implements advanced analytics capabilities. Essential requirements for the A-box include the ability to provide complex data analysis tasks, such as statistical analysis, machine learning, and predictive modeling, on the data received from the D-box. Furthermore, in the CCAM environment, it propagates a trust score that addresses the trustworthiness of components. It must also support real-time or near-real-time processing to enable timely insights and decision-making.

The primary need of the A-box lies in its capability to derive actionable insights and intelligence from the vast amounts of data ingested from the D-box. It offers advanced analytical algorithms, models, and techniques tailored to the specific domain or application context. Furthermore, the A-box must handle diverse data types and formats, ranging from structured to unstructured data and support scalability to accommodate growing data volumes and computational requirements. However, the D-box will achieve the normalization of data, and the A-box will implement its capabilities based on the data the D-box provides.

The A-box's capabilities include advanced analytics, machine learning, predictive modeling, anomaly detection, and pattern recognition. By leveraging sophisticated algorithms and techniques, the A-box enables the extraction of valuable insights and patterns from complex datasets, empowering decision-makers with actionable intelligence. Moreover, it supports iterative model training and refinement, enabling continuous improvement and adaptation to changing data dynamics.

The A-box's limitations primarily revolve around computational complexity, resource constraints, and the need for domain-specific expertise, specifically in the automotive domain. Performing advanced analytics tasks on large-scale datasets can be computationally intensive, requiring significant computational resources and infrastructure. Additionally, designing and implementing effective analytical models often necessitate expertise in data science, statistics, and domain knowledge, which may pose challenges in resource-constrained environments.

3) E-box: The E-box, or event box, is the primary system after receiving events. Essential requirements for the E-box include event processing, routing, and distribution functionalities. It must be capable of receiving events from external sources, processing them in real-time or near-real-time, and distributing them to downstream components or subsystems. In the case of the proposed CCAM VSOC, the E-box receives events from the HTTP REST. The current HTTP REST interface does not fulfill real-time requirements. However, we argue that the current implementation does not require real-time since decisions and actions are verified by humans regardless. API and distributes them to other boxes.

The primary need for the E-box revolves around its ability to effectively handle incoming events and ensure timely processing and distribution within the system. It implements robust event processing capabilities, fault tolerance, and scalability to accommodate varying event volumes and processing requirements. Furthermore, the E-box must support event routing and filtering based on predefined criteria or rules, enabling targeted distribution to relevant components.

Capabilities of the E-box include event ingestion, processing, routing, and distribution. By leveraging event-driven architecture and real-time processing capabilities, the E-box enables rapid response to incoming events, facilitating timely decision-making and action. Moreover, it supports seamless integration with external systems and data sources, enabling interoperability and data exchange across disparate systems. The seamless integration is realized through the usage of HTTP REST. As highlighted in Section IV-A, participating entities implement HTTP REST capabilities.

The E-box's limitations include scalability challenges, potential performance bottlenecks, and event processing and routing complexities. As event volumes grow, the E-box may face scalability limitations, requiring careful design considerations and optimization strategies to ensure optimal performance. Additionally, managing event streams from diverse sources and ensuring reliability and fault tolerance can introduce system design and implementation complexities.

4) R-box: The R-box, or response box, is responsible for submitting responses to external systems based on the results generated by the A-box and utilizing data from the D-box. Essential requirements for the R-box include response generation, integration with external systems, and data retrieval from the D-box for contextual information. Again, the HTTP REST API is used as a communication interface.

The primary need for the R-box lies in its ability to effectively translate insights and intelligence derived from the A-box into actionable responses for external systems. It provides seamless integration with external interfaces and protocols and data retrieval mechanisms from the D-box to enrich responses with contextual information. Furthermore, the R-box must support adaptability and reconfigurability to tailor responses based on specific requirements or preferences.

The R-box's capabilities include response generation, integration with external systems, and data retrieval from the D-box. By leveraging insights and intelligence generated by the A-box and utilizing contextual information from the D-box, the R-box enables the generation of timely and relevant responses to external stimuli. Moreover, it supports interoperability with diverse external systems, enabling seamless data exchange and communication.

The R-box's limitations primarily revolve around integration challenges, scalability constraints, and the complexity of response generation. Integrating diverse external systems and protocols can be challenging, requiring extensive customization and adaptation to ensure compatibility and seamless communication. Additionally, as response complexity and data volumes increase, the R-box may face scalability limitations, necessitating careful design considerations and optimization strategies to ensure operation.

5) F-box: The F-box, or forensics box, is particularly relevant in the context of the CCAM environment. Its primary purpose is to provide forensic capabilities tailored for event reconstruction within CCAM ecosystems. Essential requirements for the F-box include data preservation, traceability, and analysis functionalities specific to the unique characteristics of CCAM environments, such as vehicular communication networks and autonomous vehicle operations.

The need for the F-box stems from the inherent complexity and dynamic nature of CCAM environments, where interactions between connected vehicles, infrastructure, and other elements create a vast and constantly evolving data landscape. In such environments, incidents or anomalies may occur, necessitating detailed forensic analysis to reconstruct events, identify root causes, and facilitate corrective actions. The F-box must, therefore, support the preservation and collection of relevant data traces, including vehicle sensor data, communication logs, and environmental context, to enable comprehensive event reconstruction.

Capabilities of the F-box encompass a range of forensic techniques and tools tailored for CCAM environments. These include data acquisition and preservation mechanisms, data correlation and analysis algorithms, and visualization techniques for presenting reconstructed events. By leveraging advanced forensic methodologies (e.g., data normalization of vehicle data and correlation of functional as well as non-functional in-vehicle data), the F-box enables investigators to reconstruct complex sequences of events, analyze causality relationships and identify contributing factors, ultimately supporting effective incident response and mitigation efforts within CCAM ecosystems.

The relevance of the F-box in CCAM environments lies in its ability to address specific challenges inherent to vehicular communication networks and autonomous vehicle operations. In these environments, incidents or anomalies may have far-reaching implications, affecting safety, security, and operational efficiency. The F-box provides essential capabilities for reconstructing events within this context, enabling stakeholders to gain insights into the underlying causes of incidents, identify potential vulnerabilities, and enhance the resilience and robustness of CCAM systems.

We further argue that the need for a dedicated F-box lies in the relevance of CCAM environments. Investigations involving cars (i.e., touching safety aspects of participants and occupants) must be investigated with more focus on the quality of a Automotive Digital Forensics (ADF) investigation. Hence, the results of an ADF must be usable in front of a court.

6) TiMS-box: The TiMS-box is a feature in the VSOC that complements the A-box capabilities. The knowledge repository, utilized by the TiMS, collects different data sources, such as design, architectural, threat, and attack data. This data helps throughout threat hunting activities. It allows analysts to check for relevant aspects, such as critical endpoints or crown jewels of the overall architecture. Essential requirements for the TiMS-box include analysis and mapping functionalities of threat, attack, and design information within the CCAM ecosystem and its iterative application during threat-hunting activities, including the tractability of the design and threat information.

The need for the TiMS based on the dynamic and diverse CCAM ecosystem. This environment leads to complex, unique, and fast-changing threats that have to be considered to ensure safety. Instead of only waiting for alerts about incidents, active threat hunting activities complement the mainly passive and reactive activities of SOC analysts, e.g., determining the impact a compromised supplier has on systems and infrastructure. Therefore, a structured approach supports threat hunting activities within the CCAM environment. The generated, prioritized, and design-based attack paths, consisting of single steps, assist threat hunters in a guided way to detect, track, and disrupt threats as early as possible and throughout a complex threat.

The TiMS-box's capabilities include analysis algorithms, modeling, data mapping, graph theory, and knowledge representation techniques. Mapping of relevant threat (including attack and adversary) information (like Spoofing, Tampering, Repudiation, Information disclosure, Denial of service and Elevation of privilege (STRIDE), Tactics, Techniques, and Procedures (TTP)s from MITRE ATT&CK) with related design and asset information within the CCAM represents the modeled knowledge foundation [18]. Using the VSOC API and E-box allows the integration and storage of the individual sources (e.g., form threat intelligence providers) into the D-box. Coming from the D-box (via VSOC API and E-box), an analyst requests iteratively relevant attack paths for a specific adversary group on this knowledge base. As a result, the R-box submits the generated and prioritized attack paths of design information back to the analyst.

The TiMS-box's limitations primarily include mapping adversary, threat, asset, and design information. This information has heterogeneous data sources, formats, and diverse abstraction levels. The A-box assists the TiMS-box in necessary analysis and prepossessing tasks, e.g., due to different formats of sources. However, input data integration, mapping, and representation face complexity challenges, including the complexity of attack path generation. Moreover, mapping attack and design information often necessitate expertise in threat hunting, security architecture, graph theory, and domain knowledge, which may pose challenges in resource-constrained environments. Finally, the quality of the generated attack paths and their abstraction level depend on the quality and abstraction of the available design and attack information as input for the TiMS.

C. Technical realization

The technical implementation is realized using Docker. Figure 3 illustrates the different docker-compose components. We further published the full VSOC implementation on GitHub [19]. Additional and in-depth implementation details can be found in the referenced GitHub repository.

The VSOC API uses HTTP REST as a communication protocol. Each tool and participant of the CCAM environment has their REST endpoint and required methods. We further use OpenTelemetry to generate metadata for the HTTP REST requests. It is an open-source and widely used tool that suits our requirements within the VSOC. It identifies user agents and other telemetry data that the A-box can use for anomaly detection. The OpenTelemtry logs are gathered using OTL Collector (an OpenTelemtry utility), which transmits the logs to an APM server. The APM server stores the data in the SIEM of the VSOC. In case of this implementation, we use the ELK Stack as a SIEM. The ELK Stack is open-source, widely used in SIEMs, and well documented, which makes it a suitable technology for the VSOC. We use Elasticsearch as a search engine and Kibana for data visualization. Both are integrated in the ELK Stack out of the box. In the case of the Docker implementation, each part of the ELK Stack holds certificates for secure communication and the data in their corresponding Docker volumes. This approach separates the data from each system and makes the VSOC tool-agnostic to change the SIEM solution or other technical parts.

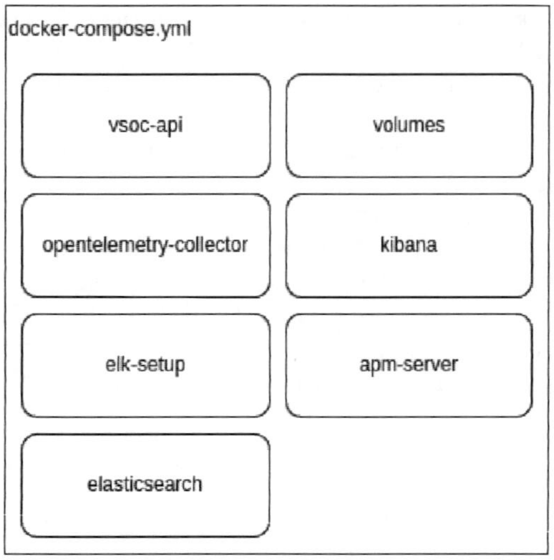

Figure 3. Docker compose components.

The different boxes (E-box, R-box, A-box, D-box, and F-box) are realized within the ELK Stack. For example, the Docker volumes used by the ELK Stack realize the D-box and F-box as storage units. The A-box is implemented within Kibana and Elastic search. Analysts can utilize both tools to evaluate events, visualize logs, and perform actions. The E-box and R-box are part of the VSOC API, while the ELK Stack realizes tasks such as event classification and verification.

We argue that, nevertheless, which SIEM technology is used (e.g., Splunk, ELK Stack, etc.), our proposed methodology can be adapted. In the case of this publication, we utilize the ELK Stack and highlight the implementation of our methodology. Other SIEM solutions might need additional adaptation to certain boxes.

V. Evaluation

We address the highlighted criteria from Langer et al. [2], Hofbauer et al. [5], Menges et al. [8], and our own to evaluate the highlighted VSOC for the CCAM environment. Table II presents the metrics and their fulfillment. The checkmark (✓) illustrates their complete fulfillment, and the bullet (•) is their partial fulfillment.

Our VSOC partially fulfills the **reaction time** metric by implementing alerting and automation within internal boxes. These features facilitate prompt identification and response to potential security threats, enhancing responsiveness. However, there is room for improvement in optimizing reaction times under real-world conditions.

TABLE II
USED CRITERIA AS EVALUATION METRICS.

Fulfillment	Metric	Source
•	Reaction time	Langer et al. [2]
✓	Criticality	Langer et al. [2]
✓	Autonomy	Langer et al. [2]
✓	Data aggregation	Langer et al. [2]
✓	Control-flow	Langer et al. [2]
✓	Coverage	Hofbauer et al. [5]
•	People	Hofbauer et al. [5]
✓	Technical	Hofbauer et al. [5]
✓	Governance and compliance	Hofbauer et al. [5]
•	Data privacy	Menges et al. [8]
✓	Physical assets	Our contribution
•	Real-time safety	Our contribution
•	Complex supply chain	Our contribution
•	Attack vectors	Our contribution

The VSOC fully meets the **criticality** requirement by effectively flagging events with criticality tags in Kibana (ELK stack). This capability ensures that incidents are prioritized based on severity, allowing for efficient resource allocation and swift resolution of critical issues.

Autonomy is another area where our VSOC excels. The system incorporates a high level of automation within its internal processes, minimizing the need for constant human intervention. Human operators oversee critical aspects and events, ensuring essential decisions are scrutinized appropriately.

Our **data aggregation** capabilities are robust. We leverage the VSOC HTTP REST API alongside OpenTelemetry and the ELK stack. This combination enables comprehensive monitoring and analysis of security events across various data sources, fully meeting the data aggregation metric. We further tested the load using the Locust.

The VSOC's **control-flow** capabilities are robust. The implemented VSOC HTTP REST API, as well as the internal boxes, enables a simple way to communicate and control data between the diverse CCAM participants, independent of the endpoint, e.g., OEM or a vehicle-component.

The VSOC API is designed to collect data comprehensively from vehicles and the CCAM ecosystem. In addition, IT metadata is gathered using OpenTelemetry, providing extensive **coverage** and insight into the security landscape. This thorough approach ensures that we meet the coverage requirement.

The **people** metric is partially fulfilled due to the limited capacity to test the VSOC in real-life settings with an entire team of VSOC analysts. Despite this, integrating the ELK stack demonstrates the system's ability to augment human analysts' capabilities, enhancing overall performance.

We fully meet the **technical** metric by successfully collecting and analyzing technical information from various sources, including ECUs, wireless and wired communications, consumer electronics, vehicle components, and sensors. The VSOC does not perform automated blocking or reactions; instead, it provides suggestions to tools, maintaining a human-in-the-loop setup for critical decision-making.

Our VSOC adheres to UNECE R155 standards and incorporates identity and asset management through ontologies as a knowledge repository. This ensures that our operations comply with regulatory requirements and follow best governance practices, fully meeting the governance and **compliance** metrics.

Implementing the different boxes with their dedicated responsibilities partially fulfills the **data privacy** metric. Depending on the box, e.g., the D-box, the recommended requirements by Menges et al. to ensure legal compliance of the VSOC can be applied individually. However, the evaluation of detection performance and necessary near-real-time data in combination with, e.g., pseudonymization still needs to be concluded.

Collecting data from the ecosystem, including **physical attributes**, is another area where our VSOC excels. Tools like safety monitoring and collaboration tools (e.g., to propagate information using car-to-car messages) exemplify our ability to gather comprehensive data from various physical assets, fully satisfying the physical assets metric.

Our human-in-the-loop approach partially fulfills **real-time safety** by minimizing the risk of unintended consequences from automated reactions. While this conservative approach ensures safety, it limits the system's real-time safety impact.

Our use of ontologies to store and manage the complex relationships within the **supply chain** partially meets this metric. The effectiveness of this approach depends on the availability and accuracy of knowledge within the system.

The VSOC partially addresses various **attack vectors** by utilizing the TiMS. This feature considers diverse threat information about design information of CCAM technologies and generates prioritized attack paths. The provided knowledge informs and guides analysts about how CCAM-based attack vectors (e.g., GPS spoofing in a platooning) can occur. A step-by-step path and the related context information facilitate analysts' detection and response to these threats. However, the effectiveness of these features depends on the availability and quality of threat and design data. The evaluation of effectiveness and associated tests still need to be concluded.

In summary, our VSOC demonstrates strong performance across multiple metrics, with particular strengths in criticality, autonomy, data aggregation, control flow, coverage, technical capabilities, governance and compliance, and physical assets. Areas for improvement include reaction time, real-time safety, people, data privacy concerns, the management of complex supply chain relationships, and attack vector management.

VI. Conclusion and Further Work

We presented a VSOC architecture for the CCAM environment. It consists of six boxes to provide event processing, analysis, data storage, forensic, response propagation, and threat hunting capabilities. We implemented a proof-of-concept using Docker, the ELK Stack, and OpenTelemetry.

Our implementation highlights the relevant data streams for a VSOC (RQ1) in between the presented boxes. Furthermore, the architecture introduced the TiMS and F-box to address CCAM-specific requirements (RQ2). Finally, the API implementation and description of the boxes highlight relevant information that should be shared with other CCAM participants (RQ3).

Our present work does not yet consider Machine Learning (ML) approaches to assist VSOC analysts their decision-making. As various existing publications suggest applying ML algorithms for the detection, analysis, and automatic response to incidents in the IT environment, future work can investigate to which extent machine or deep learning can increase the performance of our proposed VSOC architecture. For that, the data that serves as input and output to the different VSOC components conceptualized in our work need to be processed and prepared for the respective learning task. Hence, further research has to be performed on feature extraction and selection. As it is crucial for the SOC analyst to understand the proposals of the ML model, further work should also consider the explainability and transparency of possible solutions.

Acknowledgment

This project has received funding from the European Union's Horizon Europe research and innovation program under grant agreement No 101069748.

References

[1] European Partnership, *Ccam - connected, cooperative, and automated mobility*, url: https:www.ccam.eu, Accessed: 2024-09-19, Sep. 2024.

[2] F. Langer, F. Schüppel, and L. Stahlbock, "Establishing an Automotive Cyber Defense Center", in *17th Escar Europe: Embedded Security in Cars (Konferenzveröffentlichung)*, Oct. 2019. DOI: 10.13154/294-6652.

[3] International Organization for Standardization, "ISO/SAE 21434:2021 - Road vehicles - Cybersecurity engineering", International Organization for Standardization, Tech. Rep., Aug. 2021.

[4] UNECE, "UN Regulation No. 155 - Cyber security and cyber security management system", United Nations Economic Commission for Europe, Tech. Rep., 2020.

[5] J. Hofbauer, K. K. Gomez Buquerin, and H.-J. Hof, "From SOC to VSOC", in *21th Escar Europe : The World's Leading Automotive Cyber Security*, Ruhr-Universität Bochum, Oct. 2023. DOI: 10.13154/294-10389.

[6] V. S. Barletta *et al.*, "V-SOC4AS: A Vehicle-SOC for Improving Automotive Security", *Algorithms*, vol. 16, no. 2, p. 112, Feb. 2023, Collecting CAN logs, converting them to JSON (syslog representation), and send it to the SIEM (IBM Qradar). VSOC. DOI: 10.3390/a16020112.

[7] R. Bader, R. Katyal, and F. Capocasale, "Automotive Cyber-security - An End-to-End Automotive Cybersecurity Solution Combining NTT DATA's Intrusion Detection System for CAN Bus with its State-of-the-Art Vehicle-Security Operation Center", NTT DATA Deutschland GmbH, Tech. Rep., 2021.

[8] F. Menges *et al.*, "Towards GDPR-compliant data processing in modern SIEM systems", *Computers & Security*, vol. 103, p. 102 165, Apr. 2021, ISSN: 0167-4048. DOI: 10.1016/j.cose.2020.102165.

[9] R. B. Misra, "Global IT Outsourcing: Metrics for Success of All Parties", in *Journal of Information Technology Cases and Applications*, p. 21, vol. 6, 2004.

[10] L. Yang and A. Shami, "A Transfer Learning and Optimized CNN Based Intrusion Detection System for Internet of Vehicles", in *ICC 2022 - IEEE International Conference on Communications*, IEEE, May 2022. DOI: 10.1109/icc45855.2022.9838780.

[11] I. Ahmed, G. Jeon, and A. Ahmad, "Deep Learning-Based Intrusion Detection System for Internet of Vehicles", *IEEE Consumer Electronics Magazine*, vol. 12, no. 1, pp. 117–123, Jan. 2023, ISSN: 2162-2256. DOI: 10.1109/mce.2021.3139170.

[12] M. D. Hossain, H. Inoue, H. Ochiai, D. Fall, and Y. Kadobayashi, "LSTM-Based Intrusion Detection System for In-Vehicle Can Bus Communications", *IEEE Access*, vol. 8, pp. 185 489–185 502, 2020, ISSN: 2169-3536. DOI: 10.1109/access.2020.3029307.

[13] H. Li *et al.*, "POSTER: Intrusion Detection System for In-vehicle Networks using Sensor Correlation and Integration", in *Proceedings of the 2017 ACM SIGSAC Conference on Computer and Communications Security*, ser. CCS '17, ACM, Oct. 2017. DOI: 10.1145/3133956.3138843.

[14] A. Leandros, "A Novel Distributed Intrusion Detection System for Vehicular Ad Hoc Networks", *International Journal of Advanced Computer Science and Applications*, vol. 6, no. 4, 2015, ISSN: 2158-107X. DOI: 10.14569/ijacsa.2015.060414.

[15] D. Kosmanos *et al.*, "Intrusion Detection System for Platooning Connected Autonomous Vehicles", in *2019 4th South-East Europe Design Automation, Computer Engineering, Computer Networks and Social Media Conference (SEEDA-CECNSM)*, IEEE, Sep. 2019. DOI: 10.1109/seeda-cecnsm.2019.8908528.

[16] R. Bidou, "Security Operation Center Concepts & Implementation", Semantic Scholar, 2005.

[17] F. Menges *et al.*, "Introducing DINGfest: An architecture for next generation SIEM systems", 2018, Initial architecture of DINGfest (SIEM)
Privacy aware SIEM. DOI: 10.18420/SICHERHEIT2018_21.

[18] T. Volkersdorfer and H.-J. Hof, "A Concept of an Attack Model for a Model-Based Security Testing Framework", in *SECURWARE 2020, The Fourteenth International Conference on Emerging Security Information, Systems and Technologies*, 2020.

[19] Security in Mobility, *SELFY VSOC*, https://github.com/securityinmobility/selfy-vsoc-api, Sep. 2024.

SEC-AIRSPACE: Addressing Cyber Security Challenges in Future Air Traffic Management

Karin Bernsmed and Per Håkon Meland
Dep. of software engineering, safety and security
SINTEF
Trondheim, Norway
{karin.bernsmed,per.h.meland}@sintef.no

Tim H. Stelkens-Kobsch
Dep. of ATM Simulation
German Aerospace Center (DLR)
Braunschweig, Germany
tim.stelkens-kobsch@dlr.de

Alessandra Tedeschi
Research and Innovation
Deep Blue srl
Rome, Italy
alessandra.tedeschi@dblue.it

Carlo Dambra and Irene Buselli
ZenaByte s.r.l.
Genova, Italy
{carlo.dambra,irene.buselli}@zenabyte.com

Enrico Frumento
Cybersecurity Research Lead
Cefriel - polytechnic of Milano
Milan, Italy
enrico.frumento@cefriel.com

Davide Martintoni and Valerio Senni
Dept. of Applied Research & Technology
Collins Aerospace
Trento and Rome, Italy
{davide.martintoni,valerio.senni}@collins.com

Andrei Gurtov and Gurjot Singh Gaba
Dep. of Computer and Information Science
Linköping University
Linköping, Sweden
{andrei.gurtov,gurjot.singh}@liu.se

Alejandro Sastre García
Technical Directorate
Skyway Air Navigation Services, S.A.
Madrid, Spain
asastre@skyway-ans.com

Supathida Boonsong
Research and Innovation
Air Navigation Services of Sweden
Norrköping, Sweden
supathida.boonsong@lfv.se

Abstract—**Digitalisation offers many benefits to Air Traffic Management (ATM). Yet, with technological innovations come challenges in managing new cyber security threats and risks. This paper presents a comprehensive review over challenges faced in ATM when protecting critical assets, and outlines how the newly established exploratory research project SEC-AIRSPACE will address these challenges.**

***Keywords*-cyber security; threats; vulnerabilities; security risk assessment; Learning Analytics; Air Traffic Management; SESAR.**

I. INTRODUCTION

Air Traffic Management (ATM) is a complex global infrastructure that enables a safe and efficient flow of air traffic. However, as the ATM systems become more interconnected and complex, the risks towards these systems are increasing. Emerging technologies are including a future data-sharing service delivery model, the deployment of infrastructure through a service-oriented architecture, and increased sharing of data between different actors. The new technologies required for achieving a more dynamic airspace management and ATM service provision will expose the ATM systems to new cyber security threats. In the worst-case, this can have catastrophic consequences if not properly addressed. To address these challenges, this paper briefly describes the approach of the recently established Horizon Europe project SEC-AIRSPACE [1], which aims to enable a more resilient ATM, by focusing on reducing the cyber security risks of the ATM systems and increase the awareness of the ATM stakeholders of such risks.

Section II of this paper provides a comprehensive review and discussion of challenges to cyber security in current and future ATM systems. In Section III, we present the SEC-AIRSPACE approach, which aim to address these challenges. Finally, Section IV concludes the paper.

II. CHALLENGES

This section outlines a set of distinct challenges that the project will address.

A. Cyber security risk assessment of ATM systems

Cyber security risk assessment is nowadays *the* established approach to identify, assess, and mitigate cyber security threats in any sector that relies on digital information, data-sharing and service-oriented architectures, including critical infrastructure. Aviation, and more specifically the dynamic, integrated management of air traffic and airspace, known as ATM, is no exception. In Europe, a significant part of the Research & Development (R&D) activities in the ATM sector is performed as part of the SESAR Joint Undertaking [2]. Their cyber security strategy [3] recognises that the key to deliver secure and cyber-resilient solutions for ATM is to focus the efforts where they are most effective, and points out that security risk assessment needs to be performed already under the R&D phase, in particular when technologically complex architectures and new technologies are being introduced. The state of the art for applied risk assessment in ATM is still scattered though, as there is no "one-size-fits-all" solution for its various systems. The majority of the ATM (R&D) projects in Europe follow the Security Risk Assessment Methodology (SecRAM) [4], which has been developed and is being maintained by SESAR for many years. Similar approaches are being used in other sectors and in different contexts;

two widely used standards are ISO/IEC 27005 [5] and NIST SP 800-30 [6]. Regardless of which methodology is being applied, it is necessary to fully understand the architecture of the system and its intended operation and to understand which are the critical assets that needs protection. This is a prerequisite for a correct understanding of the cyber risks and for identifying suitable countermeasures for reducing the risk to an acceptable level. However, a recent published interview study of SecRAM practitioners [7], identified that many of them struggle in the process, in particular when trying to identify critical assets and when trying to understand what will be the relevant threats and risks for the technologies and processes that they will deliver.

Additional issues also arise when ATM systems become more complex. The SESAR 2020 cyber security strategy [3] explicitly states that security risks are to be managed by the individual R&D projects. This may be an appropriate strategy for today's ATM systems, but may become a risk in itself in the (not so distant) future, when the systems are expected to become more interconnected, with increased data sharing and realised through virtualised services where the boundaries between actors and systems become "blurred". This risk has already been recognised by key stakeholders in Europe, as documented in the report on ATM cyber security challenges published by EUROCOM [8]. A new proposal for rationalisation and harmonisation of the regulatory framework, issued by the European Union Aviation Safety Agency (EASA) and a number of aviation stakeholders in the European Strategic Coordination Platform (ESCP), therefore promotes international cooperation and harmonisation in risk management, risk information-sharing between organisations, and points out the need for more holistic risk assessment methods [9].

Charitoudi and Blyth [10] recognises that current cyber risk models need to be improved: (i) from the process point of view because the threats change very rapidly, they need efficiency to enable a continuous update of estimations, (ii) from the model point of view, consider that cyber threats are no longer limited to the IT systems, but they also include humans, and cyber-physical systems, and (iii) from the comprehensiveness point of view, failing to include both tangible and intangible assets along the entire supply chain. Systems can be attacked through the humans operating the systems, through the cyber-physical systems or through the suppliers. Further, as pointed out by the FP7 GAMMA project, "any security solution [for ATM] must consider the changes in security risk profiles due to the new security threats faced by the ATM system that can spread their negative effects; an attack to one particular node could compromise, in a very short time with domino effect, the functionality of the whole ATM system and the air transportation system" [11]. Such aspects are not sufficiently covered in SecRAM. For example, there is little or no support for identifying critical assets in virtualised environments, for analysing cascading effects of cyber-attacks, or for dynamic analysis of security risks.

Further, cyber security risk assessments are rarely performed; usually only once during the development of a system, and/or once a year when it has been deployed [12]. At the same time, the need to perform risk assessments more frequently, or ideally to be able to monitor risks dynamically has been recognised, not only in the ATM domain but also in other domains where the threat picture is constantly changing [13]. Erdogan et al. have recently published a systematic mapping study [14] providing an overview of security risk assessment approaches that use automatic support, including Artificial Intelligence (AI), to identify, estimate, and/or evaluate cyber risks. The study shows that on average, the number of papers on AI-supported security risk assessment has increased with the growth rate of 133% between 2010 and 2020. The approaches reported have mainly addressed cyber-risks related to intrusion detection, malware detection, and industrial systems. They focus mostly on identifying and/or estimating security risks and use primarily Bayesian networks and neural networks for the AI part. Nevertheless, the usage of AI for cyber-risk assessment is relatively new, particularly in the ATM community, where this research topic is still at its infancy.

B. Vulnerabilities and threats to ATM systems

The vision of the future ATM implies an increased connectivity and integration of systems and services, enabling Air Navigation Service Providers (ANSPs), airlines, airports, and future ATM data service providers to share information and access to services in new and innovative manners. This will inevitably increase the potential attack surface to the ATM systems, which have previously been "shielded" from attacks through their use of proprietary standards and isolated systems. Further, the need to increase interoperability while reducing costs imply an increased use of Commercial-Off-The-Shelf (COTS) components. It is well known that the use of COTS poses a serious risk to security when such software is integrated with other software products to create new composite services or systems-of-systems [8]. A well-known example for ATM is the introduction of the IP protocol suite in the Future Communication Infrastructure (FCI). Another issue that may increase risk in future ATM systems is the integration between different civil and military actors, and ground and space-based communication, navigation, and surveillance systems [8].

During the last decade, we have seen an increased interest in ATM security from the hacker community. For example, "white-hat" security researchers have demonstrated on several occasions that it is both easy and inexpensive to manipulate existing air-to-ground safety-related data transmission protocols [15], [16]. Already in 2014, IOActive revealed that SATCOM firmware from several different vendors contain multiple vulnerabilities, including hard-coded credentials, undocumented protocols, insecure protocols, back doors, and weak password reset mechanisms [17]. According to IOActive, these vulnerabilities may allow an attacker to take control of the air-to-ground SATCOM link, thus posing a direct threat to flight safety due to the lack of cyber security. Similar experiments have since been performed at Linköping University (LiU) in Sweden, where researchers have found weaknesses and demonstrated potential attack scenarios to both the surveillance technology Automatic Dependent Surveillance–Broadcast (ADS-B) and to the communication protocol Controller Pilot Data Link Communications (CPDLC) [18]. To add to this, the increased occurrence of jamming of GPS-based navigation systems is having an increasingly serious effect on air traffic, in particular in the Baltic area [19]. All in all, the cyber risks and threats towards ATM systems are expected to increase.

C. Cascading effects of cyber-attacks in ATM systems

Many systems for airport and airspace management have grown historically and were never designed to be connected to complex global systems. The growing passenger and freight volumes require new systems that enable more effective operations. Furthermore, exponentially growing amounts of data provide opportunities for new business models, which can only be utilised efficiently by increasing the connections to other sectors. To advance the optimisation of airport management for the growing challenges, data and isolated systems will require more interconnection.

The progressive transition from traditional air traffic control systems to improved monitoring and communication systems in modern data networks will significantly change the safety assessment of the aviation environment [20]. However, this makes legacy systems that were rarely considered and developed from a security but rather from a safety perspective vulnerable and could provide a gateway to malicious actors. This system integration will lead to expanded supply chains in which each party is dependent on the services of their counterparts and on the interaction between ATM stakeholders, their industrial partners and the related supply chains.

In summary, as reported by Wynsma and Sulliva [21], *"The security of the supply chain within aviation poses a great risk as it allows multiple points for malicious actors to subvert the activities of an organisation or its products. Attacks can impact both electronic components as well as data and non-electronic components such as structural items. Thus, supply chain security can appear to be an indistinct problem in comparison to securing systems in operation – whether these are enterprise systems, servers or electronic components installed on aircraft. The view of supply chain should consider more than just the operational systems but instead include all systems that are used to support the products and operations"*. As highlighted by Haan [11], two challenges have received insufficient attention: ATM architectures and their supply chains. Therefore, by assessing and understanding the ATM architecture, its components and the related vendors, ATM supply chain security can become a crucial part of a cyber risk assessment, allowing practitioners to identify possible cascading effects, implement appropriate measures and build trust.

D. Security controls for mitigating threats to ATM systems

Cyber security in aviation is explicitly addressed in the ICAO Standards and Recommended Practices Annex 17 [22], which in Europe has been implemented in the Common Requirements Regulation in the form of requirements for ANSPs. Since the ANSPs are considered to be "providers of essential services", they also need to comply with the NIS2 Directive [23] and the Cybersecurity Act [24]. The regulatory framework is complex, but, as explained in EUROCONTROL's report on ATM cyber security, it "forces operators to adopt a broad-based, holistic approach to security, addressing people, processes, and technology" [8].

For the ATM organisations that apply SecRAM to manage their security-related risks, the mitigation strategies for managing high- and medium level risks are usually selected from the SESAR Minimum Set of Security Controls (MSSC) [25]. As discovered in the study by Bernsmed et al. [7], this approach is problematic, since the MSSC is based on the ISO/IEC 27002 standard, which implies that it contains high-level security controls for *information systems*, which in turn could cause conflicts with *safety* if proper care is not taken when the security controls are implemented and deployed in the ATM systems. Further, as shown in the paper by Bernsmed, Jaatun and Meland [26], there is no guidance material available on how to ensure that subcontractors implement the necessary security controls. This is particularly concerning in the aviation domain where there are few, if any, obligations on 3rd party software providers to deliver secure software, not even when their software is integrated into safety-critical systems.

E. Personalised cyber security training and awareness for ATM organisations

Resilience requires a holistic approach to cyber security, which includes not only reducing risk through technical security controls, but to also include the social, human and organisation factors when protecting the systems. It is well known that humans can be a significant source of cyber risk. A newly released report by the World Economic Forum shows that 95% of cyber security incidents occur due to human errors [27]. Similarly, a recent study performed by the Boston Consultancy showed that of 50 major data breaches, only 23% were caused by inadequate security technology and that in most cases (77%) the breach was the result of an organizational failure, a process failure, or a human error [28]. These findings are relevant for all IT-enabled sectors, including ATM, because, as shown by Frumento et al. [29], humans are a significance source of cyber risk in any business context they operate. Many cyber security attacks therefore target humans, by exploiting their lack of training or awareness. Hence, human interventions with technology is a crucial element in both attack and defence strategies. Inducted errors (e.g., convincing people to do something they should not do using social engineering tactics) or mistakes (e.g., underestimating a threat or not blocking a website) are common examples. No IT-enabled sector is safe. For this reason, cyber security technology nowadays utilizes automation, AI systems, and logic to assist or even remove humans from the loop. However, there is one category of security defence where this is not possible and which is at the same time not evolving at a similar pace compared to other cyber security areas: training. With an unprecedented number of employees working in hybrid or fully remote environments, such as in virtualised centres [30], there has never been a more critical time to effectively create and maintain a cyber-secure ATM workforce and an engaged security culture. Today, training and awareness campaigns are already performed with the purpose to reduce severe cyber risk. However, the evolution of training methodologies is not proceeding as desired. Often, the best option is still to train people in traditional ways, through courses, classes, and training tracks. This approach has two problems: first, the lessons are often loosely tied to current cyber risk and the critical assets at stake: second, the tangible impact on risk reduction is hard to measure and the Return of Training Investment (ROTI) is uncertain. In other words, the problem is to monitor how people's skills and awareness evolve and to measure the impact on ROTI and the corresponding cyber risk reduction. At professional level, there is a lack of accessible tools for continuous awareness, training, and skills development on cyber security aspects [31].

In ATM, simulation of real air traffic scenarios is part of the practical training for both pilots and air traffic controllers. However, it is very rare that cyber security threats are included in the exercises. As shown by Strohmeier et al. [32], neither pilot nor air traffic controllers are prepared to handle cyber-attacks, and many of them are not even aware that commonly used communication protocols, such as CPDLC, lack integrity and authenticity protection. Similar results have been shown by researchers at LiU, who have developed a tool for simulating ADS-B and CPDLC attacks and used it to demonstrate and evaluate how air traffic controllers react to such attacks [33].

III. The way forward: The SEC-AIRSPACE approach

To address the challenges identified in the previous section, the SEC-AIRSPACE project has formulated the following objectives: 1) improving the cyber security risk management of existing and future ATM systems, and 2) increasing the cyber security awareness and maturity amongst the ATM stakeholders. The overall ambition and long-term vision is to enable a more cyber-resilient ATM, focusing on reducing the risks of virtualisation and increased data-sharing between all components of the ATM infrastructure and the relevant stakeholders.

A. Improving ATM cyber security risk management

SEC-AIRSPACE will enhance the existing methodologies and the good practices currently adopted in ATM with prominent building blocks for cyber security risk management. Our baseline will be the typical steps that one may find in most cyber security risk assessment methodologies, including but not limited to ISO/IEC 27005 and SecRAM. The intention is not to propose a new methodology, but rather to provide the necessary extensions that will be needed to provide better estimations of the cyber risks in future ATM scenarios.

First, SEC-AIRSPACE will deliver a taxonomy for modelling the elements of future ATM systems. The taxonomy will be based on a holistic vocabulary that facilitates the representation of the complete ATM supply chain, including

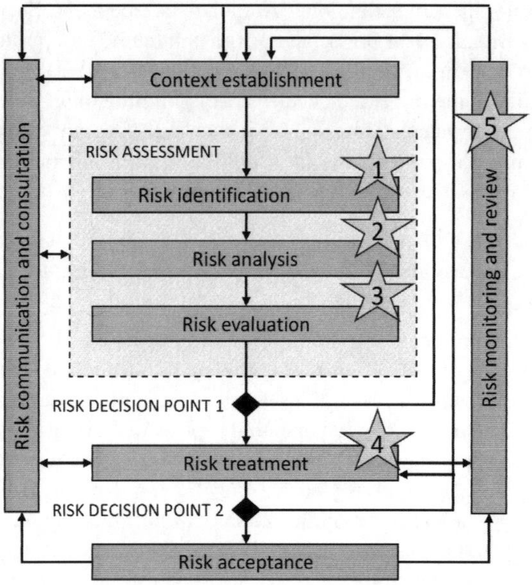

Figure 1. Overview over the key contributions for improving established security risk management processes (figure adapted from ISO/IEC 27005 [5]).

tangible and intangible assets and human, procedural and organisational aspects. It will also support the representation of risks related to complex systems-of-systems and service-oriented architectures, the use of virtualized elements, and interfaces for data sharing between ATM actors. The ambition is to facilitate better and more accurate cyber risk assessment of complex ATM systems and, in a later step, also help analysing the potential impacts of cyber-attacks with cascading effects. As illustrated by the first golden star in Figure 1, the taxonomy will support the context establishment phase of the security risk assessment, where the identification of critical assets at risk is one of the main outputs.

Second, to be able to combat cyber threats, modern cyber security risk management life-cycles must be holistic, meaning they need to consider all the possible sources of risks, including those arising from the integration of IT systems with cyber-physical and control systems, and from humans. Indeed, some security issues are generated by human malicious intents or errors and should therefore be modelled considering the interactions among people, organizations, and the technologies they use [34]. Moreover, a comprehensive cyber risk assessment should include any type of asset at risk. For example, the recent EU project HERMENEUT [35] demonstrated that intangible assets, e.g., brand, reputation and human capital are crucial elements. Another recent EU project DOGANA [36] studied a cyber risk estimation methodology for human-related risks derived from social engineering. However, integrated and holistic cyber risk models and life-cycle are still rarely used, and SecRAM is no exception. SEC-AIRSPACE will deliver guidelines to identify vulnerabilities and weaknesses of the considered ATM systems, including human, procedural and organisational factors. This will enable the ATM security risk assessment practitioners to create a holistic picture of the cyber threat landscape and identify and analyse relevant risks (second golden star in Figure 1).

Third, in the highly interconnected ATM world, virtualisation among the systems within this world, cascading effects, i.e., secondary consequences of an attack on other organizations and/or sectors become an emerging issue. SEC-AIRSPACE will review established approaches to prevent such events and provide a novel analysis of identification, correlation, and mitigation mechanisms. The main contribution will be a model for analysing dependencies between different ATM system components, and between ATM systems and other (critical) infrastructures. As illustrated by the third golden star in Figure 1, the output will support the risk analysis and evaluation phases of the security risk assessment process.

Fourth, once cyber security risks are identified, specific security controls must be applied to reduce the risks to an acceptable level. SEC-AIRSPACE will provide a new set of "recommended security controls" for ATM, to mitigate the threats identified in the earlier steps (fourth golden star in Figure 1). These security controls will be based on existing best practices, such as the ISO/IEC 27002 standard [37] and the SESAR Minimum Set of Security Controls (MSSC) [25], but adapted to the needs of the future ATM systems. SEC-AIRSPACE will also analyse the cyber-related human factors and organisational aspects in the ATM supply chain to identify key areas where mitigations, such as training and awareness, redesign of tools and procedures, and increasing engagement of operators can be more effective. The recommended security controls will be tagged with cost indicators to help the risk analyst prioritise different mitigation strategies. Special care will be taken to avoid conflicts between safety and security, which otherwise tend to occur when IT security specialists formulate requirements on safety critical systems [38].

Finally, SEC-AIRSPACE will improve the reviewing and monitoring of the risks, by providing a method for dynamic monitoring and assessment of risks, which will be specially crafted for ATM (fifth golden star in Figure 1). The method will use the data models of the ATM systems as input and schematically translate these into risk assessment algorithms, which will be connected to risk indicators to dynamically measure and visualize the current level of risk.

B. Increasing cyber security awareness and maturity

To increase the cyber security awareness and maturity amongst the ATM stakeholders, the SEC-AIRSPACE project will utilize a cutting-edge application of the general concept of People Analytics (PA) [39], [40], applied to cyber risk mitigation. PA is originally a human resources analytics approach for managing people at work, which has been successfully used in many different settings to develop data-driven insights to improve workforce processes and promote employee experiences. The hypothesis in SEC-AIRSPACE is that PA can also be successfully used to increase cyber security awareness while keeping training costs at a minimum. The intention is to deliver contextualised and personalised cyber security training, by integrating analytics and visualization techniques to support the reduction of human-related cyber risks. The project will first apply the core concepts of PA to Learning Analytics [41], and then take the results further to generate Learning Analytics for cyber security. This means generating the most appropriate cyber security awareness recipe, i.e., *what to teach, to whom and how*, with the goal of developing and growing the ATM organisations' cyber security culture based on their current exposure to cyber risk. Awareness and training will then become a tool to reduce human-related cyber risks. An overview of the key elements in the application of PA in the SEC-AIRSPACE project is provided in Figure 2. As can be seen, the output of this research activity will be training suggestions for groups of employees, such as air traffic controllers, selected from the available catalogue of courses in the ATM organisation and specifically targeted for protecting the organisation's assets at risk. These can then be delivered as recommendations to (other) organisations providing the training.

C. Project use cases

The SEC-AIRSPACE use cases serve multiple purposes. First, they will be used to establish the context and the baseline for the research activities outlined in Section III-A and III-B. Then, they will be used to validate the key results from this research. Finally, the use cases will be utilized in the demonstration, exploitation, and communication of the project results.

In the first use case, we will investigate the end-to-end data flow between air traffic controllers and pilots in a future scenario of 4D trajectory-based operations [42], where voice instructions are replaced by digital messaging utilizing existing, publicly available, IP-based communication infrastructures. Here, CPDLC clearances will be sent in advance of horizontal, vertical and longitudinal trajectory changes, thereby enabling an optimal path for the airborne aircraft. In the second use case, we will analyse a conceptual architecture of a virtual centre. The virtual centre will be built upon a number of elements, including System-Wide Information Management (SWIM) principles of data exchange protocols and open service-oriented architectures.

The two use cases have been carefully selected; they are both scenarios that illustrate evolving ATM scenarios with digital infrastructures and services provisioning, with associated cyber security threats and risks, and they are both in line with the vision of the development of ATM in the coming decade, as outlined in the SESAR Strategic Research and Innovation Agenda for the Digital European Sky [3]. Needless to say, cyber security is a hot topic of interest in both these use cases.

IV. Conclusion

The ATM world is becoming more complex. As outlined in this paper, the introduction of new actors, new services, integrated technologies, virtualization, and increased data sharing will expose ATM systems and their critical assets to new cyber threats and risks. To efficiently protect aviation

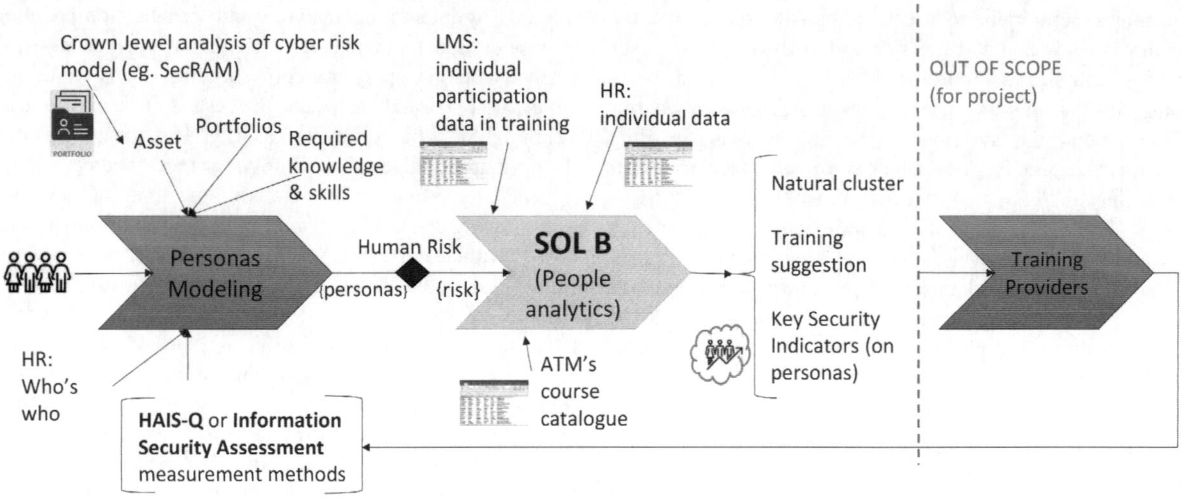

Figure 2. Overview over the key elements in the application of People Analytics.

systems, operators must perform security risk assessments and implement security controls to mitigate the identified risks. However, technology, in the form of security controls will not be enough to combat the threats. When defences are compromised, operators must detect these breaches, alert personnel, contain the effects of the breaches, and identify recovery and mitigation actions based on contingency plans. Cyber resilience hence requires a holistic view of security risk assessment, which also includes increased focus on awareness and training for the humans operating these systems.

The main impact of the SEC-AIRSPACE project will be increased cyber resilience; our system-wide holistic approach to cyber security risk management means that cyber-attacks will be more likely to be identified (and mitigated) at an early stage. In the longer term, the project results will contribute to a continued safe delivery of ATM services, despite eventual cyber-attacks and unwanted variations in the digital information chain. This will ensure that air transportation remains the safest way to travel, also in the future.

ACKNOWLEDGMENT

This project has received funding from the SESAR Joint Undertaking under the European Union's Horizon Europe research and innovation programme under grant agreement no 101114635 and 101114676.

REFERENCES

[1] *Exploratory research project. SEC-AIRSPACE - Cyber Security Risk Assessment in virtualized AIRSPACE scenarios and stakeholders' awareness of building resilient ATM*, https://www.sesarju.eu/projects/sec-airspace, [retrieved: 09, 2024].

[2] *The Single European Sky ATM Research Joint Undertaking (SESAR-JU)*, https://sesar.eu/, [retrieved: 09, 2024].

[3] SESAR Joint Undertaking, *SESAR 2020 cybersecurity strategy*, Oct. 2017.

[4] *SecRAM 2.0. Security Risk Assessment Methodology for SESAR 2020*, Sep. 2017.

[5] *ISO/IEC 27005:2018 — Information technology — Security techniques — Information security risk management (third edition).*

[6] NIST SP 800-30, "Guide for conducting risk assessments," en, National Institute of Standards and Technology, Gaithersburg, MD, Tech. Rep. NIST SP 800-30r1, 2012. DOI: 10.6028/NIST.SP.800-30r1.

[7] K. Bernsmed, G. Bour, M. Lundgren, and E. Bergström, "An evaluation of practitioners' perceptions of a security risk assessment methodology in air traffic management projects," *Journal of Air Transport Management*, vol. 102, p. 102 223, 2022, ISSN: 0969-6997. DOI: https://doi.org/10.1016/j.jairtraman.2022.102223.

[8] EUROCONTROL, *Air traffic management - a cybersecurity challenge*, https://www.eurocontrol.int/sites/default/files/2021-12/eurocontrol-atm-cybersecurity-report.pdf, [retrieved: 09, 2024].

[9] European Union Aviation Safety Agency, *Opinion no 03/2021. management of information security risks*, https://www.easa.europa.eu/en/document-library/opinions/opinion-032021, [retrieved: 10, 2024].

[10] K. Charitoudi and A. Blyth, "A socio-technical approach to cyber risk management and impact assessment," 2013. DOI: 10.4236/jis.2013.41005.

[11] J. de Haan, "Specific air traffic management cybersecurity challenges: Architecture and supply chain," in *Proceedings of the IEEE/ACM 42nd International Conference on Software Engineering Workshops*, ser. ICSEW'20, Seoul, Republic of Korea: Association for Computing Machinery, 2020, pp. 245–249, ISBN: 9781450379632. DOI: 10.1145/3387940.3392223.

[12] G. Falco and E. Rosenbach, "Why is cyber risk an issue?" In *Confronting Cyber Risk: An Embedded Endurance Strategy for Cybersecurity*. Oxford university press, Jan. 2022, pp. 1–15, ISBN: 9780197526545. DOI: 10.1093/oso/9780197526545.003.0001.

[13] M. S. K. Awan, P. Burnap, O. Rana, and A. Javed, "Continuous monitoring and assessment of cybersecurity risks in large computing infrastructures," in *2015 IEEE 17th International Conference on High Performance Computing and Communications, 2015 IEEE 7th International Symposium on Cyberspace Safety and Security, and 2015 IEEE 12th International Conference on Embedded Software and Systems*,

2015, pp. 1442–1447. DOI: 10.1109/HPCC-CSS-ICESS.2015.224.

[14] G. Erdogan, E. Garcia-Ceja, Å. Hugo, P. H. Nguyen, and S. Sen, "A systematic mapping study on approaches for ai-supported security risk assessment," in *2021 IEEE 45th Annual Computers, Software, and Applications Conference (COMPSAC)*, 2021, pp. 755–760. DOI: 10.1109/COMPSAC51774.2021.00107.

[15] A. Costin and A. Francillon, "Ghost in the air (traffic): On insecurity of ads-b protocol and practical attacks on ads-b devices," *Black Hat USA*, pp. 1–12, 2012.

[16] H. Kelly, "Researcher: New air traffic control system is hackable," *Cable News Network (CNN), Jul*, 2012.

[17] R. Santamarta, *A Wake-up Call for SATCOM Security*, https://ioactive.com/wp-content/uploads/2018/05/IOActive_SATCOM_Security_WhitePaper.pdf, [retrieved: 09, 2024].

[18] S. Eskilsson, H. Gustafsson, S. Khan, and A. Gurtov, "Demonstrating ads-b and cpdlc attacks with software-defined radio," in *2020 Integrated Communications Navigation and Surveillance Conference (ICNS)*, 2020, 1B2-1-1B2–9. DOI: 10.1109/ICNS50378.2020.9222945.

[19] Financial Times, *Russian gps jamming threatens air disaster, warn baltic ministers*, https://www.ft.com/content/37776b16-0b92-4a23-9f90-199d45d955c3, [retrieved: 09, 2024].

[20] G. Lykou, G. Iakovakis, and D. Gritzalis, "Aviation cybersecurity and cyber-resilience: Assessing risk in air traffic management," in *Critical Infrastructure Security and Resilience: Theories, Methods, Tools and Technologies*, D. Gritzalis, M. Theocharidou, and G. Stergiopoulos, Eds. Cham: Springer International Publishing, 2019, pp. 245–260, ISBN: 978-3-030-00024-0. DOI: 10.1007/978-3-030-00024-0_13.

[21] H. Wynsma and S. Sullivan, "Civil aviation cybersecurity supply chain recommendations report," Civil Aviation Cybersecurity Subcommittee, Tech. Rep., 2020.

[22] International Standards and Recommended Practices, *ICAO Annex 17 to the Convention on International Civil Aviation, Safeguarding International Civil Aviation Against Acts of Unlawful Interference*, Jul. 2022.

[23] *Directive (EU) 2022/2555 on measures for a high common level of cybersecurity across the Union, amending Regulation (EU) No 910/2014 and Directive (EU) 2018/1972, and repealing Directive (EU) 2016/1148 (NIS 2 Directive).*

[24] *Regulation (EU) 2019/881 of the European Parliament and of the Council of 17 April 2019 on ENISA (the European Union Agency for Cybersecurity) and on information and communications technology cybersecurity certification and repealing Regulation (EU) No 526/2013 (Cybersecurity Act).*

[25] SESAR Project 16.02.03, *Minimum Set of Security Controls*, Aug. 2013.

[26] K. Bernsmed, M. G. Jaatun, and P. H. Meland, "Safety critical software and security - how low can you go?" In *2018 IEEE/AIAA 37th Digital Avionics Systems Conference (DASC)*, 2018, pp. 1–6. DOI: 10.1109/DASC.2018.8569579.

[27] World Economic Forum, *The Global Risks Report 2022, 17th edition (insight report)*, https://www3.weforum.org/docs/WEF_The_Global_Risks_Report_2022.pdf, [retrieved: 09, 2024].

[28] Boston Consultancy Group, *Building Cybersecurity Skills*, https://www.bcg.com/capabilities/digital-technology-data/building-cybersecurity-skills, [retrieved: 09, 2024].

[29] E. Frumento et al., *The role of Social Engineering in evolution of attacks*. 2016. DOI: 10.6084/m9.figshare.12369248.v1.

[30] *Smart ATM Virtual Centres*, https://www.sesarju.eu/virtual-centres, [retrieved: 09, 2024].

[31] European Cyber security Organisation, *Strategic Research and Innovation Agenda, WG6 SRIA*, https://ecs-org.eu/ecso-uploads/2022/10/59e615c9dd8f1.pdf, [retrieved: 10, 2024], Jun. 2017.

[32] M. Strohmeier, M. Schäfer, R. Pinheiro, V. Lenders, and I. Martinovic, "On perception and reality in wireless air traffic communication security," *IEEE transactions on intelligent transportation systems*, vol. 18, no. 6, pp. 1338–1357, 2016.

[33] A. Blåberg, G. Lindahl, A. Gurtov, and B. Josefsson, "Simulating ads-b attacks in air traffic management," in *2020 AIAA/IEEE 39th Digital Avionics Systems Conference (DASC)*, 2020, pp. 1–10. DOI: 10.1109/DASC50938.2020.9256438.

[34] PACAS deliverable D3.1, *Gap analysis of existing modelling methodologies for the ATM domain and requirements*, Nov. 2016.

[35] *Horizon 2020 project. Enterprises intangible Risk Management via Economic models based on simulation of modern cyber attacks (HERMENUT)*, https://www.hermeneut.eu/, [retrieved: 09, 2024].

[36] *Horizon 2020 project. aDvanced sOcial enGineering And vulNerability Assessment (DOGANA)*, https://www.dogana-project.eu/, [retrieved: 09, 2024].

[37] *ISO/IEC 27002:2022 — Information technology — cybersecurity and privacy protection — Information security controls.*

[38] C. W. Johnson, "Cyber security and the future of safety-critical air traffic management: identifying the challenges under NextGen and SESAR," in *10th IET System Safety and Cyber-Security Conference 2015*, IET, 2015, pp. 1–6.

[39] A. Tursunbayeva, S. Di Lauro, and C. Pagliari, "People analytics—a scoping review of conceptual boundaries and value propositions," *International journal of information management*, vol. 43, pp. 224–247, 2018.

[40] F. Pagnozzi, "People analytics and human resource management: How the use of smart data can improve the training processes," *puntOorg International Journal*, vol. 7, Aug. 2022. DOI: 10.19245/25.05.pij.7.2.2.

[41] T. Elias, *Learning analytics: Definitions, processes and potential*, 2011.

[42] SKYbrary, *4d trajectory concept*, https://skybrary.aero/articles/4d-trajectory-concept, [retrieved: 09, 2024].

Evaluating Performance Characteristics of Threshold Fully Homomorphic Encryption for Distributed Analytics Scenarios

Svetlana Boudko, Kristian Teig Grønvold
DART,
Norwegian Computing Center
Oslo, Norway
e-mail: svetlana@nr.no | kristegro@gmail.com

***Abstract*—Distributed analytics, such as federated learning, involve collaborative computation across multiple decentralized devices. This approach not only reduces data transfer costs but also offers some degree of protection for privacy-sensitive information. To achieve a higher level of privacy protection, it is recommended to use more advanced privacy-preserving technologies, such as homomorphic encryption. However, the use of homomorphic encryption schemes results in high computational costs. In this study, we evaluate the performance characteristics of threshold fully homomorphic encryption, a technique that can be effectively applied in multi-user environments and distributed analytics scenarios. We present results from the performance evaluation of the Cheon-Kim-Kim-Song scheme.**

Keywords-privacy; data security; threshold homomorphic encryption; multi-party computation; distributed analytics.

I. INTRODUCTION

Homomorphic encryption [1] is a form of encryption that allows computations to be carried out on ciphertext, generating an encrypted result which, when decrypted, matches the result of operations performed on the plaintext. This unique property of homomorphic encryption makes it highly valuable in the field of data privacy and distributed analytics, e.g. federated learning, where sensitive data are processed.

The first practical Fully Homomorphic Encryption (FHE) scheme was proposed by Craig Gentry in 2009 [2]. Subsequently, various homomorphic encryption schemes have been introduced in the literature, all aiming to enhance computational efficiency [3]–[6]. Initially, these schemes were proposed as single-key homomorphic encryption methods. While these schemes are useful for several scenarios, they are not suitable for distributed analytics. In distributed analytics, different clients need their own unique secret keys to ensure protection of their data, making single-key systems inapplicable.

This problem is attempted to be addressed through Multi-Key Homomorphic Encryption (MKHE) [7]–[9], where each client holds its own secret key. However, current MKHE schemes are not yet practical for most applications due to their high computational cost. The key generation is computationally expensive, and the size of the generated ciphertext increases in proportion to the number of clients.

Threshold homomorphic encryption [10]–[13] is another multi-key scheme that addresses the issue of ciphertext expansion. As a result, it can be effectively utilized in distributed analytics. Currently, several standardization bodies, such as the National Institute of Standards and Technology (NIST), the International Organization for Standardization (ISO), and Homomorphic Encryption Standardization, have initiated their efforts on threshold cryptography and homomorphic encryption with the goal of establishing guidelines and recommendations for threshold cryptosystems and promoting wider adoption of these technologies [14]–[16]. While extensive research has been done exploring this approach, its practical application remains limited thus far. Hence, it is important to assess the practical applicability of threshold homomorphic encryption schemes.

In our previous work [17], we outlined the main components and directions for implementing privacy-preserving federated learning using threshold homomorphic encryption. In this ongoing study, we have evaluated a number of parameters to understand the practicality of this approach. These parameters include the size of the keys used in the threshold process, the runtime differences between computations on encrypted and plaintext data, and the key generation runtime for varying multiplicative depths.

The remainder of the paper is organized as follows. After presenting an overview of related work in Section II, we discuss a representative scenario in Section III. Evaluation setup and results are given in Section IV, before discussing future work and concluding in Section V.

II. RELATED WORK

The threshold multi-key encryption methods are based upon Learning With Errors (LWE) problem [18] and its more efficient version the Ring-LWE problem [19]. These problems belong to the category of lattice-based cryptography, also known to be post-quantum resistant.

In these methods, each party contributes a portion of the encryption key, and a specific threshold number of parties must be established before the data can be decrypted.

The clients generate their own secret key shares and collaborate to generate evaluation and joint public keys. The evaluation keys are sent to the server to perform calculations on encrypted data, and the generated joint public key is shared among the participants and used for data encryption. Each data owner encrypts their data using the joint public key, and the result is computed by the server in encrypted form using the evaluation keys. The clients collectively decrypt the result using their own secret key shares.

Several threshold multi-key homomorphic encryption schemes have been introduced in the literature and are available as open-source libraries [20], [21]. The Brakerski-Gentry-Vaikuntanathan (BGV) [3] and the Brakerski/Fan-Vercauteren (BFV) [4], [22] schemes rely on the Ring-LWE problem. The BGV scheme optimizes homomorphic operations by effectively managing the ciphertext's noise, primarily through enhancing the modulus switching technique. The BFV scheme is a scale-invariant construction with the same noise growth as in the BGV scheme. Both schemes are designed to support computations over integer arithmetic circuits.

The Ducas-Micciancio (FHEW) [23] and the Chillotti-Gama-Georgieva-Izabachene (CGGI) [5] schemes support the encryption of small bit-width integers and are constructed for Boolean circuit evaluation. In the FHEW scheme, the authors introduced a new bootstrapping technique that reduces the noise level. The CGGI scheme achieves faster bootstrapping by implementing programmable bootstrapping, which is a computational operation on a ciphertext performed during bootstrapping. This reduces the noise while processing ciphertexts.

Another threshold homomorphic encryption scheme, known as the Cheon-Kim-Kim-Song (CKKS) scheme [24], features approximate homomorphic computations over real and complex numbers. This scheme uses a rescaling operation to reduce noise growth from multiplications. Due to its support for arithmetic operations on real or complex numbers, the CKKS scheme is particularly well-suited to tackle a wide range of data analytics problems and is therefore chosen for the purpose of this study.

III. Representative Scenario

To demonstrate the applicability of threshold homomorphic encryption schemes, we consider a federated learning scenario where a group of clients collaboratively participates in the training and updating of machine learning models. Federated learning is a distributed machine learning approach that enables on-device model training using client-specific data, with further aggregation of the obtained local model updates on a central server, as depicted in Figure 1. Instead of sending data for centralized processing, this data is used locally to train the model. Subsequently, the model updates are sent to the central server to refresh the central model. The updated model is then sent back to the clients for the next update step.

Federated aggregation is a key process in federated learning. Cross-silo aggregation and cross-device aggregation are two concepts used in federated learning architectures. Cross-silo refers to the process of integrating, sharing, or collaborating on data and information across different departments or organizations (silos). On the other hand, cross-device aggregation involves the collection and integration of data from multiple devices, such as those in the Internet of Things (IoT).

These two approaches have different requirements. In the case of IoT devices, computing power and storage capacities are crucial. However, these parameters do not pose a challenge for institutions involved in cross-silo aggregation.

Federated averaging and weighted federated averaging are the most commonly used aggregation algorithms due to their efficiency [25]. In these methods, a subset of clients is selected to perform updates using stochastic gradient descent over several iterations. The process alternates between multiple local stochastic gradient updates and the exchange of their averaged weights for updates of the global model. Since these updates could potentially expose sensitive information and are susceptible to privacy attacks [26], [27], we employ homomorphic encryption to secure the data.

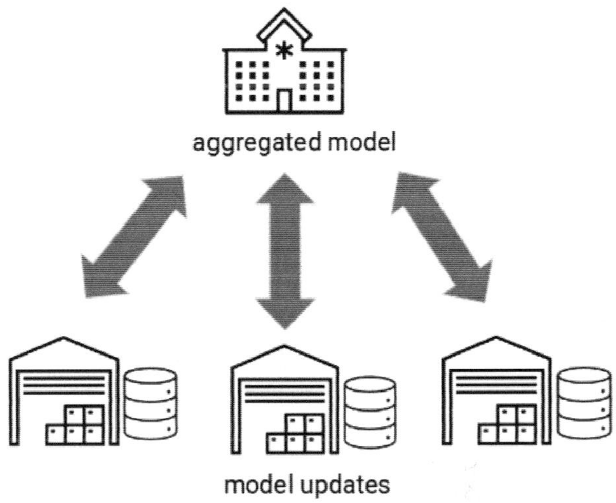

Figure 1. Cross-silo federated aggregation involving three clients and a central unit. The clients calculate their model updates using their own data and share these updates with the central unit. The central unit then generates a new model, which is sent back to the clients for the next iteration.

IV. Evaluation

A. Evaluation Setup

To perform the evaluation, we used the OpenFHE library [20]. This library is implemented in C++ and includes Python bindings, which simplify its integration with machine learning and data analytics platforms. The library supports threshold FHE for BGV, BFV, and CKKS schemes.

In our evaluation, we utilized the CKKS scheme. This scheme supports computations over real numbers and, therefore, can serve as a basis for developing data protection mechanisms for distributed analytics applications

B. Evaluation Results

Both key generation and general computations have been evaluated. Key generation was assessed for sets of 3, 4, 5, 6, 7, and 8 keys, across multiplicative depths of 5, 10, 15, and 20. The multiplicative depth refers to the maximum number of sequential multiplications that can be performed. Table I below shows the runtime for key generation in seconds at different multiplicative depths.

A larger multiplicative depth increases the time required to generate the same amount of keys. Additionally, it enlarges the size of the serializations of the cryptocontext and various keys, introducing further overhead for most applications since the

TABLE I. RUNTIME FOR DIFFERENT MULTIPLICATIVE DEPTHS.

Number of keys generated	Runtime in seconds			
	MultDepth 5	MultDepth 10	MultDepth 15	MultDepth 20
3	12.28	17.02	48.93	61.67
4	14.98	22.80	64.58	82.07
5	18.23	27.88	81.28	101.52
6	21.52	33.59	98.63	123.64
7	25.11	39.02	112.34	141.71
8	28.55	44.47	129.62	163.07

cryptocontext and keys must be deserialized before use. Storage space might also become an issue, as each user must store the cryptocontext, the joint public key, the multiplication key, and their own secret key. See Table II below for a breakdown of file sizes at various multiplicative depths. Due to the costs

TABLE II. FILE SIZES FOR DIFFERENT MULTIPLICATIVE DEPTHS.

Multiplicative depth	5	10	15	20
Cryptocontext	21 KB	30 KB	40 KB	49 KB
Joint public key	41 MB	66 MB	189 MB	238 MB
Multiplication key	131 MB	209 MB	600 MB	757 MB
Secret key	14 MB	23 MB	65 MB	84 MB

associated with higher multiplicative depths, it is recommended to keep them as small as possible. Even if large computations are needed, it is possible to save on multiplicative depth by employing more efficient techniques, such as computing powers of two. OpenFHE also supports bootstrapping to reduce the depth of a ciphertext; however, the bootstrapping process itself requires some available depth and further increases runtime.

Evaluation has been done for computing averages, both on plaintext and encrypted data, using both weighted and unweighted approaches. Ten datasets were used, each containing from 1 to 10 elements, with values ranging from 1 to 100. Across all tests, the sum of the values was 2976, and the total number of elements across the datasets was 55. Table III presents a breakdown of the runtime in seconds and the estimated precision for the encrypted results.

TABLE III. RUNTIME AND PRECISION ESTIMATION FOR PLAINTEXT AND CIPHERTEXT

Operation	Runtime (s)	Estimated precision (bits)
Average on ciphertext, total	11.71	42
Average on ciphertext, computations only	1.19	
Average on plaintext	0.017	N/A
Weighted average on ciphertext, total	15.43	28
Weighted average on ciphertext, computations only	6.29	
Weighted average on plaintext	0.017	N/A

The runtime on encrypted data does not include the time needed to generate the keys, which are assumed to have been generated in advance. The runtime marked with 'computations only' also does not include the time needed to load the cryptocontext and keys, nor the time used for encryption and decryption. Thus, while the runtime is higher for encrypted data, much of the increase comes from other processes that are not directly related to the computation itself.

Both types of averages utilize the OpenFHE function EvalMult, and the weighted average also utilizes the function EvalDivide. EvalMult takes a ciphertext and either another ciphertext, a plaintext, or a constant, and computes the product of these. This computation is done per element for inputs that contain more than one element. Meanwhile, EvalDivide takes a ciphertext and computes its inverse.

In the unweighted average, EvalDivide is not used since the number of elements in a dataset is not encrypted. Based on the runtime results shown in Table III, it can be concluded that EvalDivide is slower than EvalMult. Moreover, using EvalDivide negatively affects the estimated precision of the results: the unweighted average has an estimated precision of around 42 bits, while the weighted average has an estimated precision of about 28 bits.

The precision of EvalDivide can be improved by increasing the degree parameter; however, this also increases the runtime. Additionally, a larger degree parameter requires a higher multiplicative depth, which, as previously noted, increases overhead for most applications.

V. CONCLUSION AND FUTURE WORK

This paper introduces an ongoing study that utilizes threshold fully homomorphic encryption to protect sensitive data within the context of distributed analytics applications. It presents preliminary results from the performance evaluation of the CKKS scheme, as implemented in the OpenFHE library. The aim was to evaluate the efficiency of computing averages and weighted averages for federated aggregation on encrypted data.

The results show that due to a large size of cryptocontext data and time required for encryption and decryption, applying this method is challenging for cross-device aggregation. For IoT devices, which have limited processing power and memory, handling large cryptocontext data can be unfeasible. Cross-silo scenarios, on the other hand, involve the collaboration of various institutions where processing power and storage capabilities do not pose a bottleneck. Therefore, they can effectively apply these methods.

Future work will involve several steps, including: (1) further design and analysis of extended scenarios and use cases; (2) development of a testing platform to evaluate the applicability of threshold homomorphic encryption schemes to various scenarios; and (3) analysis, implementation, and testing of communication protocols, mechanisms, and key generation processes.

Distributed analytics and homomorphic encryption require significant computational resources and may be slower compared to conventional methods. As the number of devices and the volume of data grow, scaling these technologies presents a substantial challenge. Research is needed to develop methods for scalable, decentralized learning and efficient homomorphic encryption. Therefore, a more comprehensive analysis and evaluation of available threshold fully homomorphic encryption schemes and libraries will be conducted, alongside integration with existing federated aggregation methods, and modification of these methods if required.

ACKNOWLEDGMENT

This work has been carried out in the context of the Center for Research-based Innovation NORCICS, funded by the Research Council of Norway, grant number 310105/F40.

REFERENCES

[1] R. L. Rivest, L. Adleman, and M. L. Dertouzos, "On data banks and privacy homomorphisms", *Foundations of Secure Computation, Academia Press*, pp. 169–179, 1978.

[2] C. Gentry, "Fully homomorphic encryption using ideal lattices", in *Proceedings of the Forty-First Annual ACM Symposium on Theory of Computing*, ser. STOC '09, Bethesda, MD, USA: Association for Computing Machinery, 2009, pp. 169–178, ISBN: 9781605585062. DOI: 10.1145/1536414.1536440.

[3] Z. Brakerski, C. Gentry, and V. Vaikuntanathan, "(leveled) fully homomorphic encryption without bootstrapping", in *Proceedings of the 3rd Innovations in Theoretical Computer Science Conference*, ser. ITCS '12, Cambridge, Massachusetts: Association for Computing Machinery, 2012, pp. 309–325, ISBN: 9781450311151. DOI: 10.1145/2090236.2090262.

[4] Z. Brakerski, "Fully homomorphic encryption without modulus switching from classical gapsvp", in *Advances in Cryptology – CRYPTO 2012*, R. Safavi-Naini and R. Canetti, Eds., Berlin, Heidelberg: Springer Berlin Heidelberg, 2012, pp. 868–886, ISBN: 978-3-642-32009-5.

[5] I. Chillotti, N. Gama, M. Georgieva, and M. Izabachène, "Faster fully homomorphic encryption: Bootstrapping in less than 0.1 seconds", in *Advances in Cryptology – ASIACRYPT 2016*, J. H. Cheon and T. Takagi, Eds., Berlin, Heidelberg: Springer Berlin Heidelberg, 2016, pp. 3–33, ISBN: 978-3-662-53887-6.

[6] C. Gentry, A. Sahai, and B. Waters, "Homomorphic encryption from learning with errors: Conceptually-simpler, asymptotically-faster, attribute-based", in *Advances in Cryptology – CRYPTO 2013*, R. Canetti and J. A. Garay, Eds., Berlin, Heidelberg: Springer Berlin Heidelberg, 2013, pp. 75–92, ISBN: 978-3-642-40041-4.

[7] A. López-Alt, E. Tromer, and V. Vaikuntanathan, "On-the-fly multiparty computation on the cloud via multikey fully homomorphic encryption", in *Proceedings of the Forty-Fourth Annual ACM Symposium on Theory of Computing*, ser. STOC '12, New York, New York, USA: Association for Computing Machinery, 2012, pp. 1219–1234, ISBN: 9781450312455. DOI: 10.1145/2213977.2214086.

[8] M. Clear and C. McGoldrick, "Multi-identity and multi-key leveled fhe from learning with errors", in *Advances in Cryptology – CRYPTO 2015*, R. Gennaro and M. Robshaw, Eds., Berlin, Heidelberg: Springer Berlin Heidelberg, 2015, pp. 630–656, ISBN: 978-3-662-48000-7.

[9] Z. Brakerski and R. Perlman, "Lattice-based fully dynamic multi-key fhe with short ciphertexts", in *Advances in Cryptology – CRYPTO 2016*, M. Robshaw and J. Katz, Eds., Berlin, Heidelberg: Springer Berlin Heidelberg, 2016, pp. 190–213, ISBN: 978-3-662-53018-4.

[10] D. Boneh *et al.*, "Threshold cryptosystems from threshold fully homomorphic encryption", in *Advances in Cryptology – CRYPTO 2018*, H. Shacham and A. Boldyreva, Eds., Cham: Springer International Publishing, 2018, pp. 565–596, ISBN: 978-3-319-96884-1.

[11] Y. Desmedt, "Threshold cryptography", in *Encyclopedia of Cryptography and Security*, H. C. A. van Tilborg and S. Jajodia, Eds. Boston, MA: Springer US, 2011, pp. 1288–1293, ISBN: 978-1-4419-5906-5. DOI: 10.1007/978-1-4419-5906-5_330.

[12] B. Schoenmakers, "Threshold homomorphic cryptosystems", in *Encyclopedia of Cryptography and Security*, H. C. A. van Tilborg and S. Jajodia, Eds. Boston, MA: Springer US, 2011, pp. 1293–1294, ISBN: 978-1-4419-5906-5. DOI: 10.1007/978-1-4419-5906-5_13.

[13] R. Bendlin and I. Damgård, "Threshold decryption and zero-knowledge proofs for lattice-based cryptosystems", in *Theory of Cryptography*, D. Micciancio, Ed., Berlin, Heidelberg: Springer Berlin Heidelberg, 2010, pp. 201–218, ISBN: 978-3-642-11799-2.

[14] *Multi-party threshold cryptography*, Online: https://csrc.nist.gov/projects/threshold-cryptography, accessed: 2024-10-01, National Institute of Standards and Technology, 2024.

[15] *ISO/IEC 18033-6:2019, IT Security techniques – Encryption algorithms – Part 6: Homomorphic encryption*, Online: https://www.iso.org/standard/64772.html, accessed: 2024-10-01, International Organization for Standardization, 2019.

[16] M. Albrecht *et al.*, "Homomorphic encryption security standard", HomomorphicEncryption.org, Toronto, Canada, Tech. Rep., Nov. 2018.

[17] S. Boudko, "Towards implementation of privacy-preserving federated learning aggregation using multi-key homomorphic encryption", in *2024 Congress in Computer Science, Computer Engineering, & Applied Computing (CSCE)*, In press, 2024.

[18] O. Regev, "On lattices, learning with errors, random linear codes, and cryptography", in *Proceedings of the Thirty-Seventh Annual ACM Symposium on Theory of Computing*, ser. STOC '05, Baltimore, MD, USA: Association for Computing Machinery, 2005, pp. 84–93, ISBN: 1581139608. DOI: 10.1145/1060590.1060603.

[19] V. Lyubashevsky, C. Peikert, and O. Regev, "On ideal lattices and learning with errors over rings", in *Advances in Cryptology – EUROCRYPT 2010*, H. Gilbert, Ed., Berlin, Heidelberg: Springer Berlin Heidelberg, 2010, pp. 1–23, ISBN: 978-3-642-13190-5.

[20] A. A. Badawi *et al.*, *OpenFHE: Open-source fully homomorphic encryption library*, Cryptology ePrint Archive, Paper 2022/915, accessed: 2024-10-01, 2022.

[21] *Lattigo v5*, Online: https://github.com/tuneinsight/lattigo, accessed: 2024-10-01, Nov. 2023.

[22] J. Fan and F. Vercauteren, *Somewhat practical fully homomorphic encryption*, Cryptology ePrint Archive, Paper 2012/144, accessed: 2024-10-01, 2012.

[23] L. Ducas and D. Micciancio, "Fhew: Bootstrapping homomorphic encryption in less than a second", in *Advances in Cryptology – EUROCRYPT 2015*, E. Oswald and M. Fischlin, Eds., Berlin, Heidelberg: Springer Berlin Heidelberg, 2015, pp. 617–640, ISBN: 978-3-662-46800-5.

[24] J. H. Cheon, A. Kim, M. Kim, and Y. Song, "Homomorphic encryption for arithmetic of approximate numbers", in *Advances in Cryptology – ASIACRYPT 2017*, T. Takagi and T. Peyrin, Eds., Cham: Springer International Publishing, 2017, pp. 409–437, ISBN: 978-3-319-70694-8.

[25] H. B. McMahan, E. Moore, D. Ramage, and B. A. y Arcas, *Federated learning of deep networks using model averaging*, accessed: 2024-10-01, 2016. arXiv: 1602.05629.

[26] V. Mothukuri *et al.*, "A survey on security and privacy of federated learning", *Future Generation Computer Systems*, vol. 115, pp. 619–640, 2021, accessed: 2024-10-01, ISSN: 0167-739X. DOI: https://doi.org/10.1016/j.future.2020.10.007.

[27] R. Gosselin, L. Vieu, F. Loukil, and A. Benoit, "Privacy and security in federated learning: A survey", *Applied Sciences*, vol. 12, no. 19, 2022, ISSN: 2076-3417. DOI: 10.3390/app12199901.

Blue Team Fundamentals: Roles and Tools in a Security Operations Center

Jenny Hofbauer *, Kevin Mayer †
CARISSMA Institute for Electric, Connected, and Secure Mobility
Technical University Ingolstadt
Germany
e-mail: *jeh7703@thi.de, †kevin.mayer@carissma.eu

***Abstract*—The evolution from low-impact malicious code in the mid-70s to current Denial-of-Service (DoS) attacks, widespread malware campaigns, and Advanced Persistent Threats (APTs) shaped the furtherance of Information Technology (IT) security services that Security Operations Centers (SOCs) provide to protect against cyberattacks. Despite the ever-growing importance of SOCs, there is little academic and fundamental research. Terminology and the associated definitions are highly influenced by companies developing proprietary software and training and are mostly not standardized. This paper closes part of the gap and provides a suitable research base regarding people and technologies. For this purpose, literature research was conducted using academic literature and industry data, such as advertising material, company white papers, and employment advertisements. A survey with 24 experts in various areas of IT security was conducted to validate and expand the identified roles and tools, allowing the creation of an overview of roles and tools currently utilized in the industry. These can be seen as building blocks, whereas the company's individual needs determine its presence, capabilities, and association within SOCs. The percentage of participants who classified the defined roles and tools as part of SOCs is detailed. The survey furthermore captured the affiliation of roles between SOCs and Computer Emergency Response Teams (CERT) or Computer Security Incident Response Teams (CSIRT), often seen as specialized sub-capabilities that work on data SOCs provide. The common terminology creates a uniform basis for further research and more efficient communication and defines roles and technologies in SOCs that can be used to identify possible gaps.**

Keywords-Security Operations Center; SOC; SOC Roles; SOC Tools; Blue Team.

I. INTRODUCTION

In its annual report *The State of IT Security in Germany* [1], the Federal Office for Information Security describes the current threat situation in Information Technology (IT) security as tense to critical with the highest level of cybercrime ever recorded. Cyberattacks' quantitative and qualitative development has grown in recent years, making cybersecurity increasingly crucial for businesses. Security Operations Centers (SOCs) utilize people, technologies, and processes to protect against cyberattacks [2]. Software tools and knowledge needed to operate efficient SOCs are primarily proprietary. There is little public and objective information, standardization, and fundamental research, not only because most cybersecurity software is not freely accessible but also because of paid training courses. This work closes part of the gap by providing a suitable research base of the industry's current SOC roles and tools. It compiles an overview of standardized terminology for enterprise IT SOC roles and tools and defines their capabilities. First, the definition of SOCs in the context of this paper is established in Section II. Based on this definition, Section III highlights already conducted SOC research and places this paper within the context. Section IV details the research methodology of this paper, which is based on literature research and surveys with experts. The developed SOC roles and tools are listed and provided with context in Sections V and VI. Section VII gives insights and reasoning behind some of the classifications, while the final Section VIII concludes the results of the research.

II. DEFINITION OF A SECURITY OPERATIONS CENTER

The systematic study by Vielberth et al. [2] defined SOCs as an IT security service provider that protects against cybersecurity threats and information loss. It identifies, detects, and mitigates cyberthreats through people, processes, and technologies. As highlighted by Hofbauer et al. [3], there is no standardized definition of enterprise IT SOCs. Affiliations and tasks differ between individual companies and sub-organizations. Functions traditionally assigned to Computer Emergency Response Teams (CERT) or Computer Security Incident Response Teams (CSIRT) are also considered in this paper since companies often do not have dedicated resources or responsibilities overlap. All aspects of product security are excluded. This paper lists roles and tools that implement the primary SOC capabilities defined by [3]:

- Change and Asset Management
- Threat Intelligence Management
- Vulnerability Management
- Data Collection and Management
- Security Event Management
- Incident and Crisis Management
- Forensic and Investigation of Security Incidents
- Compliance Management and Reporting
- Recommendations and Advice
- Security Awareness Training

III. RELATED WORK

To the best of our knowledge, no research paper addresses the terminology and definition of roles and tools in SOCs in detail. Olt [4] published a rough overview of SOC roles and their interactions, which has been used as the basis of numerous other papers [2], [5], [6]. These include a paper published in 2020 by Vielbert et al. [2] that uses a holistic approach to define the state of the art of SOCs and open challenges, especially in the collaboration between people and technology. The individual aspects of the paper are examined in greater detail in the books from Knerler et al. [7] and Nathans [8]. Nathans' work from 2014 includes a detailed list of SOC tools divided into organizational, operational, and support infrastructure, with the umbrella terms still used similarly in current general SOC works [5], [9]–[13]. Many works deal with individual tools or roles in SOCs, but do not provide a general overview. Since a large part of the further development of SOCs is done by companies, product portfolios and information from SOC as a service providers show the current state of SOC roles and tools in the industry. However, such articles are primarily designed to sell software solutions or services and do not correspond to scientific standards.

IV. Research Methodology

The research methodology for establishing roles, responsibilities, and tools in a traditional enterprise IT SOC is divided into two phases. In the first phase, a detailed literature review was carried out. Since the literature is limited, the findings were expanded and validated through a survey in the second phase. People and technologies considered part of the SOC by at least one expert were included. Quick and Hall [14] suggested an appropriate sample size of 4-50 participants in their study about qualitative research, a range we adhered to. The experts were selected based on their involvement in previous SOC-related research projects and peer-reviewed publications or needed to be at least fairly confident in one of the areas of IT security. During the selection, we strived to achieve diversity across industry (Figure 1), age (Figure 2) and experience (Figure 3). The survey was conducted over two months via the survey platform SoSci [15]. Each participant was presented with an overview of roles, tools and their descriptions in SOCs established through the literature research. They were given the option to confirm, deny, or not answer whether every role and tool belonged in SOCs and encouraged to provide additional comments on their choice and suggest any missing assets. This approach ensured transparency and allowed for a comprehensive understanding of the participants' perspectives. Unfinished surveys or ones that did not meet the requirements of an expert were not considered. Twenty-four valid interviews were conducted; the raw data from the interview can be found at [16].

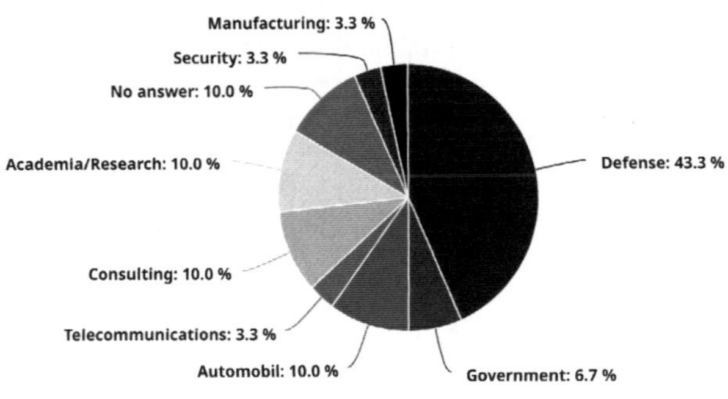

Figure 1. SOC Survey Participant Industry.

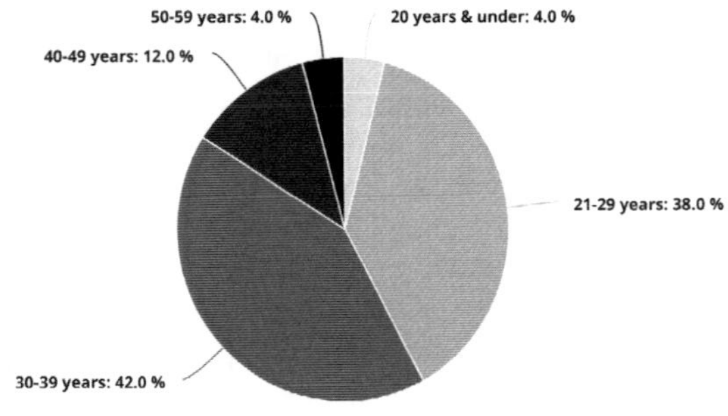

Figure 2. SOC Survey Participant Age.

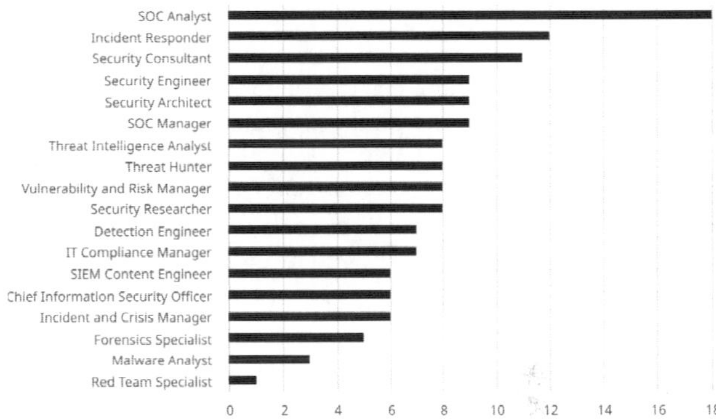

Figure 3. SOC Survey Participant Experience.

V. Roles in an Enterprise SOC

The following roles and descriptions were compiled from academic literature [2], [4], [7], [9], [12], [17]–[21], SOC provider advertising material [22]–[25] and appropriate job listings from employment website marked with the search terms "Security Operations Center", "Computer Emergency Response Team", "Computer Security Incident Response Team", "Blue Team" and excluded any listings related to product security and penetration testing. Due to the limited academic literature and the widespread implementation of SOCs in the industry, advertising material was assessed for reliability and is considered equivalent to reputable sources. Company-specific role titles were not considered. During the literature research and the interviews, other terms for roles with the insert "Chief" were occasionally found; this is primarily used in American companies where the word "Chief" indicates seniority. Roles and their descriptions were grouped into technical (Table I), management (Table II), and consulting (Table III). The literature research was expanded and validated by interviews described in Section IV.

A. Technical SOC Roles

This section examines the technical roles in SOCs. Table I lists the role name and description. Figure 4 shows the percentage of survey participants who consider each role part of the SOC. Various literature works [2], [17], [19], [22] refers to a tier 1 SOC analyst as a triage or alert specialist, tier 2 as an incident responder, and tier 3 as a threat hunter. The roles established in this paper do not follow those labels. It was noted several times in the interviews that the division of SOC analysts into tiers is only theoretical and not implemented in practice. The forensics analyst was generally attributed to a CERT/CSIRT and an often outsourced role since continuous practice is needed that a single company environment can rarely provide. Through the increase of modern tools like Endpoint Detection and Response (EDR) and the need for fast response, forensic analysts are commonly restricted to disk forensics and finding legal evidence. The Security Information and Event Management (SIEM) content engineer is often not a specifically dedicated role but rather done by the SOC analyst or architect. Since many companies are moving away from the single platform strategy of only using a SIEM, the role will be called security tool content engineer in this paper. The incident responder is also typically attributed to a CERT/CSIRT. The role overlaps with a forensic expert or SOC analyst on a technical basis; they are usually the interface between technical roles and the supporting teams, such as server operations and management. Based on the literature research, the red team specialist was initially categorized as a technical role but was attributed to the consulting roles due to survey comments.

TABLE I. TECHNICAL SOC ROLES

Role	Description
SOC Analyst	Review and triage real-time alarms and alerts and determines if they are a false or true positive. Conduct in-depth analyses of security incidents, contain them, and introduce recovery mechanisms. Perform vulnerability assessments and penetration testing to proactively identify and treat threats and vulnerabilities.
Threat Intelligence Analyst	Collect, analyze, produce, and share cyberthreat intelligence.
Malware Analyst	Analyze malware functionality to collect necessary information for detection and incident response.
Forensics Specialist	Investigate incidents to collect legally sound evidence.
Detection Engineer	Design, test, and maintain threat detection logic.
Security Engineer	Develop, integrate, and maintain tools the Security Operations Center uses.
Security Tool Content Engineer	Manage, parse, correlate, and enrich logs and data for the security tools.
Threat Hunter	Proactively search the network and infrastructure to detect unknown threats.
Incident Responder	Discover intrusion artifacts to mitigate and provide technical support to resolve cyberincidents and act as an interface between involved parties.

B. Management SOC Roles

All established management roles are listed in Table II with the corresponding Figure 5 visualizing the belonging to a SOC. Regarding the management roles, the IT compliance manager can be seen as part of SOCs or the company since aspects such as data protection are relevant outside of IT security. A security incident and crisis manager is usually part of a CERT/CSIRT and has a corresponding non-security, general incident, and crisis manager role in the organization. The vulnerability and risk manager is located in the CERT/CSIRT and can be split into separate cybersecurity-only vulnerability and risk manager roles. The cybersecurity awareness officer was added as a separate role since survey comments stated that it is common practice in larger companies.

TABLE II. MANAGEMENT SOC ROLES

Role	Description
Chief Information Security Officer	Define strategies, policies, and goals for the security operations of the entire company.
SOC Manager	Manage and supervise the Security Operations Center team's daily operations and tactical direction.
IT Compliance Manager	Organize compliance aspects such as data protection and information security.
Security Incident and Crisis Manager	Coordinate all aspects regarding security incident and crisis response.
Vulnerability and Risk Manager	Identify, assess, manage, prioritize, contextualize, and prevent vulnerabilities.
Cybersecurity Awareness Officer	Understand and triage human risks and take measurements to mitigate those behaviors.

C. Consulting SOC Roles

The following roles listed in Table III are often located outside SOCs or entirely outsourced and only provide services for SOCs. Figure 6 shows the percentage of survey participants who consider each role part of the SOC.

TABLE III. CONSULTING ROLES

Role	Description
Security Architect	Research and design a robust security infrastructure.
Red Team Specialist	Attack systems to identify vulnerabilities and possible evasions for cybersecurity defenses.
Security Consultant and External Personnel	Provide independent audits and consulting in specific areas, for instance, cloud or artificial intelligence security consulting or expertise from a security tool manufacturer.

VI. TOOLS IN AN ENTERPRISE SOC

Technologies are the second central pillar, including tools that SOCs do not directly manage but leverage functionalities or data. Few academic publications exist in this area [5], [8]–[13], which is why advertising material from companies [26]–[37] was primarily used. The researched tools were categorized with the help of the infrastructure chapter of Nathans' work [8], the primary SOC capabilities, and the structure of cybersecurity company websites. Table IV and Figure 7 highlight the tools responsible for the collection and management of data. Every tool involved in the organization and analysis of incidents is depicted in Table V and Figure 8. Security solutions that protect the infrastructure are separated into their area of application. This includes the security of the network (Table VI and Figure 9), endpoints (Table VII and Figure 10), and the combination of both labeled infrastructure (Table VIII and Figure 11). Table IX and Figure 12 highlight security applications running on servers and endpoints. Tools used to manage the security of a company are depicted in Table X and Figure 13. Lastly, tools that are not directly managed but influenced or leveraged by SOCs are combined under the categories of identity attestation

(Table XI and Figure 14) and security awareness (Table XII and Figure 15).

TABLE IV. DATA COLLECTION AND MANAGEMENT

Tool	Description
Security Information and Event Management (SIEM)	Aggregates event data from infrastructure and endpoints, correlates events, and compares them to behavior rules to detect potential threats.
Threat Intelligence Platform (TIP)	Platform to collect, aggregate, enrich, and organize threat intelligence.
Vulnerability Scanner, Penetration Testing Tools, and Breach and Attack Simulation (BAS)	Scans infrastructure and endpoints for vulnerabilities and misconfigurations.
Threat Hunting Tools	Enables the proactive search for cyberthreats that have bypassed established security solutions.
Log Collection and Management Tool	Collects and manages log data not limited to security-relevant data.
Honeypot	A system that is purposefully insecure to gather threat intelligence, detect attackers, and deflect from real systems.

TABLE V. INCIDENT ANALYSIS

Tool	Description
Malware Analysis Sandbox / Platform	Dynamic or static analysis and execution of malware in a secure environment.
Digital Forensics and Incident Response Tools (DFIR)	Hardware and software tools for recovering and preserving digital evidence and attacker methodologies to contain, remediate, and testify in case of an incident.
Security Orchestration, Automation and Response (SOAR)	Automates the contextualisation of security-relevant data and processing of security events/incidents.

TABLE VI. NETWORK SECURITY

Tool	Description
Firewall	Blocks traffic to prevent unauthorized access to and from networks. The SOC usually leverages the tool's logs and does not manage/maintain it.
Network Access Control (NAC)	Restricts unauthorized hardware and users from accessing networks. The SOC usually leverages the tool's logs and does not manage/maintain it.
Network-Based Intrusion Detection System (NIDS)	Monitors connections, data traffic, and activity on the network for malicious activity and reports it.

TABLE VII. ENDPOINT SECURITY

Tool	Description
Endpoint Detection and Response (EDR)	Modern term for a Host-Based Intrusion Detection System that records activities and monitors for suspicious behavior on endpoints.
Host-Based Intrusion Detection System (IDS)	Monitors connections, data traffic, and activity on endpoints for suspicious behavior and reports it.
Intrusion Prevention System (IPS)	Uses mitigation measures to contain suspicious behavior detected by an IDS.
User and Entity Behavior Analytics (UEBA)	Uses various data streams, such as logs and packet captures, to identify anomalies in the behavior of users and non-human entities.
Virus Scanner	Automatically detects and quarantines malware. The SOC usually leverages the tool's logs and does not manage/maintain it.

TABLE VIII. INFRASTRUCTURE SECURITY

Tool	Description
Extended Detection and Response (XDR)	Extension of an EDR system that adds vendor-specific capabilities.

TABLE IX. APPLICATION SECURITY

Tool	Description
Email Security and Protection	Protection and control of email accounts as well as incoming and outgoing email communication. The SOC usually leverages the tool's logs and does not manage/maintain it.
Web Application Firewall (WAF)	A firewall specifically designed to filter and monitor web traffic. The SOC usually leverages the tool's logs and does not manage/maintain it.
Runtime Application Self-Protection	Detects and blocks attacks on software in real-time with insight from inside the running software.

TABLE X. MANAGEMENT PLATFORM

Tool	Description
Asset Management and Discovery Platform	Network scanner that detects hardware and software in the network and extracts and stores detailed information about the asset.
Device Configuration, Update, and Patch Management Platform	Platform to organize and perform device configuration, updates, and patches. The SOC usually leverages the tool's logs and does not manage/maintain it.
Ticketing System	Platform to create and manage work tasks between different people and teams.
Change Management Platform	Supports the planning, implementation, authorization, and non-repudiation of security-relevant organizational changes, often integrated with the general IT or business.
Vulnerability Management Platform	Platform to keep track of identified vulnerabilities and corresponding mitigation measures.
Cybersecurity Risk Management Software	Platform to keep track of identified risks and corresponding mitigation measures.
Knowledge Management Platform	Used to document, manage, and share cybersecurity knowledge within the organization.
Case and Incident Management Platform	Platform for organizing and managing security cases, incidents, and associated context information.
Supplier Management Platform	Consolidates supplier data to have a single knowledge point in case of a supplier alarm.
Compliance Scanner	Monitors if system configurations are compliant with security policies.
Information Security Management System (ISMS)	Platform to establish, improve, and monitor policies and procedures to manage information security.

The security awareness and identity attestation tools documented in Table XI and XII are the responsibility of the information security officer. Parts of the execution, use of log data, and administration can fall under the responsibility of SOCs.

TABLE XI. IDENTITY ATTESTATION

Tool	Description
Public Key Infrastructure (PKI)	Creates, revokes, manages, and distributes a digital certificate and corresponds to the owner.
Identity and Access Management System	Administration, maintenance, and authorization management of user accounts and resources in a network.
Password Manager	A program that stores and manages usernames and passwords securely.

TABLE XII. SECURITY AWARENESS

Tool	Description
Bug Bounty Platform	Allows users and external security researchers to report identified vulnerabilities for a reward.
Security Awareness Platform	Platform to enhance cybersecurity user awareness.

VII. HIGHLIGHTS

This section captures highlights, trends, and reasoning behind some classifications based on the survey comments. Survey takers suggested specialized roles like cloud or artificial intelligence security analysts. The paper did not include these since they can be categorized as security architects or consultants. This highlights the importance of specializations, as no definitive distinction between roles often exists in the industry. A shortage of skilled workers forces SOC employees to take on several roles simultaneously, or individual capabilities are not needed or outsourced. Automation is frequently utilized to counteract the shortage of workers and to free up capacity for other activities. Moreover, job titles can differ between countries or even individual industry sectors. Regarding tools, their capabilities depend heavily on the manufacturer partly due to the increase of specialized solutions replacing the previously predominant single-platform SIEM approach.

VIII. CONCLUSION

SOCs are as flexible as the cyberattacks they protect against, adapting to the company's or industry's requirements. The industry mimics this and tries to stand out from the competition through convoluted marketing that promises that their newly coined terminology solves cutting-edge security problems. Fostering a need for standardized terminology and definitions to allow for objective comparison and better communication in security operations. Based on literature and expert interviews, our research defines the roles and tools that can be part of individual SOCs. While our listing is not exhaustive, it provides an overview and standardized vocabulary of the most common roles and tools used in the industry. Even though the SOC field is dominated by the industry, academic research, as a critical and neutral observer, can add significant value. Further research could include the establishment of standardized SOC frameworks for areas like SOC processes.

ACKNOWLEDGEMENTS

We want to extend a special thank you to all survey participants for their input and insights, which made this paper possible. This project has received funding from the European Union's Horizon Europe research and innovation program under grant agreement No 101069748.

REFERENCES

[1] Federal Office for Information Security, "The State of IT Security in Germany 2023", 21/11/2023, [Online]. Available: https://www.bsi.bund.de/SharedDocs/Downloads/EN/BSI/Publications/Securitysituation/IT-Security-Situation-in-Germany-2023.html?nn=1021082.

[2] M. Vielberth, F. Böhm, I. Fichtinger, and G. Pernul, "Security Operations Center: A Systematic Study and Open Challenges", *IEEE Access*, vol. 8, pp. 227 756–227 779, 2020. DOI: 10.1109/ACCESS.2020.3045514.

[3] J. Hofbauer, K. Mayer, and H.-J. Hof, "From SOC to VSOC: Transferring Key Requirements for Efficient Vehicle Security Operations", Oct. 2023. DOI: 10.13154/294-10389.

[4] C. Olt, "Establishing Security Operation Centers for Connected Cars", *ATZelectronics worldwide*, vol. 14, no. 5, pp. 40–43, 2019. DOI: 10.1007/s38314-019-0050-4.

[5] A. Reisser, M. Vielberth, S. Fohringer, and G. Pernul, "Security Operations Center Roles and Skills: A Comparison of Theory and Practice", in *Data and Applications Security and Privacy XXXVI: 36th Annual IFIP WG 11.3 Conference, DBSec 2022, Newark, NJ, USA, July 18–20, 2022, Proceedings*, Newark, NJ, USA: Springer-Verlag, 2022, pp. 316–327, ISBN: 978-3-031-10683-5. DOI: 10.1007/978-3-031-10684-2_18.

[6] C. DeCusatis, R. Cannistra, A. Labouseur, and M. Johnson, "Design and Implementation of a Research and Education Cybersecurity Operations Center", in Jun. 2019, pp. 287–310, ISBN: 978-3-030-16836-0. DOI: 10.1007/978-3-030-16837-7_13.

[7] K. Knerler, I. Parker, and C. Zimmerman, *11 Strategies of a World-Class Cybersecurity Operations Center*. The MITRE Corporation, 2022, ISBN: 979-8-9856450-4-0.

[8] D. Nathans, *Designing and Building Security Operations Center*. Waltham, MA: Syngress, 2014, ISBN: 9780128010969.

[9] S. C. Sundaramurthy, J. Case, T. Truong, L. Zomlot, and M. Hoffmann, "A Tale of Three Security Operation Centers", in *SIW '14 : proceedings of the 2014 ACM Workshop on Security Information Workers : November 7, 2014, Scottsdale, Arizona, USA*, R. Biddle, Ed., ACM, 2014, pp. 43–50, ISBN: 9781450331524. DOI: 10.1145/2663887.2663904.

[10] P. Jacobs, A. Arnab, and B. Irwin, "Classification of Security Operation Centers", in *2013 Information Security for South Africa*, 2013, pp. 1–7. DOI: 10.1109/ISSA.2013.6641054.

[11] N. Miloslavskaya, "Security Operations Centers for Information Security Incident Management", in *2016 IEEE 4th International Conference on Future Internet of Things and Cloud (FiCloud)*, 2016, pp. 131–136. DOI: 10.1109/FiCloud.2016.26.

[12] S. Schinagl, K. Schoon, and R. Paans, "A Framework for Designing a Security Operations Centre (SOC)", in *2015 48th Hawaii International Conference on System Sciences*, 2015, pp. 2253–2262. DOI: 10.1109/HICSS.2015.270.

[13] J. Hajny *et al.*, "Framework, Tools and Good Practices for Cybersecurity Curricula", *IEEE Access*, vol. 9, pp. 94 723–94 747, 2021. DOI: 10.1109/ACCESS.2021.3093952.

[14] J. Quick and S. Hall, "Part two: Qualitative research", *Journal of Perioperative Practice*, vol. 25, no. 7-8, pp. 129–133, 2015, ISSN: 1750-4589. DOI: 10.1177/1750458915025007-803.

[15] SoSci Survey GmbH, "SoSci Survey – the Solution for Professional Online Questionnaires", 27/05/2024, [Online]. Available: https://www.soscisurvey.de/en/index.

[16] GitHub, "Survey-data/blue-team-fundamentals at main · securityinmobility/survey-data", 31/05/2024, [Online]. Available: https://github.com/securityinmobility/survey-data/tree/main/blue-team-fundamentals.

[17] M. Shutock and G. Dietrich, "Security Operations Centers: A Holistic View on Problems and Solutions", in *Proceedings of the 55th Hawaii International Conference on System Sciences*, T. Bui, Ed., ser. Proceedings of the Annual Hawaii International Conference on System Sciences, Hawaii International Conference on System Sciences, 2022, pp. 7555–7564. DOI: 10.24251/HICSS.2022.907.

[18] D. Crémilleux, C. Bidan, F. Majorczyk, and N. Prigent, "Enhancing Collaboration Between Security Analysts in Security Operations Centers", in *Risks and Security of Internet and*

Systems. Springer Berlin Heidelberg, Jan. 2019, pp. 136–142, ISBN: 978-3-030-12142-6. DOI: 10.1007/978-3-030-12143-3_12.

[19] F. Kokulu *et al.*, "Matched and Mismatched SOCs: A Qualitative Study on Security Operations Center Issues", in *CCS'19*, Association for Computing Machinery, Nov. 2019, pp. 1955–1970, ISBN: 978-1-4503-6747-9. DOI: 10.1145/3319535.3354239.

[20] B. Hámornik and C. Krasznay, "A Team-Level Perspective of Human Factors in Cyber Security: Security Operations Centers", D. Nicholson, Ed., ser. Advances in Intelligent Systems and Computing, vol. 593, Springer, Jul. 2018, pp. 224–236, ISBN: 978-3-319-60584-5. DOI: 10.1007/978-3-319-60585-2_21.

[21] E. Agyepong, Y. Cherdantseva, P. Reinecke, and P. Burnap, "Towards a Framework for Measuring the Performance of a Security Operations Center Analyst", in *2020 International Conference on Cyber Security and Protection of Digital Services (Cyber Security)*, 2020, pp. 1–8. DOI: 10.1109/CyberSecurity49315.2020.9138872.

[22] Palo Alto Networks, "Security Operations Center (SOC) Roles and Responsibilities", 13/11/2023, [Online]. Available: https://www.paloaltonetworks.com/cyberpedia/soc-roles-and-responsibilities.

[23] Cybersecurity and Infrastructure Security Agency CISA, "Cyber Defense Incident Responder", 13/11/2023, [Online]. Available: https://www.cisa.gov/careers/work-rolescyber-defense-incident-responder.

[24] SANS Institute, "Common and Best Practices for Security Operations Centers: Results of the 2019 SOC Survey", 13/11/2023, [Online]. Available: https://www.sans.org/white-papers/39060/.

[25] Indeed, "12 Types of Cybersecurity Roles (With Duties and Salaries)", 13/11/2023, [Online]. Available: https://www.indeed.com/career-advice/finding-a-job/types-of-cyber-security-roles.

[26] Splunk, "Splunk Products", 22/05/2024, [Online]. Available: https://www.splunk.com/en_us/products.html.

[27] Mandiant, "Threat Intelligence Solutions | Cyber Security Services & Training", Tue, 09/07/2021, [Online]. Available: https://www.mandiant.com/.

[28] Proofpoint, "2023 Human Factor Report: Analyzing the Cyber Attack Chain", 2023, [Online]. Available: https://www.proofpoint.com/.

[29] Kaspersky, "Kaspersky Security for Business Portfolio", 27/05/2024, [Online]. Available: https://www.kaspersky.com/small-to-medium-business-security/resources/products/kaspersky-security-for-business-portfolio.

[30] Fortinet, "Global Leader of Cybersecurity Solutions and Services", 27/05/2024, [Online]. Available: https://www.fortinet.com/.

[31] Cloudflare, "Cloudflare Product Portfolio", 27/05/2024, [Online]. Available: https://www.cloudflare.com/cloudflare-product-portfolio/.

[32] CrowdStrike, "CrowdStrike: Stop breaches. Drive business", 13/05/2024, [Online]. Available: https://www.crowdstrike.com/en-us/.

[33] Palo Alto Networks, "Products a-z", 22/05/2024, [Online]. Available: https://www.paloaltonetworks.com/products/products-a-z.

[34] Trend Micro, "Products", 27/05/2024, [Online]. Available: https://www.trendmicro.com/en_us/business/products.html.

[35] Darktrace, "AI Cyber Security Solutions", 27/05/2024, [Online]. Available: https://de.darktrace.com/products.

[36] SentinelOne DE, "The Enterprise Security AI Platform | Securing Endpoint, Cloud, Identity, and Data", 7/05/2024, [Online]. Available: https://de.sentinelone.com/.

[37] CyberArk, "Product Datasheets", 27/05/2024, [Online]. Available: https://www.cyberark.com/resources/product-datasheets.

APPENDIX

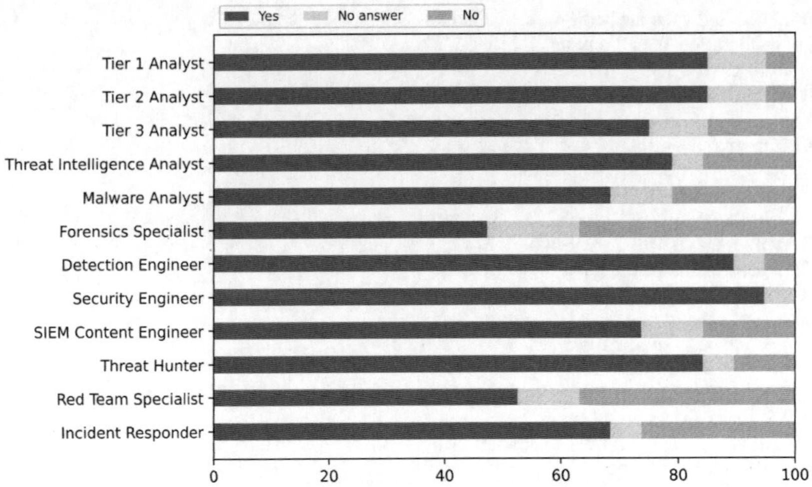

FIGURE 4. CLASSIFICATION OF TECHNICAL SOC ROLES.

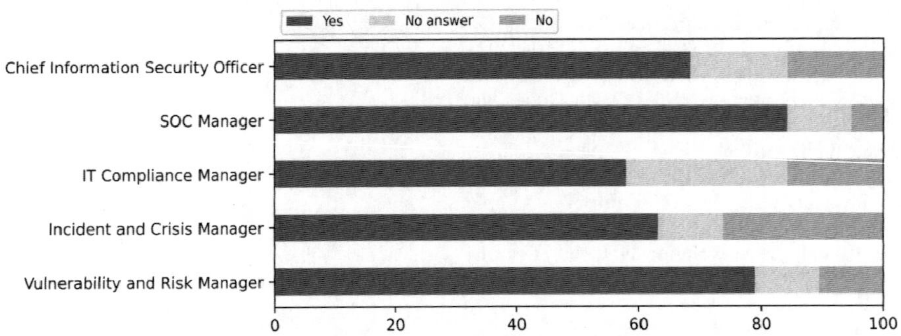

FIGURE 5. CLASSIFICATION OF MANAGEMENT SOC ROLES.

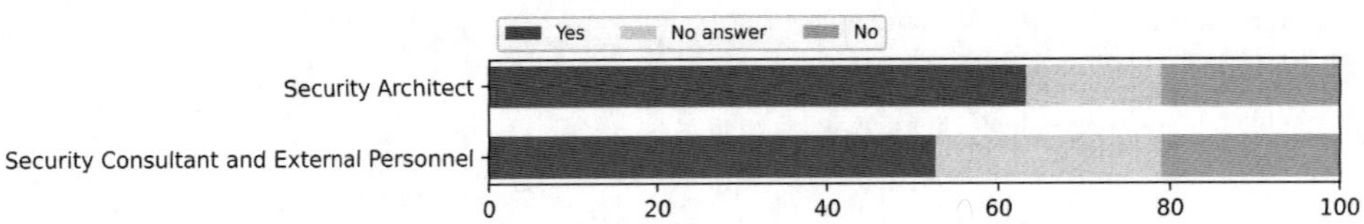

FIGURE 6. CLASSIFICATION OF CONSULTING SOC ROLES.

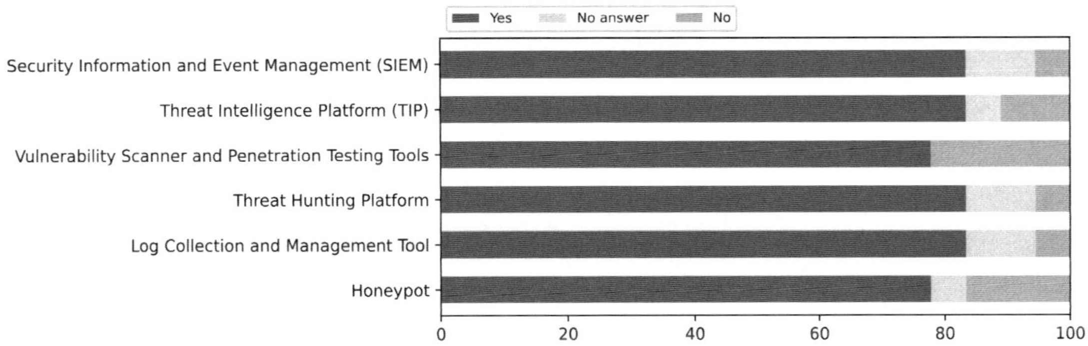

FIGURE 7. CLASSIFICATION OF DATA COLLECTION AND MANAGEMENT SOC TOOLS.

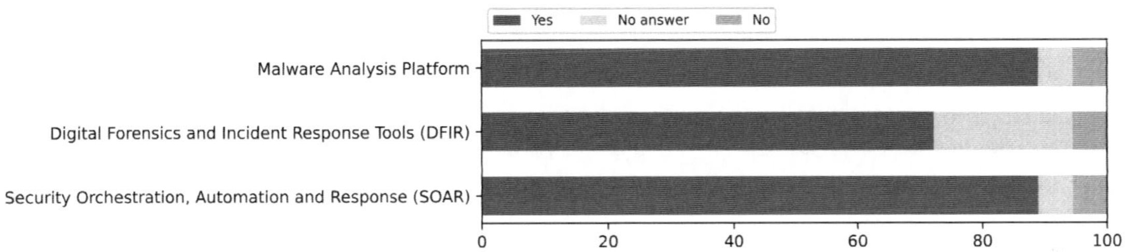

FIGURE 8. CLASSIFICATION OF INCIDENT ANALYSIS SOC TOOLS.

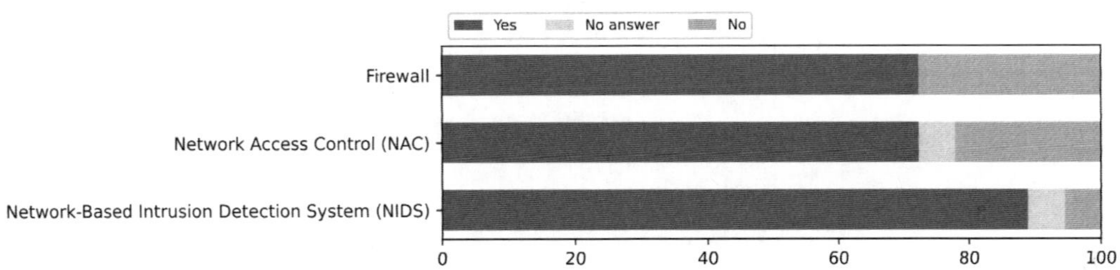

FIGURE 9. CLASSIFICATION OF NETWORK SECURITY SOC TOOLS.

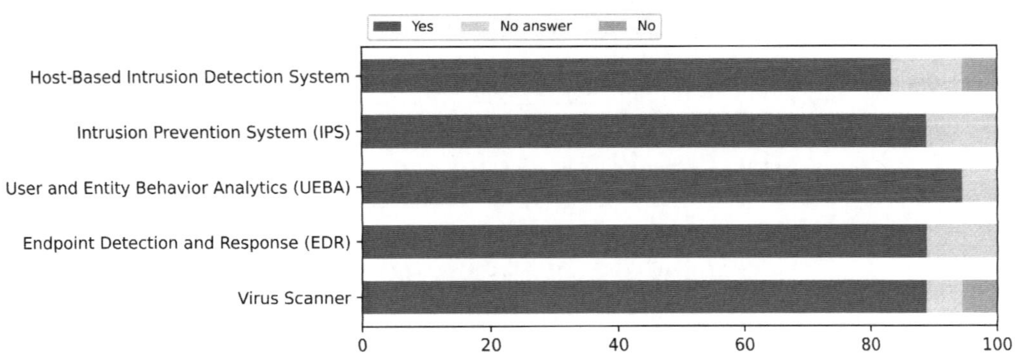

FIGURE 10. CLASSIFICATION OF ENDPOINT SECURITY SOC TOOLS.

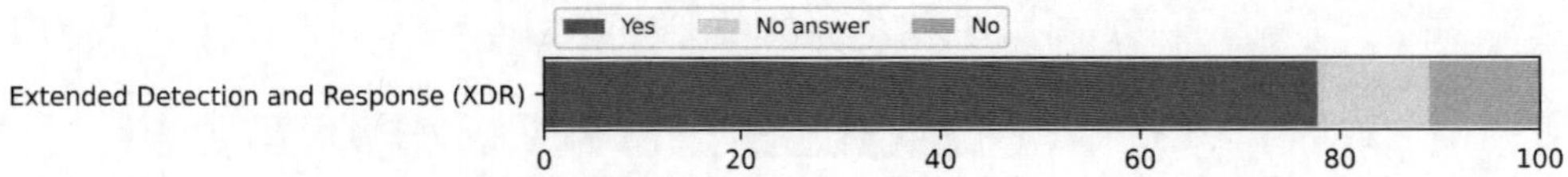

FIGURE 11. CLASSIFICATION OF INFRASTRUCTURE SECURITY SOC TOOLS.

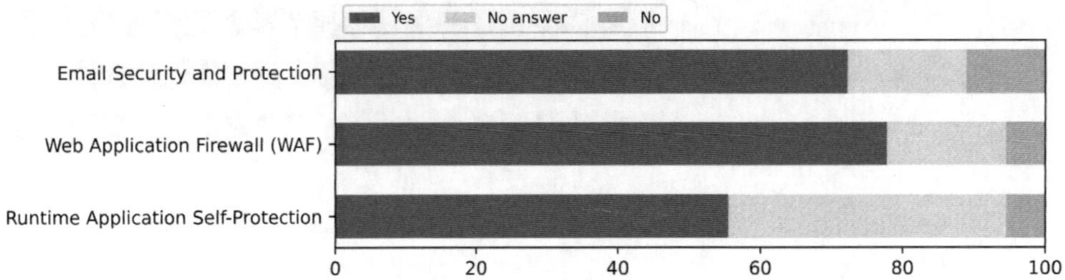

FIGURE 12. CLASSIFICATION OF APPLICATION SECURITY SOC TOOLS.

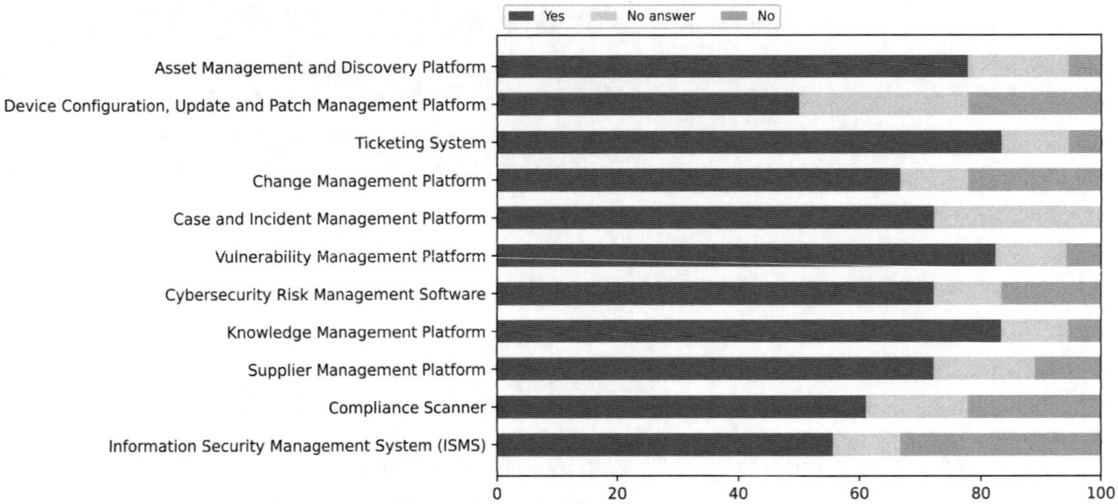

FIGURE 13. CLASSIFICATION OF MANAGEMENT PLATFORM SOC TOOLS.

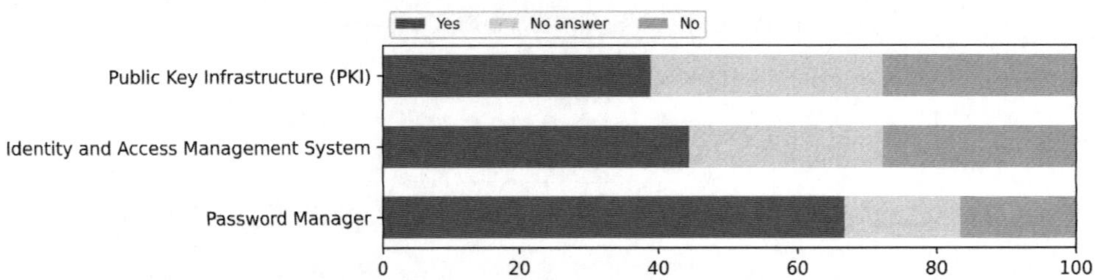

FIGURE 14. CLASSIFICATION OF IDENTITY ATTESTATION SOC TOOLS.

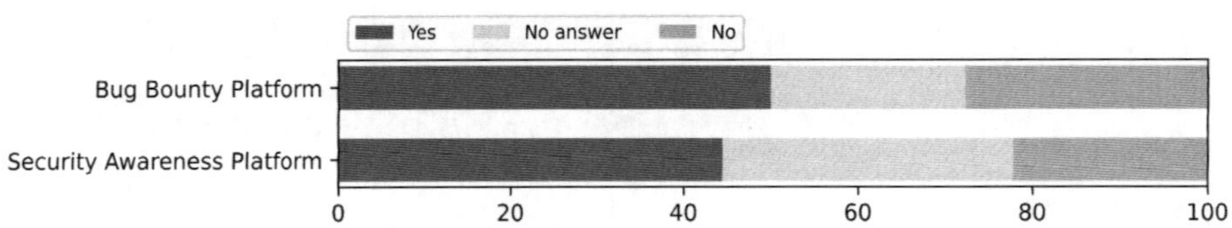

FIGURE 15. CLASSIFICATION OF SECURITY AWARENESS SOC TOOLS.

Cryptocurrency Integration in Qatar's Financial Markets Analyzing the Opportunities, Issues, and Regulatory Implications

Asma Nasser Al-Nassr
Dept. of Computing and Data Science
Oryx Universal College in Partnership
with Liverpool John Moores University
in Qatar
Doha, Qatar
e-mail: 102452@oryx.edu.qa

Moutaz Alazab
Dept. of Computing and Data Science
Oryx Universal College in Partnership
with Liverpool John Moores University
in Qatar
Doha, Qatar
e-mail: moutaz.a@oryx.edu.qa

Abstract— **In recent years, digital currencies have prompted discussions about their potential impact on global financial systems. While cryptocurrencies present challenges and opportunities for innovation in secure and efficient transactions, their role remains debatable. This research examines the potential implications of increased cryptocurrency adoption in Qatar. Muslim Sharia law, regulatory standards, and Islamic banking principles influence the country's conservative stance towards cryptocurrencies. Concerns about price volatility and security risks also contribute to this position. However, factors such as the growing expatriate population and technological advancements have initiated conversations about the potential benefits of cryptocurrency ecosystems. These discussions explore possibilities such as reduced transaction fees and more efficient cross-border payments while acknowledging significant remaining hurdles. This study focuses on perceptions of cryptocurrencies in Qatar and explores potential approaches to align cryptocurrency use with Sharia law and regulatory requirements. Employ a hybrid-method design incorporating a comprehensive literature review, stakeholder interviews, surveys, and economic analysis. This study aims to contribute to a balanced assessment of the potential costs and benefits of modifying Qatar's current stance on digital currencies. The goal is to inform decision-making processes and regulatory frameworks, striking a delicate balance between financial innovation and the stability of Qatar's financial services sector. Our findings illuminate the economic, ethical, and legal considerations for responsible cryptocurrency implementation. This approach prioritizes careful consideration and prudent evaluation of all factors involved.**

Keywords- financial innovation; blockchain technology; fintech; economic analysis; cryptocurrency; Islamic finance; sharia law; regulatory framework.

I. INTRODUCTION

The advent of cryptocurrency and blockchain technology has significantly disrupted established financial systems, facilitating faster, cheaper, and more transparent cross-border transactions. This paper examines the dichotomy of support and skepticism surrounding cryptocurrencies, particularly in Qatar, where Islamic finance principles and Sharia law are crucial in shaping the regulatory landscape. The study explores the legitimacy of cryptocurrencies within the Islamic framework, the potential benefits of their adoption, and the implications for Qatar's financial sector. The integration of cryptocurrency into global economic systems has elicited varied responses from nations. While some countries embrace cryptocurrencies, others, including Qatar, have taken a firm stance against them due to their incompatibility with Islamic financial principles. This paper aims to analyze the current state of cryptocurrency in Qatar, the challenges of Sharia law, and the potential for regulatory harmonization.

The legitimacy of cryptocurrency remains a contentious issue within the Islamic world. Many clerics oppose cryptocurrencies, citing their lack of intrinsic value and decentralized nature, which contradicts Islamic principles that emphasize trade based on tangible assets. The absence of reliable authority and risk management mechanisms further complicates the adoption of cryptocurrencies in Islamic finance, as excessive uncertainty in transactions is prohibited. The theological perspective that value creation is a divine prerogative adds to the resistance against cryptocurrencies, which are perceived as creating value from nothing. Despite the prevailing skepticism, discussions regarding the reevaluation of cryptocurrency bans in Qatar have emerged, driven by the influx of expatriates and the need for financial innovation in the rapidly globalizing fintech sector. The potential benefits of reduced transaction costs and enhanced cross-border payment efficiency are significant considerations for policymakers. However, the challenge remains whether cryptocurrency can align with Islamic finance norms.

Cryptocurrencies, including Bitcoin and Ethereum, utilize cryptography and blockchain technology, providing enhanced security and anonymity in transactions. Unlike traditional fiat currencies, cryptocurrencies operate outside the interest-based financial system, which aligns with Sharia law prohibitions against interest. Ethereum, as a versatile platform for decentralized applications and smart contracts, and Monero, which offers additional anonymity, exemplify the diverse functionalities of cryptocurrencies. The growth of cryptocurrency services, such as Binance, reflects a burgeoning crypto-favored culture that could benefit Qatar's economy. Qatar could mitigate wealth leakage and enhance its Gross Domestic Product (GDP) by fostering domestic cryptocurrency trading and tokenization initiatives. The study highlights the importance of developing a regulatory framework that accommodates cryptocurrency while adhering to Sharia law, thereby increasing public confidence and understanding of the associated risks and benefits. This paper represents a pioneering effort to explore cryptocurrency adoption in Qatar, addressing this emerging technology's legal, ethical, and financial dimensions. By analyzing the potential for harmonizing cryptocurrencies with Shariah regulations, the study aims to inform decision-making processes and contribute to the establishment of a robust regulatory framework in Qatar's financial sector. The findings underscore the necessity for ongoing dialogue and research to navigate the complexities of cryptocurrency adoption in a context governed by Islamic finance principles.

A. *Contributions of the study*

The main contributions of this study are as follows:

i. This study investigates the potential for enhancing cryptocurrency adoption in Qatar, examining the implications of lifting the current ban and addressing associated legal, moral, and financial issues related to its use.
ii. This study highlights the need to align cryptocurrency usage with Islamic legal principles. It explores whether embracing virtual currencies can promote financial inclusivity and creativity within the Qatari fintech ecosystem.
iii. The research emphasizes the benefits of digital currencies in expediting cross-border payments and reducing transaction costs while acknowledging counterarguments against their adoption.
iv. By gathering insights from various stakeholders, including government officials and religious scholars, the study aims to suggest the development of new regulations that balance innovation with stability, contributing to the discourse on cryptocurrency governance in Islamic contexts.

This paper is organized as follows: Section 2 discusses the related work. Section 3 outlines the methodology, including data collection, analysis, significance, and ethical considerations. Section 4 presents the proposed framework, including integrating anti-money laundering measures with traditional banking and lessons learned from neighboring industries. In Section 5, we compare our work with existing research. Finally, Section 6 discusses the conclusions.

II. LITERATURE REVIEW

This literature review, with a unique geographical focus on the Middle East and surrounding regions, delves into the implications and adoption of cryptocurrencies. It explores how technological innovation, religious principles, and regulatory frameworks shape the acceptance and integration of digital currencies within these settings, offering a fresh perspective on this emerging field.

This literature review outlines the complex nature of cryptocurrency adoption and regulation across the Middle East and surrounding regions. Despite the potential to transform financial systems into more efficient ones and drive economic growth, integrating cryptocurrencies with religious doctrines, legal uncertainty, and socio-economic factors remains a significant obstacle. However, the potential of blockchain technology to overcome these obstacles and revolutionize the financial landscape in the Middle East is a cause for optimism.

Khan et al. [15] examine the intersection of blockchain, cryptocurrency, and Shariah compliance, highlighting the tension between high-return investments and Islamic economic principles. Although many scholars agree that blockchain technology meets Shariah requirements, cryptocurrency is widely considered haram. The study has two main objectives: to examine the technological framework of blockchain and its application in cryptocurrencies and to assess Shariah's governance of cryptocurrencies and digital tokens, such as Bitcoin. This study provides valuable insights into the compatibility of emerging financial technologies with Islamic principles.

In February 2023, Ammy et al. [5] studied library research, "Investing in Cryptocurrency through the Lens of Islamic Economics," studied library research, examined the Quran, Hadith, Ijtihad, and Qia in cryptocurrency investing, and concluded that the government should protect cryptocurrency investors through appropriate regulations [5]. In Islamic finance, some cryptocurrencies are considered illegal due to gharar (uncertainty) and maysir (gambling), but cryptocurrency transactions are considered permissible under muamalah (transactions).

The study, 'Trade Economy in Qatar: Blockchain and Economic Diversification' in 2020 [2], discusses the initial resistance to cryptocurrencies in the Gulf. However, as technological development and investment skills improved, cryptocurrencies gained global traction, leading to rapid adoption in the Gulf countries. This recognition led to transformative changes in various sectors, highlighting the potential of cryptocurrencies in the Gulf.

Several studies have highlighted the importance of cryptocurrencies in the Gulf. For example, Abdeldayem et al. [11] survey on cryptocurrency in the GCC economy highlighted its potential benefits in the Gulf Cooperation Council (GCC), where remittances are essential. By introducing cryptocurrencies, networks can be streamlined, resulting in faster, more efficient, and safer operations than traditional fiat currency channels.

Foreign remittances play a crucial role in the Gulf countries, including key economic transactions that cross international borders. In their analysis of governance in the context of the rise of blockchain technology in Qatar, Ibrahim and Truby [8] highlight the increasing demand for efficient and cost-effective financial solutions. As foreign entrepreneurs send money back home, the surge of interest in cryptocurrencies in the Gulf becomes more pronounced.

"Trade Finance in Qatar: Blockchain and Financial Diversity" [7] explores how blockchain technology can transform trade finance, which is critical to Qatar's economic transformation. He highlights the challenges MSMEs face in traditional trade finance, which is often complicated and inefficient. Blockchain's decentralization, security, transparency, and immutability provide a solution to facilitate trade finance, increase the competitiveness of MSMEs, and foster FinTech growth. The paper highlights blockchain as a critical driver of Qatar's financial and commercial economic transformation.

In "Blockchain-Based Supply Chain Financing Solutions for Qatar," Charfedin and Umlai [9] address the significant challenges SMEs face in accessing traditional finance, facing limited financial resources and limited credit history. The ADB and the WTO cite ICC and requirements reports, indicating that the trade deficit is expected to widen, exacerbated by the COVID-19 pandemic. The authors propose blockchain-based solutions to provide more flexible financing options for SMEs in Qatar and highlight the importance of addressing trade finance gaps and the potential of blockchain technology to harness them in addressing these challenges.

Truby et al. [16], in "Global Blockchain-Based Trade Finance Solutions: An Analysis of Governance Patterns and the Impact of Local Laws in Six Jurisdictions," explores blockchain's potential to transform trade finance, reducing inefficiencies and risk, especially for SMEs. The study examines regulatory frameworks in the US, UK, Australia, Singapore, Hong Kong, and Qatar, focusing on various blockchain integration approaches. The authors stress the urgent need for supportive regulatory reforms and harmonized regulatory mechanisms to utilize the benefits of blockchain to ensure full compliance, and ultimately, the economic prospects of SMEs worldwide have increased.

Cryptocurrencies offer potential benefits, such as lower transaction costs, faster processing times, and improved security compared to traditional remittance methods. This has spurred the adoption of new financial technologies, such as cryptocurrency, which is included in this section. Moreover, Dahdal et al. [2], in their "Review of Trade Finance in Qatar," discuss how factors such as faster cross-border exports, reduced transaction costs, and improved security are associated with cryptocurrencies.

III. RESEARCH METHODOLOGY

The research methodology of this study is illustrated below:

A. *Research Design*

Regarding the research objectives, this study adopts a mixed-method research design, as shown in Figure 1. It involves using qualitative and quantitative methods to examine cryptocurrency adoption in Qatar. Thus, it has an objective ontology. It acknowledges the consideration of quantitative and qualitative positivism and interpretivism epistemological perspectives.

B. *Data Collection*

This study's primary data collection methods were face-to-face interviews and structured questionnaires issued to various stakeholders in Qatar's financial markets. Primary quantitative data was attained through surveys and questionnaires targeted at a sample Qatari population. We also received economic statistics from official reports.

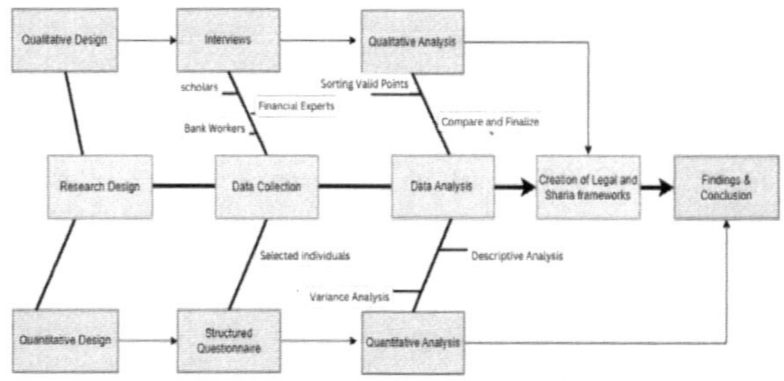

Figure 1. Research Methodology Chart.

C. *Data Analysis*

Quantitative data from questionnaires was analyzed to examine participants' responses. Qualitative narration from interviews provided rich information for further elaborating on the subjects' responses. Descriptive statistics analysis was applied to quantitative data. It offered viability in determining the effect of cryptocurrency adoption on the economy of Qatar.

D. *Sample Size and Techniques*

Three face-to-face interview respondents. Questionnaires were provided online, and tools such as Google Forms were used. Economic analysis also entailed information from official bodies like Qatar's central bank and the Ministry of Finance.

E. *Ethical Considerations*

In the research process, ethical issues were considered. The participants' privacy was preserved, and their identity was not disclosed. Participants had the right to drop out of the exercise at any time. They also had the right to provide informed consent. The study conformed to the directions of the IRB (Institutional et al.) of Qatar University and other relevant bodies.

F. *Significance*

Thus, through qualitative and quantitative data analysis and observing ethical practices, this study aims to research cryptocurrency usage in Qatar following the Sharia law and regulations.

G. *Statistical Measures*

The integration of cryptocurrencies in Qatar has garnered significant interest, prompting varied responses from stakeholders in the financial sector. This analysis explores attitudes towards cryptocurrency integration, focusing on overall sentiment and the critical role of regulatory frameworks. Utilizing JASP (Jeffrey's Amazing Statistics Program) statistical software, as shown in Table 1, the study employs descriptive analysis and graphical representation of frequency distributions, incorporating measures of central tendency (mean, median, mode) and variance (standard deviation, sample variance, skewness, kurtosis).

Statistical measures include the mean, which represents the average value of the dataset. In a Likert scale context, values less than or equal to two point ninety-nine indicate negative responses, three denotes neutrality, and values greater than three reflect positive responses. The median serves as the middle value of the dataset, interpreted as one (strongly disagree) to five (strongly agree) on a Likert scale. The mode represents the most frequently occurring value in the dataset, indicating the prevalent response without numerical assignment. Standard deviation measures response variability: a higher standard deviation suggests more excellent dispersion from the mean. Sample variance quantifies the spread of data around the mean, with higher values indicating more variability. Standard error reflects the precision of the sample mean; lower values suggest more excellent reliability. Skewness assesses data distribution asymmetry, where positive skewness indicates a rightward tail and negative skewness suggests a leftward tail. Kurtosis describes the "peakedness" of the distribution, where positive kurtosis indicates a leptokurtic distribution (more peaked), while negative kurtosis suggests a platykurtic distribution (flatter).

IV. Summarized Results of the Survey Study

The survey results, a crucial source of information, offer a comprehensive view of Qatari attitudes toward cryptocurrency integration. Through descriptive statistical analysis, key themes emerged from each variable, revealing stakeholders' varied opinions and concerns. The following sections outline the primary insights gathered from each question in the survey, providing a valuable resource for policymakers and financial institutions. We are interested in cryptocurrency and its implications in Qatar.

The first question concerns integrating blockchain-based cryptocurrencies to exchange goods and services in Qatar. The number of respondents is 162. The mean value of this distribution is 3.27, which indicates that most respondents are marking neutral opinions. The mode result shows that most respondents want to refrain from specifying their views. In variability analysis, the standard deviation of 1.14 shows moderate response variability, meaning the responses are not tightly clustered around the mean. The sample variance of 1.30 also indicates that the variances of responses are mild and do not impact the results meticulously. The standard error value of 0.089 shows that the accuracy of the sample mean compared to the population mean is precise. The negative kurtosis value of 0.51 indicates a flatter distribution of data, which means fewer extreme values and lighter tails. The near-zero skewness of -0.13 indicates that the distribution is nearly symmetrical.

The second question of the study is related to lifting the current ban and amending the existing law to include cryptocurrency in Qatar. The mean response is approximately 3.76, which means the responses are above the midpoint of the Likert scale. The mode value of 4 is assigned to the 'Agree' attribute. The median value of 4 also indicates a positive study result—the Standard Deviation of 1.18 shows only moderate variability. The sample variance of 1.40 also confirms the moderate spread of the responses. The relatively low standard error (0.093) shows that the sample mean is a precise estimation of the population mean. The kurtosis value of 0.432 indicates a slightly flatter distribution than a normal distribution. The skewness value of -0.727 indicates a left skewness. The data set generally reflects a positive trend, which means the people from Qatar are recommending amending the existing law and lifting the ban.

Table 1 presents the descriptive statistics of the collected data to help provide a clearer understanding of the participant's responses and overall trends in the dataset. The analysis was conducted using JASP, an open-source statistical software widely used for data analysis in social sciences and other fields.

TABLE I. DESCRIPTIVE STATISTICS - PERFORMED ON JASP (JEFFREYS'S AMAZING STATISTICS PROGRAM)

Variables	Valid	Mode	Median	Mean	Std. Error of Mean	Std. Deviation	Variance	Skewness	Kurtosis
Blockchain aligns with Sharia principles	162	3	3	3.265	0.09	1.141	1.302	-0.131	-0.514
Amending the law for cryptocurrency	162	4	4	3.759	0.093	1.184	1.401	-0.727	-0.432
Adoption of cryptocurrency	162	4	3	3.265	0.094	1.199	1.438	-0.198	-0.894
Readiness of financial market for crypto	162	3	3	3.235	0.09	1.145	1.311	-0.12	-0.774
Acceptability by vendors and investors	162	4	4	3.525	0.087	1.11	1.232	-0.38	-0.592
Jeopardy to security and transparency	162	3	3	3.222	0.086	1.092	1.193	-0.076	-0.66
Advantages of financial inclusion	162	4	3.5	3.426	0.084	1.074	1.153	-0.308	-0.539
Financial infrastructure for crypto	162	3	3	3	0.088	1.115	1.242	0.164	-0.717
Regulatory exclusion of crypto	162	3	3	3.481	0.07	0.886	0.785	0.084	-0.197
Islamic banking cultural views	162	3	3	3.222	0.086	1.092	1.193	-0.192	-0.454
Decentralized crypto impact	162	3	4	3.568	0.087	1.103	1.216	-0.4	-0.502
Blockchain security concerns	162	4	4	3.395	0.089	1.128	1.272	-0.406	-0.518
Cryptocurrency and illegal use	162	4	4	3.846	0.08	1.019	1.038	-0.755	0.225
Impact on financial transparency	162	4	4	3.636	0.074	0.938	0.879	-0.584	0.214
Financial privacy concerns	162	4	4	3.512	0.084	1.065	1.133	-0.361	-0.485
Smart contracts and execution	162	4	4	3.617	0.075	0.96	0.921	-0.318	-0.276
Regulatory uncertainty impact	162	4	4	3.796	0.079	1.004	1.008	-0.699	0.222

The following variable is cryptocurrency adoption into Qatar's financial market. The average responses are around 3.27 (Mean), almost like the first variable. This indicates that most reactions are coming near the midpoint value with a slightly positive trend. The median value of 3 also shows a neutral position. However, the mode value 4 gives a positive trend rather than neutrality. The standard deviation of 1.20 and sample variance of 1.44 indicate a moderate spread of responses around the mean value, which shows a diversified opinion. The relatively low standard error (0.094) suggests that the sample mean is precise compared to the population mean value. The negative kurtosis value (-0.894) indicates a platykurtic with few extreme values and lighter tails. The skewness of - 0.198 shows a slight leftward skewness. We suggest that QCB should develop more policies to minimize the risks involved in cryptocurrency transactions.

The fourth variable discusses whether the Qatar financial market is ready or not to use cryptocurrency in the present scenario. This variable provides more fictional values as the government has not lifted the cryptocurrency ban yet. The mean value of 3.23 suggests a small positiveness with most central point responses. The mean value and mode value of 3 also indicate the same results. The standard deviation value of 1.15 and sample variance value of 1.31 indicate moderate variability, indicating the spread of data is around the mean value only. The standard error of 0.090 shows a precise estimation of the sample mean compared to the population mean. The kurtosis is platykurtic here with a negative value of 0.774. The skewness of - 0.120 indicates left-skewed data, which means more responses on the higher end with a tail extending towards the lower back. This suggests that the respondents do not know whether Qatar's financial system is ready to include cryptocurrency.

The following variable concerns the acceptability of cryptocurrency by Qatar's usual vendors and investors to do their financial transactions. The central tendency measures show a positive response with a mean value of 3.52 and a median and mode value of 4. Though the mean value is slightly positive, the median and mode values show a more positive response trend. The univariate analysis (S.D of 1.11 and sample variance of 1.23) shows only a moderate variance. The kurtosis value is – 0.592, which shows a platykurtic, and the skewness of – 0. 380 shows a left skewness. The data set reflects a slightly positive response with moderate variability and a skewed distribution. The responses show that the vendors and investors of Qatar are ready to accept cryptocurrency to do their financial transactions.

The next question was to comment on whether integrating cryptocurrency could jeopardize security, privacy, and financial transparency in the Qatar financial market. The mean response of the variable is 3.22, and the median value is 3. The value of mode is also 3, which means most of the responses are centered on neutrality with slight positiveness. The variance analysis shows moderate variability only. The standard deviation of 1.09 and sample variance of 1.19 show a diverse but centered set of responses around the mean value. The kurtosis value of – 0.659 shows that the data distribution is slightly flatter than the normal distribution, meaning fewer extreme values exist. The skewness value of – 0.076 is close to zero, which indicates a nearly symmetric distribution. The data set shows generally neutral to slightly positive sentiment among the respondents. This suggests that the respondents somewhat lean towards the agreement but are primarily neutral. More discussions and research should be conducted to establish a new regulatory framework to address cryptocurrency's privacy and security issues, inviting the audience to contribute to this important process.

The following variable is the study related to the significant advantages of cryptocurrency for Qatar's financial inclusion. The mean value (3.43) is slightly above the midpoint, indicating that cryptocurrency substantially benefits Qatar's economic inclusion. The median value of 3.5 indicates a slight lean toward the positivity of the given variable. The mode value of 4 indicates that many respondents believe cryptocurrency adoption is helpful for Qatar's financial inclusion. The variance analysis shows moderate variability. The standard deviation of 1.07 and sample variance of 1.15 denotes a moderate spread of values around the mean value. The standard error of 0.084 is comparatively less; therefore, the sample mean's preciseness is very close. In short, the statistical results show that the responses to the statement "Cryptocurrency offers significant advantages for financial inclusion in Qatar" are optimistic but moderate, suggesting a promising future for cryptocurrency in Qatar.

The eighth variable is related to Qatar's financial infrastructure for integrating cryptocurrency, especially as a medium of exchange. The statistical data provided for this variable shows a neutral trend among the respondents. The mean value is precisely 3 in this analysis. Moreover, the median and mode values are also 3. This shows that the respondents are balanced in their answers. The relatively lower standard error (0.084) also indicates the same because the mean value of the sample is exact compared to the population mean. This neutrality suggests that the respondents neither strongly agree nor disagree with the statement. This specifies a balanced result with no robust lean towards either side of the spectrum. The positive skewness and negative kurtosis explain a symmetric data distribution with neither positive nor negative responses.

The following variable checks whether the regulatory entity in Qatar led to the banning of cryptocurrencies following an exclusion. The mean value of 3.48 shows a slight positiveness to the statement. The median and mode values stand at 3, which is due to the generality of the respondents. The standard deviation is less than 1 (0.89), indicating that the Variance is very low in the data set. The sample variance of 0.79 also confirms the low variability of the data set. The value of standard error is also less in this data set. The mistake of 0.069 is merely negligible. The negative kurtosis shows a significantly flatter data distribution, and the slight positive skewness shows a slight rightward skew of the distribution. The positive skew towards agreement (mean>3) indicates that the regulatory entity in Qatar played a vital role in banning cryptocurrency. However, due to its slight positive value, it cannot be strongly pronounced.

The subsequent variable is related to the cultural and ethical views of Islamic banking regarding the adoption of cryptocurrency. The mean score of 3.22 indicates that the respondents are generally neutral to slightly favorable to the statement. The median and mode values are the same (3), reinforcing the neutrality trend; the standard deviation of 1.092 and sample variance of 1.192 show moderate variability in the data set. The standard error is lower (0.086) in this data set, which means the central tendency measures are precise to the population data. Here, both kurtosis (-0.454) and skewness (-0.192) are slightly negative and near to symmetry. In short, the cultural and ethical views of Islamic banking are critical in the adoption of cryptocurrency in Qatar. However, the neutrality of the data set may be one of the obstacles.

The following dataset concerns cryptocurrency's unregulated/ decentralized use and its effect on Qatar's financial market. The mean value of 3.57 shows a lean towards agreeing that the unregulated/ decentralized use of cryptocurrency could adversely affect the monetary market in Qatar. Both median and mode values are 4 (more significant than the mean value), which establishes that most respondents agree with the statement. The skewness value of – 0. 400 indicates a slight left skewness, meaning the values towards agreement are higher than those towards disagreement. The negative kurtosis value of – 0. 502 also suggests that the distribution is near symmetrical with light tails and few extreme figures. In a nutshell, the central tendency measures show that a significant portion of the respondents believe that the unregulated/ decentralized use of cryptocurrency could adversely affect the financial market in Qatar.

The following variable for analysis is related to the security concerns of the blockchain system in which the cryptocurrencies are working. The mean value (3.40) is slightly above the mid value (3.00), which indicates that the blockchain system is a significant drawback of cryptocurrency. Both median and mode have the same value (4), more than the mean (3.40), so most respondents have concerns about cryptocurrency security matters. The standard deviation is 1.13, which indicates a moderate variability among respondents. Skewness (-0.41) and Kurtosis (-0.52) are harmful as they also show some response variations.

The following variable is whether cryptocurrency can easily be used in illegal activities. The mean value of 3.85 is significantly above the mid value of 3.00, which states that respondents agree with the above statement. The median and mode are the same (4), above the mean (3.85). So, most respondents believe that the illegal use of cryptocurrency is a significant issue. The standard deviation of 1.02 indicates nominal variability, which does not create a substantial discrepancy in opinion. The skewness of -0.76 indicates a left skew, which means more responses are gathered towards the higher end of the scale, representing a more substantial agreement with the statement. The kurtosis value is (0.23) positive, which means a few more extreme responses on both ends of the scale, though the central tendency remains towards agreement.

The following analysis of the statement "the pseudonymous nature of cryptocurrency transactions impacts financial transparency/tax evasion." Here, the mean (3.64) is above the mid value (3.00), indicating that the respondents agree with the statement. The median (4) and mode (4) show that at least half of the respondents agree or strongly agree with the statement. The Standard Deviation is 0.94. There is some variability among the respondent's opinions, but the responses are almost identical, and there is a fair level of consensus. Skewness is (-0.58), with a slight skew to the left, indicating that more responses are on the higher end of the scale, which also agrees with the statement. A positive kurtosis (0.21) indicates a few insignificant extreme reactions. So, we can conclude that most respondents believe cryptocurrency transactions' pseudonymous nature negatively impacts financial transparency.

The next question is: Does the adoption of cryptocurrency enhance financial privacy due to the transparency of blockchain technology? Here, the mean is 3.5 above the midpoint 3. Median and mode are the same values (4) and positively respond to the matter. Standard deviation (1.06) and Variance (1.13) indicate moderate response variability, showing some diversity in their opinions. Kurtosis (-0.49) and Skewness (-0.36) indicate negative values. Overall, the analysis of the responses on this matter is somewhat favorable but varied, reflecting the topic's complexity and nuanced nature.

Statistical analysis of the statement 'smart contracts' in cryptocurrency enable automatic execution of contractual agreements without the need for intermediaries is the next. The mean of the responses is 3.62, which shows that more opinions agree with the statement. The median and mode are the same values (4), indicating a favorable agreement toward intelligent contracts enabling automatic execution without intermediaries. Standard deviation (0.96) and Variance (0.92) show only moderate variability in opinions, indicating some degree of consensus. Kurtosis (-0.28) shows a negative value and is a relatively flat distribution. Skewness (-0.32) is also negative, indicating a leaning towards lower values, which means the responses are more neutral or disagree.

The last variable is the statistical interpretation of the response's regulatory uncertainty regarding the impact of cryptocurrency on investor confidence. The study's mean is 3.80, which shows that most respondents agree with the matter. Median and mode are the same value (4), indicating that regulatory uncertainty highly affects investor confidence. Standard deviation (1.00) and Variance (1.01) show only a moderate variability in responses and some diversity in opinions. The positive kurtosis (0.22) represents the responses indicating moderate agreement only. The negative skewness (-0.70) shows the responses are left-tailed; fewer responses are disagreements.

The analysis reveals cautious optimism among respondents regarding cryptocurrency integration in Qatar, highlighting the need for robust regulatory frameworks to address concerns about privacy, security, and transparency.

V. PROPOSED FRAMEWORK

A. *Cryptocurrency and Sharia Law*

This discussion is on Cryptocurrency and its relationship with Islamic Law (Sharia). The viewpoint is mainly from the angle of Qatar's legislation.

1) Creation of Stablecoins: Stablecoins are digital currencies like Bitcoin or Ethereum. The critical difference is that the currency is backed by something of value, which makes these currencies more stable. Sharia law recommends trade based on something of value. The main issue that Islamic countries are backing from cryptocurrencies is the lack of value behind the coins. Stablecoins can be the answer to such matters. If a country's central bank creates these currencies, the problem of lack of authority can also be eliminated. There are several types of Stablecoins, such as fiat currency-based Stablecoins, commodity-based Stablecoins, crypto-collateralized Stablecoins, etc.

2) Creation of Central Bank Digital Currency (CBCD): The central bank can create its version of digital currency using cryptography technology. The volatile nature of cryptocurrency is a significant reason for rejection, per Sharia law. By creating a currency, the central bank can control uncertainty. The issue of lack of authority can also be eliminated by introducing such currencies. The use of cryptocurrency for criminal activities can be mitigated with strategy. Since the currency is issued and managed by government authorities, there will be a structured regulatory framework. Many countries have issued such currencies. It can improve digital currency circulation and reduce the need to carry cash for everyday use.

3) Regulation through application: Cryptocurrencies are traded using third-party applications such as Binance. Cryptocurrency provides anonymity. However, via legal regulation, a country can regulate these platforms to prevent the use of digital currency in criminal activities and reduce the anonymity of its users. The central authority can impose laws that specifically stress the need to conduct KYC (know your customer) and occasionally furnish those details to the legislator. The authority can also draw a framework that compels the platform to submit detailed user activity reports. Money laundering, terrorist funding, and other illegal activities can be mitigated via these strategies.

4) *Global system for cryptocurrency transactions:* Cryptocurrencies like Bitcoin, Ethereum, etc., have unique features that enable them to be used globally. Real-time settlement and transaction speed make them suitable for the current globalized economy. Creating such currency worldwide with the supervision of an international organization, such as the United Nations (UN) or the Arab League, can boost the global economy. Since this currency is created and managed by an international organization in partnership with various countries, it can leverage the technology of multiple participants.

5) *Cryptocurrency and Global Finance:* Cryptocurrency is a decentralized digital currency based on blockchain technology. It started in 2009 with Bitcoin. Its advantages include being safeguarded against inflation, cost-effective, and allowing global transactions without boundaries. Conversely, some challenges include high volatility, the potential for criminal use, and difficulties in monetary policy regulation.

From commodity-backed to fiat currencies, which can be unstable and easily affected by inflation rates that result in the evolution of money, there is an alternative decentralized financial system (DeFi). Cryptocurrency attracts people who do not believe in central banks' effectiveness. Nevertheless, there are barriers to its diffusion, such as limited public awareness or knowledge.

6) *Sharia, Cryptocurrency, and Global Finance:* Islamic scholars have no strong stand on whether cryptocurrency complies with Sharia law. Some support it because of the historical development of currencies, from barter trade to precious metal exchange to paper currencies. They also propose that cryptocurrency is worth it due to its market price and acceptance as a medium of exchange.

Enthusiasts have claimed that cryptocurrency is harmonious with Islamic finance since it does not partake in interest and could lead to justice in the business context. They also point out that one can own and keep it, so it fulfills the conditions of a valid transaction according to Shariah laws.

Nevertheless, some scholars fight against cryptocurrency because it contains uncertainty(gharar). It is not identified from intrinsically valuable items, and its management is not central. Cryptocurrencies have high volatility and unreasonable changes in value. A group of scholars argue that the above and the use of ICOs exempt them from Shariah compliance.

7) Blockchain Technology and Sharia Compliance:

Blockchain is the technology that underpins cryptocurrencies. It offers features that could align with Sharia principles:

- **Transparency:** Each transaction is documented, and there is transparency in that all the network participants can view these records.
- **Elimination of intermediaries:** For peer-to-peer transactions, one can be done away with or have little or no charges on interest.
- **Immutability:** Unlike in a cheque system, where a transaction can be easily forged, one cannot alter a recorded transaction in a way that would lead to unlawful use of the money.
- **Tokenization:** Putting physical assets on the market electronically makes transactions more accessible and less costly.
- **Privacy in charitable giving:** With blockchain, anonymity can be achieved during a contribution while still maintaining records and ensuring that the funds are allocated as required.

8) Cryptocurrency Legislation in Qatar: Qatar's attitude toward cryptocurrency has advanced.

- **2018**: Qatar Central Bank banned the use of cryptocurrencies. It was because of their modification and use for illegal purposes.
- **2020:** The Qatar Financial Authority Charter prohibits the deduction of specific discounts on similar assets in the Qatar Financial Authority.
- **2022:** After a crypto trading platform opens in Qatar, people are advised not to deal with unlicensed companies.
- **2024:** Qatar is already investigating the possibility of having a legal tender status for cryptocurrency, its legalization and categorization, the combating of money laundering through cryptocurrencies, and consumer protection.

Hence, the regulatory environment that Qatar plans to establish is supposed to reflect its global counterparts' main concerns, including fluctuations in the market, protection of consumers, and prevention of immoral activities, such as money laundering and financing of terrorism. It is also possible that the country is engrossed in developing novel and sophisticated coins acceptable under Sharia law.

9) Creating Sharia-compliant currencies: The framework proposes several approaches to create currencies that adhere to Sharia principles.

- **Stablecoins:** Stable digital currencies that are linked to another currency, metal, or another type of cryptocurrency to minimize risk. Private organizations could perform this function, provided the government gives them ample power.
- **Central Bank Digital Currencies (CBDCs):** State-backed digital money that delivers the advantages of digital money yet remains under the command of a state's central bank.
- **Regulation through applications:** Adopt severe policies and legislation for cryptocurrency trading, such as KYC checks and regular filings to the center.
- **Global partnerships:** Issuing an independent world cryptocurrency with the assistance of reliable organizations, such as The World Bank or IMF, that will be backed by the UN legislation and implemented through discussion. It could also promote the ease of cross-border business and trading and offer a substitute for the US dollar.

Currently, Cryptocurrency has a lot of potential. This is evident especially with the rising distrust of traditional banking systems. However, governments must devise sound legal requisites to ensure that investors are shielded from conducting unlawful deeds. There are possibilities for more innovative and less regulated money like stablecoins and CBDCs.

Adopting solutions like digital currencies poses dilemmas and opportunities. For a country like Qatar, this should also be done while complying with Islamic law. Qatar should promote the corresponding regulations and form an environment for innovation in this sphere.

10) Critical considerations for Moving Forward Include:

- **Consumer protection:** Well-defined rules and international collaborations are required to protect the users' interests.
- **Expert engagement:** Therefore, there is a need to engage professionals in cryptology that will give a sound understanding of how cryptocurrencies and blockchain technology work.
- **Alignment with Sharia principles:** Stress the positive role that cryptocurrencies and blockchain may play in attaining higher levels of justice and a fair financial deal.
- **Adaptation and innovation:** People are facing the challenge of accepting change, and the only way to go is to adopt advanced technologies to enhance the economy's growth while competing for space in the global financial market.
- **Broader applications:** Remember that blockchain and other technologies work not only with currencies but might also change multiple aspects of the post-industrial economy.

Lastly, the document reiterates that even though cryptocurrency and blockchain technology pose some risks, they are also opportunities for the further development of new technologies and industries that will grow the economy. Thus, countries that manage to effectively respond to constantly changing legislation and enhance the potential of these technologies may gain a competitive edge in the new world financial arena.

B. Regulatory Framework Model

Qatar is taking steps towards a more strategic approach to incorporating cryptocurrencies into its monetary policy while reducing their associated risks. Qatar's strategy has apparent implications for cryptocurrencies. They are treated like digital objects supported by their inherent value and accounting systems. The QCB does not directly regulate them. This simple definition sets the stage for how these new assets may or may not be legal under Qatari law.

Recognizing the diversity within the cryptocurrency realm,

Qatar distinguishes between three primary categories:

There are payment tokens, utility tokens, and security tokens. Payment tokens work similarly to regular money and are a means of exchange for products and services. Utility tokens provide the right to use blockchain-based products or services, as tokens are keys within related systems—real-world assets back a security token and grant holders' rights, such as shares or voting rights.

1) Blockchain Technology and Sharia Compliance: The government strictly regulates entry into the specific market of cryptocurrencies in Qatar through the Qatar Financial Centre Regulatory Authority (QFCRA), which entails a comprehensive licensing process. Some of these standards include having sufficient capital to support the entity, putting up measures to secure the users, and enshrining clear operational policies. They are already licensed and undergo periodic compliance inspections and audits. These are aimed at placing scrutiny on such organizations. Because of this, all necessary performance requirements can be established as required by law.

2) *Anti-Money Laundering (AML) and Counter-Terrorism Financing (CTF) Measures*: Qatar has prioritized strict AML and CTF procedures in addressing potential cryptocurrency risks. These processes require strict adherence to Know Your Customer (KYC) policies, which require users to verify their identity before processing cryptocurrencies. Continuous monitoring of transactions for suspicious activities ensures prompt detection and reporting to the Qatar Financial Intelligence Unit (FIU) for further investigation.

3) *Consumer Protection and Education:* Qatar understands the challenges and risks associated with cryptocurrencies. Thus, the state emphasizes consumer protection through transparency and education. The policy emphasizes the importance of clearly communicating potential risks to investors. They should be empowered to make informed decisions. In addition, Qatar plans to establish mechanisms for resolving consumer complaints and disputes under the guidelines of the QFCRA. Public education sessions will also be held to raise awareness about the benefits and risks of cryptocurrencies. It will equip individuals with the skills to confidently navigate this changing economic landscape.

4) *Integration with Traditional Banking*: Rather than seeing cryptocurrency as a separate financial system, Qatar intends to integrate digital assets into the traditional banking sector. This approach encourages banks to explore new services related to cryptocurrencies, such as digital asset manager services, the convenience of cryptocurrency payments, and leveraging traditional banks' established trust and structure to provide funds that will be invested in digital property rights.

5) International Alignment and Collaboration: Recognizing the global nature of cryptocurrencies, Qatar is committed to aligning its regulatory framework with international standards and best practices in cooperation with international regulators and guidelines issued by organizations such as the Financial Services Commission (FATF). Established compliance ensures consistency and fairness in cross-border transactions and investments. This international conference underscores Qatar's commitment to tackling illegal activities in the cryptocurrency market and strengthens its position in the global economy.

6) *Lessons from GCC Neighbors:* Drawing insights from neighboring countries in the Gulf Cooperation Council (GCC), Qatar has been exploring the legal path adopted by Bahrain and the United Arab Emirates (UAE). Bahrain and the UAE have extensive licensing policies and strict economic internal security measures; with robust legal oversight, cybersecurity measures are also being implemented to balance innovation. Qatar aims to incorporate these successful practices with the program, using local experiences to strengthen its regulatory environment for cryptocurrencies.

7) *Adaptability and Future Prospects:* Qatar's proposed regulatory framework recognizes the strengths of cryptocurrencies and anticipates continued developments in blockchain technology and global regulatory standards. Built-in strategies for continuous review and innovation ensure flexibility to adapt to emerging trends and technological developments. This flexibility allows Qatar to take advantage of cryptocurrencies' potential benefits, attract investment, foster innovation in financial technology, and maintain regulatory effectiveness over time.

8) *Challenges and Implementation:* Implementing a comprehensive cryptocurrency framework in Qatar will demand substantial effort and resources. Key priorities include investing in technological infrastructure for research and regulation, enhancing the capacity of regulators and legislators, and fostering collaboration among government agencies, financial institutions, technology companies, and international partners to promote public education. Qatar aims to adopt a balanced regulatory approach that embraces innovation while ensuring legal oversight and consumer protection, setting a benchmark for responsible cryptocurrency regulation. This will involve clearly defining cryptocurrency, enforcing stricter licensing requirements, improving Anti-Money Laundering (AML) and Counter-Terrorism Financing (CTF) processes, and prioritizing consumer protection and education.

VI. DISCUSSIONS

Religious and cultural beliefs are crucial in shaping the acceptance and regulation of cryptocurrencies in Qatar. Survey data reveal a cautious outlook towards cryptocurrencies, influenced by concerns regarding compliance with Shariah principles. This aligns with existing literature in Islamic finance, where some scholars view cryptocurrencies as permissible due to their speculative nature, while others advocate for strict regulation to establish legitimacy. Economic development goals, financial stability, and technological readiness have shaped Qatar's legal framework. Survey responses indicate a neutral to slightly positive sentiment regarding regulatory changes, reflecting a careful approach to potential shifts consistent with broader GCC strategies to reduce reliance on hydrocarbons.

The importance of stakeholder engagement is emphasized in balancing innovation with risk management. Blockchain technology is recognized for its potential to enhance efficiency and transparency in trade finance and supply chain management, particularly for Small and Medium-sized Enterprises (SMEs). However, concerns regarding budget readiness persist. Literature supports the notion that blockchain can democratize financial services for small businesses. Qatar's regulatory approach towards cryptocurrencies is primarily determined by good governance and economic openness, with survey results indicating a neutral attitude towards institutional readiness. This underscores the necessity for improved mechanisms to facilitate integration. Islamic financial institutions in Qatar are positioned to incorporate cryptocurrencies while ensuring adherence to Shariah principles and addressing security concerns. The survey data reflect a cautious yet optimistic perspective on this integration, highlighting the significance of Shariah-compliant policies for promoting financial inclusion and transparency.

VII. Conclusion and Future Work

This study explores the increasing adoption of cryptocurrency in Qatar while ensuring compliance with Shariah legal and regulatory standards. It addresses the concerns of Islamic scholars regarding uncertainty (Gharar), moneylending (Riba), and abuse. The research suggested methods through a literature review and a comprehensive analysis, including creating hard currency with assets you can see. Another idea was to support or establish a Central Banking Digital Currency (CBDC) in line with Islamic financial principles. The paper proposes a tailored regulatory framework for Qatar, covering Legal interpretation, Licensing mechanisms, Anti-Money Laundering measures, Consumer protection, Traditional banking integration, international compliance, and Periodic reviews aimed at reducing transaction risks.

This framework will provide clarity for businesses and investors. It will also ensure security and stability, encouraging cryptocurrency's complementary use. This study contributes insights to policymakers and stakeholders in navigating the complexities of cryptocurrency adoption, guiding informed decision-making and policymaking. It aims to balance innovation and strong governance, positioning Qatar to lead the burgeoning fintech scene and ensure financial stability by upholding Shariah principles. We plan to conduct further research based on this study by adding more crucial factors, such as demographic details of the respondents, and applying more rigorous statistical analysis with many samples to clarify the study.

References

[1] A. Alomari and N. Fetais, "Blockchain Technology Adoption in the State of Qatar: Qualitative Risk Analysis," Qatar University Press, 2023.

[2] A. Dahdal, J. Truby, and H. Botosh, "Trade Finance in Qatar: Blockchain and Economic Diversification," Law and Financial Markets Review, vol. 14, no. 4, pp. 223-236, 2020.

[3] A. Eaddy, "Innovation in Terrorist Financing: Interrogating Varying Levels of Cryptocurrency Adoption in al-Qaeda, Hezbollah, and the Islamic State," Doctoral dissertation, Tri-College Libraries, 2019.

[4] A. M. Z. Othman and E. M. E. Dosh, "Regulating Digital Currencies in the Emirate of Dubai: A Comparative Legislative Review," International Journal of Public Law and Policy, vol. 10, no. 2, pp. 204-225, 2024.

[5] B. Ammy, A. Soemitra, and Z. M. Nawawi, "Investing in Cryptocurrency Through the Lens of Islamic Economics," Proceeding Medan International Conference on Economic and Business, pp. 227-243, 2023.

[6] B. Najafi, M. Amra, and A. Najafi, "Exploring Global Fintech Advancement and Application: Case of Saudi Arabia, Turkey, and Qatar," in Exploring Global FinTech Advancement and Applications, IGI Global, pp. 158-211, 2024.

[7] H. Botosh, "Trade Finance in Qatar: Blockchain and Economic Diversification," 2020.

[8] I. A. Ibrahim and J. Truby, "Governance in the Era of Blockchain Technology in Qatar: A Roadmap and a Manual for Trade Finance," Journal of Banking Regulation, pp. 1-20, 2021.

[9] L. Charfeddine and M. Umlai, "Blockchain-based Supply Chain Financing Solutions for Qatar," DOI:10.13140/RG.2.2.18262.27206, 2021.

[10] L. Safina and U. A. Oseni, "Utilizing Blockchain Technology for Post-Trade Securities Settlement: A Framework for Islamic Capital Markets in the GCC Region," in Fintech, Digital Currency and the Future of Islamic Finance: Strategic, Regulatory and Adoption Issues in the Gulf Cooperation Council, pp. 187-207, 2021.

[11] M. M. Abdeldayem and S. H. Aldulaimi, "Cryptocurrency in the GCC Economy," International Journal of Scientific and Technology Research, vol. 9, no. 2, pp. 1739-1755, 2020.

[12] M. M. Babu, T. Bason, R. Porreca, P. Petratos, and S. Akter, "Fostering Trust and Overcoming Psychological Resistance Towards Cryptocurrencies and Cryptoassets," Psychology & Marketing, vol. 41, no. 1, pp. 45-68, 2024.

[13] N. J. N. AlNasr, "Adopting Fintech: The Fintech Ecosystem in Qatar with a Comparison to Other Emerging Markets," Doctoral dissertation, Hamad Bin Khalifa University, Qatar, 2022.

[14] N. M. A. Jaradt and H. A. M. B. Issa, "Electronic Money System and its Importance in Electronic Payment: Comparative Analysis of Bahrain and UK Laws," Test Engineering and Management, vol. 83, pp. 856-861, 2020.

[15] S. Khan and M. R. Rabbani, "In-depth Analysis of the Blockchain, Cryptocurrency, and Sharia Compliance," International Journal of Business Innovation and Research, vol. 29, no. 1, pp. 1-15, 2022.

[16] J. Turby, A, M Dahdal, and O, Caudevilla, "Global Blockchain-based Trade Finance Solutions: Analysis of Governance Models and Impact on Local Laws in Six Jurisdictions," Global Journal of Comparative Law, 11, p. 167-196, 2022.

[17] W. George and T. Al-Ansari, "Roadmap for National Adoption of Blockchain Technology Towards Securing the Food System of Qatar," Sustainability, vol. 16, no. 7, p. 2956, 2024.

[18] Y. C. Yeong, K. S. Kalid, K. S. Savita, M. N. Ahmad, and M. Zaffar, "Sustainable Cryptocurrency Adoption Assessment Among IT Enthusiasts and Cryptocurrency Social Communities," Sustainable Energy Technologies and Assessments, vol. 52, p. 102085, 2022.

International Academy, Research,
and Industry Association (IARIA)
412 Derby Way
Wilmington, DE 19810

ISBN 979-8-3313-1384-5

9 798331 313845

CURRAN ASSOCIATES INC.
proceedings
.com

Eleventh International Conference on eHealth, Telemedicine, and Social Medicine (eTELEMED 2019)

Held at DigitalWorld 2019

Athens, Greece
24 – 28 February 2019

IARIA